History and Memory in the Carolingian World

WITHDRAWN

The writing and reading of history in the early middle ages form the key themes of this book. The primary focus is on the remarkable manifestations of historical writing in relation to historical memory in the Frankish kingdoms of the eighth and ninth centuries. The book considers the audiences for history in the Frankish kingdoms, the recording of memory in new genres including narrative histories, cartularies and *Libri memoriales*, and thus particular perceptions of the Frankish and Christian past. It analyses both original manuscript material and key historical texts from the Carolingian period, a remarkably creative period in the history of European culture. Presentations of the past developed in this period were crucial in forming an historical understanding of the Greco-Roman and Judaeo-Christian past and, in subsequent centuries, of early medieval Europe. They also played an extraordinarily influential role in the formation of political ideologies and senses of identity within Europe.

ROSAMOND MCKITTERICK is Professor of Medieval History in the University of Cambridge. Her previous publications include *The Carolingians and the Written Word* (1989), *The Frankish Kings and Culture in the Early Middle Ages* (1995) and *The New Cambridge Medieval History*, II, *c. 700–c.900* (1995). She has presented many conference papers and lectured extensively at universities in Britain, continental Europe, North America and Australia. She is a Fellow of the Royal Historical Society.

D1160711

History and Memory in the Carolingian World

Rosamond McKitterick

Professor of Medieval History,
University of Cambridge and Fellow of Newnham College

PUBLISHED BY THE PRESS SYNDICATE OF THE UNIVERSITY OF CAMBRIDGE
The Pitt Building, Trumpington Street, Cambridge, United Kingdom

CAMBRIDGE UNIVERSITY PRESS
The Edinburgh Building, Cambridge, CB2 2RU, UK
40 West 20th Street, New York, NY 10011-4211, USA
477 Williamstown Road, Port Melbourne, VIC 3207, Australia
Ruiz de Alarcón 13, 28014 Madrid, Spain
Dock House, The Waterfront, Cape Town 8001, South Africa

http://www.cambridge.org

First published 2004

Printed in the United Kingdom at the University Press, Cambridge

Typeface Plantin 10/12 pt   *System* LATEX 2ε   [TB]

A catalogue record for this book is available from the British Library

ISBN 0 521 82717 5 hbk
ISBN 0 521 53436 4 pbk

In loving memory of
Claude Anthony Pierce,
21 November 1919–16 May 2001

Contents

Preface

This book's themes are the writing and reading of history in the early middle ages. The primary focus is on the many remarkable manifestations of historical writing in relation to historical memory in the Frankish kingdoms of the eighth and ninth centuries. I consider the audiences for history in the Frankish kingdoms and the recording of memory in various new genres, including narrative histories, cartularies and *Libri memoriales*, and thus particular perceptions of the Frankish and Christian past. I offer analyses of manuscript material and of key historical texts from the Carolingian period, a remarkably creative period in the history of European culture. Presentations of the past developed in the eighth and ninth centuries were crucial in the formation of an historical understanding of the Greco-Roman and Judaeo-Christian past, as well as for the history of early medieval Europe in subsequent centuries. They also played an extraordinarily influential role in the formation of political ideologies and senses of identity within Europe.

This book draws in part on material already published in articles or chapters in books over the past decade, but here presented in a completely revised and augmented form. I am grateful to the original publishers as listed below for their kind permission to make use of my work in this way.

In Cambridge I am fortunate in being able to draw on the wonderful resources of the Cambridge University Library, and I should like to thank all the staff in Manuscripts and Rare Books, the Periodicals Department, the West Room, the Reading Room, the Anderson Room, the Map Room, and the departments of Accessions and Cataloguing for their unfailing helpfulness over the years. I am also greatly obliged to all the assistance given me as a reader by the staffs of the manuscripts departments of Bamberg Staatsbibliothek; Berlin, Deutsche Staatsbibliothek; Brussels, Bibliothèque Royale; Copenhagen, Kongelige Bibliotek; Düsseldorf, Universitätsbibliothek; The Hague, Koninklijke Bibliotheek; Leiden, Universiteitsbibliotheek; London, British Library; Oxford, Bodleian Library; Paris, Bibliothèque nationale de France; Prague, Knihovna metropolitní Kapituli; Rome, Biblioteca Apostolica Vaticana;

St Gallen, Stiftsbibliothek; Valenciennes, Bibliothèque Municipale; Vienna, Österreichische Nationalbibliothek; Wolfenbüttel, Herzog August Bibliothek; and to many others for kindly meeting my requests for microfilms and photographs.

Much of the material in this book, moreover, was first presented at conferences, as working papers at 'workshops', or as lectures in Aix, Auxerre, Bergen, Cambridge, Chapel Hill, Cividale, Copenhagen, Laurence (Kansas), Leeds, Lille, London, Oslo, Oxford, Paris, Perth (Western Australia), Rome, Sewanee, Utrecht, Vienna, Washington, DC, York and Zwettl. I have consequently benefited greatly from the comments, suggestions and reactions from the many friends, colleagues and students who heard them, especially Sverre Bagge, Lars Boje Mortensen, Claude Carozzi, Christine Carpenter, Mayke de Jong, Flavia de Rubeis, David Ganz, Carl Hammer, Wolfgang Haubrichs, Martin Heinzelmann, Yitzhak Hen, Michael Hoeflich, Matthew Innes, Dominique Iogna-Prat, William Klingshirn, Regine Le Jan, Niels Lund, John Morrill, Ruth Morse, Marco Mostert, Jinty Nelson, Thomas Noble, Michel Parisse, Richard Pfaff, Walter Pohl, Susan Rankin, Alastair Reid, Susan Ridyard, Anton Scharer, Jonathan Shepard, Terje Spurkland, Jonathan Steinberg, Huguette Taviani-Carozzi and Chris Wickham. Many of these friends were also kind enough to send me photocopies of rare editions of texts and offprints of their own work, which have been of immeasurable help. Most of the ideas explored in this book, moreover, were initially formulated in the context of lectures and classes for undergraduates and research students in Cambridge, who provide an unfailingly stimulating and demanding audience. Despite all the efforts of government institutions to make working in a university in Britain an exhausting and demoralizing juggling act, it is the students who continue to make university teaching and research so enjoyable and worthwhile.

I was especially fortunate to be elected to a Hugh Baldson Fellowship at the British School at Rome in 2002 and should like to thank all at the School who helped to make my stay in Rome so productive and enjoyable. For assistance with visits to France (in connection with my collaborative research project with Dominique Iogna-Prat) I am indebted to the British Academy and the CNRS. I am grateful, as ever, for the support offered by the Principal and Fellows of Newnham College. I am particularly indebted to my audiences in Oxford, Paris and York in spring 2003 who commented on the material offered in the introduction. My greatest debt, however, is to my current and former graduate students in early medieval history in Cambridge, and to the gatherings of graduate students in Utrecht, Vienna and Cambridge since 1997 for the 'Texts and Identities' workshops, for the constant stimulus of their criticism and questions on all the topics discussed in this book. I should especially like to thank Helmut Reimitz, Max Diesenberger and Richard Corradini in Vienna for the work we have done together and the generous help they have given me.

As usual, I am indebted to Cambridge University Press and the unfailingly professional assistance and support they provide for their authors, but I wish here, in the year of his retirement, to acknowledge my long, happy and productive association with the History Editor William Davies. I am very grateful to Liz Hosier of the Faculty of History in the University of Cambridge, who gave me invaluable help with typing. My daughter Lucy has contributed in many ways to this book, both in practical assistance and with information and suggestions. But without my husband David the work for this book could not have been undertaken or completed; my lasting and most fervent thanks, as always, are to him.

Cambridge, September 2003

Acknowledgements

The cover picture is from the Psalterium Aureum (Golden Psalter) of St Gallen, Stiftsbibliothek MS 22, p. 140, produced in the second half of the ninth century (before 883). It depicts King David's general Joab setting out on campaign against the Syrians and Ammonites from the illustration to Psalm 59 and is one of the few historical narrative pictures to be found in Carolingian manuscripts. I am grateful to the Bibliothekar Ernst Tremp, and the Stiftsbibliothek St Gallen, for kindly permitting me to reproduce this page.

I am grateful to the following editors and publishers for kindly allowing me to make use in this book of work published in earlier versions: Paolo Chiesa, Wolfgang Haubrichs, Jörg Jarnut, Flavia de Rubeis, Marco Mostert, Meta Niederkorn, Anton Scharer, Georg Scheibelreiter and Susan Ridyard; Blackwell (*Early Medieval Europe*); Brepols and Utrecht University's Centre for Medieval Studies; Cambridge University Press; Centre d'études médiévales, Auxerre; Ecclesiastical History Society (*Studies in Church History*); Finnish Institute, Rome; Forschungsstelle für Geschichte des Mittelalters der Österreichischen Akademie der Wissenschaften, Vienna; Forum, Udine; Oxford University Press (*English Historical Review*); The University of the South (*Sewanee Medieval Studies*); Institut zur interdisziplinären Erforschung des Mittelalters und seines Nachwirkens, Paderborn; Oldenbourg Verlag; The Royal Historical Society of Great Britain (*Transactions of the Royal Historical Society*).

Abbreviations

Apart from the following, all works are cited in full at the first reference to them and susbsequently in short title form in each chapter. Full details may also be found in the Bibliography.

BAV	Rome, Biblioteca apostolica Vaticana
Bischoff, *Katalog*	Bernhard Bischoff, *Katalog der festländischen Handschriften des neunten Jahrhunderts (mit Ausnahme der wisigotischen) Teil I: Aachen-Lambach* (Stuttgart, 1998)
Bischoff, *Mittelalterliche Studien* I, II, III,	Bernhard Bischoff, *Mittelalterliche Studien*, 3 vols. (Stuttgart, 1966, 1967 and 1981)
Bischoff, *Schreibschulen*	Bernhard Bischoff, *Die Südostdeutschen Schreibschulen und Bibliotheken in der Karolingerzeit*, I: *Die Bayerischen Diözesen*, 3rd edn (Wiesbaden, 1974), II: *Die vorwiegend Österreichischen Diözesen* (Wiesbaden, 1980)
BnF	Bibliothèque nationale de France
c., cc.	capitulum, capitula
CCCM	*Corpus Christianorum, Continuatio Mediavalis* (Turnhout, 1966–)
CCSL	*Corpus Christianorum, Series Latina* (Turnhout, 1952–)
ChLA	*Chartae Latinae Antiquiores*, ed. Albert Bruckner, facsimile edition of the Latin charters prior to the ninth century 1– (Olten and Lausanne, 1954–)

CLA	E. A. Lowe, *Codices Latini Antiquiores: A Palaeographical Guide to Latin Manuscripts Prior to the Ninth Century* I–XI plus Supplement, Oxford (1935–71)
cod.	codex
CSEL	*Corpus Scriptorum Ecclesiasticorum Latinorum* (Vienna, 1866–)
DA	*Deutsches Archiv für Erforschung des Mittelalters*
EHR	*English Historical Review*
EME	*Early Medieval Europe*
fol.	folio
Innes and McKitterick 'Writing of history'	M. Innes and R. McKitterick, 'The writing of history', in R. McKitterick (ed.), *Carolingian culture: emulation and innovation* (Cambridge 1994), pp. 193–222
McKitterick, *Books, scribes and learning*	R. McKitterick, *Books, scribes and learning in the Frankish kingdoms, 6th–9th centuries* (Aldershot, 1994)
McKitterick, *Carolingians and the written word*	R. McKitterick, *The Carolingians and the written word* (Cambridge, 1989)
McKitterick, *Frankish kings and culture*	R. McKitterick, *The Frankish kings and culture in the early middle ages* (Aldershot, 1995)
McKitterick, *Migration*	R. McKitterick, *The migration of ideas in the early middle ages* (Cambridge, forthcoming)
McKitterick (ed.), *NCMH*	R. McKitterick (ed.), *The new Cambridge medieval history* II *c. 700–c.900* (Cambridge, 1995)
McKitterick, *Uses of literacy*	R. McKitterick (ed.), *The uses of literacy in early mediaeval Europe* (Cambridge, 1990)
MGH	*Monumenta germaniae historica*
AA	*Auctores antiquissimi*, 15 vols. (Berlin, 1877–1919)

Cap.	*Capitularia, legum sectio* II, *Capitularia regum francorum*, ed. A. Boretius and V. Krause, 2 vols. (Hannover, 1883–97)
Conc.	*Concilia, legum sectio* III, *Concilia*, II, ed. A. Werminghoff (Hannover, 1906–8), III, ed. W. Hartmann (Hannover, 1984)
Epp.	*Epistulae* III–VII (=*Epistulae merovingici et karolini aevi*, Hannover, 1892–1939)
Epp. Sel.	*Epistulae Selectae in usum scholarum*, 5 vols. (Hannover, 1887–91)
Fontes	*Fontes iuris germanici antiqui in usum scholarum ex Monumentis Germaniae Historicis separatim editi*, 13 vols. (Hannover, 1909–86)
Leges nat. germ.	*Leges nationum germanicarum*; ed. K. Zeumer (*Lex visigothorum*); L. R. de Salis (*Leges burgundionum*); F. Beyerle and R. Buchner (*Lex ribuaria*); K. A. Eckhardt (*Pactus legis salicae* and *Lex salica*); E. von Schwind (*Lex baiwariorum*); 6 vols. in 11 parts (Hannover, 1892–1969)
Poetae	*Poetae latini aevi carolini*, ed. E. Dummler, L. Traube, P. von Winterfeld and K. Strecker, 4 vols. (Hannover, 1881–99)
SRG	*Scriptores rerum germanicarum in usum scholarum separatim editi*, 63 vols. (Hannover, 1871–1987)
SRL	*Scriptores regum langobardicarum et italicarum saec. VI–IX*, ed. G. Waitz (Hannover, 1898)
SRM	*Scriptores rerum merovingicarum*, ed. B. Krusch and W. Levison, 7 vols. (Hannover, 1920)
SS	*Scriptores* in folio, 30 vols., Hannover (1826–1924)
MIÖG	*Mitteilungen des Instituts für Österreichische Geschichtsforschung*
MS	manuscript
ÖNB	Österreichische Nationalbibliothek
PL	*Patrologiae cursus completus, series latina*, ed. J.-P. Migne, 221 vols., Paris (1841–64)

RB	*Revue Bénédictine*
Reynolds, *Texts*	
and transmission	Reynolds, L. D. (ed.), *Texts and transmission. A survey of the Latin classics* (Oxford, 1983)
Scharer and Scheibelreiter,	
Historiographie	A. Scharer and G. Scheibelreiter (eds.), *Historiographie im frühen Mittelalter* (Munich and Vienna, 1994)
Settimane	Settimane di Studio del Centro italiano di studi sull' alto medioevo (Spoleto, 1954–)
TRHS	*Transactions of the Royal Historical Society*

1 Introduction: History and memory in the Carolingian world

History and memory in the Carolingian world, the title of both this book and this chapter, is at once a reflection of the current interest in the ways by which various medieval societies constructed and understood their pasts and an acknowledgement of the degree to which memory has become a much-explored and much-theorised topic. The book's principal themes are the writing and reading of history in the early middle ages, with a primary focus on the remarkable manifestations of historical writing in the Frankish kingdoms in the eighth and ninth centuries. Within this framework I consider what is meant by history books, and the Franks' choice of historical texts, whether of Roman, Christian, 'barbarian' or Frankish history: where they appear and where, when and for whom they were made. Further questions concern the readership of these history books and how far the physical characteristics of the Carolingian manuscripts in which the texts survive reveal anything of what contemporaries may have thought about these texts and their wider cultural context.

Historians of western, middle-eastern and oriental history have looked at the way a common past could inform what Eggert and Patzold in 1994, and in relation to Saxony in the early middle ages, called 'Wir-Gefühl', that is, a sense of 'us-ness'.[1] It has become a commonplace that ideas about the past could define societies and that the present plays a crucial role in moulding understanding of the past.[2] The focus of the study of medieval historical writing in particular, moreover, has shifted in recent

---

[1] W. Eggert and B. Patzold, *Wir-Gefühl und Regnum Saxonum bei frühmittelalterlichen Geschichtsschreibern* (Berlin, 1984).

[2] I draw in part here on M. Innes, 'Introduction', in Y. Hen and M. Innes (eds.), *The uses of the past in the early middle ages* (Cambridge 2000), pp. 1–8, but I have in mind also the early Islamic historiographical tradition: see A. al-D. al-Duri, *The rise of historical writing among the Arabs*, ed. and trans. L. Conrad (Princeton, 1983); A. Noth, *The early Arabic historical tradition: a source critical study*, 2nd edn in collaboration with L. Conrad, trans. M. Bonner (Princeton, 1994); F. Donner, *Narratives of Islamic origins. The beginnings of Islamic historical writing*, Studies in Late Antiquity and Early Islam 14 (Princeton, 1998); C. F. Robinson, *Islamic historiography* (Cambridge, 2003); B. Lewis, *History – remembered, recovered, invented* (Princeton, 1975). On government-sponsored histories and the work of the T'ang 'historiographical office' in the eighth and ninth centuries in China

1

years away from a preoccupation with sources of information and textual affiliation. Now historical narratives are studied both as constructed texts and bearers of memory which were targeted for particular audiences, and as an important element in the promotion of the political culture and identity of particular groups. Studies such as those assembled by Guenée, Magdalino, Scharer and Scheibelreiter, or Hen and Innes,[3] to cite only four among the best and most recent, have focussed above all on perceptions and uses of the past.

All take the so-called 'linguistic turn' and post-modernism into account to a greater or lesser extent, but have resisted the reduction of historiography to literary history.[4] Examination of authorial intention, of the audiences for history, and of manuscript traditions of the surviving texts to try to determine a text's meaning in context offer what Geary has described as 'escape routes' out of the 'prison house of language' and sterile notions of intertextuality.[5] But too zealous a pursuit of the escape routes threatens to undermine the potential value of historical narratives as representations of a contemporary memory of reality, as accounts of events and people and attitudes, or as powerful combinations of both objective and subjective interpretations of the past, however difficult these may be for modern historians either to reconstruct or to distinguish.

It is in this respect that memory and the imperative to record what is remembered have been invoked as well. Here the work on both the mechanisms and the rituals of remembering in the middle ages by such scholars as Carruthers, Coleman, Geary, Geuenich, Oexle, Schmid and Treitler, quite apart from the contributions of the anthropologists, have greatly enlarged our understanding of the sheer capacity for remembering as well as the creative forms mnemonic devices could take in the middle ages.[6]

---

see W. G. Beasley and E. B. Pulleybank, *Historians of China and Japan* (Oxford, 1969); D. McMullen, *State and scholars in T'ang China* (Cambridge, 1988); and D. Twitchett, *The writing of official history under the T'ang* (Cambridge, 1992).

[3] B. Guenée, *Le Métier de l'historien au moyen âge* (Paris, 1977); P. Magdalino (ed.), *The perception of the past in twelfth-century Europe* (London, 1992); A. Scharer and G. Scheibelreiter (eds.), *Historiographie im frühen Mittelalter* (Vienna, 1994); and Hen and Innes (eds.), *The uses of the past.*

[4] For a concise discussion of the 'linguistic turn' and its implications for the study of historical writing see W. Pohl, 'History in fragments: Montecassino's politics of memory', *EME* 10 (2001), pp. 343–74, especially pp. 343–54; and W. Pohl, *Werkstätte der Erinnerung: Montecassino und die Gestaltung der langobardischen Vergangenheit* (Vienna, 2001).

[5] P. Geary, 'Frühmittelalterliche Historiographie. Zusammenfassung', in Scharer and Scheibelreiter, *Historiographie*, pp. 539–42.

[6] M. Carruthers, *The book of memory. A study of memory in medieval culture* (Cambridge, 1990); J. Coleman, *Ancient and medieval memories. Studies in the reconstruction of the past* (Cambridge, 1992); P. Geary, *Phantoms of remembrance. Memory and oblivion at the end*

If historical narratives are statements about what people remember of the past as well as what they choose to forget, then the degree to which texts reflect collective memories needs to be further explored. Halbwachs's notion of the part shared memory plays in the self-definition of a social group has been wholeheartedly accepted by most historians and underpins Fentress and Wickham's rich account of what people in the past have done with respect to social memory.[7] I myself have taken the notion of 'shared memory' in the chapters of this book as something established by communication, whether oral or written. I have considered how recalled past experience and shared images of the past are the kinds of memories that have particular importance for the constitution of social groups.[8] I have also looked at the 'construction of the past', that is, the creation of accounts of past events that drew on memory but selected from it in distinctive ways that became accepted and thereafter shared by a group.[9] Nevertheless, the notion of 'shared memory' can only really be useful if tested, first of all, against the articulated memories of a specific group. Secondly, we should confront the problematic issues and methodological difficulties it raises, not least how we might be able to document how, or even whether, such accounts were indeed disseminated, known and accepted. It is with these issues in particular that this introductory chapter is concerned.

Because we are bound to concentrate on the surviving written evidence for the memory-keeping and historical composition of any group in the past, it may be helpful to look at an extract from the royal Frankish annals, first written at the end of the eighth century, in order to identify some of the main questions and methodological difficulties to which I have alluded.

In the entry for the year 788 which recounts the downfall of Tassilo, duke of Bavaria, and the annexation of his realm by his cousin Charlemagne, the annalist tells us that Charlemagne called an assembly

---

of the first millennium (Princeton, 1994); and *idem*, 'Land, language and memory in Europe, 700–1100', *TRHS* sixth series 9 (1999), pp. 169–84; K. Schmid and J. Wollasch (eds.), *Memoria. Der geschichtliche Zeugniswert des liturgischen Gedenkens im Mittelalter*, Münstersche Mittelalter-Schriften 48 (Munich, 1984); D. Geuenich and O.-G. Oexle (eds.), *Memoria in der Gesellschaft des Mittelalters*, Veröffentlichungen des Max Planck Instituts für Geschichte 111 (Göttingen, 1994); and L. Treitler, 'Homer and Gregory. The transmission of epic poetry and plainchant', *The Musical Quarterly* 60 (1974), pp. 333–72. For discussions of the role of gender see E. van Houts (ed.), *Medieval memories: men, women and their past 700–1300* (London, 2001). See also M. Innes. 'Memory, orality and literacy in an early medieval society', *Past and Present* 158 (1998), pp. 3–36.

[7] J. Fentress and C. Wickham, *Social memory* (Oxford, 1992); and see M. Halbwachs, *Les Cadres sociaux de la mémoire* (Paris, 1925) and *La Mémoire collective* (Paris 1950).

[8] See especially chapters 7 and 8.   [9] See especially chapters 3, 4, 5 and 6.

at Ingelheim (near Mainz on the Rhine) and that Tassilo came there with his *fideles*.

Bavarian *fideles* began to say that since giving his son and other hostages and taking oaths, Tassilo, incited by his wife Liutperga, had not maintained his faith (to Charlemagne) inviolate but had been seen to betray it. And Tassilo could not deny this but confessed that since then he had sent messengers to the Avars, had urged the vassals of Charlemagne to join him and had plotted their deaths. He has also ordered his *homines* to make mental reservations when they were swearing oaths and to swear deceitfully. What is more he confessed to having said that even if he had ten sons he would rather lose every one of them than accept that the agreements should remain as they were and that he would be better dead than living thus. And after he had been convicted of all these things, the Franks and the Bavarians, Lombards and Saxons, and those from every province gathered at that assembly, *remembering his earlier evil deeds and how he had even deserted the lord king Pippin on campaign* – which is called *harisliz* in German – saw fit to condemn him to death.[10] (My emphasis.)

My interest in this introductory chapter is not so much in the vivid picture of Tassilo's despair and hopeless defiance, nor how the narrative works as an account of the triumph of Charlemagne and of justice over the hapless Tassilo, for these have been fully explored by Matthias Becher and by Stuart Airlie.[11] What I wish to highlight are the implications of the phrase *reminiscentes priorum malorum eius* about remembering Tassilo's evil deeds and an earlier desertion of Pippin.

The Royal Frankish annals is the only text to refer to this remembrance on the part of the assembly. The revised version of the Royal Frankish annals, produced in the early years of the ninth century omits this statement.[12] Other texts drawing on the Royal Frankish annals, but writing later into the ninth century, such as the annals of Fulda, also omitted it. Only the more nearly contemporary 'Lorsch annal' entry for 788 refers in a more general way to how the assembly recalled all the wicked deeds Tassilo had done.[13]

The allusion in the Royal Frankish annals is to the desertion from Pippin's army in 763. Both Airlie and Becher commented on the

---

[10] *Annales regni francorum*, ed. F. Kurze, *MGH SRG*, VI (Hannover, 1895), p. 80; English translation P. D. King, *Charlemagne. Translated sources* (Kendal, 1987), p. 86.

[11] See S. Airlie, 'Narratives of triumph and rituals of submission: Charlemagne's mastering of Bavaria', *TRHS* sixth series 9 (1999), pp. 93–120; and M. Becher, *Eid und Herrschaft. Untersuchungen zum Herrscherethos Karls des Großen*, Vorträge und Forschungen Sonderband 39 (Sigmaringen, 1993).

[12] *Annales Einhardi*, ed. F. Kurze, *MGH SRG*, VI (Hannover, 1895), p. 81.

[13] *Annales lauresbamenses*, ed. G. Pertz, *MGH SS*, I (Hannover, 1826), pp. 22–39, at p. 33. See also the facsimile edition of ÖNB cod. 515: F. Unterkircher (ed.), *Das Wiener Fragment der Lorscher Annalen. Christus und die Samariterin. Katechese des Niceta von Remesiana. Codex Vindobonensis 515 der Österreichischen Nationalbibliothek Facsimile Ausgabe*, Codices Selecti 15 (Graz, 1967). See also below, pp. 104–10.

unlikelihood of either the Lombards or Saxons remembering something that had happened in 763, for neither people was even under Frankish rule, let alone part of the army. Neither Airlie nor Becher mentioned the possibility, however, that this memory was an allusion to something recorded in the annals themselves. Indeed, it is the annals which present the damning account of Tassilo's relations with his uncle Pippin III and Charlemagne, how he was given Bavaria to rule in 748, swore oaths of fidelity to Pippin III in 757, deserted the Frankish army in 763, renewed his oath of fidelity to Pippin's son Charlemagne in 781 and was forced to acknowledge his subordinate status in 787 with the handing over of hostages, including his own son.

The following questions emerge, therefore. In what sense was the memory described in the annals one that was part of collective memory? Who is included in the notion of 'collective memory'? Is the memory based on knowledge of the annals or a real memory among those at Ingelheim in 788 of disgraceful behaviour in 763? Does the allusion then support an early date for the composition of the annals? Is the 788 entry perhaps a witness to the expectation that this text would be in circulation and form the basis of subsequent knowledge? Is this why the Franks, Bavarians, Lombards and Saxons are credited with retrospective knowledge in this way? Was their knowledge formed by this particular piece of historical writing? The entry also underlines one of the fundamental difficulties in charting memory, namely that we are bound to do it from the evidence of surviving written texts and that these in their turn raise the problem of how we can determine the impact and influence of such an historical text. To suggest knowledge of the contents of a text is to make assumptions about the process of production, methods of circulation, speed of reception and the impact of the text itself, all of which must be tested. Thus we also need to consider the relevance of literacy to the extension and record of memory, and the degree to which literacy, and thus the recoverable indicators of memory, are the preserve of an elite.

It is easy to label literacy as the 'preserve of an elite' in the early middle ages but it is much harder to define it. It has, after all, become a commonplace, voiced by me as much as by everyone else, that the great majority of our sources are primarily those of the 'social elites' of early medieval Europe. These 'social elites' might be defined as the groups in society who had power or some measurable superiority in some sphere over other individuals or groups of people.[14] But what we all actually mean by saying that should be challenged. I have also maintained, for example, that the local charter evidence from centres all over western Europe and dating

---

[14] See R. Le Jan (ed.), *La Royauté et les élites dans l'Europe carolingienne (du début du IXe siècle aux environs de 920)*, Centre d'Histoire de l'Europe du Nord-Ouest 17 (Lille, 1998).

from the period from the seventh to the tenth centuries is an indication of the exploitation of literate modes by landowners down a social hierarchy that may have included peasant farmers and small-scale landowners.[15] Since 1989 a number of studies have explored the degree to which local lay communities used the written word for their legal transactions and played some role in their production or preservation in the early middle ages.[16] Even so, how great a proportion of the 'peasant' population, estimated at 90 per cent of the total in this period, had any regular access or customary familiarity with the written word?

I stress the words 'regular' and 'customary', for we should also remember that this is a world in which even a freed slave is known by the word *cartularius*, that is, 'charter man'.[17] It is a world in which religions of the book, Christianity, Islam or Judaism, predominate. In the Carolingian empire, above all, there is an insistence from the second half of the eighth century onwards on the central role of texts for the consolidation and harmonization of the Christian religious faith and practice, for the transmission of knowledge, and for the exercise of justice and government. In the course of the ninth century, even a written musical notation is developed to provide a written supplement for the transmission of melodies for the liturgical chant, hitherto passed on by cantors.[18] Certainly, the possession of the skills of writing may have been the preserve of the specially trained. Similarly, those who could read complex material, as distinct from those who could simply recognise the letters of the alphabet, may have formed an intellectual elite. This intellectual elite, owing to the limited opportunities for education, could also have been a social elite, though it is important to remember that Ebbo, archbishop

---

[15] McKitterick, *Carolingians and the written word*, pp. 77–134, in relation to the evidence of the St Gallen material.

[16] For discussions of Lorsch and Bavaria see M. Innes, *State and society in the early middle ages 400–1000* (Cambridge, 2000); and W. Brown, *Unjust seizure: conflict, interest and authority in an early medieval society* (Ithaca, 2001). For Italy see N. Everett, *Literacy in Lombard Italy, c. 568–774* (Cambridge, 2003). See also R. Schieffer, *Schriftkultur und Reichsverwaltung unter den Karolingern*, Abhandlungen der Nordrhein-Westfälischen Akademie der Wissenschaften (Opladen, 1996); and the studies emanating from the Utrecht University Centre for Medieval Studies *Pionier* Project on medieval communications: Marco Mostert (ed.), *New approaches to medieval communication*, Utrecht Studies in Medieval Literacy 1 (Turnhout, 1999); and K. Heidecker (ed.), *Charters and the use of the written word in medieval society*, Utrecht Studies in Medieval Literacy 5 (Turnhout, 2000). The new early medieval charter study project which younger scholars such as Warren Brown, Marios Costambeys, Adam Kosto and Matthew Innes are coordinating is likely to bring more valuable material to the fore.

[17] A point stressed by J. L. Nelson, 'Literacy in Carolingian government', in McKitterick (ed.), *Uses of literacy*, pp. 258–96.

[18] For the background see S. Rankin, 'Carolingian music', in R. McKitterick (ed.), *Carolingian culture: emulation and innovation* (Cambridge, 1994), pp. 274–316.

of Rheims, among others, was of humble origin and thus the extent to which the acquisition and possession of literate skills may have enabled an individual to cross other social barriers.[19]

If so many men and women in Carolingian Europe had some kind of access to written culture, however restricted in scope, right the way down the social scale, and if literacy could offer a passport into an elite group, then of what value is the concept of an elite at all? Should we rather regard access to a written culture as defining an elite? Did the possession of literate skills make one eligible to be or to become a member of the elite in the Carolingian world? To focus exclusively on levels of literacy in any social or political group defined according to criteria which do not include the criterion of literacy, therefore, is to miss the point. We should focus instead on the extent to which the exploitation of written culture provided the means for contemporaries at the time to define themselves as an elite. What really matters, therefore, is what men and women in the Carolingian world hoped to achieve by exploiting the written word and why they chose that medium of communication.

A more productive approach might be to look at the problem of the elites and written culture in the Carolingian world from the opposite direction. I propose to consider the idea of elites in relation to written culture as a phenomenon reflected in and thus defined by their use of texts, and especially historical texts. In particular I should like to pursue the possibility for the Carolingian period that there was an elite, lent cohesion by their particular use of the written word to provide that elite with a recorded memory, and thus identity, that would transcend other political or social divisions. If we consider how the past was understood by the Franks in the Carolingian period, that is, in the period from the eighth to the tenth centuries, and how a group placed itself in relation to that past, we may be able to see how that group becomes defined as an elite with special characteristics, and how the written texts act as an enabling mechanism in the expression of an elite memory and identity. In other words, the study of history and memory in the Carolingian world is a study both of the texts in which an elite defines itself and of the extant Carolingian manuscripts which provide the indications of the Franks' understanding of the past.

The understanding of history and the past in the Frankish kingdom embraced Roman, Christian and 'Germanic' (Lombard, Anglo-Saxon, Gothic and Frankish) history. Records of its past included historical

---

[19] On Ebbo see S. Airlie, 'Bonds of power and bonds of association in the court circle of Louis the Pious', in P. Godman and R. Collins (eds.), *Charlemagne's heir: new perspectives on the reign of Louis the Pious (814–840)* (Oxford, 1990), pp. 191–204.

chronological syntheses and narratives, and records of other kinds.[20] From the work recorded elsewhere in this book as well as still in progress, it seems clear that there was a concerted effort to acquire and copy history books throughout the Carolingian realm from the late eighth century onwards. There is also the well-known phenomenon of the remarkable number of contemporary histories written in the late eighth and the ninth centuries.[21] These two phenomena, that is, the copying of older history books and the writing of new history, are arguably related and interdependent. The possibility of a connection between the copying of older history, primarily in monastic scriptoria, and the composing of new history, incidentally also raises the issue of the distinctiveness of the role of the monastery itself in Carolingian record keeping and history writing, and the role monasteries may have played in the formation of Frankish perceptions of the past, but I shall have to leave detailed consideration of these to another occasion.

I have set out the evidence about the history books and history writing of the Carolingian world in the remaining chapters of this book. It is clear that, for the Franks, an understanding of the past worked at several levels and was manifested to them in a number of different textual contexts. What these Carolingian history books reveal is the interplay between memory, forms of historical record and the writing of history. It is this interplay which is an essential component of the process of defining an elite and a people. The books read and produced in Frankish centres indicate the formation of a sense of the past – biblical, Roman and Christian – to which the Franks collectively belonged and which they had inherited.

In their own history writing the Franks also show an impulse to forge an identity that explicitly placed the origin of the Franks in a far distant Roman and Trojan past. It is to the forging of this identity by means of the creation of a common memory in the form of a distinctive narrative that I now turn. There is only space to do so with specific reference to one example, the *Liber historiae francorum*, and the implications of one ninth-century copy of it now in Paris. With the *Liber historiae francorum* in this codex is the text of the *Annales regni francorum*. The association of complementary accounts of Frankish history and its implications will form the final section of this introductory chapter.

---

[20] For fuller discussion see below, chapters 7, 9 and 12.
[21] See Innes and McKitterick, 'Writing of history'; and for the general context see A. Momigliano, 'Pagan and Christian historiography in the fourth century A.D.', in A. Momigliano (ed.), *The conflict between paganism and Christianity in the fourth century* (London, 1962), pp. 79–99.

Frankish historical writing and the *Liber historiae francorum*

Although it provides evidence of the process of the reception of a complex cultural heritage, the interest in the Judaeo-Greco-Roman past needs to be used and developed in order to constitute evidence of the definition of an elite identity and the enhancement of historical memory. The *Liber historiae francorum* was one of the new Carolingian historical works produced in the eighth century and copied extensively in the ninth century. It constructs a specific past for a particular group of people. First of all, it provides them with a group memory and identity. Secondly, it places them, both culturally and historically, within the wider history of the Roman empire and Christian Roman Gaul. The *raison d'être* of this text, indeed, could be described as the definition of a people by means of its history. The *Liber historiae francorum* is customarily dated 727 due to its reference at the end to the sixth year of Theudebert (IV). From the outset the text insists that it is about both kings and the people of the Franks: let us present the beginnings of the kings of the Franks, the origins and deeds of the kings and those peoples (*Principium regum francorum eorumque origine vel gentium illarum ac gesta proferamus*).

The *Liber historiae francorum* is a short but remarkable history which has suffered unreasonable neglect. More crucially it has been underestimated as a piece of historical writing largely as a result of the way it is printed and presented in modern editions. Most of its earlier sections (apart from the first four chapters) are held to be so derivative from the sixth-century Gallo-Roman author Gregory of Tours as not to be worth mentioning. Attention has thus focussed more or less exclusively on the last eleven chapters, 43–53 (in which the *Liber historiae francorum* author writes a completely independent account of the seventh and early eighth centuries) without a consideration of how these chapters fit into the structure and message of the text as a whole.

Dependence on Gregory, however, is a misleading way in which to understand the *Liber historiae francorum* author's use of the earlier text. It would be far better to describe the process of composition as judicious selection, with some highly significant changes. Further, there are substantial additions. The changes and additions are most notable at the beginning of his work. Certainly the judicious use of Gregory is important, but more as a witness to Gregory's high status as a history book than as a symptom of derivative and impoverished history writers in the eighth century. The many small changes and larger insertions are even more significant, however. These, as we shall see, alter the emphasis in crucial ways which are entirely consistent with the opening chapters.

Above all, one needs to read the whole narrative as it is presented in the early manuscripts of the *Liber historiae francorum*. Although the whole text is undoubtedly printed in Krusch, even he diminished the impact of the text by presenting it visually as a text full of borrowings signalled in a much smaller typeface.[22] As a result he confuses the purpose of the original manuscripts. In the manuscripts, the *Liber historiae francorum* demands to be read on its own terms, for no such distinction is made. It should not be seen in terms merely of what is borrowed or new, but as a complete text with very distinctive emphases of its own. The themes of war and kingship and the elaborate account of the marriages and role of queens, of treasure, of devotion to particular saints and particular churches in Paris, are all reiterated throughout the text.

The *Liber historiae francorum* rejected Gregory's emphasis at the beginning of the work and Gregory's picture of biblical Franks as the new chosen people, with its emphatically Judaeo-Christian chronology and framework.[23] Instead, he or she (and it may well be the latter) provides a spirited alternative view of the Franks and their origins.[24] Thus the Franks' superiority in relation to other barbarian groups (Alans, Huns, Burgundians) is stressed and illustrated with the story of their origins. The text begins with a statement about the origins of the Franks. It locates them to Troy and thereafter to the refuge a group of Trojans found north-west of the Black Sea. They thus have historical, rather than mythical, origins. These historical origins are rooted in a past linked with Rome because of the association with Trojan origins. The author contrives nevertheless to convey a sense of Frankish superiority even over the early Romans.[25] Thus Aeneas, who is provided with the significantly pejorative

---

[22] *Liber historiae francorum*, ed. B. Krusch, *MGH SRM*, II (Hannover, 1888), pp. 241–328.

[23] For a useful context see M. de Jong (ed.), *The power of the word: the influence of the Bible on early medieval politics*, special issue, *EME* 7 (1998), pp. 261–357. Compare M. Garrison, 'The Franks as the new Israel? Education for an identity from Pippin to Charlemagne', in Hen and Innes (eds.), *The uses of the past*, pp. 114–61.

[24] R. Gerberding, *The rise of the Carolingians and the Liber historiae francorum* (Oxford, 1987), pp. 150–9, locates the author to Soissons but dismisses the notion that the text could have been produced at Notre-Dame, 'simply because it was a nunnery'! For an alternative view see J. L. Nelson, 'Gender and genre in women historians of the early middle ages', in Nelson, *The Frankish World 750–900* (London, 1996), pp. 183–97; and R. McKitterick, 'Frauen und Schriftlichkeit im Frühmittelalter', in H.-G. Goetz (ed.), *Weibliche Lebensgestaltung im frühen Mittelalter* (Cologne, Weimar and Vienna, 1991), pp. 65–118, and revised English version 'Women and literacy in the early middle ages', in McKitterick, *Books, scribes and learning*, chapter 13, pp. 1–43.

[25] See M. Innes, 'Teutons or Trojans? The Carolingians and the Germanic past' in Hen and Innes (eds.), *The uses of the past*, pp. 227–49; F. Graus, 'Troja und trojanische Herkunftssage im Mittelalter', in W. Erzgraber (ed.), *Kontinuität und Transformation der Antike im Mittelalter* (Sigmaringen, 1989), pp. 25–43; I. N. Wood, 'Defining the Franks: Frankish origins in early medieval historiography', in S. Forde, L. Johnson and A. V.

epithet of tyrant (*tyrannus*), fled to Italy but other Trojan leaders, Priam and Antenor, fled to the Moaetian marshes on the Don river and built the city Sicambra. It is from this branch, by implication more worthy of praise, that the Franks' history proceeds. As late as the fourth century their descendants are still called Trojans and have become allies of Rome to drive the Alans out of the Moaetian marshes (c. 2). Valentinian, the Roman Christian emperor, gives them the name of Franks (because they were hard-hearted and bold) but he taxed them once their ten-year agreement had lapsed and they thereupon revolted, with the declaration of the wish to be free. The Franks then were defeated by the Romans and fled to the Germanies (note that the phrase reflects the designation of Roman provinces) and lived under Marcomir, son of Priam, and Sumo, son of Antenor.

It is a weird chronology to be sure, but the emphases are rather interesting; they provide an alternative Roman connection and one in which Franks, although often driven hard and sometimes behaving badly, succeed in maintaining their independence.

It is that very independence and identity which is consolidated in the following chapters, in a variety of ways and not always with consistent approbation. In the early stages of their history, for example, the Roman emperor had kept his side of the bargain, namely, to remit taxes to the Franks if they assisted him against the Alans. As already remarked, the Franks rebelled when asked to pay taxes after those ten years had elapsed. Further on in the narrative, it is not just Fredegund who is criticized (though the author clearly also appreciates her wiliness, especially the godmother trick played on Queen Audovera and the successful plan to deceive the enemy army with a precursor of Birnam wood coming to Dunsinane);[26] some of the activities of the Merovingian kings are also regretted.

A full analysis of the whole import of the narrative of the *Liber historiae francorum*, especially for the portrayal of Merovingian kingship, is not possible here. For the moment, and in the context of my theme, I wish to stress a few points only. These relate most closely to the cultural identity of the Franks. First of all, in chapter 4, there is a brief account of the raising up of Faramund, Marcomir's son, as a *rex crinitus*. On the death of Faramund the Franks raised up Chlodio, his son, also with long hair, and the author claims that from this time they began to have long-haired

Murray (eds.), *Concepts of national history in the middle ages* (Leeds, 1995), pp. 47–59; and compare J. Barlow, 'Gregory of Tours and the myth of the Trojan origin of the Franks', *Frühmittelalterliche Studien* 29 (1995), pp. 86–95.

[26] *Liber historiae francorum*, cc. 31 and 36, pp. 293 and 305; compare William Shakespeare, *Macbeth*, Act V, Scene 5.

kings. We should register the significance of this being insisted upon in 727 as if to reinforce the legitimacy of the Merovingian line at a time when their actual power was beginning to be overshadowed by that of the Carolingian mayors of the palace. Throughout the text, moreover, there is a consistent acceptance of the importance of the election to the kingship and maintenance of a line of succession, most usually from father to son. The structure of the history reinforces this, in that each chapter tends to start with the death of another king by way of introducing the next phase of the story.

Secondly, it is during the reign of Faramund that the author chooses to locate the introduction of laws, expounded by four prominent men, Wisowastus, Wisogastus, Arogastus and Salegastus, who lived in villas beyond the Rhine called Bethagm, Salechagm and Widechagm. These laws, although those of the Franks and expounded by four leading men, were by implication supported and acknowledged by the kings. The same claim for the introduction of laws to the Franks is of course also made in the prologue to the law of the Franks known as the *Pactus legis salicae* in some of its redactions (though not the earliest) and embroidered further in the *Lex salica karolina*.[27] This portion of the story is indicative first of all of the close connection between historical and legal texts in general. Secondly it uncovers at least a tantalizing possibility of a link, involving the Carolingian royal court, between the author of the *Liber historiae francorum*, or a copy of his/her text, and the redactor of the *Lex salica* prologue. The conventional understanding is that this prologue was added to the *Lex salica* at some stage in the sixth century, despite the fact that it does not appear in the earliest (A, B) redactions but only in *Lex salica* manuscript 'C6' (Paris, BnF lat. 18237 from western France, s.IX/2), and various copies of the D, E and K versions, the earliest of which are the three 'E' redactions attributed to the *leges* scriptorium associated with the court of Louis the Pious and usually dated to the first quarter of the ninth century.[28] Quite apart from the difficulties the manuscript evidence presents for our understanding of the relationship between the various redactions of the *Lex salica*, the earliest manuscripts of the *Liber historiae francorum* also survive only from the late eighth and early ninth centuries. Thus the precise relationship or direction of influence between the *Lex salica* prologue and the *Liber historiae francorum*'s suggestion about the origin of the laws is difficult to determine. It is certainly very possible that the history inspired the author of the prologue rather than the other

---

[27] *Pactus legis salicae* and *Lex salica*, ed. K. A. Eckhardt, *MGH Leges nat. germ.* IV, 1 (Hannover, 1962), p. 2, and IV, 2 (Hannover, 1969), pp. 4 and 5.

[28] R. McKitterick, 'Zur Herstellung von Kapitularien: die Arbeit des Leges-Skriptoriums', *MIÖG* 101 (1993), pp. 3–16.

way about. Had the story been known to Gregory or to pseudo-Fredegar, would they not have used it?

It is also notable that a geography still conceived within the framework of Roman imperial administration is maintained. The author is anxious to stress that King Chlodio, the first real long-haired king, was based in the Roman province of Germania, that the Romans were on the west of the Rhine as far south as the Loire, that the Goths occupied the region beyond the Loire and that the Burgundians were clustered around Lyon. Chlodio subsequently settled in the region between Cambrai and the Somme river. Chlodio was there succeeded by his son Merovech, from whom the Merovingian line took its name. In keeping with the geographical ideas incorporated into many early medieval histories, recently studied by Andrew Merrills, the *Liber historiae francorum* maintains a notable insistence on political geography throughout the work.[29]

Finally, there is a signal prominence given to the role of the queens, especially Clothild (*Chrotildis*), wife of Clovis, first king of the Franks. Indeed, a veritable *gesta Clothildis* is inserted into the *Liber historiae francorum*. The *gesta* of Clothild occupy page after page in the manuscript copies. There are details of Clovis' courtship of Clothild, her marriage, her advice to rulers, the baptism of the king, the baptism of her children, her endowment of churches, her management of her sons and thus of the succession, and an insistence on pious devotion to the church and the special royal association with the churches of St Victor, St Geneviève and St Peter in Paris. Clothild also becomes a role model for subsequent queens in the narrative, with the marriage, sons, death and burial of queens faithfully recorded. The queen as a source of legitimacy for the royal line and the queen as fount of Christian piety are thus twin preoccupations of the author. This is cleverly reinforced (by dramatic repetition of phrasing as well as the actual content of the text) by Queen Clothild's unequivocal association with the baptism of the king, of the army, of his sisters and of the whole Frankish people.

The manuscript transmission: the example of Paris, BnF lat. 10911

The copying of a text is one important indicator of its reception as well as for the process of the dissemination of the particular representation of a group. Some indication of the dissemination of copies of the *Liber historiae francorum* in the early Carolingian empire can be gained from the manuscript transmission. These codices provide some hint, indeed,

---

[29] A. Merrills, *History and geography in late antiquity* (Cambridge, 2005).

that the Carolingians, if not actually promoting the text, certainly appear to have associated themselves with it and thus conceived their own history in direct relation to the story it contained. The extent to which the *Liber historiae francorum* provides an alternative, or even preferred, view of the Frankish past and of Frankish status to the ones presented in other contemporary Frankish histories needs to be addressed more fully than can be done here. I have remarked elsewhere, moreover, that so far insufficient attention has been paid to the Carolingian edition of Fredegar,[30] though Helmut Reimitz is now considering the implications of the Carolingian transmission of the six-book version of Gregory of Tours' *Historiae*.[31]

Out of thirty-two extant manuscripts of the *Liber historiae francorum*, fifteen date from the later eighth, the ninth or the early tenth centuries. All come from the westerly and Rhineland areas of the Carolingian empire. A number of these contain the *Liber historiae francorum* text only, though in at least two instances the manuscripts would appear to be incomplete. The five codices in which the *Liber historiae francorum* text is combined with other Frankish histories, such as the *Vita Karoli* or with the *Annales regni francorum* or other Frankish annals, in particular, merit further attention. They need, furthermore, to be set beside the manuscript transmission of Gregory of Tours on the one hand and of Fredegar on the other, quite apart from the massive documentation of the manuscript transmission of Einhard's *Vita Karoli*,[32] and the dissemination of the *Annales regni francorum* in composite Frankish history books. The Lorsch

---

[30] See chapter 2 below and the preliminary study by R. Collins, *Fredegar*, Authors of the Middle Ages and Religious Writers of the Latin West IV, no. 13 (Aldershot, 1996), who is preparing a new edition of Fredegar's Chronicle.

[31] Helmut Reimitz, 'Social networks and identities in Frankish historiography. New aspects of the textual history of Gregory of Tours' *Historiae*', in R. Corradini, M. Diesenberger, and H. Reimitz (eds.), *The construction of communities in the early middle ages: texts, resources and artefacts*, The Transformation of the Roman World 12 (Leiden, 2003), pp. 229–268 and plates 1–3; and H. Reimitz, 'Der Weg zum Königtum in historiographischen Kompendien der Karolingerzeit', in J. Jarnut and M. Becher (eds.), *Historiographie und Identität in den fränkischen Regna der Merowinger- und Karolingerzeit* (forthcoming). I am very grateful to Helmut Reimitz for discussion of Paris, BnF lat. 10911, his kindness in letting me read his paper 'Der Weg zum Königtum' in advance of publication, and stimulating discussions on matters to do with Frankish historiography in general. Paris, BnF lat. 10911 is one of the three codices being prepared in a digital edition by R. Corradini, K. Giesriegl and H. Reimitz, *Drei fränkische Geschichtsbücher aus der Karolingerzeit: Paris Bibliothèque nationale lat. 10911, Vienna ÖNB lat. 473, St Petersburg, NLR lat. F.v.IV.4.* See also M. Heinzelmann and P. Bourgain, 'L'Œuvre de Grégoire de Tours: la diffusion des manuscrits', in N. Gauthier and H. Galinié (eds.), *Grégoire de Tours et l'espace gaulois. Actes du congrès international Tours, 2–5 novembre 1994*, 13e supplément à la Revue Archéologique du Centre de la France (Tours, 1997), pp. 273–317.

[32] See the comprehensive study provided by M. Tischler, *Einharts Vita Karoli. Studien zur Entstehung, Überlieferung und Rezeption*, 2 vols., MGH Schriften 48 (Hannover, 2001).

fragment of the *Liber historiae francorum* (Paris, BnF lat. 7906) combines it with sections from the *Aeneid* and Dares Phrygius and thus concentrates on the origin of the Franks and the wanderings of those who survived the Trojan war. This suggests that Virgil's *Aeneid* was also a history book for the Franks.[33]

All these constitute important evidence for the exploitation of the written word, both to promote and to inculcate a particular sense of identity. I should like here to comment briefly, therefore, on only one of the examples of a composite Frankish history book, namely, Paris, BnF lat. 10911. It was written by a single scribe, possibly in Paris, in sloping early caroline minuscule and is probably to be dated to the first third or second quarter of the ninth century.[34] The consistency of the presentation of the text as well as the single hand responsible suggests that this is a very particular and deliberate design rather than a mere assemblage of related texts.

The manuscript reminds the reader forcefully of the historical context in which this history was written, for it enhances the message of the *Liber historiae francorum* as a history of Frankish kings, Frankish queens and *gens francorum* by using it to preface the *Annales regni francorum*.[35] The former text, after all, composed *c.* 727, was effectively written from the vantage point of the emergence and triumph of Charles Martel and at the point when Dagobert III, raised in the monastery of Chelles, is made king of the Franks in Neustria. To my mind this can with hindsight be seen as a premonition, if nothing more, of the rule of the Carolingian mayors of the palace and the short reign of the last Merovingian king of all. Childeric III was also taken from a monastery, and relegated to a monastery once more on his deposition in 751. Certainly the connection between the *Liber historiae francorum* and the triumph of the Carolingian mayors and kings is made in the early Carolingian period.[36] That Charles Martel is regarded as the real hero of the earlier part of the story in the eyes of the scribe at least is also indicated by the text's headings suddenly breaking out into red rustic capitals with Charles's triumph over the Saracens.

---

[33] R. A. Gerberding, 'Paris, Bibliothèque Nationale latin 7906: an unnoticed very early fragment of the "Liber historiae francorum", *Traditio* 43 (1987), pp. 381–6. For further on the *Aeneid* see McKitterick, *Migration*.

[34] For some comments on this manuscript in relation to Einhard's text see Tischler, *Einharts Vita Karoli*, pp. 1156–8. There, however, Tischler makes the palaeographically improbable suggestion that the manuscript is from Fleury and is to be dated to the late ninth century. He also does not consider what its relationship to Bern, Burgerbibliothek 599, definitely from Fleury, might be.

[35] On the *Annales regni francorum* see below, chapters 4, 5 and 6. Compare the independent comments of R. Collins, 'The "Reviser" revisited: another look at the alternative version of the *Annales regni francorum*', in A. C. Murray (ed.), *After Rome's fall: narrators and sources of early medieval history. Essays Presented to Walter Goffart* (Toronto, 1998), pp. 191–213.

[36] Gerberding, *The rise of the Carolingians*.

Incidentally, another Carolingian copy of the *Liber historiae francorum* in Paris, BnF lat. 5596 (s.IX, possibly from St Germain-des-Prés) reinforces the perception of the *Liber historiae francorum* as the pre-history of the Carolingian rulers by highlighting the names with enlarged initials and a line of red capitals or uncials. It treats the emergence of Pippin II and Charles Martel in the same way. In this codex the *Liber historiae francorum* is combined with the *Vita sancti Remigii*, which of course also gave prominence to the baptism of Clovis and the role of Clothild. It thus serves to reinforce the message in the *Liber historiae francorum*. Further, in the text of the latter, the naming of the Franks by the Emperor Valentinian, the names of the lawgivers in the reign of Faramund and the career of Clovis are highlighted, as is the emphasis on the ruler in each chapter. Notes, furthermore, have been inserted by a Carolingian reader anxious to get the lines of royal succession (and the names of the royal wives) straight. The manuscript thus contrives to place the history of the Franks as an extension of that of fifth-century Gaul by the simple expedient of visual markers and layout. It suggests that the perspective offered in BnF lat. 10911 was not an isolated one.

Krusch's edition obscures other significant elements of BnF lat. 10911's arrangement of the text. The *Liber historiae francorum* text is actually divided into chapters 1–51 and ends with the initial triumph of Charles Martel over Ragamfred and Chilperic. Krusch had created fifty-three chapters by dividing chapter 5 into two parts at *Ipse itaque Merovechus genuit filius nomine Childericum*. He also divided chapter 48 into two (= 49 and 50). The narrative is then augmented by a rearrangement of a selection of chapters from the Continuations to Fredegar's *Chronicle*, bringing the story to the death of Charles Martel. Thereafter in Paris, BnF lat. 10911, the *Annales regni francorum* continue the narrative with the first entry recording the death of Charles Martel.

The *Annales regni francorum* 741 restarts at chapter 1 on fol. 56r. This is also the beginning of a new quire, with a large DCCXLI written in red uncial and the first letter of *Carlus* written in red, as a consciously new text. At DCCL the text pauses. Six lines are left blank and so is the following verso, so that this decade-long period before the assumption of the kingship by the Carolingian family forms a short epoch in itself, recording the competition presented to Pippin by Carloman and Grifo and the emergence of Pippin alone. This section is thus also distinguished visually from the rest by isolating it in the manuscript. Entries for 751 and 752 are absent, and as far as this scribe is concerned they were missing, for space was left for them as well as chapter numbers notionally assigned; the next entry, for 753, is numbered c. 13 and thus cc. 11 and 12 are absent. The text then runs to c. 73 for 813 and the entries for 814 onwards are not numbered. This suggests that one exemplar may have offered the text either only as far as 814 or distinguished it in some way with special headings (as Vienna, ÖNB cod. 473 does).[37]

This can be set out schematically as follows:

LHF I-LI

LHF LII = Fred. Cont. 10

LHF LIII = Fred. Cont. 11 (final section), 12, 13

LHF LIIII = Fred. Cont. 14, 15, 16, 17, 18, 19

LHF LV = Fred. Cont. 20–24 (to 741)

ARF I-LXXIII = *Annales regni francorum* 741–813 (that is Charles Martel, Pippin and Charlemagne)

ARF 814–829 (Louis the Pious)

The scribe distinguished between the sections by use of different scripts and the structure of the book. Not only do the *Annales regni francorum* start on a new quire but the sections taken from the Continuations of Fredegar's *Chronicle* and conflated into a differently structured narrative are distinguished by means of capitals and elaborate headings. For chapters 52–4 there are headings in rustic capitals or half uncial, and summaries of the chapters. The famous and problematic calculation of years from the Continuations to Fredegar's *Chronicle*, chapter 16, starts a new quire (fol. 49r). Originally this quire may have contained three and a half empty folios (fols. 52v, 53–55v) which were only filled in the late twelfth or early thirteenth century with a letter purporting to be from Alexander the Great to Aristotle.[38] The *Annales regni francorum* section, therefore, which starts in the following quire, may originally have proceeded after a substantial gap in the manuscript. Although the sewing of the binding now makes it difficult to be certain, it is possible, however, that the quire containing most of the reorganized sections from the Continuations of Fredegar's *Chronicle* in fact originally ended on fol. 52v, forming a quire of four leaves. The twelfth-century scribe may then have used the final blank leaf of the original quire and added three single leaves to accommodate the rest of his own text. Whatever the case, it is clear that the Carolingian scribe distinguished codicologically between the *Liber historiae francorum* and added sections from the Continuations of Fredegar's *Chronicle* on the one hand, and the *Annales regni francorum* text on the other. Yet he also preserved the sense of continuity by maintaining the same generous margins and spacious layout throughout the manuscript. Further, the *Annales regni francorum* replicates the structure of the *Liber*

[37] See below, pp. 122 and 215.

[38] For Bibliography and context see the entry for Alexander in the *Lexikon des Mittelalters* I (Stuttgart, 1999), col. 356.

historiae francorum with its emphasis, in the first words of the initial series of chapters, on the ruler or else the main protagonist in each chapter.

1. **Carlus** maior domus defunctus
2. Quando **Carlomannus et Pippinus**
3. Tunc **Carlomannus et Pippinus**
4. Iterum **Carlomannus et Pippinus**
5. Tunc **Carlomannus** confessus est **Pippino germano suo**
6. Tunc **Carlomannus** Romam perrexit
7. **Grifo** fugivit in Saxoniam
8. **Grifo** de Saxonia ... pervenit
9. **Burghardus** ... **Fulradus**
10. **Pippinus** secundum morem francorum electus est ad regem

The addition of the *Annales regni francorum* and compression of text from the Continuations of Fredegar to this manuscript also contrives, by this clever juxtapositioning, to present the *Liber historiae francorum* from the Carolingian perspective. It belittles the succession of Merovingian kings, Chilperic, Chlothar, Theoderic son of Dagobert, mentioned in c. 53 and makes no reference to the last Merovingian king Childeric III at all.

The manuscript presentation thus makes the whole story of the origin, kingship, cleverness of queens, law making and Christianity of the Franks into a prelude to the triumph of the Carolingian house, where these themes are taken up and elaborated. It is entirely consistent, for example, that it should be only in this copy of the *Annales regni francorum* that the deaths of Queen Hildegard and Queen Bertha are noted under 783. The compilation suggests that the *Liber historiae francorum* was in fact rather greater an inspiration for the royal Frankish annalist than has hitherto been imagined.

In effect, therefore, BnF lat. 10911 presents a Carolingian history book which sets the rise and triumph of the Carolingian rulers Charles Martel, Pippin III and Charlemagne in the context of the early emergence of the Franks from a specifically Trojan, Roman and at least geographically germanic past. But it is the Franks who emerge triumphant once they occupy Gaul. The *Liber historiae francorum*, and especially this Carolingian packaging of it, thus serves as a statement of confidence in the process of Frankish identity. It records, moreover, in its emphases and omissions as well as in the adjustments and additions to Gregory's text, the kind of reception, selection and rejection of aspects of the Frankish past which were both a part of that process of a formation of identity and a reflection of it. The *Liber historiae francorum* is an uncompromising statement of the group identity of the Franks and constructs a specific past that places them, both culturally and historically, within the wider history of the Roman empire and Christian Frankish Gaul. The combination of the *Liber historiae francorum* with the triumphalist *Annales regni francorum* presents, in effect, a strong definition of an elite to contemporaries in the Carolingian world, and to posterity.

So far so good, but we then have to consider the problem of the manuscripts themselves. Who might have read them? How effective was the dissemination of the texts they contained and who was responsible? Thus this codex containing the *Liber historiae francorum* and the *Annales regni francorum* needs to be set within the context of the transmission of the latter and all the uncertainties and puzzles that arise in consequence.

The major problem with the *Annales regni francorum* 741–829 is that not one of the surviving manuscripts can be regarded as the original. What we have are copies from the time of Charlemagne's grandsons. Although there are a number of ninth-century copies, none survives from the late eighth century and the earliest copy, Paris, BnF lat. 10911 discussed above, dates from *c.* 830. The *Annales regni francorum* purportedly survive in five versions, known as A, B, C, D and E, defined by their late nineteenth-century editor Kurze according to the groups of manuscripts with related portions of the texts (A up to 788, B up to 813, C and D up to 829 but with particular variants: thus D is distinguished from C (and A and B) because it includes the notes about the conspiracies of 785 and 792 against Charlemagne led by Hardrad and Pippin the Hunchback respectively. The revised version of the *Annales regni francorum*, that is, the 'E' or 5th redaction, was once known as the *Annales Einhardi*. It actually only revises the text from 741–801. Kurze thought the E version from 802 to 829 was dependent on D. All the (many) manuscripts of E were thought by Kurze to go back to one archetype, 'Ex', in which the Annals were linked with the *Vita Karoli* of Einhard.

The oldest of these manuscripts, Vienna, ÖNB lat. 510, is unfortunately late tenth century so the problem of the E recension in terms of its original dissemination is even worse than for all the other versions. Kurze tried to work out how the text was constructed, and thought in precisely these terms, of construction rather than composition. For him it was more a copying process and only towards the end of his discussion does he introduce the idea of the 'original' and authorship. His stemma is a clear visual presentation of the hypotheses and intermediaries he proposed in order to take account of the sequence of apparent borrowing, repetitions, errors in common and the like.[39]

---

[39] *Annales regni francorum*, pp. V–XIX; and the fuller study F. Kurze, 'Ueber die karolingischen Reichsannalen von 741–829 und ihre Ueberarbeitung. 1: Die handschriftliche Ueberlieferung', *Neues Archiv* 19 (1894), pp. 295–339; and 'Zur Ueberlieferung der karolingischen Reichsannalen und ihrer Ueberarbeitung', *Neues Archiv* 28 (1903), pp. 619–69.

The various recensions Kurze proposed in their turn have led to hypotheses about the sequence of composition. Kurze interpreted the dates at which particular recensions stopped as an indication of original batches of annals – one to 788, another taking the story to 813, later continued to 829. The manuscripts themselves certainly reflect texts truncated in this way, but whether this is as part of a larger design in the compilation of historical miscellanies, or due to the original circulation of the text in a number of recensions to which other sections were gradually added, is difficult to determine. Further, the *Annales regni francorum* are regarded as 'official' court-based history. The problem with this of course is how can we work out how or whether the court might determine either content or distribution.

The attraction of Kurze's theoretical framework for the composition of the *Annales regni francorum*, of course, is that it envisages a major effort to record the early rise to prominence of Pippin and Charlemagne, and then a further reflection on Charlemagne's reign at the end of it, around the time that his heir Louis the Pious was crowned. The degree to which the manuscripts may be able to throw light on the original conception, process of composition and dissemination of the annals nevertheless seems to me to be very limited. Despite, or because of this, it has prompted a great deal of speculation. It is important, however, to be clear about the basis on which we are speculating. An analysis based on the printed text alone, without taking the manuscripts into account, is simply inadequate. The manuscript dissemination may nevertheless be able to illuminate the perception of the Frankish past subsequently, in the reigns of Louis the Pious and his sons Lothar, Louis the German and Charles the Bald, as well as the subsequent circulation of Frankish history in the later ninth century and the course of the tenth century.[40]

What this leaves unresolved is the status of the text either as historical record, or as a statement of a particular memory of the Frankish past. If the manuscript witnesses are regarded as reflections of particular preferences in memory and the selection of what was wanted from the past to hand on to posterity, then each manuscript has a great deal to disclose. Any effort at total reconciliation of accounts and perspectives will probably be fruitless, nor is it necessarily advantageous. What the Frankish annals manuscripts point to above all is a number of alternative histories and alternative memories of the Frankish past. The early history of the Franks and Carolingians is remarkably widely circulated, in many permutations and combinations, including the *Annales mettenses priores*,[41]

---

[40] See below, pp. 101–13.
[41] See Y. Hen, 'The Annals of Metz and the Merovingian past', in Hen and Innes (eds.), *The uses of the past*, pp. 175–90.

the Annals of Fulda,[42] the *Chronicon laurissense breve*, the Continuations of Fredegar, the *Annales regni francorum*, and the dozens of so-called minor annals that remain to be analysed.[43] Such a rich dissemination is crucial for our assessment of the formation of an historical memory of the origin of the Franks and the rise and triumph of the Carolingian family.

A further questions remains: If the *Annales regni francorum* is court-based, official history, is there any discernible role played by the court in the dissemination of this particular rendering of the Frankish past? Of all the manuscripts surveyed by Kurze and discussed by everyone else since, only two, St Petersburg Saltykov-Schedrin Library F.v.IV.4 and Vienna, ÖNB cod. 473, have any links with a Carolingian court (both, as it happens, with that of Charles the Bald) and both are part of composite presentation manuscripts.[44]

There is, however, one early fragment of the *Annales regni francorum*, not known to Kurze, and apparently ignored by, or unknown to, every subsequent commentator. This is Cologne fragment Sankt Maria in Kapitol AII/18, dated s.IX 1/3 and containing the E text entry for the year 824 but with some variants.[45] It is a single leaf, desperately frail and thin, with the script made very difficult to decipher as a consequence. It witnesses to a court-associated copy of the revised text of the Frankish annals and may well be the archetype of E1–E8 whose existence was supposed by

[42] It is too often forgotten that the Annals of Fulda start in 714 with the career of Charles Martel and present in their entirety an interestingly different perspective on the career of the early Carolingian rulers: ed. F. Kurze, *Annales fuldenses sive annales regni francorum orientalis*, MGH SRG VII (Hannover, 1891).

[43] These fill G. Pertz (ed.), *MGH SS*, I and II (Hannover, 1826 and 1829) with others in *MGH SS*, XV (Hannover, 1887); and see R. McKitterick, *The Frankish kingdoms under the Carolingians, 751–987* (London, 1983), pp. 3–5. J. Davis made a start on an analysis of thirty-nine of these 'minor annals' in 'Conceptions of kingship under Charlemagne' (unpublished M.Litt. dissertation, University of Cambridge, 1999), pp. 173–83.

[44] For an account of the contents of St Petersburg F.v.IV.4, see Tischler, *Einharts Vita Karoli*, pp. 1163–76, and see note 31 above. For the Vienna codex see H. Reimitz, 'Ein karolingisches Geschichtsbuch aus Saint-Amand und der Codex Vindobonensis palat. 473', in C. Egger and H. Weigl (eds.), *Text-Schrift-Codex. Quellenkundliche Arbeiten aus dem Institut für Österreichische Geschichtsforschung*, MIÖG Ergänzungsband (Vienna and Munich, 2000), pp. 34–90, and below, chapter 5.

[45] This fragment was first signalled by B. Bischoff, 'Die Hofbibliothek Ludwig dem Frommen', in J. J. G. Alexander and M. T. Gibson (eds.), *Medieval learning and literature. Essays presented to Richard William Hunt* (Oxford, 1976), pp. 3–22, and in English translation (by M. Gorman), in B. Bischoff, *Manuscripts and libraries in the age of Charlemagne*, Cambridge Studies in Palaeography and Codicology 1 (Cambridge, 1994), pp. 76–92, at p. 90, there with the old signature of Capsula 34.I. It was also discussed by L. Kolarova, 'The transmission and dissemination of Carolingian annals' (unpublished M.Phil. dissertation, University of Cambridge, 1995). I am most grateful to Dr Joachim Oepen of the Historisches Archiv des Erzbistums Köln for his kindness in sending me information and photographs of this remarkable fragment. See also p. 130 below.

Kurze. It raises the possibility, therefore, of the royal court being directly associated with the dissemination of at least one version of the Frankish past.

I have suggested in this introductory chapter that Frankish history books, containing both new and old texts, reflect a particular exploitation of the potential of written culture in the Carolingian world. They supplied an arsenal of past precedent and knowledge and a statement about present identity. They imply a potential audience for these texts and provide the means for their dissemination. Taken together the texts and extant manuscripts constitute the self-defining action of an elite and the use of history texts to shape shared memory. In these Frankish historical texts we see the use of the written word to persuade contemporaries and posterity of the importance and status of the Franks. But in shaping memory, the Franks drew on a host of written versions and records of the past. The annals I have discussed are simply the most prominent among many variant compilations disseminated throughout the Frankish world. Fortunately we do not have to rely solely on these narratives for an understanding of their relation to reality, for there is a host of documentary, legal and epistolary material with which to compare them. Nevertheless, the great variety of reception and dissemination of history texts mirrored in the ninth-century manuscripts is an unequivocal indicator of the sheer extent of the network of a shared memory of Frankish history in the early middle ages. It is to the documentation of this shared memory and history in its extraordinary variety in the Carolingian world that the following chapters are devoted.

In the next chapter, on Carolingian history books, I take up the issue of determining the purpose and subsequent audience for early medieval historical texts on the basis of the evidence provided by surviving manuscripts and their dissemination, and develop therefore a major theme this introduction has also addressed. The manuscripts enable modern historians to assess the status of the text and to place them in an appropriate historical context. This chapter discusses the manuscript tradition of the *Liber pontificalis*, Einhard's *Vita Karoli*, the *Annales fuldenses* and Fredegar's Chronicle. It assesses the implications of the survival and record of copies in the early middle ages of Roman and early Christian historiography. Finally, it discusses the implications of three major historical miscellanies or history books, one in St Omer, one in Lucca and the third the so-called 'Verona miscellany', which is now divided into four volumes, two each in Berlin and St Petersburg. Here the agenda of the compiler is crucial for determining the purpose of the collection as a whole and suggesting its possible audience. I argue that all historical writing can be transformed to serve a particular author's or compiler's specific purpose in relation to whatever audience or audiences the author or compiler may have had in mind.

In the third chapter, I turn to the question of the particular audience initially envisaged for a particular text in relation to Paul the Deacon's *Historia langobardorum* (History of the Lombards). The conquest of Lombardy in 774 is universally recognized, both by contemporaries and by modern historians, to have been one of the most momentous events in Charlemagne's reign. Yet the process by which Charlemagne consolidated his rule in the Lombard kingdom of Italy, and the cultural and religious consequences of 774 for both Franks and Lombards, are far less easy to determine. In this chapter I argue that it is in the context of Paul the Deacon's political involvement both before and after the Frankish conquest that all his writings, and especially the *Historia langobardorum*, should be seen. I look at both the content of the *Historia langobardorum* and the manuscript tradition and transmission of the work. I suggest that Paul's history might be better understood as a very skilful piece of image-making about the Lombards' past and identity on behalf of the Lombards for the Franks, either in Francia itself or for the Franks and Lombards at the court of Pippin of Italy. The History was designed to serve a particular function, namely, to instruct the Franks about the Lombard past and provide some measure of legitimation of Carolingian rule. What can be put together about its reception suggests that it was successful. In short, the *Historia langobardorum* is a very active contribution to the shaping of Frankish and Lombard relations and the understanding of kingship in the aftermath of 774.

The next three chapters form a group. They continue the discussion of the shaping of perceptions of kingship already touched on in chapter 3 but concentrate in particular on the forging of Frankish identity. In chapter 4, 'The Carolingians on their past', I argue that the *Annales regni francorum* forge a Frankish identity by constant reiteration and triumphal narrative. The ruler and the Franks are the achievers and together create the great realm. Consolidated within an historical and Christian framework, this is the message passed on to their contemporaries and to posterity. The insistence on precise chronology according to the year of the Incarnation is a deliberate device to enhance a very determined expression of the Franks' identity and cultural affiliations. I am concerned with the construction of a past by the Franks, its coherence and consistency, and the degree to which such a construction constitutes the formation of the collective memory of the newly formed Frankish people under Carolingian rule. I focus on the *Annales regni francorum* as one highly influential historical narrative that constructed so powerful an image of Frankish society and its events, and evoked such a convincing sense of identity, that it is their version of the Frankish past that has been remembered, and believed, ever since.

Chapter 5, 'Politics and history' serves as a companion piece to the preceding chapter, for it takes up the issue of the dissemination of the *Annales regni francorum* within the Carolingian empire in the ninth century. It also takes up one of the challenges I offered in chapter 2 concerning historical compilations. It begins as a study of a single manuscript but it implicates all other Carolingian codices containing historical texts. It focusses in particular on a royal history book, Vienna, ÖNB cod. 473, probably written in 869. It included the Frankish annals with other historical texts (such as the *Liber pontificalis*, the *Liber historiae francorum* and *Vita Karoli* of Einhard) to create an extraordinarily significant and important book. Such a collection exposes the necessity to explore the implications of the dissemination of Carolingian historiography in terms not only of the specific political impetus for the initial production of each text but also of their subsequent impact and use.

In chapter 6, 'Kingship and the writing of history', I examine the creation of a particular image of royal and Frankish power. I test the hypothesis that the writing of history in the Frankish world was not simply a matter of an observer recording, or even selecting judiciously, disingenuously or with deliberate intent to mislead, from events as they happened. I make the case for the need to register the formation of an historical sensitivity by means of the other texts which a particular author of an historiographical work might have encountered, as well as the formation of a collective memory, understanding and interpretation of what had happened. My particular focus is the account in the royal Frankish annals of the usurpation of the Merovingian throne by the Carolingian mayor of the palace Pippin III. I argue that the claim that the Pope had sanctioned the deposition of the last Merovingian king in 751 is a piece of creative mythmaking on the part of the annalist for political and ideological reasons. This claim had an astonishing resonance in political thinking and ideas about the French constitution thereafter. I suggest, therefore, that the pope's first involvement in the political affairs of the Frankish kingdom was not until 753/4 and that Pippin's apologists created a very particular understanding of the making and early years of Carolingian royal power that has misled historians and political theorists ever since.

The following two chapters then take up the wider themes of social memory and history and the different manifestations of their expression that can be observed in surviving Carolingian documents. Both in chapters 7 and 8, therefore, I discuss cartularies and *Libri memoriales*, where there is a conjunction of an historical sense of the past, attachment to geographical place, commemoration, record and writing. *Libri memoriales*, first written in the Carolingian period, survive from Brescia, Durham, Passau, Pfäfers, Reichenau, Remiremont, Salzburg, St Gallen and Winchester. I examine the continental books in particular, notably the *Liber memorialis* of Remiremont and the *Liber vitae* of Salzburg. These types of book constitute written forms other than historical narrative in which the past was remembered and commemorated in the early middle ages, and have much to tell us about cultural attitudes in the early middle ages. The *Libri vitae* and the cartularies augment oral modes and memory as a form of communication in the early middle ages. They also function as a symbol on many different social and spiritual levels. They illustrate, moreover, the role of writing as a form of communication over time, and it is this which is absolutely crucial to our understanding of the uses and implications of literacy in the early middle ages as a whole. The *Liber vitae* of Salzburg, first compiled in 784, is a remarkable example of the use of writing in commemoration and the recording of social memory in the early middle ages. I argue that this book reflects not only more general cultural assumptions in early medieval Bavaria in the years surrounding Charlemagne's annexation of Tassilo's duchy of Bavaria, but also specific political affiliations and social communities within Bavaria at the end of the eighth century. The *Liber vitae* of Salzburg certainly anchored the Salzburg community within its locality and immediate institutional memory. That memory itself, however, was not separated from a wider political realm represented both by Bavarian dukes and the Carolingian king, and by the links forged between the religious houses and sees of west Francia and Bavaria. It witnesses to the different strands of influence and affiliation in Agilolfing and Carolingian Bavaria.

The prayers for the dead, the *Libri vitae* and the cartularies which formed the subject of the two preceding chapters provide an ostensibly immediate conjunction between past and present time, in that the dead are remembered in terms of the commemoration of their anniversaries in the present. Yet such texts also convey a very particular sense of the historical past in which chronology has a crucial role to play. In thinking about the writing of history and the keeping of historical records of many different kinds, we also need to think about the historical mindedness of the Franks and the formation of historical sensitivity by means of reading texts. How did an author's historical 'training' and reading influence the presentation and perception of the events, issues and personalities he records? What are the implications of the presence of histories and what was made available by copying in the ninth and tenth centuries?

In the remaining chapters of the book I turn to the question of historical knowledge and the role of texts. As a case study in chapter 9, I draw in particular on the evidence, insofar as I have been able to reconstruct it from surviving manuscripts from this period, of what was read and used at the monasteries of Lorsch and St Amand in the ninth and tenth centuries. In chapter 10 I explore a particular aspect of the 'longer past' of the Franks, namely the history of the church. I aim to demonstrate that the relationship of the Carolingian Franks to the books in their libraries was not simply that of scholars to a repository of learning. The books in Frankish monastic and cathedral libraries, as part of a past which the Franks had assimilated to themselves, as discussed in chapters 7, 8 and 9, formed part of the Frankish sense of identity. In other words the Franks were not only a textual community in relation to the Bible, as has long been recognised; they were also a textual community in terms of their intellectual and textual inheritance. I use the phrase 'textual community' as defined by Brian Stock in his book: 'What was essential for a textual community was not a written version of a text, though that was sometimes present, but an individual who having mastered it, then utilized it for reforming a group's thought and action'.[46] In the case of the Franks in the Carolingian period, I am concerned both with the ruler's advocacy of particular texts but also of the Frankish scholars who mastered a precise set of texts. I explore the formation and ramifications of the very distinctive understanding of books and of the Franks' place in history within the Carolingian world and the Carolingian church. I investigate in particular the wider implications of Jerome-Gennadius' *De viris illustribus*, Eusebius-Rufinus' *Historia ecclesiastica* and Cassiodorus-Epiphanius' *Historia ecclesiastica tripartita* within Carolingian Europe. These three works played a key role in creating a context for the Franks' understanding not only of the history of the church, but also of the circumstances of the composition and dissemination of Scripture and the work of the fathers of the early church.

There are striking instances from the Carolingian period of the way in which the distinctive stress on texts, authors, authority and sacred places in the ecclesiastical histories, Jerome-Gennadius' *De viris illustribus* and a number of related texts could be drawn on by readers, scribes and artists. In a companion piece to the preceding chapter, I focus in chapter 11, 'Christianity as history', on two examples in order to explore the way in which the written tradition of the church appears to have shaped perceptions and attitudes. I suggest how the particular image of the church and the Christian faith, presented by the historical tradition outlined in chapter 10 and disseminated so zealously by the Franks, manifests

---

[46] B. Stock, *The implications of literacy. Written language and models of interpretation in the eleventh and twelfth centuries* (Princeton, 1983), pp. 89–92.

itself in the Carolingian period. My two examples are Vercelli, Biblioteca Capitolare cod. CLXV, a collection of canon law, and Munich, Bayerische Staatsbibliothek Clm 22053, the famous miscellany in a codex known as the *Wessobrunner Gebet* manuscript. Both demonstrate how images were deployed to reinforce the importance of sacred places, relics, authors and books in Christian history. They also serve to underline the importance of codicological context for our own understanding of any one text and its significance for its intended audience. They thereby add to our own knowledge of the intellectual resources of particular groups in the Carolingian world, quite apart from enlarging our understanding of the reception of late antique Christian texts in early medieval Europe.

The concluding chapter, 'History and its audiences in the Carolingian world', develops the principal theme of the preceding eleven chapters in focusing on contemporary memory and the writing of history in the eighth and ninth centuries. It takes the events of 817 and the contemporary accounts of them as a case study. It discusses how the Frankish writers constructed their past in the early middle ages and how their sense of an immediate history related to the construction of a longer past. In order to pull together the issues discussed in the preceding chapters, I look again at some of the material already considered but here from the perspective of their potential audiences. I address the following questions. What contributed to the Franks' sense of place in historical time? What did they use to construct their past? How did their own immediate history relate to this longer past? I argue that the Franks' sense of the past was a composite one. It had overlapping sequences. These comprised different local and institutional senses of identity which were expressed in terms of their own community's foundations, property, associations, dead members, benefactors and others. They were remembered, moreover, with some association with a particular place. Simultaneously there was an understanding of the chronological progression of Jewish and Christian history; of being heirs of both imperial and Christian Rome; and of their own sense of achievement as Franks, expanding ever eastwards and imposing their own composite culture on others. A sense of the past was deeply integrated into the sense of identity of the audiences for history the Carolingian world. How distinctive this Frankish sense and exposition of the past is among their contemporaries, notably in the Byzantine, Islamic and Anglo-Saxon regions, forms the subject of my concluding paragraphs.

2   Carolingian history books

The history of Alexander by Quintus Curtius Rufus was written in the first century AD. Its earliest surviving manuscript, Paris, Bnf lat. 5716, was written in the Carolingian period for Count Conrad by the scribe Haimo in the Loire region in the second half of the ninth century. How may we account for this?

Quintus Curtius Rufus is not an orthodox member of the Roman historiographical canon in the sense that he does not deal with contemporary Roman themes. Certainly his History of Alexander is sensational and emotional; it has much of the exotic and the remote in its narrative, and good character sketches. There are vivid depictions of the characteristics of different peoples – effeminate Persians, intelligent Scythians, volatile Egyptians, the Greeks, who are 'political trimmers by temperament', 'time-serving Cretans', the Sicilians' penchant for flattery and the fickleness of the mob. The speeches abound and the morals are pointed. Accounting for its attractions, therefore, is perhaps not difficult, though it risks being a subjective exercise in relation to modern tastes. Nevertheless, other ninth-century copies of Quintus Curtius Rufus of different origin besides that of Count Conrad's book do indeed suggest some popularity of the text. Further, the text tradition these various manuscripts represent is very diverse. It might be natural to postulate a mutilated archetype as the original from which the others stemmed, for all texts omit Books 1–2, the end of Book 5 and the beginning of Book 6.[1] The other copies, however, are sufficiently different from the Conrad manuscript to indicate the possibility of a number of independent exemplars and varying milieux of production in the Carolingian period and later in the middle ages. Thus the surviving manuscripts can suggest, firstly, that there was a dispersed audience for this particular classical historical text at a particular time. Secondly, in one case we encounter a ninth-century lay official in the

---

[1] McKitterick, *Carolingians and the written word*, p. 261; K. Müller, *Q. Curtius Rufus Geschichte Alexanders der Großen* (Munich, 1954); pp. 783–802; Reynolds, *Texts and transmission*, pp. 148–9. It is illustrated in E. Chatelain, *Les Classiques Latins*, II (Paris 1894–1900), plate 188.2.

Loire region apparently commissioning this history for his own pleasure and instruction.

What of contemporary history in the ninth century? It might seem a straightforward task to discover for whom and within what milieu any one historical text was written. Some of the problems have already become apparent in the preceding chapter with reference to the *Liber historiae francorum* and the *Annales regni francorum*, but another obvious example might be Einhard's *Vita Karoli* (Life of Charlemagne). In determining the exact relationship between this text and the court of Louis the Pious and the intended contemporary political impact the dating of Einhard's composition has proved to be of paramount importance.[2] Now a decade after Matthew Innes and I first argued the case for the date of *c*. 817, it is disappointing all the same that discussion subsequently has focused more on the date itself rather than on the contemporary political circumstances that would make the date of *c*. 817 most likely. Apart from Karl Heinrich Krüger's very interesting case for a date of composition in 823, many aspects of our argument have simply been overlooked.[3] In particular, we suggested that the agenda for rulership implicit in the *Vita Karoli*, with its stress on consensus and Frankishness, as well as its attempt to define what the imperial title might mean, is best seen as a manifesto in support of the settlement of 813–14 at a time when it would, together with the great reform endeavours of 816 and 817 and the *Ordinatio imperii* of 817, have the greatest political impact.

If written *c*. 817 therefore, Einhard's *Vita Karoli* had the immediate purpose of consolidating Louis the Pious's position as the rightful

---

[2] For a full discussion of the dating of Einhard see Innes and McKitterick, 'Writing of history', pp. 203–8; with reference to the earlier literature, especially H. Löwe, 'Die Entstehungszeit der *Vita Karoli* Einhards', *DA* 39 (1963), pp. 85–103, in favour ultimately of 827–9; and F. L. Ganshof, 'Einhard, biographer of Charlemagne', in F. L. Ganshof, *The Carolingians and the Frankish monarchy*, trans. Janet Sondheimer (London, 1971), pp. 1–16, who fell back on any time between 817–830. I am grateful to Matthew Innes for kindly allowing me to draw on our joint work in what follows. For further discussion of Einhard see M. Innes, 'The classical tradition in the Carolingian Renaissance: ninth-century encounters with Suetonius', *International Journal of the Classical Tradition* 3 (1997), pp. 265–82.

[3] K. H. Krüger, 'Neue Beobachtungen zur Datierung von Einhards Karlsvita', *Frühmittelalterliche Studien* 32 (1998), pp. 124–45. See also M. S. Kempshall, 'Some Ciceronian apects of Einhard's life of Charlemagne', *Viator* 26 (1995), pp. 11–38; D. Ganz, 'The preface to Einhard's "Vita Karoli"', in H. Schefers (ed.), *Einhard. Studien zu Leben und Werk* (Darmstadt, 1997), pp. 299–310; P. Depreux, *Prosopographie de l'entourage de Louis le Pieux (781–840)*, Instrumenta 1 (Sigmaringen, 1997), p. 181, n. 60; M. Tischler, *Einharts Vita Karoli. Studien zur Entstehung, Überlieferung und Rezeption*, 2 vols., *MGH* Schriften 48 (Hannover, 2001), pp. 163–4. For more general observations on the genre of biography as a whole see W. Berschin, *Biographie und Epochenstil im lateinischen Mittelalter*, Quellen und Untersuchungen zur lateinischen Philologie des Mittelalters 8–10, 12, 4 vols. (Stuttgart, 1986–99).

and appropriate heir to his father's dominion. A date of 823 would alter the initial purpose as Krüger has suggested, but the expected immediate audience would still have been the political elite associated with the royal court. When Walafrid Strabo composed a preface to Einhard's history for the second and later redaction of the text, however, he addressed himself to a later generation as well as to posterity.[4] By then the *Vita Karoli* had become not only a portrayal of Charles the Great but also a model portrait of a king. Undoubtedly written by a man who had been impressed by Suetonius' *Lives of the Caesars*, it contrives to enlist the virtues of Suetonius' twelve Roman emperors in order to stress the superiority of one Frankish ruler. It does so in Latin of a level much admired by contemporaries as the closest a Carolingian writer came to Ciceronian Latin. The text survives in an extraordinary number of manuscripts, and in those of the ninth and tenth centuries it is accompanied by other texts dealing with the history of the Franks.[5]

Einhard's *Vita Karoli*, therefore, together with the popularizing History of Alexander by Quintus Curtius Rufus, raises three interlocking issues which are of relevance for our understanding of the reception of early medieval history texts. These issues extend the themes of the reception and dissemination of history texts in the Carolingian world outlined in chapter 1 above. Firstly, there is the degree to which Carolingian history writing is a taught mode of organizing memory derived from classical and late antiquity. This involves matters of form, content, method and purpose. Thus the role played by the linguistic, grammatical and rhetorical traditions of pagan and early Christian historiography needs to be considered. These traditions are coupled with particular attitudes to truth and convention which are rather different from ours.[6] Added to this there is the question of the degree to which past imagining and word pictures fired the imagination of the Franks. That is, how much did the copying of older texts and emulation of classical authors provide a structure or leave room for independent imagination on the part of later authors? In presenting narratives of the past, to what extent did pagan and early Christian texts offer a set of models, conventions and genres? How far did the Franks develop new methods of recording the past? As Matthew Innes and I have stressed, the writing of history was not simply a matter of keeping a record for posterity. Its purpose was also to make the past comprehensible and to relate it in some way to the present. Thus the

---

[4] Walafrid Strabo, Preface to ed. O. Holder-Egger, *Einhardi Vita Karoli Magni, MGH SRG*, XXV (Hannover, 1911), pp. XXVIII–XXIX.
[5] See Tischler, *Einharts Vita Karoli*, and below, chapter 4.
[6] R. Morse, *Truth and convention in the middle ages: rhetoric, representation and reality* (Cambridge, 1991).

past could provide support for contemporary political ideology or explain God's purpose for humanity.[7] Any consideration of the possible role of precedents and models in the Franks' perception of the past, is complicated by the fact that, as we shall see in chapter 9, the older texts were being copied at precisely the same time as the new ones were being created. The Franks' sources formed part of a written tradition, but so did their own work. Literacy and education for a Frank in the eighth and ninth centuries entailed acquiring knowledge of the Bible and other works and an active engagement with and response to them. The texts they studied brought the Carolingians into contact with a different past, a new perception of man's role in relation to God, and within the scheme of things. They offered a set of models, conventions and genres for the presentations of the past. Thus it is essential to understand the Franks' models, and the forms and context in which they may have encountered them in order to understand their own construction of their past. It is for this reason that an understanding of the manuscript sources on which the Franks themselves drew is so crucial.

Language is the second issue to be addressed, for these texts are in Latin. As mentioned in the previous chapter, there has been considerable debate about the early medieval audience, and specifically the Carolingian audience in the ninth century, for whom any text in Latin could have been intended. There are many different ways in which a particular text could be communicated, by private reading, reading aloud, paraphrase, or even translation. Latin itself remained comprehensible in different degrees from Antiquity until late into the ninth century. Within the Frankish empire it may have been the second language rather than the mother tongue of many people, especially in the German-speaking regions. We should also not underestimate the extent of bilingualism. Everyday Latin speech only gradually became distinct from the Latin of the educated and developed into the early forms of French, Italian and Spanish. Occasionally in the manuscripts there are indications, such as varied word order and orthography, of these different levels and varied pronunciations of Latin.[8]

---

[7] See especially chapters 9 and 10 below.

[8] M. van Uyhtfanghe, 'Histoire du Latin, protohistoire des langues romanes et histoire de la communication. A propos d'un recueil d'études, et avec quelques observations préliminaires sur le débat intellectuel entre pensée structurale et pensée historique', *Francia* 11 (1983), pp. 579–613; R. Wright, *Late Latin and early Romance in Spain and Carolingian France* (Liverpool, 1982); idem (ed.), *Latin and the Romance Languages in the early middle ages* (London, 1991, and Philadelphia, 1996); idem, 'Complex monolingualism in early Romance', in W. J. Ashby (ed.), *Linguistic perspectives on the Romance languages: selected papers from the 21st linguistic symposium on Romance languages* (Amsterdam, 1993), pp. 377–88. Compare McKitterick, *Carolingians and the written word*, pp. 1–22; and M. Banniard, *Viva Voce: communication écrite et communication orale du IVe siècle en occident latin* (Paris, 1992); and idem., 'Language and communication', in McKitterick (ed.), *NCMH* pp. 695–708.

In linguistic terms, therefore, the audience for Latin texts, including history books in Latin, at least to the end of the ninth century, is as follows. Firstly, there was the audience provided by those who were taught to read. Secondly there were those able to use their reading skills to disseminate the content of written texts more widely by reading them aloud. Lastly, there were the hearers of such recitation. The surviving evidence makes it clear that many people, lay and cleric, male and female, to a considerable way down the social scale were literate to some degree, had access to literate modes of communication, and deployed them when necessary.[9]

The third issue raised by the works of Einhard and other Frankish writers as well as copies of pre-Carolingian historical texts (both classical and early medieval), is that of determining the purpose and subsequent audience both on and after their initial production. What, in short, do Carolingian history books look like? It is on this that I wish to concentrate for the rest of this chapter. That is, I shall focus on the manuscript tradition of a number of history texts current in the Carolingian period and the accompanying problems of dissemination. As we have seen already in the preceding chapter in relation to the *Liber historiae francorum*, the fact that some individuals or institutions regarded these texts as of sufficient interest or importance to make and distribute copies of them can be regarded as one indication of their audience. The manuscript tradition of particular texts, however, presents many puzzles, not least for the status of the text itself and how modern historians are to place them in an appropriate historical context.

The *Liber pontificalis*

Take the *Liber pontificalis*, for example, the series of papal biographies from St Peter to Pope Stephen V, whose first redaction was put together in papal circles in the 530s, with a second redaction no more than two decades later. Continuations were then added from the early seventh century onwards (and the material for the period between the 540s and 630s supplied) up to the 880s on a life-by-life basis.[10] Texts of the *Liber*

[9] McKitterick, *Carolingians and the written word*; see also above, pp. 5–7.
[10] *Le Liber pontificalis*, ed. L. Duchesne, 2 vols. (Paris, 1886 and 1892); M. Buchner, 'Zur Überlieferungsgeschichte des *Liber pontificalis* und zu seiner Verbreitung im Frankenreich im IX. Jahrhundert: zugleich ein Beitrag zur Geschichte der karolingischen Hofbibliothek und Hofkapelle', *Römische Quartalschrift* 34 (1926), pp. 141–65. See also O. Bertolini, 'Il *Liber pontificalis*', in *La Storiografia altomedievale*, Settimane 17 (Spoleto, 1970), pp. 387–455; T. F. X. Noble, 'A new look at the *Liber Pontificalis*', *Archivum Historiae Pontificiae* 23 (1985), pp. 347–58; and R. Davis, *The book of the pontiffs (Liber pontificalis to 715)* (Liverpool, 1989), pp. ii–vii, and *The lives of the eighth-century popes (Liber pontificalis)* (Liverpool, 1992), pp. xv–xviii.

pontificalis left Rome at different dates, but we have no idea precisely how, let alone why. A remarkably large contingent of the surviving ninth-century manuscripts of the *Liber pontificalis* is of Frankish origin. It is usually presumed that these copies, dating from the second quarter of the ninth century onwards, can be traced back to an exemplar from the court library. It is further surmised that a copy reached Charlemagne as one of a gift of books received by him between 800 and 814. That this surmise implicates the royal court in the dissemination of a particular history book is something to which I return below.[11]

The dissemination of the *Liber pontificalis*, however, was very wide, and various scribes altered the text in a number of significant, and less significant, ways. Among all these manuscripts of Frankish or Italian origin, not one, at least as far as the lives of the eighth- and ninth-century popes are concerned, can be regarded as the base text. The criterion of completeness gave a Farfa manuscript of the late eleventh century (BAV lat. 3734) a spurious status to *Liber pontificalis* editors before Duchesne in that it is the only one to extend to 892. Whatever it may have to tell us about later popes, however, the status of its texts for the earlier popes is doubtful, and one may simply have to select from an amalgam of versions to create an artificially complete text. With five major groups of manuscripts and the later medieval recensions, one moves ever further away from what may have been an original version penned by anonymous clerks in the Lateran. How individual scribes or compilers could alter texts to suit their own prejudices and preoccupations is clear from Lucca, Biblioteca Capitolare 490, a manuscript containing a text of the *Liber pontificalis*, to which I shall return shortly.

Annales fuldenses

The manuscripts of the *Annales fuldenses* (Annals of Fulda) present similar problems of late manuscript witnesses, multiple authorship, wide dissemination and different recensions in various locations. These Carolingian annals are usually regarded as the main narrative for the east Frankish kingdom and as a continuation (from 830) of the *Annales regni francorum* (Royal Frankish Annals) which run until 829.[12] The composite nature of the text and the presence of a number of authors have not been in question since Kurze first produced his edition at the end of the nineteenth century. There is even a significant divergence at the end of the text, with a section 882 to 901 known as the Bavarian continuation and

---

[11] Below, chapters 9 and 10.
[12] For the *Annales regni francorum* see above, chapter 1 and below, chapter 4.

an alternative account of the section 882–7 represented elsewhere in the text tradition.

All those who have studied the text are agreed that the *Annales fuldenses* were not conceived as a whole in the sense that the whole text was written at one sitting or by one author. Sections of it may be attributable to one author, however, even if not the same person who has been proposed as author in the past. When Kurze analysed the text for his Monumenta edition, he followed the marginal annotations in the eleventh-century Selestadt manuscript to which he had given priority, attributing the text up to 838 to Einhard, the portion 839–63 to Rudolf of Fulda and the narrative for 864–82 to Meginhard of Fulda. The earliest section, 714–837, remains the one to which the least attention has been paid, largely because Kurze, following the general preoccupation of nineteenth- and many twentieth-century editors with the establishing of sources and borrowing, considered it so predominantly made up of extracts from other identifiable or hypothetical sources as to fail the test of an 'original' work.

Thus the *Annales fuldenses* have generally been regarded as providing no independent witness for the rise of the Carolingians, the reign of Charlemagne or the early years of the reign of Louis the Pious. Most scholars have only paid close attention to them from 830 onwards and have tended to ignore the narrative for the text from 714 to 829, despite the fact that it clearly offers an independent, and east Frankish, perspective on the events recorded in the *Annales regni francorum* as well as other items of information.[13] Even if the authors or compilers drew on earlier texts to construct the account from 714–829, the resulting emphases in the presentation of events merit closer attention.[14] The problems of assessing the text are exacerbated by the pattern of the manuscript tradition. As Timothy Reuter has commented, the surviving manuscripts probably represent, in his words, but 'an echo of what must have been a much more extensive transmission'.[15] With those that remain, possibly an arbitrary selection, how can we determine their relative status as texts, let alone as history?

Kurze suggested that the manuscripts fell into three groups (1, 2 and 3), the third of which contains the oldest surviving manuscript witness to the Fulda annals, namely, Leipzig, Stadtbibliothek 129a of the last quarter of the ninth century. This group contains the Bavarian continuation

---

[13] The English translation by T. Reuter, *The annals of Fulda* (Manchester, 1992), runs only from 838. Reuter regarded the entries for the section 828–38 as too 'thin and uninteresting' to be worth translating.
[14] See R. Corradini, *Die annales Fuldenses – Studien zur Überlieferungsgeschichte* (in preparation).
[15] Reuter, *The annals of Fulda*, p. 2.

and the different version of events recounted for the section 882–7 from that in the group 2 manuscripts. The Leipzig text of the annals for 714–901 has considerable authority for the later years, especially from 882.[16] The divergences of the group 2 and group 3 versions, moreover, suggest a different set of priorities and assumptions on the part of the compilers. Let us assume for the moment, as all those who have ever used the annals of Fulda seem to have assumed, that the eleventh-century and later manuscripts comprising group 2 derive from a different version in circulation in the later ninth century, and do the same for the redaction represented in group 1. This would give us at least three different historical accounts, all based on a text in such a way as to suggest that an east Frankish set of annals was in circulation and adapted in particular centres, as we can see it being adapted in the Bavarian continuations. Further, the section 741–828 provides a positive indication of the circulation and adaptation of the *Annales regni francorum* in the east Frankish kingdom.

The difficulty in terms of Carolingian understanding of the past, nevertheless, is to be certain both that the adaptations are from as early as the ninth century and where they were made. Apart from the group 3 manuscripts of the *Annales fuldenses*, we have too many supposed intermediaries intervening between ninth-century compilation and eleventh- and twelfth-century copies to be at all confident. But in works compiled in the way annals were compiled, the three groups of Fulda annals' manuscripts, or the two main groups of manuscripts of Regino's *Chronicon*,[17] serve simply to alert us to the different versions potentially compiled.

The *Chronicon laurissense breve* is an even clearer example. In many ways a typical example of a 'minor' annal, it covers the years 714–817, that is, from the death of Pippin II to the *Ordinatio imperii* of Louis the Pious. There is an introductory section on Pippin II, and it combines general events within the kingdom with more local news, especially about the monastery of Lorsch.[18] Two recensions and seven phases of redaction have been identified: it was originally produced at Lorsch, was reworked and extended at Fulda in *c.* 807, where independent items up to 815 were added. Later recensions of it were made at Rheims and St Vaast.[19]

---

[16] H. Löwe (ed.), *Wattenbach-Levison. Deutschlands Geschichtsquellen im Mittelalter. Vorzeit und Karolinger. 6. Die Karolinger vom Vertrag von Verdun bis zum Herrschaftsantritt der Herrscher aus dem Sächsischen Hause. Das ostfränkische Reich* (Weimar, 1990), pp. 677–8.
[17] *Ibid.*, pp. 901–4.
[18] *Chronicon laurissense breve*, ed. H. Schnorr von Carolsfeld, *Neues Archiv* 36 (1911), pp. 13–39.
[19] R. Corradini, *Die Wiener Handschrift Cvp 430*. Ein Beitrag zur Historiographie in Fulda im frühen 9. Jahrhundert*, Fuldaer Hochschulschriften 37 (Frankfurt am Main, 2000); and R. Corradini, 'The rhetoric of crisis: *computus* and *Liber annalis* in early ninth-century

Ostensibly the same text, each manuscript of it, such as Vienna, ÖNB cod. 430* (the Fulda recension) or BAV pal. lat. 243 (the Lorsch recension) offers a local reading of, and response to, Frankish history. In the case of the Lorsch recension there is an additional section starting at the year 685, announced (fol. 55r) as based on Bede's *Chronica* (that is, chapter 66 of the *De temporum ratione*) but with material added in from other texts such as Paul the Deacon's *Historia langobardorum*. This precedes the record of Pippin II's death in 714 and thus sets Frankish history in a longer perspective with explicit connections with the Byzantine empire and Lombard kingdom.

Although historians feel the need to have *the* text of a particular history, we would be better advised, therefore, to be content with *a* text, knowing that we have a local version and perspective offered in any one manuscript and thus the impact on a local audience to assess. Indeed, our total stock of primary evidence is thereby of course very greatly increased.

It has to be said, however, that in such a manuscript context the concept of authorship becomes increasingly intangible,[20] and that of audience increasingly flexible. It is not enough to extrapolate from the internal evidence in a text for whom it might have been intended. Every manuscript containing that text has to be examined with a view to determining for whom that particular copy may have been intended. The manuscripts of Fredegar's *Chronicle* and its continuations may serve to illustrate this point further.

The *Chronicle* of Fredegar and its continuations

The four books of the *Chronicle* of Frankish history from Adam to *c.* 642 were put together by anything from one to four authors in Burgundy in the latter half of the seventh century. Like the *Liber historiae francorum* author, he, she or they made use of Gregory of Tours' *Historiae* for the narrative up to the 590s. The Continuations take the account to 768 and were apparently written under the auspices of members of the Carolingian family.[21] The surviving manuscripts contradict the simplistic notion that the oldest surviving manuscript of a history might be the closest to the

Fulda', in R. Corradini, M. Diesenberger and H. Reimitz (eds.), *The construction of communities in the early middle ages: texts, resources and artefacts*, The Transformation of the Roman World 12 (Leiden, 2003), pp. 269–321.

[20] For a discussion of the question of authorship in an early medieval context together with the wider considerations, see D. Pratt, 'Problems of authorship and audience in the writings of King Alfred the Great', in P. Wormald (ed.), *Learned laity in the Carolingian era* (Cambridge, forthcoming); see also below, pp. 110–11.

[21] See chapter 6 below.

original author and enable us to reconstruct his intended audience with the greatest precision. Although Paris, BnF lat. 10910, written 714/15, is the oldest manuscript, it is in fact not the parent of any other known copy of the *Chronicle*. No direct exemplar for Book IV of the *Chronicle* and the Continuations appears to survive. What the manuscript tradition does witness to, however, is that about fifty years after Fredegar's text was last added to in *c.* 660, it was copied and garbled by someone whom Michael Wallace-Hadrill called 'an unintelligent Burgundian cleric of the late seventh or early eighth century'.[22] Between then and the mid-eighth century a second copy reached Austrasia, the north-east region of the Frankish kingdoms. From this copy, which does not survive, all subsequent manuscripts are descended and they present what amounts to a Carolingian edition of the text.[23]

Thus interest in the Austrasian Chronicle appears to have been raised at the turn of the eighth century and the dissemination of copies began with an abundance of ninth-century texts, mostly from the Rhineland and northern France, that is, the Carolingian heartland. Which version, then is the superior one as far as historians are concerned? The one read by the Franks in the Carolingian period or the one written in the Merovingian period? Do we read Fredegar's Book IV and the Continuations in the ninth-century version with sufficient recognition of the pitfalls of so doing? Critical analysis of the current printed edition of Fredegar's text and its Continuations is certainly sophisticated, but, unlike studies of Gregory of Tours,[24] has not yet taken the implications of the manuscript transmission to heart.[25]

---

[22] J. M. Wallace-Hadrill (ed.), *The fourth book of the Chronicle of Fredegar and its Continuations* (London, 1960), p. lv, though why it should necessarily have been a cleric is not established.

[23] For a full account of the text and the manuscripts see R. Collins, *Fredegar*, Authors of the Middle Ages. Historical and Religious Writers of the Latin West IV, no. 13 (Aldershot, 1996), especially pp. 87–89 on Paris, BnF lat. 10910.

[24] M. Heinzelmann, *Gregor von Tours (538–594): 'Zehn Bücher Geschichte' Historiographie und Gesellschaftskonzept im 6. Jahrhundert* (Darmstadt, 1994), trans. C. Carroll, *Gregory of Tours: history and society in the sixth century* (Cambridge, 2001); and M. Heinzelmann, 'L'Oeuvre de Grégoire de Tours: la diffusion des manuscrits', in N. Gauthier and H. Galinié (eds.), *Grégoire de Tours et l'espace gaulois*. Actes du congrès international Tours, 2–5 novembre 1994, 13e supplément à la Revue Archéologique du Centre de la France (Tours, 1997), pp. 273–317; and H. Reimitz, 'Social networks and identities in Frankish historiography. New aspects of the textual history of Gregory of Tours' *Historiae*', in Corradini, Diesenberger and Reimitz (eds.), *The construction of communities in the early middle ages*, pp. 229–68.

[25] J. Jarnut, U. Nonn and M. Richter (eds.), *Karl Martell in seiner Zeit*, Beihefte der Francia 37 (Sigmaringen, 1994), especially R. Collins, 'Deception and misrepresentation in early eighth-century Frankish historiography: two case studies', pp. 227–47.

The assumptions modern scholars make about early medieval scribes copying other texts also need to be taken into account. Certainly casual errors, slips in copying, mishearing of dictation and misunderstanding or misreading of the exemplar can be used to help scholars identify possible exemplars or sort manuscripts into groups of related copies.[26] But there is also the problem of notions of purity versus those of corruption in a text. Should the scribes have corrected a text as they went? We should bear in mind that the Carolingians were probably dependent for their Roman historians on late antique exemplars, themselves full of variants and corrections.[27] The philologist and classical scholar A. E. Housman assumed that a scribe would edit as he went, but such an assumption gains no support from the Carolingian copies of older texts that we have and what we can deduce of their copying practices. They appear usually to have copied what they saw. In other words, the text could be excerpted, and put to alternative use by placing it in new contexts, but emendation of the actual sentences was less likely. Many studies of Carolingian manuscripts detect the nature of their exemplars from the errors preserved by the scribes. Extreme examples of excerpt compilation, furthermore, might be the *Collectanea* of Hadoard of Corbie and Heiric of Auxerre.[28]

If it is an extraordinary mixture of respect and disrespect for an exemplar, it also highlights the special relationship of the Carolingians with classical antiquity. Their use of antique exemplars provided them with immediate contact with a remote intellectual world. They preserved it and communicated it by making faithful copies of the texts they saw. These were probably very different in appearance from the kind of books they would produce themselves in their own contemporary forms of caroline minuscule script. For a start, the older exemplars were written in different scripts – rustic and square capitals, uncial and half uncial.[29] The layout of the Carolingian copies would also most usually be adapted, and alterations introduced in the use of punctuation to assist

---

[26] See, for example, M. D. Reeve, 'The place of P in the stemma of Livy 1–10', in C. A. Chavannes-Mazel and M. M. Smith (eds.), *Medieval manuscripts of the Latin classics: production and use* (Los Altos Hills and London, 1996), pp. 74–90; and D. Ganz, 'Lucretius in the Carolingian age: the Leiden manuscripts and their Carolingian readers', in *ibid.*, pp. 91–102.

[27] See chapter 9 below.

[28] B. Bischoff, 'Hadoardus and the manuscripts of classical authors from Corbie', in *Didascaliae. Studies in honor of A. M. Albareda* (New York, 1961), pp. 41–57, with a revised German version in Bischoff, *Mittelalterliche Studien*, I, pp. 49–63; and R. Quadri (ed.), *I collectanea di Eirico di Auxerre* (Fribourg, 1966).

[29] For guidance on the scripts of antiquity and the early middle ages see B. Bischoff, *Latin palaeography: antiquity and the middle ages*, trans. D. Ó Cróinín and D. Ganz (Cambridge, 1990, from the 1986 2nd revised German edition).

contemporary Frankish readers.[30] In this way Frankish scribes made the remote intellectual world of antiquity accessible for a contemporary audience. The manuscripts, as much as the texts they contain, therefore, potentially have something to reveal of the textual communities they served as well as of the people whose identity they express.

History books

This can best be assessed looking at the range of ninth-century Carolingian history books containing the historical writing of late antiquity and the early middle ages. Quite apart from the Carolingian histories and the *Liber pontificalis* already mentioned, we also have to reckon with the continuing influence not only of Roman and Christian historiography, but also the so-called histories of the *gentes* or narratives of 'barbarian history' by Gregory of Tours, Jordanes, Paul the Deacon and Bede.[31] There can be no doubt that the principal precedents for the writing of history – classical, biblical, early Christian and 'barbarian' – were all available to the Franks and that the Carolingians themselves, particularly from the royal court, did much to disseminate knowledge of them.[32] Not only that, the royal court played an important role in providing exemplars of both ancient histories such as Sallust[33] and more recent histories such as Bede.[34]

I provide below a preliminary list of histories in Latin known in the Frankish kingdoms up to and including the tenth century. I shall be discussing some of the implications of these in more detail in chapter 9 but for the present it is important simply to identify the works that were available. Not all of them may have been known to the Franks in the early middle ages by any more than name or from a quotation, but my list is based on the evidence of extant manuscripts up to *c.* 900, of inclusion of authors and titles in ninth- and tenth-century library catalogues, and of the incorporation of sections or shorter excerpts of earlier histories in other historical works.

---

[30] See the examples discussed in M. B. Parkes, *Pause and effect: punctuation in the west* (London, 1992). For more general issues of changing layout in the presentation of texts in the middle ages see H.-J. Martin and J. Vezin (eds.), *Mise en page et mise en texte du livre manuscrit* (Paris, 1990).

[31] W. Goffart, *The narrators of barbarian history (A.D. 550–800): Jordanes, Gregory of Tours, Bede and Paul the Deacon* (Princeton, 1988).

[32] For further discussion see Innes and McKitterick, 'Writing of history'.

[33] If one accepts that the list mentioning Sallust in Berlin, Deutsche Staatsbibliothek Diez B. Sant 66 is a list of the Carolingian royal library books *c.* 800: see below, pp. 80–1, and Reynolds, *Texts and transmission*, pp. 340–52, at p. 343.

[34] Cambridge University Library MS Kk.5.16 and see below, chapters 9 and 10 and p. 209.

Latin historians known to c. 900: Roman history[35]

Ammianus Marcellinus, fl. 330–93. †*Res gestae* (last sixteen books for AD 338–78) (regarded as a continuation of the Roman historian Tacitus though much has been lost)

Dares Phrygius. Greek of first century AD in a Latin version of fifth or sixth century AD †*Historia troiae*

Eutropius, fourth century AD †**Breviarium ab urbe condita* (written 364–78) (extended by Paul the Deacon, eighth century, †*Historia romana* to the mid-sixth century[36]

Frontinus, 30–104 AD †*Strategemata*

Gaius Julius Caesar, 100–44 BC †*Bellum gallicum*

†*Ilias latina*, first century AD (a Latin version of Homer)

Justinus (third century AD) †Epitome of Pompeius Trogus, *Historiae philippicae*

Livy, 58 BC–18 AD †**Ab urbe condita*, Decades I, III, IV, V: books 41–5 (the rest of the work, once 142 books in length, is lost).

Pompeius Trogus, first century BC *Historiae philippicae* (lost) but see under Justinus

Quintus Curtius Rufus, *c.* 50 AD †*Historiae Alexandri Magni Macedonis*

Sallust, 86–34 BC †**De coniuratione catilinae (Bellum catilinae)*; †**Bellum jugurthinum*; †**Historiae*

†*Scriptores historiae augustae*, end of fourth century AD

Suetonius, died after 116 AD †**De vita caesarum*

Tacitus, 55–116/20 AD †*Annales*; †*Agricola*; †**Germania*

Velleius Paterculus 20/19 BC–*c.* 29 AD †the 'Tiberian narrative'[37]

Virgil, 70–19 BC *Aeneid*, the epic poem about the flight of the hero Aeneas from Troy, his various adventures, and the foundation of Rome

---

[35] The symbol † indicates an extant Carolingian or earlier manuscript. The symbol * indicates that the title is listed in an extant Carolingian library catalogue. For details about the catalogues see McKitterick, *Carolingians and the written word*, pp. 165–210. Useful introductory surveys on Roman historians are M. Grant, *The ancient historians* (New York, 1970); and D. Rohrbacher, *The historians of late antiquity* (London, 2002); and see also J. Marincola, *Authority and tradition in ancient historiography* (Cambridge, 1997). For all details on surviving manuscripts see Reynolds, *Texts and transmission*.

[36] Also continued by Landolfus Sagax (*c.* 1000) †*Historia miscella*, to the ninth century.

[37] Reynolds, *Texts and transmission*, pp. 431–3 records that a ninth-century witness to the text in caroline minuscule from Murbach is now lost. Velleius Paterculus was a soldier who served under Gaius Caesar and under Tiberius in Germany. Book 1 of his text, to 168 BC, is missing.

The manuscript tradition of such authors as Sallust, Tacitus, Ammianus Marcellinus, Justinus, Livy, Caesar, Eutropius, Quintus Curtius Rufus, Frontinus, the *Scriptores historiae augustae* and Suetonius demonstrates that the earliest manuscript is a Carolingian one. I explore the implications of this more fully in chapter 9. For the moment, however, we need to see what these manuscripts have to tell us about the reception and transmission of these texts in the Carolingian world. I can give only a few instances here. The three earliest manuscripts of Caesar's *Bellum gallicum*, for instance, are Carolingian. All allude to late antique correctors. Thus their exemplars were probably late antique as well. These codices appear to descend from two suggested archetypes, surviving in two different parts of Gaul, with the monasteries of Fleury and Corbie playing a key role.[38]

Sallust, present in the royal library as well as at Corbie, Reichenau and Murbach, was distributed between west Francia (Soissons, Auxerre, Ferrières) and southern Germany and Alemannia, with a clear gain in popularity in the tenth century.[39] The *Historiae* provided a major inspiration, for example, for Richer of Rheims.[40] The earliest manuscript of Suetonius is Paris, BnF lat. 6115, written at Tours *c.* 820. Lupus of Ferrières, writing in the middle of the ninth century, tells us that there was a copy at Fulda and this is presumably where Einhard read it. Lupus may have copied it there and taken his own copy back to Ferrières, for Heiric of Auxerre, a pupil of Lupus, certainly made excerpts from it at Auxerre.[41] Suetonius, therefore, was the focus of scholarly interest on the part of two *litterati* who have established in their letters and other extant works how much sympathy with the works of classical antiquity they had.[42]

---

[38] *Ibid.*, pp. 35–6, and below, p. 193.

[39] It also survives in a fifth-century manuscript used at the turn of the seventh century at Fleury. See H. Bloch, 'The structure of Sallust's Historiae: the evidence of the Fleury manuscript', in S. Prete (ed.), *Didascaliae. Studies in honor of Anselm M. Albareda* (New York, 1961), pp. 61–7; and M. Mostert, 'The tradition of classical manuscripts of Fleury, Appendix: Latin classics from the Fleury library', in Chavannes-Mazel and Smith (eds.), *Medieval manuscripts of the Latin classics*, pp. 19–40.

[40] Richer, *Historia*, ed. H. Hoffman, *Richer von Saint-Remi, Historiae MGH SS*, XXXVIII (Hannover, 2000); H. Hoffmann, 'Der Historien Richer von Saint-Remi', *DA* 54 (1998), pp. 445–552; and J. Glenn, *Politics and history in the tenth century: the work and world of Richer of Reims* (Cambridge, 2004).

[41] E. K. Rand, 'On the history of the *De vita caesarum* of Suetonius in the early middle ages', *Harvard Studies in Classical Philology* 37 (1926), pp. 1–48. There is no evidence of any insular influence in the manuscript tradition.

[42] C. H. Beeson, *Lupus of Ferrières as scribe and text critic* (Cambridge, Mass., 1930); On the school of Auxerre see L. Holtz, 'L'École d'Auxerre', in D. Iogna-Prat, C. Jeudy and G. Lobrichon (eds.), *L'École carolingienne d'Auxerre de Murethach à Remi 830–908* (Auxerre, 1991), pp. 131–46.

Fulda also preserved Ammianus Marcellinus, and the *Annales*, *Agricola* and *Germania* of Tacitus. Rudolf of Fulda, for example, used the *Germania* in formulating his paragraph about the origin of the Saxons and thus demonstrates how one account could be drawn on for the creation of another in order to make sense of the past. The Jesi manuscript of Tacitus' *Germania*, Jesi lat. 8, probably written at Fulda in the second quarter of the ninth century, had an Auxerre connection; corrections made to the text have been attributed to Heiric of Auxerre.[43] Livy's monumental work appears to have been transmitted in pentads or decades (that is, groups of five or ten books) and is unusual in having so many late antique codices among its surviving copies. There is evidence that Charlemagne, and the Saxon rulers of Germany in the tenth century, Otto I, and Otto III, had copies, but Tours and Corbie also play a role in its tradition in the late eighth and the ninth centuries. The famous fifth-century uncial Puteanus Livy (BnF lat. 5730), containing the third decade, was copied at Tours in the abbacy of Alcuin. Lorsch and Fulda, as we shall see, are both implicated in the survival of the *Scriptores historiae augustae*.[44]

Apart from the complete manuscripts of the mainline Roman historians, and the inspiration they may have provided for subsequent historians, there are specific indications about the process of historical composition and the use made of earlier histories to be gained from examination of the manuscript tradition of a work. One example may serve, namely, the Roman history by Eutropius.

Eutropius is a summary in ten short books of the simple facts of Roman history from Romulus to his own time, written at the request of the Emperor Valens (364–78). A Greek version was made by a contemporary, and a later translation into Greek was made s.V/VI. It has a very complicated text tradition, but it is important to note that despite Paul the Deacon's summary and continuation, known as the *Historia romana*, Eutropius also survived in its original form.[45] The work was known to Bede and to Alcuin and a particularly important manuscript, also containing Festus and Frontinus, survives in a ninth-century codex, written at

[43] R. Till, *Handschriftliche Untersuchungen zu Tacitus Agricola und Germania* (Berlin-Dahlem, 1943) (this includes a facsimile); and R. P. Robinson, *The Germania of Tacitus* (Middletown, Conn., 1935). On Fulda see further below, chapter 9.

[44] Above p. 2 and see S. H. Ballou, *The manuscript tradition of the Historia Augusta* (Leipzig and Berlin, 1914); excerpts survive in BAV pal. lat. 886, s.IX first half from Lorsch, and Paris, BnF lat. 1750, fols. 127v–129v) s.X/XI, written in France, a compilation thought to be attributable to Sedulius Scottus of Liège; see Reynolds, *Texts and transmission*, pp. 354–6.

[45] Eutropius, *Breviarium*, ed. H. Droysen, *MGH AA*, II (Hannover, 1871), ed. F. Rühl (Vienna, 1887), and C. Santini (Vienna, 1979), and English trans. H. W. Bird (Liverpool, 1993). See also Reynolds, *Texts and transmission*, pp. 159–62.

Fulda but which was probably at Murbach.[46] Pursuing recorded extracts from Eutropius also uncovers all kinds of varied historical miscellanies, but these and their implications will be explored below. Paul the Deacon's *Historia romana* consisted of an expansion of Eutropius' *Breviarium* by means of the insertion of extra material from Orosius and Jerome and the addition of six books bringing the story to the time of Justinian.[47] This in its turn was copied and expanded by Landolfo Sagax *c*. 1000 in his *Historia miscella*, which survives in BAV pal. lat. 909, a copy made for Landolfo himself, who brought the story up to the ninth century.[48] Thus a Roman historian provided not only a springboard for the kind of topics that are treated but also reveals a perception on the part of the compilers of a certain continuity across the centuries covered by the text. There was also a *florilegium* of extracts from Eutropius and Justinus in Italy made in the ninth century or earlier. From this *florilegium*, extracts were incorporated into the great historical miscellany at Verona in the ninth century.[49]

Another Roman historian who carried some weight in the early middle ages is the third-century writer Justinus.[50] He compiled an epitome of the *Historiae philippicae* of the Augustan historian Pompeius Trogus, with a concentration on the peoples outside Italy. It is concise, factual and simple in style and survives in no less than 200 medieval manuscripts, the earliest of which is a fragment in eighth-century Northumbrian script.[51] Justinus was also among the books Gerward, *cancellarius* to the Emperor Louis the Pious, left to Lorsch.[52] The earliest Carolingian witness, Paris,

---

[46] Gotha, Forschungs- und Landesbibliothek, membr. I, 101 and see Bischoff, *Katalog* no. 1422, p. 297; and Reynolds, *Texts and transmission*, pp. 158–62.

[47] Paul the Deacon, *Historia romana*, ed. A. Crivellucci, Fonti per la Storia d'Italia 51 (Rome, 1913), and B. Cornford, 'The idea of the Roman past in early medieval Italy: Paul the Deacon's *Historia romana*' (unpublished Ph.D. dissertation, University of Cambridge, 2003).

[48] *Landolfo sagax historia romana*, ed. A. Crivellucci, I (Rome, 1912), pp. xiii–xxi.

[49] See below and R. Cessi, 'Di due miscellanee storiche medioevali', *Archivio Muratoriano* 13 (1913), pp. 69–96; and Reynolds, *Texts and transmission*, p. 61.

[50] See the translation and commentary with useful introduction by J. C. Yardley and W. Heckel, *Justin. Epitome of the Philippic history of Pompeius Trogus books 11–12: Alexander the Great* (Oxford, 1997).

[51] Reynolds, *Texts and transmission*, pp. 197–9.

[52] B. Bischoff conjectured that the Weinheim fragment was a remnant of Gerward's book: *Die Abtei Lorsch im Spiegel ihrer Handschriften*, 2nd edn (Lorsch, 1989), p. 65. Julia Crick has disputed this. She concluded from an additional leaf she discovered in the Bagford collection in the British Library in London that the idiosyncratic readings found in the Fischer-Bagford fragments single them out from the rest of the transalpine group of Justinus manuscripts and show that the original manuscript from which they came cannot hold the central position in the textual tradition which the suggestion about Gerward requires. But in any case the period of Anglo-Saxon activity on the continent provides a plausible background for the Bagford fragment. There is no reason why it

Bnf lat. 4950, was written in north-east Francia *c*. 800 and was later at Corbie. There was a text of Justinus at St Riquier by 831 and probably a copy at Fulda, for the epitome was used by Einhard, Hraban Maur (in his commentary on Maccabees) and Walafrid Strabo. It is also recorded in the catalogues of the libraries of Reichenau, St Gallen and Murbach. Thus the text was well established in the Lake Constance area.[53] St Gallen 623 is probably to be identified with the copy mentioned in the St Gallen catalogue. This particular family of the text spread west into France. Leiden, Bibliotheek der Rijksuniversiteit Voss. lat. Q.32, s.IX first half, and Paris BnF n.a. lat. 1601, s.IX second quarter or s.IX med, for example, are both of Fleury origin.[54] Other portions were included in the Verona miscellany.[55] The earliest witness to a further family of texts is Vercelli, Biblioteca Capitolare CLXXVII, s.X, from Vercelli, and Leiden Voss. lat. Q.101, possibly of west Frankish origin.[56] Thus a relatively obscure compilation of historical information continued to attract interest.

Given the knowledge subsequently displayed by Carolingian writers, history probably had some role to play in the Carolingian school curriculum. The criteria for such a role may not have been merely linguistic or literary but the evidence for this is ambiguous. One might have supposed that Lucan's *De bellum civile*, for example, would have been of interest as history to the Carolingians. It provides an account of the civil war 49–48 BC, beginning with Caesar's crossing of the Rubicon and telling of the destruction of the Roman republic. It was certainly used as a school text in the fifth and sixth centuries. There is a remarkable number of ninth-century copies extant but the manuscript transmission and codicological context appear to indicate that the Carolingians were more inclined to categorize this work as literature rather than as history.[57] This nevertheless does not preclude Lucan being understood and remembered as history by those who read or heard it.

could not be a continental production by a Northumbrian scribe rather than written in Northumbria itself: J. Crick, 'An Anglo-Saxon fragment of Justinus' Epitome', *Anglo-Saxon England* 16 (1987), pp. 181–96. See also R. McKitterick, 'The diffusion of insular culture in Neustria between 650 and 850: the implications of the manuscript evidence', in H. Atsma (ed.), *La Neustrie. Les pays au nord de la Loire de Dagobert à Charles le Chauve, 650 à 850*, Beihefte der Francia 16/2 (Sigmaringen, 1989), p. 395, reprinted, *Books, scribes and learning*, chapter 3.

53 Giessen, Universitätsbibliothek MS 233 (s.IX, third quarter) was written at Reichenau; see Bischoff, *Katalog*, no. 1390, p. 291.
54 See Reynolds, *Texts and transmission*, p. 198; but M. Mostert, *The library of Fleury. A provisional list of manuscripts* (Hilversum, 1989), p. 98 omits the Paris codex.
55 See below, pp. 52–7.   56 Reynolds, *Texts and transmission*, p. 199.
57 H. Gotoff, *The transmission of the text of Lucan in the ninth century* (Cambridge, Mass., 1971).

A further encouragement to include history among texts studied in school might have been provided by Cassiodorus' *Institutiones*. This sixth-century annotated bibliography on secular and sacred texts all educated people should know certainly recommends the reading of history, but it is specifically Jewish and Christian authors who are mentioned:

> Christian studies also possess narrators of history who, calm in their ecclesiastical gravity, recount the shifting movements of events and the unstable history of kingdoms with eloquent but very cautious splendour. Because they narrate ecclesiastical matters and describe changes which occur at various times they must always of necessity instruct the minds of readers in heavenly affairs, since they strive to assign nothing to chance, nothing to the weak power of gods as pagans have done, but to assign all things truly to the will of the Creator.[58]

Certainly it is the case that side by side with the continued copying and excerpting of Roman histories in the Carolingian period there was a wide dissemination of Old Testament history books and the works of Jewish and Christian ecclesiastical historians. I list below the principal Jewish and early Christian histories known to the Franks.

> *Latin historians known to c. 900: Jewish and Christian history*
> †*Old and New Testaments: especially Kings, Chronicles, Maccabees, Gospels, Acts, etc., more usually copied as separate books in the Carolingian period.
> Flavius Josephus †* *c.* 37–95 AD Jewish historian. †*Antiquitates* and *De bello judaico*
> Hegesippus, second century AD †*Latin version of Josephus' *De bello judaico*
> Eusebius-Rufinus: Eusebius of Caesaria (263–339), *Historia ecclesiastica* in ten books, translated into Latin by †*Rufinus of Aquileia, who boiled Eusebius' ten books down to nine and added two new ones of his own; *Chronicle* (see under Jerome). Eusebius' *Vita Constantini* was not known in any Latin version in the Carolingian period.
> Orosius of Braga, migrated to Africa *c.* 414 †*Historiae adversus paganos*.
> Jerome *c.* 342–420, born near Aquileia; †*translation of Eusebius' Chronicle into Latin and continued it to his own day.

---

[58] Cassiodorus, *Institutiones*, ed. R. A. B. Mynors, *Cassiodorus senatoris institutiones* (Oxford, 1937), I, c. 17 and English trans. L. W. Jones, *Cassiodorus Senator: an introduction to divine and human readings* (New York, 1946), p. 115–16. For discussion of the influence of Cassiodorus on the formation of a canon of knowledge in the Carolingian period see McKitterick, *Carolingians and the written word*, p. 194.

Prosper of Aquitaine 390–463 †*Chronicon* continues that of
Eusebius and Jerome and is particularly valuable for 425–55.
Epiphanius, sixth century, †*Historia ecclesiastica tripartita*, a
Latin translation of an amalgamation of the Greek ecclesi-
astical histories of Socrates, Sozomen and Theodoret of the
mid-fifth century, all of whom wrote continuations of Eusebius's *Historia ecclesiastica.*
Josephus, Eusebius, Orosius, the *Historia tripartita* of Sozomen, Socrates
and Theodoret in the translation by Epiphanius commissioned by
Cassiodorus, are all prominent in the ninth-century library catalogues.
Their reception, although part of the wider reception of the writings of the
church fathers in the Carolingian period, has distinctive features.[59] Not
only were these texts available, but they were then used and altered in various ways by different copyists and compilers to serve different purposes
from that which the original Roman and Christian historians intended.
They form the introduction to other histories, or are incorporated into
them. Alternatively, they are placed next to some other history to make
a specific point by juxtaposition.

Josephus' *Antiquitates* was written *c.* 94 AD while its author, a Jew and
Pharisee who became a Roman citizen, was in Rome. It recounted the
history of the Jews from the Creation until the Jewish wars of the later
first century AD. The text, originally in Greek, was known in the west
in a Latin translation made in the sixth century at Vivarium and was
counted, partly because drawn on by Eusebius, as Christian history.[60]
The *De bello iudaico*, however, on the Jewish wars themselves, and possibly originally written in Aramaic, was more familiar in the Latin version
and abridgement in five books circulated under the name of Hegesippus.
The *Antiquitates* was copied at Lorsch.[61] *De bello iudaico* is listed in the
catalogues of Reichenau, St Wandrille, St Riquier, St Gallen and the
list associated by Bischoff with the court of Charlemagne.[62] It was at
Freising in the tenth century. The Carolingian scholars Alcuin, Freculf
and Hraban Maur cite it and Ekkehard of St Gallen knew of it from a

---

[59] For a fuller discussion of Eusebius and the *Historia tripartita* in particular, see chapter 10
below. On the distinctive theological dimension see W. Otten, 'The texture of tradition:
the role of the church fathers in Carolingian theology', in I. Backus (ed.), *The reception of
the church fathers in the west: from the Carolingians to the Maurists*, 2 vols. (Leiden, 1997),
pp. 3–49.

[60] Flavius Josephus, *Antiquitates*, ed. F. Blatt, *The Latin Josephus, Antiquitates lib. I–V*
(Aarhus and Copenhagen, 1958); and Cassiodorus: ed. Mynors, *Institutiones* I, c. 17;
and see W. Berschin, *Greek letters and the Latin middle ages* (Washington, DC, 1988),
p. 78

[61] See below, p. 200.

[62] On the list in Berlin Diez B. Sant. 66 see above, p. 39 and below, pp. 80–1.

St Gallen copy.[63] Josephus enjoyed a wide circulation in the early middle ages. Cassiodorus c. 570 mentions a translation of the *Antiquitates* already in existence possibly made by Rufinus.[64] Like other older histories, Josephus/Hegesippus attracted contemporary historical writings of various kinds. The *Rhythmus langobardorum* of 698, for example, was written probably at Bobbio and inserted in an early Hegesippus manuscript (Milan, Ambrosiana C.105inf).[65]

The *Historia ecclesiastica* of Eusebius written in the fourth century and narrating the history of the early Christian church, and his World Chronicle in Jerome's translation with Continuation, are equally well documented and are discussed in detail in chapter 10. A relatively large group of nine seventh- and eighth-century manuscripts of Orosius' *Seven books of history against the pagans* survives. Orosius's work was written in the early fifth century and it is conventionally understood as an apologetic addressed to those who thought that Rome's troubles were due to her abandonment of the pagan gods.[66] These codices are from Italy and Francia, and the earliest of them, Florence Biblioteca Medicea Laurenziana plut. 65.1, an uncial codex of the late sixth century, is perhaps the most famous. It was possibly written at Ravenna; it bears the inscription *Confectus codex in statione magistri Uiliaric antiquarii ora pro me scribtore sic DNM* in the same sloping uncial script as the marginalia. Uiliaric is thought to have been either the scribe or the master of the book shop in which the book was produced.[67] The volume thus sheds a dim light on the processes of book production and distribution in sixth-century Ravenna.

---

[63] T. Rajak, *Josephus: the historian and his society*, 2nd edn (London and Philadelphia, 2002). See also P. Bilde, *Flavius Josephus between Jerusalem and Rome. His life, works and their importance. Journal for the Study of Pseudepigrapha*, Supplement series 2 (Sheffield, 1988), pp. 61–5. On the transmission of his writing, see H. Schreckenburg, *Die Flavius-Josephus-Tradition in Antike und Mittelalter* and *Rezeptionsgeschichtliche und textkritische Untersuchungen zu Flavius Josephus*, Arbeiten zum Literatur und Geschichte des hellenistichen Judentums 5 and 10 (Leiden, 1972 and 1977). The oldest Greek manuscripts, apart from a fragment Vienna, ÖNB P. Graec. 29810, date from the ninth to the eleventh centuries and thus the Latin versions are the earliest witnesses to the text.

[64] Cassiodorus: ed. Mynors, *Institutiones* I, c. 17. See W. Berschin, *Greek letters*, p. 302, note 23. The older Latin versions survive in a printed edition made of them in 1524.

[65] Milan Ambrosiansa C. 105inf. fols. 121–121v, *CLA*, III (Oxford, 1938), no. 323a and 323b.

[66] See Orosius, *Historiae adversus paganos*, ed. M. P. Arnaud-Lindet, *Histoires (contre les païens) Orose*, 3 vols. (Paris, 1990–1), pp. LXVII–XCVII, which replaces Karl Zangemeister (ed.), *Pauli Orosii Historiarum adversus paganos* (Leipzig, 1889). See also J. Bately and D. J. A. Ross, 'A check list of manuscripts of Orosius *Historiarum aduersum paganos libri septem*', *Scriptorium* 15 (1961), pp. 329–34.

[67] *CLA*, I (Oxford, 1938), no. 298. On Uiliaric see P. Amory, 'A prosopography of Goths in Italy, 489–554', in P. Amory, *People and identity in Ostrogothic Italy, 489–554* (Cambridge, 1997), pp. 438–9.

The manuscripts from the pre-Carolingian period together with those of the ninth century, moreover, witness to a wide dispersal of the text, especially north of the Alps, with many variants emerging in the text tradition as a whole. A curious instance of the use of Orosius in the Carolingian period is by the Breton writer Wrmonoc. In his account of the Life of Paul Aurelian (c.18) the count Witures describes a terrible serpent menacing his island and which is destroyed by the saint. The account of the serpent and its destruction is taken from Orosius' account of a battle between Regulus, a Roman consul, and a huge serpent in the First Punic war.[68] Another is the abridged version, probably made at Lorsch and surviving in a manuscript once in Wrocław and known as Rehdigeranus 107, now in Berlin, which merits further study.[69] More straightforward use of the text is made by the Carolingian historian Freculf of Lisieux.[70]

The *Historia tripartita* was not just for reading as far as the Carolingians were concerned. Its text and information were also exploited, as we can see from its use by those involved with the synod of Paris in 825. We also find it being incorporated into historical accounts and into discussions of the church and tracts on rulership of the Carolingian period, by, for example, Alamannus in the *Vita et translatio helenae*, by Freculf of Lisieux in his *Chronicle*,[71] by Walafrid Strabo in his *De exordiis et incrementis rerum ecclesiasticarum*,[72] by Sedulius in his *Liber de rectoribus christianis*, by Anastasius Bibliothecarius,[73] and by Hincmar in his *De regis persona et regio ministerio*. Chapters 5 and 14 are cited by the author of the *Miracula sancti Gorgonii* in 965 in support of one of his historical incidents. It was also used in the twelfth century. All these citations are to provide information or historical precedent and support for some other event that is being described.[74]

The circulation of the so-called barbarian histories is just as well attested as that of Christian and Roman historiography, as can be seen from

---

[68] N. Wright, 'Knowledge of Christian Latin poets and historians in medieval Brittany', *Études Celtiques* 23 (1986), pp. 163–85 at pp. 182–3.
[69] Reported by Arnaud-Lindet (ed.), *Orose*, pp. LXXVI–LXXVII.
[70] See M. I. Allen, *Frechulfi Lexoviensis episcopi opera omnia. Prolegomena. Indices*, CCCM, CLXIX (Turnhout, 2002), pp. 214*–216* and 317*–326*.
[71] *Ibid.*, pp. 204*–205* and 285*–288*.
[72] See A. L. Harting-Correa (ed.), *Walafrid Strabo's Libellus de exordiis & incrementis quarundam in observationibus ecclesiasticis rerum. A translation & liturgical commentary* (Leiden, 1996), p. 40.
[73] See C. Leonardi, 'Anastasio Bibliotecario e le traduzioni dal greco nella Roma alto medievali', in M. W. Herren (ed.), *The sacred nectar of the Greeks: the study of Greek in the west in the early middle ages* (London, 1988), pp. 277–97.
[74] See W. Jacob, *Die handschriftlichen Überlieferung der sogenannten Historia tripartita des Epiphanius Cassiodor*, Texte and Untersuchungen 59 (Berlin 1954).

the following list:

Latin historians known before c. 900: 'barbarian' history

Victor of Vita, *Historia persecutionis africanae provinciae* on the Catholic church under the Vandal rulers Gaiseric and Huneric in the period 429–84, written *c.* 485

Jordanes, **Getica* and †**Romana*, histories of the Romans (to 552) and of Goths (to 540)

Isidore (560–636), †**Historia de regibus gothorum, vandalorum et suevorum* and **Chronica maiora* (Creation to AD 615)

Bede (*c.* 673–735), †**Historia ecclesiastica gentis anglorum*, on the conversion of the English to Christianity

Paul the Deacon (*c.* 720–799), †**Historia langobardorum* (History of the Lombards)

Gregory of Tours (*c.* 540–94), †**Historiae*, in ten books with Book V onwards on the period 575–91, mostly about the Franks

There are some evident 'national' concentrations among the extant early medieval copies of these texts. Generally, however, the manuscript tradition of some of these works is more widely dispersed and in these cases indicates an interest in the text in regions other than that in which the author wrote. Bede's *Historia ecclesiastica gentis anglorum*, for example, was disseminated on the continent even more widely than in England. A copy made at Jarrow in the third decade of the eighth century (Cambridge University Library MS Kk.5.16) found a place at the court of Charlemagne, and many of the extant continental manuscripts belong to the same family.[75] Most of the earliest manuscripts of Paul the Deacon's *Historia langobardorum* are of Frankish or North Italian origin.[76] Copies of Isidore of Seville's *History of the Goths, Sueves and Vandals* survive in manuscripts of Frankish origin. Codices containing Gregory of Tours, on the other hand, are exclusively Frankish and the *Getica* of Jordanes appears rarely outside the regions once ruled by Goths.[77]

Such distribution patterns suggest that the stress on the growth of the church and Christianity in Bede appears to have found a wider audience, assisted no doubt by the number of Anglo-Saxons in centres on the continent who wished to acquire copies. The readership and

[75] See B. Colgrave and R. A. B. Mynors (eds.), *Bede's ecclesiastical history of the English people* (Oxford, 1969), pp. xlii–lxx; and R. McKitterick, 'Kulturelle Verbindungen zwischen England und den fränkischen Reichen in der Zeit der Karolinger: Kontext und Implikationen', in J. Ehlers (ed.), *Deutschland und der Westen Europas im Mittelalter*, Vorträge und Forschungen 56 (Stuttgart, 2002), pp. 121–48.

[76] See below, pp. 77–83.

[77] See P. Bourgain and M. Heinzelmann, 'L'Oeuvre de Grégoire de Tours: la diffusion des manuscrits', in Gauthier and Galinié (eds.), *Grégoire de Tours et l'espace gaulois*, pp. 273–318.

distribution of the other texts is more difficult to explain. It may be that the specific provision of an historical identity of most of the other texts may have been the most important aspect of the text as far as its later audiences were concerned. The questions of historical identity, knowledge and audience, however, also need to be explored with reference not just to complete texts and all that they have indicated, but also to extracts and compilations.

Historical miscellanies

Certainly the varied use made of excerpts and extracts may expand our knowledge of the audience for historical texts. These can be epitomes of texts or extracts from particular texts within other works. At Lorsch in the first half of the ninth century, for example, what have been described as excerpts were made from the *Scriptores historiae augustae* (BAV pal. lat. 886) (that is, on Hadrian, Commodus, Marcus Aurelius, Severus, Caracalla, etc.) but it appears to have more of the character of a short epitome than just of random excerpts and would merit further study. Then there is a further series of excerpts which has been attributed to Sedulius Scotus incorporated into his *Collectaneum* and possibly serving as a source of ideas for his *De rectoribus christianis*.[78]

Rather more fruitful are the historical miscellanies. I turn therefore to questions raised by particular 'history books' from the ninth century, one from northern Francia and two from northern Italy.

St Omer, Bibliothèque Municipale 706 is famous for containing the *Annales Bertiniani* (Annals of St Bertin), that is, the continuation of the *Annales regni francorum* from 830–82 directly after a 'C' text of the *Annales regni francorum* themselves.[79] The codex is dated to the late tenth century, and is possibly a copy of an earlier compilation made at St Vaast that may in its turn go back to an original Rheims compilation. As Felix Grat pointed out, however, these Frankish annals for the years 741–882 are part of a very large historical miscellany, for St Omer 706 was originally the second half of St Omer 697. The whole book contained the following texts in this order: Eutropius, *Historia romana*, the *Chronicon* of Marcellinus Comes, the *Notitia galliarum*, the *Historiae* of Gregory in a

---

[78] See S. Hellmann, *Scottus, Quellen und Untersuchungen zur lateinischen Philologie 1*, 1 (Munich, 1906).

[79] I am reliant in this instance on the full descriptions and account of the manuscript in *Catalogue générale des manuscrits des Bibliothèques publiques des départements 3* (Paris, 1861), pp. 305 and 309–10; F. Kurze, 'Ueber die fränkischen Reichsannalen und ihrer Ueberarbeitung 1: Die handschriftliche Ueberlieferung', *Neues Archiv* 19 (1894), p. 315 (it is Kurze's MS 'C3'); and F. Grat, L. Vielliard and S. Clémencet (eds.), *Annales de Saint-Bertin* (Paris, 1964).

Carolingian reworking, Fredegar's *Chronicle*, Book IV and Continuations (but only the material covering 584–741 adding to an expanded 'Book X of Gregory'), the *Annales regni francorum* and the *Annales Bertiniani*. The compendium may also have included an excerpt from Bede's *Chronica*, the *Chronicon laurissense breve* and the *Annals of St Vaast*.

St Omer 697 + St Omer 706, therefore, present a continuous history from the foundation of Rome to the Carolingians, with a special emphasis on Gaul, and with, most crucially, the version of the events between 741 and 768 in the *Annales regni francorum* substituted for that presented in the Continuations of Fredegar. It is, in short, a Frankish history book very much in sympathy with Paris, BnF lat. 10911 discussed in the previous chapter, though it lacks the Trojan element. The juxtaposition of older Roman and Frankish history with court-centred Carolingian history is significant, and is a remarkable witness to the consistency and longevity of the association of Roman and Frankish history in Carolingian perceptions of the past.[80]

A further example is the core of historical texts contained in the late eighth- and early ninth-century codex from Lucca, Biblioteca Capitolare 490. It was put together between 787 and 796 and various hands, judging from the variety of pre-caroline minuscules and uncials, at Lucca were responsible. The Isidore and the *Liber pontificalis* sections are written in uncial and mixed pre-caroline minuscule scripts. Some b-d uncial in this part may indicate legal training on the part of the scribe, for this type of uncial is usually associated with legal codices in Italy. An attempt has been made to identify one of the scribes with Bishop John I (780–800) and one scribe (fol. 211v) seems to be identical with the *presbiter Danihel* whose signature is found in Lucca charters as late as 816.[81]

Lucca 490 also includes a fragment of recipes for pigments, and portions of the *Canonum collectio hispana* and *Collectio canonum sanblasiana*. Bede's *De natura rerum* and the *Genealogiae totius bibliothecae* in uncial of the late eighth or early ninth century are accompanied by excerpts from Eusebius's *Historia ecclesiastica* in Rufinus' version, Easter Tables and the *Liber pontificalis*. It is the *Liber pontificalis* text in this manuscript that contains the most salutary warnings to the historian studying these texts and endeavouring to piece together the significance of the manuscript tradition and who the texts were for.

As mentioned earlier, by the beginning of the eighth century, the *Liber pontificalis* (Book of the Popes) was being updated on a Life-by-Life basis,

---

[80] Above, pp. 13–19.
[81] L. Schiaparelli, *Il codice 490 della biblioteca capitolare di Lucca e la scuola scrittoria Lucchese sec. VIII–IX. Contributi allo studio della minuscola precarolina in Italia*, Studi e Testi 36 (Vatican City, 1924).

sometimes while the subject was still living. The compilation was, therefore, being made by compilers who can be presumed to have had some first-hand knowledge of what they were recording. But it can also be presumed that the compilers of at least the official manuscript version would be loyal. If the political activities of a particular pope threw less than reputable light on his career, it might be that other aspects of his career, such as the register of sumptuous material provision for the churches of Rome, would gain more space.[82] The *Liber pontificalis* text, of course, left Rome at different stages to go into circulation[83] so that only six manuscripts include the Life of Leo III (Life 98) and from then on there are gaps and missing portions so that the last paragraph of Life 112, Pope Stephen V, is known only from an incomplete manuscript. Davis comments that the manuscript variants are a sure witness to the fact that the text had no sacrosanctity. He goes on to suggest that the very fact of the *Liber pontificalis*' anonymity may have encouraged interpolations in and modifications to the text. The most striking variants are in Life 91 (Gregory II), which we have both in the original and in a much revised form produced about twenty years later. Life 94 of Stephen II, moreover, exists in what is known as the 'Lombard recension'; it makes the text more palatable to Lombard readers by excising the opprobrious comments about Lombards. It is this version which survives in Lucca 490.

Thus in Lucca 490 a unique, pro-Lombard, version of a particular text about the popes is combined with canon law material springing from two independent and non-papal sources, namely the decrees of the councils of Merovingian Gaul and Visigothic Spain and the early Italian collection which included material from fifth-century popes. Neither the sacrosanctity nor the integrity of the texts used concerned the compiler who had his own objectives in creating an historical and legal compilation with its own internal logic and train of thought. Audience and purpose can, therefore, alter the emphasis of the texts compiled.

An even more striking example is the famous 'Verona miscellany'. This is a book that appears to offer an opportunity to reconstruct both the knowledge of history in early Carolingian north Italy and its particular emphases, at least on the part of its compiler. At Verona in the first half of the ninth century a large historical miscellany was compiled of material

[82] See the points on material wealth raised by T. F. X. Noble, 'Paradoxes and possibilities in the sources for Roman society in the early middle ages', in J. M. H. Smith (ed.), *Early medieval Rome and the Christian west. Essays in honour of Donald Bullough* (Leiden, 2000), pp. 55–84.

[83] In addition to the comments made on the manuscript transmission by L. Duchesne, *Le Liber pontificalis*, I, pp. CLXIV–CCIII, see R. Davis, *The lives of the eighth-century popes* (*Liber pontificalis*) (Liverpool, 1992), pp. xv–xviii.

relating to the late antique and early medieval history of Italy. This appears to have been donated to the newly founded monastery of St Vincent at Metz in *c.* 984 by Bishop Deodericus of Metz. Other Verona manuscripts were given at the same time, notably Berlin, Deutsche Staatsbibliothek Phillipps 1676 (50), the famous Egino Homiliary codex of the late eighth or early ninth century with corrections and additional fulminations by the controversial tenth-century bishop, Rather of Verona, and Berlin, Deutsche Staatsbibliothek Phillipps 1831 (128) a collection of texts to do with time including Easter cycles, Bede's *De temporibus, De natura rerum* and *De temporum ratione,* a list of Greek emperors to 820, school texts on astronomy, *computus* and arithmetic, and a discussion of the names of the days and months.

The historical miscellany, however, was an even more elaborate collection than the other codices in this group. Now dismembered and split into four volumes, it is divided between Berlin and St Petersburg. Its original sequence of contents was reconstructed by Valentin Rose.[84] Two volumes are in Berlin (Deutsche Staatsbibliothek, Preussischer Kulturbesitz Phillipps 1885+1896) and St Petersburg State Library Q.v.Class. No. 9 and Q.v.IV.5.[85] When I first referred to this manuscript in 1994, before I had seen the Berlin sections, I characterized it as 'a compilation of material relating to the late antique and early medieval history of Italy'. It is certainly that, but it is also far more than that. I stressed then how important this miscellany was for the north Italian compiler's understanding of the past and what he wished to understand or what he hoped his patron and readers would understand. Certainly the book serves as an exemplum of one of the major problems of historical writing, namely, the context of each manuscript witness to a particular text and how we are to interpret the complicated messages it provides. Yet more needs to be said about this north Italian choice of extracts.

It is important to understand that the four volumes we now have comprise quires 4 to 36 of a book which once contained at least thirty-seven quires, or gatherings of eight leaves, each. Secondly, the quires in these codices, fortunately for us, mostly possess quire marks on the last leaf of each gathering. I say 'fortunately' because the medieval binder who

---

[84] V. Rose, *Die Handschriftenverzeichnisse der Königlichen Bibliothek zu Berlin. Verzeichnis der lateinischen Handschriften,* II, part 3 (Berlin 1905), nos. 136 and 137.

[85] I have so far only been able to examine the Berlin portions in the flesh. For the St Petersburg portions I have studied a microfilm, and printout from the microfilm, assisted with a full description made of the St Petersburg portion in the Berlin and St Petersburg catalogues. I have also benefited greatly from notes on the codicology of the St Petersburg portions kindly provided by Helmut Reimitz, to whom I am very grateful for these and for the loan of the St Petersburg microfilm.

gathered the quires together appears to have done so in a haphazard order. They now survive as follows.

Quires I–III   **missing**
Quires IV–VII   St Petersburg Q.v.IV.5
Quires VIII–X   St Petersburg Q.v.Class. No. 9
Quires XI–XIV   Berlin Phillipps 1885
Quires XV–XX   Berlin Phillipps 1896
Quires XXI–XXVII   Berlin Phillipps 1885
Quires XXVIII–XXXIIII   Berlin Phillipps 1896
Quires XXXV–XXXVI   Berlin Phillipps 1885

Altogether there are 75 + 89 = 164 folios in Berlin and 50 in St Petersburg, giving a total of 214 folios. There is an estimated further additional forty-three leaves missing, comprising twenty-four folios (that is, the missing first three quires assuming they were regular quires of eight leaves each) plus nineteen lost from the existing quires. Originally therefore, before it was broken up, the manuscript was a substantial volume of at least 257 folios, or 514 pages. The page format is not strikingly large. Although the page size differs between the four different volumes, between 197–183 × 140 mm, the writing block is 150–115 mm. There are twenty-three lines to the page. The script is a markedly clear, even, slightly sloping and well-spaced early caroline minuscule of c. 800, with open and minuscule **a**, uncial and straight **d**, a **g** whose underneath curve is sometimes detached from the rest of the letter, the ascender of **f** coming below the line and a very sparing use of both abbreviations and ligatures. The gatherings in St Petersburg lat. Q.v.IV.5 are far from regular; many leaves are singletons slotted in.

But what of the content? With the reconstruction of the volume suggested by Valentin Rose, the compilation of texts in their original sequence shows a consistent emphasis. I give now the contents in the sequence in which they would have been in the original manuscript (and here differ from Rose in some respects), not as they now are.

In the St Petersburg portion Quire IV, St Petersburg Q.v.IV.5 starts with Justinus' epitome of Pompeius Trogus Books I and II, and thus includes the kingdoms of the Assyrians and Scythians (*De regno assyriorum*; *De scitharum regno*). This was marked out with a large **P** at the beginning of the text after a heading written in red uncial script. Justinus is followed by a comprehensive selection, from Eutropius' *Historiarum romanorum breviarium* up to the civil war period and Julius Caesar. Again this is distinguished by fancy capital headings and a large four-line initial at the beginning of the text. The passing of time throughout the text is emphasized by writing the words *deinde, post hanc, eodem anno*, etc. in red uncial at the beginnings of sections. In the Berlin portions, an account of the Goths running as far as the Gothic king Wallia *Rex* from Isidore of Seville's History of the Goths, Sueves and Vandals, that is, chapters 1–22, is set out with dating according to era and imperial regnal years. There is a particularly ornate beginning for the section on the Vandals and it includes the account of the conversion of the Goths by Ulfilas and the creation of the Gothic alphabet.

Thereafter (in Berlin Phillipps 1896) come extracts from Jordanes' *Romana* with the narrative from the descent from Adam, the Persian kings in whose reign famous Jewish leaders lived, reaching Romulus by fol. 8v. There are large red headings for the kings of the Persians, Assyrians, Macedonians and Alexander the Great. The extracts from Jordanes' *Getica* which follow introduce Theodoric to Italy. These are then complemented by extracts concerning Theodoric from the Anonymous Valesianus and Gregory the Great's *Dialogues* and then more from Jordanes' *Getica* concerning Theodoric's later career.

To this was added a selection from all six books of Paul the Deacon's *Historia langobardorum* that contrives to omit most of the especially Lombard material. What is does include, however, is the section about the Saracens in Sardinia and the bringing of St Augustine's relics from thence by Liutprand, king of the Lombards, to Pavia.[86] This section ends with Charles Martel and Liutprand, the famous account of Pippin III's haircut when he was a boy being brought up at the Lombard court and Charles Martel's victory over the Saracens. In other words, the stress Paul contrives to place on the links between Lombards and Franks is similarly highlighted by the compiler.[87] Thus what appears to be the first part of the codex concentrates on ethnographic history, with many people and the background to the history of Italy and its peoples outlined. There is a clear insistence on chronological sequence, even when the chronology occasionally goes back to a period before that which a text has just covered. But it is a background for a Lombard-Frankish kingdom with roots in the kingdoms of the Assyrians, Persians, Greeks, Romans and Goths.

The second part of the manuscript selects texts which have more to do with political structures, namely, kingship, empire and conquest.

Berlin, Phillipps 1896 opens with Quire XXVIII and some of Jerome's commentary on Daniel's vision which in fact includes many reflections on the kings Balthasar, Darius and his satraps, Cyrus, Nebuchadnezzar. Here, there may be a thematic reminiscence of, and an intention to imply

---

[86] This is the story that was included in the BAV pal. lat. 243 version of the *Chronicon laurissense breve* as well, see above pp. 35–6.

[87] See chapter 3 below and the brief comments by P. Chiesa, 'Caratteristiche della trasmissione dell' "Historia langobardorum"' in *Paolo Diacono e il Friuli altomedievale (secc. VI–X)* (Spoleto, 2001), pp. 61 and 65–6.

parallels between, the Jews under the Assyrians and the Jewish kings under Romans in Israel with the Lombards under the Franks. The text then reinforces this with extracts from the Book of Kings concerning the Old Testament kings, set out with their names forming the headings. Thereafter comes the Chronicle of Eusebius-Jerome, written out as prose rather than in the normal columns. But the compiler has read down the columns vertically rather than across horizontally, and forms thereby sequences of the kingdoms of Israel, Egypt, Macedonia, Assyria and Syria. It is thus not a direct visual transfer of the history such as is made by other authors who made use of the Jerome-Eusebius *Chronicle*, such as Prosper of Aquitaine in his *Chronicle*. In Prosper's text, the items once juxtaposed in columns are placed in sequences of sentences and curious information emerges, such as that Aeneas was supposedly a contemporary of Samson.[88] An extract from Isidore of Seville's *Etymologiae* on Kings provides a comment on the vicissitudes of political power and on *regna, reges, consules imperatores* and *tyranni*. The compiler then returns to the chronicle to set out the *origo constantini imperatoris*, with emphasis on Helena, Constantine's mother. Finally, there is a section from the Anonymous Valesianus on Constantine's death and burial in Constantinople.

At a basic level the compiler has been able to draw on a well-stocked library, with the Bible, Eusebius, Jerome, Isidore, Jordanes, Anonymous Valesianus and Paul the Deacon's works. But he has used his material to present the past of many peoples as a continuum from Assyrians to Lombards and Franks. The latter are squeezed in because of the inclusion of extracts from Paul's *Historia longobardorum*. Many rulers are singled out, most prominently Zeno, Anastasius, Theodoric, Justinian, Liutprand and Charles Martel.

A contemporary reader, writing in a rather more cursive hand than the main text, moreover, has annotated the text here and there. These mostly indicate attentive rather than partisan reading. For example, in part of the text in Berlin, Phillips 1885 fol. 4r concerning the third year of the emperor Valens and the description of the division of the Goths under Athanaric and Fridigerius, the annotator has noted *atanaricus rex*. He insists elsewhere that Alaric was *rex* as well (fol. 5r) and that when Alaric entered Rome the Romans remained *inviolatos et securos*. With reference to the hair cutting of Pippin the annotator has noted that this is *scala*

---

[88] For background on Eusebius, see R. Burgess with W. Witakowski, *Studies in Eusebian and post-Eusebian chronography* (Stuttgart, 1999); and see the edition by G. Brugnoli, *Curiosissimus excerptor: gli 'Additamenta' de Girolamo ai 'Chronica' de Eusebio* (Pisa, 1995). On Prosper, see R. Markus, 'Chronicle and theology: Prosper of Aquitaine', in C. Holdsworth and T. Wiseman, (eds.), *The inheritance of historiography, 350–900* (Exeter, 1986), pp. 31–44.

next to the passage, while in the Jordanes text the capture of Troy and the career of Attila are noted. Above the account of the conversion of the Goths by Ulfilas, the annotator notes that the Goths were heretics. In the Justinus and Eutropius portions brief notes of the names of principal protagonists and events provide a short marginal guide to the contents of the text.

Thus this book is primarily an ethnographic history, linking the peoples of Italy, and especially the Lombards both by implication and juxtaposition, with the peoples of the Old Testament and with the Romano-Greek world. It is also a book reflecting on political power and on rulership. Given the probable political context in which the books which supplied these excerpts were collected together, and from which this collection was compiled, it suggests that the question of Frankish rule was not entirely clear cut. A further illustration of this will be considered in the following chapter in relation to Paul the Deacon's *Historia langobardorum*. The Berlin-St Petersburg codex emerges as a strong and rather unexpected statement of historical identity which has many facets, not least the marked interest in the history of the Goths. Yet the approach of this compiler is arguably within the Frankish mode of historical compilation. There is a perception of the continuation of contemporary affairs reinforced by the simple but effective method of text extracts and juxtaposition. Let us not forget, moreover, that the book is written in caroline minuscule, another sign of the speedy adoption of a Frankish import.

From all these compilations it is but a short step to the historical amalgamations we now accord such titles as Fredegar's Chronicle, or from a later period, the *Gesta normannorum ducum* of William of Jumièges, Orderic Vitalis and Robert of Torigni, which draws heavily also on Dudo of St Quentin.[89] William of Jumièges, furthermore, was often included with earlier histories such as Einhard's *Vita Karoli*. This had the effect of placing the Normans in a legitimate succession of authority. Such compilations and schemes of composition demonstrate a very different conception of authorship and historical composition from the one we encounter in an author such as Bede or the ninth-century Carolingian annalists such as Nithard or Hincmar of Rheims. In these compilations there is not one master mind, one perspective or one set of sources of information but several. The more sophisticated the selection and stitching together of texts, the more particular emphases may be observed.

[89] See the Introduction in E. M. C. van Houts (ed. and trans.), *The Gesta normannorum ducum of William of Jumièges, Orderic Vitalis and Robert of Torigni*, Oxford Medieval Texts, 2 vols. (Oxford, 1992–5); and M. Chibnall (ed. and trans.), *Ecclesiastical history of Orderic Vitalis*, Oxford Medieval Texts (Oxford, 1969–80).

But we gain the impression also of the past as continuous process, with each successive author making or being selected by a compiler to make, a particular contribution to a chosen theme. It is of crucial significance for the determination of the particular significance and appreciation of the message of any one particular text that its inclusion in composite historical manuscripts be recorded and observed and that the specific circumstances not only of the texts but of each manuscript containing the text, be established as far as this is possible.

Thus, as I stressed in the previous chapter, the codicological context and manuscript tradition of a particular work may well have as much to tell us about the general milieu in which the manuscript was produced as the text it contains. Generally we can learn much from the grouping of particular texts about what its status as history may have been, quite apart from the associations created by juxtaposition. The codicological context in which both Gregory of Tours and other contemporary histories such as the Chronicle of Fredegar are found underlines how fully these works stood in the tradition of Eusebius and Jerome's Chronicle. As we have seen from a book such as St Omer, Bibliothèque Municipale 697 + 706, Fredegar, Gregory and abridgements of Gregory are found as parts of composite works of history drawing on earlier chronicles. Other compilations of historical works, such as Vienna, ÖNB cod. 473, provide crucial indications of a compiler's intentions and perceptions of the past, as well as the possible audience's expectations.[90] The Astronomer's Life of Louis the Pious for instance has virtually no codicological existence independent of Einhard's *Vita Karoli*. Many of these manuscripts also include the Royal Frankish annals or other Frankish history texts as well.[91] St Petersburg, F.v.IV.4 combines the *Liber historiae francorum* (including the end section drawn from the Continuations of Fredegar), the *Annales regni francorum*, Einhard's *Vita Karoli*, the Astronomer's *Vita Hludowici imperatoris*, and the text known as the *Genealogia regum francorum*.[92]

Certainly the early medieval interest in the so-called barbarian histories was part of a wider interest in the histories of various peoples – Romans and Greeks as well as Goths and Franks. But to presume that this was all it was does not entirely accord with the Carolingian evidence provided by library catalogues and extant historical collections such as the ones examined in this chapter. These show that the Frankish interest in history was not indiscriminate: it was concentrated for the most part on the three

[90] On the Vienna codex see chapter 5 below.
[91] See E. Tremp, *Die Überlieferung der Vita Hludowici imperatoris des Astronomus*, MGH Studien und Texte 1 (Hannover, 1991).
[92] *Ibid.*, pp. 50–3.

peoples, Trojans, Romans and Jews, whose history was seen to stand in direct continuity with that of the Franks.[93]

What the extant manuscripts do indicate is that not one historical text – Roman, Christian or early medieval – can be regarded as an unchanging entity. All historical writings could be transformed to serve a particular author's or compiler's specific purpose in relation to whatever audience, or audiences, that author or compiler had in mind. Thus the miscellanies discussed in this chapter serve as exempla of one of the major problems of the transmission of historical writing, namely, the context of each manuscript witness and how we are to interpret the complicated messages it provides. Location and immediate purpose become crucial considerations. It is not possible simply to address the content of each historical writer while ignoring the manuscript tradition and codicological context from which it derives. Only by detailed examination of the manuscripts concerned can we begin to gain some notion of what those audiences might have been. It may rarely be as close a connection as the one between Quintus Curtius Rufus and Count Conrad with which I began this chapter. Nevertheless, we should endeavour to establish how a text may have been read, the associations an early medieval reader may have been expected and intended to make, and the consequences for our appreciation of this text as an historical source. I pursue these issues further in the following chapters.

---

[93] See the further discussion in chapters 9 and 10.

3 Paul the Deacon's *Historia langobardorum* and the Franks

The conquest of Lombardy in 774 is universally recognized, both by contemporaries and by modern historians, to have been one of the most momentous events in Charlemagne's reign. As an action it can easily be understood as one in a succession of campaigns and incorporations of territory by the Frankish ruler, from the subjugation of Aquitaine to the annexation of Bavaria, the oppression of the Saxons and the destruction of the Avars. All these conquests are presented in the Frankish sources as divinely supported victories and the bringing of many people under Frankish rule. Yet the process by which Charlemagne consolidated his rule in the Lombard kingdom of Italy, and the cultural and religious consequences of 774, for both Franks and Lombards, are far less easy to determine. In the past, moreover, much excellent research has been done, first of all to establish the state of Lombard culture in the second half of the eighth century and, secondly, what in cultural and artistic terms Lombards were able, either potentially or actually, to contribute to Frankish culture.[1] In the case of San Vincenzo in central Italy, moreover, recent confidence in the strength of Carolingian, as distinct from Lombard and Beneventan, influences in the development of the abbey would appear to be misplaced.[2] A focus on the reception of Frankish culture in northern and central Italy and the nature of Franco-Lombard cultural relations, especially in the immediate aftermath of 774, has been less constant and it is this which is my concern in this chapter.

[1] See the survey by L. Capo, 'Paolo Diacono e il problema della cultura dell'Italia Longobarda', in S. Gasparri and P. Commarosano (eds.), *Langobardia* (Udine, 1990), pp. 169–235; and C. Villa, 'Cultura classica e tradizione Longobarde; tra latino e volgari', in P. Chiesa (ed.), *Paolo Diacono e l'origine dell'Europa medievale: uno scrittore fra tradizione longobarda e rinnovamento carolingio* (Udine, 2000), pp. 575–600.

[2] R. Hodges, *Light in the dark ages: the rise and fall of San Vincenzo al Volturno* (London, 1997). Compare R. McKitterick, review in *The Times Literary Supplement*, 5 September 1997, p. 12.

The need for questions about the interaction between Franks and Lombards is nowhere more apparent than in discussions of Paul the Deacon and his historical writing. I have been fascinated, like, in a sense, a Frankish outsider invading the Lombard world of the eighth century, at the assumptions about Paul and the Lombards that have dominated discussions hitherto. The impact of 774 upon modern scholarship and the feeling that somehow the Lombards ought not to have let themselves be conquered by the Franks does a great disservice to the strengths of Lombard culture in this period and distorts our understanding of the Franks' role in Italy. The so-called 'Lombard failure' in 774, as Paolo Delogu points out, has been seen as 'throwing doubt on the political cohesion and moral determination of the Lombards at a moment when they should have been defending their own survival as a sovereign people'.[3] The social complexity and loose political organization of Lombard society, the existence of aristocratic opposition to Desiderius, king of the Lombards (757–74), political links with Francia, the Lombards in some sense treacherously renouncing their national identity, and the Lombards having apparently lost their taste for war, have all been stressed by way of excusing the events of 774.

What did the Franks think of the conquest? It may have offered the Frankish magnates opportunities but it also surely represented a considerable challenge to their resources and energies. The Frankish sources, notably the Royal Frankish Annals, present the assumption of the Lombard throne as a self-evident victory.[4] It was not the conquest of the perfidious people who were long-standing enemies of the Franks but a political coup. Charlemagne is successful again. Another *gens* is added to those already within the Frankish realm.[5] The annalists speak in terms of a political coup and change of leadership as distinct from a major invasion, though it should be noted that the revised version of the annals makes more of the oppression of the Romans by the Lombards and Charlemagne's strenuous exertion in dealing with Desiderius. Charlemagne usurped the Lombard throne and won the loyalty of the Lombards much as his father Pippin had usurped the Merovingian throne and won the loyalty of the Franks.

On his return from Rome the lord king Charles came again to Pavia and captured the city and Desiderius with his wife and daughter and the whole treasure of his

---

[3] P. Delogu, 'Lombard and Carolingian Italy', in McKitterick (ed.), *NCMH*, pp. 290–319, at p. 301.

[4] *Annales regni francorum*, ed. F. Kurze, *MGH SRG*, VI (Hannover, 1895), s.a. 773, 774, pp. 34–40.

[5] See further below, chapter 4.

palace besides. All the Lombards came from every city of Italy and submitted to the rule of the glorious lord king Charles and of the Franks... After subduing Italy and setting it to rights, the lord king Charles left a Frankish garrison in the city of Pavia and by God's help returned triumphantly to Frankia with his wife and the rest of the Franks.[6]

Rotgaud of Friuli's rebellion is presented in Frankish sources from a characteristically Frankish point of view as breaking faith and not keeping oaths: 'Charles placed the cities he had captured under Franks, that is, Cividale, Treviso and the other places which had revolted and returned again to Francia, successful and victorious.' Again, the revised version supplies far more detail and alleges that Rotgaud aspired to the kingship.[7]

Thereafter, the Lombard dimension of Charles' activities is simply incorporated into the annalist's narrative. He records how the duke of Spoleto arrived with many presents in 779, and that in 780 Charles celebrated Christmas at Pavia.[8] Of greater significance were the events of 781. Pippin, Charlemagne's four-year-old son, was baptised by Pope Hadrian in Rome and anointed king of Italy. At Milan, Charlemagne's newly born daughter Gisela was baptised by Archbishop Thomas of Milan (759–83), who also acted as sponsor.[9]

These can be read as graceful ways of stressing that the Lombard kingdom was close to the Carolingian family's interests and respected, though one could also see at least the creation of Pippin as king as a hostile demonstration to the Lombards of who now was boss. On the other hand, giving a newly added territory and potentially diasaffected people a (sub)king of their own was a policy Charlemagne deployed in Aquitaine as well and one that can be interpreted positively as affording a measure of independence and clear identity.[10] The separate identity of the Lombard kingdom was confirmed in 813. The later appointments of Lothar (Charlemagne's grandson) as king in 817, and of Lothar's own son Louis II as his successor in 839, marked a maintenance of Italy's autonomy.

---

[6] *Annales regni francorum*, s.a. 774, ed. Kurze, p. 38, trans. B. Scholz, *Carolingian chronicles* (Ann Arbor, 1970), p. 50; and see *Annales q.d. Einhardi*, s.a. 773, *Annales regni francorum*, ed. Kurze, p. 37.

[7] *Annales regni francorum*, s.a. 775–6, pp. 42 and 44; trans. Scholz, *Carolingian chronicles*, p. 53., *Annales q.d. Einhardi*, s.a. 776, *Annales regni francorum*, ed. Kurze, pp. 43 and 45.

[8] *Annales regni francorum*, s.a. 779 and 780, ed. Kurze, pp. 52, 54 and 56.

[9] *Ibid.*, s.a. 781, ed. Kurze, p. 56.

[10] See B. Kasten, *Königssöhne und Königsherrschaft. Untersuchungen zur Teilhabe am Reich in der Merowinger- und Karolingerzeit*, MGH Schriften 44 (Hannover, 1997); and M. Tillotson, 'Carolingian sub-kings and kingship, 781–864' (unpublished M.Phil. essay, University of Cambridge, 2003).

Desiderius' immediate family, not least Adalperga of Benevento herself, who has been the subject of a fine recent study by Janet Nelson,[11] may have reacted to the Carolingian takeover in a very different way from other Lombard magnates. Carolingian impositions of rule on Lombard Italy have been interpreted negatively in the modern historiography.

With the seizure of the Lombard throne by Charlemagne in 774, it could be said that he had potentially bitten off far more than he could hope to chew. Yet the coup, apart from the rebellion of Rodgaud of Friuli and the continued disaffection of the dukes of Benevento, was remarkably peaceful. It stands, for example, in stark contrast to the bloody and protracted conquest of Saxony. One is reminded, indeed, of Paul the Deacon's own account of the successive invasions of Italy in his *Historia romana*.[12] Just as the Lombards had no less right in the peninsula than anyone else, so could this be thought of the Franks in their turn.

Many questions spring to mind. To what extent was an integration of the Lombard kingdom in the Carolingian realm achieved? How far was its identity preserved? What did the Franks know, or seek to know about the Lombards? Can a search for knowledge and understanding in any way be interpreted as part of the process of conquest and integration? Were Lombards actively involved in the process of integration? Just as there are traces in the surviving evidence of thought being given by Charlemagne and his advisers to the process of the consolidation of Carolingian rule in the Saxon lands and in Bavaria, so also we should investigate whether we can detect any signs of a persuasion of the Franks about the future place of Lombard Italy within the Carolingian realm. Is there any indication of the promotion of the Lombard's historical identity and traditions? It is in this respect that Paul the Deacon seems to me to play a crucial role, but not quite in the way that has been understood hitherto.

In this chapter, therefore, I offer an hypothesis about the purpose and audience of Paul the Deacon's *Historia langobardorum* within the context of the political and cultural consequences of the Frankish conquest of 774. My first presentation of this hypothesis was as the opening lecture in Cividale in May 1999. Even at the second phase of the celebration of

---

[11] J. L. Nelson, 'Making a difference in eighth-century politics: the daughters of Desiderius', in A. C. Murray (ed.), *After Rome's fall: narrators and sources of early medieval history. Essays presented to Walter Goffart* (Toronto, 1998), pp. 171–90.

[12] Paul the Deacon, *Historia romana*, ed. A. Crivellucci, Fonti per la Storia d'Italia 51 (Rome, 1913); and A. Crivellucci, 'Per l'edizione della Historia Romana di Paolo Diacono', *Bullettino dell'Istituto Storico* 40 (1921), pp. 7–103. See also W. Goffart, *The narrators of barbarian history (A.D. 550–800): Jordanes, Gregory of Tours, Bede, and Paul the Deacon* (Princeton, 1988), pp. 347–56, esp. p. 356; and B. Cornford, 'The idea of the Roman past in early medieval Italy: Paul the Deacon's *Historia romana*' (unpublished Ph.D. dissertation, University of Cambridge, 2003).

the 1,200th anniversary of Paul's death, in September 1999, and thus before my lecture had been published, reactions to my suggestions (mostly positive but with some interesting extra considerations) were articulated, and are recorded in the proceedings with reference to the Italian version of my Cividale lecture, then still in the press.[13] Some of these I anticipated in the English version of my Cividale lecture, published in a special issue of the journal *Early Medieval Europe* devoted to early medieval Italy, and also while the Italian version was in the press. I have done my best in what follows, therefore, to take these generous and various comments into account.

Let us look first at ecclesiastical disputes and church reform, for this is one sphere in which Lombard reactions to Frankish infuences can be documented. This takes us, moreover, to the diocese of Aquileia and to Paul the Deacon's home town of Cividale itself in 796. In that year, Paulinus of Aquileia (*c*. 726–802), archbishop of Aquileia from 787, convened a provincial church council.[14] The discussion at this synod took up the two major themes of the Council of Frankfurt of 794 and impressed them upon Paulinus' suffragans, namely the battle against the Spanish heresy about Christ being merely the adopted son of God, known as Adoptionism, and the reform of the kingdom and the church.[15] Here we see Frankish decisions being applied within the north Italian arena where they are clearly regarded as no less relevant. Paulinus' own contributions to the Adoptionism debate were the *Contra felicem libri tres* (on which Alcuin, another contributor to the debate, may have drawn) written in response to Felix of Urgel's own treatise,[16] and the *Liber sacrosyllabus* of the bishops of Italy, written and later revised by Paulinus. Both these were

---

[13] See, for example, L. Capo, 'Paolo Diacono e il mondo franco: l'incontro di due esperienze storiografiche', in Chiesa (ed.), *Paolo Diacono*, pp. 39–74, at pp. 73–4 and note 47; and C. Leonardi, 'La figura di Paolo Diacono', in *Paolo Diacono e il Friuli altomedievale (secc. VI–X)*, Atti del XIV congresso internazionale di studi sull'alto medioevo, 2 vols. (Spoleto, 2001), I, pp. 15–24.

[14] *Capitulare episcoporum*, ed. A. Werminghoff, *MGH Conc.* II.i (Hannover, 1906), No. 21, pp. 179–95.

[15] *Ibid.*, no. 19G, pp. 165–71. On Adoptionism and its principal advocate, Felix of Urgel, see the excellent study by J. Cavadini, *The last Christology of the West. Adoptionism in Spain and Gaul, 785–820* (Philadelphia, 1993); H. Nagel, *Karl der Grosse und die theologischen Herausforderungen seiner Zeit*, Freiburger Beiträge zur mittelalterliche Geschichte, Studien und Texte 12 (Bern, 1998), pp. 75–85; and the recently discovered text of the 809 synod on the related issue of the procession of the Holy Spirit and the *filioque* phrase added to the Creed by the Franks, ed. H. Willjung, *Das Konzil von Aachen 809*, *MGH Conc.* II, Supp. 2 (Hannover, 1998).

[16] Paulinus of Aquileia, ed. D. Norberg, *Paulini Aquileiensis opera omnia pars I: Contra felicem libri tres*, CCCM, XCV (Turnhout, 1990); and see also *MGH Epp.*, IV, ed. E. Dümmler (Hannover, 1895) pp. 522–5.

appended to the Frankfurt proceedings.[17] The further confirmation in 796 of Aquileia's support for the Frankish position on Adoptionism and the double procession of the holy spirit, regardless of the Pope's position on it, is a crucial indication of Paulinus' own acceptance of the *filioque* clause. It symbolized an alignment with the Frankish church. Paulinus's letter reporting the synod, moreover, makes it clear that Charlemagne had asked that this provincial elaboration and reiteration of the Frankfurt decisions be held. Paulinus welcomed the chance peaceful times now gave him to concentrate on the consolidation of church reform in his own ecclesiastical province.[18]

Paulinus had apparently identified himself with the Frankish enterprise and shared the particular image of the church and Christianity formed through the liturgical and canon law collections, biblical study, knowledge of the church fathers and early histories of the church that it promoted.[19] Equally important are the indications that as far as the assembled bishops at Frankfurt were concerned, the Italian bishops were part of the Frankish church. A contemporary comment in the Lorsch annals, moreover, stressed the attendance of the papal *missi* and the Italian archbishops Paulinus of Aquileia and Peter of Milan and their suffragans at this synod.[20] The church was one major sphere in which the Lombards appear to have become integrated into the Frankish world, at least in the diocese of Aquileia. Evidence from elsewhere in northern Italy, especially in the sphere of secular and canon law, however, suggests that Italian and Frankish traditions could be combined.[21] The Vercelli canon law collection discussed below in chapter 11, for example, is a local compilation from northern Italy to be dated no later than the second quarter of the ninth century and probably to be located to the church of S. Felice in Pavia.[22] This manuscript shows the north Italian compiler responding to

---

[17] *Concilium francofurtense* a. 794, ed. Werminghoff, *MGH Conc.* II.i, no. 19D, *Libellus sacrosyllabus episcoporum italiae*, pp. 130–42.

[18] Paulinus, ed. Dümmler, *MGH Epp.*, IV, pp. 517–20.

[19] See below, chapter 10, and G. Brown, 'Introduction: the Carolingian Renaissance', in R. McKitterick (ed.), *Carolingian culture: emulation and innovation* (Cambridge, 1994), pp. 1–51; J. Contreni, 'The Carolingian Renaissance: education and literary culture' in McKitterick (ed.), *NCMH*, pp. 709–57; and R. McKitterick, 'Das Konzil im Kontext der karolingischen Renaissance', in R. Berndt (ed.), *Das Frankfurter Konzil von 794. Kristallisationpunckt karolingischer Kultur*, 2 vols., Quellen und Abhandlungen zur mittelrheinischen Kirchengeschichte 80 (Mainz, 1997), II, pp. 635–76.

[20] Lorsch annals, ed. G. Pertz, *MGH SS*, I, pp. 22–39, s.a. 794 and see below pp. 104–10. The *Annales regni francorum* report that the papal *missi* were Bishops Theophylact and Stephan, *Annales regni francorum*, ed. F. Kurze, *MGH SRG*, VI (Hannover, 1895) s.a. 794, p. 94.

[21] See below, chapter 11.

[22] See K. Zechiel-Eckes, *Die Concordia canonum des Cresconius. Studien und Edition*, Freiburger Beiträge zur mittelalterlichen Geschichte 5 (Frankfurt am Main, 1992),

emphases and concerns that were arguably an outcome of the involvement of the north Italian church in Frankish affairs.

In the Italian bishops' response to Adoptionism at Cividale, and in the early medieval manuscript evidence from Italy, it is clear that Lombard clerics brought to their discussion, or had access to, a knowledge of the same works by patristic and Gallo-Roman theologians as their Frankish colleagues. These included Hilary of Poitiers, Augustine, Orosius, Gregory the Great, Jerome, Ambrose, Isidore of Seville, Maximus of Turin, Ambrosiaster and Cyprian. It follows that the religious and intellectual bedrock upon which the decisions at Frankfurt were based were also shared by the Lombard clerics of northern Italy.[23] They may themselves, of course, have added their own learned contributions to discussion in addition to those we can clearly observe in Paulinus' writings.

This was no accident. Charlemagne gathered a number of prominent Lombard intellectuals to his court. This was arguably with the express intention of using them as his 'task force' in the promotion of the Christian religion and culture which was so prominent a part of his political enterprise. The Lombard scholars clearly had something to contribute to the Franks. Equally, however, Paulinus' activities indicate that the intention may well have been for them to return home and introduce Frankish perspectives to the Lombards. Carolingian rule did not only mean assuming the kingship and placing Franks or local magnates whose loyalty could be relied upon in local administration. A full integration of Lombard concerns into those of the Franks, together with the Frankish acknowledgement of the importance of Lombard concerns, had to be achieved. Paulinus of Aquileia was summoned to the Frankish court as early as 776, presumably in the wake of the suppression of rebellion in Friuli. Peter of Pisa was another so honoured after 774. So of course, was Paul the Deacon, who was in touch with, if not actually at the Frankish court by 782.

Paul the Deacon

It may be helpful to rehearse the few certainties of Paul's life. There seems to be no clear indication that Paul was not at the court of Charlemagne in Francia from 776 with Paulinus of Aquileia, for in that year Paul's

pp. 172–84. This provides an essential supplement to F. Maassen, *Bibliotheca latina iuris canonici manuscripta* (Vienna, 1866) pp. 418–19, and *idem.*, *Geschichte der Quellen des canonischen Rechts im Abendlande bis zum Ausgange des Mittelalters* 1 (Graz, 1870), pp. 799–802.

23 See Berndt, *Das Frankfurter Konzil*; and W. Hartmann, *Die Synoden der Karolingerzeit im Frankenreich und in Italien* (Paderborn, 1989), pp. 105–15 and 116–27.

own brother Arichis had been taken prisoner for his part in the rebellion of Rotgaud of Friuli. The six years between this incident and Paul's somewhat tardy poem petitioning the Frankish ruler for Arichis' release have not been accounted for and it is one of the many puzzles of Paul's career. Some landmarks in his career before Paul took up residence at the Frankish court can be established nevertheless.

Paul had seen Ratchis, king of the Lombards, and therefore he was born by *c.* 735. He dedicated a poem to Adalperga, the daughter of King Desiderius and wife of Duke Arichis of Benevento, in 763 when she had one child. Paul dedicated the *Historia romana* to her when she had three children, and this is thought to have been somewhere around 773. (In 787 Adalperga is recorded as having five grown children.) Paul appears to have been in Francia by 783 when he wrote his poetic petition to Charlemagne about Arichis his brother. The *Gesta episcoporum mettensium* was written in 784 at the request of Bishop Angilram of Metz. Some time after that, according to his epitaph written by his pupil Hilderic the grammarian, Paul retired to Monte Cassino. This was possibly as early as 786 or 787 and Paul is thought to have died in 799, though I have found no early evidence in support of this date.[24]

Paul's sense of a larger past incorporating the later Roman empire and a respect for the papacy as exemplified by Pope Gregory the Great emerges from many of his writings.[25] Paul's close involvement in and contributions to the religious and liturgical reforms of the Carolingian church, moreover, are as important as those of Paulinus of Aquileia. Indeed, it is striking how much Paul wrote and compiled for essentially political reasons and both Frankish and Lombard royal patrons. There is the poem for Adalperga, an epitaph for duke Arichis datable to September 787–May 788 and other poems and epitaphs; the continuation to Eutropius known as the *Historia romana* was dedicated to Duchess Adalperga;[26] the *Gesta episcoporum mettensium* of 784, with its strong emphasis on the legitimation of Carolingian rule and the Carolingian family inheritance, was commissioned by the head of the Carolingian royal chapel, Bishop Angilram of Metz; a collection of forty-seven sermons of Gregory the Great was presented by Paul to Adalhard of Corbie, Charlemagne's cousin; Paul's epitome of the Lexikon of Festus was presented to Charlemagne;[27] his

[24] W. Pohl discusses this fully in 'Paolo Diacono e la costruzione dell'identità longobarda', in P. Chiesa (ed.), *Paolo Diacono* (Udine, 2001), pp. 413–26.

[25] See, for example, G. Gandino, 'La dialettica tra il passato e il presente nelle opere di Paolo Diacono', in *Paolo Diacono e il Friuli altomedievale*, pp. 67–98.

[26] See L. Boje Mortensen, '*Impero romana, Historia romana e Historia langobardorum*', in Chiesa (ed.), *Paolo Diacono*, pp. 355–66.

[27] Reynolds, *Texts and Transmission*, pp. 163–4; and W. M. Lindsay (ed.), *S. Pompei Festi de verborum significatu quae supersunt cum Pauli epitome* (Leipzig, 1913); see also R. Cervani,

Homiliary compiled for use throughout the Carolingian realm was a royal commission.[28] The hymns, grammar and the Life of Gregory the Great may have been unsolicited pieces of work. We should remember, however, Paul's own comment in one of his poems addressed to Peter of Pisa: 'Unless I earn my living by what I write, I have nothing to give.'[29] In the light of this pattern of Paul's output, it is likely that the *Historia langobardorum* was also written for a political purpose and patron.[30]

All Paul's works have been fitted into the chronology of Paul's life according to assumptions about his piety, the peace and seclusion needed for writing, his relationship with Adalperga, his sojourn at Monte Cassino and where he was at the time of writing particular works. Paul's activities in the political world of the later eighth century have been unnecessarily obscured by the false assumption that he was a monk at Monte Cassino, and based in Monte Cassino, for most of his adult life. Adalperga may have been taught by Paul when a girl at her father Desiderius' court and was married to the Friulan Arichis, duke of Benevento. It would make sense for Paul to stay in touch with her and a former Friulan and to seek her patronage. Yet there is no necessity for him to have been in Benevento himself to do this. Still less was it necessary for him to have entered Monte Cassino's community itself. Goffart's reasoning on this account is specious. That Paul refers to himself in his preface to the *Historia romana*, also dedicated to Adalperga, as *exiguus* and *supplex*, is insufficient to identify him as a monk.[31] Piety and humility, especially in relation to royal patrons, is hardly the prerogative of those who have entered the religious life. The epitaph for Arichis need not have been written by a monk. Nor does Paul's career, or what little we know of it,

---

L'*Epitome di Paolo del 'de verborum significatu' di Pompeo Festo. Struttura e metodo* (Rome, 1978); and S. Lanciotti, 'Tra Festo e Paolo', in Chiesa (ed.), *Paolo Diacono*, pp. 237–50.
[28] *MGH Cap.*, I, ed. A. Boretius (Hannover, 1883), no. 30, pp. 80–1, trans. P. D. King, *Charlemagne. Translated sources* (Kendal, 1987), pp. 208–9. This appears, despite the entry in *The Oxford Dictionary of the Christian Church*, ed. E. A. Livingstsone, 3rd edn (Oxford, 1997), p. 1241, to be a reference to the Homiliary rather than to any additional work. See also R. Grégoire, *Homéliaires liturgiques médiévaux. Analyse des manuscrits* (Spoleto, 1980), pp. 423–86; and Y. Hen, 'Paul the Deacon and the Frankish liturgy', in Chiesa (ed.), *Paolo Diacono*, pp. 205–23; I am grateful to Yitzhak Hen for discussing this Homiliary with me.
[29] Ed. and trans. P. Godman, *Poetry of the Carolingian renaissance* (London, 1983), p. 89.
[30] See also W. Pohl, 'Paulus Diaconus und die "Historia langobardorum": Text und Tradition' in A. Scharer und G. Scheibelreiter (eds.), *Historiographie*, pp. 375–405; and Gandino, 'La dialettica tra il passato e il presente', p. 91, n. 80; and Capo, 'Paolo Diacono e il mondo franco', pp. 73–4, n. 47.
[31] *Historia romana*, ed. Crivellucci, p. 3; and see Goffart, *Narrators of barbarian history*, pp. 332–47, who rehearses the evidence with reference to earlier literature. For slightly different emphases but similar hypotheses and assumptions concerning the pattern of Paul's career see D. Bullough, 'Ethnic history and the Carolingians: an alternative reading of Paul the Deacon's *Historia langobardorum*', in C. Holdsworth and T. Wiseman (eds.), *The inheritance of historiography 350–900* (Exeter, 1986), pp. 85–106.

indicate that he was a professed monk from Monte Cassino at this stage. Charlemagne's reference to him in his letter of advice to the lectors, dated *c.* 786–801, refers to him as *diaconus* and *clientulus*.[32]

Further, Paul's epitaph, written by his pupil, the grammarian Hilderic, maintains that Paul retired to Monte Cassino on his return from the Frankish court.[33] There seems no good reason to doubt Paul's epitaph by Hilderic,[34] though it certainly does not exclude the possibility that Paul had taken refuge with the community, if not actually taking his vows, at an earlier stage. In this respect one ought, of course, to register Paul's letter to Theodemar, usually dated 783 and extant in Paris, BnF lat. 528, fols. 127–8, a Frankish manuscript of the ninth century.[35] Yet this letter is less explicit than many commentators have thought.[36] In it, Paul simply says he will return to Monte Cassino and implies, in his concern for monks who may have died, that he has been part of the community in some way.

It should be noted too that only two of the poems in Paul's entire corpus have directly to do with monasticism, namely nos. VI and VII. The greater proportion of poems and epitaphs are for lay members of the Carolingian and Lombard royal houses and most of these are for the Carolingians. The manuscript tradition of these poems is also significant for its earliest phase is largely north Italian and Frankish.[37] We need to recall, moreover, the number of public figures – Wala of Corbie is an obvious example – who at one time or another had taken refuge from political calamities in monasteries, had been incarcerated in monasteries by their political opponents, or who had retired to monasteries at the end of their careers. Monastic exile could be very flexible.[38]

---

[32] *MGH Cap.*, I, ed. Boretius, p. 81; and compare H. Mordek, *Biblioteca capitularium regum francorum manuscripta. Überlieferung und Traditionszusammenhang der fränkischen Herrscherlasse*, MGH Hilfsmittel 15 (Munich, 1995), pp. 185–6.

[33] Hilderic, *Epytaphium Pauli diaconi*, ed. G. Waitz, *Pauli historia langobardorum*, MGH SRG, XLVIII (Hannover, 1878), pp. 15–16 and *MGH SRL* (Hannover, 1878), pp. 23–4; and compare L. Bethmann, 'Paulus Diaconus Leben und Schriften', *Archiv der Gesellschaft für ältere deutsche Geschichtskunde* 10 (1851), pp. 247–334, at p. 259.

[34] Goffart, *Narrators of barbarian history*, p. 335, n. 25, states baldly that Hilderic was wrong, without giving any reasons.

[35] *MGH Epp.*, IV, ed. Dümmler, pp. 506–8.

[36] Compare M. Costambeys, 'The monastic environment of Paul the Deacon', in Chiesa (ed.), *Paolo Diacono*, pp. 127–38, for counter arguments concerning the extent of Paul's monastic career.

[37] K. Neff, *Die Gedichte Paulus Diaconus, Quellen und Untersuchungen zur lateinischen Philologie des Mittelalters*, III, 4 (Munich, 1908), pp. 69–73. See also F. Stella, 'La poesia di Paolo Diacono: nuovi manoscritti e attribuzioni incerte', in Chiesa (ed.), *Paolo Diacono*, pp. 551–74.

[38] See L. Weinrich, *Wala. Graf, Mönch und Rebell. Die Biographie eines Karolingers* (Lübeck, 1963); D. Ganz, 'The *Epitaphium Arsenii* and opposition to Louis the Pious', in P. Godman and R. Collins (eds.), *Charlemagne's heir. New perspectives on the reign of*

There can be no doubt that Paul wrote the *Historia langobardorum* within a specific context, but Goffart's notion that Paul wrote the history of the Lombards for the Lombards, and especially the Lombards of Benevento is unconvincing.[39] Paul's attitude to Grimoald of Benevento, who was, after all, a Friulan, is accounted for by his loyalties no doubt being somewhat torn. The contemporary situation of Benevento in relation to Charlemagne may well have been uppermost in Paul's mind. One could not expect someone like Paul to have become so completely Frankish in his outlook. Yet Paul may well have acknowledged the potential benefits of Frankish rule. Indeed, I suggest that Paul wrote the *Historia langobardorum* as a consequence of the events of 774 for the Carolingians and Lombard supporters of the Carolingians. His history was probably intended for the Carolingian court in Italy, if not for the Frankish court in Francia. It was conceivably written at the specific request of the Frankish ruler, who had asked him to write so much else.

The active link with the Frankish court has not, to my knowledge been considered as a possibility before. The unwarranted assumption that Paul wrote the *Historia langobardorum* at the end of his life and that his writing came to a halt at the end of Book VI (which is itself undoubtedly complete) when death intervened has become well entrenched. Erchempert of Benevento maintained, on the other hand, that Paul did not finish his history because he could not bear to chronicle the downfall of the Lombards.[40] Modern scholars have followed him in this, or taken the view that a proper history of the Lombards should have taken the story up to 774 rather than stopping with the death of Liutprand in 744. Much has been made to support the idea of a truncated text, furthermore, of Paul's brief reference to Baodilinus the holy man and a certain miracle Baodilinus performed, where Paul says he will give an account of this at a later time in its proper place.[41] It has been assumed by most historians of Paul the Deacon that this is a reference to an intended later portion of the *Historia langobardorum*. It could equally well be, however, that Paul had it in mind to write a *Miracula* collection or *Vita* of Baodilinus.

Louis the Pious (Oxford, 1990), pp. 537–50; and M. de Jong, *In Samuel's image. Child oblation in the early medieval west* (Leiden, 1996), pp. 252–66; and *idem.*, 'Monastic prisoners or opting out? Political coercion and honour in the Frankish kingdoms', in M. de Jong, F. Theuws with C. van Rhijn (eds.), *Topographies of power in the early middle ages* (Leiden, 2001), pp. 291–328.

[39] Goffart, *Narrators of barbarian history*, pp. 343–7.
[40] *Historia langobardorum beneventanorum*, ed. G. Waitz, *MGH SRL* (Hannover, 1878), p. 234.
[41] *Historia langobardorum*, VI, 58, ed. G. Waitz, *MGH SRG*, XLVIII (Hannover, 1878), p. 241.

It is important to keep an open mind about where Paul was when he wrote his particular works, what connections he maintained, and with whom, and to whom his works were addressed. Whether or not the *Historia langobardorum* was written at Monte Cassino or was the last of Paul's works, I do not see the necessity for positing that Paul's history is incomplete.[42] It seems to me to have a strong internal structure and a very skilfully worked-out message which entirely accords with the possibility that the work was intended for the Franks and Lombards in the new regime after 774. In this respect, a case can be made for its ending with Liutprand's reign being highly appropriate and an essential reinforcement of the work's ideological and historical meaning. Indeed, in the other five books the king as a central figure acts as a connecting link with the next book. Alboin links Books I and II; Authari is in Books II and III; Agilulf connects Books III and IV; Grimoald is in IV and V; Cunincpert straddles V and VI. In Book VI, however, Liutprand is both introduced and dies and no other king or potential king is mentioned.[43]

There is not space here to argue the case for the ideological and historical coherence of Paul's narrative in all the detail it deserves. Let me nevertheless single out a few points by way, first of all, of illustration, and, secondly, to reinforce my suggestion of the specific political objectives of the composition of the work as a whole.

First of all there is throughout the text an evident pride in the Lombard rulers who followed what are arguably Carolingian models of kingship.[44] Each Lombard king is prevented by one attribute or another from matching that model. Rothari, for example, is brave and strong and followed the path of justice but he was an Arian.[45] Liutprand was all that was praiseworthy in a king save that he was illiterate.[46] Indeed, the praise of Liutprand's peculiarly royal virtues is particularly significant: not only did he appoint dukes in the duchies; he also built churches and monasteries. Even more interestingly Liutprand can be demonstrated to be a ruler on the Carolingian model for did he not also establish a palace chapel and appoint priests and churchmen to perform the daily service for him? No

[42] In this I follow the MGH editors Waitz and Bethmann.

[43] See also C. Leonardi, 'La figura di Paolo Diacono', in *Paolo Diacono e il Friuli altomedievali*, pp. 22–3, who also argues for the work ending fittingly with the reign of Liutprand. In addition, I am grateful to my 1999 group of first-year undergraduates in a class on Paul the Deacon and the Lombards, especially Laura Diener, for lively discussion of this point.

[44] As Paolo Delogu kindly suggested when he first read the earlier version of this chapter, Paul's presentation could conceivably also mirror an independent Lombard model of Christian kingship. Paul's text is, of course, our only witness to such a model.

[45] Paul, *Historia langobardorum*, IV, 42.   [46] *Ibid.*, VI, 58.

other Lombard king had done this. In every respect, therefore, Liutprand, at least as far as Paul's presentation is concerned, is a ruler on the Carolingian model. But like Rothari before him he also does not quite measure up to Charlemagne who surely was the king Paul had in mind. Liutprand was a 'man of much wisdom, very religious and a lover of peace, shrewd in counsel, powerful in war, merciful to offenders, chaste, modest, prayerful in the night watches, generous in charities'. Then comes the slightly defensive 'ignorant in letters indeed' – again there is the implicit unspoken comparison with Charlemagne invoked – 'yet worthy to be likened to philosophers, a supporter of his people, an increaser of the law.[47] At the beginning of his reign he took many fortresses of the Bavarians. He relied always more upon arms and always with the greatest care kept peace with the Franks and the Avars.'[48]

To a Frank or a Lombard the message would be clear. These portrayals, read with the powerful stress on Lombard kingship in Book V, would convey a reader's understanding that these were good kings, but not quite as great as Charlemagne. Liutprand in particular was a worthy predecessor of Charlemagne and the Frankish ruler would be understood as continuing the excellent traditions of the Lombards. What better way to integrate Lombards ideologically into the Carolingian realm than by acknowledging their identity in a text which contrived to remind them of bad Franks in the past and the excellence of the new Carolingian dynasty. Defeats of the Franks by Lombards recorded by Paul are, of course, defeats of the Franks under the Merovingians and highlight the triumphs of the Franks under Carolingian rule.

It is part of Paul's purpose, therefore, that in Book VI he provides an account of the Merovingian kings of the Franks, who were 'degenerating from their wonted courage and skill' and at this time 'those who were regarded as stewards of the palace began to administer the kingly power and to do whatever is the custom for kings, since it was ordained from heaven that the sovereignty of the Franks should be transferred to the race of these men'.[49] This is the standard Carolingian presentation of the takeover from the Merovingians in Frankish Gaul. The positive accounts of Charles Martel enhance this emphasis on Carolingian excellence. Paul makes certain that the Lombards and Franks understand that

---

[47] Compare Paul's presentation of Theodoric the Ostrogoth in the *Historia romana*, 16, 3–4, 8–10 and Goffart, *Narrators of barbarian history*, pp. 365–7.

[48] Paul, *Historia langobardorum*, VI, 58; English trans. W. D. Foulke, *Paul the Deacon, History of the Lombards* (Philadelphia, 1907), p. 306; and see also. L. Capo (ed.), *Paolo Diacono Storia dei Longobardi* (Verona, 1992) pp. 363, 365, and her commentary pp. 610–12.

[49] Paul, *Historia langobardorum*, VI, 16, trans. Foulke, *Paul the Deacon*, p. 262.

the Lombards were important assistants to, and allies of, the Carolingians and in every way admirable. Goffart's point that Paul cast the lingering remnants of the line of Theodelinda, Perctarit and Cunincpert as *rois fainéants* on the Merovingian pattern, if perhaps a little overstated,[50] is also entirely consistent with the view that this text was initially intended for Franks and Lombard loyalist supporters of Carolingian power. This would have been something that the Franks would have understood and appreciated: strong rulers did away with those who were useless kings.[51]

Book VI goes on to stress the connections between the Carolingian family and the Lombard kings in the earlier eighth century. Paul relates how Charles Martel, the ruler of the Franks, sent his son Pippin (Charlemagne's father) to Liutprand 'so that Liutprand would take his hair according to custom. And the king, cutting his hair became a father to him and sent Pippin back to Charles enriched with many royal gifts'.[52] This is another indication that the text was written for Franks. It seems to be a reference to the *barbatoria* or *capillaturia*. Yitzhak Hen has traced the development of this custom and its incorporation into the Frankish liturgy of the eighth century.[53] He argues that Pippin's ritualistic *barbatoria* in 738 is in fact the last specific indication of *barbatoria* in the sources. In 791 it is the arming of the young Louis the Pious rather than a *barbatoria* which is the ceremony used to mark his entry into adult life. Even more important, however, is the story's indication of the special symbolic kinship created between Pippin and the Lombard ruler.[54]

The Lombards and the Carolingians are also portrayed as allies. Paul recounts Charles Martel's defence of Gaul against the Saracens and the assistance rendered Charles by the Lombards.[55] Further, the stories of Byzantine treachery would have been justifications for Carolingian policy in Italy and the Franks' continuation of Lombard attempts to deal militarily with the threat they posed. The portrayal of the Byzantines impinges on both the question of Venice and theological matters. Venice had been

---

[50] Goffart, *Narrators of barbarian history*, p. 412.
[51] See chapters 4 and 6 below for the Franks' own presentation of the events of the eighth century; compare Einhard, *Vita Karoli*, cc. 1 and 2, ed. R. Rau, *Quellen zur karolingischen Reichsgeschichte*, I (Darmstadt, 1974), pp. 166–8; and *Annales regni francorum*, ed. F. Kurze, *MGH SRG*, VI (Hannover, 1895), s.a. 749, p. 8.
[52] Paul, *Historia langobardorum*, VI, 53.
[53] Y. Hen, *Culture and religion in Merovingian Gaul, AD 481–751*, Culture, Beliefs and Tradition. Medieval and Early Modern People 1 (Leiden, 1995), pp. 137–43; and R. Bartlett, 'Symbolic meanings of hair in the middle ages', *TRHS* sixth series 4 (1994), pp. 43–60.
[54] This is analogous to the spiritual kinship created by godparenthood: see A. Angenendt, 'Das geistliche Bündnis der Päpste mit den Karolingern (754–796)', *Historisches Jahrbuch* 100 (1980), pp. 1–94; and J. H. Lynch, *Godparents and kinship in early medieval Europe* (Princeton, 1986).
[55] Paul, *Historia langobardorum* VI, 54.

taken by the Lombards and recovered by the Venetians and Franks. Yet the relations with Venice remained rather tense and the Byzantines also had a keen interest in the lagoon area.[56] Paul's discussion of the Three Chapters, moreover, touches on the context of the discussion of Adoptionism which, as we have seen, was still an issue in Lombard Italy and the diocese of Aquileia in the late eighth century as well.[57]

It is also significant that Paul provides full details of Liutprand as ruler within the Lombard kingdom, most notably in appointing dukes and in his dealings with Spoleto and Benevento. It is as if the royal role in appointing dukes, taken over by Charlemagne, is also being justified and legitimated. The Franks' relations with Spoleto and difficulties with the Beneventans are in some sense prefigured by those of the earlier Lombard kings.

Paul in effect was urging his audience to remember the Lombards at their best, and the old alliance with the Franks. He did this by the simple expedient of omitting any reference to any ruler after Liutprand, and leaving out Aistulf, Ratchis and Desiderius, whose relations with both the papacy and the Carolingian rulers cannot be said to have been amiable. The Carolingians were not alien interlopers at all, but connected with the greatest of the Lombard kings. Paul encourages his readers, by his silences and omissions, to reduce the place of more recent history in their memories. Instead, he makes his readers create a Lombard place in Frankish history which entirely accorded with the presentation of the past the Franks themselves were creating, as we shall see in the following three chapters of this book.

What can be said of the relationship between Paul's narrative and that of the royal Frankish annalist and the other immediate influences on his work?[58] Paul's continuation of, and additions to, the *Historia romana* c. 773 are indications of his familiarity with, and understanding of, the potential ideological force of historiography. In particular, as Benjamin Cornford has shown, the *Historia romana* did not draw simple boundaries between the Roman past and Paul's present but contributed to making

[56] For the context of Carolingian relations with Byzantium and the Venetians see J. M. H. Smith, '*Fines imperii*: the marches', and M. McCormick, 'Byzantium and the west, 700–900', in McKitterick (ed.), *NCMH*, pp. 169–89 and 349–80; and J. Sassel, 'L'organizzazione del confine orientale d'Italia nell'alto medioevo', in *Aquileia e le Venezie nell'alto medioevo*, Antichità alto adriatiche 32 (Udine, 1988), pp. 107–14.

[57] Paul, *Historia langobardorum* III, 20 and 26. See M. Herren, 'Theological aspects of the writings of Paul the Deacon', in Chiesa (ed.), *Paolo Diacono*, pp. 223–36; and above, p. 65. The matter would merit further study, especially in the light of the important set of articles assembled in C. Chazelle (ed.), *The three chapters* (Turnhout, forthcoming).

[58] On Paul's working practices see P. Delogu, 'Longobardi e Romani: altre congetture', in P. Cammarosano and S. Gasparri (eds.), *Langobardia* (Udine, 1990), pp. 112–67; and L. Capo, 'Paolo diacono e il mondo franco', pp. 35–74.

information available about the Roman past. Such information was to prove an important resource for political legitimation and cultural reform in the eighth century.[59] At Charlemagne's court, however, Paul would have encountered those responsible for the Frankish annals at about this time (and the historians may have influenced each other).[60] He may also have seen, for he seems to have read at least some of it, the *Historia ecclesiastica* of Bede, which we know was at the royal court in the codex now known as the Moore Bede in Cambridge University Library.[61] If Paul had not encountered it already in Italy, it is conceivable that a copy of the *Liber pontificalis*, as far as Life 94 (Stephen II), would also have been available.[62] Paul had clearly read Gregory of Tours' *Historiae*.[63] He had probably read the Carolingian edition of the *Chronicle* of Fredegar, and possibly its Continuations.[64]

These historiographical works together provided a heady mixture. All present, in their different ways, a great stress on the Christian identity of a particular community, whether the English, the Franks or the Romans, on God's guidance in the exercise of Christian kingship, and on the providential nature of kingship. More specifically in the case of Bede, his account of the 'Germanic' origins of the English and of the geography of Britannia surely offered ideas to Paul.[65] Equally, however, his view of where the past started may have been influenced by the *Origo gentis*

---

[59] Cornford, 'The idea of the Roman past in early medieval Italy'. See also L. Boje Mortensen, '*Impero romano, Historia romana e Historia langobardorum*', in Chiesa (ed.), *Paolo Diacono*, pp. 355–66.

[60] See chapters 4, 5 and 6 below.

[61] Cambridge University Library, Kk.5.16, facsimile ed. P. Hunter-Blair, *The Moore Bede*, Early English Manuscripts in Facsimile 9 (Copenhagen, 1959). See also B. Bischoff, 'Die Hofbibliothek Karls des Grossen', in *Mittelalterliche Studien*, III (Stuttgart, 1981), pp. 149–69, at pp. 160–161; and trans. M. Gorman, 'The court library of Charlemagne', in B. Bischoff, *Manuscripts and libraries in the age of Charlemagne* (Cambridge, 1994), pp. 56–75, at pp. 67–8. I do not follow Bullough, 'Ethnic history and the Carolingians', pp. 98 and 105, n. 47, in his rejection of this possibility on the grounds that the spelling, with one consonant different, of one word in a quotation in Paul's *Historia langobardorum* taken from Bede is not that of the Moore Bede. With no extant autograph original of Paul's text or even one demonstrably close to him in date or place, this can hardly be taken as a compelling argument.

[62] The Frankish manuscript, Leiden, Bibliotheek der Rijksuniversiteit, Voss. lat. Q. 60, of the late eighth century, probably from Rheims, for example, has the 'Lombard version' of Life 94 and goes no further. For the implications of the manuscript transmission of the *Liber pontificalis* see briefly chapter 2 above.

[63] See H. Reimitz, 'Social networks and identities in Frankish historiography. New aspects of the textual history of Gregory of Tours' *Historiae*', in R. Corradini, M. Diesenberger and H. Reimitz (eds.), *The construction of communities in the early middle ages: texts, resources and artefacts*, The Transformation of the Roman World 12 (Leiden, 2003), pp. 229–68.

[64] See Goffart, *Narrators of barbarian history*, pp. 370–73, 396, 402.

[65] I have learnt much from A. Merrills, *History and geography in late antiquity* (Cambridge, 2005).

langobardorum which Walter Pohl has linked with Theodelinda's family.[66] The *Liber pontificalis* provided Paul and the Franks with an unequivocal image of Rome, its saints and the rule of the popes, as well as a portrayal of the Lombards for which Paul might have wished to offer a different perspective. The *Annales regni francorum*, as I argue in the following chapter of this book,[67] are a skilfully constructed and highly selective triumphal narrative. They offer a subtly nuanced portrayal of the Carolingian rulers whose success is identified with the Frankish people. The Franks in the *Annales regni francorum* were identified and stressed as a *gens*, just as the Lombard's identity as a *gens* is highlighted by Paul in the *Historia langobardorum*.[68]

It is in the context of the remarkable production of Carolingian historiography in the eighth and ninth centuries, all of which reflects an urgent political purpose in the interpretation of contemporary events, that Paul's *Historia langobardorum* should be seen. Paul added to this corpus of historical narratives in a very distinctive and apposite way. Paul consolidated the Franks' collective memory of the Lombards. He even managed to join in the systematic Carolingian derogation of the Merovingian rulers and the celebration of the eighth century as the Golden Age from which Charlemagne's great kingdom sprang. Frankish and Lombard representations and memory of the past are connected and thereby the two peoples are associated. Paul provides a particular representation and Christian interpretation of the Lombards' past to which the contemporary history of the Franks could now be added. It is thus no accident that Paul completed his history with the death of Liutprand, Charles Martel's ally, in 744 and that the *Annales regni francorum* start with the death of Charles Martel in 741. Hereafter the history of the two peoples, by historiographical suggestion, could be seen as connected. This historiography was designed to justify and even to legitimate particular courses of action and manifestations of political power in relation to specific historical circumstances. It is entirely consistent that Paul's own *Gesta episcoporum mettensium*, commissioned by Bishop Angilram of Metz in 784, commemorated events of vital concern to the entire Frankish church and kingdom. Paul omitted all

---

[66] W. Pohl, 'Paolo Diacono e la costruzione dell'identità longobarda', in Chiesa (ed.), *Paolo Diacono*, pp. 413–26; and see also *Origo gentis langobardorum Introduzione, testo critico, commento*, ed. A. Bracciotti, Biblioteca di cultura Romanobarbarica 2 (Rome, 1998).

[67] See especially pp. 113–18.

[68] For further examples and discussions see the essays assembled in Corradini, Diesenberger and Reimitz (eds.), *The construction of communities*, and H.-W. Goetz, J. Jarnut and W. Pohl (eds.), *Regna and gentes. The relationship between late antique and early medieval peoples and kingdoms in the transformation of the Roman world*, The Transformation of the Roman World 13 (Leiden, 2003), especially J. Jarnut, '*Gens, rex* and *regnum* of the Lombards', pp. 409–27.

reference to the Merovingian kings and church. His text, as Goffart has argued, serves to reinforce the legitimacy of the Carolingians' succession and claim to rule.[69]

The *Historia langobardorum*: transmission and dissemination

The questions remain of when and where Paul wrote the *Historia langobardorum* and for whom? There can be no certainty about the date of composition, but everything adduced in this chapter so far is consistent with a date in the mid-780s.[70] The indications of Paul having derived some of his information from books known to have been at the court of Charlemagne makes the court at least a possibility, though equally of course he could have relied on his memory. The transmission and dissemination of the *Historia langobardorum* may throw some light on its origin, purpose and audience.

Certainly the *Historia langobardorum* was a text which was widely and energetically disseminated throughout western Europe in the middle ages. There are over twenty manuscripts dating from before the eleventh century, and over eighty thereafter. The gargantuan task of sorting out the intensely complicated text history of the more than one hundred manuscripts of the *Historia langobardorum* was tackled over a hundred years ago first by Bethmann and more definitively by Georg Waitz in 1876 for his *MGH* edition.[71] Laura Pani has now provided a definitive list of 115 manuscripts.[72] Inevitably, some of the palaeographical judgements about dates made in 1876 may need to be revised and it may be possible now to give far more precise a notion of attributions in many instances.[73] Any comments made now, without full re-examination of the earliest copies from the late eighth to the late tenth century, therefore, let

---

[69] Paul, *Gesta episcoporum mettensium*, ed. G. Pertz, *Liber de episcopis mettensibus*, *MGH SS*, II (Berlin, 1829), pp. 260–88; and W. Goffart, 'Paul the *Deacon's Gesta episcoporum mettensium* and the early design of Charlemagne's succession', *Traditio* 42 (1986), pp. 59–94. See also M. Sot, 'Le *Liber de episcopis mettensibus* dans l'histoire du genre "Gesta episcoporum"', in Chiesa (ed.), *Paolo Diacono*, pp. 527–50.

[70] See W. Pohl, 'Paulus Diaconus und die "Historia langobardorum"; Text und Tradition', in Scharer and Scheibelreiter, *Historiographie*, pp. 375–405, at p. 376.

[71] G. Waitz, 'Ueber die handschriftliche Ueberlieferung und die Sprache der Historia Langobardorum des Paulus', *Neues Archiv* 1 (1876), pp. 533–66; and see also *Historia Langobardorum*, ed. Waitz, *MGH SRG* XLVIII (Hannover, 1878), pp. 23–48; G. Waitz (ed.), *MGH SRL* (Hannover, 1878), pp. 28–45.

[72] L. Pani, 'Aspetti della tradizione manoscritta dell'Historia langobardorum', in Chiesa (ed.), *Paolo Diacono*, pp. 367–412, at pp. 404–12, though unfortunately without including indications of date in the list as distinct from in her preceding discussion.

[73] See Bischoff, *Katalog*, pp. 299 and 412, who revises a few of Waitz's dates and attributions, most notably for Waitz's G5, s'Gravenhage MS 74.J.19, which is not late ninth

alone the significance of the distribution of later copies, can only be tentative. Nevertheless, the apparent patterns of distribution of Paul's text are striking.[74]

Above all, the manuscript tradition of the *Historia langobardorum* cannot be said to lend any support to the assumption, already challenged, that Paul the Deacon wrote it once he had retired to Monte Cassino on leaving the court of Charlemagne. Not one extant manuscript can be associated with the scriptorium of Monte Cassino or any other writing centre in southern or central Italy.[75] The earliest references to manuscripts of the *Historia langobardorum* at Monte Cassino are Leo of Ostia's mention of a copy written under Abbot Theobald (1022–35) and Peter the Deacon's information that a further copy was made under Abbot Desiderius. There are certainly earlier references to the text in the later ninth and the tenth centuries.[76] Both Erchempert of Monte Cassino[77] and the author of the *Chronicon salernitatum* knew the work, though the latter never expressly mentions Paul's *Historia langobardorum* even if it is clear that he borrowed extensively from it. It is significant, moreover, that the text group to which the *Chronicon salernitatum*'s author's text belonged is very difficult to pin down and was related to the text as it is found in manuscripts from northern Italy and Francia.[78] Monte Cassino itself, therefore, would appear to have played no role in the dissemination of the *Historia langobardorum* even if the text were known there in the ninth century.[79]

North Italian manuscripts, on the other hand, are strongly represented among the surviving copies. Certainly among the eleven classes of text Waitz identified on the basis of variant readings, four (A, B, E and F),

century but late tenth or early eleventh century, and Copenhagen Gl. Kgl. 2158 4o, which is a French tenth-century codex, not late ninth or early tenth century. For useful comments and revision of the dating and location of some of the manuscripts see also Pani, 'Aspetti della tradizione manoscritta'.

[74] See Pohl, 'Paulus Diaconus'.

[75] For important observations on this issue see P. Chiesa, 'Caratteristiche della transmissione dell' "Historia langobardorum"', in *Paolo Diacono e il Friuli altomedievale (Secc. VI–X)*(Spoleto, 2001), I, pp. 45–66.

[76] Leo of Ostia and Peter the Deacon, *Chronica monasterii casinensis* II, 53, and III, 63, ed. H. Hoffmann, *MGH SS*, XXXIV (Hannover, 1980).

[77] Erchempert, *Historia langobardorum beneventana*, c. 1, commends Paul's History in his introductory chapter, ed. G. Waitz, *MGH SRL* (Hannover, 1878), pp. 234–64; and see U. Westerbergh, *Beneventan ninth-century poetry*, Studia latina Stockholmensia 4 (Stockholm, 1957).

[78] U. Westerbergh (ed.), *Chronicon salernitanum. A critical edition with studies on literary and historical sources and on language*, Studia latina Stockholmensia 3 (Stockholm, 1956), at pp. 199–202. See also W. Pohl, 'History in fragments: Montecassino's politics of memory', *EME* 10 (2001), pp. 343–74, and *Werkstätte der Erinnerung: Montecassino und die Gestaltung der langobardischen Vergangenheit* (Vienna, 2001), who establishes a tenth-century stress at Monte Cassino on the link with Paul the Deacon.

[79] See also Pohl, 'Paulus Diaconus', pp. 388–405.

appear to be predominantly north Italian in origin, though in the cases of B and E the earliest manuscripts are late ninth/early tenth century and late tenth/early eleventh century respectively. Each will need to be placed in its proper historical context and circumstances of production if we are to understand the reception of Paul the Deacon's *Historia langobardorum* and his potential impact in later decades. Waitz's classes H–L comprise late manuscripts, from the eleventh century onwards. Representatives of each class seem assignable to particular regions: H is French, I is Bavarian and the others contain indications of a later medieval circulation and recopying or reception of the text in England, western Germany and France.

The earliest surviving copy of the *Historia langobardorum* is the famous palimpsested Assisi uncial fragment (San Francesco 585) of the late eighth century.[80] The placing hitherto of its origin in northern or central Italy to some degree has rested on the assumptions about where Paul was when he wrote the text and from whence copies were disseminated. On palaeographical grounds, however, this seems to me to be a north Italian book.[81] Claudia Villa has commented, moreover, on the prevalence of uncial script in codices from northern Italy.[82] From the late eighth or early ninth century is St Gallen, Stiftsbibliothek 635. It is also from northern Italy with an early Milanese provenance before it arrived in Reichenau and went from thence to St Gallen.[83] Both this and the early ninth-century Cividale manuscript (the only book of identifiably regional character in Bischoff's opinion),[84] are also from north-east Italy and clearly postdate the Carolingian conquest of 774. Further, the famous Verona miscellany

---

[80] *CLA*, III (Oxford, 1938,) no. 279; and see R. Morghen, 'Il palinsesto Assisiense dell' "Historia langobardorum" di Paolo Diacono', *Bullettino dell'Istituto Storico Italiano* 38 (1918), pp. 7–23 and plates 1–26.

[81] See B. Bischoff, 'Panorama der Handschriftenüberlieferung aus der Zeit Karls des Grossen', in B. Bischoff, *Mittelalterliche Studien*, III (Stuttgart, 1981), pp. 5–38, at pp. 28–38, and 'Frühkarolingische Handschriften und ihre Heimat', *Scriptorium* 22 (1968), pp. 306–14. Bischoff includes the Assisi fragment in his list of 'late uncial manuscripts written in Italy'. For an English translation of 'Panorama' and the list of uncial manuscripts see 'Manuscripts in the age of Charlemagne', trans. M. Gorman, in Bischoff, *Manuscripts and libraries*, pp. 20–55, at pp. 44–55.

[82] C. Villa, 'Lay and ecclesiastical culture,' in C. La Rocca (ed.), *Italy in the early middle ages* (Oxford, 2002), pp. 189–203, at p. 193. There she has apparently written Perugia instead of Assisi, unless she meant to allude to the ninth-century copy of Justinian in Perugia, Biblioteca Capitolare 32, which she mentions in Villa, 'Cultura classica e tradizioni Longobarde; tra latino et volgari', in Chiesa (ed.), *Paolo Diacono*, pp. 575–600, at p. 591.

[83] *CLA*, VII (Oxford, 1956), no. 945; see Pani, 'Aspetti della tradizione manoscritta', pp. 385–95 and fig. 1; and Pohl, 'Paulus Diaconus', pp. 389–91, where by mistake he gives the St Gallen manuscript the shelf number 736. See also Chiesa, 'Caratteristiche della trasmissione', pp. 60–1.

[84] Cividale del Friuli, Museo Archeologico Nazionale, Ms XXVIII: Bischoff, 'Panorama', p. 30; and Pani, 'Aspetti della tradizione manoscritta', pp. 385 and 396–7 and fig. 2.

of the first half of the ninth century discussed in the preceding chapter of this book, and also from northern Italy, includes extracts from all the books of the *Historia langobardorum*.[85]

It has to be acknowledged that the palaeography of Italian manuscripts of the later eighth and early ninth centuries, together with the sporadic persistence of uncial script, has made it very difficult for certainties to be reached about the origin of most of the extant codices. What indications we have do not exclude either Cividale or Aquileia as possible centres of production of the earliest extant witness to Paul's text. A further possibility is the court of Pippin of Italy itself. On analogy with the various scribes responsible for the books of Charlemagne's supposed 'court school' manuscripts, I should add that Cividale, Aquileia or Verona could well have been one of the north Italian centres from which books for use at the Carolingian Lombard court were acquired, quite apart from being the source of books transported across the Alps.[86] Alternatively, scribes from any of these places could have worked at court. There are in fact a number of books that have been associated by Bernhard Bischoff with the court of Pippin of Italy and a number of different script types and hands are represented among them. The splendid *Liber comitis* (Paris, BnF lat. 9451), for use presumably in the palace chapel, is written in large elaborate monumental minuscule and uncial.[87] The script of Pelagius' commentaries on the Epistles of Paul (Paris, BnF lat. 653) is a very different early caroline minuscule and a strong uncial.[88] St Gallen Stiftsbibliothek 108 and 227, containing texts falsely attributed to Isidore and Jerome on the end of the world and on the psalms,[89] the *Lex alemannorum* in Wolfenbüttel (Herzog August Bibliothek, Helmsted. 513),[90] the Karlsruhe copy of Jerome's Commentary on Matthew (Karlsruhe, Landesbibliothek, Aug. CCLXI)[91] and a special selection of sermons in Vienna, ÖNB cod. 1616),[92] all contain similar strong uncial and minuscule scripts.

The standing of Pippin's court as a cultural centre has recently been substantially enhanced with Claudia Villa's suggestion that Berlin,

---

[85] See above, pp. 52–7, and R. Cessi, 'Di due miscellanee storiche medioevali', *Archivio Muratoriano* 13 (1913), pp. 69–96.

[86] For further comment see chapter 9 below, especially in relation to the *Historia augusta*, p. 205.

[87] *CLA*, V (Oxford, 1950), no. 580.   [88] *Ibid.*, no. 527.

[89] *CLA*, VII (Oxford, 1956), nos. 905 and 930.

[90] *CLA*, IX (Oxford, 1959), no. 1382. See also R. Kottje, 'Zum Geltungsbereich der Lex Alamannorum', in H. Beumann and W. Schröder (eds.), *Die transalpinen Verbindungen der Bayern, Alemannen und Franken bis zum 10. Jahrhundert*, Nationes, Historische und philologische Untersuchungen zur Entstehung der europäischen Nationen im Mittelalter 6 (Sigmaringen, 1987), pp. 359–78, at p. 373, who dates the book 'c.800'.

[91] *CLA*, VIII (Oxford, 1959), no. 1111.   [92] *CLA*, X (Oxford, 1963), no. 1563.

Deutsche Staatsbibliothek Diez B. Sant. 66 might have been used at the Frankish court in Italy. This contains a collection of texts mostly by north Italian authors, including the grammar of Peter of Pisa and the poem celebrating Pippin of Italy's victory over the Avars (792–6).[93] But it also includes, written in a north Italian hand, the famous list of books Bischoff suggested was a list of volumes in the library of Charlemagne but which Villa has challenged.[94] Although her initial suggestion of a close link with Verona has been disputed, this association of the book list with Pippin's court in the context of my discussion in this chapter is a very exciting possibility and one that makes excellent sense. It has the merit of retaining the list as one connected with a Frankish royal court, and leaves room for the other important aspects of Bischoff's original thesis, namely, the evidence of connections between the book list and subsequent north Frankish copies of the particular texts it records.[95] Villa also associates another miscellany, Paris, BnF lat. 7530, along with Berlin, Deutsche Staatsbibliothek Diez B. Sant 66, with the education of court officials.[96] Her conception of a political and lay public for texts at Pippin's court also entirely accords with my suggestion about the initial audience intended for Paul's *Historia langobardorum*.

These books indicate the supply to the Carolingian court in the Lombard kingdom of texts from local resources, if not the royal patronage of book production in the great cultural centres of northern Italy at the end of the eighth century. Very little otherwise is known of the court of Pippin of Italy, but this group of manuscripts at least suggest an interest in, and promotion of, religious culture comparable with that of other centres north of the Alps. It is conceivable that the hitherto unlocated Assisi

---

[93] Villa, 'Cultura classica e tradizioni longobarde', p. 578; and see also, Villa, 'Lay and ecclesiastical culture', p. 197.

[94] See below, pp. 208–9, and B. Bischoff (ed.), *Sammelhandschrift Diez B. Sant 66. Grammatici latini et catalogus librorum*, Codices selecti (Graz, 1973), and his discussion, 'Die Hofbibliothek Karls des Grossen', in W. Braunfels (ed.), *Karl der Grosse. Lebenswerk und Nachleben*, II, *Das Geistige Leben*, ed. B. Bischoff (Düsseldorf, 1965), pp. 42–62, revised in *Mittelalterliche Studien*, III, pp. 149–69; English trans. M. Gorman, 'The court library of Charlemagne', in Bischoff, *Manuscripts and libraries*, pp. 56–75. See C. Villa, 'Die Horazüberlieferung und die "Bibliothek Karls des Grossen": zum Werkverzeichnis der Handschrift Berlin, Diez B. 66', *DA* 51 (1995), pp. 29–52; and in Italian: 'La tradizione di Orazio e la "Biblioteca di Carlo Magno": per l'elenco di opere nel codice Berlin Diez B.Sant 66', in O. Pecere and M. Reeve (eds.), *Formative stages of classical traditions: Latin texts from antiquity to the Renaissance* (Spoleto, 1995), pp. 299–322, at p. 316 and note 41.

[95] Internally contradictory support for Villa's suggestion about Verona is to be found in M. Gorman, 'Peter of Pisa and the *Quaestiunculae* copied for Charlemagne in Brussels II 2572', *RB* 110 (2000), pp. 238–60; but see the effective counter-argument by T. Licht, 'Additional note on the "Library catalogue of Charlemagne's court"', *Journal of Medieval Latin* 11 (2001), pp. 210–13. For further discussion see below, pp. 208–9.

[96] Villa, 'Cultura classica e tradizioni longobarde', pp. 580–1.

uncial fragments of Paul the Deacon's *Historia langobardorum* should be added to this group; a court association with its production would be consistent with the other suggestions I have made about the purpose of the text so far.[97] A Franco-Lombard court context by north Italian scribes would account, moreover, both for the initial production of Paul's text and for its subsequent dissemination in both Italy and north of the Alps. It is of the greatest significance that, of the non-Italian classes of the text of the *Historia langobardorum*, the earliest association of three (C, D and G) from France and Germany, with many ninth-century manuscripts among them, go back to Corbie, Rheims, Auxerre and Fulda. All were centres with strong links with the Carolingian court.[98] The Verona miscellany, moreover, came to Metz in the tenth century and Metz, as we have seen, also had particular reason to respect Paul's memory.

The manuscript dissemination of Paul's *Historia langobardorum* uncovers the possibility that it was originally produced in northern Italy, possibly in association with the court of Pippin of Italy. It was subsequently disseminated both in northern Italy and the Carolingian realms north of the Alps. Thus the initial audience for the *Historia langobardorum* is indicated. The *Historia langobardorum* can be read as an *admonitio* for the Franks both at home and serving in the former Lombard kingdom. It provided the Lombards with a history and identity just as the Franks had a history and identity. Further, in his text Paul provided an informative history for the instruction of the young Frankish ruler, Pippin of Italy, and his Franco-Lombard entourage. The text also presented an exposition of Christian kingship for any ruler.[99] There were Lombard traditions that needed to be known, respected and maintained. The Carolingians needed to know about the Lombards in order to rule them successfully. The Lombard kingdom, as I stated at the beginning of this chapter, was a very different proposition from any that had been attempted by the Franks before. Hitherto the Franks had primarily annexed areas of Gaul that had once been ruled by, or which had paid tribute to, the Merovingians. In

---

[97] See also Villa, *ibid.*, p. 593, who suggests a link with the Codex Salmasianus, Paris, BnF lat. 10318; *CLA*, V (Oxford, 1950), no. 593, containing the *Anthologia latina*.

[98] Heidelberg, Universitätsbibliothek MS pal. lat. 912, Corbie, third quarter of the ninth century: Bischoff, *Katalog* 1, no. 1515; Staatsbibliothek zu Berlin, Preussischer Kulturbesitz, Phillipps 1887, Auxerre, third quarter of the ninth century, Bischoff, *Katalog* 1, no. 442; Kassel, Gesamthochschulbibliothek MS hist 72a–c (2 leaves), Fulda, second half of the ninth century: Bischoff, *Katalog* 1, no. 1792. Giessen, Universitätsbibliothek 688 of the third quarter of the ninth century is from St Bertin: Bischoff, *Katalog* 1, no. 1391, and the eleventh-century copy in the later portion of Bern, Burgerbibliothek MS 83, from fol. 104 onwards, is from Rheims; see further below, pp. 111–13.

[99] For suggestions concerning the text's subsequent audience see Capo, 'Paolo Diacono e il mondo franco', especially pp. 73–4, n. 47, and Chiesa, 'Caratteristiche della trasmissione', especially 60–1.

the case of the Saxons and Avars, the Franks were attacking pagans. In the case of the Lombard kingdom, however, the Franks were annexing a powerful, highly cultured, Christian and catholic neighbour that had been an independent part of the Roman world with its own established laws and traditions, church, and social networks.

The legislative and administrative efforts of the Carolingians in Italy indicate that they did their utmost to incorporate their new territory as rapidly as possible. It is striking, for example, how many of the new capitularies and diplomas issued after 774 are in fact intended for Italy.[100] Carolingian *missi* were operative in Italy in attempting to impose justice.[101] We have seen also that in the sphere of religious organization and doctrinal orthodoxy, Italy was part of the Carolingian church. The task of incorporation was enormous. The persuasion that the Lombards were part of the Frankish world had to be strong.

I have suggested in this chapter that the Franks, just as much as the Lombards under Carolingian rule, needed instruction and persuasion of the essential rightness of the joining of the Frankish and Lombard kingdoms, the legitimacy of Carolingian rule and of the strength of Lombard identity. There would be no credit or advantage to the Carolingians in oppressing the Lombards, or in making them feel like a conquered people. The recruitment of Paul, a highly intelligent, well-informed and politically experienced Lombard, to add a distinctive contribution in the form of his *Historia langobardorum*, was masterly. It constituted an active contribution to the shaping of Frankish and Lombard relations and to the understanding of kingship in the aftermath of 774. It was also a significant use of the genre of history to provide political legitimation, to further Frankish instances of which I now turn.

---

[100] A useful compendium is C. Azzara and P. Moro (eds.), *I capitolari italici. Storia e diritto della dominazione carolingia in Italia* (Rome, 1998). See also J. Davis, 'Conceptions of kingship under Charlemagne' (unpublished M.Litt. thesis, University of Cambridge, 1999).

[101] See F. Bougard, 'La Justice dans le royaume d'Italie aux IX–Xe siècles', in *La Giustizia nell'alto medioevo (secoli IX–XI)*, Settimane 44 (Spoleto, 1997), pp. 133–76; and R. McKitterick, 'Perceptions of justice in western Europe in the ninth and tenth centuries', in *La Giustizia*, pp. 1075–1102; and also F. Bougard, *La Justice dans le royaume d'Italie de la fin du VIII siècle au début du XI siècle*, Ecole Française de Rome (Paris, 1995).

4   The Carolingians on their past

Human beings are in a perpetual dialogue with the past from their vantage point in the present. St Augustine of Hippo (†430) put this most succinctly when he discussed what he thought of as 'three times', that is, 'a present concerning past things; a present concerning present things and a present concerning future things. For these three are in the spirit and I do not see them elsewhere: the present concerning past things is memory; the present concerning present things is perception; the present concerning future things is expectation.'[1]

To record and explain the past, men and women in history have resorted to many means. In calendars, necrologies and martyrologies, for example, past and present time are organised in conjunction with each other, for past time is remembered in terms of the commemoration of anniversaries in the present.[2] Memories may even be heightened and given the impetus to record them in writing by contemporary crises.[3] In our own profession of the writing of history, particular constraints are in evidence. We all construct a past which we try to make as faithful to our evidence as possible.[4] Yet limitations of memory (both our own and that of the authors of our sources)[5] and the chronological framework, quite

---

[1] Augustine, *Confessions*, XI, c. 20, ed. M. Skutella, H. Jürgens and W. Schaub, *S. Aurelii confessionum libri XII*, Bibliotheca scriptorum graecorum et romanorum (Stuttgart, 1981), p. 281; *praesens de praeteritis memoria, praesens de praesentibus contuitus, praesens de futuris expectatio*: English trans. R. S. Pine-Coffin (Harmondsworth, 1961), pp. 269. See J. Coleman, *Ancient and medieval memories. Studies in the reconstruction of the past* (Cambridge, 1992), pp. 101–12; and R. Corradini, *Zeit und Text. Studien zum Tempus-Begriff des Augustinus*, Veröffentlichung des Instituts für Österreichische Geschichtsforschung 33 (Munich, 1997).

[2] M. Carruthers, *The book of memory. A study of memory in medieval culture* (Cambridge, 1990).

[3] G. Althoff, 'Zur Verschriftlichung von Memoria in Krisenzeiten', in D. Geuenich and O.-G. Oexle (eds.), *Memoria in der Gesellschaft des Mittelalters*, Veröffentlichungen des Max Plancks Institut für Geschichte 3 (Göttingen, 1994), pp. 56–73.

[4] R. Morse, *Truth and convention in the middle ages: rhetoric, representation and reality* (Cambridge, 1991).

[5] See P. Geary, *Phantoms of remembrance. Memory and oblivion at the end of the first millennium* (Princeton, 1994) on the importance of what is forgotten.

apart from the nature of the discipline and conventions associated with historiography as a genre, play a crucial role in producing distinctive interpretations of the past of varying degrees of plausibility and conviction.[6]

In constructing an account of the past a writer can either work within the confines of a particular genre or create new conventions of his or her own for the record of memory.[7] He or she is dependent on information within his or her own and other people's memories and the communication of that information in oral or written form. Thus the concerns of literacy, orality and historiography come together as the record of memory.[8] Bearing in mind Halbwachs's view that social groups construct their own images of the world by establishing an agreed version of the past,[9] it is the fact that these memories are established by communication that is so important for our understanding of written history in whatever period historians study.[10] Just as we need to determine the degree to which many of one's own ostensibly private memories are social memories and shared in general terms with many others, so too the apparently individual authorship of an historical text may express a shared social memory of a particular group. Recalled past experience and shared images of the past are kinds of memories that have particular importance for the constitution of social groups. Within these, the creation of accounts of past events that draw on memory but select from it in distinctive ways that become accepted, and thereafter shared, by a group is part of 'constructing the past'. Thus the Franks in the early middle ages, their construction of their identity and an agreed version of their past in the form of narrative histories are a striking illustration of the dialectic between oral and written, and between private and group, memories.[11]

---

[6] See the seminal J. Vansina, *Oral tradition. A study of historical methodology*, trans. H. M. White (London, 1965), and the suggestions made by H. White, *The content of the form: narrative discourse and historical representation* (Baltimore and London, 1987); and W. Goffart, *The narrators of barbarian history (A.D. 550–800): Jordanes, Gregory of Tours, Bede, and Paul the Deacon* (Princeton, 1988). See also the essays in Scharer and Scheibelreiter, *Historiographie*; and L. Boje Mortensen, 'The texts and contexts of ancient Roman history in twelfth-century western scholarship', in P. Magdalino (ed.), *The perception of the past in twelfth-century Europe* (London, 1992), pp. 99–116.

[7] See L. Boje Mortensen, 'Stylistic choice in a reborn genre: the national histories of Widukind of Corvey and Dudo of St Quentin', in P. G. A. degli'Innocenti (ed.), *Dudone de S. Quintino* (Trento, 1995), pp. 77–102.

[8] J. Fentress and C. Wickham, *Social memory* (Oxford, 1992) and see chapter 1, above, and below, chapter 7.

[9] M. Halbwachs, *Les Cadres sociaux de la mémoire* (Paris, 1925) and *La mémoire collective* (Paris, 1950).

[10] On communication generally see M. Mostert (ed.), *New approaches to medieval communication*, Utrecht Studies in Medieval Literacy (Turnhout, 1999).

[11] Discussion of identity, sometimes implicated in ethnicity in the early middle ages, abound: see, for example, P. Amory, *People and identity in Ostrogothic Italy, 489–544*

In the Carolingian period, moreover, a new narrative genre, namely annals, was devised to express feelings and beliefs about the immediate past by the elite. These Frankish annals provide a year-by-year account of events, dated according to the Christian era. Questions of time and the way these written records were produced within a particular chronological framework have all kinds of symbolic resonances; they are a vital part of the organisation of memory according to received conventions. The Franks inherited historical traditions from the Jews, the Romans and the early Christians but exploited them within their own chronological and political schemes for their own ends. It is on these schemes that I wish to focus in this and the following two chapters in this book. Thereby I shall bring together the manipulation of chronology and time, questions of memory and the construction of the past in the context of the Franks and their annals in the eighth and ninth centuries.

Time and chronology

Time is something that can be measured, but it is also something that can be controlled and manipulated. This is particularly evident in the construction of the past in early medieval historiography. Indeed, attitudes towards time in Frankish sources are so fundamental a part of our historical evidence that there is a danger that we may omit to consider their significance or implications. To examine time and its functions in the early middle ages, therefore, may yield something very specific about the perception of the past, present and even future on the part of any group. As this is expressed and embodied in writing designed to record the past in one way or another, time, numeracy and literacy become inextricably linked. The concerns of the *trivium* and the *quadrivium*, with writing and speech on the one hand and numbers and calculation on the other, are united.

Let me first give some indication of the perceptions of time in the early middle ages. Bede in his *De temporum ratione* commented that time for all mortals was divided up into moments, hours, days, months, years, centuries and eras.[12] Some of these rhythms of time passing are natural

(Cambridge, 1997), and his references to the earlier literature; W. Pohl and H. Reimitz (eds.), *Strategies of distinction. The construction of ethnic communities, 300–800*, Transformation of the Roman World 2 (Leiden, 1998); R. Miles (ed.), *Constructing identities in late antiquity* (London, 1999); and A. Gillett (ed.), *On barbarian identity. Critical approaches to ethnicity in the early middle ages*, Studies in the Early Middle Ages 4 (Turnhout, 2002).
12 Bede, *De temporum ratione*, c. 2, ed. C. W. Jones, *Bede Opera didascalica*, 3 vols., CCSL, CXXIII A–C (Turnhout, 1975–80), I (CXXIII B), p. 274. For an English translation with comprehensive introduction and commentary see F. Wallis, *Bede: the reckoning of time* (Liverpool, 1999), especially p. 13.

and regulated by the sun and moon, such as years, months and days. The perception of days and months, moreover, is influenced by biological cycles in humans. Superimposed upon this natural base, however, are the man-made elements of hours, weeks, centuries and eras of the world. Generations were used, as so often in the Old and New Testaments; so was the Olympiad, a cycle of four years starting in 776 BC, or a reckoning from the foundation of Rome in 753 BC. Alternatively there was a reckoning by consulships and magistracies. In the fourth century the indiction, a fifteen-year interval between the levying of taxes and starting in AD 297, was used. These reckonings and their functions have everything to do with human mentalities. Jacques Le Goff chose to describe the early middle ages as observing 'church time' and the later middle ages as following merchant's time.[13] This is self-evidently too schematic and too simplistic. It omits to take into account that church time is also *historical* time, in that it orients itself in relation to a specific event. Initially this was the year of the Passion but it subsequently became the year of the Incarnation. Further, Christian time is also *theological* time in that it sees whatever smaller or larger units man may devise in relation to eternity. Thirdly, in terms of specific calculations during the year, Christian time observes variable *liturgical* time, and thus cyclical time, for it is the Christian festivals – Easter, a moveable feast, and Christmas, a fixed day – which determine the cycle of feasts for the entire year. All these are linked to *astronomical* time. On a day-to-day basis Christian time can also be divided up in a specific context, such as *monastic* time, where the division of days into 'hours' yields variable lengths of time according to the season.[14] Further, any particular society could add its own artificial rhythms, related to seasonal, military, administrative or daily needs. The Franks, for example, convened each spring assembly of the leading men of the kingdom which could also serve as a mustering of the host,[15] and the Alemannian laws stipulate that a judicial court should be held once a fortnight (or once a week in troubled times).[16] Thus in the early middle ages we have to consider political time, as well as social and economic time, as separate or separable from Christian time.

An obvious instance of recording political time is the narrative of the passing of years in most early medieval historical writing, where the terms

---

[13] J. Le Goff, 'Time, merchant's time and church's time in the middle ages', in idem, *Time, work and culture in the middle ages*, trans. A. Goldhammer (Chicago, 1980), pp. 29–42.
[14] See further below, p. 88.
[15] For example, *Annales regni francorum*, s.a. 767, ed. F. Kurze, *MGH SRG*, VI (Hannover, 1895), p. 24.
[16] *Lex alemannorum*, XXXVI, ed. K. Lehmann, *MGH Legum sectio I. Leges nat. germ.*, V, 1 (Hannover, 1885), p. 94.

of office or reign of particular individuals (kings, consuls, dukes, emperors) serves as the dating mechanism. Further, there is the use of regnal years in the dating of documents. Christian time as a dating scheme in the form of the year of the Incarnation was not introduced into documents until the late seventh or eighth centuries. In Anglo-Saxon England, for example, the earliest original charter preserving the year of the Incarnation appears to be the Ismere charter of 736;[17] copies preserved of charters from the kingdom of the Hwicce of earlier date (676 and 680) may indicate that the practice was evident there by the 730s if all elements are to be regarded as authentic.[18] The year of the Incarnation was not used to date Frankish royal documents until the 870s, though in 'private' or non-royal charters it appears in the early ninth century.[19] The diplomata of Charlemagne for 783, 788 and 791 survive in later copies and like the copies of Anglo-Saxon material may reflect later assumptions about the form dating clauses should take.[20] Ecclesiastical councils and synods, on the other hand, are dated according to the year of the Incarnation both in England and on the continent from the 740s onwards.

The passing of apparently simple chronological time, therefore, comprised a whole series of other measurements, interests and symbols. All these are necessarily linked with the means by which time is calculated and measured for the co-ordination of social activity. For most people in the early middle ages, the passing of time during the day was measured by the movements of the sun. Few would have had clocks or would have experienced time regulated by bells. Sunlight (that is, daylight) was a natural determinant and could be linked with religious observance. Monastic rules further regulated the daily routine of praying, working, eating, sleeping. The *Rule of Benedict*, for example, adjusted the length of hour in relation to the amount of daylight in winter and summer.[21] Longer days yielded longer day hours. The time for prayer had also to be determined, and at night it was governed by the position of the stars.[22]

---

[17] London, British Library Cotton Augustus II.3, facsimile in A. Bruckner, *ChLA* 3 (Olten and Lausanne, 1963), no. 183, pp. 22–3.

[18] See K. Harrison, *The framework of Anglo-Saxon history to A.D. 900* (Cambridge, 1976), pp. 65–75, discussing W. Birch, *Cartularium saxonicum* (Oxford, 1885), nos. 43 and 51 dating from 676 and 680. Compare the comments in S. Kelly, revised edition of P. H. Sawyer, *Anglo-Saxon Charters. An annotated list and bibliography*, typescript (Cambridge 1994), nos. 51 and 52 and see http://www.trin.cam.ac.uk/chartwww.

[19] See H. Bresslau, *Handbuch der Urkundenlehre*, 2 vols. (Berlin, 1931), II, pp. 427–8.

[20] E. Mühlbacher (ed.), *MGH Diplomatum Karolinorum*, I, *Pippini, Carlomanni, Caroli Magni Diplomata* (Munich, 1979), pp. 202–3, 218–19, 226–8.

[21] *Rule of Benedict*, c. 8, ed. and trans. J. McCann (1952), pp. 48–9, and his notes pp. 175–6.

[22] See, for example, Gregory of Tours, *De cursu stellarum*, ed. B. Krusch, *MGH SRM*, I (Hannover, 1885), pp. 854–72; and S. C. McCluskey, 'Gregory of Tours, monastic timekeeping and early Christian attitudes to astronomy', *Isis* 81 (1990), pp. 9–22.

Interest in time measurement led to various calculations and inventions of mechanical means – sundials, clepsydra, clepsammia, the famous candle clock of King Alfred[23] – to record the passing of time, not all of which would yield equal hours.[24] In calculating months and years, on the other hand, the moon plays as important a role as the sun. The division of the months into the Christian week is essentially that of the Jews, defined in the first chapter of the book of Genesis; the Romans had grouped days in eight.

Conversion to Christianity, therefore, meant, first of all, adjustment to a new *daily* cycle, reinforced by a religious symbolism attached to Sunday to which Constantine's degree concerning Sunday observance on the *dies dominica*, differentiating it clearly from the Jewish Sabbath, contributed. Gregory of Tours, for example, maintained that the Sunday of the Resurrection was the first day of the week, not the seventh.

This is the day of the resurrection of our Lord Jesus Christ, which we rightly call Sunday because of the holy rising again. In the beginning this was the first day to see the light, and it deserves to be the first to see our Lord rise from the tomb.[25]

Secondly, as is well known, Christian time is a combination of Hebrew lunar and Roman solar elements, and thus a new *yearly* cycle was created which contained within it the commemorative festivals of Christ's birth and Passion and the preparatory seasons for each such as Advent and Lent. The moveable feasts such as Easter are derived from Jewish festivals and the fixed remainder of the calendar is Roman. The associations behind these are both astronomical and historical and again have both Roman and Jewish elements. Christmas coincides with the old Roman winter solstice, and the Crucifixion and Conception coincide with the vernal equinox. There are, of course, historical reasons for the choice of the date of Easter linked with the cycle of Jewish religious festivals. The Jewish Passover, 14th Nisan, the first month of the Hebrew religious calendar, was celebrated on the first full moon after the vernal equinox. The Christians by about 120 AD had fixed Easter on the Sunday following the 14th Nisan, but many disputes remained; Quartodecimans, for example,

---

[23] Asser, *Vita Alfredi regis*, cc. 103, 104, ed. W. H. Stevenson, *Asser's Life of King Alfred* (Oxford, 1904; repr. 1959), pp. 89, 91, English trans. S. Keynes and M. Lapidge, *Alfred the Great, Asser's Life of King Alfred and other contemporary sources* (Harmondsworth, 1983), pp. 107–9.

[24] E. J. Bickerman, *Chronology of the ancient world* (1980); R. Sorabji, *Time, creation and the continuum* (London, 1983); and D. Landes, *Revolution in time, clocks and the making of the modern world* (Cambridge, Mass., 1983).

[25] Gregory of Tours, *Historiae*, I, 23, ed. B. Krusch, *MGH SRM*, I (Hannover, 1885) p. 44; English trans. L. Thorpe, *Gregory of Tours. The history of the Franks* (Harmondsworth, 1974), p. 83.

continued to observe Easter on 14th Nisan regardless of on what day of the week it fell. If Easter were to be a moveable feast, calendars were needed to determine the correct day. Cyclic tables like our Julian calendar were regarded as the most useful, for these combined movements of sun and moon.[26] All this was to orient time in relation to Christian anniversaries such as the Crucifixion and Resurrection.

So far, so familiar. But different calculations abounded in late antiquity and the early middle ages as dates and the conjunction of moon and sun were calculated according to various methods and cycles. How was anyone to ensure that Easter was celebrated each year on the correct and, above all, on the same day? The earlier solution for the pope in relation to the churches under his jurisdiction appeared to be the announcement of the day of Easter in the subsequent year, much as universities or schools publish the dates of term in advance. One or two such announcements have survived, such as Pope Leo's Paschal Letter of 454 addressed to the churches of Gaul and Spain.[27] This followed the Alexandrine calculations associated with Cyril and announced the day of Easter for 455 as Sunday 24 April, to be observed for the sake of unity with the apostolic sees (Alexandria and Rome). Observing the date of Easter at the same time as everyone else thus became a straightforward symbol of unity.

An alternative solution might be the circulation of approved tables on which Easter had been calculated well in advance so that everyone would be able to see what the date would be. Thus Victorius of Aquitaine, the *scrupulorum calculator*, produced tables in about 457 based on the nineteen-year Alexandrian cycle and projected his cycles for 532 years. But he created muddle in such a way as to produce a different date of Easter from the Alexandrian calculations for thirteen years out of the nineteen. This prompted Victorius to dub the dates the Latin and the Greek Easters and to leave the choice of which date to observe to users of

---

[26] For lucid explanations see K. Harrison, *The framework of Anglo-Saxon history to A.D. 900* (Cambridge, 1976), and Wallis, *Bede*. One lunar month = 29.5306 days; one solar year = 365.2422 days; excess lunar months in a solar year, 0.3683. To reconcile lunar and solar years the computist or calendar maker must intercalate 3 lunar months every 8 years; 4 lunar months every 11 years; 7 lunar months every 19 years (this is the Alexandrine cycle, which is the most nearly accurate); 31 months every 84-year cycle (a cycle of 532 years, that is, the Victorine, was also used). Even the 19-year cycle needed correction and adjustment because it came to a total of 6440.75 days, one day more than the 19 Julian years = 6939.75 days. To correct it, the *saltus lunae*, one lunar day, was omitted at the end of the nineteenth year. This fixed lunar XIV. See also G. J. Whitrow, *Time in history. Views of time from prehistory to the present day* (Oxford, 1988); and E. G. Richards, *Mapping time. The calendar and its history*, (Oxford, 1998).

[27] Leo the Great, letter 138, *PL*, LIV, cols. 1101–2.

his table.[28] He also related his cycle to the year of the Passion of Christ (calculated as AD 28) (= *annus mundi* 5229).[29]

A further effort to get matters straight was made by Dionysius Exiguus, who composed his famous *Libellus de cyclo magno paschae* between 525 and 532 in order to cover the years 532 to 625.[30] He introduced the use of the year of the birth of Christ, rather than the year of the Passion, as his fixed point, but the main function of his work was to fix the date of Easter each year and to advocate the nineteen-year cycle for such calculations. It was Dionysius therefore who advocated the use of the Christian era. Perhaps inevitably, the Victorine and Dionysian (as well as other) methods of calculation were adopted by different regions, with the consequences that Bede, in his account of Easter observance in Northumbria and the debate at Whitby in 664, has made very familiar.[31]

If the tables in circulation established the principles clearly enough, then a third way of ensuring the proper and simultaneous observance of Easter was to teach people how to do the necessary calculations. The skills of arithmetical computation or *computus* became an established part of the school curriculum. Thus a sense of the annual Christian cycle in relation to the movements of sun, moon and stars, to liturgy, to history (in that the nineteen-year cycles began with the year of the Incarnation) was instilled in all those receiving basic training in the schools. The Franks regarded *computus* as an essential part of clerical training. Thus in the *Admonitio generalis* in 789 issued by Charlemagne it was enjoined that the clergy should know *computus* and that it should be taught in the schools.[32] Tracts on *computus*, comprising short astronomical and computistical discussion and tables applied to the skill in creating and understanding ecclesiastical calendars, survive in abundance. So do Easter tables, yearly calendars, lists of calculations, tables to help the process of calculation,

[28] Compare Columbanus, letter 1, ed. G. S. M. Walker, *Sancti Columbani opera*, Scriptores Latini Hiberniae 2 (Dublin, 1970), pp. 1–7.

[29] Victorius, ed. T. Mommsen, *Victorius aquitanus cursus paschalis CCCVII, MGH Chronica minora*, I (Berlin, 1892), pp. 676–84. See also C. W. Jones, 'The Victorian and Dionysiac Paschal Tables', *Speculum* 3 (1934), pp. 408–21; and B. Krusch, 'Studien zur christlichmittelalterlichen Chronologie', *Abhandlungen der Preußischen Akademie der Wissenschaften, phil. hist Klasse* 8, 1937 (Berlin, 1938), pp. 4–57. For a clear account see Wallis, *Bede*, pp. l–lii.

[30] Dionysius, *Libellus de cyclo magno paschae/cyclus paschalis*, PL 67, pp. 483–508, especially col. 487, and also Krusch (ed.), 'Studien', pp. 59–87. See also G. Declercq, *Anno domini. Les origines de l'ère chrétienne* (Turnhout, 2000).

[31] Bede, *Historia ecclesiastica gentis anglorum*, III. 25, ed. and trans. B. Colgrave and R. A. B. Mynors, *Bede's ecclesiastical history of the English people*, Oxford Medieval Texts (Oxford, 1969), pp. 295–309.

[32] *Admonitio Generalis* 789, c. 72, ed. A. Boretius, *MGH Capitularia regum francorum*, I (Hannover, 1883), p. 60.

verses for memorising, dialogues for school catechism, and multiplication tables.[33]

The Northumbrian scholar Bede (†735) provided the most substantial and influential of the text books on *computus*. Bede wrote his tract *De temporibus* in 703, the *De temporum ratione* in 725, and his letter to Plegwin on the problem of computing in 708. In the *De temporum ratione*, Bede dealt fully with every aspect of time, tides and methods of dating. He calculated a new *annus mundi* (that is, the year of the Creation and age of the world) and got a different answer from everyone else, viz. 3952 years, that rejuvenated the world by 1200 years. He made a very strong case for the use of the year of the Incarnation (*annus domini*) as a means of dating Easter. Further, he himself used the year of the Incarnation in his *Historia ecclesiastica* as a reference system. It is Bede who is currently credited with the introduction of dating according to the year of the Incarnation onto the continent.[34] This dating according to *anno domini* (AD) is associated with the adoption of the Dionysian method for calculating Easter, with the consequence that uniformity in the rhythm of the Christian year was achieved in western Europe.

Bede's *De ratione temporum* may well have enhanced the Franks' understanding of the importance of the year of the Incarnation, but it is unlikely that he provided the primary impulse behind its adoption as a dating mechanism. It is much more likely that the Franks' interest in AD dating was derived directly from the work of Dionysius Exiguus. This becomes clear, appropriately enough, once the precise chronology of the dissemination of Bede's *De temporum ratione* on the continent on the one hand and, on the other, the Franks' familiarity with the year of the Incarnation and Dionysian calculations of the date of Easter are considered.

Tracing Bede's influence would appear to be straightforward. Hitherto, however, it has rested on some unproven assumptions. Firstly, it was supposed that everyone in England knew and accepted Bede's system and thus that any Englishman joining the English missionaries in Frisia, Hesse or Thuringia would naturally use and promote it on the continent.[35] Secondly, it was assumed that Bede's works were instantly circulated on the continent and had immediate impact.[36] Hence, on these

---

[33] On all these, particularly manuscripts from Fulda and the Reichenau, see W. Stevens, *Cycles of time and scientific learning in medieval Europe* (Aldershot, 1995), chapters 1, 6–11.

[34] See for example, D. Whitelock, *After Bede* (Newcastle, 1960).

[35] Still the best introduction to English activity on the continent is W. Levison, *England and the continent in the eighth century* (Oxford, 1946), but see also I. Wood, *The missionary life. Saints and the evangelisation of Europe 400–1050* (London, 1999).

[36] On the dissemination of Bede's works on the continent see R. McKitterick, 'Kulturelle Verbindungen zwischen England und den fränkischen Reichen in der Zeit der Karolinger:

preconceptions, the English missionary Boniface would have introduced AD dating and the Dionysian Easter to the Franks because he knew and accepted Bede's work. It is thought that this hypothesis is corroborated by the fact that the *Concilium germanicum* is dated according to the year of the Incarnation (742/743) convened in Austrasia under the auspices of the Carolingian mayor of the Frankish palace and presided over by Boniface.

It is important, however, to keep the issue of Easter calculation and the year of the Incarnation separate. The Dionysian method of calculating Easter was undoubtedly accepted in England and on the continent by the latter half of the seventh century. What remains uncertain is, first of all, whether the idea of dating the passing of time from the year of the Incarnation was extended to other contexts in which dating played a role. Secondly, is Dionysius or Bede the more influential example? As we have seen, the dating of documents on the continent is inconsistent and AD dating does not become common until the ninth century. Bede uses, as I said earlier, the year of the Incarnation in his *Historia ecclesiastica*. He also undoubtedly provides an account of the year of the Incarnation in the *De temporum ratione* and uses the Dionysian Paschal table to introduce the chronicle which forms Chapter 66 of *De temporum ratione*. But he uses the *annus mundi* (that is, counting the Creation as year 1) as his dating scheme in that chronicle and thus cannot be said to have advocated the use of the year of the Incarnation in the writing of history in this work.[37]

The earliest manuscript witnesses to Bede's *De temporum ratione* are from the mid- and late eighth century and have a provenance associated with Anglo-Saxon missionary centres in Germany. Malcolm Parkes placed the surviving fragments from a single copy of the *De temporum ratione* in the group of manuscripts written in what Lowe described as 'capitular uncial'.[38] This was a special small and simpler form of English uncial which Parkes argues was developed at Wearmouth-Jarrow as a regular book hand in the first half of the eighth century and used until it was superseded by insular minuscule.[39] Thus these fragments of the *De*

Kontexte und Implikationen', in J. Ehlers (ed.), *Deutschland und der Westen Europas im Mittelalter*, Vorträge und Forschungen 56 (Stuttgart 2002), pp. 121–48.

[37] See *De temporum ratione* cc. 47 and 65, trans. Wallis, *Bede*, pp. 126–9 and 155–6. See also Wallis, *ibid.*, pp. lxvii–lxxi, 33–68 and 353–66.

[38] Darmstadt, Hessische Landes- und Hochschulbibliothek MS 4262, and Bückeburg, Niedersächsisches Staatsarchiv dep. 3, Bedafragment III–VI B + Münster-in-Westfalen, Staatsarchiv MSC I 243, fols. 1v and 12v (Easter tables): M. B. Parkes, *The Jarrow scriptorium* (Jarrow, 1982), reprinted in M. B. Parkes, *Scribes, scripts and readers. Studies in the communication, presentation and dissemination of medieval texts* (London, 1991), pp. 92–120.

[39] *Ibid.*, p. 111.

temporum ratione were produced within two decades of the completion of the work, probably around 750. An earlier fragment from a different copy of the text, possibly dating from Bede's lifetime, is Darmstadt, Hessische Landes- und Hochschulbibliothek 4262.[40] It is less easy to date the arrival of these fragments on the continent. To associate them with Lull (†786) of Mainz's demands for books (though these did not include the *De temporum ratione*) from England would suggest that he was sent books written in a hand that might have been regarded by then, in Jarrow at least, as old-fashioned.[41] That remains a possibility, given the great demands requests from the continent placed on the resources at Jarrow around the middle decades of the eighth century, but it could also be feasible to think in terms of a copy being sent to the continent earlier.[42]

If we look at the distribution of other early copies of the *De temporum ratione*, there are hints of a late eighth- and early ninth-century Irish, Breton, Beneventan and Bavarian element in the manuscript tradition in the last two decades of the eighth century.[43] Other witnesses to the text are from the late eighth century and early ninth century onwards.[44] Thus the manuscripts indicate that Bede's *De temporum ratione* was known, at least on the fringes of the Frankish empire, by the last two decades of the eighth century. In the missionary areas of Hesse and Thuringia it may have been known earlier. What cannot be established from the surviving manuscript evidence is whether Bede's work was known in the Frankish heartlands before the ninth century. There is, however, use made of some chapters from Bede's text in an improved version of a Frankish manual on *computus c.* 760 from the Rhineland, though even here Jerome's calculation for the age of the world is preferred to Bede's. This might nevertheless be a remnant of a much more widely dispersed knowledge. All the same, there is no strong support for any argument in favour of Bede's *De temporum ratione* playing a dominant role in persuading the Franks to adopt the Dionysian method of calculating the date of Easter, even if Bede's text became more influential within the school curriculum subsequently. Still

---

[40] See the discussion of these fragments in Wallis, *Bede*, pp. lxxxvi–lxxxvii.

[41] Lull letters, ed. M. Tangl, *Die Briefe des heiligen Bonifatius und Lullus, MGH Epp. Sel.*, I (Hannover, 1916), letters 124–7, pp. 260–5; and see R. McKitterick, *Anglo-Saxon missionaries in Germany: personal connections and local influences*, Vaughan Paper 36 (Leicester, 1991), reprinted in McKitterick, *Frankish kings and culture*, chapter 1.

[42] On the context see R. McKitterick, 'The Anglo-Saxon missionaries in Germany: reflections on the manuscript evidence', *Transactions of the Cambridge Bibliographical Society* 9 (1989), pp. 291–329, reprinted in McKitterick, *Books, scribes and learning*, chapter 4; and Wood, *The missionary life*, pp. 57–78.

[43] Wallis, *Bede*, p. lxxxvii.

[44] W. Stevens, *Bede's scientific achievement* (Newcastle, 1986 revised 1995), reprinted in W. Stevens, *Cycles of time and scientific learning in medieval Europe* (Aldershot, 1995), chapter 2, pp. 54–8.

less does Bede's work appear to have been in a position to play a role in encouraging the Franks to adopt the year of the Incarnation in the early stages of Frankish annal writing.

The much stronger indications of Dionysian influence indicate that the Franks' interest in AD and their Easter calculations were not derived from Bede but directly from Dionysius Exiguus. As far as the Franks were concerned, the authority of Dionysius' calculations, knowledge of which they undoubtedly had, was probably reinforced by the facts that he was also associated with the authoritative collection of canon law and papal decretals known as the *Dionysiana* with which they had long been familiar, and that it was the system used in Rome.[45] There is ample evidence of independent Frankish, and especially Carolingian, recourse to papal authority in ecclesiastical matters in the course of the later seventh and first half of the eighth centuries without the use of Anglo-Saxon intermediaries.[46]

Apart from Easter tables and calendars in early eighth-century Frankish manuscripts, we need also to take into account the evidence for Frankish arithmetical reckoning and compilations which include time calculations. In about 737 a Frankish manual directed against the 'Latin' reckoning of Victorius and preferring Dionysius was compiled. It also advocates beginning the year on 1 March. It consists of thirty short chapters and was designed for teaching at some level for it is addressed to children and the laity. It is extant in only one manuscript, Berlin, Deutsche Staatsbibliothek, Phillipps 1831, fols. 138r–42r.[47] The improved version of this text of *c.* 760 considered computing the date of Easter and arithmetical calculations, explained lunar months, the cycle of the years and seasons, and advocated the use of AD dating. In 792 this text was further extended and Archbishop Hildebold of Cologne had it copied into his manual on time

---

[45] Dionysius Exiguus, ed. H. Wurm, *Studien und Text zur Dekretalsammlung des Dionysius Exiguus, Kanonistische Studien und Texte* 16 (Bonn, 1939; reprinted Amsterdam, 1964); and W. B. M. Peitz, *Dionysius Exiguus Studien* (Bonn, 1960). For the background see R. McKitterick, 'Knowledge of canon law in the Frankish kingdoms before 789: the manuscript evidence', *Journal of Theological Studies*, n.s. 36 (1985), pp. 97–117, reprinted in McKitterick, *Books, scribes and learning*, chapter 2.

[46] See, for example, Pippin's queries directed to Pope Zacharias, reported by Zacharias to Boniface in 747, in M. Tangl (ed.), *Die Briefe des heiligen Bonifatius und Lullus*, no. 77, *MGH Epp. Sel.*, I (Berlin, 1916), pp. 159–61, and responded to by Zacharias, ed. W. Grundlach, *Epistolae merovingici et karolini aevi*, *MGH Epp.* III (Hannover, 1892), pp. 479–87.

[47] B. Krusch, 'Das älteste fränkische Lehrbuch der dionysianischen Zeitrechnung', *Mélanges offerts à Emile Chatelain* (Paris, 1910), pp. 232–42. For details on this and the other Carolingian 'encyclopaedias of time', see A. Borst, 'Alkuin und die Enzyklopädie von 809', in P. L. Butzer and D. Lohrmann (eds.), *Science in western and eastern civilization in Carolingian times* (Basle, Boston and Berlin, 1993), pp. 53–78.

in 805.[48] Other miscellaneous texts were produced at the end of the eighth century, attributed in the *Patrologia latina* to 'pseudo-Bede', though some are Frankish and one or two are now thought to be Irish.[49] In the 780s a *Libellus annalis* was composed[50] which acted as the precursor of what Borst has called the 'A' version of a Carolingian Encyclopaedia on time produced in 793, possibly in Verona under the aegis of Bishop Egino. (It is from thence that its oldest and fullest manuscript comes.) The text of this Encyclopaedia offers verbal explanations of time reckoning rather than tables. It draws on Bede's *De ratione temporum*, but does not cite him by name. The 'B' version of this Encyclopaedia, compiled at Aachen in 809, included in Book II practical formulae for reckoning the existing year according to the year of the Incarnation. It is this Encyclopaedia, in its 793 and 809 versions, which is regarded as having ruled European thinking about time for the next 300 years.[51]

The Carolingian manuals and Encyclopaedia on time indicate a strong interest in the year of the Incarnation and in the reckoning of time, as well as an affirmation of Dionysius's calculations on the part of the Franks and the Frankish royal court from at least 737 onwards. The insistence of Charlemagne on time reckoning and the necessity for the clergy to know the *computus*, together with the king's own wish to be taught computation recorded by Einhard,[52] suggest more than arithmetical games with numbers on the part of monks of mathematical bent in isolated monasteries. The issue of deciding on the date for Easter to be recognised and observed, as well as the promotion of the necessary training for the making of the calculations, involves jurisdiction of central and of local government. It entails the acknowledgement of personal or party affiliation to that government and its own religious and political loyalties. It enhances the authority of those who insist on a particular observation of time and accounts for the interest of the king in it. Here we see ecclesiastical, and especially monastic, learning in conjunction with Frankish political power

---

[48] Cologne, Dombibliothek MS 83, II, fols. 59r–69r. There are two copies of it from the middle of the ninth century: Karlsruhe, Landesbibliothek Aug. CLXVII, fols. 6r–12r and St Gallen, Stiftsbibliothek 248, fols. 76–82. See A. Cordoliani, 'Une encyclopédie carolingienne de comput: les Sententiae in laude computi', *Bibliothèque de l'École des Chartes* 104 (1943), pp. 237–43, and 'Les traités de comput du haut moyen âge 526–1003', *Archivum latinitatis medii aevi* 17 (1942), pp. 51–72.

[49] *De ratione computandi*, ed. D. Ó Cróinín and M. Walsh, Studies and Texts (Toronto, 1988).

[50] Borst, 'Enzyklopädie', p. 54, credits Alcuin with this.

[51] Borst, 'Enzyklopädie', pp. 71–3.

[52] *Discebat artem computandi*: Einhard, *Vita Karoli*, c. 25, ed. O. Holder-Egger, *MGH SRG*, XXV (Hannover, 1911); and R. Rau, *Quellen zur karolingishe Reichsgeschichte*, I (Darmstadt, 1974), p. 196; see also A. Borst, *Die karolingische Kalendarreform*, *MGH* Schriften 46 (Hannover 1998), for full discussion.

keeping to a strict liturgical model of time. The rulers thus were associated with the exertion of authority over the daily lives of all Christians by a control of explicitly Christianized time in the present and future. Such control of Christian time in association with the Carolingian royal court can also be observed in the organisation and recording of the past. The *Annales regni francorum* (Royal Frankish Annals), produced in close association with the Carolingian royal court, are the first to use the year of the Incarnation as the organising principle of the narrative on a yearly basis. It is to the Frankish annals, therefore, that I now turn.

The Frankish annals and Easter tables

Annals as an historical form have been generally accepted in historical scholarship as having been developed from notes in Easter tables.[53] In St Gallen Stiftsbibliothek MS 250, for example, a set of Easter tables compiled in the 'Hartmut' period in the second half of the ninth century, and Munich, Bayerische Staatsbibliothek Clm 14641, fols 38r–40r, there are brief notes in the margins.[54] In other, later, manuscripts a page of dates was laid out and subsequently filled in with various notes by a number of hands in an unsystematic manner.[55] The space is controlled by the layout and thus what is written is controlled as well. It would be a rather attractive irony that tables designed to set out both the rhythm for the future and chart the cyclical liturgical year should have given rise to notes about the past. Although annal entries in Easter tables (that is, 'Paschal annals') are attested to in extant manuscripts dating from the ninth century onwards, I no longer think that this is how annals originally developed.[56] The traditional view has been supported by Daibhi Ó Cróinín, but his case for a very early manifestation of historical notes

---

[53] See B. Krusch, 'Ueber eine Handschrift des Victorius', *Neues Archiv* 9 (1883/4), pp. 269–82; R. L. Poole, *Chronicles and annals: a brief outline of their origin and growth* (Oxford, 1926); C. W. Jones, *Saints' lives and early chronicles in early England* (Ithaca, 1947); and M. McCormick, *Les Annales du haut moyen âge*, Typologie des sources du moyen âge occidental, fasc. 14 (Turnhout, 1975), especially p. 27. I too repeated this old orthodoxy in my *The Frankish kingdoms under the Carolingians, 751–987* (London, 1983), pp. 2–6.

[54] The notes in the former were edited by G. Pertz, *Annales S. Gallensis brevissimi, 718–889, MGH SS*, I (Hannover, 1826), p. 69. For the latter see R. Corradini, 'The rhetoric of crisis. *Computus* and *Liber annalis* in early ninth-century Fulda', in R. Corradini, M. Diesenberger and H. Reimitz (eds.), *The construction of communities in the early middle ages: texts, resources and artefacts*, The Transformation of the Roman World 12 (Leiden, 2003), pp. 269–323, plates 1–5.

[55] See, for example, the tenth-century codex Einsiedeln, Stiftsbibliothek MS 356, illustrated in Poole, *Chronicles and annals*, opposite p. 6.

[56] Harrison, *Framework of Anglo-Saxon history*, p. 45, also voices scepticism about the connection between Paschal annals and annals.

in Easter tables is undermined by his assumption that extant Easter tables were copied from older exemplars and take over any annal entries
from the exemplars.[57] There would be no necessity for a full exemplar
when compiling a new set of Easter tables. The annal entries we find
against earlier dates in tables in late ninth-, tenth- and eleventh-century
manuscripts may be the result of a quite different interest in relation to
the historical associations of the centre in which the tables were compiled. The copy of the *Canon paschalis* of Victorius and Easter tables
now in Gotha but written at Jouarre in the eighth century, for example,
has the note *Gundubadus fuit in Abinione* against the year 501.[58] Another
manuscript belonging to this Jouarre group of eighth-century codices,
namely, Paris, BnF lat. 17654, containing Gregory of Tours' *Historiae*,
describes this event, so the notes in the Gotha book could represent a
reader's cross-reference rather than a record of an event taken over from
an older exemplar.

One difficulty with the traditional 'notes in Easter Tables to annals'
hypothesis is that the manuscripts containing Easter tables with annal
entries, with the exception of the Gotha Victorius codex, postdate the
earliest annal manuscripts by some decades. Secondly, their codicological
context is usually that of canon law, *computus*, necrologies and liturgy.[59]
St Gallen, Stiftsbibliothek 250, mentioned above, is just such a miscellany. The earliest ninth-century manuscript containing Paschal annals
(Leiden, Universiteitsbibliotheek MS Scaliger 28), on the other hand,
does reflect a codicological association between Easter chronology and
historical record.[60] Generally considered to have been written at Flavigny
about 816, that is, some twenty-five or so years after the first portion of
the Royal Frankish Annals is thought to have been completed, it includes

---

[57] D. Ó Cróinín, 'Early Irish annals from Easter Tables: a case restated', *Peritia* 2 (1983),
pp. 74–86. For a useful brief survey see D. P. McCarthy, 'The chronology and sources
of the early Irish annals', *EME* 10 (2001), pp. 323–41.

[58] Gotha, Landesbibliothek Membr. I.75, fols. 70–122, which has single non-historical
entries in eighth-century Merovingian cursive on fols. 77v and 89v. See B. Krusch, 'Ueber
eine Handschrift der Victorius', p. 277. On the manuscript's origin see R. McKitterick,
'Nuns' scriptoria in England and Francia in the eighth century', *Francia* 19/1 (1992),
pp. 1–35, at p. 5, reprinted in McKitterick, *Books, scribes and learning*, chapter 7.

[59] See the codices listed by A. Cordoliani, 'Contribution à la littérature du comput
ecclésiastique au moyen âge', *Studi Medievali* 3rd series, 1 (1960), pp. 107–37, and 2
(1961), pp. 169–73, and *idem.*, 'Les Traités de comput du haut moyen âge (526–1003),
Archivum latinitatis medii aevi 17 (1942), pp. 51–72.

[60] G. I. Lieftinck, *Manuscrits datés conservés dans les Pays-Bas. Catalogue paléographique
des manuscrits en écriture latine portant des indications de date, I. Les manuscrits d'origine
étrangère (816–c.1550)* (Amsterdam, 1964), pp. 91–2 and plates 1–3. I am very grateful to
Dr. D. Th. Bouwman of the Leiden Universiteitsbibliotheek for kindly answering my
queries about this manuscript and sending me photographs in 1996. I have since
examined Scaliger 28 myself and have a study of it in preparation.

Bede's *De temporum ratione* and Victorius, excerpts from various texts concerned with the calculation of Easter and chronological questions, and the text known as the *Chronicon universale* to 741 ascribed in the manuscript to Bede.[61] The Paschal annals are inserted in the margins of fols. 3–21.[62]

Thirdly, to designate the Frankish annals simply as a development from notes in Easter tables downgrades them as a form of historical writing to too great an extent. The link with the year of the Incarnation which makes such an explicit association between the history of the Franks and the linear progression of Christian history should be separated from the essentially historical liturgical cycle represented by Easter. Easter tables with annal entries seem to me a legitimate adaptation of the idea of annals. Annals, on the other hand, belong to the extraordinary revolution in historical writing to be observed in the Carolingian period,[63] and the sense of history so evident in a wide variety of sources,[64] coupled with the Carolingian preoccupations with time reckoning outlined above. The Frankish annals, and especially the *Annales regni francorum*, explicitly linked the Frankish present to the whole course of Christian history and the life of Christ.

Such a development needs to be related to a wider change in the interaction of church and society. In many ways the early middle ages witnessed the triumph of the saints' cult as a fundamental preoccupation of society.[65] Local saints and the churches which controlled the cult of their memories increasingly became the foci of community action.[66] There is an obvious connection between the necrologies and memorial books providing networks of association and memory over the entire Frankish realm and the writing of history.[67] The cult of the dead and a sense of history were inextricably entwined. Easter tables, necrologies and martyrologies were the texts by which the church Christianized and endeavoured to control time and space.

---

[61] Ed. G. Waitz, *MGH SS*, XIII (Hannover, 1881), pp. 1–19.

[62] *Annales flaviniacenses et lausonenses*, ed. G. Pertz, *MGH SS*, III (Hannover, 1839), pp. 149–52.

[63] Innes and McKitterick, 'Writing of history'.

[64] See the comments by T. F. X. Noble, 'Tradition and learning in search of ideology: the *Libri carolini*', in R. Sullivan (ed.), *'The gentle voice of teachers': aspects of learning in the Carolingian age* (Columbus, Ohio, 1995), pp. 227–60, and chapter 7 below.

[65] I draw in this paragraph on Innes and McKitterick, 'Writing of history'. See also J. Howard-Johnson and P. A. Hayward (eds.), *The cult of saints in late antiquity and the early middle ages. Essays on the contribution of Peter Brown* (Oxford, 1999).

[66] A. Thacker and R. Sharpe (eds.), *Local saints and local churches in the early medieval west* (Oxford, 2002).

[67] See below, chapters 7 and 8, and K. Schmid, *Gebetsgedenken und adliges Selbstverständnis im Mittelalter: ausgewählte Beiträge, Festgabe zu seinem 60. Geburtstag* (Sigmaringen, 1983).

The Frankish annals are a further, and largely secular, reflection of the same mentality and might be described, from one perspective, as a very literate form of timekeeping. Yet there might be thought to be no particular reason why the annals should use the Christian era dating scheme rather than any others. As a literary form their structure was determined by the annual cycle of a community. For the *Annales regni francorum* in particular, however, the peripatetic rhythm of the political court was fitted *into* the liturgical cycle, with the place at which the court spent Christmas and Easter frequently recorded and a year's cycle according to the year of the Incarnation established.[68]

The extraordinary structure of the *Annales regni francorum* is particularly striking when seen in conjunction with the disorderly treatment of time in the so-called Continuations of the Chronicle of Fredegar completed in the second half of the eighth century. There the passing of kings (and to a lesser extent, of mayors) comprises the dating scheme, but in some chapters many years pass and in others only one. Thus thirty years pass in chapter 6. In chapter 8, Pippin II's death in 714 is recorded. He had ruled over the Franks for twenty-seven and a half years. Sometimes, as in chapter 12, we are told that a year passed. In chapter 14 the events are recounted as occurring in the course of the following year. In the chapter concerning Charles Martel's campaign in Aquitaine the chronology is most compressed. From chapter 24, however, the chapters are set down more or less on a yearly basis though inexact phrases are used, such as *eodem anno; Quo peracto tempore; His transactis sequente anno; post haec; evolutur igitur anno*. In *c.* 50, an entry relating to 768, there is the first record of where the ruler spent the Christmas period.[69] Generally a time *sequence* is clear, but the length of time between events and the duration of certain affairs are very much less than clear. It is possibly significant, moreover, that the more precise section of Fredegar in chronological terms is precisely that covered by the *Annales regni francorum*.[70] As I commented in chapter 1 above, it has always been assumed hitherto that the Royal Frankish Annalist drew on Fredegar. From a practical point of view it is easier to write a chronologically diffuse account drawn from a precise year-by-year record than vice versa.[71] It may well be, therefore, that the relationship for the section covering the years 741–68 should be reversed.

---

[68] For example, *Annales regni francorum*, ed. F. Kurze, *MGH SRG*, VI (Hannover, 1895), s.a. 771 and 772, pp. 32 and 34.

[69] Fredegar, ed. and trans. J. M. Wallace-Hadrill, *The fourth book of the Chronicle of Fredegar and its Continuations* (London, 1962), pp. 85, 86, 87, 90, 91, 24, 117, 18.

[70] See R. Collins, *Fredegar*, Authors of the Middle Ages 4, no. 13 (Aldershot, 1996), and my further observation below, chapter 6.

[71] See also pp. 138–41.

The Frankish annals: composition

The *Annales regni francorum*, therefore, make significant comments on the context in which contemporary Frankish history is to be understood, but they remain also an astonishingly under-appreciated source in terms of their content and potential propaganda value.[72] Attention has been largely focused hitherto, apart from the efforts to establish the text in the early years of the last century, on the ostensibly fuller and more sophisticated continuations of the annals known as the *Annals of St Bertin* and *Annals of Fulda*.[73] This may be due to these texts' being capable of association with particular authors or centres. All the same, the identity of the author and precise place of production of the *Annales regni francorum* still elude us, even if a writer associated with the royal court be accepted. Further, the *Annales regni francorum* have appeared to be a straightforward text that can be quarried safely for facts. Appearances, however, can be deceptive.

By way of reminder, here are some practical details. In discussions of the annals as genre, the *Annales regni francorum* have been regarded as the most representative of the so-called major annals. Originally known to editors as the *Annales laurissenses maiores*, their name was changed when Leopold von Ranke drew attention to their 'official' nature and the Carolingian point of view they express.[74] They have been associated in consequence with the royal court and thus were produced 'when the keeping of an official record of political and public events appears to have been the responsibility of the archchaplain, or someone working for him, at the royal court'.[75] The production of the *Annales regni francorum* coincides with the creation by Charlemagne of a large public court,

---

[72] A notable exception is M. Becher's comprehensive exposure of the lies woven together in the *Annales regni francorum*'s account of Tassilo of Bavaria: *Eid und Herrschaft. Untersuchungen zum Herrscherethos Karls des Großen*, Vorträge und Forschungen, Sonderband 39 (Sigmaringen, 1993), especially pp. 21–77. See also the comments by R. Collins, 'The "Reviser" revisited: another look at the alternative version of the *Annales regni francorum*', in A. C. Murray (ed.), *After Rome's fall. Narrators and sources of early medieval history. Essays presented to Walter Goffart* (Toronto, 1998), pp. 191–213, though Collins had been unable to take my own contribution into account: R. McKitterick, 'Constructing the past in the early middle ages: the case of the royal Frankish annals', *TRHS* sixth series 7 (1997), pp. 101–30.

[73] For valuable discussions of these texts, see, on the Annals of St Bertin, J. L. Nelson, 'The Annals of St Bertin', in *Charles the Bald. Court and Kingdom*, ed. J. L. Nelson and M. Gibson (2nd edn, 1990), pp. 23–40, also reprinted in J. L. Nelson, *Politics and ritual in early medieval Europe* (1986), pp. 173–94, and her Introduction to her translation, *The Annals of St Bertin* (Manchester, 1991); on the Annals of Fulda see T. Reuter's Introduction to his translation, *The Annals of Fulda* (Manchester, 1992).

[74] L. von Ranke, 'Zur Kritik fränkisch-deutscher Reichsannalen', *Abhandlungen der königlichen Akademie der Wissenschaften* (Berlin, 1854), pp. 415–56; and McCormick, *Les annales du haut moyen âge*.

[75] Innes and McKitterick, 'Writing of history', p. 208.

focused on the new palace at Aachen. If there was no attempt at 'public' record-keeping before then,[76] this is possibly due to the court not being, until Charlemagne's later years, a public forum with a centripetal political force.[77]

The *Annales regni francorum* run from 741 to 829 and begin with the death of Charles Martel. Up to 788 the annal entries, according to the current orthodoxy, supposedly drew on earlier, so-called 'minor annals' but are presenting their own view. Louis Halphen suggested eighty years ago that these minor annals were in fact derived from the *Annales regni francorum* and thus that the *Annales regni francorum* were original rather than derivative compositions from 768.[78] This suggestion has hitherto been largely disregarded.[79] I wish now not only to revive Halphen's conclusion but also to expand it to embrace the entire narrative from its chronological starting point in 741. There is simply no need for them to have been derived from (an) earlier account(s), as distinct from having been deliberately created with a miscellany of material, oral and written, contributing information.[80] The traditional view of the lack of originality of the entries before 788 cannot be substantiated; it rests on a contorted understanding of the original text's composition in relation to the surviving manuscripts and should be discarded.

The very conception of the *Annales regni francorum*'s narrative is at stake. Rather than thinking of the annal entries as year-by-year jottings, they should be recognised as a skilfully constructed and highly selective portrayal of the careers of the Carolingian rulers whose fortune and success is identified with that of the Frankish people. I leave aside the issue of the 'revised version' of the annals for the moment. The narrative of the 'original' version has been attributed to a number of different authors responsible for blocks of year entries. Analysis of authorship has depended on stylistic features and has been, therefore, inevitably somewhat subjective. It is striking, nevertheless, that a distinctive tenor of the text is

---

[76] On the possible understanding of 'public' and 'private' in the ninth century see M. Innes, *State and society in the early middle ages: the middle Rhine Valley 400–1000* (Cambridge, 2000), especially pp. 94–111 and 254–9.

[77] See, for example, the comments in J. L. Nelson, 'Kingship and royal government', in McKitterick (ed.), *NCMH*, pp. 383–430, esp. p. 417; and J. L. Nelson, 'Aachen as a place of power', in M. de Jong and F. Theuws with C. van Rhijn (eds.), *Topographies of power in the early middle ages*, The Transformation of the Roman World 6 (Leiden, 2001), pp. 217–42.

[78] L. Halphen, *Études critiques sur l'histoire de Charlemagne* (Paris, 1921).

[79] W. Wattenbach, W. Levison and H. Löwe, *Deutschlands Geschichtsquellen im Mittelalter. Vorzeit und Karolinger*, II (Weimar, 1953), pp. 245–58, provide the general view and see also McKitterick, *Frankish Kingdoms*, pp. 3–4.

[80] See H. Hoffman, *Untersuchungen zur karolingische Annalistik*, Bonner Historische Forschungen 10 (Bonn, 1958), who also summarises the discussion up until then.

maintained overall. There are many attempts in the post-801 entries to keep alive themes addressed in the earlier texts, notably the interaction on the part of the Franks with a host of non-Franks, some more exotic than others. Further, there is extraordinary sympathy between the pre-788 and the post-788 sections; they are coherent and their emphases are markedly similar.

The narrative from 741 to 788 is generally agreed to have been written down by one person at one go, and then continued, possibly by different people. Even this view, as I indicated in chapter 1 above, is too dependent on Kurze's presentation of the text in relation to his understanding of the manuscript tradition. The entries for *c.* 807–20, however, have been judged to have a certain unity of tone and style,[81] and those for 820–9 have been attributed to Hilduin, abbot of St Denis. Certainly a different individual is at work in the entries from 820 onwards. Neil Wright has identified a peculiarity of style, including a propensity to finish sentences with a compound perfect form of passive verbs, that pinpoints a change of author between 819 and 820.[82] Not everyone accepts the attributions of author to particular sections, largely because the dates of apparent stylistic continuity do not coincide with the known dates of those to whom the work is usually attributed, notably, members of the royal writing office.

The manuscripts present major problems for any attempt to work out how the *Annales regni francorum* were composed, for no original or autograph manuscript has been identified. The earliest copies of the complete text, as we have seen in chapter 1, date from *c.* 830 and later. Later manuscripts containing incomplete sections of the annals, such as 741–88 or 741–813, may well reflect stages of composition in 788 or 813 but could equally well represent a selection process on the part of the later compilers. Whatever the case, it offers no assistance in determining whether the technique of composition was as a year-by-year record or at the end of several years as a process of narrative reconstruction. Paul Dutton envisaged annal composition as follows:

The annalist rarely saw the events he recorded . . . instead he gathered reports of these events throughout the year and fashioned them into a single annal entry in February. He would note the date, make some comment on the weather of that

---

[81] I have benefited here from the comments made by the late Timothy Reuter in his paper, 'The limits of Quellen- und Ideologie-Kritik: the case of the revised *Annales regni francorum* and its implications for Carolingian historical writing', at the George Macaulay Trevelyan Colloquium, 'New perspectives on ninth-century Francia', Cambridge, 30 November 1996, and wish to record my gratitude for his permission to cite them here.

[82] I have recorded Dr Wright's observations included in the study by M. Tillotson, 'Frankish diplomatic relations in the reign of Louis the Pious' (unpublished M.Phil. dissertation, University of Cambridge, 2003). I offer warm thanks also to Mark Tillotson and Christina Pössel for discussion of the annals.

winter and describe in a roughly chronological and regional progression the main event of the year. Last the annalist would place information of general interest at the end of the entry... There was no necessary order... He ordered disorder.[83]

This may not be too fanciful a scenario for some later ninth-century annal writing, but whether it can be applied to the *Annales regni francorum* needs further consideration. A possible approach would be to compare the *Annales regni francorum* with a set of Frankish annals for which a manuscript contemporary with the composition of the text survives. Fortunately, such a thing exists in the form of the Vienna copy of the 'Lorsch' annals (Vienna, ÖNB cod. 515), written around the year 800. It is worth looking at these 'Lorsch' annals and the manuscript in which they are preserved in a little more detail, therefore, to see how much light they really do throw on the year-by-year entry idea and thus on the possible mode of composition of the Frankish annals.

While the manuscript of the 'Lorsch' annals has enhanced the importance of the text in any annal discussion by the simple fact of its being so early in date, the text itself speaks with an interestingly independent voice. It is famous for its comment on the coronation of Charlemagne, in that it is the only one to offer the opinion that Charlemagne's elevation to the imperial title was due to the name of emperor being lacking among the Greeks at the time because of female rule (*femineum imperium*) (of empress Irene). In comparison with the account of the *Annales regni francorum* of the same years, however, there are many interesting differences in terms of the events included or omitted. In the 'Lorsch' annals there is not so much emphasis on diplomacy, the visits of embassies, and what was happening at court, but more on military campaigns and assemblies. Under 794, the 'Lorsch' annals concentrate on the Synod of Frankfurt and how it dealt with the heresy of Adoptionism. They also mention that Tassilo, duke of Bavaria, whose duchy had been annexed by his cousin Charlemagne six years earlier, came to Frankfurt and renounced Bavaria. The *Annales regni francorum* omit all mention of this.[84] Similarly under 796 there is a campaign into Spain recorded by the 'Lorsch' annalist and under 797 it is the Frisians as well as the Saxons from whom Charlemagne receives hostages. The account of the events in Rome in 799 and 800 is far more laconic in the 'Lorsch' annals, apart from the independent justification offered for Charlemagne's assumption of the imperial title already mentioned. Under 802 it is the Lorsch annals which give an account of the assembly of that year and provide the narrative background from which

---

[83] P. E. Dutton, *The politics of dreaming in the Carolingian empire* (Lincoln, Nebr., and London, 1994), pp. 86–7.
[84] See Becher, *Eid und Herrschaft*, pp. 72–3.

the programmatic *Capitulare missorum generale* of 802 was issued.[85] The entry also describes how the various secular laws of the realm were read out, expounded and emended, and that the emended law was written down. Judges were able to judge according to written law; at the October Synod clerics had defined the authoritative body of canon law and the abbots and Monks undertook to live according to the *Rule of Benedict*. All of this is absent from the *Annales regni francorum*. The narrative has the tone of being by someone who is greatly interested in secular and ecclesiastical politics and rather less concerned with building up the image of Charlemagne. It also reads like the summary of news heard or gathered with very occasionally an opinion added for good measure. It is striking how rarely any name save that of a major player – Charlemagne, the pope or other rulers by title – is mentioned. The Lorsch annals thus appear to provide an indication of how the process of the dissemination of information might be received and recorded by someone not at court though not necessarily ignorant of court ways. Whether they can clarify the actual process of composition, on the other hand, is another matter.

The text in the form in which it has survived is the only surviving original fragment of any Frankish annals to appear to indicate a close connection between the composition and the writing down of the text; in it four different scribes have been identified altogether and all were writing at the turn of the eighth century.[86]

The label 'Lorsch' annals is unfortunately probably a misnomer, for the script in which the text is written is not a Lorsch script from the middle Rhine Carolingian monastery of that name. This by *c.* 800 was producing books written in distinctive scripts of its own.[87] Instead it is an Alemannian script type, the precise origin of which has still not been satisfactorily established.[88] But the scribe(s) was/were not necessarily the author(s). Indeed, autograph copies of most of our texts from the early middle ages simply do not exist.[89] It would also be mistaken to assume

---

[85] Compare *Capitulare missorum generale*, A. Boretius (ed.), *MGH Cap.*, I (Hannover 1883) no. 33, pp. 91–9.

[86] F. Unterkircher (ed.), *Das Wiener Fragment der Lorscher Annalen, Christus und die Samariterin. Katechese des Niceta von Remesiana. Codex Vindobonensis 515 der Österreichischen Nationalbibliothek Facsimile Ausgabe*, Codices Selecti 15 (Graz, 1967).

[87] See chapter 9 below; and B. Bischoff, *Die Abtei Lorsch im Spiegel ihrer Handschriften*, 2nd edn (Lorsch, 1989).

[88] *CLA*, X (Oxford, 1963), no. 1482. Compare the discussion in Bischoff, *Schreibschulen*, I, pp. 145–6, who identifies Hand A of the Vienna fragment with the first hand of Munich, Bayerische Staatsbibliothek Clm 6330, a miscellany of ecclesiastical texts.

[89] An exception is the autograph manuscript of the work of the tenth-century Rheims historian Richer in Bamberg, Staatsbibliothek E.III.3, ed. H. Hoffmann, *Richer von Saint-Remi, Historiae, MGH SS*, XXXVIII (Hannover, 2000); and J. Glenn, *Politics and history in the tenth century: the world and work of Richer of Reims* (Cambridge, 2004).

that the origin of the scribes and the origin of the author of the text
must be one and the same. There are too many instances of the movement
of scholars, scribes and even script types from one part of the Frankish
empire to another, even in this early period, for the possibility of different
scribes writing different script types and working side by side in one place
to be discounted. Examples are the links between St Amand in northern Francia and Salzburg in Bavaria,[90] the scribes writing Rhaetian and
Alemannic minuscule visible on the St Gall charters,[91] and the even earlier example of a Frankish and an insular scribe working together in Trier
Domschatz 61.[92] There are in any case indications in the orthography,
such as 'b' for 'p' and the omission of the initial aspirate 'h' and in the
corrections to the text over erasures in Vienna, ÖNB cod. 515 that the
scribes were working from dictation. This suggests either someone settling down with an amanuensis at the end, or in the course, of a year to
compose a brief account or someone with a longer composition dictating
it in instalments. Franz Unterkircher was certainly of the opinion that the
entries were made at the end of each year and in fits and starts, judging
from the changes of hand and ink colour. He insisted, moreover, that this
text was the first written version and thus an original composition rather
than a copy of an existing text.[93] According to his analysis, apart from
the changeover between Hands A and B, there is a correspondence of
year entries with different scribes: thus Hand A wrote 794–795 line 18
and 798; Hand B wrote the last seventeen lines of the entry for 795, and
all of 796 and 797; Hand C wrote 799, 800 and 801 and Hand D wrote
802, 803. The change from A to B comes after the account of the king's
dealings with the Saxons and the Obodrites. B's section begins with the
visit to Aachen of a *tudun* or *regulus* from the lands of the Avars and also
relates the decision of the king to commission a marble slab with an epitaph for Pope Hadrian inscribed upon it. There is no difficulty, in other
words, in envisaging this year entry being written in two stages, though
whether these stages were half an hour or half a year apart is impossible
to determine.

   The manuscript containing the Lorsch annals now comprises only eight
leaves with the annal entries occupying fols. 1–5r line 10. These leaves
themselves are made up of three single leaves followed by a bifolium. A
tenth-century Reichenau hand has then added the Old High German
text about Christ and the Samaritan woman on the rest of fol. 5r. On
the verso are some lines of liturgical *responsiones* with neumes, also of the

---

[90] Bischoff, *Schreibschulen*, II, pp. 61–73 and 98–140.
[91] McKitterick, *Carolingians and the written word*, pp. 85–90.
[92] N. Netzer, *Cultural interplay in the eighth century. The Trier Gospels and the making of a scriptorium at Echternach* (Cambridge, 1994).
[93] Unterkircher, *Das Wiener Fragment*, pp. 18–20.

tenth century. Fols. 6–7 are another bifolium to which fol. 8, a single leaf, has been added, and these contain the Catechism associated with Nicetas of Remesiana in a script of *c.* 800 very similar, if not identical, to that of Hand A in the annal entries. The text on fol. 1r starts in the middle of a sentence of the entry for 794 and runs to the end of a short entry for the year 803 which records that Charlemagne celebrated Easter at Aachen and held an assembly at Mainz but let the year pass without a military campaign. We have in Vienna, ÖNB cod. 515 a tantalising fragment of an independent Frankish account of the years 794–803. Where is the rest of it and what did the whole text contain? That this is part of a larger text is suggested by the copy made of it still extant in St Paul in Lavanttal, Stiftsarchiv cod. 8/1. It fills most of one quire of eight leaves which may replicate the format of its exemplar. It was made *c.* 835 in Reichenau, where the text runs from 703–803, though some minor changes of spelling or choice of words were made by this copyist.[94] The text is written by one scribe in a book of modest size (313 × 232 mm). It starts with a short proömium (ornamented with a nine-line initial P) referring to the dating scheme in Orosius' *Seven books of history against the pagans*, the number of years from the Creation to the birth of Christ as 5199 and the years since the Incarnation. In the entry for 785 a further dating mechanism is introduced, namely the number of years since the pontificate of Pope Gregory I. The first events recorded from 703–68 are written in continuous prose rather than a new line for each year entry. For the year 703, the *translatio* of St Benedict from Monte Cassino is the sole entry. Thereafter follow for 704 the death of Bishop Canon (possibly Bishop Colman of Lindisfarne, who retreated to Iona), 705 the death of Abbot Domnan (possibly Abbot Adomnan of Iona), 706 the death of Abbot Cellanus, 707 the *dormicio* of Tigermal (?Tigernach) and for 708 the death of Drogo (son of Pippin II). These early entries merit further work than can be attempted here, for they present a number of puzzles. From 768, however, the text is divided into both year entries and chapters, each starting a new line and beginning at chapter 1 for 768 and running to chapter 36 and the year 803. A fourth component of the manuscript is the Calendar on fols. 5r–7r, running from Adam to the year 835.

It would appear, therefore, that by 835 the Vienna fragment was at Reichenau. Eberhard Katz, however, thought that the St Paul in Lavanttal codex and Vienna, ÖNB cod. 515 were not so related but independent copies of a further exemplar. Resolving this depends on the implications

---

[94] See C. Stiegemann and M. Wemhoff (eds.), *799 Kunst und Kultur der Karolingerzeit. Karl der Große und Papst Leo III. in Paderborn* (Mainz, 1999), Katalog Band 1, no. II.3, pp. 38–40.

of the slight variations and corrections. The entry for 800 in the former, in particular, has a large erasure and odd layout. Close links between its text and that of the *Annales mosellani* associated with Metz or Gorze led Fichtenau to suggest that the former influenced the latter. He also discerned possible links with two other annal texts, namely the so-called *fragmentum chesnii* which he thought drew on the *Annales laureshamenses* but only up to 790, at which point it preferred to follow the *Annales regni francorum*.[95] This is not the place to follow the labyrinth of hypothetical exemplars, conjectures about directions of influence or location, made all the more uncertain by the late ninth- and tenth-century date of the manuscripts in which these texts have been preserved. But at least it can be said that there is an indication, first of all, of a wider readership and use for the 'Lorsch' annals after their initial production which appears to extend to the middle Rhine region. Secondly it looks as if copies of portions of the annals might have been circulated in batches of year entries before they were finished. One indicator of this occurs in the 'York' or first set of 'Northern annals' from Northumbria. These cover the years 732–802 and survive as a section of the *Historia regum* of Simeon of Durham. The entry for 795 in these 'Northern' annals refers to the golden lettering of the verse epitaph on the inscribed marble slab that Charlemagne commissioned to commemorate the death of Pope Hadrian as well as to the Avar treasure. The 'Lorsch' annals is the only continental narrative source to go into an equivalent amount of detail. Joanna Story suggests that the two accounts share a common source.[96] It is as likely, however, that one, the 'Lorsch' annals, could as feasibly have supplied the source of information for the York annals. The St Paul copy of the 'Lorsch' annals presents a supplementary, or complementary, possibility. Its eight-leaf-format suggests that the 'Lorsch' annals were circulated in the form of a *libellus* or, if in batches of entries, in *libelli* (rather like liturgical *libelli*). Such piecemeal circulation would help to explain the patchwork quality of the structure of some of the other Frankish annals.

The difficulty remains of determining how, when and where the annals were composed. If the St Paul copy of the 'Lorsch' annals survives in a form covering the years 703–803 in a manuscript written 835, and what is clearly an incomplete section runs from mid-794 to 803 in a manuscript contemporary with the last few year entries, then the possibility of

---

[95] See H. Fichtenau, 'Abt Richbod und die *Annales Laureshamenses*', in *Beiträge zur Geschichte des Klosters Lorsch*, 2nd edn, Geschichtsblätter für den Kreis Bergstraße, Sonderband 4 (Lorsch, 1980), pp. 277–304, a reprint with Afterword of H. Fichtenau, 'Karl der Große und das Kaisertum', *MIÖG* 61 (1953), pp. 287–309.

[96] J. Story, *Carolingian connections: Anglo-Saxon England and Carolingian Francia, c. 750–870* (Aldershot, 2003), pp. 95–114.

year-by-year compilation from 703 has to be considered. Those who have worked closely on the text have suggested that it is only from 785 that the 'Lorsch' annals offer an independent narrative, and that its contents were dependent on other resources up to then. This has led to the proposal that the 'Lorsch' annals were begun in 785 and prefaced with a preliminary section comprising short entries for the years 703–84. It was thereafter updated each year until 803 and all its entries are from a single mind. The end point of 803 is the real conclusion of the text and suggests that its author departed or died thereafter.

Rather than accepting the customary view of the fragment as indicating year-by-year composition, at least from 785, one might have to envisage it as an alternative and independent history of the Franks composed in 803, circulated within the Rhineland region with the possibility of distribution in sections remaining open. Given that Canisius's lost manuscript of the *Annales regni francorum* was from Lorsch and that the entries for the years 789–93 in that text closely resemble the 'Lorsch' annals,[97] it opens up the possibility that the 'Lorsch' annals were actually conceived in reaction to the account offered in the royal *Annales*. As such it would have the character of an interpretative narrative in annal form prompted by the major achievements of Charlemagne up to 802 and masterminded by someone sufficiently close to events to provide informed opinions and emphases. Against the idea of composition in 803, it has to be said that while the entry for 803 is indeed very short, the last two entries, with 802 ending with the mention of the arrival of the elephant in Francia and 803 simply recording that Charlemagne had celebrated Easter at Aachen, held an assembly at Mainz and let the year pass without going on campaign, does give the impression that there was an expectation, or hope, that the sequence of records would be continued.

Inevitably, there has been a search for an author. Fichtenau argued that the author who dictated the content to his scribes or secretaries was Richbod, a pupil of Alcuin, member of the court circle until 784, abbot of Lorsch from 785 and bishop of Trier from 791 until his death in 804.[98] Fichtenau pointed to the close knowledge of Adoptionism and the Synod of Frankfurt in 794, in which Richbod was closely involved, and a host of other minor features, such as an interest in Worms and Lorsch, and the indications from the related derivative texts that 785 and 791 were points at which the text was seen and used by others. Cumulatively at least these arguments are attractive. The major obstacle to accepting the

---

[97] H. Canisius, *Antiquae Lectiones*, III (Ingolstadt, 1603), pp. 187–217; his text is based on a transcript in the Bavarian ducal library of an 'old manuscript from Lorsch'.
[98] Fichtenau, 'Abt Richbod', pp. 286–99.

idea of Richbod as author has been seen as the Alemannian script of the Vienna fragment as if the work of scribes could prove anything about an author, let alone that it was nothing to do with Richbod.[99] Richbod, able to draw on the services of scribes trained to write an Alemannian minuscule, remains a possible candidate; we should also remember that nothing is known of his own background before he turned up at the court of Charlemagne. On the other hand it might be logical to take the Reichenau provenance of the Vienna fragment, and the St Paul copy, together with the Alemannian script of both, as pointing also to an author with upper, rather than middle, Rhineland connections, and associated with the monastery of Reichenau.

Altogether, the manuscripts of the 'Lorsch' annals, therefore, have suggested when and where the text might have been produced, but how it was composed remains obscure. This examination of the value of the evidence provided by the contemporary Lorsch annals and its surviving contemporary manuscript and later copy has also demonstrated that there are alternative possibilities, either of composition year by year, or a creative single narrative structured in annal form. Even here a narrative could then be continued either year by year or in groups of years. The possibilities presented by the manuscript evidence simply cannot be resolved in favour of one or the other possible mode of composition.

It is with these in mind that the *Annales regni francorum* have to be considered, for which, as already mentioned previously, the earliest extant manuscripts are contemporary with the last few entries in the 820s. The notion of an annual process of writing up does not look as if it can be applied to the *Annales regni francorum* and especially not to the sections 741–88, 789–93, 794–807. It is claimed by past editors that these were written in two or three bursts. Certainly they were designed to present a very particular narrative. I shall return to this point below.

The purportedly original manuscript, now lost, was reported to have contained the annals to 788 with a few entries added up to 793 by Canisius, its seventeenth-century editor, and that is what he reproduced in his text.[100] It is self-evidently incomplete, however, for the text breaks off in the middle of the entry for 793 and the editor adds *Caetera desunt*. This casts doubt on the high status accorded this version, on the significance of the customary 793 date surmised for this lost manuscript and the general understanding of a first bout of annal writing at *c.* 788.

[99] For example, D. Bullough, '*Europae pater.* Charlemagne's achievement in the light of recent scholarship', *EHR* 85 (1970), pp. 59–105, at pp. 64–5. See his comments on Hoffmann, *Untersuchungen*, but compare the reviews by J. M. Wallace-Hadrill, *EHR* 75 (1960), p. 326, and H. Fichtenau, *MIÖG* 67 (1959), pp. 173–5.

[100] Canisius, *Antiquae Lectiones*, pp. 187–217.

The content of the 'original' text is impossible now to determine. Even in Kurze's edition however, differences both in relation to Canisius, and other codices, have crept in. Whatever the original author(s) may have written, later copyists and compilers felt at liberty to alter sentences, change tenses and adjectives, insert extra words and omit others. The most radical and systematic changes to the entire sequence of entries from 741 to 801, formerly ascribed to Charlemagne's biographer Einhard, produced the so-called revised version. It was recognised as a separate entity even in 1898,[101] and is extant in the so-called 'E' group of manuscripts. (Stylistic changes up to 812 have been noted by some though others are not persuaded.) The existence of this 'E' version is one of the strongest indicators of the earlier and stage-by-stage composition of the original version of the annals.[102] The puzzle of the annals becomes still more complicated on examination of the classic *MGH* edition of Friedrich Kurze. It was published in 1898 and based on that of Georg Pertz in 1826. It is clear that what the printed edition of 1898 represents is a composite text, in which many ninth-century scribes as well as nineteenth-century editors have played a role.

The Frankish annals: dissemination

A full re-examination of the manuscript tradition of the annals and all the problems they raise cannot be embarked on here. It should be clear, however, that the immensely complicated dissemination of the manuscripts of the *Annales regni francorum*, and the succession of extensions, borrowings, excerpts and supposed influence with which the text is credited mirrors the process of reception and attests to an audience throughout the ninth century. As I have already commented in chapter 1, five different groups among the thirty-nine surviving *Annales regni francorum* manuscripts, fragments or reports and transcripts of others once extant were differentiated by F. Kurze in 1895; no one has yet improved on his work, though he himself did not explore the implications of his groupings nor of the individual representatives within them.[103] The 'A' and 'D' groups have only a handful of surviving representatives and some are

---

[101] Kurze printed the revised version on the recto pages of his edition. The English translation by B. Scholz preserved this differentiation, by printing the main additions, of the Reviser in indented paragraphs in relation to the main text: B. Scholz, *Carolingian Chronicles* (Ann Arbor, 1970). P. D. King, *Charlemagne. Translated sources* (Kendal, 1987) translated the entire text from 768 to 801 which gives a much better sense of the difference between the 'E' and the other versions. Kurze lists the 'E' manuscripts, pp. xii–xv.

[102] See R. Collins, '"The Reviser" revisited'.

[103] *Annales regni francorum*, ed. Kurze, pp. vii–xix, and see above pp. 19–22.

lost, notably, as mentioned earlier, the original 'A' codex, possibly from Lorsch. The 'B' group manuscripts only go as far as 813 and may all stem from a common exemplar. The 'C' group, from the west Frankish kingdom and with one representative (St Petersburg, Saltykov-Schedrin Library F.v. IV.4) that was apparently based on a codex compiled for King Charles the Bald himself,[104] continues to 829, but is divided into two different families: in one of these the annals were appended by the scribes to copies of the earlier histories known as the *Liber historiae francorum* and the Continuations of the *Chronicle* of Fredegar. In the other they were later continued by Prudentius of Troyes and Hincmar of Rheims and form the text now known as the Annals of St Bertin. This second family is at present the most highly regarded by modern historians, but this appears to be only because it includes St Omer, Bibliothèque Municipale MS 706, that is, the main manuscript of the Annals of St Bertin.[105] That is to say, the status of one group has been highlighted at the expense of another for possibly inappropriate reasons. More importantly, the assessment of the *Annales regni francorum* has apparently been made hitherto with the reflection of hindsight from the later text, not the earlier, with the consequence that its own achievement in writing history and strongly influential interpretation have been overshadowed. Members of the 'D' group were used in centres from Worms on the Rhine to Altaich on the Danube near Passau, that is, roughly speaking western and eastern Germany. The 'E' or revised version circulated from the Rhineland eastwards. The greater majority of its manuscripts postdate the ninth century; two or three are from the eleventh and twelfth century. The version of Frankish history propounded by the annals, whether in the original or the revised version, was also incorporated in some form into the histories written in the twelfth century and thereby extended the Frankish historians' influence throughout the middle ages.

The codicological context of the annals is also of significance for they were rarely transmitted on their own. The annals are implicated in the transmission of Fredegar's Continuations (class D and E manuscripts), the *Liber historiae francorum* and the Lorsch annals ('B' group).[106] Further, the *Annales regni francorum* are often found in conjunction with the *Vita Karoli* of Einhard, the Astronomer's Life of Louis the Pious and Thegan's Life of Louis the Pious. In other words, the Frankish annals form the base text of a large number of composite Frankish history books, each of which was compiled to serve a particular author's or compiler's

---

[104] R. McKitterick, 'Charles the Bald (823–877) and his library: the patronage of learning', *EHR* 95 (1980), pp. 28–47; reprinted in McKitterick, *Frankish kings and culture*, chapter 5.

[105] On St Omer 706 see above, pp. 50–1.   [106] See Collins, *Fredegar*, pp. 119–31.

purpose in relation to whatever audience, or audiences, that author or compiler had in mind. They were disseminated throughout the Frankish realm, east and west, from St Bertin to Altaich. Despite additions or omissions, and rearrangements or attachments to other historical texts which enable differentiation between the different groups, the text of the common elements remains remarkably stable. Many writers, scribes and manuscript compilers were familiar with the *Annales regni francorum*. If it is to be identified with the *Gesta francorum* mentioned in the ninth-century library catalogues, a still wider dissemination of this text is indicated, possibly initially promoted by the Frankish court itself.[107]

The Frankish annals: the text and its message

Thus the *Annales regni francorum* reached a remarkably wide audience throughout the Frankish kingdoms. The host of ninth-century copies and extensions to the *Annales regni francorum*, together with the new emphases lent the text by the juxtaposition with other history narratives, reflect the engagement of many scribes and readers with its contents. The message of the *Annales regni francorum* thus has to be understood not just as the clever construction as it once was, but also as a collaborative piece of image-making by many Frankish scribes over a number of decades and throughout the Frankish realm. Certainly in some of the later manuscripts of the annals scribes add titles to sections as they will. In Vienna, ÖNB cod. 473, for example, the text is divided at 814, the year of the death of Charlemagne, and has the title *Gesta domini Karoli magni et praecellentissimi francorum imperatoris*. The next section, running from 814, when Louis the Pious succeeded his father, to 829, has been given the title *Gesta hludovici imperatoris*. Such a small change in fact alters entirely the focus of the work as well as being a telling indication of what this ninth-century scribe thought the annals were really about.[108]

The wide dissemination is undoubtedly a consequence of the powerful story the annals tell. There is the rhythmic insistence on the year of our Lord, which with the record of where the court spent Easter and Christmas, reinforces the narrative's Christian framework. The fact that God is presented as being on the side of the Franks further enhances their supremacy and legitimacy. Secondly, there is the complete absence of the Merovingian rulers in the section before 751. The military campaigns

---

[107] See above, pp. 21–2.
[108] See H. Reimitz, 'Ein fränkisches Geschichtsbuch aus Saint-Amand und der Codex Vindobonensis palat. 473', in C. Egger and H. Weigl (eds.), *Text-Schrift-Codex. Quellenkundliche Arbeiten aus dem Institut für Österreichische Geschichtsforschung*, *MIÖG* Ergänzungsband (Vienna and Munich, 2000), pp. 34–90, and below, pp. 121–3.

were led by the Carolingian mayors of the palace and the mayors are supreme in all non-military matters as well.

Thirdly, and most prominently, there is the stress on Franks. As one reads it becomes something close to overkill. The Carolingian rulers Pippin, Carloman and Charlemagne do everything in concert with, with the consent of, or with the support of, the Franks. Pippin goes on campaign with the Frankish army in 747: *cum exercitu francorum*. In 751 he is elected *secundum morem Francorum et elevatus a Francis in regno in Suessionis civitate*. In 755 Pippin with the *Franks* is the victor against the Lombards in Italy and returns to Francia *(Pippinus rex cum Francis victor extitit)*. Pippin consults the Franks, he holds assemblies with the Franks. In 757 Pippin held an assembly *in compendio cum Francis* and again in 760 *consilium fecit cum Francis*. In 774 the Lombards came and submitted to the glorious lord King Charles and the Franks; in 775, it is the Franks who are led against the Saxons by Charlemagne. Peoples, territories and cities are conquered and placed under Frankish rule.

Such stress on the Franks as a *gens* (a people) is unprecedented either in Merovingian or in other eighth-century narrative sources. For the *Liber historiae francorum* the term 'Franks' refers quite clearly to the Neustrians, that is, those living in the area in western France between the Seine and the Loire, though as we have seen, it appears that the text could have been understood to have wider resonance in the Carolingian period.[109] In Fredegar's *Chronicle* and its Continuations it is less clear to whom the author is referring when he mentions Franks in the narrative though *Franci* are distinguished from Austrasians. It is only in the latter part of the Continuations that it is possible to understand Francia as the entire region north of the Loire across to the Rhine, peopled by the Franks.[110]

One might suppose this to be an indication of a general view by the middle of the eighth century that all those ruled by the Carolingians are Franks. On this reading the authors of the *Annales regni francorum* are reflecting some degree of consensus by the time they are writing. On the other hand, the manuscripts in which the Continuations of Fredegar are copied are ninth-century Carolingian versions. These may have been adapted in the light of an understanding, propagated by the Frankish annal writers, of the word Franks as pertaining to all those, whether Neustrian or Austrasian, under Carolingian rule. The authors of the *Annales regni francorum*, therefore, created a far more comprehensive idea of Frankish identity than had ever been used before. It was a notion of

---

[109] See above, chapter 1.

[110] E. Ewig. 'Descriptio Franciae', in H. Beumann (ed.), *Karl der Große. Lebenswerk und Nachleben I Persönlichkeit und Geschichte* (Düsseldorf, 1965), pp. 143–77.

the *gens Francorum* specifically associated with the Carolingian mayors and kings.[111]

It is significant in this respect that the text builds up a strong sense of the Franks in opposition to other people. When one reads the *Annales regni francorum* for information about the expansion and consolidation of the Frankish realm, it is easy to focus on conquest rather than the clever way the author(s) describe(s) how the Franks systematically, so it seems, set out to swallow up all other *gentes* (peoples) who in due course become appendages to the Franks. From 741, when, according to the reviser of the annals, Carloman and Pippin set out to recover the areas lost to the Franks after Charles Martel's death, there is a battery of reiterations of Pippin and Charles and the Franks in opposition to Aquitanians, Lombards, Bavarians, Saxons, Bretons, etc.; throughout the whole text I have counted thirty-seven different peoples with whom the Franks collectively, plus their ruler, have dealings. The greater majority of these dealings are as opponents of the Franks and duly conquered, defeated or brought into submission to them. They are subsequently added to the list of those acting in concert with the Franks. Reading the account steadily to 807, taking in 800 on the way, is instructive. Becoming an emperor of the Romans is simply the term used to denote becoming the ruler of the Romans or one ruler over many subject peoples; the latter is the standard sense of *imperium* in the middle ages and it is certainly how both Bede and Alcuin use it. Thus the description of the coronation of Charlemagne as emperor in 800 in the *Annales regni francorum* can be read as just one further instance of another people, the *Romani*, brought under Charlemagne and Frankish rule. It is soon said and passed over. Less space is in fact accorded the *Romani* than the *Aquitani*, the *Baiuuuarii* and above all the *Saxones*, the *Wascones*, the *Wilzi* and the *Brittani*. Rather, it is the incorporation of all these peoples into an all-encompassing Frankish *gens* that the *Annales regni francorum* really stress.[112]

The dramatic adjustments to the text in the revised version heighten this emphasis still further. The Latin was made more stylish and various

---

[111] This is in contrast to the Anglo-Saxons, who lack the emphasis on a particular family: see S. Foot, 'The making of Angelcynn: English identity before the Norman conquest', *TRHS* 6th series (1996), pp. 25–49. On questions of identity see W. Pohl, 'Tradition, Ethnogenese und literarische Gestaltung: eine Zwischenbilanz', in K. Brunner and B. Merta (eds.), *Ethnogenese und Überlieferung. Angewandte Methoden der Frühmittelalterforschung* (Vienna and Munich, 1994), pp. 9–26; and R. Corradini, M. Diesenberger and H. Reimitz (eds.), *The construction of communities in the early middle ages: texts, resources and artefacts*, The Transformation of the Roman World 12 (Leiden, 2003).

[112] Hraban Maur takes up this theme in his *Liber de oblatione puerorum*, where he insists on the *gens francorum* as the legitimate succession of other imperial *gentes*, *PL* 107, col. 432.

small amendments were introduced as well as extra information added here and there which is of considerable importance. Under 796, for example, to the rather brief account of Pope Hadrian's death, the 'E' version added information about the requirement that the Roman people should make their submission and swear an oath of fidelity to the king through his representatives. Further, the details added about Carloman and Pippin and their intentions on accession to power in 741 give glimpses of greater political tensions than the main text would allow, though it is arguable that the expansions serve primarily to elucidate and reinforce the text and make it more intelligible rather than altering the main thrust of the Royal Frankish annalists' message. Nevertheless, the Reviser also permits us to observe a further process of constructing the past on the foundations of a predecessor.

Thus, under the year 741, the anonymous author of the *Annales regni francorum* started its account with the laconic observation that Charles, mayor of the palace died: *Carolus maior domus defunctus est*. The next entry, for 742, records how Carloman and Pippin, mayors of the palace, divided the kingdom of the Franks among themselves, and mounted a campaign against Hunuald, duke of the Aquitainians. Carloman also laid Alemannia waste. In 743 both Pippin and Carloman started a war against Odilo, duke of the Bavarians. Carloman advanced into Saxony and the following year Pippin and Carloman together invaded Saxony and captured Duke Theodoric. Not until 747 is a man called Grifo mentioned who required a great deal of effort on Pippin's part to subdue.[113]

The original annalist had set a brisk pace for his narrative. The fact that he may have been writing as many as forty years after these events may have contributed to his brevity and selectivity, though other historians recounting events long before their own lifetimes before and since, such as Bede or Gregory of Tours, have not felt so inhibited. The 'Reviser' of these same annals, working many years later, added to the entry for 741 at some length, not only the incidental information that Carloman and Pippin had a half brother called Grifo who disputed the succession with them, but also further detail that serves to fill in the context for the first annalist's bald account of campaigns against Bavarians, Saxons, Alemans and others. It is the Reviser who asserts that from quelling Grifo's bid for a share of the kingdom in 741 onwards, Carloman and Pippin applied themselves to restoring order in the kingdom and to recovering the provinces which had fallen away *from the Franks* after their father's death. It is the Reviser who alerts us to the degree to which the original annalist constructed a very particular version of the Frankish past. He also allows

---

[113] *Annales regni francroum*, s.a. 741, 743, 747, pp. 2, 4, 6.

us to observe the reception and augmentation of that construction during the reigns of Pippin's son and grandson, Charlemagne and Louis the Pious. Many other insertions add circumstantial details of Charlemagne's campaigns, with the names of his generals and his opponents, especially in the expeditions against the Saxons, the Avars and the Byzantines in Benevento.

By the time the revisions were made, however, it appears to have been possible to acknowledge, and thus to locate in the past, opposition to Carolingian rule. In 768, for example, when Pippin III had died, his kingdom was divided between his two sons, Charles (Charlemagne) and Carloman. Three years later, Carloman died and Charlemagne was left as sole ruler. The original version of the annals mentions that Charles and Carloman were raised to the kingship. In 769 Charlemagne, the 'glorious lord king Charles (*gloriosus domnus Carolus rex*)', went on campaign in Aquitaine and joined his brother at *Duasdives*. From there Carloman suddenly returned to Francia (*inde Carlomannus se revertendo Franciam item arripiens*). Carloman is mentioned again in 770 as meeting his mother Bertrada. In 771 the annalist noted laconically that Carloman died at the villa of Samoussy and that his wife with a few Franks departed for Italy.[114] The Reviser, on the other hand, provides a long account of the invasion of, and campaign in, Aquitaine, and that Carloman, because of the evil counsel of his *proceres*, refused to assist his brother. The next year the dowager Queen Bertrada's visit is extended to a journey to Italy 'in the interest of peace'. In 771 the Reviser adds the gloss that the king 'bore patiently' with the departure of Carloman's wife and retinue for Italy and 'thought it was needless'.[115]

The Reviser is still a staunch admirer of Charlemagne. Indeed, if anything, the additions serve to make Carloman's doings murkier and more treacherous. The portrayal of blamelessness on Charlemagne's part nevertheless conveys something of his ruthlessness as well. So too, the accounts of further opposition, notably the revolt of Charlemagne's eldest son, the officially illegitimate Pippin the Hunchback in 792 and the conspiracy among the 'eastern Franks' in 785 led by Count Hardrad are recorded as past aberrations in the Franks' loyalty to their ruler. In the entry for 817, moreover, the annalist responsible for this section noted that the leaders of the rebellion of Bernard of Italy included Reginhar, son of Count Meginhar, whose maternal grandfather Hardrad once conspired against Charles. He thereby links this passage with the Reviser's note for 785 and acknowledges a tradition of disloyalty and opposition to

---

[114] *Ibid.*, s.a. 768, 769, 770, 771, pp. 26, 28, 30, 32.
[115] *Ibid.*, s.a. 768, 770, 771, pp. 27, 29, 31, 33.

the ruler within a particular family.[116] He can now afford to take a high moral stance and use it to highlight legitimate power.

The moral indignation conveyed by the Reviser when noting opposition and the bold way he emphasises Charlemagne's difficulties with the treachery of, and lack of co-operation from, his brother, his son and some of his leading magnates are of a piece with the interpretation offered for the revolt of Louis the Pious's nephew Bernard against Louis. That is, the indication that close members of the family had rebelled against the head of the family before, and were quite clearly in the wrong, provides a context of vindication in which to understand not only the revolts but the way Charlemagne and Louis dealt with them. There is such distinct coherence between the revised version and this later portion, 808–20, of the annals in tone and style, that it may well be to the author of this section that we may attribute the revised 'E' version of the Royal Frankish Annals. The revised version and these later portions represent a skilful augmentation of the collective memory of the Franks and a masterly enhancement of the righteousness of the Carolingian rulers. Read in this context the 'revised annals' enhance further the legitimacy of the Carolingian rulers and Louis's succession, as well as the *imperium*, that is, rule, of the Franks over many peoples.

The Royal Frankish Annals in both the original and the revised versions forge a Frankish identity by constant reiteration and triumphal narrative. The ruler and the Franks are the achievers and together create the great realm. Consolidated in an historical and Christian framework, this is the message passed on to their contemporaries and to posterity. The insistence on precise chronology is a deliberate device to enhance a very determined expression of the Franks' identity and cultural affiliations. Self-image is as important as perceived image. Whether or not the history constructed by the Royal Frankish Annalists for the Franks bore any relation to reality is to some degree irrelevant, for what has concerned me in this chapter is the construction of a past, its coherence and consistency, and the degree to which such a construction constitutes the formation of the collective memory of the newly formed Frankish people under Carolingian rule. Although many different categories of text could yield an understanding of the Franks and their sense of history, I have deliberately focused here on one highly influential historical narrative because of the very particular message it conveys. The authors of the *Annales regni francorum* in fact constructed so powerful an image of their society and its events, and evoked such a convincing sense of identity, that it is

---

[116] *Ibid.*, s.a. 785, p. 71 and McKitterick, *Frankish kingdoms*, p. 135.

their version that has been remembered, and believed, ever since.[117] In the next two chapters, therefore, I turn to further specific aspects of the annalists' narrative, namely their presentation of political ideology and of kingship.

[117] Preliminary versions of different parts of this chapter were presented to the workshop 'Tracking down the Franks' in King's College, London, Denys Hay Seminar of the University of Edinburgh and the conference for Dutch graduate students in Medieval Studies in Driebergen, organised by the University of Utrecht, in February and March 1996. I am particularly grateful to my audiences on these occasions, and to the Fellows of the Royal Historical Society assembled in Leeds in May 1997 for their lively discussion and suggestions.

5 Politics and history

An idea can hold a people together and sustain it. A shared political memory and an inspiring history of the Franks as the centre of the world, such as is presented in the *Annales regni francorum* and disseminated from the royal court may have done much to buttress Carolingian rule. Recalled past experience and shared images of the past are the kinds of memories that have special importance for the constitution of social groups. Within these, the creation of accounts of past events that draw on memory but select from it in distinctive ways that become accepted, and thereafter are shared by a group, is the process of constructing the past.[1] The Franks' historical writing, as we have seen, served to reinforce the Franks' own sense of place in the framework of history and in relation to the past.[2] Much has already been written about the role of the past in the political and cultural consciousness of the Franks.[3] Their interest in the Roman imperial and Christian past is clear from the surviving manuscripts and library catalogues,[4] but it is vital to set this beside the evidence for contemporary history provided by the annals, for it is in the image of the immediate past that the Carolingian political ideology is presented at its most fervent, backed up by telling circumstantial detail and stories of success. The exegesis of past events was provided as a way of indicating the proper political positions of the present and the shaping of the future. We have already seen that investigation of the manuscripts containing the

---

[1] Chapter 4 above, p. 85.
[2] It is in histories written in the eleventh and twelfth centuries that the Carolingians become part of a much simplified and glorious past with heroic attributes increasingly distanced from reality: A. R. Remensnyder, *Remembering kings past: monastic foundation legends in medieval southern France* (Ithaca, 1995); P. J. Geary, *Phantoms of remembrance. Memory and oblivion at the end of the first millennium* (Princeton, 1994); and K.-E. Geith, *Carolus Magnus. Studien zur Darstellung Karls des Großen in der deutschen Literatur des 12. und 13. Jahrhunderts*, Bibliotheca Germanica 19 (Bern and Munich, 1977).
[3] T. F. X. Noble, 'Tradition and learning in search of ideology: the *Libri carolini*', in R. E. Sullivan (ed.), *'The gentle voices of teachers': aspects of learning in the Carolingian age* (Columbus, Ohio, 1995), pp. 227–60, esp. 248–9; and R. McKitterick (ed.), *Carolingian culture: emulation and innovation* (Cambridge, 1994).
[4] See above, chapter 2, and below chapters 9 and 10.

Annales regni francorum can shed light on the audience for Frankish history. As a coda to the discussion in the preceding chapter I shall focus here, therefore, on one of these manuscripts and its implications.

At the monastery of St Amand in northern Francia in the second half of the ninth century, a compilation of historical texts was prepared with a very particular agenda. The manuscript was in the cathedral library of Worms by the thirteenth century and survives in Vienna, ÖNB cod. 473. It contains the following texts. First of all (fols. 1v–85v) there is the *Liber pontificalis*. This is followed by the *Liber historiae francorum* (fols. 91r–107v), the Continuations to the *Chronicle* of Fredegar (fols. 108r–114v) and the *Annales regni francorum*, in the 'D', that is, unrevised version (fols. 116r–143v and 152v–169r). There is a portion of Einhard's *Vita Karoli* (fols. 144r–151v) and the manuscript concludes with a truncated version of the *Genealogia domus carolingicae*, divided into two sections: *Genealogia sancti Arnulfi* and *Historia francorum epitomata et origine gentis ad Ludovicum pium* (fols. 169v–172r).[5]

This codex is among many compilations of Frankish history produced in the ninth century all over the Frankish empire. As mentioned above, the most common combinations of text include the *Annales* themselves and the *Vita Karoli* of Einhard, but we also find them juxtaposed with the Continuations of the *Chronicle* of Fredegar, the *Liber historiae francorum*, or the Lives of Louis the Pious by Thegan or the Astronomer.[6] For any one of these compilations the pertinent questions relate to who compiled this volume, why the selection it contains was made, for whom and for what purpose. An analysis of the St Amand collection and examination of the specific place in the notoriously complicated stemma of each of the texts help us to focus on these questions. A codex such as Vienna, ÖNB cod. 473, therefore, makes it necessary to explore the implications of the dissemination of Carolingian historiography in terms not only of the specific political impetus for the initial production of each text but also of their subsequent impact and use.

Let us look more closely, therefore, at the texts assembled in Vienna, ÖNB cod. 473. Its version of the *Liber pontificalis* is that classified by

---

[5] The texts of the genealogy are edited by G. Pertz, *MGH SS* 2 (Berlin, 1829), pp. 308–12. Since the publication (in French) of my preliminary observations on this codex, a full study has been made by H. Reimitz, 'Ein fränkisches Geschichtsbuch aus Saint-Amand und der Codex Vindobonensis palat. 473', in C. Egger and H. Wiegl (eds.), *Text-Schrift-Codex. Quellenkundliche Arbeiten aus dem Institut für Österreichische Geschichtsforschung* (Vienna, 1999). I am very grateful to Helmut Reimitz for our many discussions of this codex since 1997.

[6] See above, pp. 111–13 and E. Tremp, *Die Überlieferung der Vita Hludowici imperatoris des Astronomus*, *MGH* Studien und Texte 1 (Hannover, 1991) and his *Studien zu den Gesta Hludowici imperatoris des Trierer Chorbischofs Thegan*, *MGH* Schriften 32 (Hannover, 1988).

Duchesne as the B text and runs to Life 94, that is, Stephen II (d. 757).[7] It is closely related to the three copies of the *Liber pontificalis* made at Laon in the first half of the ninth century, the earliest of which (Cologne, Dombibliothek 164) is possibly a copy of an exemplar sent by Pope Leo III to Charlemagne. The Vienna recension, however, is essentially a Frankish one. It incorporates significant additions, notably in the lives of the eighth-century popes Gregory III and Stephen II, which are pertinent to Frankish affairs or offer a Frankish dimension to papal affairs. In the life of Gregory III, for example, an appeal from Gregory to Charles Martel for help against the Lombards is recorded. Inserted into the life of Stephen II are references to Duke Hunuald of Aquitaine's perfidy, Pippin's embassy to the pope, led by Pippin's brother Jerome, and the pope's granting of the archiepiscopal pallium to Chrodegang of Metz.[8] Thus the history of the popes in the eighth century is deployed in this codex as an adjunct and historical context for that of the Franks. It serves to reinforce the associations of the Carolingians and the Franks with Rome and papal authority, and provides essential justifications of the Frankish conquest of Italy.

Having provided the Roman and papal background, the compiler of Vienna, ÖNB cod. 473 then added excerpts concerning the Trojan origins of the Franks, ending with the burial of Dagobert at St Denis and before the account of Grimoald's coup, from the *Liber historiae francorum* in its 'B' or Austrasian recension.[9] Unlike other Carolingian copies of the Continuations of Fredegar, this one, Class 5 (f),[10] subsequently takes the text only as far as the death of Charles Martel and distinguishes that portion as the *Historia rerum gestarum Carli maioris domus*.

Similarly, the *Annales regni francorum* in Vienna, ÖNB cod. 473 are divided into two sections. The one ending at 814 is described in red rustic letters as the *Gesta domni Karoli magni*, and the other, from 814–829, is headed *Gesta Hludowici*. In a style reminiscent of the *Liber pontificalis*, it adds at 814 that while Charlemagne was passing the winter at Aachen he

---

[7] L. Duchesne (ed.), *Le Liber pontificalis*, 2 vols. (Paris, 1886 and 1892); see the introduction to R. Davis, *The lives of the eighth-century popes (Liber pontificalis)* (Liverpool, 1992).

[8] Duchesne, *Liber pontificalis*, pp. 420 (interpolated section XIV); p. 441 (addition to section IV); p. 451 (addition to section XXXCIII); p. 356 (interpolation to section LIII); and compare pp. ccxxvii–ccxxix.

[9] *Liber historiae francorum*, c. 43, ed. B. Krusch, reprinted in a revised edition by A. Kusternig under the direction of H. Wolfram, *Quellen zur Geschichte des 7. und 8. Jahrhunderts*, Ausgewählte Quellen zur deutschen Geschichte des Mittelalters 4a (Darmstadt, 1982), p. 364.

[10] The Fredegar manuscripts are discussed in detail by B. Krusch, *Chronicarum quae dicuntur fredegarii scholastici libri IV cum continuationibus*, MGH SRG 2 (Hannover, 1888), summarised in Kusternig and Wolfram, *Quellen zur Geschichte*, pp. 33–8, and see Roger Collins, *Fredegar*, Authors of the Middle Ages 4, no. 13 (Aldershot, 1996), p. 129.

died aged seventy-one, in the forty-seventh year of his kingship, the forty-third year of his rule in Italy and the fourteenth year of his rule as emperor, on 28 January. The portions of Einhard's *Vita Karoli* inserted between these two parts include the section in which Charlemagne repudiates the daughter of Desiderius and marries Hildegard. Louis the Pious, of course, was the only surviving son of Hildegard.[11] It thus serves to reinforce both the legitimacy of Carolingian succession, and the theme of the genealogy which completes the collection, where the Carolingian line from father to son, from its origins in the Trojan and Gallo-Roman past to Louis the Pious, is elaborated.

The *Annales regni francorum*, specifically described as the deeds of Charlemagne and Louis, emerge as the principal history in the arrangement of the book's contents; all the other texts complement and enhance it. It would appear that this was the deliberate intention of the compiler. It is necessary to dwell a little longer on the content of the *Annales*, themselves, for they have been too little appreciated for the forceful political ideology they convey. As I argued in the previous chapter, the *Annales* present a skilfully constructed and highly selective triumphal narrative with a subtly nuanced portrayal of the Carolingian rulers, whose success is identified with that of the Frankish people. This narrative needs, furthermore, to be seen in the context of the remarkable production of Carolingian historiography in the eighth and ninth centuries, all of which reflects an urgent political purpose in the interpretation of contemporary events;[12] much of it was designed to justify, and even to legitimate, particular courses of action and manifestations of power on the part of the Carolingian rulers in relation to specific political circumstances. Indeed, the more conventional treatises on political thought, such as those by Sedulius Scotus or Jonas of Orleans, drew in fact on ideas elaborated in the historical justifications for the actions of the Carolingian rulers.[13]

The most familiar aspect of the late eighth-century historical texts is of course the systematic derogation of the Merovingian rulers and, indeed, of Merovingian ecclesiastical and lay elites, church, religion and culture. In matters of doctrine, church organisation, Christian observance and governmental control, Carolingian legislation skilfully belittled

---

[11] Einhard, *Vita Karoli*, c. 18, ed. R. Rau, *Quellen zur karolingischen Reichsgeschichte*, I (Darmstadt, 1974), pp. 188–90, and chapter 1 above, p. 18.

[12] Innes and McKitterick, 'Writing of history'.

[13] Sedulius Scotus, *Liber de rectoribus christianis*, ed. S. Hellmann, Quellen und Untersuchungen zur lateinischen Philologie 1,1 (Munich, 1906), pp. 1–91; and Jonas of Orleans, *De institutione regia*, ed. J. Reviron, *Les Idées politico-religieuses d'un évêque du IXe siècle: Jonas d'Orléans et son De institutione regia* (Paris, 1930), pp. 119–94. See the classic survey by H. H. Anton, *Fürstenspiegel und Herrscherethos in der Karolingerzeit*, Bonner Historische Forschungen 32 (Bonn, 1968).

the Merovingian period and celebrated the great achievements of the Carolingians.[14] Similarly the Continuations of the *Chronicle* of Fredegar, disseminated widely throughout the Carolingian realm in its ninth-century version, present, from the vantage point of a family member and supporter, the steady accumulation of power and territory on the part of the Carolingian mayors, especially Charles Martel and Pippin III, at the expense of the Merovingian puppet kings.[15] As Collins has suggested, the Continuations as far as 751, where there appears to be a clear break (signalled by the famous colophon in BAV reg. lat. 213 concerning Childebrand's patronage of its composition),[16] might appear to indicate that the expansion of Fredegar's *Chronicle* to this point was undertaken in 751 to mark the inauguration of the new *rex francorum*. The subsequent portion from 751 to 768 could be seen as an updating of the work to honour Pippin III's successors, possibly for Carloman alone rather than for Pippin as well. I have argued below, however, that the continuator could have put the whole text together after 768 and that this tenth-century colophon, added only to one manuscript of the Continuations, may not be as definitive as has hitherto been assumed.[17] Nevertheless, the impact on a late ninth-century reader of the continuator's account as a whole would be to enhance an understanding of the Carolingian family's power and prestige.

Further, the *Gesta episcoporum mettensium* by Paul the Deacon, commissioned by Bishop Angilram of Metz in 781, does not celebrate the bishops of one diocese so much as commemorate, however discreetly, events vitally concerning the entire Frankish church and kingdoms.[18] Paul simply omits all reference to the Merovingian kings or church. The text, with what Walter Goffart has described as its 'four-part allegory of the Carolingian achievement' and simplified genealogy of the Carolingian rulers, was designed to reinforce the legitimacy of Carolingian succession from father to son, and especially that of Charles the Younger, eldest son

---

[14] R. McKitterick, *The Frankish church and the Carolingian reforms, 789–895*, Royal Historical Society, Studies in History 2 (London, 1977); I. Wood, *The Merovingian kingdoms, 450–751* (London, 1994); Y. Hen, *Culture and religion in Merovingian Gaul, AD 481–751*, Culture, Beliefs and Tradition. Medieval and Early Modern Peoples 1 (Leiden, 1995), pp. 198–205.

[15] R. Collins, 'Deception and misrepresentation in early eighth-century Frankish historiography: two case studies', in J. Jarnut, U. Nonn and M. Richter (eds.), *Karl Martell in seiner Zeit*, Beihefte der Francia 37 (Sigmaringen, 1994), pp. 227–48; see also chapter 2 above, pp. 36–9.

[16] Fredegar, Continuations, c. 33, ed. J. M. Wallace-Hadrill, *The fourth book of the Chronicle of Fredegar and its Continuations* (London, 1960), p. 102.

[17] Chapter 6, below, and compare Collins, *Fredegar*, pp. 113–16.

[18] *Gesta episcoporum mettensium*, ed. G. Pertz, *Liber de episcopis mettensibus*, MGH SS 2 (Berlin, 1829), pp. 260–8.

of Hildegard and Charlemagne, descended from Arnulf's son Anschisus. The name Anschisus, comments Paul, 'is believed to be derived from Anchises father of Aeneas, who long ago came from Troy to Italy. For as ancient tradition has it, the Frankish people traces its origins to Trojan stock.'[19] Thus Paul links the Carolingian house with the Trojans. In subsequently describing Charlemagne as the conqueror of Italy and ruler of Rome, he reunites the two branches of the Trojan diaspora.[20]

Preoccupation with the succession of the Carolingians is also the main point of the *Annales mettenses priores*.[21] It is now generally acknowledged that this was written as a justificatory dossier for the *Divisio regnorum* of 806. It was most probably composed at Chelles under the auspices of Gisela, Charlemagne's sister. Like Paul the Deacon's *Gesta*, it had a specific concern for the inheritance of Charles the Younger.[22] Paul Fouracre and Richard Gerberding have doubted that the *Annales mettenses priores* were written by a woman because, they claim, the author voices virulent criticism of Plectrude and is therefore a (male) misogynist.[23] Women are surely no less discerning than men when it comes to recognising the failings of members of their own sex.[24] To my mind, this reinforces the link posited between the *Annales* and Gisela at Chelles, for Plectrude was the *stepmother* of Charles Martel and had done her best to prevent Charles coming into his father's inheritance. The *Annales mettenses priores* certainly are far more concerned with division and succession than they are with an idea of imperial unity, but their most important theme is the historical justification for the ruling position of the Carolingian family, loyally upheld by their *fideles*. Each successive Carolingian ruler fulfilled an element of God's plan for the Franks which culminated in the glorious

---

[19] *Ibid.*, p. 264: *cuius Anschisi nomen ab Anchise patre Aeneae, qui a Troia in Italiam olim venerat, creditur esse deductum. Nam gens Francorum, sicut a ueteribus est traditum, a Troiana prosapia trahit exordium.*

[20] See W. Goffart, 'Paul the Deacon's *Gesta episcoporum mettensium* and the early design of Charlemagne's succession', *Traditio* 42 (1986), pp. 59–94.

[21] *Annales mettenses priores*, ed. B. von Simson, *MGH SRG* 10 (Hannover and Leipzig, 1905).

[22] H. Hoffmann, *Untersuchungen zur karolingischen Annalistik*, Bonner Historische Forschungen 10 (Bonn, 1958); and I. Haselbach, *Aufstieg und Herrschaft der Karolinger in der Darstellung der sogenannten Annales Mettenses Priores. Ein Beitrag zur Geschichte des politischen Ideen im Reiche Karls des Grossen*, Historische Studien 412 (Lübeck, 1970), pp. 1–208. See also Y. Hen, 'The Annals of Metz and the Merovingian past', in Y. Hen and M. Innes (eds.), *The uses of the past in the early middle ages* (Cambridge, 2000), pp. 175–90.

[23] P. Fouracre and R. Gerberding, *Late Merovingian France: history and hagiography 640–720* (Manchester, 1996), p. 338.

[24] For other arguments see J. L. Nelson, 'Gender and genre in women historians of the early middle ages,' in J. L. Nelson, *The Frankish world* (London, 1996), pp. 183–97; and R. McKitterick, 'Women and literacy in the early middle ages,' in *Books, scribes and learning*, chapter 13.

rule of Charlemagne. The language to describe the early Pippinids is also replete with connotations of imperial and royal rule.[25]

The *Annales regni francorum*, as we have seen, run from 741 to 829, were conceived in 788 or so, and thereafter continued in instalments, from a miscellany of both oral and written information.[26] In the *Annales regni francorum* the Merovingian rulers are also conspicuous by their absence, but there is a difference of crucial importance in the presentation of Carolingian success: it is always in concert with the triumph of the Franks. As I stressed earlier, the *Annales* constitute a major contribution to the formation of the collective memory of the people under Frankish rule. It is the Carolingian mayors who lead the Franks before 751. The Carolingian leaders do everything with the consent and support and on the advice of the Franks, that is, the lay and ecclesiastical elites. There is a remarkable stress on the Franks as a *gens*. The annalist created a far more encompassing idea of Frankish identity than ever before and a notion of the *gens francorum* specifically associated with the Carolingian mayors and kings and the legitimacy of Carolingian rule. The *Annales regni francorum* forge a Frankish identity by constant reiteration and triumphal narrative consolidated within a Christian chronological framework. The link with the year of the Incarnation first used by the royal Frankish annalist makes an explicit association between the history of the Franks; the progression of Christian history, and the secular rhythm of the court was fitted into the liturgical cycle.

The continuators of the *Annales regni francorum* after 788 add skilfully to the effect created. Year after year sees the visits of embassies from Sicily, Rome, Huesca, Persia, Jerusalem, Dalmatia and Venice, Cordoba, Byzantium, Galicia and the Asturias who seek out the Franks and their rulers, bringing gifts, offering or confirming alliances and friendship or suing for peaceful terms after 'rebellions' swiftly dealt with by the emperor's magnates.[27] Although embassies come to the court, it is the magnates who deal with the peripheral peoples in the field. Thus Eric of Friuli wins victory against the Avars and sends the treasure to Charlemagne, though Eric is subsequently killed in an ambush. Much of this Avar treasure was distributed among Charlemagne's *optimates*, ecclesiastical as well

---

[25] This is pointed out by Fouracre and Gerberding, *Late Merovingian France*, p. 346. They also highlight the contrast between the stress on divine plan in the *Annales mettenses priores* and that on family and politics in the *Liber historiae francorum*.

[26] Above, chapters 1 and 4.

[27] For a different perspective on embassies and historical texts, see J. Shepard, 'The uses of "history" in Byzantine diplomacy: observations and comparisons', in C. Dendrinos, J. Harris, E. Harvalia-Crook and J. Herrin (eds.), *Porphyrogenita. Essays on the history and literature of Byzantium and the Latin east in honour of Julian Chrysostomides* (Aldershot, 2003), pp. 91–115.

as lay, and his other *fideles*. Count Gerold also was killed in battle against the Avars. Count Wido 'conquered' Brittany for the Franks in 799. Count Aureolus was killed on the Spanish border in 809. Again it is twelve Frankish magnates who in 811 conduct the negotiations for peace with the Danes after the systematic series of campaigns conducted in an effort to contain the Danish attacks under Godofrid. Support is given to Frankish allies, such as Obodrites, by the leading men of Charlemagne and Louis the Pious. Saxon and Sorb rebellions are quelled; the Nordliudi, Wilzi and Bohemians are dealt with by the magnates or by the king's son. In all these details of international embassies, reference to internal matters is rare, but it is significant that it should be in 806 that the succession and division of the kingdom were discussed and that the annalist insists that the decisions were confirmed by an oath of the Frankish magnates. After Louis is established on the throne the annalist is quick to point out that it is 'business as usual'. Again, however, it is the magnates, the king's staunch supporters, who put agreed measures into effect. After a general assembly at Aachen, for example, Louis sends envoys to all parts of the kingdoms to render justice and relieve the oppression of the people. The annalist addressed his audience in 813 concerning the decisions made at the reform councils of that year. They have been distributed to the cities, he says, but anyone who wants to see them can also consult the palace archives. The years after 823 are replete with the record of assemblies being held after which decisions made are carried out. Occasionally the *Annales* can be recognised as having an admonitory role in pointing out the evils ensuing from military weakness or administrative incompetence.

The Continuations of Fredegar's *Chronicle*, the *Gesta episcoporum mettensium*, the *Annales regni francorum* and the *Annales mettenses priores* have in common the presentation of the eighth century as the Golden Age in which all the virtues and political strength of the Franks were elaborated. Within the framework of nostalgic triumphalist narrative, Carolingian legitimacy and clear principles about the succession to the throne are stressed. Legitimacy of succession and the ruler's relationship with his elites are also the common themes of the principal historical writing of the first half of the ninth century. These include the revised or 'E' version of the *Annales regni francorum*, possibly produced towards the end of Charlemagne's reign or in the aftermath of the first restoration of Louis,[28]

---

[28] The revised section of the Annals needs further work, for there is still no consensus about when or in what circumstances it was produced. L. Kolarova, 'The transmission and dissemination of Carolingian annals' (unpublished M.Phil. dissertation, University of Cambridge, 1995), suggested that the E version can be linked to the initiative of Gerward of Lorsch and the sponsorship of Louis the German. For some interesting observations see R. Collins, 'The "Reviser" revisited: another look at the alternative version of the

Thegan the Astronomer and finally Nithard. Keeping faith and fidelity are the dominant concerns. This historiography is not just about the Frankish rulers but about the ruling elites. It elaborates the importance of the rule of the *gens francorum*, and the position of the Carolingian rulers together with the Franks, in relation to a Christian, ancient Frankish and Trojan past; it constantly reiterates the role of the clergy and the magnates in ensuring political success. There can be few parallels for such a concerted effort on the part of the elites to ensure the necessity for their support. This is not purely monarchical historiography at all. It articulates an ideology of consensus[29] and Frankish rule, in which the elites are just as important as the ruler himself.

The St Amand codex is thus no random assemblage of texts on Frankish history. Headings, colophons and bridging passages from one text to the next are added to direct the reader. It was produced at a centre under the patronage of Charles the Bald and presided over by no less a personage than Charles the Bald's arch-chancellor Gauzlin.[30] It serves, in its account of his illustrious predecessors, to underpin Charles the Bald's own rule and the importance of the support of the Frankish secular and ecclesiastical elites. Helmut Reimitz, indeed, has made a convincing case for this manuscript's being associated with Charles the Bald's coronation at Metz in 869. It makes sense of all the Metz connections in the codex and is a reminder of all the historical reasons which made such a political move comprehensible.[31]

Yet the St Amand compilation also raises important questions about the way in which the annals were produced and disseminated. Modern scholars have tended to think of the *Annales* in a conventional nineteenth-century way. That is, the many different recensions, most of them in ninth-century manuscripts from different centres throughout the Frankish realm, and organised into a stemma with five branches,[32] are

---

Annales regni francorum', in A. C. Murray (ed.), *After Rome's fall. Narrators and sources of early medieval history. Essays presented to Walter Goffart* (Toronto, 1998), pp. 191–213.

[29] On consensus, see J. Hannig, *Consensus fidelium. Frühfeudale Interpretationen des Verhältnisses von Königtum und Adel am Beispiel des Frankenreiches* (Stuttgart, 1982); and J. L. Nelson, 'Legislation and consensus in the reign of Charles the Bald', in P. Wormald *et al.* (eds.), *Ideal and reality in Frankish and Anglo-Saxon Society* (Oxford, 1983), pp. 202–27.

[30] R. McKitterick, 'Charles the Bald and his library: the patronage of learning', *EHR* 95 (1980), pp. 28–47, reprinted in R. McKitterick, *Frankish kings and culture*, chapter 5. On Gauzlin, see K.-F. Werner, 'Gauzlin von Saint Denis und die westfränkische Reichsteilung von Amiens (März 880). Ein Beitrag zur Vorgeschichte von Odos Königtum', *DA* 35 (1979), pp. 395–462.

[31] H. Reimitz, 'Ein Karolingisches Geschichtsbuch'; and J. L. Nelson, *Charles the Bald* (London 1992), especially pp. 221–53.

[32] See F. Kurze, 'Ueber die Karolingishen Reichsannalen von 741–829 und ihre Ueberarbeitung', *Neues Archiv* 19 (1894), pp. 295–339 and 28 (1903), pp. 619–69.

understood to provide witnesses to a text that are simply judged as faithful or deviant copies. Instead, we should think of them as the deliberate deployment of the text to serve some new purpose. That new purpose is certainly related to the original import of the text, but it gives any scribe or compiler a licence to alter it, and more crucially, to 'bolt it onto' other related texts according to a particular agenda. Past assessments of the *Annales* have rested on a contorted understanding of the original text's composition in relation to the surviving manuscripts. Whatever the original authors may have written, the later copyists and compilers felt at liberty to alter sentences, change tenses and adjectives, insert extra words and omit others. These changes are no doubt very minor, in that the main thrust of the narrative remains remarkably stable. Nevertheless, any alterations are more than merely useful clues for locating a centre of production. They point to a positive engagement with the text on the part of the scribe and compiler.

The *Annales* text on which we now depend, I repeat, is a composite text, created by ninth-century scribes as well as by modern editors. But there is a far more positive way to assess this manuscript evidence, and that is to acknowledge that the text of the *Annales*, as represented in the manuscripts from the Carolingian period, mirrors its reception and attests to an audience in the ninth century. It is an audience of people who were impressed by its political message and wished it to be propagated further.

For whom the various recensions and compilations of the *Annales* were intended is to be deduced from the internal evidence of the many composite history books for which the *Annales regni francorum* form the base text. Here I wish to stress that, important as the *Annales regni francorum* are they must be seen in relation to the specific political impetus for most of the major works of Carolingian historiography. Hitherto each text has been strangely disembodied. That is, the annals, biographies and chronicles exist, we read them, and studies have been made of them as individual texts.[33] To think of them exclusively as separate texts is to deprive them of

[33] For the *Liber historiae francorum*, Fredegar, *Gesta episcoporum mettensium*, *Annales mettenses priores*, *Annales regni francorum*, and Einhard, Thegan and Astronomer, see above. For Nithard and Annals of St Bertin, see J. L. Nelson, 'The Annals of St. Bertin', in M. Gibson and J. L. Nelson, 'Public histories and private history in the work of Nithard', *Speculum* 60 (1985), pp. 251–93, reprinted in her *Politics and ritual in early medieval Europe* (London, 1986), pp. 195–238. For Notker, see H. Löwe, 'Die Geschichtsschreibung der ausgehenden Karolingerzeit', *DA* 23 (1967), pp. 1–30, H.-W. Goetz, *Strukturen der spätkarolingischen Epoche im Spiegel der Vorstellungen eines zeitgenössischen Mönchs. Eine Interpretationen des Gesta Karoli Notkers von Sankt Gallen* (Bonn, 1981); and D. Ganz, 'Humour as history in Notker's *Gesta Karoli magni*', in E. B. King, J. T. Schaefer and W. B. Wadley (eds.), *Monks, nuns and friars in medieval society*, Sewanee Medieval Studies 4 (Sewanee, 1989), pp. 171–83.

their collective power. Instead, they should be regarded as a concentrated effort on the part of a group of associated members of an elite to deploy history in the service of politics and to present posterity with a very specific image of royalty and their own position in the Carolingian world. I say 'associated members of an elite' because all the major historiographical sources of the Carolingian period produced in the century between 780 and 880 can be linked with the royal court in one way or another. As we saw in chapter 1, for example, copies of the *Annales regni francorum*, at least in its revised version, emanated from the court itself.[34] The Cologne fragment of the *Annales* from the scriptorium of Louis the Pious comes from what was once a handsome, large-format book. The text agrees with Kurze's text for the entry for 824 almost exactly. Although it has some unique readings it also shares slight variations in spelling with the manuscripts containing the *Annales regni francorum* classified by Kurze as C3, D3, and no less than five of the E group manuscripts. This increases the likelihood that the E text itself is to be closely associated with the royal court and was disseminated from it. Another court-connected book is the St Amand codex itself, produced in a monastery patronised by Charles the Bald. Other codices containing the annals have been linked with the royal monastery of Lorsch[35] and with Gerward of Lorsch, formerly at the court of Louis the Pious.[36]

It is striking how many extant manuscripts of the *Annales* and related texts are from the Rhineland and the east Frankish kingdom. How many Franks, newly conquered peoples and *exteriores gentes* were the Carolingians able to persuade of the rightness of their cause? It may be that the *Annales regni francorum* not only recount the integration of many peoples such as the Saxons, Bavarians or Wilzi, but were themselves a crucial means of persuasion to assist its very progress. Political change and disintegration can be the consequence of the breakdown of political loyalties, but a sense of a shared past would have great value in forging bonds between the many peoples under Carolingian *imperium*.

---

[34] See above, pp. 21–2 and on the general context and 'court consumers', see J. L. Nelson, 'History writing at the courts of Louis the Pious and Charles the Bald', in Scharer and Scheibelreiter, *Historiographie*, pp. 435–42.

[35] Vienna, ÖNB cod. 510 is a tenth-century copy of the *Annales regni francorum* which includes the *Vita Karoli* and was produced at Lorsch. The 'original' text of the *Annales* is also associated with Lorsch, though how precisely it is impossible now to establish. Lorsch also had the *Annales mettenses priores* by 807. Here the ties with Louis the German's court as well as Louis's are important in the person of Gerward and his interest in history. See also above, p. 19 and on Vienna, ÖNB cod. 510, M. Tischler, *Einhart's Vita Karoli, Studien zur Entstehung, Überlieferung und Rezeption*, MGH Schriften 48, 2 vols. (Hannover, 2001), I, pp. 599–607.

[36] L. Kolarova, 'The transmission and dissemination of Carolingian annals'.

The creation of a collective memory could have played as important a role as Christianisation in fostering a sense of harmony and cohesion. Distribution out from the court was not for the promotion of the king's interest alone but also for those elites in whose interests it was to support the strong mutual bond between king and magnates. What needs to be emphasized, moreover, is the cumulative and comprehensive effect of this historiographical campaign on the part of the writers associated with the Carolingian family and the Carolingian court. All of this historical writing taken together is astonishing in its consistency and its import. These texts are the voice of the elite. Reiterated over such a long period of time, the implicit and explicit statements of Carolingian political ideology contained in the historical writings of the court elites are far more than a narrative of events; they articulate a clear ideology of political power and a very particular presentation of the past that certainly achieved far wider currency than the more conventional treatises on kingship.

I have stressed elsewhere that the sources of the Carolingian period are for the most part not designed to present us with a narrative interpretation of events.[37] The historiography, on the other hand, so abundant and so forceful, was so designed. The Carolingians created their own image of their past and offered it to posterity. But they also offered it to their contemporaries, who treated their own history as part of a larger progression of the history of the Franks, and set it in the context of deeds of the great and powerful whose success redounded to their credit as well.

A number of factors have emerged in this chapter. It began as a study of one single manuscript but it implicates all other Carolingian codices containing historical texts. This is for the simple reason that it is the compilations of Frankish history in the ninth century which provide us with the clearest evidence for the impact of the texts and dissemination of the ideas they contain. Our presentations of ninth-century history in the surviving manuscripts are almost invariably an adjunct to the glories of the eighth century, the noble origins of the Franks in antiquity and Carolingian triumph. Thus the codices illuminate the role of the eighth-century Golden Age in the political ideology of the Franks in the ninth century. In them the following themes are elaborated: the narrative of Carolingian triumph; the emphasis on Roman and Trojan origins; God's divine plan for the Franks as His new chosen people; the legitimacy of Carolingian rule and the secure succession from father to son; the insistence on the role of the ruler as warlord and as centre of a vast empire; the support of the ruler by loyal *fideles* and *potentes*. These were an

---

[37] R. McKitterick, 'Introduction', in McKitterick (ed.), *NCMH*, pp. 1–17.

inspiring legacy which ninth-century Franks clearly treasured. Far more was achieved in the annals than shaping the past. Even a cursory reading of the Frankish annals establishes a clear political agenda focused on the present, and on the power and self-perception of the Carolingian secular and ecclesiastical elites. This will become even more apparent in the following chapter.

6 Kingship and the writing of history

On the death of Charles Martel in 741, his sons Pippin and Carloman assumed control, as mayors of the palace, of the territory of the Merovingian rulers of Frankish Gaul over which Charles Martel had established his authority. In 743 Carloman installed the last Merovingian king, Childeric III, on the throne,[1] but Carloman himself relinquished secular power in 747 and departed for the monastery of Mount Soracte in Italy. In 751 Pippin usurped the Frankish throne for himself and became the first member of the Carolingian family to occupy it. It was Pippin's son Charlemagne who expanded the Frankish realms to embrace most of western Europe.

The Carolingian accounts of Pippin's takeover stress that Pippin III had the consent of his supporters and the approval, if not the actual authority, of the pope for his assumption of the Frankish throne. Thus Einhard in the first chapter of his Life of Charlemagne, written in about 817, comments (I use Paul Dutton's translation):

The family of the Merovingians, from which the Franks used to make their kings, is thought to have lasted down to King Childeric whom Pope Stephen ordered deposed. His long hair was shorn and he was forced into a monastery. Although it might seem that the [Merovingian] family ended with [Childeric III] it had in fact been without any vitality (*vigor*) for a long time and had demonstrated that there was not any worth in it except the empty (*inanis*) name of king. Both the riches and power of the kingdom (*opes et potentia regni*) were in the possession of the prefects of the palace who were called mayors of the palace (*maiores domus*), and to them fell the highest command (*imperium*) . . . Moreover, Pippin, who had been mayor of the palace, was established as king by the decision of the Roman pope and he ruled the Franks by himself for fifteen years or more.[2]

---

[1] For Carloman's role see R. McKitterick, *The Frankish kingdoms under the Carolingians, 751–987* (London, 1983), p. 34.

[2] Einhard, *Vita Karoli*, cc. 1 and 3, ed. O. Holder-Egger, *MGH SRG*, XXV (Hannover, 1911), reprinted R. Rau (ed.), *Quellen zur karolingischen Reichsgeschichte*, I (Darmstadt, 1974), p. 166, trans. Paul E. Dutton, *Charlemagne's courtier. The complete Einhard* (Peterborough, Ontario, 1998), pp. 16 and 18. Note that Dutton's translation in this work differs from that which he provides in *Carolingian civilization. A reader* (Peterborough,

Later commentators reiterated particular elements of the Carolingian accounts. In 1081, for example, Pope Gregory VII drew on Frankish history to reinforce his argument supporting the power of prelates to excommunicate sinful Christians. He described how

another Roman pontiff deposed a king of the Franks not so much on account of his evil deeds as because he was not equal to so great an office, and set in his place Pippin, father of the emperor Charles the Great, releasing all the Franks from the oath of fidelity which they had sworn to him.[3]

To buttress a rather different constitutional position, namely the antiquity of the public council of the nation 'in later times called the assembly of the three estates', François Hotman in his *Francogallia*, published in 1573, addressed the question of whether Pippin was made king by the authority of the pope or by that of the 'Francogallican council'.[4] He offered the view that

when Childeric acquired the kingdom, Pippin, the mayor of the palace who had waged long and great wars in the king's name and had crushed the Saxons, concentrated power in his own hands, and did not let slip the opportunity to seize the royal title, especially since the conquering and glorious army was still in its array.

Hotman then remarked that 'It is appropriate to enquire by whose authority the kingdom was passed onto him'. He quoted with disapproval the very sentence from Pope Gregory VII's letter (which had been incorporated into the *Corpus iuris canonum*, c.3 XC.XV. q 6) and referred also to all the authors thereafter who agreed with Gregory's dictum. In opposition, Hotman cited many commentators.[5] Papal opinion had been

Ontario, 1993), pp. 25–6. On the phrase *ac detonsus atque in monasterium trusus est* see M. de Jong, 'Monastic prisoners or opting out? Political coercion and honour in the Frankish kingdoms', in M. de Jong and F. Theuws, with Carine van Rhijn (eds.), *Topographies of power in the early middle ages*, The Transformation of the Roman World 6 (Leiden, 2001), pp. 291–328, especially pp. 323–6.

[3] Gregory VII, *Registrum* VIII, 21, ed. R. Caspar, *MGH Epp. Sel.* II, 2 (Berlin, 1920), pp. 553–5, trans. E. Emerton, *The correspondence of Pope Gregory VII* (New York, 1932), cited and discussed thoroughly by E. Peters, *The shadow king. Rex inutilis in medieval law and literature 751–1327* (New Haven and London, 1970), pp. 34–47; compare W. Ullmann, *Principles of government and politics in the middle ages*, 2nd edn (London, 1966), p. 68.

[4] D. R. Kelley, *Foundations of modern historical scholarship* (New York and London, 1970); and R. McKitterick, 'The study of Frankish history in France and Germany in the sixteenth and seventeenth centuries', *Francia* 8 (1981), pp. 556–72, reprinted in R. McKitterick, *Frankish kings and culture*, chapter 13.

[5] F. Hotman, *Francogallia* (Geneva, 1573): *Francogallia by François Hotman*, ed. and trans. by R. E. Giesey and J. H. M. Salmon (Cambridge, 1972), pp. 360–2.

received but, as Hotman remarked, this is different from papal authority. Thus,

although Pippin was created king by the Franks after seeking the opinion of the pope, he was not so created by the sovereignty and authority of the pope. For it is one thing to create a king and another to give counsel about creating him.[6]

In his tract *De feudis* Hotman accords Pippin the initiative in persuading Pope Zacharias to depose Childeric and there is no mention of the public council. It might be thought that Hotman was being inconsistent on the pope's role, but it is again the opinion of the pope, not his authority, that is being stressed. Hotman then appealed to a host of authorities, including Marsiglio of Padua, to support his resistance to the idea of papal authority in deposing kings. The pope himself

did not depose the Frankish king but merely agreed with those who did. For such a deposition of a king does not belong to any bishop whatsoever ... but rather to the whole body of citizens living in a particular region or to the whole body of nobles, or the majority of them.[7]

Edward Gibbon, incidentally, preserved the line of argument that the *opinion* of the pope was sought.

An answer so agreeable to their wishes was accepted by the Franks as the opinion of a casuist, the sentence of a judge or the oracle of a prophet; the Merovingian race disappeared from the earth and Pippin was exalted on a buckler by the suffrage of the free people accustomed to obey his laws and march under his standard. His coronation was twice performed with the sanction of the popes.

Medieval and modern commentators on events in Francia in the middle of the eighth century have thus disagreed both about the role of the pope and the nature of Carolingian kingship.[8] Their readings, like those of Einhard, Gregory VII and Hotman, quite obviously are influenced by their own constitutional preoccupations and determination of prerogatives; they serve incidentally to remind us how often history can be drawn on and distorted in new political arguments. Certainly the use of Frankish

---

[6] Hotman, *Francogallia*, pp. 364 and 365.

[7] Marsiglio of Padua, *Defensor pacis*, quoted by Hotman, *Francogallia*, pp. 366–7. Hotman also (p. 368/9) cites a letter which Regino of Prüm included in his Chronicle, *MGH SS* I, p. 556 under the year 753 giving an account of the pope's vision of Saints Peter and Paul and how Stephen had anointed King Pippin and his sons and his wife.

[8] E. Gibbon, *The decline and fall of the Roman empire*, ed. J. B. Bury (London, 1898), V, p. 269. For a comprehensive summary of the voluminous literature see W. Affeldt, 'Untersuchungen zur Königserhebung Pippins. Das Papsttum und die Begründung des karolingischen Königtums im Jahre 751', *Frühmittelalterliche Studien* 14 (1980), pp. 95–187.

history in this respect deserves further investigation.[9] Yet precisely because they were so influential the events of the mid-eighth century merit
closer examination. It is the Huguenot lawyer Hotman who provides the
cue in his warning that caution should be used in reading these records.
'Since it seems likely', he wrote, 'that both Pippin and his sons incurred
much envy for seizing the kingdom from Childeric, they sought out men
of ingenuity *(homines ingeniosi)* to exaggerate the inactivity of Childeric
and the slothfulness of the earlier kings.'[10]

It is with Hotman's *homines ingeniosi* that I shall be concerned in this
chapter. One of them, of course, is Einhard, writing seventy years after
the event and in very different political circumstances. He has been used,
quite incorrectly, as if he were a reliable political commentator on what
happened. But the same criticism might be levelled at the later eighth
century accounts on which all subsequent commentaries, from Einhard
onwards, have depended. The narratives of the political changes of the
eighth century, most notably the *Annales regni francorum* (Royal Frankish
Annals), construct a version of events that all historians ever since, until
recently myself included, have accepted as more or less accurate. I should
affirm at once that I do not doubt that Pippin did become king. What is
in question is that it happened in quite the way, with quite the political
emphases that are described, or that the pope was involved in 751 at all.
In this chapter, therefore, I assess the validity of the claims in the eighth-
century Frankish narrative sources in relation to the attribution of royal
power and the pope's role, and their implications for modern historians'
understanding of Carolingian royal power.[11] Our current understanding
of Carolingian kingship, which in its turn was the foundation for medieval

---

[9] See McKitterick, 'The study of Frankish history', where I made a beginning,
R. McKitterick, 'Gibbon and the early middle ages in eighteenth-century Europe', in R.
McKitterick and R. Quinault (eds.), *Edward Gibbon and empire* (Cambridge, 1997),
pp. 162–89; for the wider context see J. Voss, *Das Mittelalter im historischen Denken
Frankreichs. Untersuchung zur Geschichte des Mittelalterbegriffs und der Mittelalterbewertung
von der zweiten Hälfte des 16. bis zur Mitte des 19. Jahrhunderts* (Munich, 1972).

[10] Hotman, *Francogallia*, pp. 354–5.

[11] For a reassessment of the events of 751, in which the famous anointing of Pippin is also
discussed, see J. Semmler, *Der Dynastiewechsel von 751 und die fränkische Königssalbung*,
Studia humaniora. Düsseldorfer Studien zu Mittelalter und Renaissance, series minor
6 (Düsseldorf, 2003). I omit from consideration the *Annales mettenses priores*, written
c. 806, ed. B. von Simson, *MGH SRG*, X (Hannover and Leipzig, 1905), p. 63. This
account is in any case dependent on the *Annales regni francorum* and presents the 751
takeover and Pippin's becoming king as a brief and indisputable fact: *ex consulto Zachariae
papae Pippinus princeps a Bonifacio archiepiscopus unctus rex francorum constituitur*. A telling
comment is added: *Unde rumor potentiae eius et timor virtutis transiit in universas terras*. On
the *Annales mettenses priores* see Y. Hen, 'The Annals of Metz and the Merovingian past',
in Y. Hen and M. Innes (eds.), *The uses of the past in the early middle ages* (Cambridge,
2000), pp. 175–90.

kingship and an inspiration for subsequent rulers in Europe, ultimately rests on developments in the second half of the eighth century and the historical record of them the Franks created soon thereafter.[12]

The eighth-century evidence

Up until now, the eighth-century evidence, especially for the appeal to the pope in 751, has seemed sufficiently contemporary to historians to inspire confidence. It is curious to equate contemporaneity with truth. In any case this evidence is not even contemporary enough to justify the confidence that is usually placed in it, as we shall see.

The three earliest accounts of Pippin III's usurpation provide the following details:

1. The Continuator to the Chronicle of 'pseudo-Fredegar' tells us that 'with the consent and advice of all the Franks the most excellent Pippin submitted a proposition to the Apostolic see, and having first obtained its sanction... was made king and Bertrada queen'. The text adds that Pippin was elected by all the Franks, received the homage of the great men (*principes*) and consecration at the hands of the bishops.[13]

2. The *Annales regni francorum* in the unrevised version mentioned that Burchard of Würzburg and Fulrad the chaplain were sent as legates to Pope Zacharias, and that they asked him whether it was good that their kings should not have royal power, *non habentes regalem potestatem*, with the satisfactory answer being received that it was better to call him king who had the royal power than he who did not.

Further, so as not to disturb the order of things (*ut non conturbaretur ordo*) the pope ordered that Pippin should be made king (*per auctoritatem apostolicam iussit Pippini regem fieri*).[14] The *Annales regni francorum* author comments further that Pippin was elected king at Soissons[15] according to the custom of the Franks *secundum morem francorum* and that he was anointed by no less a person than Boniface of saintly memory. Childeric, 'falsely called king', was tonsured and sent to a monastery.

---

[12] See J. L. Nelson, 'Kingship and empire in the Carolingian world', in R. McKitterick (ed.), *Carolingian culture: emulation and innovation* (Cambridge, 1994), pp. 52–87.
[13] *Fredegarii Chronicorum liber quartus cum continuationibus*, ed. and trans. J. M. Wallace-Hadrill, *The fourth book of the Chronicle of Fredegar with its Continuations* (London, 1960), Continuations, c. 33, p. 102: *una cum consilio et consensu omnium francorum missa relatione ad sede apostolica, auctoritate praecepta, praecelsus Pippinus electione totius Francorum in sedem regni cum consecratione episcoporum et subiectione principum una cum regina Bertradane, ut antiquitus ordo deposcit, sublimatur in regno.*
[14] *Annales regni francorum*, ed. F. Kurze, *MGH SRG*, VI (Hannover, 1895), *s.a.* 749, p. 8.
[15] See below, p. 152 and n. 70.

3. The *Clausula de unctione Pippini* reiterates this information, namely that 'This most prosperous lord and pious King Pippin had been raised to the throne of the kingdom by the authority and commandment of the lord Pope Zacharias of holy memory, and by unction with the holy chrism at the hands of the blessed priests of Gaul and election by all the Franks'.[16] Its main theme, however, is an account of the re-anointing of Pippin and his family at the hands of Pope Stephen in 754. I shall discuss the significance of this in a moment. In the meantime it should be noted that the *Annales regni francorum* record only that Pope Stephen confirmed Pippin as king and anointed his two sons, Charles and Carloman. The Continuator of Fredegar's *Chronicle* mentions Pope Stephen's visit to Francia in some detail but not the reanointing. Einhard, as noted above, attributed the deposition of Childeric to an order from Pope Stephen.[17]

Before considering the implications of these texts, let me reiterate the current opinion as far as their dating is concerned.

1. **The Continuations to Fredegar's Chronicle**. One manuscript of the Continuations of Fredegar's Chronicle (Rome, BAV, reg. lat. 213, from Rheims s.IX/X) includes after the account of 751 the chapter stating that the section covering the years 751–68 (that is, from after the consecration of Pippin as king) was commissioned by Count Nibelung and that what went before it was commissioned by his father Childebrand, uncle of Pippin.[18] It has been assumed that the first part of the Continuations stopped in 751 (and Childebrand without any other evidence is presumed to have died about then) and that the section commissioned by Nibelung was written after 768. Thus the deposition of Childeric would be a strictly contemporary account. This late ninth-century note, if we accept that it is authentic, is nevertheless susceptible to a different interpretation. There is no reason why the whole text could not have been composed after 768 with the narrative signalling where the author had reached in his text before his first patron was replaced by the second. This is all the text permits us to conclude, for there is no hint either that Childebrand died or that the phrase *usque nunc* with which the note begins necessarily

---

[16] *Clausula de unctione Pippini*, ed. B. Krusch, *MGH SRM*, I (Hannover, 1885), pp. 465–6; trans. B. Pullan, *Sources for the history of medieval Europe from the mid-eighth to the mid-thirteenth century* (Oxford, 1966), pp. 7–8; and see the new edition by A. Stoclet, 'La "Clausula de unctione Pippini regis"', *Francia* 8 (1980), pp. 1–40: *Ipse praedictus domnus florentissimus Pippinus rex pius per auctoritatem et imperium sanctae recordationis domni Zacharie papae et unctionem sancti chrismatis per manus beatorum sacerdotum Galliarum et electionem omnium Franchorum ... in regni solio sublimatus est.*

[17] Einhard, *Vita Karoli*, c. 3, ed. Holder-Egger, p. 166 and trans. Dutton, p. 18.

[18] Fredegar's *Chronicle* and Continuations, ed. Wallace-Hadrill, c. 34, p. 102.

indicates more than a note of where someone had reached in the process of composition. It also functions as a neat literary device both to mark an important change of direction in the fortunes of its chief protagonists and to claim a special relationship and therefore special knowledge of the events and people in the story. The possibility remains, moreover, that this neat literary device was the contribution of the compiler of the Rheims manuscript and has little to do with the original composition. Manuscripts of other historical texts, such as the compilation of Frankish history in Vienna, ÖNB cod. 473, discussed in the previous chapter, inserted directive headings and phrases in the texts.[19]

Neither the language of the Continuations nor the manuscript transmission militates against a later date of composition for the Continuator's narrative. Editors have been divided as to whether there are one, two or three authors responsible for different sections. Monod and Hahn favoured a single author.[20] Roger Collins has also argued the case for single authorship of the Continuations, albeit in two stages, up to 751 and 751–68, linked with the succession of Pippin and of Charles and Carloman respectively.[21] Michael Wallace-Hadrill observed that on stylistic grounds there might be something to be said for single authorship though he maintained that the earlier portion was likely to be a work of the Continuator's youth.[22] It would certainly be possible for someone in later life to have forgotten some of the stylistic and grammatical rules he had learnt at school, though the portion cc. 34–54 is by someone who has forgotten rather a lot. What does seem clear is that the author was, or authors were, too old to have benefited from the Latin reforms associated with the Carolingian renaissance.[23]

All in all, this may not enable us to date the text much later than the 780s and it may have been completed soon after 768. Charter evidence, moreover, suggests a death date for Nibelung before 786 which gives us

---

[19] On this codex see above, chapter 5, below, pp. 121–3, and H. Reimitz, 'Ein fränkisches Geschichtsbuch aus Saint Amand und der Codex Vindobonensis palat. 473', in C. Egger and H. Weigl (eds.), *Text-Schrift-Codex: Quellenkundliche Arbeiten aus dem Institut für Österreichische Geschichtsforschung*, MIÖG Ergänzungsband 35 (Vienna and Munich, 1999), pp. 34–90.

[20] Fredegar's *Chronicle* and Continuations, ed. Wallace-Hadrill, p. xxvii.

[21] R. Collins, *Fredegar*, Authors of the Middle Ages. Historical and Religious Writers of the Latin West 4, no. 13 (Aldershot, 1996), who also stresses the systematic revision and streamlining of the entire Chronicle in the Carolingian period (labelled in the Rome manuscript, BAV reg. lat. 213: *Historia vel gesta francorum*) in order to mark the later inauguration of the new *rex francorum*.

[22] Fredegar's *Chronicle* and Continuations, ed. Wallace-Hadrill, pp. xliii–xlv.

[23] See R. Wright, *Late Latin and early Romance in Spain and Carolingian France* (Liverpool, 1982); R. Wright (ed.), *Latin and the Romance languages in the early middle ages* (London, 1991, and Philadelphia, 1996); and M. Banniard, 'Language and communication in Carolingian Europe', in McKitterick (ed.), *NCMH*, pp. 695–708.

a possible date of between 768 and 786 for the text.[24] The manuscripts offer little assistance. No eighth-century manuscript of the Continuations survives. The earliest extant copies appear to be of the mid- to late ninth century and these are in the context of composite Frankish history books which have, as I reiterate below, a significant effect on the implications and function of the text. It should also be stressed that the Continuations do not provide any precise indication of the dates of events. The course of events has been worked out by comparison with other texts, most notably the *Annales regni francorum* which provide a very precise chronology and a great deal of detail omitted by the Continuators to Fredegar's *Chronicle* (see below). One does wonder why an apparently contemporary author should write so spare an account whereas someone like the *Annales regni francorum* author writing thirty years after the events is able to supply so much; one response, in the light of the comments made in chapter 4 above, might be that he was very inventive and creative.[25] Even so, the sense of security about the contemporaneity and independence of the Continuation of Fredegar's account of the elevation of Pippin to the throne seems to me to be misplaced.

2. *Clausula de unctione Pippini.* The claim of the author of the *Clausula de unctione Pippini* is that he wrote the text in the year of Our Lord 767. Indeed the author expends a remarkable amount of energy in establishing the date, for he notes that it is written in the sixteenth year of Pippin's reign, in the fifth indiction, and in the thirteenth year of the reign of his sons Carloman and Charles. Such according of a regnal year calculation to Charles and Carloman before 768 is anachronistic, for none of Charlemagne's or Carloman's charters dates their reigns back to 754; it is the one point with which none of Max Buchner's critics has dealt satisfactorily.[26] Whatever else has been said about the *Clausula*, this

---

[24] L. Levillain, 'Les Nibelungen historiques et leurs alliances de famille', *Annales du Midi* 49 (1937), pp. 337–407, at p. 343, discussing a property dispute settled in favour of the abbey of St-Germain-des-Prés, ed. R. Poupardin, *Recueil des Chartes de l'abbaye de Saint-Germain-des-Prés*, I (Paris, 1909), no. 22, p. 35.

[25] If the tyranny of a date of composition in 751 is lifted, then my suggestion above, p. 100, that the Continuations were based on the Annals rather than the other way about, gains added support.

[26] See M. Buchner, *Die Clausula de unctione Pippini, eine Fälschung aus dem Jahre 880*, Quellenfälschung aus dem Gebiete der Geschichte 1 (Paderborn, 1926). Buchner's other points are less telling if taken on their own (though equally criticisms of them are not totally conclusive). The accumulation of different dating methods in one clause in *Clausula*, however, has the smack of overkill. Compare L. Levillain, 'De l'authenticité de la *Clausula de unctione Pippini*', *Bibliothèque de l'Ecole des Chartes* 88 (1927) pp. 20–42, but also the phrasing of the salutations in the letters of Pope Stephen II (who was not necessarily an expert on Frankish diplomatic formulae) to Pippin in the *Codex epistolaris carolinus*, ed. W. Gundlach, *MGH Epp.*, III, nos. 6, 7, 9 and 10 where Pippin, Charles and Carloman are all referred to as kings.

dating clause does not ring true and is a serious bar to our accepting the text as a near contemporary account. At best, the dating is a later attempt to add verisimilitude to an already embroidered account of Pope Stephen's visit.[27] At worst the *Clausula* is, as Buchner argued, a completely fabricated piece of propaganda, though whether of the 830s, as Irene Haselbach suggested,[28] or the 880s, which was Buchner's position, is an open choice.[29] It is a context in which the word 'forgery' is not helpful, for the essential basis of the text, Pope Stephen's anointing of Pippin and his sons, undoubtedly took place and to that degree those who have pleaded the case for the text's essential authenticity are correct. The text's purpose is to relate the story of Pope Stephen's anointing of Pippin and it reproduces the Zacharias story to reinforce its effect and provide a plausible and continuous context for the papal involvement in Frankish affairs. Even if indeed written in 767, however, it would still be a fifteen-year old story at the time of writing.

3. *Annales regni francorum*. These were first put together in the late 780s and revised some time after 801 with further entries added in instalments to cover the years to 829.[30] As I demonstrated in chapter 4, the manuscript distribution is remarkably wide across both the whole of the Frankish empire and the ninth century, with five main manuscript

---

[27] The surviving manuscript is Brussels, Bibliothèque royale MS 7666–71, of the late tenth century, where the text is used as a colophon to Gregory of Tours, *De gloria confessorum*. See M. Coens, 'La provenance du MS Bruxelles 7666–71', in J. P. Gumbert and M. J. M. de Haan (eds.), *Litterae textuales. Varia codicologica. Essays presented to G. I. Lieftinck*, I (Amsterdam, 1972), pp. 25–34, who makes the case for a connection between the *Clausula* and St Denis. A possible context for the copying of this account would be St Denis in the time of Hilduin. On Hilduin, see G. Brown, 'Politics and patronage at the abbey of St Denis (814–898). The rise of a royal patron saint' (unpublished D.Phil. dissertation, University of Oxford, 1989). In Stoclet's edition, *Francia* 8 (1980), pp. 1–42, and J. Fleckenstein, 'Clausula de unctione Pippini', in R. Auty and R.-H. Bautier (eds.), *Lexikon des Mittelalters*, II (Munich and Zürich, 1983), col. 2134–5, another manuscript is mentioned which was written between 1130 and 1140 in Zwiefalten. It is now in Stuttgart, Württemburgische Landesbibliothek MS theol. et phil. Fol. 188. In the Stuttgart manuscripts' catalogue the *Clausula* is not mentioned: compare S. von Borries-Schulten, *Die romanischen Handschriften der Württemburgischen Landesbibliothek Stuttgart. Teil 1: Provenienz Zwiefalten* (Stuttgart, 1987), no. 51 (Gregory of Tours, *Vitae sanctorum*), pp. 82–3. Presumably the text of the *Clausula* is at the end of Gregory *Libri VIII miraculorum* (fols. 1v–164r), that is, on fol. 163v or 164v, but I have been unable to ascertain this.
[28] I. Haselbach, *Aufstieg und Herrschaft der Karolinger in der Darstellung der sogenannten Annales Mettenses Priores. Ein Beitrag zur Geschichte des politischen Ideen im Reiche Karls des Grossen*, Historische Studien, 412 (Lübeck, 1970), Exkurs II, pp. 193–200, and compare also her account of 751, pp. 111–18. See also the discussion by T. F. X. Noble, *The republic of St Peter. The birth of the papal state 680–825* (Philadelphia, 1984), pp. 67–71.
[29] See also Affeldt, 'Königserhebung', pp. 103–9.
[30] See above, chapter 4 and H. Hoffmann, *Untersuchungen zur karolingischen Annalistik*, Bonner Historische Forschungen 10 (Bonn, 1958).

families, though unfortunately no original text, in any persuasive sense of the term, survives.

All three texts, therefore, were written at best nearly two decades after the events they describe, and none survives in a manuscript close in date to the proposed dates of composition. Although I have gone into such detail about the dating it is not the most important aspect of the texts. Whether contemporary or written two decades later, what really matters is the overall context in which the Zacharias story is cast, and its implications.

The *Liber pontificalis*

Apart from the very imprecise chronology, there are many significant omissions from the Continuator's account, not least the elevation of King Childeric III in 743 and Pippin's half-brother Grifo's opposition to his rule. Yet there are also details added, such as Carloman supposedly having handed over his kingdom and son Drogo to Pippin[31] and the famous appeal to the pope. But it must be stressed that in the case of the latter the continuator provides no names; he simply reports that Pippin sent an embassy to the pope and obtained his agreement.

It seems curiously haphazard to acknowledge that an author can omit important detail and can add other details on which doubt has been cast, yet accept the most significant detail of the appeal to the sanction of the pope without demur. In a work which is unequivocally supportive of the Carolingian family and especially of Charles Martel and Pippin, one can only surmise that anything to add to the legitimacy of Pippin's position was invoked. The pope is deployed in similar fashion in the *Annales regni francorum* and the *Clausula*, and this time he is named as Zacharias (pope from 3 December 741 to 15 March 752). The annals also identify the legates as Fulrad, abbot of St Denis and Burchard, the Anglo-Saxon bishop of Würzburg, and claim that the bishop who had anointed Pippin in consequence of the papal response was none other than Boniface, the Anglo-Saxon archbishop of Mainz.[32]

There is one other possible witness from the papacy itself, and this is the *Liber pontificalis*. As we have seen in chapter 2, it was first put together c. 530 and revised c. 540. Thereafter, this series of papal biographies was mostly written on a life-by-life basis during or immediately after each pontificate until the late ninth century. In the Life of Zacharias, Life 93, the only reference to Frankish affairs is to the visit of Carloman to Rome

---

[31] Fredegar's *Chronicle* and Continuations ed. Wallace-Hadrill, c. 30, p. 100.
[32] On the unlikelihood of the bishop being Boniface see below, p. 150.

after he had relinquished his secular power. No mention is made of the visit of Burchard of Würzburg and Fulrad to Rome, nor of Zacharias's opinion of Pippin in relation to royal power.[33] The *Liber pontificalis* is otherwise not slow to credit the pope with taking the initiative, as the account of the year 800, to give an obvious example, testifies. Further, there is only one letter from Zacharias on any subject, let alone this one, to the Carolingian mayors of the palace or vice versa in the *Codex epistolaris carolinus*, that is, the collection of papal and Carolingian correspondence compiled in the early ninth century.[34] This is the response from Zacharias in 747 to an earlier request made by 'Pippin, mayor of the palace', and the Frankish bishops and god-fearing *principes in regione francorum* concerning various points of ecclesiastical discipline, canon law and Christian social behaviour. Zacharias's response coincides with Carloman's visit to Rome and it is tempting to surmise that it may have been Carloman himself who took Pippin's request to Rome.[35] The letter from the Franks appears, moreover, to have been the outcome of an assembly rather than an indication of any personal relationship between Pippin and Pope Zacharias.[36] This request for guidance from Pippin and his leading men was of crucial importance for Frankish ecclesiastical policy. It asks the pope to offer advice which was within the compass of the pope's practical ability to exert influence on the church outside Rome and does not offer a precedent for communication on a secular issue.

Perhaps this papal silence about the deposition of 751 is of no great significance, for such a great deal, no doubt, has been lost.[37] I state this as a general observation: we rarely know what has been lost and

[33] *Liber pontificalis*, ed. L. Duchesne, *Le Liber pontificalis*, 2 vols. (Paris, 1886–1892) and see the translation with invaluable commentary by R. Davis, *The book of the pontiffs (Liber pontificalis to 715)* (Liverpool, 1989), *The lives of the eighth-century popes* (Liverpool, 1992) and *The lives of the ninth-century popes* (Liverpool, 1995).

[34] Extant in Vienna, ÖNB cod. 449 in a copy apparently made for Willibert of Cologne, 870–89. Facsimile ed. F. Unterkircher, *Codex epistolaris carolinus*, Codices selecti 3 (Graz, 1962). See the analysis of this collection by B. Coffin, 'The production of the *Codex carolinus* in its historical context' (unpublished M.Phil. essay, University of Cambridge, 2003).

[35] *MGH Epp.* III, pp. 479–87. Note that Zacharias reported having received the request to Boniface, *Die Briefe des heiligen Bonifatius und Lullus*, ed. M. Tangl, *MGH Epp. Sel.*, I (Berlin, 1916), no. 77, p. 160. It was at least on subjects with which Carloman had already associated himself, as we know from the *Concilium germanicum* of 742/3, ed. R. Rau, *Briefe des Bonifatius. Willibalds Leben des Bonifatius nebst einigen zeitgenössischen Dokumenten* (Darmstadt, 1968), pp. 376–83.

[36] For the context and Pippin and his adviser Bishop Chrodegang of Metz's area of operations see Eugen Ewig, 'Saint Chrodegang et la réforme de l'église franque', in *Saint Chrodegang* (Metz, 1967), pp. 25–53 and M. Klaussen, *The reform of the Frankish church: Chrodegang of Metz and the Regula canonicorum in the eighth century* (Cambridge, 2004).

[37] Davis, *Eighth-century popes*, p. 29; Noble, *The republic of St. Peter*, p. 68; and R. Collins, *Charlemagne* (Basingstoke, 1998), p. 35.

merely suppose, perhaps without foundation, that something has. It might appear that Life 93, of Zacharias, in the *Liber pontificalis* is truncated; and Davis suggests that the author 'effectively gave up his task' two years before Zacharias's death. It should be noted that this suggestion stems partly from the fact that Pippin's supposed appeal to the pope is not mentioned. Tom Noble and Roger Collins were also worried about the absence of references to Carolingian contact with Zacharias. Nevertheless, the upshot is that we only have Frankish and specifically later Carolingian sources to vouch for Pippin having made an appeal to Pope Zacharias. That the *Annales regni francorum* include the story, moreover, is entirely in keeping with their general purport. Collins also observes, though without following up the implications, firstly that the early ninth-century Byzantine chronicler Theophanes, possibly dependent on eighth-century diplomatic exchanges, records Pippin's elevation (under the wrong year, viz. for 723/4) and secondly, that it was Pope Stephen who released Pippin from his oath of obedience to Childeric III. This information seems to be concerned with the exchanges between Pippin and the pope which led to the papal anointing of Pippin in 754.[38]

More crucially, what the *Liber pontificalis* does record, in considerable detail, is the association between Pippin and Zacharias's successor, Pope Stephen (Life 94) 26 March 752–26 April 757,[39] and how Stephen crossed the Alps and anointed Pippin and his two sons, 'by Christ's grace, kings of the Franks'.[40] The *Clausula*, as we have seen, affirms this, adds that Stephen also anointed Pippin's wife Bertrada and forbade the Franks ever to choose their kings from any other family.[41] This Franco-papal link is further reinforced in the Life of Paul (Life 95, 29 May 757–28 June 767), Pope Stephen's brother.[42] Visits of Fulrad of St Denis are also recorded in Pope Stephen's Life but not in that of Pope Zacharias.[43] It should be noted that the *Codex epistolaris carolinus* includes six letters

---

[38] R. Collins, *Charlemagne*, p. 35. See C. Mango and R. Scott (trans.), *The Chronicle of Theophanes Confessor. Byzantine and near eastern history AD 284–813* (Oxford, 1997), pp. 556–7, who suggest that the account was based on a western source, perhaps originating in the Greek colony of Rome.

[39] *Liber pontificalis*, ed. Duchesne, pp. 440–56.

[40] *Ibid.*, p. 448. *Sed quia tempus inminebat hyemalis eundem sanctissimum papam cum suis omnibus in Parisio apud venerabilem monasterium beati Dionisii ad exhibernandum pergere rogavit. Quo peracto et eo in eodem venerabile monasterio cum iamfato christianissimo Pippino coniugente, Domino annuente, post aliquantos dies hisdem christianissimus Pippinus rex ab eodem sanctissimo papa, Christi gratia, cum duobus filiis suis reges uncti sunt francorum.*

[41] This element of the story may be more embroidery on the part of the author of the *Clausula*.

[42] *Liber pontificalis*, ed. Duchesne, pp. 463–5.

[43] *Ibid.*, pp. 447, 454, 455. On Fulrad of St Denis see A. Stoclet, *Autour de Fulrad de Saint-Denis (v.710–784)* (Geneva and Paris, 1993).

from Pope Stephen to Pippin and thirty-one from Pope Paul to Pippin. The series starts in 753 and Paul constantly reiterates in his letters the close relationship established between his brother Stephen and Pippin with no allusion to a relationship with Paul and Stephen's predecessor Zacharias at all.

The authenticity of the Zacharias story, therefore, should be reconsidered in the light of the sheer importance of the claim it makes in relation to the attribution of royal power and the pope's role. Why did it apparently suit the Carolingians to invoke papal authority in this way? Why is an appeal to Pope Zacharias incorporated into the narratives? Frankish respect for papal spiritual authority in the eighth century in ecclesiastical and doctrinal matters is well documented. But this apparent invocation of effective *secular* power of the pope needs to be accounted for more comprehensively than the partial explanation usually offered, namely, that the pope was appealed to as an outside moral authority.[44]

In the next section of this chapter, I should like to suggest that a possible context and explanation for the creation of the Zacharias story is to be found precisely within the recorded events of the next three years and the apparent role of Pope Stephen of Rome in the support of Carolingian royal power. I have no intention of discussing the whys and wherefores of the usurpation itself, nor of the events at Ponthion or Quierzy and the so-called Donation of Pippin. All these have been exhaustively discussed elsewhere.[45] What concerns me is the construction of the narrative of these years and how the Pope, and thus St Peter, are implicated in the presentation and legitimation of royal power.

Pope Stephen II (III) and the Franks

In order to understand the Zacharias story, therefore, we need to focus on Pope Stephen II (III) and his relationship with Pippin. Stephen's visit across the Alps was unprecedented, and the support he sought from the Lombards is well attested. Life 94 of Stephen II (III) in the *Liber pontificalis* constitutes an extraordinary piece of justification for Frankish attitudes to the Lombards and their support of the papacy against the Lombards and a remarkable emphasis on the role of the *christianissimus* Pippin. The objection might be made that the *Liber pontificalis* is a papal source but two points need to be made in this respect. In the first place, as we saw earlier, the manuscript transmission of the *Liber pontificalis*, even of the

---

[44] McKitterick, *Frankish kingdoms*, p. 35; Noble, *The republic of St. Peter*, p. 70.
[45] See Affeldt, 'Königserhebung' and Noble, *The republic of St. Peter* for judicious summaries of the various issues and the copious literature on them.

so-called Lombard recension, is almost exclusively Frankish. Further, the most influential and widely circulated version of the *Liber pontificalis* is the Frankish recension or 'B' and 'D' groups of manuscripts.[46] This Frankish recension is the one copied into a number of important compilations of Frankish historical texts. In one of these, Vienna, ÖNB cod. 473, the history of the popes in the eighth century is deployed as an adjunct to, and historical context for, that of the Franks.[47] It serves to reinforce the associations of the Carolingians and the Franks with Rome and papal authority, and provides essential justification of the Frankish conquest of Italy. It incorporates, as I have stressed above, substantial additions, notably in the lives of the eighth-century Popes Gregory III and Stephen II (III), which are pertinent to Frankish affairs or which offer a Frankish dimension to papal affairs.

One of the most significant additions to the *Liber pontificalis* in the Frankish recensions is at the end of Life 94. It starts with an account of Pope Stephen's apparent restoration of the canopy of the atrium of St Peter's and proceeds, in Davis's translation, as follows:

> also close to St Peter's and on the other side of St Andrew's in the place called the Mausoleum, he made a basilica in honour of St Petronilla – in Francia he had promised the kindly king Pippin that it was there he would place St Petronilla's body; and there he put many silver canisters and many other adornments that he dedicated.[48]

This Frankish version, therefore, establishes a crucial link not only with the Popes but also with St Peter, via St Peter's supposed daughter, Petronilla. Petronilla was celebrated as a martyr, and in the early middle ages was acknowledged as the daughter of St Peter as a result of a misunderstanding. Her sarcophagus had been in the cemeterial basilica of Nereus and Achilleus in the catacomb of Domitilla, dedicated to her and restored by Pope John I (523–6). Gregory III appears to have instituted her feast (31 May) and an annual *statio* for Petronilla herself at the cemetery.[49] It was Pope Paul I, Stephen II (III)'s successor, however, who brought Petronilla's relics to the basilica of St Peter in 757. Again it is

---

[46] *Liber pontificalis*, ed. Duchesne, pp. clxiv–ccxxx and Davis, *Eighth-century popes*, pp. xv–xviii, discuss the manuscripts, the latter in summary form.

[47] See chapter 5 above and Reimitz, 'Ein fränkisches Geschichtsbuch'.

[48] Davis, *Eighth-century popes*, p. 76; and *Liber pontificalis*, ed. Duchesne, XCIII, cc. 51–3, pp. 455–6; *Fecit autem et iuxta basilicam beati petri apostoli et ab alia parte beati Andreae apostoli, in loco qui mosileus appellabatur, basilicam in honore sanctae Petronillae, quae praedicto benignissimo Pippino rege in francia spoponderat ut beatae Petronillae corpus ibidem conlocaret, ubi posuit canistra argentea multa et ornamenta alia plura quae dedicavit.*

[49] Davis, *Eighth-century popes*, p. 25; and *Liber pontificalis*, ed. Duchesne, XCII, c. 13, p. 420.

the Frankish recension of the *Liber pontificalis* which provides the relevant details:

To fulfil his elder brother and holy predecessor pope Stephen's advantageous arrangements, immediately the pontiff had died, this blessed pontiff gathered the sacerdotes, the whole clergy and this city of Rome's entire people, and began operations at the cemetery outside the Appian gate some two miles from Rome where St Petronilla had once been buried. From there he removed her venerable and holy body along with the marble sarcophagus in which it lay and on which were carved letters reading 'To Aurea Petronilla, sweetest daughter'. This made it certain that the carving of the letters could be identified as engraved by St Peter's own hand out of love for his sweetest child. The holy body and the sarcophagus were laid on a new carriage and brought by his Beatitude (sic) with hymns and spiritual chants to St Peter's; he placed the holy body in the mausoleum close to St Andrew's, whose dedication in honour of this St Petronilla, Christ's martyr, had been decreed by his brother the holy pope Stephen while yet living. There he made an adequate provision of adornment in gold, silver and brocades; he restored the church itself and in St Petronilla's honour he embellished it with wondrously beautiful pictures.[50]

Petronilla appears at this stage to have been adopted as the special saint of the Carolingian royal family and her commemoration was rapidly incorporated into the litanies of the Frankish liturgy.[51] The day chosen for

[50] Davis, *Eighth-century popes*, p. 81; and *Liber pontificalis*, ed. Duchesne, p. 464. *Hic namque beatissimus pontifex praefati sui senioris germani et praedecessoris pontificis sanctissimi Stephani papae salutifera adimplens praecepta, continuo post eius decessum aggregans sacerdotes et universum clerum atque cunctum populum istius Romanae urbis, operansque in cymiterium ubi prius beata Petronilla sita quiescebat, foris porta appia, miliario ab urbe Roma, plus minus secundo, exinde eius venerabile ac sanctum corpus cum sarcofago marmoreo in quo reconditum inerat abstulit, sculptum litteris eodem sarcofago legente: Aureae Petronillae filiae dulcissimae. Unde non dubium est quia sculptura illa litterarum propria beati Petri apostoli manu designata esse dinosci ob amore suae dulcissimae natae. Eundemque sanctum corpus cum praefato sarcofago inposito super plaustrum novum in ecclesia beati Petri apostoli cum hymnis et canticis spiritalibus eius beatitudo deportavit et in musuleo illo iuxta ecclesiam beati Andreae apostoli, quem prefatus beatissimus Stephanus papa eius germanus, dum adhuc superstes erat, ecclesia in honore ipsius sanctae Christi martyris Petronillae fieri decreverat, ipsum sanctum collocavit corpus. Ubi et ornatum tam in aurum et argentum atque palleis sufficienter tribuit; eandemque ecclesiam restaurans ad honorem sanctae Petronillae picturis miro decore inlustravit.* In fact as Davis points out, p. 81, n.6, the inscription actually read AVR. PETRONILLAE FILIAE DULCISSIMAE, that is, Aureliae, and Aurelia Petronilla was therefore an unknown member of the Aurelian family and not a martyr at all, let alone the daughter of St Peter. It has been conjectured that the paintings referred to were those described in 1458 which depicted the story of Constantine: see Davis, *Eighth-century popes*, p. 81, n. 6.

[51] Thus Paris, BnF lat. 13159; and see also the description in *CLA*, V (Oxford, 1950) no. 652, and comments by Bernhard Bischoff, 'Panorama der Handschriftenüberlieferung aus der Zeit Karls des Grossen', *Mittelalterliche Studien* 3 (Stuttgart, 1981), pp. 5–38, at p. 14 and compare the English translation by M. Gorman, 'Manuscripts in the age of Charlemagne', in B. Bischoff, *Manuscripts and libraries in the age of Charlemagne* (Cambridge, 1994) p. 29; M. Coens, 'Les Litanies carolines de

the dedication of her new shrine, 9 October, was also that of another patron of the Carolingian family, St Denis, and incidentally is the day in 768 on which Charlemagne and Carloman started their reigns.[52] It was at the monastery of St Denis that Pippin had been educated. Petronilla was closely associated in the spiritual bond of *compater*, that is the bond between spiritual and actual parents in godparenthood, established between the new Frankish king and Pope Stephen from 754 and reinforced thereafter, which Arnold Angenendt has elucidated.[53] Letters record that Pope Paul, godfather of Gisela and therefore also *compater* of Pippin, received the shawl used at Charlemagne's sister Gisela's baptism in 757 and used it for the altar in Petronilla's shrine; the shrine became a *memoria aeterna* for the king.[54] Paul's pontificate also saw the honouring of another arrangement made between Pippin and Pope Stephen, namely Pippin's donation of an altar to St Peter himself.[55]

It is in this context that the promotion in Frankish Gaul by Pippin of what was claimed to be Roman liturgical chant is to be understood. Stephen's retinue in 754 may have included members of his *scola cantorum* to enable him to celebrate mass in the papal manner. The *Liber pontificalis* records them singing hymns and spiritual chants and Walafrid Strabo, writing nearly a century later, preserves a memory of 'when Pope Stephen came into Francia to Pippin, Emperor Charles the Great's father, to seek justice for St Peter against the Lombards, his clergy brought the more perfect knowledge of plain-chant (*cantilena*) which almost all Francia now loves, to Pippin at his request. From that time onward its use was validated

Soissons et du Psautier de Charlemagne', *Recueil d'études bollandiennes*, Subsidia Hagiographica 37 (Brussels, 1963), p. 297; F. Masai, 'Observations sur le Psautier dit de Charlemagne', *Scriptorium* 6 (1952), pp. 299–303; and E. H. Kantorowicz, *Laudes regiae: a study in liturgical acclamations and medieval ruler worship* (Berkeley, Calif., 1946), pp. 31–53. This is also the codex containing the fragmentary tonary of St Riquier which is 'the first known use of the system of the eight tones – a means of classifying chants according to their melodic characteristics rather than their liturgical function'. See J. Bellingham's exposition of 'Music and the Carolingian church *c*. 750–*c*. 850', in 'Musical thought in antiquity and in the medieval west to the end of the Carolingian era' (unpublished D.Phil. thesis, University of Oxford, 1998), chapter 4, p. 1 and n. 3. My comments on the liturgy and Pippin have benefited greatly from her analysis. See also the brief comment, unfortunately without taking recent work in English into account, in R. Schieffer, 'Charlemagne and Rome', in J. M. H. Smith (ed.), *Early medieval Rome and the Christian west. Essays in honour of Donald Bullough* (Leiden, 2000), pp. 279–96, at pp. 287–8.

[52] A point made by U. Nonn, 'Zur Königserhebung Karls und Karlmanns', *Rheinische Vierteljahrsblätter* 39 (1975), pp. 386–7.

[53] A. Angenendt, 'Das geistliche Bündnis der Päpste mit den Karolingern (754–796)', *Historisches Jahrbuch* 100 (1980), pp. 1–94. On the importance generally of the godparenthood relationship in early medieval society see J. H. Lynch, *Godparents and kinship in early medieval Europe* (Princeton, 1986).

[54] *MGH Epp.*, III, *Codex epistolaris carolinus*, no. 14, p. 511.

[55] *Ibid.*, no. 21, pp. 522–4.

far and wide'.[56] Chrodegang of Metz is described by Paul the Deacon in *c.* 783 as having introduced Roman chant to Metz, and Remedius, bishop of Rouen (757–68), sent men to Rome to learn Roman chant.[57] Pippin himself is credited by Walafrid Strabo and others with the initiation of Roman 'reforms'. Pope Paul I sent Pippin copies of Roman liturgical books, namely an Antiphonary and Responsory,[58] and Pippin has been linked with the production of the so-called eighth-century Gelasian Mass book.[59]

Pippin III's connection with the pope in Rome, therefore, was not with Zacharias, but with Zacharias' successor Stephen. It came about as a result of Stephen's seeking Frankish assistance against the Lombards. Stephen's visit to Francia enabled him to forge a special relationship with a no-doubt-willing fledgling Frankish ruler by means of the papal anointing of Pippin and his sons and the rituals of papal blessing at the Carolingian abbey of St Denis. One of the Frankish magnates who escorted the pope from the monastery of St Maurice d'Agaune near the Alps was no less a person than Fulrad, abbot of St Denis. Pippin also became the protector of the papacy and was accorded the title *patricius* (about which there has been much debate). He was apparently presented with two purple porphyry columns by the pope as a further indication of his status.[60] Pippin thus entered into a political and secular relationship with the papacy, whose political advantages and disadvantages could

---

[56] *Liber pontificalis*, ed. Duchesne, pp. 446–7; and compare Walafrid Strabo, *Walafrid Strabo's Libellus de exordiis et incrementis quarundam in observationibus ecclesiasticis rerum. A translation and liturgical commentary*, ed. A. L. Harting-Correa (Leiden, 1996) c. 26, p. 168 and translation p. 169.

[57] Chrodegang, *Gesta episcoporum mettensium*, ed. G. Pertz, MGH SS, II, pp. 260–70, at p. 268; and Paul I to Pippin, *MGH Epp.*, III, *Codex epistolaris carolinus*, no. 41, pp. 553–4. On liturgy and chant see Cyril Vogel, 'Saint Chrodegang et les débuts de la romanisation du culte en pays franc', in *Saint Chrodegang* (Metz, 1967), pp. 91–109, Susan Rankin, 'Carolingian Music', in R. McKitterick (ed.) *Carolingian culture: emulation and innovation* (Cambridge, 1994), pp. 274–316, esp. 275–6; K. Levy, *Gregorian chant and the Carolingians* (Princeton, 1998); my review in *Early Music History* 19 (2000), pp. 279–90; and P. Bernard, *Du chant romain au chant grégorien (IVe–XIIIe siècle)* (Paris, 1996).

[58] *MGH Epp.*, III, no. 24, p. 529.

[59] See R. McKitterick, *The Frankish church and the Carolingian reforms, 789–987*, Royal Historical Society, Studies in History 2 (London, 1977), pp. 125–6; B. Moreton, *The eighth-century Gelasian Sacramentary. A study in tradition* (Oxford, 1976); C. Vogel, *Medieval Liturgy. An introduction to the sources*, revised edition and translation of the 1981 edition, by N. K. Rasmussen and W. G. Storey (Washington, D.C., 1986); Y. Hen, *Culture and religion in Merovingian Gaul, AD 481–751*, Culture, Beliefs and Tradition. Medieval and Early Modern Peoples 1 (Leiden, 1995); and *idem, The royal patronage of liturgy in Frankish Gaul to the death of Charles the Bald (877)*, HBS Subsidia 3 (London, 2001).

[60] See Noble's summary, *The republic of St. Peter*, pp. 278–80; and Angenendt, 'Das geistliche Bündnis', p. 40. The porphyry columns 'of St Peter and St Paul' are now in Paris, Musée du Louvre, Département des sculptures, inv. nos. MR 1078–1079.

hardly have been seen from anything other than a short-term perspective at the time. But Pippin's interest in Rome was also strongly religious. He formed a spiritual relationship with the Pope and with St Peter, and it is this special bond which consequently becomes such a crucial part of Carolingian political ideology. The Carolingian king was above all a Christian king. He acted as a Christian monarch was to act thereafter in the name of a higher, divine, authority.

The *Vita Stephani* in the *Liber pontificalis*, of course, is no less of a creative narrative than the other texts with which I have been concerned. Its importance lies not only in its portrayal of the formation of the bond between the Frankish ruler and the pope but also in its contribution to the collective memory of the Franks;[61] it did much to determine the Frankish construction of the events of 751–4 and was crucial for the three texts I discussed earlier. The strong association between Pope Stephen and Pippin, expressed in the anointing and the adoption as *auxiliatrix* of St Petronilla, could be extrapolated backwards to provide the Carolingians with still further unanswerable support for their actual usurpation in 751. Pope Zacharias, portrayed in the *Liber pontificalis* as so successful in dealing with the Lombards, who were subsequently conquered by the Franks, could thereby be accorded a role as well. The *Annales regni francorum*'s implausible allocation of the 751 anointing to Boniface may have been intended to corroborate the Zacharias connection, for Boniface and Zacharias can be associated in other sources.[62] Boniface's very limited contacts with Pippin were not notably cordial, as is attested in Boniface's letters. In one, dated 752, Boniface asks Fulrad, abbot of St Denis, to intercede for him with Pippin on behalf of Boniface's Anglo-Saxon brethren and in the second, dated 753, Boniface asks Pippin's permission to attend an assembly. These are hardly letters from a leading bishop who has just performed a vital anointing of a new king.[63] It was in any case Carloman who was Boniface's patron and Bishop Chrodegang of Metz who was Pippin's ecclesiastical adviser;[64] it is much more likely to have been Chrodegang, and conceivably some of his fellow Frankish bishops, who crowned Pippin. The Continuator of Fredegar and the *Clausula* both refer merely to the consecration of Pippin by Frankish bishops.

---

[61] See McKitterick, *Migration*.

[62] See T. Reuter, 'Saint Boniface and Europe', in T. Reuter (ed.), *The greatest Englishman* (Exeter, 1980), pp. 69–94; but see my discounting of Boniface's role in the 751 anointing in McKitterick, *Frankish kingdoms*, p. 40, n. 49.

[63] *Briefe des heiligen Bonifatius*, ed. Tangl, nos. 93 and 107, pp. 212–13 and 232–3. Pope Zacharias' role in Frankish history merits fuller investigation. I am very grateful to Mayke de Jong for comments on Zacharias, in relation to her own work on purity and *correctio* in the Frankish world.

[64] On Chrodegang's career see the essays in *Saint Chrodegang* (Metz, 1967) and Klaussen, *Chrodegang of Metz*.

Carolingian kingship

Pippin's apologists of the later eighth century, therefore, created a very particular understanding of the making and early years of Carolingian royal power. How the Continuator of Fredegar portrayed Pippin's reign must be left for another occasion (and in any case it was not nearly so influential as the *Annales regni francorum*). With the entire narrative organised according to the Christian era,[65] the Royal Frankish annalist's account of Pippin's reign, on the other hand, was the essential prelude to the narrative of the early reign of Charlemagne. Not only is Pippin's right to rule as heir of Charles Martel established by omitting all reference to the Merovingian rulers and diverting Carloman to the religious life. Pippin is also presented most positively supporting and honouring his brother. He does not even conduct a campaign that year in order better to prepare for Carloman's departure. Yet Pippin's triumphal partnership with the Franks as a *gens* of great military might is one of the strongest themes of Carolingian kingship. Pippin and Carloman had together fought Bavarians, Saxons and Aquitainians. After Carloman's departure it is the Franks with whom Pippin defeats their enemies.

The events between 749 and 754 were apparently obscure to the annalist, for these years spread the usurpation and its lessons thinly. It is significant that there is no entry at all for two years of this period, the usurpation itself also covers the entries for two years, and the visit of Pope Stephen a further two.[66] Research in the past two decades or so, however, has helped us to understand far more about the tensions and opposing political factions in the eighth-century world of the Franks and their neighbours, and thus to guess at some of the difficulties the annalist arguably deliberately ignored.[67] There are six years effectively unaccounted for in the *Annales regni francorum* or any other narrative source during which Pippin had made himself king and had had conceivably to deal with resistance or opposition on a scale similar to that encountered by his father Charles Martel between 714 and 718.[68] As Collins has commented, the risky move of deposing Childeric III while still engaged in

---

[65] See p. 16 and chapter 4 above.   [66] *Annales regni francorum*, ed. Kurze, pp. 8–13.
[67] See M. Becher, *Eid und Herrschaft. Untersuchungen zum Herrscherethos Karls des Großen*, Vorträge und Forschungen, Sonderband 39 (Sigmaringen, 1993); Affeldt, 'Königserhebung'; C. Willsdorf, 'Le Monasterium scottorum Ettonau et la famille des ducs d'Alsace au VIIIe siècle. Vestiges d'un cartulaire perdu', *Francia* 3 (1975), pp. 1–87; K. Brunner, *Oppositionelle Gruppen im Karolingerreich* (Vienna, 1979); I. Wood, *The Merovingian Kingdoms, 450–751* (London, 1994); P. Fouracre, 'Frankish Gaul to 814', in McKitterick (ed.), *NCMH*, pp. 85–109.
[68] J. Jarnut, U. Nonn and M. Richter (eds.), *Karl Martell in seiner Zeit*, Beihefte der Francia 37 (Sigmaringen, 1994).

trying to quell the political ambitions of his half-brother Grifo and of his nephew Tassilo, may have been an attempt further to enhance Pippin's position in a period of great conflict.[69] But of all this the original annalist gives no hint. The clever choice of Soissons for Pippin's election, or the annalist's placing of the election at Soissons, moreover, made a strong political point. Soissons had been the rural palace *par excellence* of the last Merovingians and Clovis had made Soissons a principal residence after his defeat of the Aegidii. In the use of Soissons there may be here reflected a knowledge of Gregory of Tours' *Historiae* and the prominence he accords Soissons in Clovis's career and that of his successors.[70]

Again, the reference to particular legates – Fulrad a leading abbot of a Neustrian abbey and Burchard, an Anglo-Saxon with connections with the royal convents of Jouarre and Chelles who might have been counted as an Austrasian representative – may be the annalist's device to symbolize sufficient Neustrian and Austrasian agreement in Pippin's seizure of the royal title and everything that went with it. It must be admitted that too little is known about Burchard to make Stoclet's suggestion of his representative status very compelling. On the other hand, the pairing of Burchard with Fulrad should at least give us pause as a possible crucial indication of his status that is otherwise obscure. Burchard may well have been among the supporters of Pippin and someone who was resistant to Boniface's influence in Franconia and Hesse.[71]

The annalist is careful to provide the inspired juxtaposition of the impossibility of a real king wielding no royal power and how it was better to

[69] Collins, *Charlemagne*, p. 34.

[70] See R. A. Gerberding, *The rise of the Carolingians and the Liber historiae francorum* (Oxford, 1987), pp. 150–1 on Soissons in the eighth century, and for details about its importance to the Merovingians see C. Brühl, *Palatium und Civitas I: Gallien* (Cologne, 1975), R. Kaiser, *Untersuchungen zur Geschichte der Civitas und Diözese Soissons in römischer und merowingischer Zeit*, Rheinisches Archiv 89 (Bonn, 1973); and E. Ewig, 'Résidence et capitale pendant le haut moyen-âge', *Revue Historique* 230 (1963), pp. 25–72, reprinted in E. Ewig, *Spätantikes und fränkisches Gallien*, I (Munich, 1976), pp. 362–408. See also K. Hauck, 'Von einer spätantiken Randkultur zum karolingischen Europa', *Frühmittelalterliche Studien* 1 (1967), pp. 3–93. On the Carolingian knowledge of Gregory of Tours see P. Bourgain and M. Heinzelmann, 'L'Œuvre de Grégoire de Tours: la diffusion des manuscrits', in N. Gauthier and H. Galinié (eds.) *Grégoire de Tours et l'espace gaulois. Actes du congrès international Tours, 2–5 novembre 1994*, 13e Supplément à la *Revue Archéologique du Centre de la France* (Tours, 1997), pp. 273–318; M. Sot, 'Les dix livres d'Histoire chez les écrivains carolingiens', *ibid.*, pp. 319–30; and H. Reimitz, 'Social networks and identities in Frankish historiography. New aspects of the textual history of Gregory of Tours' Historiae', in R. Corradini, M. Diesenberger and H. Reimitz (eds.), *The construction of communities in the early middle ages: texts, resources and artefacts* The Transformation of the Roman World 12 (Leiden, 2003), pp. 229–68.

[71] See Stoclet's discussion, *Autour de Fulrad de Saint-Denis*, pp. 454–62. On Fulrad's role see also J. M.Wallace-Hadrill, *The long haired kings and other studies in Frankish history* (London, 1962), p. 242.

call him king who had the royal power than he who did not. This was the annalist's claim for Pippin, buttressed in the context of military success, ecclesiastical blessing, papal approval and the consent, by election, of the Franks. The narrative consolidates this position by augmenting Pippin's actions with other indications of his status. There are his dealings with Aistulf, king of the Lombards, who is every bit as villainous in the *Annales regni francorum* as he is in the Frankish recension of the *Liber pontificalis*. There is Pippin's receipt of fine presents, including the imperial gift of an organ, from the Byzantine emperor.[72] There is the preparation for the Carolingian annexation of Bavaria with the account in 757 of the commendation of Tassilo of Bavaria and his magnates to Pippin and Tassilo's subsequent repudiation of the oath in 763.[73] There are the initial campaigns in Saxony. There is the steady battering of the Aquitainians, already, in 761, with Pippin's son Charles at his side. There is the council at Gentilly in 767 on images. All these – Tassilo and the Bavarians, the Saxons, the Aquitainians and the image question – culminate triumphantly in Charlemagne's reign. Charlemagne proves himself the mighty successor to his father, justifying the holding both of his royal title and royal power.

To its earliest audience in the late 780s all this was presumably heady stuff. The annalist was singlemindedly presenting every amount of persuasion possible about Pippin's position, that of his son Charles, and of the Franks who had acquiesced in Carolingian rule.[74] Pippin's special relationship with the pope in the spiritual and ecclesiastical sphere provided the ideal context. We should therefore treat the narrative of Pippin's takeover and his early establishment of royal power as the political and ideological creation it was. It may have been a fiction of power yet it was, as the ideologues quoted at the beginning of this chapter indicate, a powerful and influential fiction.

The Reviser of the *Annales regni francorum*, who augmented, amended and often rewrote the text, allows us to observe the reception and augmentation of this clever construction of the past, probably during the early part of the reign of Louis the Pious. There is more inserted about family opposition to Pippin's rule from Grifo, supporters of Carloman and others

---

[72] On the importance of the organ see J. Herrin, 'Constantinople, Rome and the Franks in the seventh and eighth centuries', in J. Shepard and S. Franklin (eds.), *Byzantine diplomacy* (Aldershot, 1992), pp. 91–108; and P. Williams, *The organ in western culture, 750–1250*, Cambridge Studies in Medieval and Renaissance Music (Cambridge, 1993), pp. 137–42.

[73] For full discussion see Becher, *Eid und Herrschaft*, and the critique of Becher offered by P. Depreux, 'Tassilon III et le roi des Francs: examen d'une vassalité controversée', *Revue Historique* 593 (1995), pp. 23–73. See also above, pp. 3–5.

[74] See above, chapter 5.

and indications provided of the subsequent greatness of Charlemagne in succession to Pippin.[75] The earlier version notes that Charles, first born son of Pippin, accompanied his father on campaign. The reviser adds that Charles had supreme rule over the whole empire after his father's death: *In hac expeditione fuit cum rege filius eius primogenitus Karlus, ad quem post patris obitum totius imperii summa conversa est.* Essentially, however, the portrait of Pippin and the representation of Carolingian royal power remains as persuasive as in the earlier version.

As I have suggested in the two previous chapters, the annalist's presentation of the past formed a crucial element in the collective memory of the newly formed realm under Frankish and Carolingian rule and constitutes a vital element in the self-perception of the Carolingian secular and ecclesiastical elites. The manuscript evidence altogether witnesses to a remarkably wide dissemination of the annalist's version of the past. Yet one of the greatest problems in assessing the history of the Franks in the second half of the eighth century is that our evaluation rests, in relation to the narrative sources, on texts which, although dated to before 800, survive almost entirely in manuscripts written considerably after that date, with a concentration during the period of rule of Charlemagne's grandsons Charles the Bald, Lothar and Louis the German. They thus represent a major and widespread effort to transmit a particular political message, not only at the time of composition but also in the mid- and later ninth century, most notably about Frankish rule and the Carolingian kings. They mirror an extraordinarily focused sense of the past which is of the utmost importance in any assessment of the strength, perceived or real, of Carolingian royal power at that time.

Our understanding of Carolingian royal power and its practical manifestations is a skilful creation of a few individuals on the winning side, designed at a later stage not only to convince posterity but, more importantly, contemporaries, of the inevitability of Carolingian and Frankish success. It is also necessary to consider the commitment of these individuals to the support of monarchy at all. It is self-evident that a very different picture of royal power emerges from the narrative sources and from the material evidence, such as the coinage and royal palaces,[76] from

---

[75] *Annales regni francorum*, ed. Kurze, s.a. 761, pp. 18–21. For further comments on the Reviser see R. Collins, 'The "Reviser" revisited: another look at the alternative version of the *Annales regni francorum*', in A. C. Murray (ed.), *After Rome's fall: narrators and sources of early medieval history. Essays presented to Walter Goffart* (Toronto, 1998), pp. 191–213.

[76] Still the best guide to the coinage of the early Carolingian rulers is P. Grierson and M. Blackburn, *Medieval European coinage, I, The early middle ages (5th–10th centuries)* (Cambridge, 1986), pp. 190–210. On the palaces see the useful summary by G. Binding, *Deutsche Königspfalzen von Karl dem Grossen bis Friedrich II (765–1240)* (Darmstadt, 1996), and his references.

that which is expressed in the Capitularies and charters, not least in the areas of Frankish royal activity which the annals simply do not mention.[77] A variety of early medieval genres are bound, of course, to give different impressions about a particular subject. Each no doubt is valid in its own terms and forms part of the total picture (insofar as a 'total' picture can be reconstructed) that we try to piece together and understand. But there is a risk that we may forget the first twenty years of the construction of Carolingian royal power in both textual and actual terms and the extent to which our appraisal of Carolingian rulership is based on sources designed to persuade us that Carolingan kingship was fully formed in 751. That it was then so formed is, however, an illusion.

My examination of the creation of a particular image of royal and Frankish power has been based on the premise that the writing of recent history in the Frankish world was not simply a matter of an observer recording, or even selecting judiciously, disingenuously or with deliberate intent to mislead, from events as they happened. We also need to register the formation of an historical sensitivity by means of the other texts a particular author of an historiographical work might have encountered. The texts reflect the formation of a collective memory, understanding and interpretation of what had happened. These two themes are addressed in detail in the remaining chapters of this book.[78]

---

[77] See J. Davis, 'Conceptions of kingship under Charlemagne' (unpublished M.Litt. dissertation, University of Cambridge, 1999); and J. Davis, 'The conception of kingship in Charlemagne's capitularies' (unpublished undergraduate thesis, Harvard University, 1997); and on Carolingian kingship generally J. L. Nelson, 'Kingship and royal government', in McKitterick (ed.), *NCMH*, pp. 383–430, and her references.

[78] Earlier versions of this chapter were presented to the Colloquium 'Herrschaft und Integration im Frühmittelalter' in Vienna in March, 1998 and to the Anglo-American conference on 'Monarchy' at the Institute of Historical Research in London in July 1998. I am particularly grateful to my respective hosts, Walter Pohl and David Cannadine, for their invitations to speak, to my audiences, especially Jinty Nelson, Matthew Innes, Chris Wickham and Mayke de Jong, for their questions and comments, and to John Maddicott and the anonymous referee of *EHR*, in which the earlier version of this chapter was published, for their helpful suggestions as well as to the useful points made by the translators of the German version, Helmut Reimitz and Peter Erhart.

7 Social memory, commemoration and the book

In this chapter I shall explore the theme of history and memory by looking at two further kinds of book created in the Carolingian period. The first of these is the cartulary. Cartularies are generally regarded as straightforward collections of the legal records and rights to property of a religious foundation. They survive in great abundance from the eleventh and twelfth centuries from all over Europe and incorporate copies of older documents which were then for the most part discarded. Recent work such as that of Barbara Rosenwein and Constance Brittan Bouchard, however, has established that the charters also record the social bonds created between the donors (for the most part members of the local community) and the monastery or local church.[1] Further, Patrick Geary has noted how the exchanges of property recorded in the cartularies both altered and clarified relationships among the living and the bonds with the dead; they created an image of social stability in which the church was involved. Cartularies, therefore, had a commemorative and liturgical as well as legal function.[2]

The second type of book is the confraternity book, also known as a *Liber vitae* or *Liber memorialis*. This listed names of the living and the dead to be prayed for in a number of institutions. Study of these remarkable books, notably by the 'Freiburg school', has made them yield evidence touching on the history, structure and kinship of local families, the personnel of monasteries in the Frankish realms and the network of spiritual and written communications between them.[3] The entries witness

---

[1] B. Rosenwein, *To be the neighbor of St Peter. The social meaning of Cluny's property, 909–1049* (Ithaca and London, 1989); C. B. Bouchard, *Sword, miter and cloister. Nobility and the church in Burgundy, 980–1198* (Ithaca and London, 1987).

[2] P. J. Geary, *Phantoms of remembrance: memory and oblivion at the end of the first millennium* (Princeton, 1994).

[3] The fundamental studies are those of G. Tellenbach, 'Liturgische Gedenkbücher als historische Quelle', *Mélanges E. Tisserant* V, Studi e testi 235 (Rome, Vatican City, 1964), pp. 389–99, and 'Der Liber Memorialis von Remiremont. Zur kritische Erforschung und zum Quellenwert liturgische Gedenkbücher', *DA* 25 (1969), pp. 64–110; and K. Schmid, 'Über das Verhältnis von Person und Gemeinschaft im früheren Mittelalter',

to connections stretching across Europe as well as local bonds. Further, strong links were created between the living and the dead by means of such organised commemorative prayer. Commemoration was designed to incorporate the souls of the dead into the community of the blessed in the other world and the *Libri vitae* therefore also witness to the creation of a liturgical community on earth.[4]

Interpretations of these two kinds of book have not so far attempted a connection between them. Yet both can be understood as different ways of writing history and creating an historical record which functioned on many different levels. The implications of these books and the cultural assumptions which were behind their creation need to be investigated. Thus I shall focus here on the social memory embodied in the cartularies and *Libri vitae* newly compiled in the Carolingian period. I shall consider the implications of the role of writing and books in their creation and transmission. I shall suggest that these books need to be understood within a wider context of the Carolingian perceptions of time and history and their sense of the Franks' place in relation to a very particular past. The rest of this chapter, therefore, is divided into two parts, namely discussions of the cartularies and of the *Libri vitae*. I conclude with some brief comments on the wider context.

The cartularies

At Fulda in the third decade of the ninth century, a cartulary estimated to have contained over 2000 charters documenting the monastery's

---

Frühmittelalterliche Studien 1 (1967) pp. 225–49, and K. Schmid and J. Wollasch, 'Die Gemeinschaft von Lebenden und Verstorbenen in Zeugnissen des Mittelalters', *Frühmittelalterliche Studien* 1 (1967) pp. 365–405, especially Schmid's section 'Probleme der Erforschung frühmittelalterlicher Gedenkbücher', pp. 366–89. See also G. Althoff, *Amicitiae and Pacta. Bündnis, Einung, Politik und Gebetsgedenken im beginnenden 10. Jahrhundert*, *MGH* Schriften 37 (Hannover, 1992). Althoff has examined the many tenth-century entries documenting *amicitia* and *pacta*, that is, social and political connections sanctified by being placed in the codex along with everything else in the confraternity books of Reichenau and St Gallen, the necrologies of Fulda and the *Liber memorialis* of Remiremont, from the Bodensee, Main and north Burgundian, Lotharingian and Alsacian regions respectively.

[4] O.-G. Oexle, 'Die Gegenwart der Toten', in H. Braet and H. Verbeke (eds.), *Death in the Middle Ages* (Louvain, 1983), pp. 19–77; D. Sichard, *Le Liturgie de la mort dans l'église latine des origines à la réforme Carolingienne* (Münster, 1978); A. Ebner, *Die Klösterlichen Gebetsverbrüderungen bis zum Ausgange des karolingischen Zeitalters. Eine kirchengeschichtliche Studie* (Regensburg, New York and Cincinnati, 1890); M. McLaughlin, *Consorting with saints. Prayer for the dead in early medieval France* (Ithaca and London, 1994); and R. Rappman and A. Zettler, *Die Reichenauer Mönchsgemeinschaft und ihr Totengedenken im frühen Mittelalter, Archäologie und Geschichte*. Freiburger Forschungen zum ersten Jahrtausend in Südwestdeutschland 5 (Sigmaringen, 1998).

landholdings was compiled under the aegis of the abbot, Hraban Maur.[5] Only eighty-six folios of this vast compilation survive, but information from later references, not least those of Eberhard of Fulda in the twelfth century, makes it clear that the copies of charters it comprised were organised geographically with the charters of each Gau grouped together. Within each Gau, although only the section for Alsace and Worms now survives, a quasi-chronological arrangement was imposed in that the charters were grouped according to the abbacies of the successive abbots of Fulda – Sturm, Baugulf, Ratgar, Eigil and Hraban. Modern editors have destroyed this deliberate arrangement by insisting upon overriding both the Gau and the abbot order and imposing a strict but artificial chronological sequence.

The Fulda cartulary simultaneously recorded rights to property, details of the monastic estates with the different plots for wine, pasture, crops, woods, fish and the names of the benefactors in the local community. Thus the cartulary also served as a memorial to many named individuals and their families who were crucial for the support of the monastery and whose sons in many instances became monks within the Fulda community.[6] The charters record far more than the fact and personnel of legal transactions; they provide records of associations, personal friendships and obligations. Further, because of their arrangement and their inclusion of all the names and places associated with the abbey's existence since its foundation, a sense of the history of the abbey and of the society to which it belonged was built into the legal and memorial functions of the cartulary. The past was thus anchored in the local community by means of legal title and of family and institutional memory. The cartulary mirrors the reciprocal ties that bound the monastery to its social, geographical and chronological position and allows historians to reconstruct something of the social fabric of the community. As a statement about its property and all the individuals associated with it, the cartulary is a distinctive reflection of the monastery's historical identity.

In the Freising cartulary compiled by the deacon Cozroh for Bishop Hitto (811–35), moreover, Cozroh was explicit about the significance of his work. In his prefatory explanation he stressed the importance of preserving the *memoria* of the benefactors of Freising. The charters recording their gifts were copied so that 'the memory of those who had enriched this house with their property and made it their heirs might remain in

[5] E. E. Stengel (ed.), *Urkundenbuch des Klosters Fulda*, I.1 (Marburg, 1913), and, I.2 (Marburg, 1956). See also E. F. J. Dronke, *Codex diplomaticus fuldensis* (Aalen, 1962 reprint of 1850 edition).

[6] K. Schmid (ed.), *Die Kloster Gemeinschaft von Fulda im früheren Mittelalter*, Münstersche Mittelalterschriften 8 (Munich, 1978).

perpetuity'.[7] Further, Cozroh had had it impressed upon him by Bishop Hitto that he was not to alter, augment or abbreviate the charters in any way when copying them, except to correct scribal errors. Written records of transactions made on the part of the largely lay donors to Freising for the redemption of their souls were transformed, as Joachim Jahn and Patrick Geary have commented, into a collection to celebrate the memory of benefactors in a manner reminiscent of *Libri vitae*; the cartulary thus also played a liturgical role.[8] Yet a legal function remained, in that the compilation was intended to facilitate consultation in matters of dispute over rightful title.[9]

Cozroh provided a table of contents preceding the texts of the charters in the original Freising manuscript (Munich, Hauptstaatsarchiv, Hochstift Freising, Lit. 3a).[10] He organised the compilation historically, with the charters arranged according to the chronological sequence of bishops under whom these grants were made. He created, therefore, an account of the early history of the bishops of Freising from the perspective of their links with the local community and the accumulation of their material wealth, just as the Fulda cartulary provided a basic framework for the history of the abbots of Fulda.[11]

Similarly, the cartulary of Mondsee (Vienna, Handschriftensammlung des Haus-, Hof-, und Staatsarchivs, Blau 70, fols. 1–52) compiled in the second half of the ninth century, was organised by Gau and then according to places within the Gau.[12] This arrangement not only probably corresponds to the original archive order but also is even more tightly

---

[7] T. Bitterauf, *Die Traditionen des Hochstifts Freising* 1 *(744–926)*, Quellen und Erörterungen zur bayerischen Geschichte NF 4 and 5, 2 vols. (Munich, 1905), I, pp. 1–2.

[8] P. Geary, *Phantoms of remembrance*, pp. 95–6; and J. Jahn, 'Virgil, Arbeo and Cozroh: Verfassungsgeschichtliche Beobachtungen an bairischen Quellen des 8. und 9. Jahrhunderts', *Mitteilungen des Gesellschaft für salzburger Landeskunde* 130 (1990), pp. 201–91.

[9] See S. Molitor, 'Das Traditionsbuch: zur Forschungsgeschichte einer Quellengattung und zu einem Beispiel aus Südwestdeutschland', *Archiv für Diplomatik* 36 (1990), pp. 61–92.

[10] Although Bitterauf rearranged the charters in his edition, the manuscript's table of contents is printed, so that Cozroh's original arrangement can still be appreciated. For a description of the manuscript see B. Bischoff, *Schreibschulen*, I, pp. 112–13.

[11] See also J.-P. Genet, 'Cartulaires, registres et histoire: l'exemple anglais', in B. Guénée (ed.), *Le Métier d'historien au moyen âge. Études sur l'historiographie médiévale*, Publications de la Sorbonne. Série "Études" 13 (Paris, 1977), pp. 95–129; and H. Wolfram, 'Political theory and narrative in charters', *Viator* 26 (1995), pp. 39–52.

[12] G. Rath and E. Reiter (eds.), *Das älteste Traditionsbuch des Klosters Mondsee*, Forschungen zur Geschichte Oberösterreichs 16 (Linz, 1989), have fortunately preserved the original cartulary arrangement. For another example, from the twelfth century, see C. B. Bouchard, *The Cartulary of Flavigny 717–1113*, Medieval Academy Books 99 (Cambridge, Mass., 1991), p. 6, though the significance of the arrangement is not fully discussed.

related to location than the cartularies of Fulda and Freising. A gift for the souls of Dukes Tassilo and Odilo made in 777 is the first in the cartulary. Further, the dates of all the charters are preserved, just as they were in the Fulda and Freising compilations. The cartulary provides a social history of and memorial to the benefactors of Mondsee as well as a vital sense of the monastery's own past, linked to particular places. Its compilation may possibly be associated with the coming of the monastery under the jurisdiction of the bishops of Regensburg. Then it became essential for the Mondsee community to reinforce the sense of its own identity by recording its past in terms of its material possessions and the names of those individuals in the Mattigau, Kanzig, Salzburg and other Gaue in the region who had associated themselves with the monastery in this particular way, quite apart from the importance of the records for claims to legal title. In that the cartulary compiler stated the simple fact that these were the gifts of men to this holy place, the link is also made between human property and the holy. The abbey's property, formed by a multitude of small gifts from the faithful, was thus no ordinary estate but was sanctified in a special way.

Passau's cartulary of the middle of the ninth century comprises a host of legal transactions as well as records of royal *placita* (nos. 50 and 54). Geary has suggested that Passau's collection is particularly indicative of concern for the consequences of Tassilo's downfall in 788 and that it functioned primarily as a declaration of rights which extended back into Bavaria's ducal past, a declaration reinforced by the brief history it incorporates on fols. 28v–29r concerning the founding, consecration and deposition of relics in Passau's church. The making of the cartulary itself may have been a response to events in the early reign of Louis the Pious. Certainly the striking element in all the Bavarian cartularies extant is the decisions taken, well into the Carolingian period, to preserve the documentation of the foundation and support given each monastery by the members of the Bavarian ducal house.[13] The affirmation and declaration of legal rights is also a statement of the Bavarian monasteries' pride in their pre-Carolingian past.

In the Fulda and Bavarian cartularies, therefore, there is a conjunction of an historical sense of the past, attachment to geographical place, commemoration, record and writing. Although there have been many studies of commemoration and attitudes towards the dead,[14] I wish to stress the

---

[13] This cartulary is discussed by Geary, *Phantoms of remembrance*, pp. 90–1.

[14] F. S. Paxton, *Christianizing death. The creation of a ritual process in early medieval Europe* (Ithaca, 1990); M. McLaughlin, *Consorting with saints*; D. Geuenich and O.-G. Oexle (eds.), *Memoria in der Gesellschaft des Mittelalters*, Veröffentlichungen des Max-Planck-Instituts für Geschichte 111 (Göttingen, 1994); O.-G. Oexle (ed.), *Memoria als Kultur*, Veröffentlichungen des Max-Planck-Instituts für Geschichte 121 (Göttingen, 1995).

importance of the cartularies as constituting written forms other than historical narrative in which the past was remembered and commemorated in the early middle ages, and what these have to tell us about the different strands of early medieval cultural attitudes.

Given that memory plays so central a role in human cognition, and that the writing of history acts as a formal organisation of social memory,[15] it is hardly to be wondered that the recent spate of articles and books 'taking stock' of modern medieval studies[16] coupled with the critical sensitivity to texts, especially historiographical texts,[17] has also prompted so many fine studies of the function and recording of memory in the middle ages[18] and of historical writing.[19] As a consequence of these recent studies it is fully acknowledged first of all, that literacy, because it covers both the content of the written tradition and the levels of individual or collective achievement in it, must be discussed in terms of its diverse historical contexts if it is to be understood. Secondly, literate modes of communication and record are not dissociated from oral modes in any way, for they are interdependent and interactive, not antagonistic. Thirdly, literacy, as

[15] J. Fentress and C. Wickham, *Social memory* (Oxford, 1992), and compare chapter 1 above.

[16] See, for example, D. H. Green, 'Orality and reading: the state of research in medieval studies', *Speculum* 65 (1990), pp. 267–80; J. van Engen (ed.), *The past and future of medieval studies*, Notre Dame Conferences in Medieval Studies 4 (Notre Dame, 1994); and the series of *Speculum* assessments: 'The New Philology', ed. S. G. Nichols, *Speculum* 65 (1990), pp. 1–108; 'Studying medieval women', ed. N. F. Partner, *Speculum* 68 (1993), pp. 305–471; and 'Approaches to early medieval art', ed. L. Nees, *Speculum* 72 (1997), pp. 959–1143.

[17] For example, J. Vansina, *Oral tradition. A study in historical methodology*, trans. H. M. White (London, 1965); J. Vansina, *Oral tradition as history* (Madison, Wis., 1985); H. White, 'The historical text as literary artefact', in R. H. Canary and H. Kozicki (eds.), *The writing of history: literary form and historical understanding* (Madison, Wis., 1978), pp. 41–62; and H. White, *The Content of the form. Narrative discourse and historical representation* (Baltimore and London, 1987); W. Goffart, *The narrators of barbarian history (A.D. 550–800). Jordanes, Gregory of Tours, Bede and Paul the Deacon* (Princeton, 1988); and R. Morse, *Truth and convention in the middle ages: rhetoric, representation and reality* (Cambridge, 1991).

[18] I refer in particular to *Temps, mémoire, tradition au moyen âge*. Actes du XIIIe Congrès de la Société des historiens médiévistes de l'enseignement supérieur public, Aix-en-Provence, 4–5 juin 1982 (Aix-en-Provence, 1983); M. Carruthers, *The book of memory. A study of memory in medieval culture* (Cambridge, 1990); J. Coleman, *Ancient and medieval memories. Studies in the reconstruction of the past* (Cambridge, 1992); Fentress and Wickham, *Social memory*, especially pp. 144–72; Geary has reconstructed the process by which some people in the early eleventh century went about remembering, and forgetting, their early medieval past, notably in relation to the cartulary evidence in *Phantoms of remembrance*; see also A. Remensnyder, *Remembering kings past: monastic foundation legends in medieval southern France* (Ithaca, 1995).

[19] Scharer and Scheibelreiter, *Historiographie*; P. Magdalino (ed.), *The perception of the past in twelfth-century Europe* (London, 1992); C. Holdsworth and T. Wiseman (eds.), *The inheritance of historiography 350–900* (Exeter, 1986); Y. Hen and M. Innes (eds.), *The uses of the past in the early middle ages* (Cambridge, 2000); and chapters 1 and 4 above.

Isidore of Seville recognised, acts as an adjunct to and extension of the power of memory at a basic level: letters were invented 'in order to remember things. For lest they fly into oblivion, they are bound in letters. For so great is the variety of things that all cannot be learned by hearing, nor contained only in memory'.[20] Because of the way and the contexts in which literate skills were exercised in the middle ages, writing was more than a straightforward means of communication.[21] It is within this wider context that the cartularies and *Libri Vitae*, both very particular manifestations of literate record and group memory, need to be considered.

Libri vitae

Let us now take up the cue offered by Cozroh of Freising. He told us that one aim of his cartulary was to act as a memorial to the benefactors of his monastery. Thus the cartulary resembles a *Liber vitae*, the most obviously commemorative text of the Carolingian world. The idea of a Book of Life is expressed many times in the Old and New Testaments, such as in Exodus 32, v. 33, when the Lord says unto Moses 'Whosoever hath sinned against me, him will I blot out of my book' (*Qui peccaverit mihi, delebo eum de libro meo*) and in Psalm 68, v. 29: 'Let them be blotted out of the Book of Life, and not be written with the righteous' (*deleantur de libro viventium et cum iustis non scribantur*) taken up by John the Divine in the Book of Revelation, chapter XX, vv. 12, 15:

And I saw the dead, small and great, stand before God; and the books were opened; and another book was opened which is the Book of Life: and the dead were judged out of those things which were written in the books, according to their works ... And whosoever was not found written in the Book of Life was cast into the lake of fire.[22]

---

[20] Isidore of Seville, *Etymologiae* I, 3, 2, ed. W. M. Lindsay, *Isidori Hispalensis episcopi, Etymologiarum sive originum Libri XX* (Oxford, 1911): *Usus litterarum repertus propter memoriam rerum. Nam ne oblivione fugiant, litteris alligantur. In tanta enim rerum varietate nec disci audiendo poterant omnia, nec memoria contineri.* See the discussion and translation by Carruthers, *The Book of Memory*, p. 111. For a forceful affirmation of the link between orality and literacy and acute critique of earlier discussions, see M. Innes, 'Memory, orality and literacy in an early medieval society', *Past and Present* 158 (1998), pp. 3–36.

[21] For various illustrations of this see McKitterick, *Carolingians and the written word*; A. Bowman and G. Woolf (eds.), *Literacy and power in the ancient world* (Cambridge, 1994); and M. Aston and P. Biller (eds.), *Heresy and literacy, 1000–1530* (Cambridge, 1994).

[22] I have argued elsewhere that Revelation was central to the Carolingians' understanding of the role of the book and writing in relation to their Christian faith and practice, in R. McKitterick, 'Text and image in the Carolingian world', in R. McKitterick (ed.), *Uses of literacy*; and see below, pp. 258–9.

The Book of Life therefore is a heavenly book, God's book, containing the names of the elect. Patristic and Carolingian exegetes interpreted this book both literally and allegorically. It is illustrated, for example, in the Utrecht Psalter, Utrecht, Bibliotheek der Rijksuniversiteit MS 32, fol. 38v, with a huge book set by angels before Christ.[23] The heavenly Book of Life became linked, as Koep has established, with the recitation of diptychs in the early Christian church, that is, with the lists of those who were to be remembered in prayer in the liturgy. Evidence for these survives in the early Mass books.[24] Thus the names in the liturgical Book of Life laid on the altar would also be inscribed in God's heavenly Book of Life.

From the Synod of Attigny (762) it is possible to document with some precision the creation of confraternities of prayer or prayer associations, particularly between monastic communities.[25] The bonds involved reciprocal prayer and the exchange of names living and dead. From the seven so-called confraternity books, *Libri vitae* or *Libri memoriales* which survive from before the tenth century, we can see that lists of names were made, and the decision taken in some centres to enter these lists into codices as earthly counterparts to the heavenly Book of Life. Names of the dead were also recorded, specifically in close association with the living as another category of member of their communities and kin groups. Such lists, if confined to the names of members of one house and perhaps a few close neighbours, would constitute the corporate memory of a religious community. As the bonds of prayer associations were extended, and the lists of names occupied an ever-increasing number of pages, so the community became larger, but was still bound within the pages of one book. Scrutiny of the extant *Libri vitae*, furthermore, reveals many suggestive differences between them which merit closer consideration.

St Peter's Salzburg, founded *c.* 700, began its *Liber vitae* (Salzburg St Peter, Archiv MS. A 1) as early as 784 under Bishop Virgil.[26] Some further names, and whole sheets (such as the list of monks from Schwarzach between pp. 2 and 3) were added from time to time in the later ninth and

---

[23] See the discussion by A. von Euw, *Liber viventium fabariensis. Das Karolingische Memorialbuch von Pfäfers in seiner Liturgie- und Kunstgeschichtlichen Bedeutung*, Studia Fabariensia. Beiträge zur Pfäferser Klostergeschichte 1 (Bern and Stuttgart, 1989), p. 212.

[24] *Ibid.*, p. 213; and L. Koep, *Das himmlische Buch in Antike und Christentum. Eine religionsgeschichtliche Untersuchung zu altchristliche Bildersprache*, Theophaneia. Beiträge zur Religions- und Kirchengeschichte des Altertums 8 (Bonn, 1952), p. 100.

[25] The classic article is O.-G. Oexle and K. Schmid, 'Voraussetzungen und Wirkung des Gebetbundes von Attigny', *Francia* 2 (1975), pp. 71–122.

[26] K. Forstner, *Das Verbrüderungsbuch von St Peter in Salzburg. Vollständige Faksimile-Ausgabe im Originalformat der Handschrift A1 aus dem Archiv von St Peter in Salzburg* (Graz, 1974); and see chapter 8 below.

early tenth centuries and another section was added under Abbot Tito in 1004, with names organised by place. In the eleventh and twelfth centuries lists of relics and a few copies of charters were also entered. The whole book, therefore, constituted a carefully controlled (it is remarkably neat and tidy in comparison with some of the others) and continuous record of the clergy and laity commemorated in Salzburg.[27] The prayer on fol. 28r reinforces the identification of this book, placed on the altar with prayers offered for those listed in it, with God's heavenly Book of Life.

From 813/14, the St Gallen *Liber vitae* (St Gallen, Stiftsarchiv C3 B55) replaced what the editor regarded as possible earlier fragments with lists of monks from a host of houses largely in the Alemannian and Bavarian regions, though Tours, Langres, Prüm and Weissenburg are represented as well. There are also the names of many bishops, such as those of Constance, Chur, Mainz, Worms, Chalons, Milan, Strasbourg and Cremona, many names of lay women (pp. 50–62) and names which are probably those visitors to the abbey asked to have included, such as those of King Aethelstan of England and some English bishops. The names were placed within double arcades with painted decoration. The second portion of the book, added *c.* 890, comprises the professions of the St Gall monks, and acts therefore as a Register as well as an entry in the *Liber vitae*.[28]

Some of the *Libri vitae* make their sacred and liturgical function more explicit. The Pfäfers *Liber viventium*, for example, the work of a single scribe and artist, is unique in placing its name lists in conjunction with the lections from the four Gospels. The Gospel lectionary section has richly painted portraits of the evangelists, and the *Liber viventium* is written out within elaborately decorated arcades which resemble canon tables in their layout. From the second half of the ninth century inventories of the treasure of Pfäfers, lists of books, relics and other precious artefacts were added. The Pfäfers *Liber viventium* comprises some 4500 names, including those of the men and women of the Carolingan royal house. It seems to incorporate whole lists of laymen and their families as well as the names of many monks. The codex thus embodies the abbey and

---

[27] In that the book remains in St Peter's, where it was written 1200 years ago, the *Liber* is still part of the community. See K. Schmid, 'Probleme der Erschließung des Salzburger Verbrüderungsbuches', in E. Zwinke (ed.), *Frühes Mönchtum in Salzburg*, Salzburg Diskussionen 4 (Salzburg, 1983), pp. 175–96; and see chapter 8 below.

[28] P. Piper (ed.) *Libri confraternitatum sancti galli, augiensis, fabariensis, MGH Necrologia germaniae* [Supplementum] (Munich, 1983 reprint of 1884 Berlin edition). See also M. Borgolte, D. Geuenich and K. Schmid, *Subsidia Sangallensia*, I, *Materialien und Untersuchungen zu den Verbrüderungsbüchern und zu den älteren Urkunden des Stiftsarchivs St Gallen*, St Galler Kultur und Geschichte 16 (St Gallen, 1986).

the local society in which it was embedded. It serves as a further forcible reminder not only of the liturgical function of the book in which the names to be commemorated were inscribed, but also of the sheer physical and ritual symbolism represented by the book itself. It was a sacred text.[29]

The *Liber memorialis* of Reichenau (Zürich, Zentralbibliothek MS Rh.hist.27) is, with the St Gallen volume, perhaps the purest example of the genre of confraternity book. The Reichenau book is certainly the most disciplined and consistent in its layout and contents, for it is more or less entirely made up of lists of members of monastic communities. Most of the entries appear to have been made at the same time, copied in from lists received and assembled from all those to be joined together in the association of prayer.[30] Begun *c.* 820 and probably compiled by Reginbert, scribe, teacher and librarian of Reichenau (d. 848), the Reichenau confraternity book comprises a total of approximately 40,000 names neatly set out page after page with separate headings indicating to which house the brethren or sisters belonged. It is preceded by a list of all the houses represented. These include, apart from the brothers of the Reichenau itself, monks and nuns of about fifty monasteries east of the Rhine and north of the Seine (only Flavigny, Conques and Manglieu in Burgundy and Provence are outside this web) and the clergy of the churches of Basel, Constance and Strasbourg. After the initial massive task of compilation, other names were added from time to time, reflecting possible contacts, visits made or benefactors. Certainly laymen and laywomen are among them. The list of monastic professions appended (as at St Gallen), furthermore, serves as a continuous record of the monastic community, for it was maintained until the fifteenth century.

Carolingian profession registers have also been found elsewhere. A case in point is the register of new monks from the abbey of St Remi, Rheims in the late ninth century. This included the texts of the oblation charters with the names of the new members, their donors and the witnesses. This register had more than an administrative function: Mayke de Jong has rightly argued that 'it united all newcomers to the community in one codex . . . whenever the register was deposited upon the altar at the occasion of another oblation or profession, all those contained within its covers . . . were repeatedly brought in contact with the sacred'.[31]

---

[29] *Ibid.*; and see A. von Euw, *Liber viventium fabariensis*.

[30] J. Autenrieth, D. Geuenich and K. Schmid (eds.), *Das Verbrüderungsbuch der Abtei Reichenau, MGH Libri memoriales et necrologia, nova series* 1 (Hannover, 1979).

[31] M. de Jong, *In Samuel's image. Child oblation in the early medieval west*, Studies in Intellectual History 12 (Leiden, 1996), pp. 100–25 esp. p. 113.

From San Salvatore in Brescia (founded 760), the *Liber vitae* (Brescia, Biblioteca Queriniana cod. G. VI. 7) of the mid-ninth century (*c.* 854) combines its small number of confraternity lists (of the Reichenau and Murbach monks, the abbots and brothers of the monastery of St Eufemia in Brescia, and the clergy of the cathedrals of Soissons, Bergamo and Brescia) with an extensive set of liturgical texts pertinent to the oblation of new entrants and the ritual commemoration of the dead nuns.[32] Further, there are many entries recording the gifts of daughters to the house by their families and pages of dedications of the living and recently dead of the families of particular individuals, according to the formula: *N. cum omnibus parentibus vivis atque defunctis, cum omnibus suis vivis et mortuis.*[33]

The convent of Brescia was rich in its royal connections. Founded in the 750s by King Desiderius of the Lombards and Queen Ansa, its first abbess was their daughter Anselperga. After the Carolingian conquest of the Lombard kingdom, the monastery was presided over by women of the Carolingian royal house and richly endowed with various possessions and privileges. San Salvatore's position in relation to the routes customarily traversed by visitors from the northern Frankish realms over the Alps seems to have ensured a stream of distinguished visitors (it would not be the first or last royal convent to function as a high-class guest house).[34] Among Brescia's guests were Aethelwulf, king of the West Saxons, Burgred, king of the Mercians, and other Englishmen, whose names were duly recorded in the *Liber.*[35] Further, many names of those related to the nuns had their names entered, not least many Carolingian rulers and their wives, so that the book is less a *monastic* confraternity book than one mirroring the network of social and political affiliations of the nuns and the series of connections, as they were formed over time, with particular individuals or institutions.[36] All are joined together in this codex and in the prayers the book symbolises.

---

[32] A. Valentini, *Codice necrologico-liturgico del monasterio di S. Salvatore o S. Giulia in Brescia* (Brescia, 1887); and D. Geuenich and U. Ludwig, *Der Memorial- und Liturgiecodex von San Salvatore/Santa Giulia in Brescia*, MGH Libri memoriales et necrologia, nova series 4 (Hannover, 2000).

[33] For a description and criticism of Valentini's edition see E. Mühlbacher's review in *MIÖG* 10 (1889), pp. 469–79, which also offers views on the book's status as a confraternity book rather than as a *Liber memorialis* or Necrology.

[34] J. W. Bernhardt, *Itinerant kingship and royal monasteries in early medieval Germany, c. 936–1075* (Cambridge, 1993).

[35] On the English entries see Simon Keynes, 'Anglo-Saxon entries in the "Liber Vitae" of Brescia', in J. Roberts and J. L. Nelson, with M. Godden (eds.), *Alfred the Wise: Studies in honour of Janet Bately on the occasion of her sixty-fifth birthday* (Cambridge, 1997), pp. 99–119.

[36] H. Becher, 'Das königliche Frauenkloster San Salvatore/San Giulia in Brescia im Spiegel seiner Memorialüberlieferung', *Frühmittelalterliche Studien* 17 (1983), pp. 299–392.

From England the *Liber vitae* of Durham from the middle of the ninth century (London, British Library, Cotton Domitian A.VII)[37] and of Winchester of the later tenth and eleventh centuries (London, British Library, Stowe 944) have survived. The latter contains indications that there had been earlier examples of commemorative lists. It incorporated many other texts of central importance to the history of the abbey, not least its foundation charter from King Edgar and the will of King Alfred the Great.[38]

Commemorative entries also appear in other codicological contexts and can serve similar purposes. Sometimes, therefore, a liturgical or biblical book was transformed into a *Liber vitae* or *Liber memorialis* by later additions. Thus the ninth-century Hadrianum sacramentary from Essen has commemorative lists of names added to it. They include names of nuns and members of the laity and secular church associated with Essen.[39] At Cividale (Museo Archeologico, s.n.), Lombard and Slav names were entered from the eighth century onwards into a sixth-century Gospel book. They function in a similar way to the pilgrim's graffiti at Gargano, for they appear to be the names entered on behalf of pilgrims to Aquileia. No doubt some gift would be offered in exchange for the prayers offered for the named individuals by the clergy thereafter.[40] Even for the simple faithful and travellers, therefore, the inscribing of their names in a sacred book was of the utmost importance.

The most complex example of a *Liber vitae* is the so-called *Liber memorialis* of Remiremont (Rome, Biblioteca angelica cod. 10). It was begun as a result of an agreement made by Abbess Thiothild in 820/1 to commemorate the living and the dead in a daily mass and to continue this practice under her successors. This agreement is recorded in the *Liber* (fol. 1v). A further undertaking to commemorate the founding abbots Romarich and Amatus on Sundays and feast days is also noted (fol. 19r). Lists of the names of the living, the dead, donors and benefactors together

---

[37] J. Gerchow, *Die Gedenküberlieferung der Angelsachsen*, Arbeiten zur Frühmittelalterforschung 20 (Berlin, 1988), with full details of the commemorative tradition in England; and ed. J. Stevenson, *Liber vitae ecclesiae dunelmensis*, The Publications of the Surtees Society 136 (London, 1923). See D. Rollason, A. Piper, M. Harvey and L. Rollason (eds.), *The Durham Liber vitae and its context* (Woodbridge, 2004).

[38] S. Keynes (ed.), *The Liber vitae of the New Minster and Hyde Abbey, Winchester*, Early English manuscripts in facsimile 26 (Copenhagen, 1996).

[39] V. Huth, 'Die Düsseldorfer Sakramentarhandschrift D 1 als Memorialzeugnis. Mit einer Wiedergabe der Namen und Namengruppen (Tafs. XIV–XXXII)', *Frühmittelalterliche Studien* 20 (1986), pp. 213–98.

[40] *CLA*, III (Oxford, 1938), no. 285; see L. Bethmann, 'Die Evangelien Handschrift zu Cividale', *Neues Archiv* 2 (1877), pp. 111–28, at p. 113. On the Gargano inscriptions see N. Everett, *Literacy in Lombard Italy, c. 568–774* (Cambridge, 2003), pp. 265–74. See also von Euw, *Liber viventium fabariensis*, pp. 211–12.

with texts of the masses to be said for them were all copied into a book. The initial conception, therefore, was one which was of a straightforward commemorative and liturgical text. The present codex was produced perhaps four decades later, however, probably using an older exemplar (and conceivably discarding earlier material at that stage). This codex comprises an older (fols. 32–6, 42–3, 45–7) and younger (fols. 1–5 and 10–26) portion. The whole of the former has still not been precisely dated but the latter was added in 862/3. The presence of scribe 5's hand in both portions suggests that they were written not long after each other.

Well over 100 scribes, of astonishingly varying degrees of competence, have been identified in the book, mostly of the ninth and tenth centuries. As well as the evidence of the nuns' ability, in the form of copies of charters of sufficient organisation of legal records and charter production, to cope with their own business, there is the provision of lists of other *fratres* and *sorores*. The latter implies a network of literate communication. Indeed, this process of compilation and what it reveals of written communications in this period is something the editors of the confraternity books have not considered sufficiently. We may imagine an abbot, abbess or some other official in the monastery (such as Thiothild of Remiremont, Virgil of Salzburg or Reginbert of Reichenau) deciding to set about the formation of prayer associations in a systematic way, and to extend these links as far as the collective knowledge and contacts of the abbey may make possible. Letters would then be sent to all these places, asking for lists to be sent and the response would be in the form of single sheets such as we observe from Prüm and Reichenau bound into the *Liber memorialis* of Remiremont or the leaf from Schwarzach in the *Liber vitae* of Salzburg. The lists would then be inserted or copied into the new book created for the purpose. They could have been left in single sheets and kept in a box, but these monks and nuns chose to create a special kind of codex which served as a reminder of the duty to commemorate collectively, whether silently or out loud,[41] the names recorded in it within the liturgy. That they did so is entirely in keeping with the attitude towards the book as sacred text and authority in the Carolingian world. They constitute, in other words, a highly sophisticated manifestation of the symbolic importance

---

[41] Giles Constable, 'The *Liber memorialis* of Remiremont', *Speculum* 47 (1972), pp. 261–77, at p. 263, follows A. Hamilton-Thompson on the *Liber vitae* of Durham in regarding this as a wholly silent text. On the other hand there are Mass texts which refer to the reciting of the names: see McLaughlin, *Consorting with the Dead*, pp. 91–2, who cites Paris, BnF MS lat. 9434, fol. 338r. To extrapolate from views about the purpose and use of the Durham book to the function of the Carolingian books, therefore, may not be appropriate.

of the written word and a further instance of the creation of an 'enduring community on parchment'.[42]

The older portion of the *Liber memorialis* of Remiremont comprises the following: a necrology from January to December; the names of the abbesses and nuns of Remiremont before it accepted the Rule of Benedict after the 816/17 Aachen decrees of Louis the Pious had urged observation of the Rule on all the religious communities of the realm; the names of the present nuns of Remiremont; the brothers of Murbach; a further necrology running from March to December; and a list of names of members of the Carolingian house and their supporters (fol. 43r). In a brilliant piece of historical reconstruction, Schmid established that this last-mentioned entry had probably been made in December 861 on the occasion of a meeting between Lothar II and Louis the German (with their sons, wives, daughters, concubines (Lothar's concubine Waldrada was also there) and lay and ecclesiastical *potentes* in their entourage) in order to discuss the sending of an embassy to Charles the Bald to protest against his invasion of Provence in the autumn of 861.[43]

The younger portion of the book includes the following: the copy of the announcement of the original intention of 820/1; the mass texts; the so-called kings' diptych with the names of Merovingian and Carolingian rulers up to and including Charles the Bald and his wife Ermentrude;[44] and a list of those apparently attending another special meeting held at the abbey sometime between 847 and 913. On this occasion the Hatto mentioned is either Bishop Hatto of Verdun (after 846–70) or Hatto of Mainz (891–913). Count Haimo presided. There is also a further list of the living nuns of Remiremont. Folios 10–26 begin with a list of the brothers of Lobbes. There is then a third necrology from Christmas day through to the following 23 December (fols. 10v–19r). This is succeeded by the memorial mass texts. On fols. 21r and 22v–26v decorated arcades were prepared for lists of brethren and sisters in other monasteries, which in due course got filled in with names of members of the communities of Murbach, Prüm, Annegray, and others. On fol. 22v the names of some popes (Gregory IV, Sergius II, Benedict II and Nicolas I), together with those of Bishops Radoald (of Porto) and Johannes (of Cervia) were entered at the top of the first column. The two bishops came to the Synod

[42] The phrase is M. de Jong's, *In Samuel's image*, p. 125.
[43] K. Schmid, 'Ein karolingischer Königseintrag im Gedenkbuch von Remiremont', *Frühmittelalterliche Studien* 2 (1968), pp. 96–134.
[44] F.-J. Jakobi, 'Diptychen als frühe Form der Gedenk-Aufzeichnungen. Zum "Herrscher-Dipychon" im Liber memorialis von Remiremont', *Frühmittelalterliche Studien* 20 (1986), pp. 186–212. The continuance of interest on the part of the members of the abbey in the kings of Lotharingia and Francia into the tenth century is recorded not just in the kings' dyptych but also in the plea to pray *pro Rodulfo rege cum Ludouuico fratre suo* on fol. 5r.

of Metz in the winter of 862/3 held in connection with the case of Lothar II's divorce. They may even have visited Remiremont itself.

For the most part, the calendars when first laid out had no entries. The death notes were subsequently filled in over the years thereafter against appropriate days. They provide the names of men and women associated with the abbey, both nuns and others. When the day was not known, entries of names were made on other pages. In addition to these two main portions, single sheets were inserted into the book from time to time. More substantial sections were added in the form of notes of charters recording gifts of property (both of land and of humans) from the later ninth century onwards, and the polyptych or *censier* was compiled in *c.* 965 (fols 65r–68v). Although the original design was in the tradition of the *Liber Vitae* format[45] with quadruple decorated arcades on each page (of some elegance in the earlier part if rather cruder in the later portion), the layout was thereafter constantly overridden by other scribes inserting names wherever they could find space. On every page of the book, both in its original portions and on the later leaves, names are recorded. The book contains some 11,500 names in all. Mostly these are single names but sometimes there is more detail. Bishop Dado of Verdun (880–923) and his dependants had their names entered on fol. 4r. Seven men – Sendradus amd his brother Gottiscaddus, Rodulfus VVilgierus (sic), Gotseramnus, Saleco and Bernardus – who died for their faith, killed by pagans (presumably in an attack by Magyars) are remembered on fol. 57v; Ermintrude and her children, redeemed by her relatives Rotbertus and his wife Dodana from the Magyars and given to the abbey, have their ordeal briefly chronicled on fol. 33v. As a result of his paying for the restoration of the church, the names of Duke Gislebert, his wife and children and his *fideles* were entered on fol. 6r. Indeed, the very great number of lay people recorded, especially of counts, suggests that Remiremont was a centre of local, possibly judicial, activity of some kind, and that it acted as a focal point for the surrounding population in much the same way that Lorsch did further to the east.[46]

Most of the names in the book are the names of the Remiremont nuns themselves and of the devoted laity, male and female, who bestowed land and servants, daughters and portable property on the abbey to the glory of God and for the sake of their immortal souls in a spiritual exchange mechanism by which prayers were given in return for material gifts. Thus the gifts and their record are in effect witnesses to the good deeds of the

---

[45] On the different precursors of this format such as canon tables in Gospel Books, see von Euw, *Liber viventium fabariensis*, pp. 107–51 and 209–14.

[46] M. Innes, *State and society in the early middle ages. The middle Rhine valley 400–1000* (Cambridge, 2000).

devout. All names, even those of the unfree who were given by donors, are recorded. Their names are listed as part of the transactions recorded or simply as single names with no identifiable association with any other. As we have seen, the abbey also received visitors and was apparently a venue for political meetings (as in the winters of 861 and 862/3).

The abbey's political prominence and interests are no doubt to be attributed to the family connections of Abbess Thiothild. She presided over the abbey from 819/20 until 862/5,[47] and was related to Adalhard the seneschal of Charles the Bald and to Judith, Charles the Bald's mother. Charles the Bald's wife was Adalhard's niece. We are familiar with the prominence of royal convents in the Ottonian period but clearly at least Remiremont, Chelles and Brescia were useful to the Carolingians and many of the nuns were from the leading families of the realm.

Even more explicitly than the other *Libri vitae*, the *Liber memorialis* of Remiremont, therefore, is a history book. It is far more than just a set of records or list of names. Collectively these names certainly constitute the identity of the community. For some *Libri vitae*, such as that of the Reichenau, this community stretches across Europe. In Remiremont's case it is predominantly local. The local rhythm of life is reflected in the steady arrival of gifts and new oblates for the abbey, but so occasionally are the affairs of the wider world. Those killed in Magyar attacks are cases in point. Just as in any parish church in Europe where the names of those killed in the First World War from that particular parish are recorded, with the evocation of the families and neighbours who shared their grief and their collective loss, and of the particular moments when the affairs of the outside world impinged so terribly on the small worlds of the village communities,[48] so the Remiremont *Liber memorialis* records small and more cataclysmic events in the history of the society supporting the monastery in remembering the names of those involved. It preserves the history of the key phases of the community in terms of its acceptance of the Rule of Benedict and of the reforms of Louis the Pious. It was a venue for those taking political decisions. It was possibly a refuge for those for whom public life was no longer an option, such as Lothar II's beloved but forcibly discarded concubine Waldrada, who may have ended her career there. The individuals mattered. The names acted as a mnemonic for the events in which the individuals were involved. Each person recorded was subsumed into the collective memory and identity created by the book. The book thus serves both to form and to symbolise the identity of a

---

[47] E. Hlawitschka, *Studien zur Äbtissinnenreihe von Remiremont*, Veröffentlichungen des Instituts für Landeskunde des Saarlandes (Saarbrücken, 1963).

[48] See in particular J. M. Winter, *Sites of memory, sites of mourning. The Great War in European history* (Cambridge, 1995).

living community. The recording of the names of the dead and the effort to pray for their souls functioned as a preservation of collective memory. Writing was exploited to develop this identity and reinforce this memory. A new kind of book was created.

Commemoration and memory: the wider context

The immediate context for the creation of the *Libri vitae* can be recognised in the development of the ritual response to death in the early middle ages documented by Frederick Paxton. The Carolingian period was one in which fundamental changes in the rites associated with the last illness and death of men and women were effected. These rites were observed throughout the Carolingian empire.[49] Prayers were composed and recorded in the sacramentaries of the eighth and ninth centuries. Choices were made for and against materials by compilers involved in the process of transmission. It seems to have been in the Seine Basin and Picardy in particular that the elaboration and standardisation of the ritual of death in written form was encouraged. Abbots Adalhard and Gauzlin of St Amand are associated with this development. Simultaneously there was an effort within the Carolingian empire, promoted from Charlemagne's *Admonitio generalis* of 789 onwards, to establish harmony, if not actual uniformity, of Christian observance by means of the promotion of authoritative and authorized versions of particular texts.[50] Just as Christians throughout the Frankish empire were to be united through their common observance of ritual, so too would the prayer bonds create unity by spiritual association, and in both cases this unity was effected by writing. All these books were maintained by a multiplicity of scribes over long periods of time and thus were part also of a continuity of worship in textual form.

Dennis Green commented that any society with a sense of self-awareness has to store essential information about its past. In an oral society this has to be done by memory rather than by writing.[51] In a literate society writing serves as an adjunct to memory.[52] In the Carolingian world many new ways were devised, as we have seen, of storing social memories by writing them down. The cartularies and the *Libri memoriales*

---

[49] Paxton, *Christianization of death*.

[50] R. McKitterick, *The Frankish church and the Carolingian reforms, 789–895*, Royal Historical Society, Studies in History 2 (London, 1977); and *idem*, 'Unity and diversity in the Carolingian church', in R. Swanson (ed.), *Unity and diversity in the Christian church*, Studies in Church History 32 (1996), pp. 59–82.

[51] D. Green, 'Orality and reading: the state of research in medieval studies', *Speculum* 65 (1990), pp. 267–80, at p. 272.

[52] As Isidore of Seville affirmed: see above, note 20.

constitute further evidence that literacy was indeed central in Carolingian society.[53]

This does not mean that oral modes of communication were not also crucial within Carolingian society. Orality and literacy are not mutually exclusive, nor is an oral culture a preliminary stage before the triumph of literacy.[54] Oral modes of discourse and communication complement literate ones.[55] In the eighth and ninth centuries in particular they interacted with each other constantly and creatively. They coexisted. The *Libri vitae* and the cartularies have demonstrated that writing not only augmented oral modes and memory as a form of communication in the early middle ages, but also functioned as a symbol on many different social and spiritual levels. These books illustrate the role of writing as a form of communication over time, and it is this which is absolutely crucial to our understanding of the uses and implications of literacy in the early middle ages as a whole. It is of the utmost significance therefore that it was precisely in the Carolingian period that these Books of Life were first produced. They provided written records to commemorate the dead of local communities and ensured them of a place in the memories of the living.

---

[53] It is astonishing to me, for example, that McLoughlin, *Consorting with saints*, p. 236, and n. 183 can still persist in maintaining, despite her close study of so many Carolingian texts, their impact and significance, that Carolingian society was a 'society dominated by orality'.

[54] The flaw in M. Richter, *The formation of the medieval west. Studies in the oral culture of the barbarians* (Dublin, 1994) is to assume that this is the case and that what he conceives of as 'oral (secular) culture' is actually in opposition to his notion of a 'literate (clerical) culture' in the Carolingian period. The orality debate has also tended to get tangled unprofitably in discussions about the emergence of 'German' vernacular poetry. For a clear-headed assessment of the language issue see E. Hellgardt, 'Zur Mehrsprachigkeit im Karolingerreich. Bermerkungen aus Anlaß von Rosamond McKittericks Buch "The Carolingians and the Written Word"', *Beiträge zur Geschichte der deutschen Sprache und Literatur* 118 (1996), pp. 1–48.

[55] See above all the good sense of D. H. Green, 'Orality and reading: the state of research in medieval studies', *Speculum* 65 (1990), pp. 267–80, and his book *Medieval listening and reading. The primary reception of German literature 800–1300* (Cambridge, 1994). K. Dailinger, 'Voicing the written word' (Cambridge Ph.D. dissertation in preparation) offers much new material.

8 History and memory in early medieval Bavaria

The *Liber vitae* or confraternity book of Salzburg is a remarkable example of the use of writing in commemoration and the recording of social memory in the early middle ages discussed in the preceding chapter. As is well known, it is essentially a book full of lists of the names of living and dead people for whom the religious community wished to pray. The date of production at the end of the eighth century in Salzburg, and the names included in the lists, however, are potentially peculiarly placed in relation, firstly, to Frankish and Carolingian interests in Bavaria just before Charlemagne's annexation of Tassilo's duchy in 788 and, secondly, to its immediate aftermath.[1] Texts can work simultaneously at many different levels of communication and understanding, and they can help to forge ideas and identities as well as mirror them. In addition, historians are not confined to narrative texts (despite post-modernist assumptions that they are). The texts themselves are of an extraordinary diversity and some, such as the Salzburg *Liber vitae*, are not usually regarded as ways of writing history. The Salzburg *Liber vitae*, like the other *Libri vitae*, however, is essentially a history book and thus a very distinctive way of creating an historical record.[2] It reflects not only cultural assumptions but also specific political affiliations and social communities within Bavaria at the end of the eighth century.

It is important to see the *Liber vitae* of Salzburg in the context of historical record making in early medieval Bavaria. It is well known how complex the Bavarian annalistic tradition in the Carolingian period is, and how much work is still needed to clarify the connections between the various local annals extant.[3] Besides the late eighth-century Lives of Corbinian

---

[1] See S. Airlie, 'Narratives of triumph and rituals of submission: Charlemagne's mastering of Bavaria', *TRHS* sixth series 9 (1999), pp. 93–120.

[2] K. Forstner, *Das Verbrüderungsbuch von St Peter in Salzburg. Vollständige Faksimile-Ausgabe im Originalformat der Handschrift A1 aus dem Archiv von St Peter in Salzburg* (Graz, 1974).

[3] See W. Wattenbach, W. Levison and H. Löwe, *Deutschlands Geschichtsquellen im Mittelalter*, II, *Vorzeit und Karolinger* (Weimar, 1953), pp. 180–92, for the older literature. See also H. Wolfram, *Grenzen und Räume. Geschichte Österreichs vor seiner Entstehung*

and Emmeram by Arbeo of Freising, there remains the possibility of a contemporary narrative account of Tassilo III's reign having once existed.[4] Most of our other manifestations of historical writing of any kind postdate Charlemagne's annexation of Bavaria and the Salzburg *Liber vitae* itself. Because of the relative dearth of conventional historical narrative from Agilolfing Bavaria in the late eighth century we are obliged to observe Bavarian affairs for the most part in terms of particular pieces of Bavarian eighth-century 'news' preserved in other sources, such as the *Liber pontificalis*'s reference to Duke Theodo of Bavaria's visit to Rome[5] and a letter of Pope Gregory II, dated 716, concerning the reorganisation of the church in Bavaria in response to Theodo's plea.[6] Further, there are the famous distortions of Bavarian politics and Tassilo's career constructed by the writers of the *Annales regni francorum* and its revised versions.[7]

There was, nevertheless, a well-developed historical consciousness within Agilolfing and early Carolingian Bavaria. This manifests itself in a variety of non-narrative or quasi-narrative sources, such as the ninth-century cartularies from Freising, Mondsee and Passau. These, as we have seen, incorporate earlier legal and historical records. Their affirmation and declaration of legal rights is a statement of the Bavarian monasteries' pride in their Agilolfing and pre-Carolingian past.

Yet that very Agilolfing past had long been linked with the Merovingian kingdoms to the west. A further, and crucial, factor is the Bavarian ducal family's own close blood relationship with the Carolingian family. Self-evidently, family and political rivalries as well as competing conceptions of royal and ducal power were involved in the increasingly acrimonious relations between Tassilo and Charlemagne in particular. It is not my intention to rehearse these political issues, for many have addressed them fully and illuminatingly elsewhere.[8] Yet the Salzburg *Liber vitae* was begun

---

(Vienna, 1995), pp. 71–6; F. Losek, '*Notitia arnonis* und *Breves notitiae*', *Mitteilungen der Gesellschaft für Salzburger Landeskunde* 130 (1990), pp. 5–192; J. Jahn, *Ducatus Baiuvariorum. Das bairische Herzogtum der Agilolfinger*, Monographien zur Geschichte des Mittelalters 32 (Stuttgart, 1991); A. Lhotsky, *Quellenkunde zur mittelalterlichem Geschichte Österreichs*, *MIÖG* Ergänzungsband 19 (Vienna, 1963); and Karl Schmid, 'Probleme der Erschließung des Salzburger Verbrüderungsbuches' in E. Zwinke (ed.), *Frühes Mönchtum in Salzburg*, Salzburg Diskussionen 4 (Salzburg, 1983), pp. 175–96.

[4] Wattenbach, Levison and Löwe, *Geschichtsquellen*, p. 191, n. 77.

[5] *Liber pontificalis*, 91.4, ed. L. Duchesne, *Le Liber pontificalis*, 2 vols. (Paris, 1886 and 1892), I, p. 398. See also R. Davis, *The lives of the eighth-century popes (Liber pontificalis)* (Liverpool, 1992), pp. 5–6.

[6] 15 May 716, *MGH Leges*, III, p. 451.

[7] For full discussion see M. Becher, *Eid und Herrschaft. Untersuchungen zum Herrscherethos Karls des Großen*, Vorträge und Forschungen, Sonderband 39 (Sigmaringen, 1993).

[8] In addition to the work cited above, note 4, see C. Hammer, *Charlemagne's months and their Bavarian labors. The politics of the seasons in the Carolingian empire*, BAR International series

in the 780s, that is, during the most difficult period of Franco-Bavarian relations. Consequently, the following questions arise. First of all, what cultural assumptions and affiliations does the *Liber vitae* reflect? Secondly, does the *Liber vitae* throw any light on any of the immediate political sympathies and tensions of the time it was written, most notably the careers of Virgil and Arno in Salzburg itself? Thirdly, and more generally, to what degree does the book help us to understand the record of memory and the formation of an historical record in early medieval Bavaria, or for that matter, western Europe as a whole, in the early middle ages?

Let us now look at the Salzburg *Liber vitae* itself. The community of St Peter's Salzburg, founded *c.* 700, by the Frank St Rupert, began its *Liber vitae* or *Liber memorialis* (Salzburg, St Peter Archiv A1) as early as 784. It is in fact the earliest of the confraternity books extant. It comprises two parts, the first forty pages of which, divided into three quires, constitute the *Liber vitae*. The remainder of the book, quires 4–9, consists of charters of Salzburg, bound with the *Liber memorialis* by the fifteenth century. The first four pages, in a separate bifolium, contain materal relating to the see of Salzburg from the eleventh and twelfth centuries. The second quire, of twelve leaves (twenty-four pages), contains the eighth- and ninth-century *Liber vitae*. A further section, quire 3, comprising six leaves or twelve pages, was a new confraternity book added under Abbot Tito in 1004. This section was arranged in columns under arches like the Carolingian *Libri memoriales* from St Gallen, Reichenau and Pfäfers and, also like other Carolingian books, with names of individuals recorded in sections for the most part by place, though it preserves the earlier section's distinction by *ordo* of person as well.[9]

The original *Liber vitae* in quire 2 was added to at the end of the eighth century and from time to time throughout the ninth century, with a relic list entered in the second half of the ninth century and a small leaf with the names of the monks, laymen and laywomen of Schwarzach in the second half of the ninth century inserted at some stage. In the eleventh

---

676 (Oxford, 1997); *idem.*, 'The social landscape of the Prague Sacramentary: the prosopography of an eighth-century mass book', *Traditio* 54 (1999), pp. 41–80; and W. Brown, *Unjust seizure: conflict, interest and authority in an early medieval society* (Ithaca, 2001); and K. Pearson, *Conflicting loyalties in early medieval Bavaria: a view of socio-political interaction, 680–900* (Aldershot, 1999).

[9] See A. von Euw, *Liber viventium fabariensis. Das karolingische Memorialbuch von Pfäfers in seiner liturgie- und kunstgeschichtlichen Bedeutung*, Studia Fabariensia. Beiträge zur Pfäferser Klostergeschichte 1 (Bern and Stuttgart, 1989); E. Hlawitschka, K. Schmid and G. Tellenbach (eds.), *Liber memorialis von Remiremont*, MGH Libri memoriales, I (Munich, 1981); and J. Autenrieth, D. Geuenich and K. Schmid (eds.), *Das Verbrüderungsbuch der Abtei Reichenau, MGH Libri memoriales et necrologia, nova series* 1 (Hannover, 1979).

and twelfth centuries, moreover, poems by Alcuin on the church of St Rupert were copied onto blank leaves in the book.

As it appears now the book might be thought to be a mess. In fact it is a tapestry of great historical intensity. With its steady accumulation of names associated with the abbey, many of them also recorded in the charters of St Peter's, it is a history book rather than a mere set of records or list of names. Collectively these names constitute the identity of the community over time. It is an identity in which the historical dimension plays a crucial role, for the whole point is that it is cumulative and evokes the local rhythm of gift, association, gratitude and pious devotion expressed towards the abbey. The book as a whole, including all the additions, serves both to form and to symbolise the identity of a living community in which the dead and the effort to pray for their souls functioned as a preservation of collective memory and a very special rendition of the past of the Salzburg community.

Yet we should also consider the book as it was when first produced, when it was a statement at a particular moment rather than the cumulative commemorative and liturgical text as it now appears. Precisely what that statement was is difficult to decode, but I offer here some suggestions. As it was first designed and laid out in 784, the book left many pages and spaces blank for later additions. The first entries appear to have been the work of the scribe known as 'H1' and it is by tracing his hand that the original conception can be discerned. In the book, all the names are grouped into *ordines*. On the first page (p. 5 in the present manuscript) there are the *ordines* of patriarchs and Old Testament prophets and of Apostles, martyrs and confessors. On the left of this page, therefore, the list includes Abel, Seth, Enoch, Noah, Melchisadech, Abraham, Isaac, Jacob, Joseph, Job, Moses, Samuel and David. The New Testament list starts with John the Baptist and the Virgin Mary, and proceeds with some, but not all, of the twelve apostles, the evangelists, early popes and Roman saints, including Peter, Paul, Matthew, Mark, Luke, Stephen, Silvester, Clement, Laurence and Gregory. Further, a five-line prayer is added invoking the memory of all those whose names are recorded in the Book of Life.

The next page (p. 6) lists the living monks of St Peter's Salzburg. Some names were erased and moved to the list of dead members of the community. Ample space was left for additions (p. 6). On p. 9 in the second half of the page the *pulsantes* of St Peter (probably adult novices, but their precise religious status is not clear) were listed.[10] On p. 10 are the

---

[10] See P. Quinn, *Better than the sons of kings: boys and monks in the early middle ages*, Studies in History and Culture 2 (New York, Bern, Frankfurt am Main and Paris, 1989), pp. 46–7,

entries that have contributed most helpfully to the dating of the manuscript, namely the *ordo* of living kings and their wives and children, the order of living dukes (of Bavaria) and their wives and children and of living priests, bishops, priests and abbots from elsewhere in Bavaria and Francia. Pages 11–13 were allocated to living nuns and monks from other communities, though hardly any entries were made on these pages initially. On p. 14 the lists of the dead begin, with for the most part the same sequence of categories as we found with the lists of the living. Here, however, the dead start with bishops and abbots of Salzburg (and the names of Virgil of Salzburg and of Alcuin were added in the time of Arno, Virgil's successor) before the monks and *pulsantes*. On p. 20 the dead kings, dukes and foreign bishops and abbots are listed.

It is here that the famous list of Irish saints and abbots, starting with St Patrick and Columba, is to be found. Most of these names are those of dead abbots of Iona, from Columba to Adomnan and from Conaman to Slebteene, up to 772, but they are interspersed with the names of Ciaran of Clonmacnoise (an opponent of Iona), Columbanus of Luxeuil and Dorbeni, the copyist of the *Vita Columbani* of Adomnan (who in the Martyrology of Tallaght is given the title of abbot).[11] Next to these abbots, however, is a list of primarily Bavarian bishops, such as Emmeram, Corbinian, Vivilo, Sidonius, Willibald of Eichstätt and Arbeo of Freising, and it also includes Lull of Mainz. Thereafter there are dead 'foreign' priests and nuns and the last seven pages of the book are allocated to dead laymen and laywomen associated with Salzburg, rounded off with a prayer complementing the beginning prayer which starts with the words *Dignare domine*.

The book has many extraordinary features and oddities which distinguish it from the other confraternity books discussed in the previous chapter. First of all, each category is called an *ordo*. The sequence is of Old and New Testament figures and Roman saints, the Salzburg community and thereafter the world outside. There is thus a very particular notion of hierarchy, signalled only by the order in which they are placed in the book. As Hermann has stressed, moreover, these *ordines* have a clear theological message, in that they are the representatives of mankind

but compare M. de Jong, *In Samuel's image. Child oblation in the early medieval west*, Studies in Intellectual History 12 (Leiden, 1996), pp. 130–1.
11   P. Grosjean, 'Virgile de Salzbourg en Irlande', *Analecta Bollandiana* 78 (1960), pp. 92–123; M. Coens, 'Les litanies bavaroises du "Libellus precum" dit de Fleury (Orléans MS 194)', *Analecta Bollandiana* 77 (1959), pp. 373–91; J. Hennig, 'Scottorum gloria gentis. Erwähnungen irischer Heiliger in festländischen Liturgietexten des frühen Mittelalters', *Archiv für Kulturgeschichte* 52 (1970), pp. 177–91; and D. O. Riain-Raendel, 'Aspects of the promotion of Irish saints' cults in medieval Germany', *Zeitschrift für celtische Philologie* 39 (1982), pp. 1–15.

redeemed by Christ recorded in the Book of Life. As the prayers at the beginning and end of the book reiterate, they are in God's book of life too.[12] They are a triumphant, or potentially triumphant, community of the saved.

Yet the sequence embodies more than this. In its juxtaposition of the ancient biblical as well as early Christian past with Salzburg's present, the community is placed in the longer perspective of Christian history. A reinforcement of this perception is that a mere decade after the translation of St Rupert's relics from Worms to Salzburg, Rupert's name is not in the list of saints at the beginning but simply recorded among the dead abbots and bishops of Salzburg. The Salzburg book constitutes, therefore, an expression of both local and universal identity.

Further, if we concentrate on p. 10, the political affiliations of Salzburg are expressed. In the *ordo* of living kings there are the names of Charlemagne and his wife Fastrada, his sons Pippin, Louis, Charles and Pippin and his daughter Hrodrud. In the *ordo* of living dukes the names of Tassilo, his wife Liutperga, and son Theodo and daughters Cotani and Hrodrud are listed. The Carolingian ruler and by implication his subordinate duke, therefore, are acknowledged. How this apparently clear commemoration of the Carolingian ruler and of Tassilo before he lost his duchy should be interpreted depends in part on the identification of the individuals responsible for the original compilation of the book.

The Salzburg *Liber vitae* also represents a statement of links with Francia and the Frankish church in the time of Tassilo. The book needs to be seen as mirroring attitudes of some at least of the establishment of Bavaria and their Frankish sympathies. Such a statement of political loyalty is not to be found in any of the other extant Carolingian *Libri memoriales*. In Remiremont, for example, as we have seen, the names record visitors to the abbey.[13] By contrast, the Salzburg entries of king and duke and their wives and offspring were part of the original conception.[14] From the Bavarian council of Dingolfing (*c.* 770–*c.* 776/7), held under the auspices of Duke Tassilo, we can see the extension of the Frankish idea of prayer association, expressed at Attigny in 762, among the churches of Bavaria.[15] The book at Salzburg is a direct, as well as the

---

[12] K. F. Hermann, 'Zum Geleit', in Forstner, *Das Verbrüderungsbuch von St Peter in Salzburg*, p. 11.

[13] K. Schmid, 'Ein karolingischer Königseintrag im Gedenkbuch von Remiremont', *Frühmittelalterliche Studien* 2 (1968), pp. 96–134; and see above, chapter 7.

[14] Compare, however, F.-J. Jakobi, 'Diptychen als frühe Form der Denk-Aufzeichnungen. Zum "Herrscher-Diptychon" im Liber memorialis von Remiremont', *Frühmittelalterliche Studien* 20 (1986), pp. 186–212.

[15] Synod von Dingolfing and *Notitia de pacto fraternitatis episcoporum et abbatum bawaricorum*, ed. A. Werminghoff, *MGH Conc.* II.1, no. 15 (Hannover, 1906), pp. 96–7. For

earliest, embodiment of the apparently Frankish idea of the prayer association coupled with that of the earthly counterpart to the heavenly Book of Life. Virgil, bishop of Salzburg, had attended the synod of Dingolfing, for he is recorded as being there. It would seem that he or people close to him thought of this way of putting the ideas into practice and thus providing a further practical manifestation of the status of the written word in the early middle ages.[16] That the book is indeed to be associated with Salzburg in the time of Virgil is established from the names included or not included among the living and dead. Forstner has narrowed the date of compilation down to between 4 May and 16 July 784.

The identity of neither the scribe nor the compiler is known. They may not be one and the same, for the scribe could have been working under the direction of someone else. This is most likely. The script of the original entries points to a scribe with west Frankish training, if not origin, for it is a west Frankish caroline minuscule whose closest links are with St Denis. Indeed, the Salzburg book is one of the three earliest dateable examples, all from the early 780s, of caroline minuscule extant.[17] The west Frankish and, for its time very new, character of the script has generally been regarded as excluding the possibility that Virgil himself was the scribe, for he is thought to have been Irish. It is assumed, therefore, that he would have written insular minuscule. In any case the main scribe clearly continues to work after Virgil's death so the script is neither here nor there in relation to Virgil himself.

The alleged Irish connections of Virgil merit some consideration. The earliest indication of Virgil's connection with Ireland is the epitaph on him by Alcuin written in the time of Arno, Virgil's successor as bishop of Salzburg, and presumably, therefore, from information supplied by Arno.[18] The *Conversio bagoariorum*, moreover, written in 870 to legitimise Salzburg's efforts to convert lower Pannonia, records that Virgil, wise and very learned, came from Ireland to the court of Pippin III at Quierzy. There he remained at the king's request for two years. As Pippin

the wider context see K. Schmid and O.-G. Oexle, 'Voraussetzungen und Wirkung des Gebetbundes von Attigny', *Francia* 2 (1974), pp. 71–122; O.-G. Oexle, 'Memorial und Memorialüberlieferung im früheren Mittelalter', *Frühmittelalterliche Studien* 10 (1976), pp. 70–96; and J. Gerchow, *Die Gedenkbücher der Angelsachsen*, Arbeiten zur Frühmittelalterforschung 20 (Berlin, 1988).

[16] See McKitterick, *Carolingians and the written word*; McKitterick (ed.), *Uses of literacy*; and R. Schieffer (ed.), *Schriftkultur und Reichsverwaltung unter den Karolingern* (Opladen, 1996).

[17] Bischoff, *Schreibschulen*, II, pp. 83–4. Forstner, *Das Verbrüderungsbuch von St Peter*; and K. Forstner, 'Das Salzburger Skriptorium unter Virgil und das Verbrüderungsbuch von St Peter', in H. Dopsch and R. Juffinger (eds.), *Virgil von Salzburg. Missionar und Gelehrter* (Salzburg, 1984), pp. 135–40.

[18] Alcuin, *Carmina* 109, ed. E. Dümmler, *MGH Poetae* I, p. 340.

recognised that Virgil was so learned, Pippin sent Virgil to Odilo in Bavaria and gave him the bishopric of Salzburg.[19] The *Breves notitiae* of Salzburg, on the other hand, refer to Virgil as *peregrinus* (the word is also used of others who had come from Francia to Bavaria) and state that Odilo made Virgil bishop.[20] This is not the place to get engrossed in the debate about whether or not Virgil did indeed originally come from Ireland or was a Frank or Bavarian who had studied in Ireland. Nor do I wish to get embroiled in the associated argument about whether he is to be identified with Aethicus Ister and his extraordinary *Cosmographia*, though that discussion has undoubtedly been clouded by assumptions about Virgil's origins.[21] The recently discovered late eighth-century bifolium containing a fragment of the *Cosmographia* in Salzburg script indicates at the very least that Salzburg played a role in the early dissemination of the *Cosmographia*.[22] This must be set alongside the earliest complete text of the *Cosmographia* which was produced in Freising in the time of Arbeo (764/5–782/3).

It is conceivable that Virgil was himself in fact a Frank or a Bavarian. He had studied in Francia as well as Ireland. There are also so many links between Bavaria and Francia in the early eighth century, especially in the political sphere, that it is hardly a matter for surprise if men from Francia like Rupert, or perhaps Virgil too, are seen to be playing a role, often sponsored by the Frankish kings or Carolingian mayors, in Bavaria.[23] As far as the script is concerned, it remains a possibility that Virgil himself, whether an Irishman or a Frank, had learnt to write the newly evolved formal book

---

[19] *Conversio bagoariorum et carantanorum*, ed. H. Wolfram (Vienna, 1979), p. 40.

[20] *Breves notitiae*, ed. F. Losek, 'Notitia arnonis und Breves notitiae', *Mitteilungen der Gesellschaft für Salzburger Landeskunde* 130 (1990), pp. 5–192, at p. 114. For a full discussion see H. Wolfram, *Salzburg, Bayern, Österreich. Die conversio Bagoariorum et Carantanorum und die Quellen ihrer Zeit* (Vienna, 1995), pp. 252–74.

[21] For the identification of Virgil as the author of the *Cosmographia* see H. Löwe, 'Ein literarischer Widersacher des Bonifatius. Virgil von Salzburg und die Kosmographie des Aethicus Ister', *Abhandlungen der Akademie der Wissenschaften und der Literatur in Mainz. Geistes- und sozialwissenschaftliche Klasse 1951*(Wiesbaden, 1952), pp. 899–988; and the summary of the debate in F. Brunhölzl, *Histoire de la littérature latine au moyen âge I/I L'époque mérovingienne* (Turnhout, 1990), pp. 251–2. For arguments against this identification see M. Draak, 'Virgil of Salzburg versus "Aethicus Ister"', *Dancwerk. Opstellen angeboden aan Prof. Dr D. Th. Enklaar ter gelegenheid van zijn vijfenzestigste verjaardag* (Groningen, 1959), pp. 33–42. Draak's work was not noted by Löwe or Brunhölzl. See also the new edition by O. Prinz (ed.), *Die Cosmographie des Aethicus*, *MGH Quellen zur Geistesgeschichte des Mittelalters* 14 (Munich, 1993), who casts strong doubts on the alleged Irish elements in the *Cosmographia*.

[22] W. Selzer, 'Ein alt-Salzburger Fragment der Kosmographie des Aethicus Ister aus dem 8 Jht', *MIÖG* 100 (1992), pp. 132–49.

[23] See for example, H. Wolfram, 'Der heilige Rupert und die antikarolingische Adelsopposition', *MIÖG* 80 (1972), pp. 7–34; and J. Semmler, 'Zu den bayrisch-westfränkischen Beziehungen', *Zeitschrift für bayerische Landesgeschichte* 29 (1966), pp. 372–85.

hand at St Denis during his time spent studying in Francia. It is also noteworthy how meagre the insular influence in Salzburg manuscripts is apart from the close connection between the Englishman Alcuin, based in Francia, and Arno the Bavarian.[24]

Stronger support for Virgil's Irish links, if not origin, might appear to be the names of Irish abbots in the left-hand column on p. 20 of the *Liber vitae*. This is weakened by the juxtaposition in the right-hand column of the names of Bavarian and continental Anglo-Saxon bishops such as Willibald of Eichstätt and Lull of Mainz. Further, on this page are also to be found the names of Charles Martel, Swanhild, Pippin, Karloman, Desiderius the Lombard king and others. The names could thus be attributed as much to a Bavarian as to an Irish compiler. It is noteworthy that the abbatial reign of Slebteene runs to 772 and by this time Virgil had long been in Bavaria as bishop. Certainly connections existed between Salzburg and Iona, but they may not have been due to Virgil. Other Irish monks were in Salzburg in the time of Virgil's abbacy and died during that period, namely Baithanus and Mailprech.[25] They might originally have come from Iona and might have brought the Iona list with them, if the list had not been sent independently from Iona itself. There are thus alternative explanations for the presence of the list of Irish abbots in the Salzburg *Liber vitae*, as there are for the references to Irish saints in the Bavarian litany.[26]

What is clear, however, is the strong Frankish association reflected in the *Liber vitae* itself, not just in the concept of the book as a whole, and the script in which it is written, but also in the names included. This is a book compiled by people with strong links and sympathies with the west Frankish world. This may not necessarily extend, however, to strong

---

[24] Bischoff, *Schreibschulen*, II, pp. 52–61.

[25] Bischoff, *Schreibschulen*, II, p. 56; and *Liber vitae* p. 14 (grid. ref. Cd7; C2). Compare Forstner, 'Das Salzburger Skriptorium', p. 135.

[26] Coens, 'Les litanies bavaroises'; and see M. Niederkorn, 'Das Sanctorale Salzburgs um 800. Liturgie zwischen Norm und Praxis', Habilitationsschrift Universität Wien (Vienna, 1999). The Irish saints in the ninth-century Fleury *libellus precum* (Orléans, Bibliothèque Municipale 184) and in the Salzburg litany, however, could have reached Salzburg from a number of directions – Francia, Rome and elsewhere in Bavaria. It is equally possible that the whole list was taken over from an Irish liturgical text like the Stowe Missal or Martyrology of Tallaght. Fursey, for example, is mentioned in the Bavarian litany. One could posit Péronne or Echternach, both havens for Irish monks in the seventh and eighth centuries, as sources. See *The Stowe Missal*, ed. G. F. Warner (London, 1906); *The Martyrology of Tallaght*, ed. R. I. Best and H. J. Lawlor (London, 1931); and L. Traube, 'Perrona Scottorum', in L. Traube, *Vorlesungen und Abhandlungen*, II: *Kleine Schriften* (Munich, 1920), pp. 95–119. The literature on Echternach is extensive: see most recently M. Polfer (ed.), *L'Évangelisation des régions entre Meuse et Moselle et la fondation de l'abbaye d'Echternach (Ve–IXe siècle)*, (Luxembourg, 2000), and the bibliographical references therein.

political sympathies. The inclusion of Charlemagne and his immediate family was as much a recognition of Tassilo's blood ties as of the political relationship between Bavaria and the rest of the Frankish realms.[27] Both could be seen as an enhancement of Tassilo's own status as well as the reflection of the historical situation of Bavaria in relation to the rest of the Frankish world since the sixth century. With hindsight, of course, we know that the kinship with Charlemagne proved fatal to Tassilo's political ambitions. But this was not known when the *Liber vitae* of Salzburg was compiled, nor when Arno succeeded Virgil as bishop of the see. In this respect, therefore, it is an oversimplification to see Virgil as a Bavarian-oriented pre-Carolingian Tassilo supporter, and Arno as his pro-Carolingian successor. I can see no reason, moreover, why Arno should be regarded as Charlemagne's nominee in the see of Salzburg. His subsequent career after 788 should not be allowed to influence our understanding of Arno's position before 788. Arno would not be the first or the last turncoat bishop who had had to adjust to a new regime.[28] It was Arno, after all, who with Abbot Hunric of Mondsee went on Tassilo's behalf to Rome in 787 to beg the pope to intercede with Charlemagne.[29] The *Liber vitae* evidence, furthermore, suggests that both Virgil and Arno are at least Francophile, if not pro-Carolingian, nominees. It indicates that the political situation in Bavaria in the last two decades of Tassilo's rule, as well as the relations Tassilo and his followers enjoyed with his cousin and neighbour Charlemagne, were even more complex than has hitherto been realised.

It is significant that the foreign abbots listed, apart from those elsewhere in Bavaria, are primarily those of places such as Tours, St Denis and St Amand. Unlike the lists of brethren of other houses familiar from other Carolingian confraternity books, the Salzburg entries content themselves with a reference to the name of an abbot 'and his congregation'. These, I suggest, are very particular and personal links rather than an indication of general communication. We should note too the significance of the Old Testament prophets listed on p. 5 of the *Liber vitae*. These might simply be an indication of the Bavarian association with the Frankish assertions of their special role as the new children of Israel and the role of the Bible in politics.[30] Equally the list could represent an independent

---

[27] Airlie, 'Narratives of triumph'.

[28] See, for example, Wulfstan of Worcester in the aftermath of the Norman Conquest of England: E. Mason, *St Wulfstan of Worcester c. 1008–1095* (Oxford, 1990).

[29] *Annales regni francorum*, s.a 787, ed. F. Kurze, *MGH SRG*, VI (Hannover, 1895), p. 74.

[30] M. de Jong (ed.), *The power of the word. The influence of the Bible on early medieval politics*, special issue, *EME* 7 (1998).

proclamation on Salzburg's part of the special role of the Old Testament prophets in their perception of the past.[31] Such an independent claim would certainly accord with the famous preface to the *Lex baiuvariorum* and its association of Bavarian lawmaking with the laws of the Hebrews, the Greeks, the Romans, and the Merovingian Frankish kings of the sixth and early seventh centuries.[32]

Just as Virgil of Salzburg is associated with the Frankish court of Pippin III in the *Conversio bagoariorum*, so his successor Arno, originally from Bavaria, had also spent time in Francia and received the abbacy of St Amand in northern Francia before becoming bishop of Salzburg.[33] It has been customary to think of Arno's arrival as marking a very clear cultural and political reorientation of the diocese, and subsequently archdiocese, of Salzburg. By implication, his elevation is thought to signal the location of Bavaria within the Carolingian orbit. The *Liber vitae* itself contradicts this view; it has clear evidence of Arno's explicit and apparently immediate association of himself with the *Liber vitae* and all that it stood for. On page 6 of the *Liber vitae*, as Karl Forstner has observed, and under the heading related to living bishops and abbots, the name *Arn* is written on top of an original entry in uncial which appears to be the name VGLUS EPIS (*Virgilius episcopus*).[34] Almost as soon as it had been completed, in other words, the living bishop's name was altered to that of Arno, and Virgil's name was inserted into the list of the dead. Arno is therefore associated with the book in its original format and content as represented in the work of the scribe 'H1'. It is likely that Arno assumed the overseeing of the book's compilation on Virgil's death.

The cultural affiliations in the Salzburg *Liber vitae* are thus common to both Virgil and Arno. Arno's support of Tassilo, his Bavarian loyalties, his links with Frankish culture and his uneasy position as intermediary between Charlemagne and Tassilo, and between Francia and Bavaria, are just as clearly manifested in the *Liber vitae* as in the Frankish annals. The fact that the *Liber vitae* continued to provide the written expression of the Salzburg community's memory thereafter, moreover, explicitly continued Salzburg's associations with the very complex network of political sympathies and cultural affiliations recorded in the original book.

---

[31] I owe the latter suggestion to Tony Moore, of Churchill College, Cambridge.

[32] *Lex baiuvariorum*, ed. E. von Schwind, *MGH Leges nat. germ.* V, 2 (Hannover, 1926), pp. 198–203. The first redaction of the laws is usually attributed to Tassilo's period of rule; for discussion see R. Kottje, 'Die Lex Baiuvariorum – das Recht der Baiern', in H. Mordek (ed.), *Überlieferung und Geltung normativer Texte des frühen und hohen Mittelalters*, Quellen und Forschungen zum Recht im Mittelalter 4 (Sigmaringen, 1986), pp. 9–24.

[33] See M. Niederkorn and A. Scharer (eds.), *Arn von Salzburg* (Vienna, 2004); and Wolfram, *Salzburg, Bayern, Österreich*, pp. 290–5.

[34] Forstner, *Das Verbrüderungsbuch St Peter*, p. 18.

The *Liber vitae* of Salzburg is certainly a book anchoring the Salzburg community within its locality and immediate institutional memory. That memory itself, however, was not separated from a wider political realm represented both by the Bavarian dukes and the Carolingian king, and by the links forged between the religious houses and sees of west Francia and Bavaria. The book remained at the heart of the Salzburg community, with names added, most substantially, in the time of Arno. It stands therefore as a memorial to that community and as a record of it. It is a witness to the different strands of influence and affiliation in Agilolfing and Carolingian Bavaria.

9 The reading of history at Lorsch and St Amand

The prayers for the dead, the *Libri vitae* and the cartularies which formed the subject of the preceding two chapters in this book provide an immediate conjunction between past and present time; the dead are remembered in terms of the commemoration of their anniversaries in the present. Yet such texts also convey a very particular sense of the historical past in which chronology has a crucial role to play. The historical precedents for the records of the *Libri vitae*, furthermore, reinforce the sense of historical memory being formed in relation to particular books. Anton von Euw has uncovered precursors of the page layout with columns of the *Liber viventium* of Pfäfers in calendars and lists such as as the Calendar of 354 (BAV Barberini lat. 2154, fol. 7r) and its list of *natales caesarum*.[1] The Cologne canon law collection (Cologne, Dombibliothek MS 212, fols 168v–169r) of the late sixth or early seventh century similarly places its list of *pontifices romanorum* in double arcades. The names of the popes from Peter to Gregory the Great are accompanied by a precise indication of their pontificate in years, months and days. A further influence, both conceptually and in the visual layout of the *Libri vitae*, may have been exerted by ivory diptychs such as the *Diptychon barberini* with its list of members of the Merovingian royal family (612–75) and Merovingian bishops from the fourth to the seventh centuries. Jakobi, indeed, has emphasised the 'diptych' in the *Liber memorialis* of Remiremont as a written record kept for memorial purposes which was used in the liturgy and appears to have been a reuse of an antique form.[2]

---

[1] A. von Euw, *Liber Viventium Fabariensis. Das karolingische Memorialbuch von Pfäfers in seiner Liturgie- und Kunstgeschichtlichen Bedeutung*, Studia Fabariensia. Beiträge zur Pfäferser Klostergeschichte 1 (Bern and Stuttgart, 1989), pp. 209–214.

[2] H. Thomas, 'Die Namenliste des Diptychon Barberini und der Sturz des Hausmeiers Grimoald', *DA* 25 (1969), pp. 17–63; and F.-J. Jakobi, 'Diptychen als frühe Form der Gedenk-Aufzeichnungen. Zum "Herrscher-Diptychon" im Liber memorialis von Remiremont', *Frühmittelalterliche Studien* 20 (1986), pp. 186–212. See also A. Ebner, *Die klösterlichen Gebetsverbrüderungen bis zum Ausgange des karolingischen Zeitalters. Eine kirchengeschichtliche Studie* (Regensburg, New York and Cincinnati, 1890).

Yet this visual perspective needs to be joined to those of text reception and the transmission of ideas. It is not just that the dates of papal reigns provided in the Cologne *Collectio canonum* correspond exactly with those in the *Liber pontificalis*, a book of the utmost importance to the Franks in their historical education. The idea of the provision of such lists in the *Collectio canonum* is more than one of how to set it out in columns; it is indicative of an historical mentality and a strong sense of chronological position. The names are placed precisely in time but bear in addition an eternal memorial function, like an inscription.

The *Libri vitae* and cartularies, therefore, need to be set beside the more conventional narrative representations of the past composed in the Carolingian period, not least the remarkable number of contemporary histories written in the late eighth and the ninth centuries discussed elsewhere in this book.[3] In thinking about the writing of history, however, and the keeping of historical records of many different kinds, we also need to think about the historical mindedness of the Franks and the formation of historical sensitivity by means of reading texts. How did an author's historical training (as it were) and reading influence the presentation and perception of the events, issues and personalities they record? More generally, we need to explore the implications of the presence of histories and what was made available by copying in the ninth and tenth centuries. The perceptions of the past and of layers of time in the Carolingian world are peculiarly distinctive and their formation needs to be investigated. This can only be done in concert with a recognition that humans do make creative leaps and connect previously unrelated ideas in ways we cannot now document, even though we can observe and analyse some of the results. Nevertheless, elements of what enabled such connections to be made can be unravelled.

One major element in the formation of both a sense of the past and knowledge of history is of course what any individual or group of people may have read and what was available to them. It is this wider context of the Carolingian association of history and the book which I wish to explore in this chapter, using the evidence in particular of what was read and used at the monasteries of Lorsch in the middle Rhineland and of St Amand in northern France in the ninth and tenth centuries as case studies. Whereas my principal focus in the preceding chapters has been on Frankish and contemporary history, most of the following discussion concerns ancient Roman and early Christian history texts.

---

[3] See Innes and McKitterick, 'Writing of history'; and for the general context see A. Momigliano, 'Pagan and Christian historiography in the fourth century A.D.', in A. Momigliano (ed.), *The conflict between paganism and Christianity in the fourth century* (London, 1962), pp. 79–99.

Let me first offer some general considerations. As Cozroh of Freising himself tells us, the creation of the Freising cartulary was part of the concerted effort by Bishop Hitto to augment both the cathedral library and the texts for use in the liturgy.[4] We have ample evidence of the success of these efforts on the part of Hitto and his successors Erchanpert (835–54), Anno (854–75), Arnold (875–83) and Waldo (883–906) in the extant manuscripts from Freising dated to the ninth century.[5] Hitto's episcopate, indeed, marked a striking shift of emphasis in the books produced in Freising's scriptorium. There is a growing concentration not only of contemporary works but also of the works of Augustine (compared with an apparently older preference for Gregory the Great) and a manifestly rapid response to the Carolingian rulers' recommendations for correct and authoritative texts in the provision of the *Dionysio-Hadriana* collection of canon law and the homiliary of Paul the Deacon. At Freising, therefore, the commemoration of benefactors and the wish to provide a history of the bishops' activities are to be seen in the context of concentrated literate activity of a very particular kind.[6] It is part of the gathering together and production of books concerned with Christian learning and the maintenance of the Christian faith and ritual within a framework of Christian history. Canon law in the *Dionysio-Hadriana* collection, moreover, was organised in chronological sequence, with the great oecumenical councils of the early church and decretals of subsequent popes providing a sense of the historical development of ecclesiastical law. Knowledge of history was augmented by the copy of the seven books of history against the pagans by Orosius made at Freising (Munich, Bayerische Staatsbibliothek Clm 6308) quite apart from the foundation provided by the historical books of the Bible such as the Book of Kings (Munich, Bayerische Staatsbibliothek Clm 6220).

This conjunction of literacy, history and memory was not of course confined to Freising. At Fulda it is even more striking and is particularly to be associated with Hraban Maur, abbot of Fulda (824–42) and archbishop of Mainz (847–56).[7] Hraban's command of biblical history and

---

[4] Cozroh, ed. T. Bitterauf, *Die Traditionen des Hochstifts Freising*, Quellen und Erörterungen zur bayersichen und deutschen Geschichte NF 4 and 5, 2 vols. (Munich, 1905) I, pp. 1–2 and see the discussion by P. Geary, *Phantoms of remembrance. Memory and oblivion at the end of the first millennium* (Princeton, 1994), pp. 93–6, as well as above, pp. 158–9.

[5] B. Bischoff, *Schreibschulen*, I, pp. 58–130.

[6] See R. McKitterick, 'Unity and diversity in the Carolingian church', in R. Swanson (ed.), *Unity and diversity in the church*, Studies in Church History 32 (Woodbridge, 1996), pp. 59–82, at pp. 74–7.

[7] See above, Introduction, and R. Corradini, *Die wiener Handschrift Cvp* 430. Ein Beitrag zur Historiographie in Fulda im frühen 9. Jahrhundert*, Fuldaer Hochschulschriften 37 (Frankfurt am Main, 2000); and J. Raaijmakers, 'Sacred time, sacred space: history and

his application of it to Frankish history is now being explored by Mayke de Jong.[8] It was again under the aegis of Hraban Maur as archbishop of Mainz that a dossier of the life of St Boniface was compiled. An earlier archbishop of Mainz, Lull, had commissioned the *Vita* by Willibald and prepared a collection of Boniface's letters in two groups, represented in two extant manuscripts.[9] A third collection of letters, extant in Vienna, ÖNB cod. 751, is attributed to Hraban Maur's interest. Further it was Hraban who devised a Martyrology, organised in historical sequence and with careful details supplied as to when and where each martyr had lived.[10] We should also remember that Einhard was educated at Fulda, and Rudolf was a monk and author based at Fulda.[11] Both give clear indications in their own work of their knowledge of the histories of Tacitus, Ammianus Marcellinus, Suetonius and Justinus' *Epitome* of Pompeius Trogus' *Historiae philippicae*.[12] Within this context, therefore, it is not surprising to find so many extant history books which can be associated with Fulda in this period, as can be seen from table 9.1 below. There are, furthermore, many other instances of Carolingian historical mindedness, not least the historical organisation of the authors in chronological sequence in Carolingian library catalogues. What we are observing is a more general phenomenon of the reception of a host of ideas and their

identity at the monastery of Fulda (744–856)' (Ph.D. thesis, University of Amsterdam, 2003; Akademisch Proefschrift).

[8] See M. de Jong, 'Old law and new found power: Hrabanus Maurus and the Old Testament', in J. W. Drijvers and A. A. MacDonald (eds.), *Centres of learning: learning and location in pre-modern Europe and the near East* (Leiden, New York and Cologne, 1995), pp. 161–76. See also M. Rissel, *Rezeption antiker und patristischer Wissenschaft bei Hrabanus Maurus. Studien zur karolingischen Geistesgeschichte* (Bern and Frankfurt, 1976).

[9] Munich, Bayerische Staatsbibliothek Clm 8112, a copy of an original collection, dating from the end of the eighth century copied at Mainz, and probably at Fulda by the eleventh century. A second collection, represented by Karlsruhe, Landesbibliothek Rastatt 22, was also produced on Lull's commissioning, compiled at Mainz and a copy of it was made at Fulda. See M. Tangl, 'Studien zur Neuausgabe der Briefe des hl. Bonifatius und Lullus Teil I', in M. Tangl, *Das Mittelalter in Quellenkunde und Diplomatik. Ausgewählte Schriften* 1, Forschungen zur mittelalterlichen Geschichte 12 (Berlin, 1966), pp. 60–175.

[10] *Rabani Mauri martyrologium*, ed. J. McCulloh, CCCM, XLIV (Turnhout, 1979); and J. Dubois, *Les Martyrologes du moyen âge latin*, Typologie des sources du moyen âge occidental 26 (Turnhout, 1978).

[11] On Einhard see the useful compilation by Paul E. Dutton, *Charlemagne's courtier. The Complete Einhard* (Peterborough, Ontario, 1998), and his references, as well as above, pp. 29–30. On Rudolf see B. Krusch, 'Die Übertragung des H. Alexander von Rom nach Wildeshausen durch den Enkel Widukinds 851. Das älteste niedersächsische Geschichtsdenkmal', *Nachrichten der Gesellschaft der Wissenschaften zu Göttingen*, II, 13 (Göttingen, 1933), pp. 405–36.

[12] For Hraban Maur of Fulda and history see M. de Jong, 'The empire as *ecclesia*: Hrabanus Maurus and biblical *historia* for rulers', in Y. Hen and M. Innes (eds.), *The uses of the past in the early middle ages* (Cambridge, 2000), pp. 191–226.

Table 9.1 *History manuscripts associated with Fulda (from Carolingian library catalogues, extant manuscripts and the citation of earlier historians made by Carolingian authors at Fulda)*

---

1. BAV lat. 1873 s.IX/1
   Ammianus Marcellinus, *Res gestae*[13]
2. Florence, Biblioteca Laurenziana MS plut. 68.1
   Tacitus (*Annales*, 1–6, *Germania* and *Agricola*)
3. Jesi lat. 8 (Tacitus, *Germania* and *Agricola* with Dictys Cretensis, *Bellum Troianum*)[14]
4. Eutropius *Historia romana*[15] (Fulda copy now lost)
5. Rufius Festus, *Breviarium*
6. Frontinus, *Strategemata*[16]
7. Bamberg, Staatsbibliothek, Class. 54 of s.IX 2/4 copied by a Fulda scribe from Vat. pal. lat. 899 s.IX from northern Italy (see also under Lorsch)
   Scriptores historiae augustae[17]
8. Fulda, Hessische Landesbibliothek, Fragm. 24 is from western Germany and may have been in Fulda's library in the ninth century
   Josephus, *Antiquitates*
9. Kassel, Gesamthochschulbibliothek, 4o Ms. hist. 72a-c. (fragment)
   Paul the Deacon, *Historia langobardorum*
10. Kassel, Gesamthochschulbibliothek, 4o Ms. theol. 2
    Bede, *Historia ecclesiastica gentis anglorum*, in a copy written in a Northumbrian script
11. Kassel, Gesamthochschulbibliothek, 2o Ms. astron. 2
    Annales breves fuldenses[18]
12. Vienna, ÖNB 430*
    Chronicon laurissense breve[19]

---

[13] Bischoff, *Katalog*, no. 1798, notes that the exemplar of the Fulda manuscript BAV lat. 1873 was probably Kassel, Landesbibliothek 2o Ms. philol. 27 from Hersfeld.

[14] Bischoff, *Katalog*, no. 1237. The Jesi manuscript has disappeared since the Second World War, but see R. Till, *Handschriftliche Untersuchungen zu Tacitus Agricola und Germania* (Berlin-Dahlem, 1943) for a facsimile, and Reynolds, *Texts and Transmission*, p. 410.

[15] See Reynolds, *Texts and transmission*, p. 159. Compare Gotha, Forschungsbibliothek, membr. I.101 from ninth-century Murbach.

[16] *Ibid.*, p. 159.

[17] Bischoff, *Katalog*, no. 216; see also Reynolds, *Texts and transmission*, pp. 354–5.

[18] Bischoff, *Katalog*, no. 1338 (Josephus), 1792 (Paul the Deacon), *CLA*, VIII (Oxford, 1959), no. 1140 (Bede). See also Bischoff, *Katalog*, no. 1790 (*Annales breves fuldenses*).

[19] See H. Schnorr von Carolsfeld (ed.), 'Das Chronicon laurissense breve', *Neues Archiv* 36 (1911), pp. 13–39; and R. Corradini, *Die Wiener Handschrift Cvp 430*. *Ein Beitrag zur Historiographie in Fulda im frühen 9. Jahrhundert*, Fuldaer Hochschulschriften 37 (Frankfurt am Main, 2000); and R. Corradini, 'The rhetoric of crisis: *computus* and *Liber annalis* in early ninth-century Fulda', in R. Corradini, M. Diesenberger and H. Reimitz (eds.), *The construction of communities in the early middle ages: texts, resources and artefacts*, The Transformation of the Roman World 12 (Leiden, 2003), pp. 269–321. I am very grateful to Richard Corradini for discussing this manuscript and its relationship with BAV pal. lat. 243 with me.

location in time and space right across the Carolingian empire. It is manifest in the creation of many new kinds of book and text in which historical orientation is a guiding principle. Such precise location of ideas in time and place as part of the Carolingian sense of the past has not yet been charted. Janet Coleman, for example, has focused most productively on the relation between theory and memory in twelfth-century historiography and Richard Southern in a famous series of lectures also documented a development of historiography that largely omitted Carolingian historical writing.[20]

It is one of the underlying convictions of this book that the developments of the ninth century were in every sense formative and crucial for subsequent conceptions and understandings of the past. Studies of the twelfth century which ignore the developments in the ninth century, therefore, are doing more than passing over an earlier century. They are actually neglecting to register the foundations of the twelfth-century understandings of the past. The sheer historical precision and orientation of the Carolingians need emphasis, for they had a strong ideological underpinning. Tom Noble, for example, has demonstrated that the *Libri carolini*, written c. 793 by Theodulf of Orléans as part of the Frankish response to iconoclasm, is a 'metahistory' that seeks to locate the Franks in their own time.[21] This was more than the adjustment in Christian historiography when Christians had been obliged to locate themselves in relation to a new past and when conversion to the Christian faith meant the discovery of a whole new history from Adam and Eve, or at least from the birth of Abraham. The Franks' careful placing of themselves in a Christian past was closely related to their sense of relationship with Rome as well. Hence their insistence on defining the place of the eastern Roman empire or Byzantium not only in relation to themselves, but also in relation to this same biblical and Christian past.

In the Carolingian period, as in any other, therefore, we can observe one outcome of what people read in what they wrote themselves and how it oriented their thinking. Many medievalists are exploring many different aspects of reading and understanding, not least the methods of communicating a text, an image, or a building, by private reading, reading

---

[20] J. Coleman, *Ancient and medieval memories. Studies in the reconstruction of the past* (Cambridge, 1992), pp. 274–324; and R. Southern, 'Aspects of the European tradition of historical writing. I. The classical tradition from Einhard to Geoffrey of Monmouth', *TRHS* fifth series 20 (1970), pp. 173–96, though his preliminary remarks are very much to the point. See also G. M. Spiegel, *The past as text: the theory and practice of medieval historiography* (Baltimore, 1999).

[21] T. F. X. Noble, 'Tradition and learning in search of ideology: the *Libri Carolini*', in R. Sullivan (ed.), *'The gentle voices of teachers': aspects of learning in the Carolingian age* (Columbus, Ohio, 1995), pp. 227–60.

or singing aloud, paraphrase, excerpting or translation. Annotation provides evidence of reading and how texts were understood. Translation is also a means by which a text is mediated through the reading and comprehension of one person to a different audience.[22]

A further manifestation of reading which I want to discuss in this chapter is what was copied and preserved in manuscripts, and how reading placed Roman and early Christian history into a new context. Copying a text rests on a network of actions and decisions. Someone must have the knowledge of the existence of a text already, and also the knowledge of where a copy of that text might be in order to furnish an exemplar. A decision must be taken to expend precious materials and time in order to have that particular text, or, lacking resources at home to make a copy himself/herself/themselves in a particular centre. There must be the means of purchase or exchange in order to procure the text that is wanted. The letters of Lupus of Ferrières are famous for the number of times he asks to borrow a particular book in order to copy it, such as the papyrus codex containing the commentaries on the *Topica* of Cicero by Boethius he borrowed from Tours or an additional copy of Cicero's *De rhetorica* in order to compare it with the one he had already in order to check its accuracy.[23]

A vital source of information about books was Jerome-Gennadius' *De viris illustribus*, also organised in chronological sequence.[24] The library catalogues from the ninth century, some of which we can establish were exchanged between various monastic libraries, such as the Reichenau and St Gallen, Fulda and Lorsch, St Denis and St Gallen, attest to the knowledge and zeal of monastic librarians in stocking their libraries with what was needed, either by procuring exemplars for copying in the house scriptorium or by gift and exchange. It is not difficult to understand how a core of books everyone should have, that is, a canon of knowledge or literary Noah's Ark, was formed in the ninth century.[25] Certainly from copies of older classical and patristic texts made in the late eighth and the ninth centuries it is clear that there was a process of deliberate selection and salvage of ancient learning in train.

---

[22] See, for example, the papers in Susan J. Ridyard (ed.), *Reading and the book in the middle ages*, Sewanee Medieval Studies 11 (Sewanee, 2001); and especially the chapters on classical antiquity in G. Cavallo and R. Chartier (eds.), *A history of reading in the west* (Oxford and Amherst, 1999).

[23] Lupus, ed. L. Levillain, *Loup de Ferrières, Correspondance*, Les Classiques de l'histoire de France au moyen âge 10 (Paris, 1964), nos. 53 and 1; I, pp. 214 and 8.

[24] Jerome-Gennadius, ed. E. C. Richardson, *Hieronymus, Liber de viris inlustribus. Gennadius de viris inlustribus* (Leipzig, 1896); and see McKitterick, *Carolingians and the written word*, pp. 200–5, and below, chapter 10.

[25] *Ibid.*, pp. 115–220.

It is against this background that we can set the transmission of pagan and early Christian history books in the early middle ages. Particular histories became part of the canon of required knowledge. As I have already suggested above, the manuscript transmission of such Roman histories as those by Sallust, Tacitus, Ammianus Marcellinus, Justinus, Livy, Caesar, Eutropius, Quintus Curtius Rufus, Suetonius and the authors of the *Historiae augustae*, indicates that there was an extraordinarily creative cultivation of an interest in Roman history and 'pagan historiography' in the late eighth and the ninth centuries.[26] Similarly, there was a wide dissemination of Old Testament history books and the works of Jewish and Christian ecclesiastical historians such as Josephus,[27] the *Historia ecclesiastica* of Eusebius, known in the Latin west in the augmented translation by Rufinus,[28] the *Historia tripartita* of Epiphanius commissioned by Cassiodorus and Orosius. The latter includes the famous descriptions of the world in Book 1, so important for the transmission of geographical ideas in the middle ages, and of the sack of Rome in 410 by Alaric and his Visigoths. Orosius' description of the events of 410 culminates in the triumphal procession of the Arian Christian Goths and Roman Catholics to restore the treasures of St Peter's to the basilica. It also contains, of course, a wealth of information about the history of Rome.[29]

A few examples may serve to illustrate the extent of the dissemination of pagan and Christian history in the Frankish realms. At Corbie in Picardy, texts available included Livy, Caesar and Justinus.[30] Tours possessed the sister of the Corbie Livy in Florence.[31] Associated with Fleury we find fifth-century palimpsested leaves of Sallust as well as a ninth-century text, Caesar, Quintus Curtius Rufus and Livy's First Decade.[32] According to

---

[26] Reynolds, *Texts and transmission*, and see also above, chapter 2.

[27] Hegesippus/Josephus: ed. V. Ussani, *Hegessipi qui dicitur Historiae libri V*, CSEL 66 (Vienna, 1932); see also H. Schreckenburg and K. Schubert (eds.), *Jewish historiography and iconography in early and medieval Christianity* (Assen and Minneapolis, 1992).

[28] E. Schwartz and T. Mommsen (eds.), *Eusebius Werke, II, Die lateinische Übersetzung des Rufinus*, ed. T. Mommsen (Leipzig, 1908); and see below, chapter 11.

[29] Orosius, ed. C. Zangemeister, *Historiarum adversum paganos libri VII* (Leipzig, 1889); ed. M. P. Arnaud-Lindet, *Histoires (contre les païens) Orose*, 3 vols. (Paris 1990–1); English trans. I. W. Raymond, *Seven books of history against the pagans*, Columbia Records of Civilization, Sources and Studies (New York, 1936) and R. J. Deferrari, *Orosius, seven books of history against the pagans*, Fathers of the Church 50 (Washington, D.C., 1964).

[30] Livy, First Decade, fragment in Copenhagen, Kongelige Bibliotek F84 and F86; Third Decade, Paris, BnF lat. 5730, of s.V; see *CLA*, V (Oxford, 1950), no. 562, plus Florence, Biblioteca Medicea Laurenziana, plut. 63.20, the copy made of it; Caesar, BAV lat. 3864; Justinus, Epitome, Paris, BnF lat. 7950. See D. Ganz, *Corbie in the Carolingian Renaissance*, Beihefte der Francia 20 (Sigmaringen, 1990).

[31] BAV reg. lat. 762, *c.* 800, also copied from Paris, BnF lat. 5730.

[32] Sallust (s.V palimpsested leaves e.g. Berlin, Deutsche Staatsbibliothek lat. Qu. 364, and Paris, BnF lat. 16024, s.IX/2); Caesar (Amsterdam, Universiteitsbibliotheek

the library catalogues there were copies of Eusebius-Rufinus' *Historia ecclesiastica* and the *Historia tripartita* at St Germer de Fly, Würzburg, Bobbio, St Riquier, St Gallen, Reichenau, Murbach.[33] Chelles also possessed Eusebius-Rufinus,[34] and the centre writing a-b script (Chelles? Jouarre? Soissons?) had a copy of the *Historia tripartita* made, according to an eleventh-century note, for Adalhard of Corbie.[35] Other ninth-century copies of the *Historia tripartita* are from Orléans, Constance, Regensburg and Tours. The library catalogue of Murbach had a separate heading *De historiis* under which it listed Josephus, Egesippus, Orosius, Eusebius, *Historia tripartita*, *Historia clementis* and Velleius Paterculus.[36] Lupus of Ferrières in the Loire valley in the middle of the ninth century quotes from his own reading of history from, or mentions the texts of, many Roman and Christian historians, such as Justinus, Pompeius Trogus, Livy, Aurelius Victor, Caesar, Sallust, Eusebius-Rufinus' Ecclesiastical History, Josephus and Suetonius.[37]

Further categories of historical text transmitted to the Carolingians are the more recent so-called 'barbarian histories' such as Jordanes the Goth's *Getica*, a history of the Goths from their legendary origins to the reconquest of Ostrogothic Italy by Justinian,[38] and the *Historia romana* by the same author. There are also contemporary histories which were brought up to date at regular intervals, such as the *Liber pontificalis*.[39]

With one exception (Lucca, Biblioteca Capitolare MS 490),[40] the earliest complete manuscripts (all from the ninth century) of the *Liber*

XV.G [81] s.IX 2/4, and Paris, BnF lat. 5763 s.IXin); Quintus Curtius Rufus (Bern, Burgerbibliothek 451); Iustinus Epitome of Pompeius Trogus (Bern, Burgerbibliothek 330, s.IX/2, and Leiden, Bibliotheek der Rijksuniversiteit, Voss. lat. Qu. 32 (s.IX 2/4); Livy First Decade + ab urbe condita (Paris, BnF lat. 5724 s.IX/2).

[33] For references see McKitterick, *Carolingians and the written word*, pp. 169–96.

[34] Eusebius-Rufinus (Paris, BnF lat. 18282), *CLA*, V (Oxford, 1950), no. 674; and compare Paris, BnF lat. 10399, fol. 4,5 + 14000, fol. 2,7, *CLA*, V (Oxford, 1950), no. 594.

[35] St Petersburg, Saltykov-Schedrin Library, MS F.v.1, no. 11.

[36] On Velleius Paterculus see Reynolds, *Texts and transmission*, pp. 431–3; and for the Murbach catalogue see W. Milde (ed.), *Der Bibliothekskatalog des Klosters Murbach aus dem 9. Jahrhundert. Ausgabe und Untersuchungen von Beziehungen zu Cassiodors 'Institutiones'*, *Euphorion, Zeitschrift für Literaturgeschichte*, Beiheft 4 (Heidelberg, 1968), p. 47. Murbach also possessed a copy of Bede's *Historia ecclesiastica*, but this was listed with the rest of Bede's works, just as it was at Lorsch.

[37] Lupus, ed. L. Levillain, *Loup de Ferrières, Correspondance*, nos 6, 8, 9, 33, 35, 46, 101, 104; I, pp. 52–4, 68, 78, 152, 156, 196; II, pp. 124, 130.

[38] See Walter Goffart, *The narrators of barbarian history (A.D. 550–800): Jordanes, Gregory of Tours, Bede and Paul the Deacon* (Princeton, 1988), pp. 20–111.

[39] *Liber pontificalis*, ed. L. Duchesne, 2 vols. (Paris, 1886 and 1892) and translated by R. Davis, *The book of pontiffs (Liber pontificalis to 715)* (Liverpool, 1989); *The lives of the eighth-century popes (Liber pontificalis)* (Liverpool, 1992) and *The lives of the ninth-century popes (Liber pontificalis)* (Liverpool, 1995).

[40] On this extraordinarily complex manuscript see above, pp. 51–2, Duchesne, *Liber pontificalis*, pp. clxii–clxvi, and L. Schiaparelli, *Il codice 490 della biblioteca capitolare di Lucca e*

pontificalis are of Frankish origin. Two earlier fragments witness to the *Liber pontificalis'* distribution in Italy, namely Turin, Biblioteca Nazionale F.IV.18[41] and the late seventh- or early eighth-century Italian minuscule Naples, Biblioteca Nazionale IV.A.8, fols. 40–47, important in that it contains the spurious prefatory letters between Pope Damasus and Jerome and thus establishes their existence by then.[42]

It is difficult to be certain, firstly, when the *Liber pontificalis* was introduced into Francia and, secondly, when the Frankish recension (represented by Duchesne's 'B' and 'D' groups) was made. This Frankish version, as we have seen, incorporated significant additions, notably in the lives of the eighth-century popes Gregory III and Stephen II (III), which are pertinent to Frankish affairs or offered a Frankish dimension to papal affairs.[43]

Three copies of this version of the *Liber pontificalis* were made in the early ninth century, the earliest of which, Cologne, Dombibliothek 164, was formerly proposed by Jones as a copy made at Cologne in the time of Archbishop Hildebold.[44] It is now judged to have been produced at the Laon scriptorium under Bishop Wenilo (799–814),[45] possibly from an exemplar sent by Pope Leo III to Charlemagne.[46] Where and when Frankish additions were made, in Francia or Rome, has not been satisfactorily resolved, and this is not the occasion to do so. The so-called Lombard recension (of which the most famous representative is Lucca, Biblioteca Capitolare 490 mentioned above) has an Italian origin and provenance with some Frankish representatives, and is notable for its

---

la scuola scrittoria Lucchese (sec. VIII–IX). Contributi allo studio della minuscola precarolina in Italia, Studi e testi 36 (Vatican City, 1924).

[41] Listed by Duchesne as an eighth-century palimpsested fragment of four leaves in a twelfth-century Antiphoner from Bobbio, *Liber pontificalis*, p. clxxv, but it appears to have been missed by Lowe in *CLA* and in all subsequent additions (though it is possible that it was judged by Lowe to be a little too late in date for inclusion). Davis does not mention it at all in his summary of the manuscripts, *The eighth-century popes*, p. xv.

[42] *CLA*, III (Oxford, 1938), no. 403. The manuscript is presumed to have been written at Bobbio (though it could be from elsewhere in northern Italy) and is a palimpsest. The underneath script is a sixth-century uncial copy of the *De re rustica* of Gargilius Martialis. The list of popes ending in Conon (†687) dates the upper script with the *Liber pontificalis* to 687–701.

[43] See above, chapters 5 and 6.

[44] L. W. Jones, *The script of Cologne from Hildebold to Hermann* (Cambridge, Mass., 1932), p. 20 and no. 11, pp. 47–51.

[45] J. J. Contreni, *The cathedral school of Laon from 850 to 930. Its manuscripts and masters*, Münchener Beiträge zur Mediävistik und Renaissance Forschung (Munich, 1978), pp. 50–1.

[46] See P. Lehmann, 'Erzbischof Hildebold und die Dombibliothek von Köln', *Zentralblatt für Bibliothekswesen* 25 (1908), pp. 153–8; and B. Bischoff, 'Die Kölner Nonnenhandschriften und das Skriptorium von Chelles', in B. Bischoff, *Mittelalterliche Studien*, I (Stuttgart, 1966), pp. 16–34, at pp. 18–19.

removal of the harsh criticisms and extremely negative language applied to the Lombard rulers in their dealings with the pope.

Lastly there are the contemporary histories of the Franks themselves. The *Liber historiae francorum*, written *c.* 727,[47] the Continuations of the *Chronicle* of Fredegar,[48] and the many series of annals and biographies I referred to earlier, not least the *Annales regni francorum* and Einhard's *Vita Karoli*, belong to this category.[49]

All these works were copied in Carolingian monasteries at the end of the eighth and throughout the ninth centuries.

With very few exceptions the earliest witness to all the classical or early Christian texts is a Frankish manuscript from the Carolingian period. The scriptoria of Lorsch and St Amand were especially active in the copying of Roman and early Christian history; each produced a greater concentration of these texts, with the possible exception of Fulda, than the other places mentioned above. This requires a fuller consideration of the extant manuscripts from these two places so that we can gain an understanding of the reception and reading of history in the Carolingian world.

Lorsch

The monastery of Lorsch was initially an aristocratic *Eigenkloster*, founded by Cancor, a count in the upper Rhine region, and his mother Wolliswinth in 762 or 763 on the site of Roman estate. It very soon came under the aegis of Bishop Chrodegang of Metz, the chief ecclesiastical adviser to Charlemagne's father Pippin III, who installed his brother Gundeland as abbot (764/5–78). Lorsch acquired extra religious status at about the same time because of the acquisition of the relics of St Nazarius (11 July 756) and its newly built church was consecrated by Archbishop Lull of Mainz in 774. The charters of Lorsch dating from 766 onwards reveal a huge number of gifts of land to the abbey, so that it rapidly became very wealthy.[50] Its status within the Frankish realm was further elevated by its coming under royal protection in 772. Lorsch remained closely connected with the Carolingian rulers throughout the ninth century and it is there that Louis the German was buried in a fine classicising sarcophagus and

---

[47] *Liber historiae francorum*, ed. B. Krusch, *MGH SRM*, II (Hannover, 1888) pp. 241–328; and R. Gerberding, *The rise of the Carolingians and the 'Liber historiae francorum'* (Oxford, 1987); and chapter 1 above.

[48] *The fourth book of the Chronicle of Fredegar and its continuations*, ed. and trans. J. M. Wallace-Hadrill (London, 1960); and see R. Collins, *Fredegar* (Aldershot, 1997).

[49] See chapter 1 above.

[50] K. Glöckner (ed.), *Codex laureshamensis*, Arbeiten der historischen Kommission für den Volkstaat Hessen 3, 3 vols. (Darmstadt, 1929–36); and see M. Innes, *State and society in the early middle ages 400–1000* (Cambridge, 2000).

that the famous Torhalle was built. Lorsch enjoyed connections not only with the royal court, but also with such monasteries as Fulda, St Riquier and St Vaast.[51]

Lorsch's rise to prominence as an intellectual and cultural centre was under Abbot Richbod, a member of Charlemagne's court circle, a pupil of the Englishman Alcuin of Tours, and from 791 Archbishop of Trier. It was in the time of Richbod and his successors, especially Abbot Adalung (804–37), that the scriptorium of Lorsch flourished. About 100 manuscripts survive from Lorsch from the period from *c.* 780 to *c.* 860 alone, with another concentrated period of activity later in the tenth century under Abbot Salemann (972–99).[52]

It is fortunate that an even more impressive documentation of Lorsch's activity in both copying texts and acquiring books from elsewhere is reflected in ninth-century catalogues also surviving from Lorsch. These catalogues, in different redactions, now fully elucidated by Angelika Häse,[53] essentially record the library of Lorsch as it was in the middle of the ninth century. It was, for its time, an impressive and comprehensive collection of biblical, patristic, liturgical and school texts. But what is really fascinating is the large group of history books. They are listed in the Lorsch catalogue known now as Ca (formerly Bischoff Kat. III) directly after the books of the Old and New Testaments, as follows.[54]

The evidence of the library catalogue, BAV pal. lat. 1877
(Kat. Ca, s.IXmed/2)

(identified extant Lorsch MSS in *italic*)

fol. 3r
Historia ecclesiastica eusebii libri XI in uno codice
Historia iosephi libri XI in uno codice
Isyppi lib V de eodem historiographo in uno codice
Historia orosii libri VII in uno codice
Chronica eusebii hieronimi et bedae in uno codice

---

[51] See *Beiträge zur Geschichte des Klosters Lorsch*, 2nd edn, Geschichtsblätter für den Kreis Bergstraße, Sonderband 4 (Lorsch, 1980).

[52] B. Bischoff, *Die Abtei Lorsch im Spiegel ihrer Handschriften*, 2nd edn (Lorsch, 1989), and on Richbod see above, pp. 109–10.

[53] A. Häse, *Mittelalterliche Bücherverzeichnisse aus Kloster Lorsch. Einleitung, Edition und Kommentar*, Beiträge zum Buch- und Bibliothekswesen 42 (Stuttgart, 2002).

[54] I have followed Dr Häse's edition, though she has silently expanded abbreviations, supplies capitalisation and punctuation not in the original and prints the list of books in continuous prose rather than beginning each item on a new line and in two columns per page as in the manuscript. I have adopted her expanded abbreviations but not the other features of the edition.

fol. 3v

Tripertita historia libri XII socratis zozomeni theodoriti in uno
codice[55]

Gesta pontificum romanorum in uno codice

Libri clementis X in uno codice

Gesta francorum gregorii toronensis libri V in uno codice

Historia iordanis de summa temporum seu ori
*   gine romanorum liber I*

Pompei troi epitome lib XLIIII in uno codice

Favii claudii gordiani de aetate mundi &
    hominis reservati singulis litteris per singu
    los libros ab a usque z sed desunt nobis libri XI in uno codice

Excidium troiae liber I & historia daretis frigii
    de exitu romanorum in uno codice

Liber ethyci cosmographi in uno codice

Ennei flori epitoma<de> libio<periochae> romane historiae
*   in libris CXLII in uno codice*

Libellus quinti iulii hilarionis de origine mundi
    usque ad resurrectionem Christi. Item in eodem
    libello hieronomi chronica excerpta inde
    idacii ab anno primo theodosii augusti usque
    iustinianum in uno codice

Solini poliistor de situ orbis terrarum & mira
    bilibus in uno codice

Item libri antiquitatum iosephi historiographi
    a duodecimo usque in nonum decimum in uno codice[56]

fol. 21r

BEDAE PRESBITERI

Historia anglorum libri V in uno codice

. . .

De temporibus et com
potum libri II & chronica eiusdem & circuli dionisii
in uno codice

. . .

Item de temporibus & compotum libri II
    & chronica eiusdem & circuli dionisii in alio
    codice[57]

---

[55] This survives only in s.XII copy.   [56] Häse, *Mittelalterliche Bücherverzeichnisse*, p. 137.
[57] *Ibid.*, p. 154.

fol. 27v
ISIDORE
Eiusdem <liber> prohemiorum & chronica et eiusdem de significatione nominum ad orosium in uno codice
Breviarium eiusdem super divinae historiae libros
et versus qui scripti sunt in armaria sua ab ipso
compositi & in eodem libro sermo sancti augustini
in natale iohannis baptistae et in natale apostolorum Petri
et Pauli, in uno codice
. . .

sententiae
et chronica in quarternionibus[58]

fol. 29v
Epitaphia in basilica sancti petri seu versus[59]

fol. 31r
Descriptio arculfi de situ hierusalem et locorum sanctorum in
circuitu eius
. . .

Liber einhardi de miraculis sanctorum marcellini & petri
. . .

Historia frehculfi libri VII in uno codice

fol. 31v
metrum Bedae presbiteri de virtutibus sancti cutbercti eiusdem
hymni LXXVII in uno codice
. . .

Aratoris in actibus apostolorum, libri II, in uno codice
. . .

liber annalis[60]

fol. 78ra (**Lorsch catalogue A**) added s.IX/2[61]
Vita Caroli imperatoris

BAV pal. lat. 57 (**Lorsch catalogue D**, s.IXmed)
Similar to **Lorsch III** but it omits Eusebius-Rufinus, Josephus
and the so-called 'Gregory of Tours' and adds Orosius[62]
Lorsch's manuscripts and the development of the scriptorium were
studied by Bernhard Bischoff. He established the evolution of the 'older'

---

[58] *Ibid.*, p. 161.   [59] *Ibid.*, p. 163.   [60] *Ibid.* p. 165.   [61] *Ibid.* p. 99.
[62] *Ibid.*, p. 169, lines 14–24.

and younger' Lorsch styles of script. The earlier script of the late eighth and early ninth centuries was a rounded sloping minuscule and in many of the earlier books a strong insular influence is discernible in the letter forms and style of decoration. The younger Lorsch style of the ninth century is very regular, with few abbreviations or ligatures. In the early years of the monastery's existence the scripts of Lorsch were very similar to those of Metz and Weissenburg. This is as one might expect, given the history of its foundation and early development. Bischoff also stressed that the scripts of the last two decades of the eighth century in particular were to be seen in relation to the remarkably similar scripts of books associated with the court of Charlemagne itself.[63] Methods of book production and letter forms in all these places, furthermore, reflect some very tantalising indications of insular influence. It also should be remembered that the earliest datable examples of caroline minuscule only emerge at Corbie and in association with the royal court in the 780s.[64] It is really only in the younger Lorsch style of the ninth century, therefore, that there is a distinctive house style developed at Lorsch with all that that implies as far as scribal discipline, compliance with particular norms established within the scriptorium and particular aspects of the script and book production are concerned. What we have therefore is a period of very rapid development, with a potential openness to all kinds of influence from both scribes and the books available as exemplars. Quite apart from the other Lorsch manuscripts from the early period of the scriptorium, we can see how this might be reflected in the surviving manuscripts containing history.

The history books from Lorsch which still survive are shown in table 9.2 below. There is only space here to consider one of the problems these books raise. The majority of the codices date to the early years of the Lorsch scriptorium's activity. In consequence, we need to reflect on how a monastery might set about building up its library, especially if it were, like Lorsch, a relatively new foundation with wealth only really building up in the 770s and 780s. How would it decide what books it should have? Where and how would it acquire copies? What kinds of precedents would it have to copy texts? Would it have been confronted with texts belonging to genres, or with whose contents it may not have been familiar? Would the impulse all be internal or would Lorsch also have responded to developments outside the monastery? Aside from speculations about

[63] Bischoff, *Die Abtei Lorsch*, pp. 31–8.
[64] B. Bischoff, trans. D. Ó Cróinín and D. Ganz, *Latin palaeography: antiquity and the middle ages* (Cambridge, 1990), from second revised edition of *Paläographie des römischen Altertums und des abendländischen Mittelalters* (Berlin, 1986), p. 112.

Table 9.2 *Extant history books from Carolingian Lorsch*

1. BAV pal. lat. 170 Hegesippus s.IX /1
2. BAV pal. lat. 243 Einhard (written at St Amand) and Lorsch Chronicle s.IX/2 and s.IX/X
3. BAV pal. lat. 277 Isidore *Proemium* and Chronicle s.IX/1
4. BAV pal. lat. 822 Eusebius-Rufinus, *Historia ecclesiastica* s.VIII/IX
5. BAV pal. lat. 829 Orosius, *Historiae* s.VIII/IX
6. BAV pal. lat. 814 Josephus, *Antiquitates* 1–2 s.VIII/IX
7. BAV pal. lat. 966 *Liber historiae francorum* and *Annales nazariani* s.VIII/IX ?Murbach
8. BAV pal. lat. 1448 Bede, *Computus* and *Chronica*, Calendars s.IX/1
9. BAV pal. lat. 920 Jordanes, *Romana*, and *Getica* s.IX/1
10. BAV pal. lat. 899 *Historia augusta* s.IX/1 N. Italy[65]
11. BAV pal. lat. 833 papal epitaphs s.IX/1
12. Heidelberg, Universitätsbibliothek pal. lat. 894 Florus, *Epitome* of Livy, s.IX/1
13. Luxembourg, Bibliothèque Nationale MS I:110 (olim 22), fols. 45r-128v. Freculf, *Chronicon*, s.IX2/4 written at Arras for Lorsch[66]
14. Paris, BnF lat. 7906 *Liber historiae francorum* + *Aeneid* extracts + Dares Phrygius

what the catalogue can tell us, it is only the books themselves and what they reveal of the process of copying which may help us address the problem of the source of Lorsch's exemplars.

The copying process   Some palimpsested leaves give a tantalising glimpse of Lorsch's acquisition of late antique history texts and the possible process of rescue, recopying or discard. BAV pal. lat. 24 is a copy of the Old Testament books Tobias, Judith, Job and Esther. Forty-five leaves of this book were written, probably at Lorsch on fresh parchment and completed portions of the books of Tobias and Judith. The rest of this book, however, is written in Frankish uncial of the late seventh or early eighth century on palimpsested leaves which contain on the lower script Seneca, *De amicitia* and *De vita patris* in b-d uncial of the fifth century, Lucan, *Pharsalia* in rustic capitals of the late fourth or early

[65] An indication that the books are being read is the presence of annotations. The probably early tenth-century Lorsch reader of the *Historia augusta*, for example, annotated the manuscript in such a way as to suggest a particular interest in the 'extravagant conduct on the part of bad emperors or to call attention to them'. This annotator also made extensive and rather good corrections to the text, apparently at some stage after the Fulda copy had been made. See S. Ballou, *The manuscript tradition of the Historia augusta* (Leipzig and Berlin, 1914), p. 11 on the contribution of P2 to the text. Another ninth-century manuscript from Lorsch, BAV pal. lat. 886, witnesses to the presence and reading of the *Historia augusta* there, for it contains some excerpts from it. See also below, p. 205.

[66] M. I. Allen (ed.), *Frechvlfi lexoviensis episcopi opera omnia. Prolegomena. Indices*, CCCM, CLXIX (Turnhout, 2002), pp. 147*–148*. I have not yet seen this manuscript.

fifth century, Hyginus's *Fabulae* in fifth-century uncial, a Greek medical fragment in Greek sloping uncial of the fifth century, Fronto's *Gratiarum actio pro carthaginiensibus* in tiny rustic capitals of the late fourth or early fifth century, an oratorical fragment in 'quarter-uncial' of the late fifth or early sixth century, Livy (Book XCI) in small and delicately formed fourth-century rustic capitals, Aulus Gellius, *Noctes atticae* in very fine fourth-century rustic capitals with a strong contrast between thick and thin strokes, Cicero, *Pro Fonteio*, Cicero, *Pro Rabirio* and *Pro Sexto Roscio*.[67]

The palimpsested leaves could simply be from a supply accumulated by a second-hand parchment dealer. They could, on the other hand, represent the recycled leaves of late antique books from a variety of places which had been recopied because their condition was poor and/or the texts were wanted in a modern script. Some late antique codices survived better than others. The *Virgilius palatinus*, for example, in expert rustic capitals of the late fourth or early fifth century, was at Lorsch itself in the early ninth century, as is indicated by the annotations in Lorsch caroline minuscule.[68] It may be the original survivor of a group of late antique codices, most of which were recopied. It is very difficult to identify the character of the script or the date of an exemplar from its copy, but sometimes there are particular misunderstandings a scribe makes which suggest a misreading of letters or of abbreviations in a particular script or from a particular period. The analysis of the text of Ammianus Marcellinus by Robinson, for example, has suggested that the exemplar from which BAV lat. 1873 was copied was Kassel, Gesamthochschulbibliothek 2o Ms. philol. 27, s.IX/1, written in insular script. It has been conjectured that the latter was itself based on an insular pre-archetype based on a rustic capital exemplar.[69]

The format of the copy may also provide some indication of the exemplar. That is, the unusual appearance of these late eighth- and ninth-century codices containing history texts (both pagan and Christian) from the fifth century or earlier suggests that the copies were made from late antique exemplars. In copying either page by page or, as was probably more usual, quire by quire, the Carolingian scribes may have attempted to reproduce the layout and format of their exemplars. The few complete

[67] *CLA*, I (Oxford, 1935), nos. 68a-77.

[68] BAV pal. lat. 1631, *ibid.*, no. 99. It is possibly to be identified with the manuscript of Virgil among Gerward's books and may also have had Carolingian court connections: see Häse, *Mittelalterliche Bücherverzeichnisse*, p. 168; and B. Bischoff, 'Bücher am Hofe Ludwigs des Deutschen und die Privatbibliothek des Kanzlers Grimalt', in Bischoff, *Mittelalterliche Studien*, III (Stuttgart, 1981), pp. 187–212.

[69] R. P. Robinson, 'The Hersfeldensis and the Fuldensis of Ammianus Marcellinus', *University of Missouri Studies. A quarterly of research* 11 (1936), pp. 118–140; and Reynolds, *Texts and transmission*, pp. 6–8.

late antique books we have are more often than not rather large and, more importantly, almost square, that is, almost as wide as they are tall in both the page size and the writing space, though it is the writing space, given the possibility of binders' cropping, which is the better indicator. The *Virgilius palatinus*, for example, is 305 × 235 mm (205–210 × 185–190 mm). Most manuscripts from the early middle ages, on the other hand, are far taller in relation to the width of the manuscript. It is very striking that the late eighth- and early ninth-century Lorsch copies of late antique history – Orosius, Eusebius-Rufinus, Josephus, Hegesippus, *Historia augusta*, the Fulda and Corbie copies of Ammianus Marcellinus and Caesar, and the Tours Livy – are all more or less square as well as, except for the Caesar, impressively and unusually large books. I set out the details below:

> **Eusebius-Rufinus**: BAV pal. lat. 822
> 295 × 220 mm (220 × 180 mm)
> 30 long lines to a page
> **Orosius**: BAV pal. lat. 829
> 275 × 230 mm (220 × 180 mm)
> 31 long lines to a page
> **Josephus**: BAV pal. lat. 814
> 350 × 280 mm (290 × 235 mm)
> 2 columns of 40 lines each
> **Hegesippus**: BAV pal. lat. 170
> 360 × 300 mm (285 × 245 mm)
> 2 columns of 40 lines each
> *Historia augusta*: BAV pal. lat. 899
> 307 × 240 mm (215 × 150 mm)
> 26 long lines to a page
> **Ammianus Marcellinus**: BAV lat. 1873 (Fulda)
> 275 × 235 mm (195 × 185 mm)
> **Caesar**: BAV lat. 3864 (Corbie)
> 220 × 180 mm (165 × 135 mm)
> 31 long lines to a page
> **Livy**: BAV, reg. lat. 762
> 320 × 238 mm (220 × 170 mm)
> 27–30 long lines to a page

The Tours Livy, moreover, is notable in two principal ways. First of all, the fifth-century exemplar for this manuscript, Paris, BnF lat. 5730, is still extant and this ancient exemplar also provided the text for a copy made by Corbie scribes.[70] Secondly, the scribes who copied it signed their names

---

[70] See above, p. 193.

on the portions they had completed. Even if we did not also have the exemplar, it would be clear that they copied their text from an exemplar which still maintained continuous script with little or no punctuation or word separation in the antique manner. The earlier quires of this codex, particularly those written by the scribes Gislarus and Aldo, clearly concentrated on copying letter by letter, but the scribes responsible for later portions, such Fredegarius, Ansoald and Theogrimus, were rather more successful in their efforts to modernise the layout for Frankish readers; Ansoald in particular believed in the utility of punctuation.

The size of the pages in these books, incidentally, called for very good and plentiful supplies of parchment; such lavish layout did not come cheaply and is in itself a reflection of the wealth of the scriptorium responsible for producing these books. If it had only been a case of one or two books this shape and size it might not be particularly significant, but so many very large and square codices from the Lorsch scriptorium in particular are impressive, especially when copies of other patristic and early medieval texts are smaller and more oblong. Compare, for example:

Isidore, *Liber proemiorum*, BAV pal. lat. 277, 222 × 154 mm (164 × 120 mm) of the eighth century and copying a seventh-century text

Lorsch *Chronicle* + Einhard, *Vita Karoli*, BAV pal. lat. 243, both ninth-century texts, 210 × 143 mm (146 × 101 mm);

Liber historiae francorum, BAV pal. lat. 966, 250 × 165 mm (190 × 100 mm)

Jordanes, BAV pal. lat. 920, a ninth-century copy of a later sixth-century text: 252 × 164 mm (194 × 127 mm)

Exemplars and an interest in history books   If most of the Lorsch history books are indeed copied directly from late antique exemplars at the end of the eighth and at the beginning of the ninth centuries then we need to explore the possible context in which such exemplars may have become available. From whence did they come? Older foundations in Frankish Gaul, Spain, Italy and the British Isles have all been suggested from time to time as possible origins for one or more of these codices. Given the Franks' commercial and religious links with England and Ireland, and their conquest of northern Italy and the Spanish march, all are feasible.

It is mistaken to assume that all must have come from one place as a result of a particular event. It is not necessarily the case, for example, that these exemplars have to have come from Italy. Charlemagne's conquest of the Lombard kingdom has provided a tempting event with which to associate the carrying off of war booty. Some scholars have clearly imagined late antique codices being loaded onto carts and taken across the Alps to Charlemagne's court. The *Annales regni francorum* are not usually coy about describing in gloating terms how much booty was acquired by the Franks on their military expeditions. The treasure of the Avars, for example, described by Einhard as treasure amassed by past kings over many years, was remembered for decades afterwards.[71] There are many both earlier and later examples of conquerors enriching their own culture with treasures from the conquered peoples, not least the arrival in Rome of the Lorsch manuscripts themselves. Certainly the Royal Frankish Annals mention that Charlemagne captured the city of Pavia, King Desiderius and his wife and daughter, and all the treasure of his palace.[72] This treasure might have included books, but no extant codex has yet been identified as having once been at the Lombard royal court, nor is there any secure evidence for a Lombard royal library. The earliest suggestion of a court library in northern Italy is in relation to a group of six books (none of them is a history book, however) associated with the court of Pippin of Italy and dated to the end of the eighth century.[73] Other centres in northern Italy could have been plundered. We have no certain knowledge of substantial libraries before the end of the eighth century at any centre apart from Bobbio and Verona, and in neither of these are history books prominent. The *Historia augusta* (BAV pal. lat. 899) may be from Verona, however, and there is also the so-called 'Verona historical miscellany' to take into account.[74]

Contexts other than those of conquest could also have provided the means for the exchange of books, such as the ecclesiastical links between northern Italy and Provence, Alemannia, Rhaetia and Bavaria. These remained constant throughout the early middle ages and were particularly important in the earlier decades of the eighth century. Diplomatic and papal gifts might have accounted for some, though those that are specifically

---

[71] Einhard, *Vita Karoli*, c. 13, ed. R. Rau, *Quellen zur karolingischen Reichsgeschichte*, I (Darmstadt, 1974), p. 182.

[72] *Annales regni francorum*, s.a. 774, ed. Kurze, *MGH SRG* (Hannover, 1895), p. 38.

[73] B. Bischoff, 'Panorama der Handschriftenüberlieferung aus der Zeit Karls des Grossen', *Mittelalterliche Studien*, III (Stuttgart, 1981), p. 31 and n. 132; see also the English translation of M. Gorman in B. Bischoff, *Manuscripts and libraries in the age of Charlemagne*, Cambridge Studies in Palaeography and Codicology 1 (Cambridge, 1994), p. 46; and above, chapter 3, pp. 80–2.

[74] See above, chapter 2, pp. 52–7. See also C. Villa, 'Cultura classica e tradizioni longobarde', in P. Chiesa (ed.), *Paolo Diacono: uno scrittore fra tradizione longobarda e rinnovamento carolingio* (Udine, 2000), pp. 575–600; C. Villa, 'Lay and ecclesiastical culture', in C. La Rocca (ed.), *Italy in the early middle ages* (Oxford, 2002), pp. 189–203; and *idem*., *Pacifico di Verona. Il passato carolingio nella costruzione della memoria urbana*, Istituto storico italiano per il medio evo, Nuovi studi storici 31 (Rome, 1995).

mentioned in papal letters or annalists' accounts of embassies between
the Popes, the Byzantine empire and the Frankish rulers Pippin III and
Charlemagne are all theological and liturgical books.[75] Equally, the great
Gallo-Roman episcopal centres, such as Tours, Lyons, Rheims and Trier
and their associated monastic communities could well have possessed late
antique codices which were then copied in the early decades of the Carolingian period, such as the Tours copy of Livy or the codices of the plays
of Terence.[76]

Although the precise source of exemplars for the books cannot be established, the distribution and survival patterns of the greater majority
of both the pagan Roman histories and the church histories of Eusebius
Rufinus and the *Historia tripartita* are nevertheless significant. Apart from
some palimpsest fragments of Sallust and Livy and an early codex of Livy,
some sixth-century fragments in half-uncial script of Eusebius-Rufinus,
and some sixth- and seventh-century leaves of portions of Orosius, the
earliest witnesses to these texts date from the late eighth and early ninth
centuries.[77] With the exception of the *Historia augusta* written in north
Italian script (which is not the same as saying it was written in northern Italy), the fragments of Sallust and the sixth-century fragment of
Eusebius-Rufinus, these early codices are Frankish and from centres that
are both important intellectual and religious places and can also be closely
associated with the royal court. Lorsch, Corbie and Chelles, for example,
all had close links with the court. All were 'royal' monasteries, presided
over by former members of the court circle or members of the royal family:
the abbess of Chelles, for example was Charlemagne's sister; some of the
books written at Chelles can be linked with the production of books for
the archbishop of Cologne, who was also the archchaplain at the royal
court.[78] St Amand's abbot Arno, who became bishop of Salzburg, was
a close friend of the Englishman Alcuin, abbot of Tours and a confidant
and adviser to Charlemagne.

Historians of the Carolingian reforms have long associated the dissemination of copies of essential liturgical books in 'authorised versions'
such as the mass book (the supplemented *Hadrianum*), canon law
(the *Dionysio–Hadriana* collection), antiphonary, Gospels, Psalter (the

---

[75] For the wider context see M. McCormick, 'Byzantium and the west', in McKitterick
(ed.), *NCMH*, pp. 349–80; and *idem*, *Origins of the European economy. Communication
and commerce AD 300–900* (Cambridge, 2001).

[76] For the Livy see above, p. 193; and for Terence see Reynolds, *Texts and transmission*,
pp. 412–420.

[77] I discuss the manuscript distribution of the ecclesiastical histories in more detail below,
chapter 10.

[78] B. Bischoff, 'Die Kölner Nonnenhandschriften und das Skriptorium von Chelles',
Mittelalterliche Studien, I (Stuttgart, 1965), pp. 16–34.

court edition), and Bible, homiliary (compiled by Paul the Deacon) and the promotion of what was claimed as 'Roman' chant, with the royal court.[79] In earlier work I have also linked the production and dissemination of capitularies, the germanic *leges* and the Royal Frankish annals to court initiative.[80] I argue below that it is possible that the remarkable concentration of early church history manuscripts and the very wide dissemination of ecclesiastical history texts, especially of the Eusebius-Rufinus *Historia ecclesiastica* and the *Historia tripartita* across the Carolingian empire, could reflect the deliberate promotion of these books at an early stage of the Carolingian reform movement.[81] What these ecclesiastical histories offer is a distinctive presentation of the past and of the history of the church. The history of Christianity is presented as the history of written authority, of the process of the formation of the scriptural canon and of its essential continuation by the fathers of the church in their writings. Yet they also offer a very particular perspective on Roman imperial history. This is then augmented and extended by the secular histories of Livy, Tacitus and Ammianus Marcellinus, which represent, moreover, full versions of the comparative chronology of the rise and fall of empires familiar to Christian readers from the Chronicle of Eusebius and Jerome. This is a world in which Augustus is the emperor in whose reign Christ was born and Tiberius the emperor in whose reign Christ was crucified. Titus acquires fame as the victor over the Jews and Domitian is remembered for his exile of St John to Patmos. In his additions to Eusebius' ecclesiastical history, Rufinus emphasised the precariousness of Christianity too easily jeopardised by contention among Christians and the impiety of emperors. An historical understanding of the Christian faith required a proper knowledge of those same emperors, just as the cult of the martyrs inevitably portrayed them against a backdrop of Roman imperial rule.

The interest in Roman history was thus also closely connected with the Roman imperial and early Christian past which Carolingian rulers undoubtedly sought to emulate. Historical example played a vital role

---

[79] See for example, the work by J. Deshusses, *Le Sacramentaire grégorien* (Fribourg, 1971); B. Fischer, 'Bibeltext und Bibelreform unter Karl dem Grossen', in W. Braunfels (ed.), *Karl der Grosse. Lebenswerk und Nachleben*, II, *Das Geistige Leben*, ed. B. Bischoff, (Düsseldorf, 1965), pp. 154–216; R. Gregoire, *Homéliaires liturgiques médiévaux. Analyse des manuscrits* (Spoleto, 1980); K. Levy, *Gregorian chant and the Carolingians* (Princeton, 1998); and see my review, *Early Music History* 19 (2000), pp. 279–90.

[80] R. McKitterick, 'Zur Herstellung von Kapitularien: die Arbeit des Leges-Skriptorium', *MIÖG* 101 (1993), 3–16; chapters 4, 5 and 6 above and 'Unity and diversity in the Carolingian church', in R. Swanson (ed.), *Unity and diversity in the church*, Studies in Church History 32 (Woodbridge, 1996), pp. 59–83.

[81] See chapter 10.

in Carolingian political ideology. Kings were exhorted to read history
for inspiration. For King Charles the Bald of the west Franks, Charlemagne's grandson, it was the deeds of the Roman emperors: as Lupus of
Ferrières wrote to him in 844, 'I have had a very brief summary of the
deeds of the emperors (probably a reference to the *Epitome* of Aurelius
Victor) presented to your majesty so that you may readily observe from
their actions what you should imitate or what you should avoid. I especially commend to your consideration, however, Trajan and Theodosius,
because you can most profitably find many things among their deeds to
imitate.'[82]

Thus the extraordinary concentration of Roman history books from
the late eighth and early ninth centuries, together with the copies of ecclesiastical history, represent a systematic provision of history books more
generally in the Carolingian realm. Their initial promotion is to be associated with the close links established by Charlemagne and his father
Pippin III with Rome and with the immediate aftermath of the conquest
of Lombard Italy. It certainly predates Charlemagne's coronation as emperor in Rome in 800. The Franks show in their own history writing,
as we have seen, an impulse to forge an identity that explicitly placed
the origin of the Franks in a far distant Roman and Trojan past.[83] That
the promotion of Roman and early Christian history had its origins in the
Carolingian court is certainly suggested by the coincidence that all the
centres producing them, as I have outlined above, can be demonstrated
to have had Carolingian court connections. Although the status of the
famous list of rare classical texts in the late eighth-century collection
of grammatical texts and poems from the royal court, now in Berlin,
Deutsche Staatsbibliothek, Preussischer Kulturbesitz Diez B Sant. 66,
as a list of books in Charlemagne's library[84] has been challenged by
Villa,[85] other elements of Bischoff's arguments remain firm and a Verona

---

[82] Lupus, ed. L. Levillain, *Loup de Ferrières, Correspondance*, no. 37; I, p. 164; English
translation, G. W. Regenos, *The Letters of Lupus of Ferrières* (The Hague, 1966), no. 37,
p. 55.

[83] See M. Innes, 'Teutons or Trojans? The Carolingians and the Germanic past', in Y.
Hen and M. Innes (eds.), *The uses of the past in the early middle ages* (Cambridge 2000),
pp. 227–249.

[84] B. Bischoff, 'Die Hofbibliothek Karls des Grossen', in Braunfels (ed.), *Karl der Grosse*,
pp. 42–62; revised version in *Mittelalterliche Studien*, III (Stuttgart 1981), pp. 149–171,
and English translation M. Gorman, in B. Bischoff, *Manuscripts and libraries in the age
of Charlemagne* (Cambridge, 1994), pp. 56–75.

[85] See above, pp. 80–1, and C. Villa, 'La tradizione di Orazio e la "biblioteca di Carlo
Magno": per l'elenco di opere nel codice Berlin Diez B. Sant. 66', in O. Pecere and
M. D. Reeve (eds.), *Formative stages of classical traditions: Latin texts from antiquity to the
renaissance* (Spoleto, 1996), pp. 299–322 and German version 'Die Horazüberlieferung
und die 'Bibliothek Karls des Grossen': zum Werkverzeichnis der Handschrift Berlin,
Diez B. 66', *DA* 51 (1995), pp. 29–52.

connection is also by no means established.[86] A reference by Wigbod, a member of the court circle, in a dedication of his own work to the king, to Charlemagne's *sententia* which caused books to be gathered from many countries, led Bischoff to propose that Charlemagne had sent a letter round asking for rare and old books.[87] Further, Bischoff traced (by means of palaeographical indications and text affiliation) the dissemination and distribution of texts from exemplars in the court library from the Frankish court to other centres in the realm, especially Corbie and Tours.

A famous example of such a text disseminated from the court is Bede's *Historia ecclesiastica gentis anglorum*. The manuscript known as the Moore Bede, dated *c*. 737, written in Northumbria, and now in Cambridge University Library (MS Kk. 5.16), contains at the back various canonical precepts written in the caroline minuscule associated with the court school of Charlemagne. No fewer than seven ninth-century copies of Bede contain both the history and these additions, suggesting that the court library copy served as their direct or indirect exemplar.[88] A late antique work, possibly regarded by the Franks as a history text, and connected with the court, is Virgil's *Aeneid*. Three of the famous late antique copies of the *Aeneid*, all now in the Vatican, have been linked with the Frankish centres of Lorsch and St Denis in the ninth century.[89] They may have been acquired first by Charlemagne, though there are other possibilities one might explore.

The Franks had had links with Rome before but only sporadically. There are two major differences between earlier Frankish links and the Carolingian rulers' association with Rome. First of all, there is the relationship with the Pope and with the Frankish church. Secondly, there is Charlemagne's conquest of the Lombard kingdom. From the middle of the eighth century the Franks acquired an extra dimension to their past and to their intellectual horizons. They appear to have decided to learn about Roman and early Christian history and add history systematically to the canon of texts they should know. Work done on the Carolingian rulers' receptiveness to scholarship has established how much the demand for new texts, from the *Libri carolini*'s arguments concerning images in

---

[86] See above, chapter 3, note 95.

[87] Wigbod, ed. E. Dümmler, *MGH Poetae*, I (Hannover, 1881), p. 195; and Bischoff, 'Hofbibliothek Karls des Grossen, p. 154 and n. 44.

[88] R. A. B. Mynors, 'Textual introduction', in B. Colgrave and R. A. B. Mynors (eds.) *Bede's Ecclesiastical history of the English people* (Oxford, 1969), pp. xxxix–lxxiv, particularly xlii–xlvi and lxi–lxix.

[89] *CLA*, I (Oxford, 1935), nos. 13, 19, 99 (BAV lat. 3256, 3867, pal. lat. 1631); and McKitterick, *Migration*, for further discussion.

church in response to the iconoclast controversy,[90] the debate about the *filioque* clause in the Creed,[91] no doubt related to the investigation concerning the sacrament of baptism,[92] to the texts of commentary on the Bible, came from the king. There were reading sessions at court, and argument and debate. Historical examples were entrenched in the intellectual reference system of the Franks. Mayke de Jong has established how patristic commentary in the middle decades of the ninth century, often commissioned by or dedicated to the Carolingian rulers of the historical books of the Bible, made texts such as Esther, Judith and Maccabees accessible to the powerful. Biblical commentary translated biblical truths into contemporary terms at an allegorical level but it also drew on other historical texts for its interpretation.[93] Thus Hraban Maur incorporated large chunks of Josephus into his commentary on Maccabees and offered implicit comments on society. For the Franks, salvation was also part of political history. A number of different factors were playing a role in the formation of a sense of the past and a particular perception of the past in the eighth and ninth centuries.[94]

The Lorsch history books, therefore, appear to witness to a deliberate cultivation of an interest in Roman history, secular historiography and early Christian history throughout the Frankish empire in the late eighth and the ninth centuries. The interest can be readily justified in terms of the content of the history and the use subsequently made of historical examples in political ideology and tracts on kingship, admonitions to the ruler in the form of letters and treatises, declarations on the part of the ruler to his wish to emulate famous rulers in the past, and the clear associations Frankish historical writers and compilers provide with the past.[95]

St Amand

St Amand was founded in the seventh century by the Aquitainian missionary Amandus on land given by King Dagobert.[96] By the late eighth

---

[90] A. Freeman (ed.), *Opus Caroli regis contra synodum (Libri Carolini)*, MGH *Conc.*, II. Suppl. I (Hannover, 1998).

[91] H. Willjung (ed.), *Das Konzil von Aachen 809*, MGH *Conc.*, II, Suppl. 2 (Hannover, 1998).

[92] S. Keefe, *Water and the word*, 2 vols. (Notre Dame, 2002).

[93] See M. de Jong (ed.), *The power of the word: the influence of the Bible on early medieval politics*, special issue, *EME* 7 (1998).

[94] I explore this further in my Conway lectures, University of Notre Dame, 2004, on 'Perceptions of the past in the early middle ages'.

[95] See above, chapter 2.

[96] H. Platelle, *Le Temporel de l'abbaye de Saint-Amand des origines à 1340* (Paris, 1962).

century the monastery was a wealthy and important institution and had established a scriptorium for the copying of texts.[97] Thereafter the scriptorium flourished, as did the school of St Amand, and the monastery enjoyed royal patronage under a succession of very prominent abbots and *potentes* of the realm, notably Abbot Gauzlin, archchancellor to Charles the Bald and later bishop of Paris (d. 886).[98] Notable scholars and masters of the later ninth century were Milo and Hucbald of St Amand.[99] As well as the extant manuscripts of St Amand, mostly now concentrated in the Bibliothèque Municipale in Valenciennes and the Bibliothèque nationale de France, other St Amand books, such as the Mass Books produced on commission from various Frankish episcopal sees,[100] or the multiple copies of Prudentius' *Psychomachia*, are scattered more widely and witness to an effective dissemination of texts. We have records of the contents of the library of St Amand made in the late tenth and in the twelfth centuries.[101] These lists establish how relatively little of the early collection has in fact been lost and thus make it possible to reconstruct with some confidence the contents of the Carolingian library at St Amand which is confirmed by those of its manuscripts still extant (see table 9.3 below).

From the late eighth century until about 821, St Amand is closely linked with Salzburg, both palaeographically and through Arno, Alcuin's friend, who was abbot of St Amand and who became bishop and subsequently archbishop of Salzburg. Bernhard Bischoff dubbed the script produced in this period the 'Arn-Stil' and it was during this Arno period that Leiden, Voss. lat. Q.60 was produced.[102] It is a version of the

---

[97] On the early history of the St Amand scriptorium in relation to that of Salzburg see B. Bischoff, *Schreibschulen*, II, pp. 53–161.

[98] R. McKitterick, 'Charles the Bald and his library: the patronage of learning', *EHR* 95 (1980), pp. 28–47, reprinted in McKitterick, *Frankish kings and culture*, chapter 5. On Gauzlin see K.-F. Werner, 'Gauzlin von Saint-Denis und die westfränkische Reichsteilung von Amiens (März 880). Ein Beitrag zur Vorgeschichte von Odos Königtum', *DA* 35 (1979), pp. 395–462.

[99] On Milo and Hucbald see F. Brunhölzl, *Histoire de la littérature latine du moyen âge. II De l'époque carolingienne au milieu du onzième siècle*, revised trans. from German edition of 1992 by H. Rochais (Turnhout, 1996), pp. 88–96; and J. M. H. Smith, 'A hagiographer at work: Hucbald and the library of Saint-Amand', *RB* 106 (1996) pp. 151–71.

[100] J. Deshusses, 'Chronologie des grands sacramentaires de Saint-Amand', *RB* 87 (1977), pp. 230–7.

[101] Valenciennes, Bibliothèque Municipale MS 33, and Paris, BnF lat. 1850: see L. Delisle, *Le Cabinet des manuscrits de la Bibliothèque impériale* (I) *nationale* (II and III), 3 vols. (Paris, 1868–81), II, pp. 448–58.

[102] B. Bischoff, *Schreibschulen*, II, no. 43, p. 102, and *CLA*, X (Oxford, 1963), no. 1583. According to the *ex libris* notices in the codex, it was certainly in Rheims by the late tenth or eleventh century (the two notes are of the late tenth/early eleventh and late twelfth/early thirteenth centuries respectively).

Table 9.3 *Extant history manuscripts from St Amand*

---

1. Leiden, Bibliotheek der Rijksuniversiteit Voss. lat. Q. 60
   Liber pontificalis s.VIIIex (at Rheims s.IXin)
2. Koblenz, Staatsarchiv 701/759 III + Marburg, Hessisches Staatsarchiv Hr.4, 17
   '*Hegesippus*' (= Latin version of Josephus, *De bello iudaico*) s.IXin
3. Würzburg, Universitätsbibliothek M.p.th.f.46 s.IXin/820 (after 828 in Salzburg.
   Still there in 976 but later in Würzburg)
   Bede, *De temporum ratione*; *Annales salzburgenses*
4 Valenciennes, Bibliothèque Municipale 95 (88) s.IX/1
   Jordanes, *Romana* and *Getica*; Junilius; Eucherius
5. Valenciennes, Bibliothèque Municipale 545 (499), s.IX
   Orosius, *Historiae adversos paganos*
6 Valenciennes, Bibliothèque Municipale 330bis, s.Xin
   Chronicon laurissense breve; Bede, *Chronica maiora de sex huius saeculi aetatibus*
7. BAV, pal. lat. 243 s.IX/2
   Einhard, *Vita Karoli*
8. Copenhagen, Kongelige Bibliotek Gl. Kgl. S. 163, s.IX/2
   Eusebius-Rufinus, *Historia ecclesiastica*
9. Vienna, Österreichische Nationalbibliothek lat. 473. c. 869
   Liber historiae francorum; *Liber pontificalis*; *Annales regni francorum*;
   Vita Karoli of Einhard; and genealogies; *Passio sancti Stephani*

Lombard recension of the *Liber pontificalis*, but it has additions, inserted at the beginning of the book before the main text, made in the later ninth century either at St Amand by someone trained to write at Rheims or possibly at Rheims itself. The excerpt from Jerome entered on fol. 1 and the sermon on fols. 1v–2v are in ninth-century Rheims minuscule. The connections between Rheims and St Amand are well attested, not least in the person of Hucbald himself who taught at Rheims before returning to St Amand. There are also many annotations by a number of different hands, also of the late ninth or early tenth century with one, who wrote a large, somewhat ill-formed script, predominating. These annotations are more copious for the lives of Gregory II, Zacharias and Stephen II. Many are simply very brief indications of content set in the margin or a proper name inserted above a pronoun as on fol. 104, where *Liutprandus* is written above *praedictus rex*. The names of the Carolingian rulers are noted frequently and attention is drawn to an eclipse of the moon on fol. 74v. Occasionally a note will indicate extra knowledge, such as the gloss on fol. 99r which adds that the Constantinian basilica mentioned in the text is near the Lateran. This reader may even have visited Rome. On fol. 85vr a gloss adds to the account of Pope Sergius ordaining Clemens bishop that Clemens was in fact Willibrord and that he was mentioned also by Bede. This reader therefore also knew Bede's *Historia ecclesiastica* for Bede describes Willibrord's career in Book 5, chapters 10–11.

This was a closely read manuscript and it looks as if it may have been collated with another copy of the *Liber pontificalis*, quite apart from the reader bringing other knowledge to bear upon the text. Of particular interest in the Leiden manuscript is the preliminary material. Here were the spurious letters included in some of the extant manuscripts purporting to be what Jerome wrote to Damasus and Damasus' response concerning the compilation of the history of the popes.[103] Their inclusion is significant. They stress on pseudo-Jerome's part a wish to learn which of the popes deserved the crown of martyrdom and who transgressed against the apostolic canons. Pseudo-Damasus, on the other hand, talks of the interest which *sacerdotes* show in the past and claims that he sends Jerome what he has been able to find out about the history of his see. The ninth-century copyists and readers, therefore, understood the *Liber pontificalis* to be a text produced in the pontificate of Damasus (366–84) on the urging of no less a scholar than Jerome, the translator of the Vulgate. Pope Damasus is also linked with the Vulgate in the prefatory letter from Jerome to Damasus starting with the words *Novum opus* included at the beginning of every extant Carolingian Gospel Book. The text of the *Liber pontificalis* was thus dated, placed and associated with the highest of authorities within the Christian church.

Further, there is a list of popes provided, numbered 1–94, with a note of their reigns and where they were born. In this list of popes, moreover, the same late ninth-century hand has annotated it to indicate which patristic authors were writing in the time of which pope, thus locating Jerome, Augustine, Ambrose and others in relation to the bishop of Rome and successor to St Peter. The layout of the manuscript is also noteworthy. The clarity of the layout, with the two columns of twenty-eight lines, dramatic initials, alternating lines of capitals in green, yellow and black for incipits and titles, make this a readily accessible text.

The striking layout is echoed in the Eusebius manuscript from Copenhagen (Kongelige Bibliotek Gl. Kgl. S. 163). With a very spacious format (305 × 225 mm [240 × 170 mm]), and again in two columns of twenty-eight lines, with very exact quiring in relation to divisions in the text, it reveals careful and precise calculation of the length of the text on the scribes' part (though the last twenty-two chapters of Book 11

---

[103] *Liber pontificalis*, ed. Duchesne, pp. 48 and 117 and trans. Davis, *The book of the pontiffs*, p. 1. These appear in most of the manuscripts, notably the early Naples fragment. See above p. 195 and note 42.

from this codex are now lost). A reader has added summary notes of the content in some of the margins. What is impressive, about both the *Liber pontificalis* and Eusebius/Rufinus manuscripts, in addition to the evidence of readers using the books, is their design and layout. The scribes were clearly working from exemplars, but their approach to the presentation of the text was that of scribes who knew and understood what it said and who wished to make it as accessible to the next reader as possible.

Apart from study of the manuscripts themselves, there are two further ways in which to observe the reading process. One is to look at what the scholars of St Amand wrote. If we examine Hucbald of St Amand's work, for example, he is ostensibly a disappointment, for he has left behind only hagiography and some skilful if frightful poetry. It is Hucbald who perpetrated the long poem in celebration of baldness, every word of which begins with C. Analysis of Hucbald's hagiography has revealed a distinctively historical approach to his subjects as well as the use and even quotation from particular history books he had read. He reveals how he exploited the library of St Amand and those of other institutions.[104] Hucbald had been trained at St Amand, had taught at St Bertin and at Rheims, and retired to St Amand, where he lived until his death at the ripe old age of about ninety in 930. Eight books once owned by Hucbald are still extant and some he clearly acquired on his travels in northern France (such as Bede's *Chronica maiora*). From his writing it is clear that he had absorbed such Frankish history as the account of the quarrels between the sons of Louis the Pious by Nithard, and the *Gesta Dagoberti*. Julia Smith has demonstrated how 'Hucbald also evinced a desire to set the saints about whom he wrote in as precise and specific a historical context as possible'. She has shown how, in his *Vita Lebuini*, composed between 918 and 930, Hucbald reworked an older *Vita* but drew on both Bede and the *Chronicon laurissense* (extant in a manuscript known to have belonged to Hucbald) in order to recreate the ecclesiastical politics of the mid-eighth century in which Lebuin had worked.[105]

The *Gesta Dagoberti*, a Carolingian revisionist work written at St Denis possibly by Abbot Hilduin during the reign of Louis the Pious, provided Hucbald with the necessary backdrop to Rictrudis' life and the career of her husband for his *Vita sanctae Rictrudis*. The life includes the myth of the Franks' Trojan origins, and an account of the baptism of Clovis by Remigius with oil sent from heaven. In the *Vita Lebuini*, Hucbald includes an account of the social structure of the early Saxons which he appears to have borrowed from Nithard. Hucbald, therefore, shows how he absorbed

---

[104] See Smith, 'A Hagiographer at work', on which I draw for the rest of this paragraph.
[105] See list above, no. 6, p. 212.

not only specific historical facts from his reading but also a method of thinking. This included a wish to establish an historical context.

Lastly I come to the St Amand historical compilation, now Vienna, ÖNB cod. 473, and its implications for the reading of history at St Amand. I have mentioned this manuscript in earlier chapters, so here simply reiterate the main points in order to demonstate how the processes of copying and compilation offer crucial evidence for reading and reception of history texts.[106] The manuscript contains the following:

> fols. 1v–85v *Liber pontificalis* in the 'B' text, that is, the Frankish version. It runs to life 94 of Stephen II (III) (d. 772)
>
> fols. 85v–88v *Revelatio S. Stephani*
>
> fols. 90r–91 list of descent from Adam to Noah
>
> fols. 91r–107v *Liber historiae francorum* in the 'B' or Austrasian version ending with the burial of Dagobert in 662. It includes the section about the Trojan origins of the Franks
>
> 108r–114v Continuations to the *Chronicle* of 'Fredegar' in the version called Class 5(f). It goes as far as the death of Charles Martel in 741
>
> fols. 116r–143v and 152v–169r *Annales regni francorum* in the 'D' or unrevised version, 741–829
>
> fols. 144r–151v a portion of Einhard's *Vita Karoli* concerning Charlemagne's marriage to Hildegard inserted after 814
>
> fols. 169v–170v *Genealogia Sancti Arnulfi*
>
> fols. 171r–172r *Historia francorum epitomata ab origine gentis ad Ludovicum pium*

As I have already commented, a codex such as this makes it necessary to explore not only the motives and circumstances of its compilation but also the implications for the initial production, reading and dissemination of Carolingian historiography generally. As already noted in chapter 5, the compiler used the *Liber pontificalis* text already at St Amand, for he reproduced all the preliminary material. He made it fit the B family, possibly by reference to a different exemplar from Laon or Cologne and converted it thereby into a distinctively Frankish version of the papal careers. The history of the popes in this codex, therefore, is deployed as an adjunct to and historical context for that of the Franks. It serves to reinforce the associations of the Carolingians and Franks with Rome and papal authority and provides essential justification for the Frankish conquest of Italy recorded in the annals included later in the same codex.

---

[106] See above, chapter 5, and H. Reimitz, 'Ein fränkisches Geschichtsbuch aus Saint-Amand und der Codex Vindobonensis palat. 473', in C. Egger and H. Weigl (eds.), *Text-Schrift-Codex. Quellenkundliche Arbeiten aus dem Institut für Österreichische Geschichtsforschung*, *MIÖG* Ergänzungsband (Vienna and Munich, 2000), pp. 34–90.

The Frankish history sections, the interpolation from Einhard and the genealogies together reinforce the legitimacy of the Carolingian succession. The *Annales regni francorum*, specifically described as the deeds of Charlemagne and Louis with special headings, constitute the centrepiece of the codex. All the other texts are designed to complement and enhance it.

The compiler of this history book was working at St Amand at the time it was enjoying royal patronage under the abbacy of Gauzlin, archchancellor of Charles the Bald. Helmut Reimitz has convincingly linked it to the coronation of Charles the Bald at Metz in 869.[107] It may have been compiled in order to persuade a particular individual or group of the force of its message, either within St Amand itself or elsewhere. We know from the palaeographical evidence that St Amand had a link with Mainz, as well as with such western centres as Fleury, Tours, Rheims and Corbie.[108] Vienna, ÖNB cod. 473's later provenance of Worms unfortunately throws no light on its immediate distribution, though a move from Mainz to Worms is relatively easy to contemplate.[109] Further work may shed light on this aspect of the codex's history.

A further striking message of Vienna, ÖNB cod. 473, seen in relation to the other history books copied at St Amand, is its insistence on the association of Carolingian, papal and Roman history. There are many other and enormously varied instances of the Roman orientation of Frankish historical perspectives. The Roman orientation embraced the pagan imperial past to some degree but is more devotedly focused on the early Roman martyrs and the succession of the heirs of St Peter. The Franks' relation to Rome is no less than a proclamation issuing from the pages of the Vienna codex and reflects a process of assimilation of a particular past as a consequence of reading a very diverse set of texts.

With the history manuscripts produced at Lorsch and St Amand as my examples, it can be seen that compilation and copying are themselves evidence of reading and thinking. The setting out of a particular text so that it could be read is indicative of a process of reading that has already taken

[107] Reimitz, 'Ein fränkisches Geschichtsbuch'.

[108] This information is derived from my own unpublished research on the ninth-century manuscripts of St Amand.

[109] M. Tischler, *Einharts Vita Karoli. Studien zur Entstehung, Überlieferung und Rezeption*, *MGH* Schriften 48, 2 vols. (Hannover, 2001), pp. 450–69, maintains Worms as the origin of the manuscript, despite the strong palaeographical and other indications to the contrary discussed by Reimitz, 'Ein fränkisches Geschichtsbuch'. Tischler was right, however, to point out (p. 456, n. 704) that I had mistakenly substituted Vienna, ÖNB cod. 473's contents with those of a different manuscript in *Carolingians and the written word*, p. 240, n. 101, even though I corrected this in subsequent publications.

place. Knowledge is adapted, both visually and by new juxtapositions, to serve new ideas and new priorities. Thus knowledge of the past was not only a matter of memory; it also involved the reading and understanding of texts and their redeployment for new purposes. When we are reading medieval texts, therefore, we should try and think backwards from that text to consider the formation of the author's thinking. We should investigate what the author may have read, in what contexts and formats, and for what purposes. We should also consider the development of knowledge and understanding on the part of the scribes and compilers and how they used the texts they inherited. Lastly we should consider the readers' attitude towards, and definition of, the textual and historical authority of the texts available to them; it is this which is my focus in the following chapter.

10 Texts, authority and the history of the church

In 849, Gottschalk of Orbais in the diocese of Soissons was summoned to the Synod of Quierzy. From his own studies of the patristic theologians he had formed views on predestination that had found little favour with the established church of his day. No text of the proceedings at Quierzy survives, but we do have reports from eye witnesses in the contemporary Annals of St Bertin – interpolated by Archbishop Hincmar of Rheims to Gottschalk's disadvantage – and by Florus the Deacon of Lyons. Hincmar is very scathing on how much Gottschalk's learning had led him astray; he was too erudite for his own good. Hincmar tells us that at the synod, Gottschalk was accused of errant views, condemned, flogged and compelled to burn the books containing his statements (*librosque suarum adsertionum*).[1] Florus the Deacon, however, provides crucial extra information. While Hincmar gave us the impression that Gottschalk went to Quierzy more or less to be publicly punished, Florus' account suggests that Gottschalk, at least as far as he, Gottschalk, was concerned, went to engage in dispute. He may even have been buoyed up with the hope of convincing his audience of bishops and abbots from the ecclesiastical province of Rheims, including Paschasius Radbertus of Corbie and Gottschalk's own abbot from Orbais, that he was justified in his views. Florus tells us that what Gottschalk had to burn were the sections from the Bible and patristic writings that vindicated his opinions and that he had brought with him to the synod.[2] Gottschalk's reference collection

---

[1] *Annales Bertiniani*, *s.a.* 849, ed. R. Rau, *Quellen zur karolingischen Reichsgeschichte*, II (Darmstadt, 1972), pp. 72–7; trans. J. L. Nelson, *The Annals of St Bertin* (Manchester, 1991); and see her argument concerning Hincmar's interpolation into Prudentius of Troyes' text, *ibid.*, p. 14, supporting, as she points out, views already put forward by scholars in the eighteenth century. Hincmar claims that Gottschalk had gone to Italy, Dalmatia, Noricum and Pannonia. Compare the *Annales fuldenses*' account of the earlier decision by bishops in Louis the German's kingdom (also recorded in the *Annals of St Bertin*) (Mainz, 848) who sent him to Hincmar, in R. Rau, *Quellen zur karolingischen Reichsgeschichte*, III (Darmstadt, 1974), p. 36. On the synods see W. Hartmann, *Die Synoden der Karolingerzeit im Frankenreich und in Italien* (Paderborn, 1989), pp. 226–8.
[2] W. Hartmann (ed.), *Die Konzilien der karolingische Teilreiche 843–859*, MGH *Conc.*, III, *Concilia aevi karolini 843–859* (Hannover, 1984), p. 197: *Quia inaudito irreligiositatis et*

sounds very much like the dossiers assembled at other councils (not least Nicaea II in 787) compiled from authoritative writings to support views maintained in discussion.[3]

Gottschalk himself was flogged almost to death and condemned to silence. Thus Gottschalk's interpretation, the writings of authority and his oral expression of his views were all done away with. More crucially the treatment of Gottschalk's sources by the Frankish bishops and abbots at Quierzy indicates also an attempt to control their meaning, to exert power over those particular texts from the Bible and church fathers, and to assert the right to exclusive understanding of them. Although the burning of books at Quierzy was a symbolic destruction, for these were only Gottschalk's copies of texts readily available elsewhere, such ritual burning was a grand and violent act of official disavowal of particular texts. Death was inflicted as if the books acted as an effigy of Gottschalk, with destruction and purification by fire. The context, moreover, is obviously one in which knowledge is gained from books. Acts against particular writers to achieve silence and prevent the dissemination of their ideas witness to the notion that the act of writing invoked a power and authority beyond that of the author himself. The Carolingian clergy who sought to destroy Gottschalk's writings and his sources out of fear of their power, therefore, clearly appreciated the potency of the written word.

The Carolingian destruction of Gottschalk's books needs to be set within the context of other instances of such violent activity from antiquity and the early middle ages. Quite apart from the burning of the prophecies of Jeremiah recorded in the Old Testament,[4] and the establishment of book burning as a form of legal punishment towards the end of the reign of the emperor Augustus,[5] the most dramatic incidents in

---

crudelitatis exemplo, tandiu ille miserabilis flagris et caedibus trucidatus est, donec (sicut narraverunt nobis, qui praesentes aderant) accenso coram se igni libellum, in quo sententias scripturarum sive sanctorum patrum sibi collegerat, quas in concilio offeret, coactus est iam pene emoriens suis manibus in flammam proicere atque incendio concremare; cum omnes retro haeretici verbis et disputationibus victi atque convicti sunt.

[3] On Nicaea II see M.-F. Auzépy, 'Francfort et Nicée II', in R. Berndt (ed.), *Das Frankfurter Konzil von 794; Kristallisationspunckt karolingischer Kultur*, 2 vols., Quellen und Abhandlungen zur Mittelrheinischen Kirchengeschichte 80 (Leiden, 1997), I, pp. 279–300, at p. 291. On predestination see J. Marenbon, 'Carolingian thought', in R. McKitterick (ed.), *Carolingian Culture: emulation and innovation* (Cambridge, 1994), pp. 171–92, esp. pp. 181–3; D. Ganz, 'Theology and the organization of thought', in McKitterick (ed.), *NCMH*, pp. 758–85, esp. pp. 767–73; and D. Nineham, 'Gottschalk of Orbais: reactionary or precursor of the Reformation', *Journal of Ecclesiastical History* 40 (1989), pp. 1–18.

[4] Jeremiah 36.23.

[5] F. H. Cramer, 'Book burning and censorship in ancient Rome. A chapter from the history of freedom of speech', *Journal of the History of Ideas* 6 (1945), pp. 157–96; and see also Acts 19.19 for the account of the burning of magical texts at Ephesus (incidentally the value of the books there burnt was estimated at 50,000 pieces of silver).

the early church are linked with the Donatists,[6] the conflicts between the Arians and the Catholics and the first recorded proscription of texts in the interests of the Catholic church. Constantine proscribed the works of Porphyry and Arius in a letter to 'the bishops and people', stating that if any treatise composed by Arius should be discovered it should be consigned to the flames in order not only that his depraved doctrine might be suppressed but also that no memorial of him might by any means be left.[7]

Implicit in such condemnation of texts, whether by pagans of political or Christian works or by Christians of heretical works, is the reaction to a set of texts defined by each group as of central importance to their identity and group self-consciousness. To destroy such a text or set of texts was to attack a community, whether spiritual or actual.[8] Conversely, the creation of a text and its dissemination in book form, owned by, or accessible to, members of a group, reinforced the sense of belonging to that group. By adopting his unorthodox reading of scripture and the fathers, therefore, Gottschalk put himself on the margin of his own textual community. He undermined not only ecclesiastical authority but also the Frankish clergy's understanding of their place as guarantors of orthodoxy and upholders of the learning and interpretations of the fathers within the Carolingian world. He challenged their own reading of books as familiar to them as they were to him. Like many original theological thinkers before him, he attempted to insert difference into an intellectual history that had been received as a solid interpretative scholarly tradition and which most of his contemporaries wished to preserve.

It is the reception and content of that tradition which is my principal focus in this chapter. What I hope to demonstrate is that the relationship

---

[6] Compare Diocletian's Edict of 297 (or 302) against the Manichees, *Comparison of the laws of Moses and the Romans*, ed. P. E. Huschke, E. Seckel and B. Kuebler, *Iurisprudentia anteiustiniana* (Leipzig, 1908–27), II, pp. 381–3; see A. D. Lee, *Pagans and Christians in late antiquity: a sourcebook* (London, 2000), pp. 66–7 for a succinct placing of the Diocletian decree in context and an English translation. For Diocletian against the Christians in 303, ordering the churches to be razed and the Scriptures destroyed by fire, see Eusebius-Rufinus, *Historia ecclesiastica*, eds. E. Schwartz and T. Mommsen, *Eusebius Werke, II, Die Kirchengeschichte*, ed. E. Schwartz, *Die lateinische Übersetzung des Rufinus*, ed. T. Mommsen, Die griechischen christlichen Schriftsteller der ersten drei Jahrhunderte: Eusebius 2,1 and 2,2, 2 vols. (Leipzig, 1903 and 1908), 8.2, pp. 742–3. For general discussion see W. Speyer, *Büchervernichtung und Zensur des Geistes bei Heiden, Juden und Christen*, Bibliothek des Buchwesens 7 (Stuttgart, 1981); and H. Gamble, *Books and readers in the early church. A history of early Christian texts* (New Haven, 1995).

[7] See W. Jacob and R. Hanslik (eds.), *Cassiodori-Epiphanii, Historia ecclesiastica tripartita*, CSEL, LXXI (Vienna, 1952), II.15, p. 109. For parallels see C. W. Hedrick Jr, *History and silence: purge and rehabilitation of memory in late antiquity* (Austin, 2000).

[8] See the stimulating discussions in P. Biller and M. A. Hudson (eds.), *Heresy and literacy, 1000–1530* (Cambridge, 1994).

of the Carolingian Franks to the books in their libraries was not simply that of scholars to a repository of learning. The books in Frankish
libraries, as part of a past which the Franks had assimilated to themselves, formed part of the Frankish sense of identity. In other words,
the Franks were indeed a textual community in relation to the Bible,
as has long been recognised,[9] but they were also a textual community
in terms of their intellectual and textual inheritance. It is the formation and ramifications of this very particular understanding of books
and place in history within the Carolingian world and the Carolingian church, therefore, that I wish to explore in the remainder of this
chapter.

De viris illustribus

Notker Balbulus of St Gallen (*c.* 840–912) is one of many Carolingian
writers who gives us a cue. In 885 he sent his *Notatio de viris illustribus*,
a guide to the study of the Bible, to Salamo, a newly made deacon who
became in due course Bishop of Constance.[10] Notker's *Notatio* provides
the basic essentials and is cast in the form of 'if you would know or understand a certain thing (fact, knowledge of a topic), you should read the
following text'. The bibliographical recommendations and comments are
organised more by subject than by author. It is not a comprehensive indication of what Notker might have had at his disposal. That is available
in the famous ninth-century library catalogue from St Gallen which includes many of his annotations and additions.[11] For the young Salamo,
however, Notker provided a concise programme of study, concentrating
on scripture and Christian learning. He offered many brusque and very
personal evaluations of particular works of the fathers and more recent
authors such as Bede, Alcuin and Hraban Maur. His range of examples

---

[9] See, for example, M. de Jong (ed.), *The power of the word. The influence of the Bible on early
medieval politics*, special issue, *EME* 7 (1998); J. J. Contreni, 'Carolingian biblical studies',
in U.-R. Blumenthal, *Carolingian essays* (Washington, 1983), pp. 71–98 and reprinted in
J. J. Contreni, *Carolingian learning, masters and manuscripts* (Aldershot, 1992), chapter 5;
and M. C. Ferrari, *Il 'Liber sanctae crucis' di Rabano Mauro. Testo-immagine-contesto* (Bern,
1999). The fruitful notion of 'textual community' is of course B. Stock's, *The implications
of literacy: written language and models of interpretation in the eleventh and twelfth centuries*
(Princeton, 1983). For a recent assessment see also C. F. Briggs, 'Historiographical
essay. Literacy, reading, and writing in the medieval West', *Journal of Medieval History*
26 (2000), pp. 397–420.

[10] E. Rauner, 'Notker des Stammlers "Notatio de illustribus viris"', *Mittellateinisches
Jahrbuch* 21 (1986), pp. 34–69; also ed. E. Dümmler, *Das Formelbuch des Bischofs Salomo
III von Konstanz* (1857, reprinted Osnabrück, 1974).

[11] See Susan Rankin, '"Ego itaque Notker scripsi"', *RB* 101 (1991), pp. 268–98; and
W. von den Steinen, *Notker und seine geistige Welt* (Bern, 1948), pp. 58–63.

of types of work and author could be parallelled in most monastic and cathedral schools and libraries throughout the Carolingian empire.[12]

Thus Notker recommended Jerome's works for understanding the Old and New Testaments and Jerome on Hebrew names. He suggested Augustine should be consulted for a refutation of the Manichees' views on creation. Ambrose's *Hexameron*, Origen on Leviticus and Exodus and Augustine's *Quaestiones* on the Heptateuch are also recommended as exegetes of the first books of the Bible. Notker proposed Eugippius on Augustine as a handy collection of extracts and indicated how many people have written about the Psalter. He tells Salamo that Gregory the Great had explained the difficult Book of Job, Jerome the Proverbs of Solomon and Bede had written on Tobit, Esdras and Maccabees. On the New Testament Notker said it would be enough if Salamo were to read Jerome and Bede on Matthew and Mark, and Augustine on John. Augustine should be consulted on the Sermon on the Mount. Eugippius's *collectaneum* of the works of Augustine was also recommended. For further reading after these basic essentials, Notker recommended Origen on the Epistle to the Romans, Ambrose on Luke's Gospel and on Paul's Epistles and on the letter to the Hebrews, Jerome on the Epistles to the Galatians, Ephesians, Titus and Philemon and Bede on the Seven canonical epistles. Then there were the homilies of John Chrysostom, Origen, Augustine, Gregory, Maximin, Leo and Bede to be read. On Revelation Notker commended the works of Augustine, Jerome, Gregory, Bede, Tychonius and Primasius. If Salamo wanted glosses, Hraban Maur (the ninth-century archbishop of Mainz) had them on the whole of scripture.

But study should not be confined to scripture and biblical exegesis. There were other things Salamo needed to read, such as Augustine's Confessions and his other works, Cassian on the monastic life, Isidore of Seville's *Etymologiae*, *Sententiae* and the *De officiis*. On pastoral care and the ministry Gregory the Great's *Regula pastoralis* was the principal guide. As for letters, Notker recommended the letters of Jerome, for they touched on a huge range of topics Salamo should know about, rather than the many letters of Alcuin (who is described as the *magister* of Charlemagne) to his friends, despite their abundance *quia tibi puerulo cum supercilio scriptae videntur*. The grammars of Donatus, Nichomachus, Dositheus and Priscian were worth reading. For poetry there were plenty of Christian works on martyrs and in praise of God, such as Alcimus Avitus, Iuvencus, Sedulius and the hymns of Ambrose. Salamo should

---

[12] See McKitterick, *Carolingians and the written word*, chapter 5: 'The organization of knowledge', pp. 164–210.

also read the passions of the saints, especially those of the time of Diocletian and the Caesars and the persecution of the church.[13] Most crucially, Notker recommended the accounts of the fathers in the desert and particular histories of the church, namely that of Eusebius and the *Historia tripartita* of Cassiodorus compiled from Socrates, Sozomen and Theodoret. For guidance on the *ecclesiastici scriptores*, Salamo should turn to the work of Jerome and Gennadius.

It is these allusions to Jerome-Gennadius' *De viris illustribus*, Eusebius-Rufinus' *Historia ecclesiastica* and Cassiodorus-Epiphanius' *Historia tripartita* which need to be investigated further in order to account for their inclusion in Notker's guide.

Jerome-Gennadius' *De viris illustribus* offers a very particular and original perspective on the early church, for he constructs what is in effect a history of the church[14] in terms of the authors who contributed the narratives and took part in the theological debates perceived as central to the establishment of the Christian faith and to the church's development. The work was first compiled *c.* 392. The earliest manuscripts extant date from the late seventh or early eighth century (BAV reg. lat. 2077 and Paris, BnF lat. 12161) and it may well be the case that some of the entries presented as those of Jerome or Gennadius are in fact later additions. Jerome's portion contains entries on 135 authors from Peter to Jerome himself. They are largely from the Mediterranean littoral and Asia Minor. Gennadius' continuation was made *c.* 480. It comprises ninety-nine authors, including notes on a little group of Gallo-Roman authors and Gennadius himself, probably made shortly thereafter.[15] Gennadius added many Gallic authors, thus incorporating his own region into Christian history and the construction of authority. He appears, moreover, to have been sympathetic to the ideas of the ascetic circles of Lérins and Marseilles as far as

[13] See F. Brunhölzl, *Histoire de la littérature latine du moyen âge. II De l'époque carolingienne au milieu du onzième siècle* (Turnhout, 1996 revised edition trans. H. Rochais from German edn of 1992), pp. 39–41; and E. Curtius, *Europäische literatur und lateinisches Mittelalter* (Bern, 1948), Excursus VI. 6, pp. 457–8; Eng. trans. W. Trask, *European literature and the Latin middle ages* (London, 1953), pp. 463–4.
[14] Brunhölzl, *Histoire*, p. 41.
[15] Jerome-Gennadius, *De viris illustribus*, ed. E. C. Richardson, *Hieronymus, Liber de viris inlustribus Gennadius de viris inlustribus*, Texte und Untersuchungen zur Geschichte der altchristlichen Literatur (Leipzig, 1896). See also C. A. Bernouilli (ed.), *Hieronymus-Gennadius De viris illustribus* (Freiburg i. Br. and Leipzig, 1895), who supplies fuller details on some of the manuscripts, though Richardson's text has been agreed by scholars subsequently to be the best. See now, however, A. Ceresa-Gastaldo (ed.), *Gli uomini illustri = De viris illustribus* (Florence, 1988); and on the manuscripts see below, pp. 238–9. I am grateful to Laurent Terrade for discussion of this point and many others in this chapter which arose in the course of his translation of an earlier version into French for presentation at the Institut historique allemand in Paris in November 2001.

his selection of authors and emphasis is concerned.[16] Isidore of Seville provided a further continuation, with thirty-three authors. Spanish writers predominated but notable Gallo-Roman, African, Greek and Italian theologians of the sixth century, most obviously Gregory the Great, were included. Indeed, given the very laconic account of Gregory's works in the *Liber pontificalis*, the stress on Gregory's wisdom and relatively detailed note on the *Cura pastoralis* and the *Moralia in Iob*, is striking.[17]

Jerome stated in his preface, addressed to his friend Dexter, that he wished to provide a Christian and ecclesiastical equivalent for Tranquillus' *De illustribus grammaticis* and *De claris rhetoribus* and

> do for our writers what Tranquillus did for the illustrious men of letters among the gentiles, namely to set briefly before you all those who have published any memorable writing on the Holy Scriptures from the time of our Lord's passion until the fourteenth year of the Emperor Theodosius . . . Let those who think the church has no philosophers or orators or men of learning, learn how many and what sort of men founded, built and adorned it, and cease to accuse our faith of such rustic simplicity and recognize their own ignorance.[18]

Jerome used words such as 'founded', 'built', 'adorned' (*fundare, struxere, adornare*), usual in the contexts of discussion of art and architecture, and applied them to the provision of texts as if to emphasise the idea of texts as a secure foundation.[19] The entries take the form of 'X living in Y in the time of Z (or who died during the reign of Z emperor) wrote the following works'. Sometimes there are additional comments about the quality of the work, aspects of an individual's career, the degree to which a work attributed to a particular author is really by him or whether the work is strictly orthodox.

---

[16] B. Czapla, *Gennadius als Litterarhistoriker. Ein Quellenkritische Untersuchung der Schrift des Gennadius von Marseille. De viris illustribus*, Kirchengeschichtliche Studien 4.1 (Münster, 1898).

[17] C. C. Merino, *El "De viris illustribus" de Isidoro de Sevilla. Estudio y edicion critica.* Theses et Studia philologica Salamanticensia 12 (Salamanca, 1964). See also Gustav von Dziatowski, *Isidor und Ildefons als Litterarhistoriker. Eine Quellenkritische Untersuchung der Schriften De viris illustribus des Isidor von Sevilla und des Ildefons von Toledo*, Kirchengeschichtliche Studien 4.2 (Münster, 1898); W. Smidt, 'Ein altes Handschriftenfragment der "Viri illustres" Isidors von Sevilla', *Neues Archiv* 44 (1922), pp. 122–35; and H. Knoeppler, '*De viris illustribus* and Isidore of Seville', *Journal of Theological Studies* 37 (1936), pp. 16–34. Compare the *Liber pontificalis*, Life 66, ed. L. Duchesne, *Le Liber pontificalis*, 2 vols. (Paris, 1886 and 1892), p. 312.

[18] Ed. Richardson, *De viris inlustribus*, p. 2. Eng. trans. E. C. Richardson, *Theodoret, Jerome, Gennadius, Rufinus: historical writings*, in H. Wace and P. Schaff (eds.), *A Select Library of Nicene and Post-Nicene Fathers of the Christian Church*, second series, 3 (Oxford and New York, 1892), p. 359. A new translation is in preparation by Mark Vessey for the Liverpool Translated Texts for Historians series.

[19] Ed. Richardson, *De viris inlustribus*, p. 2.

On St Peter, for example, he notes that he wrote two Epistles, that some ascribed Mark's Gospel to him, and books called the Acts, Gospel, Preaching, Revelation and the Judgement of Peter are rejected as apocryphal. On Mark himself he explains that he was a disciple and interpreter of Peter and wrote a short Gospel at the request of the people of Rome embodying what he had heard Peter tell him. Jerome states that the text was approved by Peter and published to the churches. In the entry for Hegesippus he adds detail about a history in which Hegesippus writes concerning the monuments of the pagans, notably, the games celebrated and city built in honour of Antinous of whom it was said that the Emperor Hadrian was enamoured. On the other hand, Jerome does not go into detail about the works of Tertullian because 'they are well known to most'. He records that Pantaenus was sent to India by Demetrius bishop of Alexandria. He found there that Bartholomew, one of the twelve apostles, was preaching according to the Gospel of Matthew and on his return to Alexandria Pantaenus brought the Gospel with him, written in Hebrew characters. He tells us that Pamphilus was so inflamed with the love of sacred literature that he transcribed the works of Origen with his own hand and that these are still in the library at Caesarea. Of Ambrose he withholds judgement as he is still alive; Jerome does not wish to appear to praise or blame Ambrose, lest in the former case he be criticised for adulation and in the latter for speaking the truth.[20]

Gennadius follows Jerome's format faithfully, saying of Rufinus, for example, that he had a fine talent for translation and opened up to the Latin-speaking church the greater part of Greek literature. Of Pelagius he concedes that before he was proclaimed a heretic Pelagius wrote books of practical value for students. He does not mention Pelagius' British origins though he does refer, in a later entry, to Bishop Fastidius of the Britons (*episcopus britannorum*) who wrote books on the Christian Life and on virginity. Fastidius was a disciple of Pelagius and probably British rather than Breton. Gennadius devotes a long entry to Orosius, who 'wrote seven books against those enemies of the Christians who say that the decay of the Roman state was caused by the Christian religion'. On the contrary, 'the Roman empire owed to the Christian religion its undeserved continuance and the state of peace which it enjoyed for the worship of God'. It was, moreover, Orosius who brought the relics of the martyr Stephen to the west.[21]

---

[20] *Ibid.*, Jerome, nos. 1, 8, 22, 36, 75, 134, pp. 6–7, 12, 20–1, 26, 41, 53.

[21] *Ibid.*, Gennadius, nos. 43, 58, 40, pp. 77, 81, 76; trans. Richardson, *Theodoret, Jerome, Gennadius*, p. 393. I am grateful to Laurent Terrade for pointing out to me that Caesarius of Arles uses Fastidius' work on the Christian life in his Sermon 20, though he attributed it to Fatalis, who was in fact the recipient of the work. See Caesarius of Arles, Sermons,

The *De viris illustribus* of Jerome-Gennadius, therefore, is an apologetic text, but it is also a polemic against paganism with an arsenal of Christian texts hurled at its readers. It is a new kind of history in its emphasis on Christian men of learning; it insists on their fame and importance because of what they have thought and what they have written rather than on what they have done. The perception of fame and orthodoxy is formed by their writing and their contributions to theological debates. Texts are defined in relation to the orthodox standard. It is essential to register, moreover, that Jerome and Gennadius also provide a clear and progressive chronology and that Jerome is punctilious, even if Gennadius and Isidore are less so, in supplying the geographical details of each author as well. Readers and hearers of *De viris illustribus*, therefore, would form a cumulative Christian geography in their mind's eye, in which the Christian landscape spanned the world from Britain to India, and in which certain places, such as Rome, Antioch, Caesarea and Alexandria assumed prominence because of what had been written there and by whom.

Yet such readers and hearers would also have had their imagination and knowledge shaped by the text to which Jerome himself was most indebted in the construction of the *De viris illustribus*, as he acknowledged in his preface, namely, Eusebius' *Historia ecclesiastica*. Not the least of Jerome's debts was that it had enabled him to construct the *De viris illustribus* in chronological order. A greater legacy of Eusebius' *Historia ecclesiastica*, however, was the way it constructed the Christian past in terms of books and authors.

Eusebius-Rufinus, *Historia ecclesiastica*

It is not necessary here to reiterate at length the enormous influence and importance of Eusebius' account of the development of the Christian church, and the dramatic transformation in historiographical method he effected in his recourse to letters, edicts and reports of the events he narrated.[22] He pioneered a new kind of written history, 'Christian

---

ed. M. J. Delage, *Césaire Sermons au peuple*, Sources Chrétiennes 175, 243, 330, 3 vols. (Paris 1971–86), I, p. 495.

[22] See the fine analysis in R. A. Markus, 'Church history and early church historians', in D. Baker (ed.), *The materials, sources and methods of ecclesiastical history*, Studies in Church History 11 (1975), pp. 1–17; and the useful survey in H. W. Attridge and G. Hata (eds.), *Eusebius, Christianity and Judaism* (Detroit and Leiden, 1992), especially the chapters by G. F. Chesnut, 'Eusebius, Augustine, Orosius and the later patristic and medieval Christian historians', pp. 687–713; and see also G. F. Chesnut, *The first Christian histories. Eusebius, Socrates, Sozomen, Theodoret and Evagrius* (Paris, 1977 and Macon, Ga., 1986).

historiography' (as against 'pagan historiography'),[23] in his concentration on the many important events in the history of the church; the leaders, heroes and heroines and martyrs of the earliest Christian communities; on heretics; on the fate of the Jews, and the eventual peace and recovery of the church.[24] It has long been assumed that Eusebius was extensively used in the early middle ages, by Gregory of Tours, by Bede, and many other writers as a guide and model for historical writing. That use, however, has not been adequately defined and appears in fact to have been rather limited; the *Historia ecclesiastica* does not seem to have acted as a powerful model for a narrative, even if its particular emphases, overall theme and methods were influential, as I hope to make clear.[25] The *Chronicle* of Eusebius-Jerome was a far more obvious model for many historical writers of the early middle ages. Many libraries possessed it in the version translated and extended by Jerome. It was subsequently continued by different continuators in the west into the sixth century. This was the standard reference book for world chronology. It provided the clearest and most influential notion of the establishment of Christianity in the Roman world for the Franks. It started with Abraham (that is, 2016 BC), and ran to Constantine's *Vicennalia* (AD 325) but was organised according to years since Abraham and the Olympiads. It set out significant events and reigns of important rulers in the different empires of the ancient world in sometimes as many as eleven synchronised parallel columns. It certainly conveyed what has been claimed as a Greek conception of universal history as a succession of empires,[26] but it also provided the chronological base for its many early and later medieval continuators.

What needs emphasis is that Eusebius' *Ecclesiastical history* was transmitted to the Latin west in the translation made by Rufinus of Aquileia, the translator of Greek texts so highly praised by Gennadius, and thus a preserver of a significant number of patristic texts.[27] Rufinus had been educated in Rome and Alexandria, spent time in Jerusalem and was such

---

[23] A. Momigliano, 'Pagan and Christian historiography in the fourth century A.D.', in *idem*. (ed.), *The conflict between paganism and Christianity in the fourth century* (Oxford, 1963), pp. 79–99.

[24] Eds. Schwartz and Mommsen, *Eusebius Werke*, II.

[25] See the useful (and qualifying) comments by W. Goffart, *The narrators of barbarian history* (Princeton, 1988), especially pp. 157, 226, 299.

[26] A. A. Mosshammer, *The Chronicle of Eusebius and Greek chronographic tradition* (Lewisburg and London, 1979).

[27] C. Hammond, 'A product of a fifth-century scriptorium preserving conventions used by Rufinus of Aquileia', *Journal of Theological Studies* 29 (1978), pp. 366–91; C. Hammond-Bammell, 'Products of fifth-century scriptoria preserving conventions used by Rufinus of Aquileia', *Journal of Theological Studies* 30 (1979), pp. 430–61; and C. Hammond-Bammell, 'Products of fifth-century scriptoria preserving conventions used by Rufinus of Aquileia', *Journal of Theological Studies* 35 (1984), 347–93.

a staunch defender of Origen's orthodoxy that he became involved in a bitter dispute with Jerome.

Rufinus changed the shape of the ecclesiastical history of Eusebius and thus its emphasis. Eusebius' ten books were extended to eleven. As Rufinus explains in his preface, addressed to Chromatius, bishop of Aquileia, in 401, after apologising for his lack of skill in translating:

I must point out the course I have taken in reference to the tenth book of this work. As it stands in the Greek it has little to do with the process of events. All but a small part of it is taken up with discussions tending to the praise of particular bishops and adds nothing to our knowledge of the facts.[28] I have therefore left out this superfluous matter and whatever in it belonged to genuine history I have added to the ninth book, with which I have made his history close. The tenth and eleventh books I have myself compiled, partly from the traditions of the former generation, partly from facts within my own memory; and these I have added to our previous books, like the two fishes to the loaves. If you bestow your approval and benediction upon them I shall have a sure confidence that they will suffice for the multitude. The work as now completed contains the events from the Ascension of the Saviour to the present time; my own two books those from the days of Constantine when the persecution came to an end, on to the death of the emperor Theodosius.[29]

At the end of the ninth book Rufinus added a note:

Thus far Eusebius has given us the record of the history. As to subsequent events as they have followed up to the present time, as I have found them recorded in the writings of the last generation, or so far as they are covered by my own knowledge, I will add them, obeying as best I may in this point also the commands of our father in God.[30]

The two new books added by Rufinus provide an account of the synod of Nicaea with a version of the creed and a summary of the decrees. Rufinus is eloquent on the subject of the Arian schism. He tells us of the conversion of India and Ethiopia, and of the setback for Christianity under Julian. He provides a remarkably detailed and dramatic description of the temple of Serapis in Alexandria and the downfall of the ancient wooden image of the God. It is Rufinus who relates the story of the finding of the True Cross by Helena, mother of the Emperor Constantine.

---

[28] This appears to be a reference to the very lengthy panegyric on the rebuilding of the church at Tyre.

[29] Eds. Schwartz and Mommsen, *Eusebius Werke*, II, p. 952; Eng. trans. W. H. Freemantle, *Life and works of Rufinus with Jerome's apology against Rufinus*, A Select Library of Nicene and Post-Nicene Fathers of the Christian Church, second series, 3 (Oxford and New York, 1892), p. 565; and see also P. R. Amidon, *The church history of Rufinus of Aquileia, books 10 and 11* (New York and Oxford 1997).

[30] Eds. Schwartz and Mommsen, *Eusebius Werke*, II, p. 957; Eng. trans. Freemantle, *Life and Works*, p. 565.

Rufinus adds also many apparently first-hand details about Egypt, including a fascinating little aside about the flood gauge of the Nile. Rufinus gives a brief, somewhat matter-of-fact, account of the penance of Theodosius. His emphasis is consistently on the precariousness of Christianity, too easily jeopardised by contention among Christians and the impiety of emperors. Chromatius had wished this translation of Eusebius to distract the citizens of Aquileia from the activities of Alaric and his Goths in Italy. Rufinus comments that the purpose of the history was 'that the mind of those who heard it read to them might be held so fast by it that in their eager desire for the knowledge of past events they might to some extent become oblivious of their actual sufferings'. The citizens' 'distraction' took the form of an expansive view of a constantly beleaguered, if nevertheless triumphant, church.

Doubt was cast many years ago on the extent to which these two new books were Rufinus' own work, as distinct from more translating of unacknowledged sources. Certainly one of the prime candidates, Gelasius of Caesarea, produced a Greek continuation of Eusebius.[31] Françoise Thelamon, however, has vindicated Rufinus and shown that he was writing according to a clear plan of his own,[32] though he is less assiduous in naming his sources than Eusebius had been. The history of the church is presented here as a progressive account.

Adding two books and cutting most of Eusebius Book X was not, however, all that Rufinus did to Eusebius' text. Rufinus was the very opposite of a literal translator of Books I–X (=I–IX in Rufinus). In the words of John Oulton, Rufinus 'was not a satisfactory or faithful translator. He is continually taking unjustifiable liberties with his original. He omits, abbreviates, expands according to taste; and perhaps his favourite method is to produce a kind of paraphrase which gives the general sense'.[33]

The modern attitude to Rufinus has been somewhat condemnatory when it has been acknowledged at all, for it has focused on the faithfulness and accuracy of the translation rather than on the nature of the new text thereby created. Even Oulton conceded, however, that many passages of Rufinus' version, such as those on Rome, Jerusalem, Philippi, Egypt or the Life of Origen and the martyrdom of Paul and Peter, contained

---

[31] F. Winkelman, 'Das Problem der Rekonstruktion der *Historia ecclesiastica* des Gelasius von Caesarea', *Forschungen und Fortschritte* 38 (1964), pp. 311–14; and *Untersuchung zur Kirchengeschichte des Gelasios von Kaisareia, Sitzungsberichte der deutschen Akademie der Wissenschaften zu Berlin* (Berlin, 1966).

[32] F. Thelamon, *Païens et chrétiens au IVe siècle: l'apport de l'histoire ecclésiastique de Rufin d'Aquilée* (Paris, 1981).

[33] J. E. L. Oulton, 'Rufinus's translation of the church history of Eusebius', *Journal of Theological Studies* 30 (1929), pp. 150–74, at p. 150.

additional matter, new facts or corrected Eusebius. In those places where Rufinus can also be checked against a third source, he is shown to be reliable. Where he is the only authority for a statement, therefore, Oulton concluded that Rufinus was 'not lightly to be set aside'. Where Rufinus introduces material from other sources to augment Eusebius' account, such as on the passions of the martyrs, he supplies additional vivid details. It is in Rufinus, as noted above, that we find the earliest account of the Finding of the True Cross by Helena, Constantine's mother, as well as the independent note about the penance of the Emperor Theodosius.

Thorben Christensen took up this more positive assessment in his definitive and posthumously published study of Rufinus' translation of Eusebius' Books VIII and IX, especially as far as Rufinus' style in comparison with that of Eusebius was concerned.[34] He criticised Eusebius's untidy, repetitious, verbose, long-winded, contradictory and very varied account. Christensen regarded Eusebius' Books VIII and IX as a mess, both from a compositional and literary point of view; he considered Rufinus' version to be a distinct improvement. Further, Rufinus merits attention precisely because he offers an independent presentation of the development of the Christian church for Latin readers. Rufinus, in short, should be regarded as an interpreter and editor of Eusebius.

Many of Rufinus' changes analysed by Christensen were in the interests of providing a clear Latin translation. Others were corrections and amplifications from his own knowledge (such as on Origen). All were to spell out the religious and moral teachings of the Christian *historia rerum gestarum*.[35]

If we focus for the moment on changes, these are most striking in Rufinus' theological adjustments to make any theologically dubious portions of Eusebius more orthodox. Oulton suggested that this is what motivated Rufinus to omit the Panegyric on the rebuilding of the church at Tyre in the original Book X. Oulton proposed that the panegyric could be read as indicating that Eusebius was inclined towards Arianism. Further, when Eusebius discussed the canon of Scripture, Rufinus slightly adjusted the definition of what is accepted in the New Testament, apparently in order to take account of the situation in his own day.[36] Thus he modified Eusebius' rejection of James and expanded the degree to which

---

[34] T. Christensen, *Rufinus of Aquileia and the Historia Ecclesiastica Lib. VIII–IX, of Eusebius*, Historisk-filosofiske Meddelelser 58 (Copenhagen, 1989). See also the summary of Christensen's conclusions, 'Rufinus of Aquileia and the *Historia Ecclesiastica*, lib. VIII–IX, of Eusebius', *Studia Theologica* 34 (1980), pp. 129–52.

[35] Christensen, *Rufinus of Aquileia*, p. 334.

[36] Eds. Schwartz and Mommsen, *Eusebius Werke*, II, pp. 174–3; see Oulton, 'Rufinus's translation', pp. 156–9.

other texts, such as Jude or 2 Peter, are accepted. He rescued Revelation from the contradictory comments Eusebius had made about it as both accepted and spurious, and classed it simply as disputed.[37] Of the Epistle to the Hebrews Eusebius wrote 'some authorities have rejected the Epistle to the Hebrews pointing out that the Roman church denies it is the work of Paul'. Rufinus is more emphatic: 'Hebrews even now among the Latins is not thought to be the Apostle Paul's'.[38]

What Oulton, Thelamon and Christensen have all emphasised, therefore, is that Rufinus' extended eleven books, together with his treatment of the original, mean that the Latin version of Eusebius known and exerting an influence in the west was very different from the Greek Eusebius. Quite apart from its extension of the story to include much of the fourth century, it was doctrinally more orthodox, its definition of the New Testament canon is more precise and the emperors, especially in Books X and XI, play a more prominent role.

In another fundamental respect, however, Rufinus faithfully transmits the emphasis of his original.[39] This is particularly the case in his translation of the early Books I–VII. In Books VIII and IX, as I have already mentioned, Eusebius had stressed his own contemporary knowledge and memory as well as his recourse to records. Rufinus preserves this and follows suit in Books X and XI. What both Eusebius and Rufinus highlight in Books I–VII, however, is the accretion of Christian writings and authoritative texts, and the definition of the Scriptural canon.

Let me illustrate my point with some examples, coupled with the further observation that Rufinus appears to transmit Eusebius without any major paraphrasing or omissions in these sections, apart from the adjustments already mentioned.

The Scriptural canon of both the Old and New Testaments is defined with deference to Irenaeus.[40] There is discussion of the twenty-two books of the Hebrew Old Testament canon. In Book III, as I have already mentioned, the discussion of the Apostolic letters and whether they can be accepted or are still disputed is retained, albeit modified. Rufinus also provides, incidentally, a far fuller and clearer account of the *Hexapla* of Origen; he had obviously seen a manuscript of it for he describes its layout in detail.[41] When sources are quoted, an account is given of

[37] Eds. Schwartz and Mommsen, *Eusebius Werke*, II pp. 250–1.
[38] *Ibid.*, pp. 190–1; and see Oulton, 'Rufinus's translation', p. 157.
[39] The attitude towards the Jews of both Eusebius and Rufinus, moreover, would merit further study. Compare Bede's commentary on the Canticle of Habakkuk and the observations on the salvation history of Jew and Gentile in S. Connolly, *Bede on Tobit and on the Canticle of Habakkuk* (Dublin, 1997), pp. 18–37.
[40] Eds. Schwartz and Mommsen, *Eusebius Werke*, II, pp. 443–4.   [41] *Ibid.*, p. 555.

that particular author and his works. Protagonists are characterized in terms of their contribution to the patristic corpus. There are lengthy lists provided in Books I–VII of many authors and their works, such as Philo in Book II, Clement of Rome, Josephus, Ignatius, Papias, Polycarp, Irenaeus and his contemporaries, Justin Martyr, Ambrose, Hegesippus, Dionysus of Corinth, Philip, Apollinaris, Melito, Musanus, Modestus, Tatian, Tertullian, Origen and many more. For his part Rufinus adds, in Books X and XI, accounts of the writings of Basil the Great and Gregory Nazianzus.

Authors, therefore, are cited as support for the information offered. More crucially these sections set up yet another writer and thinker as a pillar of the church. In all cases, moreover, there is precise attention to time and place, so that, as in Jerome-Gennadius, a Christian intellectual geography is created alongside an emphasis on sacred places and delineation of the Holy Land.[42] Eusebius' aim was faithfully preserved and extended by Rufinus. Like Eusebius, who said he would discuss the men of each generation who by preaching or writing were 'ambassadors of the divine word', Rufinus' aim was to write about those men *seu scribendo seu docendo verbum dei nobiliter adstruxere*.[43]

This extraordinary attention to authors has been feebly characterised in the past as 'Eusebius' synthesis of intellectual currents existing in the church',[44] as Eusebius giving us a 'handy definition of the Old and New Testament canons'[45] or Eusebius' intention 'to create a church history that was a literary history at the same time'.[46] Certainly Eusebius and Rufinus do all these things, but such comments reflect a failure to read Eusebius-Rufinus' history in its contemporary, let alone its early medieval, context and thereby seriously underestimate this crucial aspect of the work. To concentrate only on the information Eusebius and Rufinus provide for modern historians making inventories of early Christian texts is to miss the point. What the ecclesiastical history of Eusebius-Rufinus does is to offer a very particular presentation of the past and of the history of the church. The history of Christianity is presented as the history of written authority, of the formation of the scriptural canon and of its essential continuation by the fathers of the church in their writings. The sequence of Christian writers, teachers and preachers and the Scriptural

---

[42] R. Wilken, 'Eusebius and the Christian holy land', in H. W. Attridge and G. Hata (eds.), *Eusebius, Christianity and Judaism* (Detroit and Leiden, 1992), pp. 736–60. See also R. L. Wilken, *The land called holy: Palestine in Christian history and thought* (New Haven and London, 1992).

[43] Eds. Schwartz and Mommsen, *Eusebius Werke*, II, p. 7.

[44] M. E. Hardwick, *Josephus as an historical source in patristic literature* (Atlanta, 1989), especially p. 114.

[45] R. M. Grant, *Eusebius as church historian* (Oxford, 1980) pp. 126–41.   [46] *Ibid.*, p. 66.

canon, as Robert Markus observed thirty years ago, are 'part of the church's self-identity'.[47] The whole method of exposition within their narrative framework is designed to reinforce the perception that individuals and texts form the past and that it is only with reference to these texts that the church can be understood. It is in this respect that Eusebius and Rufinus alike are truly revolutionary. It is this aspect of Eusebius-Rufinus' work that is of far more importance for the Christians of the early middle ages even than the work's philosophy of history as continuous progress.

The *Historia tripartita*

Eusebius-Rufinus, furthermore, is substantially reinforced, not only by Jerome-Gennadius, but also by another immensely popular and influential ecclesiastical history of the early church, namely the Latin *Historia tripartita* of Epiphanius translated from three Greek ecclesiastical histories by Socrates, Sozomen and Theodoret[48] (and also making use of a Greek compilation of the same three texts that had been made by 'Theodorus Lector').[49] Despite the text's importance and interest, modern study of it has been almost solely confined to analyses of the translation methods, and particularly the errors, of Epiphanius in rendering the original Greek into Latin from the syntactical and lexical point of view.[50] The work of Epiphanius was initiated and encouraged by Cassiodorus and described by Cassiodorus himself in his *Institutiones* as part of a more general enterprise at sixth-century Vivarium in central Italy to translate essential texts from Greek into Latin.[51] Theodoret, Socrates and Sozomen had each certainly regarded himself as a continuator of Eusebius. In some respects the *Historia tripartita* covers the same ground as the additional Books X and XI of Rufinus, though for the most part it provides complementary

---

[47] Markus, 'Church history and the early church historians', p. 5.
[48] Jacob and Hanslik (eds.), *Cassiodori-Epiphanii*.
[49] J. Bidez, *La Tradition manuscrite de Sozomène et la Tripartite de Théodore le lecteur*, Texte und Untersuchungen zur Geschichte der altchristlichen Literatur 32 (Leipzig, 1908); and see also Theodoret, *Kirchengeschichte*, ed. L. Parmentier, revised by F. Scheidweiler, Die griechischen christlichen Schriftsteller 44 (Berlin, 1954); and J. Bidez, B. Grillet, G. Sabbah and A.-J. Festugière, *Sozomène Histoire ecclésiastique*, Sources Chrétiennes 306 (Paris, 1983).
[50] F. Weisengruber, *Epiphanius Scholasticus als Übersetzer zu Cassiodorus-Epiphanius Historia ecclesiastica tripartita*, Österreichische Akademie der Wissenschaften, phil.-hist. Klasse Sitzungsberichte 283, Veröffentlichungen der Kommission zur Herausgabe des Corpus der lateinischen Kirchenväter, ed. R. Hanslik, Heft 5 (Vienna, 1972); and S. Lundström, *Übersetzungstechnische Untersuchungen auf dem Gebiete der christlichen Latinität* (Lund, 1955).
[51] Cassiodorus, *Institutiones*, ed. R. A. B. Mynors, *Cassiodorus senatoris institutiones* (Oxford, 1937), I, c. 17, 1, p. 56.

material for the overlapping years of the fourth century and of course new material up to the middle of the fifth century. Certainly the *Historia tripartita* provides a dramatic presentation of the Arian conflict, much of which is particularly indebted to Theodoret's impassioned account of Constantine and Constantine's successors' conflicts with the Arians. It is in the *Historia tripartita*, moreover, that we find the account of the burning of the works of Arius recorded by Socrates,[52] of the distribution of copies of Scripture by Constantine,[53] of the concern of the Roman emperor for the Christians of Persia,[54] of the discussions and attendance at the Council of Sardica,[55] and of the dispute between the Emperor Constantius and Liberius, bishop of Rome about the condemnation of Athanasius which is presented in dialogue form with interjections by Eusebius the eunuch.[56] The dispute ended with Liberius going into exile after having refused all offers of money to pay his travelling expenses from the emperor, the empress and the eunuch Eusebius. In the *Historia tripartita* is also to be found the account of how Julian emulated Christian practices in promoting his new paganism,[57] a description of Gothic movements in Thrace,[58] the sack of Rome by Alaric[59] and the stoning to death of Hypatia.[60]

The vividness of the narrative, however, does not detract from the maintenance of the emphasis of Eusebius-Rufinus, namely, on the writers who were the pillars of the church, on the definition of authority and on the great controversies and discussion about the faith and the Trinity. That these concerns became a particular focus of writers and thinkers in the fifth century is also reflected in Gennadius' greater preoccupation with the documenting of contributors to Christological debates. Arianism remained a major issue.[61]

Jerome-Gennadius, Eusebius-Rufinus and the *Historia tripartita*, therefore, together comprise a distinctive presentation of the history of the Christian church. Symbolic resonance and historical detail go hand in hand. The close association and essential continuation of scripture within the chronological framework of the history of the church presented the development of the church as a textual history. The histories of the church written from the fourth century onwards provided both framework and context for a past and an identity built on texts.

---

[52] *Cassiodori-Epiphanii*, ed. Jacob and Hanslik, II, 15, pp. 108–9.
[53] *Ibid.*, I, 16, pp. 109–10.   [54] *Ibid.*, III, 3, pp. 138–9.
[55] *Ibid.*, IV, 24, pp. 179–91; compare V, 45, pp. 294–5.   [56] *Ibid.*, V, 17, pp. 237–41.
[57] *Ibid.*, VI, 29, pp. 345–8.   [58] *Ibid.*, VIII, 13, pp. 485–91.
[59] *Ibid.*, XI, 9, pp. 638–9.   [60] *Ibid.*, XI, 12, pp. 643–3.
[61] *Ibid.*, VIII, 13, pp. 488–9 gives the hostile version of the account of the conversion of the Goths by Ulfilas.

The Carolingians and the histories
of the Christian church

That the Carolingian church understood the significance of these histories and the texts and authors so closely interwoven into their narratives is amply indicated by the evidence of the library catalogues and the production and the dissemination of manuscripts in the Frankish realms in the later eighth and the ninth centuries. This is more than a matter of the reception of particular texts and the evidence that they were read, though these are also of great importance. A striking instance of the way both Eusebius-Rufinus and the *Historia tripartita* could be drawn on by readers, scribes and artists is the context they provided for the understanding of the development of canon law. In the Vercelli canon law collection of the second quarter of the ninth century (Vercelli, Biblioteca capitolare cod. CLXV),[62] for example, an artist in northern Italy provided a vivid portrayal on fol. 2v of the burning of the Arian books under Constantine. This, as I noted earlier, was also recorded by the Greek church historian Socrates in his ecclesiastical history and was excerpted and translated in the Latin *Historia tripartita* of Cassiodorus-Epiphanius. Another page of the same canon law collection, fol. 2r, illustrates the finding of the True Cross.[63] The only older representation of the scene known to Bierbrauer is in the Sacramentary of Gellone (Paris, BnF lat. 12048, fol. 76v), written in the diocese of Meaux at the end of the eighth century, while there is a full picture cycle of the legend in Munich, Bayerische Staatsbibliothek Clm 22053, produced *c.* 814.[64] All these would suggest that it is the Carolingian artists responding to a written story of the discovery of the cross who created these pictures, though there are significant differences between Rufinus' version and that illustrated in these pictures.[65]

There is more at stake, however, than documenting whether or not the Franks in the Carolingian period knew Jerome-Gennadius,

---

[62] See the discussion by K. Bierbrauer, 'Konzilsdarstellungen der Karolingerzeit' in R. Berndt (ed.) *Das Frankfurter Konzil von 794*, II, pp. 751–765 at pp. 759–65, who cites J. Straubinger, *Die Kreuzauffindungslegende* (Paderborn, 1912), pp. 66–76 as her source for the information that the story derives solely from a fifth-century Syriac source. I have been unable to consult Straubinger's work. See also C. Walter, 'Les dessins carolingiens dans un manuscrit de Verceil', *Cahiers Archéologiques* 18 (1968), pp. 99–107.

[63] Both illustrations are reproduced in J. Hubert, J. Porcher and W. Vollbach, *Europe in the Dark Ages* (London, 1969), pp. 142–3.

[64] This is the famous *Wessobrunner Gebet* manuscript: see K. Bierbrauer, *Die vorkarolingischen und karolingischen Handschriften der Bayerischen Staatsbibliothek. Katalog der illuminierten Handschriften der Bayerischen Staatsbibliothek* (Wiesbaden, 1990), I, no. 155, pp. 83–4, and II, plates 319–36.

[65] For a fuller discussion of these manuscripts and their implications see below, chapter 11.

Eusebius-Rufinus and the *Historia tripartita*. In order to demonstrate this, I turn now to the evidence of library catalogues and manuscript dissemination and its implications for our understanding of the Carolingian church and the book.

Most of the extant library catalogues and book lists from the Carolingian period, as I have observed above, record the presence in their libraries of Jerome-Gennadius, Eusebius-Rufinus or Epiphanius-Cassiodorus. In the principal ninth-century catalogue of the library of the Rhineland monastery of Lorsch, BAV pal. lat. 1877, fol. 3r-v, for example, there is a small group of books listed after the notes of various volumes of Maccabees, Acts, the seven canonical epistles, and letters of St Paul.[66] The list includes the *Historia ecclesiastica* of Eusebius, eleven books of the *Historia* of Josephus, that is, the *Antiquities*, a Greek text also translated into Latin in the enterprise at Vivarium initiated by Cassiodorus,[67] the history by 'Isyppi' in five books, which is presumably a reference to the Latin version of Josephus' Jewish War made by Hegesippus and notable for its account of the Fall of Jerusalem, the *Historia* of Orosius, namely Orosius' Seven books of history against the pagans written c. 417, and the Chronicle of Eusebius-Jerome and Bede. The Chronicle of Eusebius in Jerome's Latin translation ran from Abraham to 325 and was continued by Jerome and adapted by others subsequently, not least Bede, who drew on it for the world chronicle in chapter 66 of his *De temporum ratione*.[68] This Chronicle of Eusebius-Jerome was the major source for the chronology of the early church and particularly important for the events of the third and fourth centuries.

The Lorsch list continues on the top of the next page with the *Tripartita historia* in twelve books by Socrates, Sozomen and Theodoret in one volume, the *Liber pontificalis*, the pseudo-Clementine *Recognitiones*, Gregory

---

[66] See above, chapter 9 where the full list is reproduced, pp. 197–9, and B. Bischoff, *Die Abtei Lorsch im Spiegel ihrer Handschriften*, 2nd edn (Lorsch, 1989), Tafel 2 and pp. 21–5; and A. Häse, *Mittelalterliche Bücherverzeichnisse aus Kloster Lorsch. Einleitung, Edition und Kommentar*, Beiträge zum Buch- und Bibliothekswesen 42 (Wiesbaden, 2002), p. 137.

[67] *Institutiones*, ed. Mynors, *Cassiodorus*, I, c. 17, 1, p. 55. Eusebius also made copious use of Josephus, but the topic of the reading of Josephus in the early middle ages must await another occasion: see, for example, Hardwick, *Josephus*, and H. Schreckenberg and K. Schubert (eds.), *Jewish Historiography and iconography in early and medieval Christianity* (Assen and Minneapolis, 1992).

[68] See C. W. Jones (ed.), *Bedae opera didascalica 2*, CCSL, CXXIIIB (Turnhout, 1977), with chapter 66 supplied from T. Mommsen, *Chronica minora, 3, MGH AA*, XIII (Hannover, 1898), pp. 247–327, and the excellent translation and commentary provided by F. Wallis, *Bede: The reckoning of time* (Liverpool, 1999), pp. 157–237 and 353–66.

of Tours' *Histories*, Jordanes' *Historia romana*, Dares Phrygius on the history of Troy, Aethicus Ister's *Cosmographia*, an epitome of Livy, Quintus Julius Hilarion on the origins of the world up to the resurrection of Christ, Hydatius' chronicle from Theodosius to the reign of Justinian, Solinus, and Josephus' *Antiquitates*, Books 12–19. Lorsch also owned Jerome-Gennadius, *De viris illustribus*.[69]

The juxtaposition of the history books immediately after portions of the New Testament in the Lorsch catalogue is suggestive. In other catalogues the history books are sometimes listed together in groups, most commonly after the section on Jerome, or more rarely listed separately under different authors. They are certainly, therefore, seen for the most part as a genre of texts which belong together regardless of author. The Lorsch catalogue, however, makes explicit the essential continuation of scripture and New Testament authors into the writings of the early fathers of the church as documented in the early histories of the church, especially Eusebius-Rufinus and the *Historia tripartita*.

No other Carolingian library can quite match Lorsch's recorded wealth in history books, but Eusebius and the *Historia tripartita* and often Jerome-Gennadius as well were also, to cite only a few instances, at St Germer-de-Fly[70], Würzburg (where Eusebius is attributed to Jerome and which also owned Jerome-Gennadius),[71] Bobbio,[72] St Riquier,[73] Murbach, which also owned Jerome-Gennadius and many of the other history books recorded at Lorsch listed together under the heading *De historiis*,[74] St Gallen, which attributed the Latin *Historia tripartita* to Cassiodorus and also owned Jerome-Gennadius,[75] and Reichenau which also

---

[69] Häse, *Mittelalterliche Bücherverzeichnisse*, p. 162.

[70] *Gesta fontanellensis coenobii*, 13.6, ed. P. Pradié, *Chronique des Abbés de Fontenelle (Saint-Wandrille)* (Paris, 1999), p. 172. I wrongly located *Flaviacum* (St Germer) at Flavigny in McKitterick, *Carolingians and the written word*, p. 175.

[71] E. A. Lowe, 'An eighth-century list of books in a Bodleian manuscript from Würzburg and its probable relation to the Laudian Acts', *Speculum* 3 (1928), pp. 3–15, reprinted in L. Bieler (ed.), *E. A. Lowe, Palaeographical Papers 1907–1965* (Oxford, 1972), I, pp. 239–50, and Plates 27–30. See B. Bischoff and J. Hofmann, *Libri sancti Kyliani. Die Würzburger Schreibschule und die Dombibliothek im VIII. und IX. Jahrhundert* (Würzburg, 1952), pp. 143 and 146.

[72] Ed. G. Becker, *Catalogi bibliothecarum antiqui* (Bonn, 1886), p. 65; but see the discussion by P. Collura, *La precarolina e la carolina a Bobbio*, Fontes Ambrosiani 22 (Milan, 1943).

[73] Hariulf, *Chronicon Centulense*, ed. F. Lot, *Hariulf, Chronique de l'abbaye de Saint-Riquier Ve siècle–1104* (Paris, 1894), pp. 89 and 93.

[74] W. Milde, *Der Bibliothekskataloge des Klosters Murbach aus dem 9. Jht. Ausgabe und Untersuchung von Beziehung zu Cassiodors Institutiones. Beihefte zum Euphorion. Zeitschrift für Literaturgeschichte* 34 (1968), pp. 37, 43, 44, and the section '*De historiis*', p. 47.

[75] P. Lehmann, *Mittelalterliche Biblothekskataloge Deutschlands und der Schweiz. 1 Die Bistümer Konstanz und Chur* (Munich, 1918), pp. 73, 76.

had Jerome-Gennadius.[76] The *Historia tripartita* is listed in Wulfad of Bourges' personal collection of books.[77] The manuscript evidence allows us to extend the range of centres with these texts still further. Of the 114 surviving manuscripts of Jerome-Gennadius collated by Richardson, nineteen date from the ninth and tenth centuries or earlier and are distributed among a sufficient number of different types defined according to variants to indicate a wide dissemination.[78] As already noted, the two oldest manuscripts of Jerome-Gennadius, for example, are from the seventh century and are the top scripts of palimpsests. BAV reg. lat. 2077 is Italian, possibly from Rome (the underneath script is Cicero's *In Verrem*) and Paris, BnF lat. 12161 is from Corbie (the underneath texts include the Visigothic ruler Euric's law code).[79] There are three later eighth-century manuscripts from northern Italy and Francia and in the ninth century the text was often incorporated by Frankish scholars into what I have classified as bibliographical handbooks[80] and used as a guide for acquisitions for libraries; Frankish copies come from such centres as Weissenburg, Rheims and St Gallen. I have commented elsewhere on the historical ordering of the *De viris illustribus* and how it provided a definition of a canon of knowledge which was of fundamental importance for the construction of libraries and the production of books in the Carolingian period,[81] quite apart from its distinctive perception of history which I have stressed in this chapter. The production of Jerome-Gennadius and the clear evidence of its guidance being followed are indicative of the influence it had.

The earliest manuscripts containing the additional sections by Isidore of Seville survive from both Francia and the Christian kingdoms of northern Spain. Merino postulates an Irish episode in the transmission of Isidore's section, on the basis of a handful of 'Irish' symptoms (the doubled consonants in orthography and scribal confusion of 'r' and 'n') in the earliest surviving manuscript of Isidore's text, Montpellier, Ecole de Médecine H406. This is a manuscript of the early ninth century

---

[76] *Ibid.*, pp. 246 and 265. For a fuller list of early medieval library catalogues containing these works see A. Siegmund, *Die Überlieferung der griechischen christlichen Literatur*, Abhandlungen der Bayerischen Benediktiner Akademie 5 (Munich, 1949), pp. 56–7, 73–6.

[77] M. Cappuyns, 'Les *bibli Wulfadi* et Jean Scot Erigène', *Recherches de Théologie Ancienne et Médiévale* 33 (1966), pp. 137–9.

[78] Ed. Richardson, *De viris inlustribus*, pp. IX–XXXV.

[79] *CLA*, I (Oxford, 1935), nos. 114, and 5 (Oxford, 1950), no. 624.

[80] McKitterick, *Carolingians and the written word*, pp. 206–9.

[81] *Ibid.*, esp. pp. 165–209, esp. pp. 200–5.

but is possibly based on a late eighth-century exemplar.[82] In Hereford Cathedral Library O.3.2, a codex from the third quarter of the ninth century from France, Isidore is included with Jerome-Gennadius as part of a bibliographical handbook. Other Frankish copies, such as Bern, Burgerbibliothek 289, which is now part of a composite manuscript that may have originated in a different context,[83] the late ninth- or early tenth-century fragments from Werden in Wetzlar, Staatsarchiv 46,[84] Paris, BnF lat. 1791, a composite manuscript of which the Isidore text comprises the tenth-century Frankish portion, or the now-lost copy from St Gallen mentioned in the ninth-century St Gallen library catalogue, may have been free-standing. What the complex *stemma codicum* suggested by Merino establishes is a very wide distribution of Jerome-Gennadius-Isidore in Francia and northern Spain in the ninth and tenth centuries.[85]

The manuscript survival of Eusebius-Rufinus and the *Historia tripartita* is similarly significant. Among approximately forty-three extant manuscripts from before the eleventh century of the former is a copy from Chelles.[86] Chelles was the convent presided over by Charlemagne's sister Gisela and this book is one of a group that Bischoff associated with texts copied for the archbishop of Cologne by the nuns of Chelles.[87] Other copies come from Alemannia (later Freising), north-east France, the Loire region, Constance, northern Italy, Franconia, Rhaetia and St Amand as well as Lorsch itself.[88] The Lorsch manuscript (BAV pal. lat. 822), no doubt to be identified with the volume listed in the Lorsch catalogue, is to be dated to the late eighth or early ninth century, and is written in an early caroline minuscule.[89] Many of these books have markedly elaborate layouts of capitals, uncials, headings, chapter titles, incipits and the like. The opening of the Copenhagen Eusebius written at St Amand in

---

[82] The colophon added at the end of the Isidore section suggests this exemplar was written between 768 and 771, as it refers to the joint rule of Charles and Carloman after the death of Pippin: Merino, El *'De viris illustribus' de Isidoro de Sevilla*, p. 126; and see McKitterick, *Carolingians and the written word*, pp. 201–3.

[83] Bischoff, *Katalog*, no. 570, p. 121.

[84] W. Smidt, 'Ein altes Handschriftenfragment der "Viri illustres" Isidors von Sevilla', *Neues Archiv* 44 (1922), pp. 125–35.

[85] Merino, El *'De viris illustribus' de Isidoro de Sevilla*, pp. 87–128.

[86] Paris, BnF lat. 18282, *CLA*, V (Oxford, 1950), no. 674; but compare Paris, BnF lat. 10399, fol. 4,5 + 10400, fol. 27, *ibid.*, no. 594, a different redaction of Eusebius-Rufinus, and R. McKitterick, 'Nuns' scriptoria in England and Francia in the eighth century', *Francia* 19/1 (1992), pp. 1–35, at pp. 6–11, reprinted in R. McKitterick, *Books, scribes and learning*, chapter 7.

[87] See B. Bischoff, 'Die Kölner Nonnenhandschriften und das Skriptorium von Chelles', in Bischoff, *Mittelalterliche Studien*, I (Stuttgart, 1966), pp. 16–34.

[88] Siegmund, *Überlieferung*, pp. 78–80 greatly augments the list of four manuscripts provided by Schwartz and Mommsen in their edition.

[89] B. Bischoff, *Die Abtei Lorsch im Spiegel ihrer Handschriften*, p. 23 and Plate VI.

the first quarter of the ninth century is a case in point.[90] It should be noted, moreover, that no early medieval history books of any kind are illustrated, apart from the Bible itself and the historical illustrations added to the Vercelli canon law manuscript mentioned above. The manuscripts of the *Historia tripartita* are striking in their layout, but also lack illustrations. The earliest witness to the *Historia tripartita* is St Petersburg, Saltykov-Schedrin State Library MS F.v.I, no. 11.[91] It is written in the curious script known as 'a-b' once located to Corbie, still associated with Corbie, but usually now attributed to a group of nuns, perhaps at Soissons.[92] This particular copy is said, by an eleventh-century annotator, to have been made for Adalhard of Corbie, Charlemagne's cousin. Some years ago, however, I suggested that the 'a-b' script should be seen as a continuation of the 'b-minuscule' type developed in the eighth century at Jouarre and Chelles, the Carolingian royal convent par excellence.[93] Other ninth-century copies of the *Historia tripartita* are from Orléans, Constance, Regensburg and Tours. There are distinct families of the *Historia tripartita* text associated with northern France, northern Italy and southern Germany and, in a later distribution pattern, southern France, Catalonia and western Germany.[94] This is a sure indication of an early and exceptionally wide dissemination of this text.

There are two points that need to be stressed about the distribution and survival patterns of both Eusebius-Rufinus and the *Historia tripartita*. The first is that the earliest witnesses to these texts, apart from some sixth-century fragments in half-uncial script of a copy of Eusebius-Rufinus,[95] are from the late eighth and early ninth centuries. Secondly, again with the

---

[90] Copenhagen, Kongelige Bibliotek MS Gl. Kgl. S.163, illustrated in K. van der Horst, W. Noel and W. C. M. Wüstefeld (eds.), *The Utrecht Psalter in medieval art* (Utrecht, 1996), p. 11. *Pace* Bischoff, *Katalog*, no. 1981, p. 411, I consider this manuscript to have been written at St Amand rather than Saint-Germain-des-Prés but possibly used at the latter.

[91] O. A. Dobias-Rozdestvenskaja and W. W. Bakhtine, *Les Anciens manuscrits latins de la Bibliothèque publique Saltykov-Ščedrin de Leningrad, VIIIe–début IX siècle* (Paris, 1991), no. 39, pp. 98–101, and Plate VII.

[92] See D. Ganz, *Corbie in the Carolingian Renaissance*, Beihefte der Francia 20 (Sigmaringen, 1990), pp. 48–56.

[93] McKitterick, 'Nuns' scriptoria', pp. 18–20.

[94] See W. Jacob, *Die handschriftliche Überlieferung der sogenannten Historia tripartita des Epiphanius Cassiodor*, Texte und Untersuchungen 59 (Berlin, 1954). Jacob was reported as missing, presumed dead, on 1 February 1942, though the proofs of his edition had been ready in 1939. His work was therefore apparently done in ignorance of Siegmund, *Überlieferung*, also completed in 1939, under the supervision of Paul Lehmann. Siegmund was able to offer more precise indications of the date and origin of some of the manuscripts; on Cassiodorus, for example, see pp. 56–8.

[95] *CLA*, III (Oxford, 1938), no. **38. These fragments, Turin, Biblioteca Nazionale F.IV.29 (binding) + BAV lat. 5760, fols. i–ii + Milan, Biblioteca Ambrosiana C.91 inf., fols. 128, 129, were used at Bobbio for binding purposes in the fifteenth century; see also Siegmund, *Überlieferung*, p. 79.

probable exception of the sixth-century fragments of Eusebius-Rufinus, they are Frankish and more particularly from centres that can be closely associated with the royal court. Given that Lorsch, Corbie and Chelles had close links with the court, and that some of the books of Chelles can be linked with the production of books for the archbishops of Cologne,[96] it is possible that this astonishing concentration of early church history manuscripts and their remarkably wide dissemination could reflect the deliberate provision of this book at an early stage in the Carolingian reform movement. They are part, moreover, as we have seen, of a wider provision of history books more generally within the Carolingian realm. Thus the St Amand copy, for example, now in Copenhagen, was, like the history books at Lorsch, part of a comprehensive collection of history books produced and read at St Amand and still in the library in the twelfth century.[97]

Such a deliberate dissemination of particular history books would be entirely in keeping with what we know about one of the main thrusts of the reforms initiated by Charlemagne. Carolingian royal patronage was inextricably bound up with the themes of *correctio* and *emendatio*, which are a fundamental part of the cultural and religious achievement scholars have described as the Carolingian Renaissance.[98] Corrected texts, or texts copied from exemplars regarded as authoritative, were prepared under the auspices of Charlemagne and Louis the Pious, of Sacramentaries and canon law, the homiliary, the Gospels, the Bible and the Rule of Benedict as well as the secular laws of the peoples under Frankish rule. The commissioning of a correct text of the Bible has a parallel with Constantine's commissioning and circulation of codices of the Greek New Testament recorded by Theodoret in his ecclesiastical history and translated by Epiphanius in his *Historia tripartita* (II, 16). When Charlemagne was hailed as a new Constantine by Pope Hadrian, therefore,[99] it may be as much for this specific promotion of the Bible as for his more general championing of the Christian church. A new edition of the Gospels was prepared under the auspices of a Frankish ruler, initiated either by Pippin III or Charlemagne.[100] Charlemagne, Louis the Pious, Lothar, and possibly Charles the Bald as well, extended and developed what may

[96] Bischoff, 'Die Kölner Nonnenhandschriften'.   [97] See above, chapter 9.

[98] I discussed some aspects of this in 'Unity and diversity in the Carolingian church', in R. N. Swanson (ed.), *Unity and Diversity in the church*, Studies in Church History 32 (Woodbridge, 1996), pp. 59–82.

[99] *Codex Carolinus*, ed. W. Gundlach, *MGH Epp.*, III (Berlin, 1892), no. 60, p. 587, lines 16–18 (the letter is usually dated 778) and see M. Garrison, 'The Franks as the New Israel?', in Y. Hen and M. Innes (eds.), *The uses of the past in the early middle ages* (Cambridge, 2000), pp. 114–61.

[100] B. Fischer, 'Bibeltext und Bibelreform unter Karl dem Grossen', in W. Braunfels (ed.), *Karl der Grosse. Lebenswerk und Nachleben. II: Das Geistige Leben*, ed. B. Bischoff (Düsseldorf, 1965), pp. 156–216; and W. Koehler, *Karolingische Miniaturen*,

have begun as the provision of a clear text for use in the palace chapel into the provision of a Carolingian Bible text for the entire Frankish kingdom. The Christian ruler ensured that the word of God in a proper and corrected form was disseminated to all his leading monasteries and cathedrals. Charlemagne is particularly associated with the massive Frankish enterprise for the correction of the Vulgate Bible text, of which the editions produced at Tours and Orléans were the most famous and the most widely disseminated.[101] Such dedications as the Vivian Bible to Charles the Bald reflect a continuing and Constantinian association of the ruler with the dissemination of Scripture.[102]

The Carolingians wished to exert power over texts and to control both their use and their meaning. They were able to exert power through texts by using the written word to organise, control and challenge the world. For them the written word was sacred; it represented cumulative wisdom encoded. Thus for the Franks in the early middle ages the written word and the book were not only symbols of power and authority but also the practical means of exercising power and authority in the Carolingian world.

Although perhaps originally conceived in terms of the relation to the word of God and the secular legislation of rulers, moreover, the degree to which written transmission lent special authority to the status of the ideas they contained can be observed in every category of written text extant from the Carolingian period. Author portraits of evangelists and of Gregory, such as the portrayal of Gregory's inspiration by the Holy Spirit in the form of a dove in the Sacramentary fragment from Charles the Bald's palace school,[103] emphasise the divine source of inspiration for writers.

The act of writing in itself created authoritative knowledge. The methods of working of Carolingian authors show them to have worked through the medium of authority. The more their wisdom rested on the wisdom of others, the greater its power. Hraban Maur's compilatory method of exegesis, for example, created a bulwark of authority against ignorance

---

II, *Die Hofschule Karls des Grossen* (Berlin, 1958), and III, *Die Gruppe des Wiener Krönungsevangeliar. Metzer Handschriften* (Berlin, 1960).

[101] Fischer, 'Bibeltext'; Koehler, *Karolingische Miniaturen*, I: *Die Schule von Tours* (Berlin, 1935); E. Dahlhaus-Berg, *Nova antiquitas et antiqua novitas. Typologische Exegese und isidorianisches Geschichtsbild bei Theodulf von Orléans* (Cologne, 1975), esp. pp. 39–76; and R. Gameson (ed.), *The early medieval Bible: its production, decoration and use* (Cambridge, 1994).

[102] Paris, BnF lat. 1: see P. E. Dutton and H. L. Kessler, *The poetry and paintings of the first Bible of Charles the Bald* (Ann Arbor, 1997).

[103] Paris, BnF lat. 1141, fol. 3r, illustrated in F. Mütherich and J. Ghaede, *Carolingian painting* (London, 1976), p. 32.

and doubt.[104] Representation of books in Carolingian book illuminations, moreover, stress the power of the written word and by implication those who controlled and produced books.[105] The scene from the life of Jerome in the Vivian Bible, Paris BnF lat. 1, produced at Tours, and the Bible of San Paulo fuori le mura, produced at Rheims, for example, present such incidents as his departure from Rome, his intellectual activities in Palestine and the dissemination of the completed Vulgate translation of the Bible.[106] Jerome's work formed an apt parallel, as Kessler has suggested, for the enterprise at Tours in the ninth century for the production of a revised and corrected Vulgate text.[107]

Charlemagne in Alcuin's *De rhetorica* had asked 'How can our speech attain the authority which that of the ancients had?' Alcuin had responded: 'Their books ought to be read and their words well impressed upon our memory.'[108] In commenting on the importance of biblical *historia* in the Carolingian period, Mayke de Jong has elucidated how the Frankish present was enveloped in the authoritative past outlined by scripture.[109] For guidance in spoken and written expression as well as for understanding and knowledge, the Franks resorted to books. The Franks in the Carolingian period identified themselves in relation to particular texts and recognised them above all as symbols of the authority of the church and of God. I have documented elsewhere the definition of a canon of writings regarded as authoritative and of those that were perceived as a threat. The library catalogue evidence, extant manuscripts and citations in the writings of Frankish scholars together indicate the degree to which such major early medieval authors as Bede, Alcuin, Hraban

---

[104] See M. de Jong, 'Old law and new-found power: Hrabanus Maurus and the Old Testament', in J. M. Drijvers and A. A. MacDonald (eds.), *Centres of learning: learning and location in pre-modern Europe and the near East* (Leiden, 1995), pp. 161–76.

[105] A. Bowman and G. Woolf (eds.), *Literacy and power in the ancient world* (Cambridge, 1994); and R. McKitterick, 'Essai sur les représentations de l'écrit dans les manuscrits carolingiens', in F. Dupuigrenet Desroussilles (ed.), *La Symbolique du livre dans l'art occidental du haut moyen âge à Rembrandt*, Revue française d'histoire du livre 86–7 (Bordeaux, 1995), pp. 37–64.

[106] Paris, BnF lat. 1, fol. 3v, illustrated in Mütherich and Ghaede, *Carolingian painting*, p. 21 and San Paolo fuori le mura, fol. 3v, illustrated in H. L. Kessler, *The illustrated bibles from Tours*, Studies in Manuscript Illumination 7 (Princeton, 1977), Plate 131.

[107] H. L. Kessler, 'A lay abbot as patron: Count Vivian and the First Bible of Charles the Bald', in *Committenti e produzione artistico-letteraria nell'alto medioevo occidentale*, Settimane 39 (Spoleto, 1992), pp. 647–76.

[108] Alcuin, *Disputatio de rhetorica et de virtutibus sapientissimi regis Karli et Albini magistri. The Rhetoric of Alcuin and Charlemagne*, ed. with Eng. trans. W. S. Howell (Princeton, 1941), pp. 132–3.

[109] M. de Jong, 'The empire as *ecclesia*: Hrabanus Maurus and biblical *historia* for rulers', in Hen and Innes (eds.), *The uses of the past*, pp. 191–226.

Maur and many other Carolingian authors were incorporated alongside all those mentioned in Eusebius-Rufinus, Jerome-Gennadius and the *Historia tripartita* into the canon of required knowledge.[110] Notker's *Notatio de viris illustribus* and the later *Liber de scriptoribus ecclesiasticis* of Sigebert of Gembloux or Honorius Augustodunensis' *De luminaribus ecclesiae* not only catalogue the Frankish authors of the eighth and ninth centures along with the patristic authors as part of their intellectual foundations;[111] they also preserve the essential perception of Jerome-Gennadius and Eusebius-Rufinus of the history of the church being one that is built on texts.

I have explored in this chapter one further aspect of the process by which books and writing became both symbols of authority and knowledge in the Carolingian world and essential elements of Frankish identity and their sense of the past. Reading the histories of the church was then, and remains for us, not only a matter of gaining knowledge of the events and protagonists described, but also of being aware of how those histories are constructed, on what authorities they were based, how they were used and the definitions of textual and historical authority they contain. Thus what we observe is the consolidation of the Frankish textual community centered on the Bible in the context of the Franks' place in the entire textual history of the church.

---

[110] I discuss the role of Cassiodorus' *Institutiones* in this respect as well in McKitterick, *Carolingians and the written word*, pp. 200–5.

[111] Sigebert of Gembloux, *De viris illustribus*, ed. R. Witte, *Lateinische Sprache und Literatur des Mittelalters* I (1974) (and also in *PL*, CLX, cols. 547–88); Honorius Augustodunensis, *De luminaribus ecclesiae*, *PL*, CLXXII, cols. 197–234: see V. I. J. Flint, 'The place and purpose of the works of Honorius Augustodunensis', *RB* 87 (1977), 97–127.

11   Christianity as history

One of the most crucial aspects of the reception and dissemination of Christian writings in the Carolingian world was the perception of their original contexts. This perception of the original impetus for, and the time and place of, the composition of Christian theology, exegesis, moral guidance and ascetic instruction was itself shaped by a small group of seminal texts concerned with the history of the church and the Christian faith.

In the previous chapter I focused in detail on three of these texts in particular. The most influential of them was the *Historia ecclesiastica* of Eusebius in the Latin translation by Rufinus.[1] It is important to stress again that this Latin version is essentially an interpretation and edition of Eusebius and not a literal translation,[2] quite apart from the fact that Rufinus added two new books and cut most of Eusebius's Book X.[3] Eusebius had recounted the history of the Christian church to the reign of Constantine and Rufinus extended it to the death of the Emperor Theodosius. Secondly, Eusebius inspired and provided much of the information for Jerome when the latter compiled his *De viris illustribus* *c.* 392. The work, continued by Gennadius of Marseille, *c.* 480, contains short accounts of a total of 234 Christian authors, in chronological order,

---

[1] Eusebius-Rufinus, *Historia ecclesiastica*, eds. E. Schwartz and T. Mommsen, *Eusebius Werke*, II, *Die Kirchengeschichte*, ed. E. Schwartz, *Die lateinische Übersetzung des Rufinus*, ed. T. Mommsen, Die griechischen christlichen Schriftsteller der ersten drei Jahrhunderte: Eusebius 2,1 and 2,2, 2 vols. (Leipzig, 1903 and 1908).

[2] See T. Christensen, *Rufinus of Aquileia and the Historia ecclesiastica lib. VIII–IX of Eusebius*, Historisk-filosofiske Meddelelser 58 (Copenhagen, 1989).

[3] Despite F. Winkelman, *Untersuchung zur Kirchengeschichte des Gelasios von Kaisereia*, Sitzungsberichte der deutschen Akademie der Wissenschaften zu Berlin (Berlin, 1966), who argued that Rufinus translated a now-lost Greek continuation of Eusebius by Gelasius of Caesarea, Rufinus' authorship of Books X and XI has been vindicated: see F. Thelamon, *Païens et chrétiens au IVe siècle: l'apport de l'histoire ecclésiastique de Rufin d'Aquilée* (Paris, 1981); Christensen, *Rufinus of Aquileia*; and the useful summary of the debate in P. R. Amidon, *The church history of Rufinus of Aquileia, books 10 and 11* (New York and Oxford, 1997), pp. XIII–XVII.

describing where and when they lived and what they wrote.[4] Isidore of Seville in the early seventh century added a further thirty-three authors, including some notable writers of the sixth century.[5] Lastly, there is the *Historia tripartita*, a Latin compilation and abridgement by Epiphanius for Cassiodorus, of the ecclesiastical histories of three Greek writers, Sozomen, Socrates and Theodoret. There is some overlap in content between this work and Rufinus' Books X and XI, but the *Historia tripartita* takes the story up to the middle of the fifth century, provides complementary material for the fourth century, and a particularly dramatic presentation of the Arian conflict.[6] I have suggested that these three works played a key role in creating a context for the Franks' understanding not only of the history of the church, but also of the circumstances of the composition and dissemination of scripture and the work of the fathers of the early church.

The church was envisaged from the fourth century onwards primarily in terms of texts and more particularly, of the writings containing the fundamental ideas of Christian faith and practice. Such a perception was a direct consequence of the distinctive presentation of the history of the Christian church offered by Eusebius-Rufinus. Eusebius' emphasis, preserved and augmented by Rufinus, was on the writers who were the pillars of the church, on the definition of written authority and the canon of scripture, and on the great doctrinal controversies and discussions by theologians of the early church. Jerome and his continuator Gennadius consolidated this emphasis by presenting what amounts to a systematic bibliographical guide. The theme of written authority was then taken up and echoed in the *Historia tripartita* of Epiphanius-Cassiodorus. Taken together, Eusebius-Rufinus, Jerome-Gennadius and Epiphanius-Cassiodorus present a close association and essential continuation of the formation of a textual tradition within the chronological framework of the history of the church. The development of the church is thus also a textual history. I stress again that the histories of the church written in the fourth, fifth and sixth centuries provided both framework and context for a past and an identity built on texts.

Such a perception of the church and its historical development accords with the clear indications that the Franks in the Carolingian period

---

[4] Jerome-Gennadius, *De viris illustribus*, ed. E. C. Richardson, *Hieronymus, Liber de viris inlustribus. Gennadius de viris inlustribus*, Texte und Untersuchungen zur Geschichte der Altchristlichen Literatur (Leipzig, 1896).

[5] C. C. Merino, *El 'De viris illustribus' de Isidoro de Sevilla. Estudio y edicion critica*, Theses et Studia philologica Salamanticensia 12 (Salamanca, 1964).

[6] Eds. W. Jacob and R. Hanslik, *Cassiodori-Epiphanii, Historia ecclesiastica tripartita*, CSEL, LXXI (Vienna, 1952).

identified themselves in relation to particular texts. They recognised books as symbols of authority of the church and of God.[7] They themselves played a fundamental role in the definition of a canon of writings. That canon was constructed with the aid also of such bibliographical guides as Jerome-Gennadius-Isidore's *De viris illustribus* and Cassiodorus' *Institutiones*[8] and rested in its turn on the ecclesiastical histories written in the fourth and fifth centuries described above.

The Franks' understanding of the significance of these histories, and the tight interweaving of texts and authors in their narratives, is amply indicated by the evidence of the library catalogues and the production and dissemination of copies of Jerome-Gennadius, Eusebius-Rufinus and Epiphanius-Cassiodorus throughout the Frankish realms in the eighth and ninth centuries.[9] In consequence, it would be possible to argue, in this fundamental conception of the history of the church built on texts and writing, and of the Franks' place within that history, that words are all. Images appear to have little place.

Similarly, in documenting responses to the various histories of the church received and read in the Carolingian period, an overwhelming impression is of readers of texts, and of scribes copying texts. Imaginative understanding in verbal form, however, should not be underestimated. Mental images of writers, prophets, monks, bishops, martyrs, scribes, translators and scholars emerge strongly from the *De viris illustribus*, the *Historia ecclesiastica* and the *Historia tripartita*. So does a specific spatial understanding in terms of time and place. Naturally there is a danger of a modern reader making subjective and anachronistic assumptions about the way in which books may have been read in the past.[10] Yet the authors present the accounts of Christian writers with such consistent clarity of focus on precisely these issues of time, place and authority, that there would seem to be little doubt about the impression an early medieval reader might gain. Because of the location of these authors in relation to the chronological framework of the development of the Christian church as well as the geographical distribution of these various pillars of the church, an understanding of a Christian intellectual geography was

---

[7] I have discussed this at greater length in R. McKitterick, 'Essai sur les représentations de l'écrit dans les manuscrits carolingiens', in F. Dupuigrenet Desroussilles (ed.), *La Symbolique du livre dans l'art occidental du haut moyen âge à Rembrandt*, Revue française d'histoire du livre, 86–87 (1995), pp. 37–61.

[8] Cassiodorus, *Institutiones*, ed. R. A. B. Mynors (Oxford, 1937); see McKitterick, *Carolingians and the written word*, pp. 165–210.

[9] See chapters 9 and 10 above.

[10] For some attempts at reconstructions of the reading process in antiquity and the middle ages see G. Cavallo and R. Chartier (eds.), *A history of reading* (Oxford, 1999).

created alongside an emphasis on sacred places and delineation of the Holy Land.[11]

Pictorial images might reinforce these verbal pictures of authoritative writers and sacred places, but not replace them.[12] Actual images can be disassociated neither from mental images created by words nor from the texts to which the pictures are related. How text-based the Frankish understanding of the past and of historical narratives was may be underlined by the observation of how rarely historical narratives of any kind – classical, biblical, late antique or early medieval – were illustrated in the early middle ages. Where illustrations are included in history books, it is more usually in the biblical history books and more often than not as images of writers and individuals of authority in relation to scripture. A prime example is the depiction of scenes from the life of Jerome included in the Vivian Bible and the Bible of San Paolo fuori le Mura, both of which were given to Charles the Bald, king of the west Franks, 840–77. Here the scenes chosen for illustration are those of the composition and dissemination of the text of Jerome's Vulgate translation of the Bible.[13] The dramatic battle scenes in the St Gallen Golden Psalter and Leiden Maccabees codices, on the other hand, both produced at St Gallen, are straightforward exceptions to this in mirroring a direct representation of what is described in the text.[14]

There are, furthermore, some striking instances from the Carolingian period of the way that the distinctive stress on texts, authors, authority

---

[11] Compare on geographical ideas N. Lozovsky, 'The earth is our book'. Geographical knowledge in the Latin West ca. 400–1000 (Ann Arbor, 2000); A. Merrills, Geographical ideas in early medieval historiography (Cambridge, 2005); and P. Gautier Dalché, Géographie et culture. La représentation de l'espace du VIe au XIIe siècle (Aldershot, 1997). On the Holy Land see R. L. Wilken, The land called holy: Palestine in Christian history and thought (New Haven and London, 1992). See also D. Iogna-Prat, 'Lieu de culte et exégèse liturgique à l'époque carolingienne', in C. Chazelle and B. van Name Edwards (eds.), The study of the Bible in the Carolingian era, Medieval Church Studies 3 (Turnhout, 2003), pp. 215–44.

[12] I have discussed some of the issues this raises in 'Text and image in the Carolingian world', in R. McKitterick (ed.), Uses of literacy, pp. 297–318. But see also the essays in Testo e immagine nell'alto Medioevo, Settimane 41 (Spoleto, 1994); and for reflections on the wider context, C. Chazelle (ed.), Literacy, politics and artistic innovation in the early medieval west (Lanham, Md., 1992).

[13] The Vivian Bible (Paris, BnF lat.1), fol. 3v and the Bible of San Paolo fuori le Mura, fol. 3v, illustrated in H. Kessler, The illustrated bibles from Tours, Studies in Manuscript Illumination 7 (Princeton, 1977), plates 130 and 131.

[14] St Gallen, Stiftsbibliothek 22, pp. 140–1, illustrated in F. Mütherich and J. Gaehde, Carolingian painting (London, 1976), plates 46 and 47; and Leiden, Bibliotheek der Rijksuniversiteit, cod. Perizoni 17, fols 9r and 46r, illustrated in J. Hubert, J. Porcher and W. Volbach, Carolingian art (London, 1970), plates 163 and 164, pp. 177 and 178.

and sacred places in the ecclesiastical histories, *De viris illustribus* and a number of related texts, could be drawn on by readers, scribes and artists. It is on two examples of these that I wish to focus in this chapter. I shall explore the way in which this written tradition of the church appears to have shaped perceptions and attitudes. I shall explain how this particular image of the church and the Christian faith manifests itself in the Carolingian period. I suggest in this chapter that an important role in the shaping of perceptions of the past, and especially perceptions of the history of the church, was played by canon law. Canon law could do so in two ways, either by forming a canon of legislative material complementing history understood from other texts (such as the ecclesiastical histories discussed in the previous chapter) or by offering a history of the church in its own right. To illustrate these functions I shall look in detail at two manuscripts, Vercelli, Biblioteca Capitolare cod. CLXV, a collection of canon law, and Munich, Bayerische Staatsbibliothek Clm 22053, the famous miscellany in the *Wessobrunner Gebet* manuscript. Both must first, however, be set within the context of canon law in general in the early middle ages.

Canon law and Christian history

Ecclesiastical or canon law in the early middle ages comprised many texts of various dates and origins. It was gathered together in many different Christian communities and also included decisions made in local and regional church councils. Although the main element was the body of decrees from the great ecclesiastical councils of the early Christian church convened at Nicaea, Gangra, Chalcedon, Constantinople, Ancyra, Neocaesarea and Sardica, there were also what one might label national collections of African, Spanish, Gallo-Roman and Frankish church council decisions, some of which, especially those of the African church, were added to the general collections. Many of the oecumenical councils of course are famous for their consideration of the Christological controversies and the efforts to define orthodoxy which racked the church in the fourth and fifth centuries. Discussion also embraced, however, such matters as the true nature of asceticism (Gangra), discipline (Antioch), or the treatment of heretics, liturgy, penance and church order (Laodicea). Equally the regional church councils of the fifth, sixth and seventh centuries discussed matters of church organisation, episcopal jurisdiction, clerical discipline, lay piety, liturgy, lay behaviour and regulations concerning baptism, marriage and morality, as well as matters of faith. Problems once brought to a synod for discussion, from whether a eunuch could become a priest, or a priest could have a drink in a tavern (the answers to both were no!), to settling the definition of the Trinity were recorded and became part of a body of reference material for Christian communities thereafter.

A concerted effort was made by the popes in the sixth century to regularise canon law collections. The result was the *Dionysiana* put together by Dionysius Exiguus comprising the general church councils and a selection of papal decretals. This in its turn formed the basis of many subsequent compilations. In the time of Pope Hadrian in the eighth century, the *Dionysiana* was updated and became known as the *Dionysio-Hadriana*. Charlemagne attempted in 789 to promote this text as the authoritative body of canon law, with mixed success. The sixty-two complete and eight fragmentary late eighth- or ninth-century extant copies with a further eight from the tenth century and twenty from the period from the eleventh to the fifteenth centuries, witness to its wide dissemination. To this we need to add, of course, the selections from the *Dionysio-Hadriana* circulated in the sixteen extant ninth-century manuscripts of the *Admonitio generalis* of 789.[15] I shall return to the implications of this as far as the audience and reception of such texts is concerned below.

To these early conciliar decisions were added papal letters or decrees and other synods from time to time. The papal letters, mostly written in response to particular queries, became a substantial body of authoritative statements in their own right. With such an array of guidance available on all matters to do with the Christian church a bewildering variety of combinations of texts was assembled, all given names according to early editors or the homes of particular manuscripts, such as *Sanblasiana, Hispana, Vetus Gallica, Dacheriana, Herovalliana, Quesnelliana* and the like. These are listed in the table with their customary labels, imposed by Friedrich Maassen[16] and used by all subsequent historians of canon law. Unfortunately they have been preserved by Lotte Kéry.[17] It is a pity that this impressive new enterprise did not take the opportunity to question the usefulness of the initial classification, for it both creates and conceals a major problem for historians.

---

[15] H. Mordek, *Bibliotheca capitularium regum francorum manuscripta. Überlieferung und Traditionszusammenhang der fränkischen Herrschererlass, MGH* Hilfsmittel 15 (Munich, 1995), p. 1082, and his references.

[16] F. Maassen, *Bibliotheca latina iuris canonici manuscripta* (Vienna, 1866) and idem., *Geschichte der Quellen des canonischen Rechts im Abendlande bis zum Ausgange des Mittelalters* 1 (Graz, 1870).

[17] L. Kéry, *Canonical collections of the early middle ages (ca. 400–1140). A bibliographical guide to the manuscripts and literature, History of Medieval Canon Law* (Washington, D.C., 1999).

Canon law collections of the early middle ages

Titles in bold indicate that the collection survives in manuscripts from the first half of the eighth century or earlier. Titles with an asterisk * indicate that the collection survives in one manuscript only.[18]

A: *'Chronological' collections allegedly compiled before the end of the eighth century*[19]
1. Collectio frisingensis prima
2. *Collectio diessensis
3. *Collectio wirceburgensis
4. **Collectio Dionysiana** 2 recensions (poss. a third). One s.VIII in and two s.IX copies of first recension and a s.VI[2], three s.IX and three later copies of second recension are extant.
5. *Collectio Dionysiana bobiensis (two related copies)
6. Collectio Dionysio-Hadriana: sixty-two complete and eight fragmentary s.VIIIex or s.IX copies are extant, plus eight from s.X and twenty s.XI–XIV. This does not include the selections in the *Admonitio generalis* of 789.
7. Collectio Dionysiana adaucta
8. Breviarium ad inquaerendum sententias infra (= summary of Dionysio-Hadriana: includes BAV reg. lat. 1021, s. IX1/4 St Amand, possibly a different collection entirely).
9. **Collectio mutinensis*
10. Collectio vaticana
11. Collectio quesnelliana
12. **Collectio sanblasiana**
13. **Collectio novariensis**
14. *Collectio avellana
15. **Collectio theodosii diaconi*
16. **Collectio iustelliana*
17. *Collectio bigotiana
18. *Collectio parisiensis
19. *Collectio tuberensis

[18] I follow the sequence as given in Kéry despite there being no discernible rationale for it; it should be noted that she claims to have excluded those not produced 'specifically for ecclesiastical use, small collections in one manuscript, episcopal capitularies, Roman legal texts and pentitentials'. In fact some of these are included, not least Ansegis's capitulary collection; her focus is on other 'collections' from which excerpts are derived rather than on the new collections thereby created.
[19] Kéry lists sixty-one collections before s.VIIIex, of which thirty-three, as above, are 'chronologically arranged' (the rest are described as 'systematic' or 'unstructured', see below). Items 4, 9, 12, 13, 15, 16, 21, 22, 24, 28 survive in manuscripts from the first half of the eighth century or earlier.

20. *Collectio weingartensis
21. **Collectio Lugdunensis**
22. ***Collectio colonienesis**
23. Collectio sancti Mauri
24. ***Collectio corbeiensis**
25. *Collectio pithouensis
26. *Collectio laureshamensis
27. *Collectio remensis
28. **Epitome hispana**
29. Collectio hispana
30. Collectio hispana gallica
31. *Collectio weissenbergensis
32. Collectio sancti amandi
33. *Collectio bellovacensis

Kéry's next sections are 'Carolingian and post-Carolingian collections' with eleven items and 'Collections of local importance' (mostly ninth- and tenth-century in date) with forty-nine items. Of these only the following are chronologically arranged. The *Dacheriana* is a 'systematic' collection

(31 – s.IX; 11 s.X and nine later MSS).
34. Pseudo-Isidore, Decretales
35. Vercelli CLXV
36. Collectio Bonaevallensis secunda (Paris, BnF lat. 3859)
37. Collectio sangermanensis, BnF lat. 12021

B *'Systematic' collections from before the end of the eighth century*[20]
1. Corpus canonum africanum
2. **Constitutiones sirmondianae**
3. **Collectio 'concilii secundi arelatensis'**
4. **Statuta ecclesia antiqua**
5. Martin of Braga, capitula
6. **Fulgentius Ferrandus, breviatio canonum**
7. *Collectio teatina (Ingilramni) – 'unstructured'
8. *Collectio of BAV lat. 6808 – 'unstructured'
9. *Collectio colbertina
10. Cresconius, Concordia canonum
11. ***Collectio novariensis concilii chalcedonensis** (uncategorised)
12. ***Collectio albigensis** one s.VII MS and a s.IX copy of it.
13. Collectio vetus gallica
14. ***Collectio bernensis**

[20] Collections nos. 2, 3, 4, 6, 11, 12, 14 survive in manuscripts before s.VIIImed.

15. Collectio herovalliana
16. *Collectio frisingensis secunda
17. Excerpta hispana
18. Collectio Hadriano-Hispanica
19. Collectio hispana gallica augustodunensis
20. Tabulae hispanae
21. Collectio hispana systematica
22. Collectio hibernensis
23. Collectio 30 capitulorum (*De ratione matrimonii*)
24. *Collectio burgundiana ('unstructured')
25. Collectio 'pro causa iniustae excommunicationis'
26. *Collectio ecclesiae thessalonicensis

By seeing collections as integral texts and essentially as representatives of *Ur* collections, with little bundles of material traceable through manuscripts in a line of descent, Maassen concealed much of their contemporary historical significance. Only recently have historians begun to study individual canon law compilations in order to determine a precise and local reaction to the law of the church. Mordek's work on the *Vetus gallica* is perhaps the most spectacular,[21] but Zechiel-Eckes on the *Concordia* of Cresconius is also very valuable.[22]

Maassen also assumed, however, that the latest text included in any one collection provided a secure date for its compilation rather than merely a *terminus a quo*. I have indicated on the list above how very few of the collections given early dates by Maassen survive in early manuscripts. Of course, it would be absurd to be too reductionist about this. The fact that most of our texts from classical antiquity survive in manuscripts no earlier that the late eighth or ninth century does not encourage anyone to doubt that they were indeed originally composed many centuries earlier. Similarly texts with a very dispersed pattern of later manuscript witnesses can be assumed to have had an earlier wide dissemination, especially if there are many variant readings among the later copies. But with the canon law collections the situation is less clear cut. An instance of the problem is BAV Barberini lat. 679, a copy of the so-called 'Vatican collection'. It has a sizeable section right in the middle of it with texts from the eighth century. Maassen, however, was so certain that this was a sixth-century

---

[21] H. Mordek, *Kirchenrecht und Reform in Frankenreich: Die Collectio Vetus Gallica, die älteste systematische Kanonensammlung des fränkischen Gallien. Studien und Edition*, Beiträge zur Geschichte und Quellenkunde des Mittelalters 1 (Berlin and New York, 1975).

[22] K. Zechiel-Eckes, *Die Concordia canonum des Cresconius. Studien und Edition*, Freiburger Beiträge zur mittelalterlichen Geschichte 5 (Frankfurt am Main, 1992).

compilation that he dismissed the eighth-century portions of it as 'not belonging'.[23]

Subsequent scholars, therefore, have tended to think in terms of texts with a specific identity and have tried to establish relations between collections as if they were integral texts with established contents rather than the consequence of compilers drawing on a variety of different conciliar and decretal material with very specific imperatives governing their choice.

An example (among many) is to be found in Kéry's list. The *Collectio corbeiensis* in Paris, BnF lat. 12097 is a manuscript of the sixth century from southern France and contains a chronologically-arranged collection of conciliar canons and decretals written 'during the pontificate of Pope Vigilius'.[24] Kéry also notes the *Collectio pithouensis* (Paris, BnF lat. 1564), a Carolingian manuscript written between 785 and 819 from northern France, probably Chelles. This survives only as a fragment (the first eight quaternions are missing).[25] This time its contents are dated to the end of the sixth or beginning of the seventh century, located to Sens or Auxerre, and described as 'having a close relationship with the *collectio corbeiensis*'. Quite what this close relationship is, how it is reflected, and how it might have reached Chelles 200 years later is not clarified.[26] Undoubtedly there are major canonical collections formed which do merit proper names, and were indeed transmitted as complete collections, such as the *Dionysiana*, the *Hispana*, the *Collectio hibernenesis* and the *Dionysio-Hadriana*. We should not assume, however, that all the surviving canon law collections are of a similar type.

Even if such borrowings of lumps of material from one codex into another can be securely established, this should not be the end of the enquiry. What should then be asked is what new collection or combination of texts is thereby created and what it has to tell us about local perceptions of priorities and local understandings of the history of the church. Each of these collections identified by Maassen has very particular information about the transmission and formation of ideas. Many of them are quite clearly independent productions with a very restricted circulation and survive in one manuscript only. They are more likely to represent local definitions of the law of the church which merit closer study on an individual basis.

---

[23] For further discussion of this codex see my contribution to Settimane 52 (Spoleto, forthcoming).

[24] Kéry, *Canonical collections*, p. 47; see also D. Ganz, *Corbie in the Carolingian renaissance*, Beihefte der Francia 20 (Sigmaringen, 1990), p. 40.

[25] See *CLA*, V (Paris, 1950), no. 529.

[26] Compare Zechiel-Eckes, *Die concordia canonum des Cresconius*, pp. 233–6.

Historians of canon law have also accepted Maassen's two broad categories. Firstly, there are collections systematically arranged, that is, by theme. Secondly, there are compilations chronologically ordered in some kind of progression. In terms of the transmission of particular ideas, such as the church's views on matrimony or statements about papal authority, either systematic or chronological collections can make their points equally well. The greater concentration of chronologically-ordered collections in the ninth century and earlier, especially when the large numbers of copies of them, such as of the *Dionysio-Hadriana*, *Quesnelliana* and the *Hispana* are taken into account, is striking. The later and post-Carolingian collections tend to be systematic and many in any case are again local and individual attempts at ordering older material.

Chronologically-ordered collections, on the other hand, in themselves indicate historical sense and a perception of time and change. Seen in the context of many other manifestations of historical understanding and arrangement of material, from new forms of historical narrative – annals, biography, epic poems, martyrologies and cartularies – the preponderance and coincidence of historically-ordered canon law collections in the Carolingian period is significant.

My point is thus quite simple. Chronologically-ordered canon law collections are essentially history books, for they offer a progression of ideas and decisions of the church issuing from the great councils and popes of the church, all securely dated and geographically located. Access to these collections ensured that the fourth- and fifth-century discussions and decisions, and an understanding that they were enacted in places such as Rome, Constantinople, Sardica, Nicaea, Ephesus and Ancyra, were familiar and accessible and an essential part of the Frankish world as well. In addition, however, their emphasis on law and authoritative decisions emanating from a very specific series of places in an historical progression makes them texts fundamental in shaping the perception of the history of the early church. To a local priest or bishop the early church councils were an essential part of their understanding of the history of the church. They had been presided over by a succession of Roman emperors and a host of bishops and other representatives whose names were often meticulously copied into the manuscripts. Their decisions, the dramatic settlings of heresy, the judgements on questions of marriage and Christian morals, the opinions offered on discipline and organisation, and the claims for episcopal and especially papal authority made these books of immediate importance. If we consider the question of audience, then this peculiar form of history in the form of canon law was probably more widespread and known far more generally than the narratives provided by the church historians.

The sheer quantity of canon law manuscripts as a proportion of extant manuscripts from the ninth century is very great. Take the *Dionysio-Hadriana* for example. Although it is no doubt true that many centres preferred different compilations, there is nevertheless ample indication of wide knowledge. There are seventy surviving manuscripts or fragments thereof from the ninth century alone, with Francia, south-east Germany, the Rhineland, Alemannia and Northern Italy all represented. All have monastic, episcopal and possibly 'parochial' connections.[27]

In this respect canon law collections need to be seen side by side with the martyrologies, which are also history books of a special kind. There the history offered is in terms of the heroes of the church, which also contrives to set out, as I suggested in a paper in Vienna in 1999 and as I shall be arguing more fully elsewhere, a history of Rome from a very distinctive, if incomplete, perspective which was of great importance to the Franks.

Vercelli, Biblioteca Capitolare cod. CLXV

Let us now look in more detail at some examples in order to illustrate how canon law shaped the preception of the past and of the history of the church. The Vercelli canon law manuscript is a local compilation from northern Italy to be dated no later than the second quarter of the ninth century and probably to be located to the church of S. Felice in Pavia.[28] The compiler drew on a well-stocked library in terms of its canon law books. He included canons from Gallo-Roman and Merovingian church councils, papal letters, a handful of extracts from the episcopal statute of Theodulf of Orléans and rare texts from Africa. He added extracts from major canon law collections from Italy and Merovingian and Carolingian Gaul. The most notable of these are the selections from the original *Dionysiana* compiled in the sixth century by Dionysius Exiguus, the *Dionysio-Hadriana* (the eighth-century Frankish edition of the *Dionysiana*), the 'Bobbio *Dionysiana*', the so-called *Sanblasiana* collection (also from Italy), the *Breviatio canonum* compiled by Ferrandus of Carthage *c.* 535 and the sixth-century Italian compilation known as the *Concordia canonum* of Cresconius.

---

[27] On local clergy in the Carolingian period see C. van Rhijn, *Shepherds of the lord: priests and episcopal statutes in the Carolingian period* (Utrecht, 2003).

[28] I have not been able so far to consult this manuscript and am reliant on photographs and the published descriptions, notably the full analysis of its contents by Zechiel-Eckes, *Die Concordia canonum des Cresconius*, pp. 172–84. This provides an essential supplement to Maassen, *Bibliotheca*, pp. 418–9 and *idem*, *Geschichte der Quellen*, pp. 799–802. Kéry, *Canonical collections*, provides a useful updating of the information about the collections Maassen identifed and named, esp. pp. 33–7.

Altogether the compilation is a very substantial corpus indeed. It begins with the *Canones apostolorum*, and then in sequence the canons of
the councils of Nicaea, Ancyra, Neocaesarea, Gangra, Antioch, Laodicea,
Constantinople, Chalcedon, Sardica and Carthage. Thus it can be surmised that the compiler was concerned with the Christological controversies and the definition of the Christian faith as well as asceticism,
discipline, the treatment of heretics, liturgy, penance and church order.
It is to the latter more general matters that most of the remaining texts
gathered in the Vercelli collection are devoted, especially Ferrandus of
Carthage's *Breviatio canonum*.

The text of the *Breviatio* in the Vercelli collection is one of three surviving manuscript copies; one of the others is from southern France and
the other from Rhaetia; either region may have been the source of the
Vercelli compiler's exemplar.[29] The *Breviatio* is a systematic arrangement
of 232 extracts from the Greek and African councils of the fourth and
fifth centuries organised by topic with references to the relevant conciliar canon. It thus serves as a *vade mecum* to the full texts of the council
records of the earlier part of the codex. Thus there are groups of clauses on
matters concerning bishops, priests, deacons and other clerics, councils,
heretics, Jews and pagans, baptism, observance of Lent and behaviour in
church.

Number 85, for example, reads as follows:
Ut presbyter ante XXX annorum aetatem, quamvis sit dignus,
    non ordinetur.
Concilio novacaesariensi tit.10;

number 134:
Ut clerici edendi vel bibendi cause tabernas non ingrediantur,
    nisi peregrinationis necessitas coegerit.
Concilio laodicensi tit. 23, item 24, item 25. Concilio carthaginensi, tit. 35;

number 186:
Ut nullus a Iudaeis azyma accipiat
Concilio laodicensi tit. 36;

and number 228
Ut praeter scripturas canonicas nihil in ecclesia legatur
Concilio laodicensi tit. 57. Concilio carthaginensi tit. 45.[30]

---

[29] See Zechiel-Eckes, *Concordia canonum*, pp. 71–4.
[30] Ed. C. Munier, *Concilia africae, a. 345–a.535*, CCSL CXLIX (Turnhout, 1974), pp. 287–
306, at pp. 294, 298, 302, 306.

The compiler at Pavia, therefore, drew on an extensive range of material to provide a formidable compendium. Zechiel-Eckes has meticulously observed how the compiler reordered into chronological sequence some of the systematic collections he used for his compilation. That is, the chronological sequence and historical development of the church is mirrored in the ordering of his material. Not only are the conciliar canons arranged historically, but so is the decretal section from the *Concordia canonum* of Cresconius. The overall stress on the canonical books and orthodoxy, furthermore, is striking. The book as a whole is an eloquent *exemplum* of how writing and the encoding of the law of the church contains the fundamental ideas of Christian faith and practice.

The illustrations bunched together at the beginning of the Vercelli book (rather than interspersed throughout the text) are vigorous pen drawings of six scenes, namely the finding of the True Cross by Helena, the burning of the Arian books at the Council of Nicaea, images of Peter and Paul discussing the council of Nicaea, the burning of the books of the Macedonian heretics at the First Council of Constantinople, the emperor Theodosius presiding over the Council of Ephesus, and Christ in Majesty.[31]

These pictures do not simply reflect an artist's attempt to illustrate the convening of the councils recorded in the book. They mirror the themes of the crucified and triumphant Christ, faith and devotion, the role of the emperors in supporting the Christian church, the definition of orthodoxy, the historical place of the church in relation to the New Testament and the apostles, and the importance of books and writing as embodiments of the faith. Thus the pictures constitute a comment on the text which is itself enhanced by references to texts not in the collection at all. This is not simply a matter of the inclusion of a depiction of the discovery of the True Cross and of the Council of Ephesus which condemned Nestorius, neither of which figures in the compilation at all. The dramatic representations of the burning of the books are also not to be found in the canons of the relevant council but, at least in the case of the Council of Nicaea, in the account provided about this council in the *Historia tripartita* of Cassiodorus-Epiphanius.

Thus, the burning of the Arian books under Constantine portrayed on fol. 2v, for example, was recorded by Socrates in his ecclesiastical history and incorporated into the *Historia tripartita*.[32] The immolation of the Macedonian books, on the other hand, seems to be the artist's

---

[31] Illustrated in J. Hubert, J. Porcher and W. Volbach, *Europe in the Dark Ages* (London, 1969), plates 156–61, pp. 142–47; and see also the descriptions and reproductions in C. Walter, 'Les dessins carolingiens dans un manuscrit de Verceil', *Cahiers Archéologiques* 18 (1968), pp. 99–107.

[32] *Historia tripartita*, II, 15, ed. Jacob and Hanslik, p. 109.

creative assumption, an analogy with the historical account of Nicaea, for neither the very full coverage of the disputes with the Macedonians (a sub-group within the Arian party) in the *Historia tripartita*,[33] nor the canons of Constantinople itself, refer to the burning of the writings of these groups, only their anathematisation.[34] In other words, authority was seen by this artist in terms of books, and the countering of heresy was envisaged in terms of the destruction of books. Certainly, the other pictures reinforce the message of the book embodying authority. Paul displays a book in his hand, though Peter holds the two keys. In the representation of the Council of Nicaea, Constantine is depicted with a roll in his hand though the notary writes in a codex. The illustration of the first Council of Constantinople shows Theodosius holding a book in his left hand and the notaries to his right and left inscribe what he and the assembled bishops (crowding in behind the two scribes) decide in the book each holds. Similarly, Theodosius at Ephesus has his own codex in his hand and is flanked by two scribes, each writing in a book. These images associating the emperors with written authority and orthodoxy confirmed in codex form culminate in the representation of Christ himself, also holding a book. The link between Christ in Majesty in heaven, with an angel to his right and left, and the opening picture of this sequence, namely, the finding of the True Cross, instrument of Christ's passion on earth, is reinforced by placing Helena and Constantine beneath Christ in attitudes of supplication. These pictures together, therefore, express the principal preoccupations of the texts in Vercelli CLXV in a way that reflects a wider historical knowledge and understanding of the contexts from which the conciliar canons emerged.

The legend of the True Cross

The detail in the scene of the discovery of the True Cross, moreover, betrays the Pavia artist's wider range of reference. He drew not only on his historical understanding of the development of the Christian faith and practice as reflected in the law of the church and at least one ecclesiastical history. Certainly the legend of the discovery of the Cross by Helena is to be found in both Rufinus, *Historia ecclesiastica* X, 7–8 and the *Historia*

---

[33] *Ibid.*, V, 31, 41, 42, and IX, 12–16, pp. 260–2, 285–90, 506–22.

[34] C. Turner (ed.), *Ecclesiae occidentalis monumenta iuris antiquissima, canonum et conciliorum graecorum interpretationes latinae*, 2 vols. (Oxford, 1899), II, p. 409; and compare W. Speyer, *Büchervernichtung und Zensur des Geistes bei Heiden, Juden und Christen*, Bibliothek des Buchwesens 7 (Stuttgart, 1981), pp. 142–57; Speyer, p. 152, notes that that a law of Theodosius II and Valentinian in 436, incorporated into the Theodosian Code in the aftermath of the Council of Ephesus (431), did specify the burning of the works of Nestorius.

tripartita II,18.[35] Rufinus recounts simply that Helena, 'alerted by divine visions' journeyed to Jerusalem and there discovered the True Cross together with those of the two thieves. The identity of the Cross was established by a healing miracle. Subsequently the Nails were also found, and Helena had them incorporated into a helmet for her son Constantine and in the bridle of his warhorse. A church was then built on the site. The *Historia tripartita* adds little to this apart from reflecting on both a Sybilline oracle and a prophecy of Zechariah which seem to foretell the finding of the Cross and the incorporation of the Nails into war gear.

An alternative version known in the Latin west, however, was the so-called 'Cyriacus version' of the legend.[36] This introduces the character of the Jew 'Iudas', who shows Helena the spot where the Cross lay under the ground. Judas is subsequently converted, is baptised and changes his name to Cyriacus, and becomes bishop of Jerusalem. The earliest manuscript of the Cyriacus version is a fifth-century Syriac text, but a Latin version survives in Paris, BnF lat. 2769, a sixth-century uncial manuscript probably from Italy.[37] That this version was known in Gaul in the sixth century, moreover, is clear from the reference made to it by Gregory of Tours in his *Histories*.[38] Other copies of the Cyriacus legend survive in Carolingian manuscripts from St Gallen, Paris, Langres, St Amand and southern France. All can be divided into sub-groups related only distantly and thus attest to a very wide dissemination of this version of the True Cross story during the Merovingian and early Carolingian period.[39]

In many ways the Cyriacus version complements the Rufinus version, save that the dreams at the outset are attributed to Constantine, and Judas/Cyriacus plays such a prominent practical role. That both versions of the story were known but some people consciously preferred one over the other, moreover, is suggested by the comment in Sozomen's *Ecclesiastical History* to the effect that there were some who said that the crosses were first discovered by a Jew who derived his information from some documents which had been left to him by his father. Sozomen comments, however, that divine revelation in dreams and signs is to be

---

[35] Eds. Schwartz and Mommsen, *Eusebius Werke*, II, pp. 967–70; and *Historia tripartita*, ed. Jacob and Hanslik, p. 114–5.

[36] H. and J. W. Drijvers, *The finding of the true cross. The Judas Kyriakos legend in Syriac* (Louvain, 1997).

[37] *CLA*, V (Oxford, 1950), no. 550.

[38] Gregory, *Historiarum libri decem*, ed. B. Krusch and revised R. Buchner, *MGH SRM* I (Darmstadt, 1977), c. 36, p. 40.

[39] S. Borgehammar, *How the Holy Cross was found: from event to medieval legend*, Bibliotheca theologiae practicae 47 (Stockholm, 1991), pp. 208–28 on the manuscripts, and pp. 255–71 for an edition of the Latin text.

preferred to human information.[40] It is this preference which Epiphanius maintains, in his abridged Latin version of Sozomen, by omitting all reference to the Jew. The full version of the Cyriacus legend, however, introduces dreams and signs from God for both Constantine and Judas, quite apart from the miracle of raising the dead performed by the True Cross itself.

It is not necessary here to explore the origins or the further ramifications of these Syriac, Latin and Greek versions of the story, for they have been elucidated with great clarity by Han and Jan Willem Drijvers and by Stephen Borgehammar.[41] What they do indicate, firstly and on a practical level, however, is that a version of the story probably originated in Jerusalem in the first half of the fourth century at about the time that the relics of the True Cross were discovered. This was no doubt in the process of excavation for the foundations of Constantine's church of the Holy Sepulchre on Golgotha. Through Rufinus himself, who had spent many years in Jerusalem, the story reached the west but only in the form he preferred. Other variants, as recorded by others, including Sozomen, also reached the west and circulated concurrently. In the Carolingian period, a number of manuscripts containing each version were produced in widely separated centres. Secondly, the illustration in the Vercelli manuscript indicates that the legend itself was interpreted, by this artist at least, within the context of the discussions and definition of the nature and person of Christ in relation to God the Father. These discussions were precisely those given such prominence in the affairs of the early Christian church as recounted in the ecclesiastical histories.

Other contexts for the story were provided. A small decorated initial depicting the discovery of Cross and Nails in the Sacramentary of Gellone (Paris, BnF lat. 12048, fol. 76v) places it, as one might expect, within the liturgy of the feast for the *inventio sanctae crucis*.[42] A further response to the Latin version of the Cyriacus legend in the early Carolingian period was from an artist probably based in the Augsburg diocese, who provided the earliest-known cycle of illustrations to accompany the Latin version of the Cyriacus legend in the famous miscellany in the *Wessobrunner Gebet* manuscript.[43]

---

[40] Sozomen, *Ecclesiastical history*, II, 1, Greek ed. R. Hussey (Oxford, 1860), p. 103; English trans. H. Wace and P. Schaff, *A select library of Nicene and post-Nicene fathers of the Christian church*, second series (Oxford and New York, 1891), p. 258.

[41] J. W. Drijvers, *Helena Augusta, the mother of Constantine the Great and the legend of her finding of the true cross* (Leiden, 1992); and Borgehammar, *How the Holy Cross was found*.

[42] Illustrated in Hubert, Porcher and Volbach, *Europe in the Dark Ages*, plate 201, p. 191.

[43] K. Bierbrauer, *Die vorkarolingischen und karolingischen Handschriften der Bayerischen Staatsbibliothek. Katalog der illuminierten Handschriften der Bayerischen Staatsbibliothek*, I (Wiesbaden, 1990), no. 155, pp. 83–4, and II, plates 319–36.

The *Wessobrunner Gebet* codex

This codex was written in the diocese of Augsburg *c.* 814.[44] The manuscript comprises texts to do with theology, weights and measures, botany, geography, and chronology. It has been described as a 'kind of scrap book or collection of fragments of useful knowledge in the liberal arts',[45] but this is to underrate the coherence of this personal and individual compilation. The first twenty-one folios contain the *Liber de inventione s. crucis*. There follows the famous *Wessobrunner Gebet*, which is in fact both a description of the void before God created the world, the presence of the Creator and the act of creation. The title given the poem, *de poeta*, has been interpreted as 'creator' and is thought to be a Latinisation of the word used by Plato in the *Timaeus*, a text certainly available in the Carolingian period.[46] The glosses also suggest that the compiler knew Greek.

The poem has been interpreted as both the expression of the conviction of a pious Christian or possibly to be seen in a missionary context. Its language is predominantly Bavarian but some have detected in certain discrepancies in the word forms either a provenance further north or else an older stratum of the language.[47] Anglo-Saxon influence has also been discerned. Scholars have therefore looked to Fulda for Bavarian connections. This is easy enough, given that Abbot Sturm (†779) was himself a Bavarian. There are other possible centres in Franconia, and an Anglo-Saxon presence was not unknown in Bavaria itself in the early Carolingian period. A further insular and possibly Fulda link, however, is suggested by the manuscript tradition of the Cyriacus legend, for one of the other extant ninth-century copies is written in Anglo-Saxon and

---

[44] B. Bischoff, *Schreibschulen*, I, pp. 18–21. See also the discussion by U. Schwab, *Die Sternrune im Wessobrunner Gebet. Beobachtungen zur Lokalisierung des clm 22053, zur Hs. BM Arundel 393 und zu Rune Poem V. 86–89*, Amsterdamer Publikationen zur Sprache und Literatur 1 (Amsterdam, 1973).

[45] See J. Knight Bostock, *A handbook on Old High German literature*, 2nd edn (Oxford, 1976), p. 128, whose discussion of the language of the *Gebet* itself and its implications I here follow.

[46] Knight Bostock, *Handbook*, p. 128. On the *Timaeus* see R. McKitterick, 'Knowledge of Plato's *Timaeus* in the ninth century: the implications of Valenciennes, Bibliothèque Municipale MS 293', in H. J. Westra (ed.), *From Athens to Chartres. Neoplatonism and medieval thought* (Leiden, 1992), pp. 85–95, and reprinted in McKitterick, *Books, scribes and learning*, chapter 10; and more particularly, the important study of the manuscript tradition and its implications in A. Somfai, 'The transmission and reception of Plato's *Timaeus* and Calcidius's Commentary during the Carolingian Renaissance' (unpublished Ph.D. dissertation, University of Cambridge, 1998).

[47] See the useful summary by C. Edwards, 'German vernacular literature', in R. McKitterick (ed.), *Carolingian culture: emulation and innovation* (Cambridge, 1994), pp. 141–70.

early caroline minuscule,[48] which may suggest further knowledge of the legend at a place in the Main region in Germany with insular connections. It would be tempting from this perspective, as well as that of the language of the *Gebet*, to posit a link with Fulda itself. Knowledge of the historical accounts of the discovery of the Cross in both the ecclesiastical histories and the versions of the legend could then be linked to the composition of Hraban Maur's extraordinary celebration of the Cross.[49] The manuscript evidence is too ambiguous at present for this to be ascertainable.

At the least there seems to be agreement that the texts of both the Cyriacus legend and the *Wessobrunner Gebet* are copied from an older exemplar, perhaps from the late eighth century. Thus, like the compiler of the Vercelli canon law collection, the compiler of the Wessobrunner Gebet codex reveals the extent of the treasury of texts he had at his disposal for inclusion in his book. Similarly, it is the story of the True Cross, like an invocation, which starts each book. In the case of the *Wessobrunner Gebet* manuscript it is the whole text that acts in this way. It is amplified by the illustrations in direct response to its details. The artist of the Vercelli collection, on the other hand, chose to use the single but powerfully symbolic image of the actual discovery of the Cross.

The *Wessobrunner Gebet* codex's pictures are simple outline pictures with a sparing use of brownish red, yellow and blue. The pictures start with Constantine's dream. Helena is then represented in a number of pictures as she arrives in Jerusalem, talks to soldiers and to various groups of Jews. Thereafter the pictures relate how Judas emerges from the dry well into which Helena had him thrown, and excavates three crosses at Golgotha. It is then revealed, in the raising of a dead man, which cross is that of Christ. Thereafter a church is built by Helena and Judas is baptised and becomes Cyriacus. The Nails are also retrieved.

A clear association of ideas in the *Wessobrunner Gebet* manuscript is provided by the text directly following the *inventio sanctae crucis*. On fols. 22r–35v the scribe included the *De situ terrae sanctae* of Theodosius concerning

---

[48] Oxford, Bodleian Library Laud misc. 129, fols. 16v–22v, listed by Borgehammar, *Holy Cross*, p. 211. See B. Bischoff and J. Hofmann, *Libri sancti Kyliani. Die Würzburger Schreibschule und die Dombibliothek im VIII. und IX. Jahrhundert* (Würzburg, 1952), p. 51. It seems clear, however, that Laud misc. 129 itself was not written at Fulda, nor is there any indication that it was ever there: see H. Spilling, 'Angelsächsische Schrift in Fulda', in A. Brall (ed.), *Von der Klosterbibliothek zur Landesbibliothek. Beiträge zum zweihundertjährigen Bestehen der Hessischen Landesbibliothek Fulda* (Stuttgart, 1978), pp. 47–98; and *idem.*, 'Die frühe Phase karolingischer Minuskel in Fulda', in G. Schrimpf (ed.), *Kloster Fulda in der Welt der Karolinger und Ottonen*, Fuldaer Studien 7 (Frankfurt, 1996), pp. 249–84; who does not include Laud misc. 129 in her discussions.

[49] See M. Ferrari, *Il 'Liber sanctae crucis' di Rabano Mauro. Testo-immagine-contesto* (Bern, 1999).

other sacred places in the Holy Land.[50] Throughout the book, the compiler celebrated the passion of God the Son and the creation of God the Father in its many manifestations, as well as the importance of knowledge of the sacred places.

These two manuscripts and their illustrations, therefore, demonstrate how images were deployed to reinforce the importance of sacred place, relics, authors and books. They also serve to underline yet again the importance of codicological context for our own understanding of any one text and its significance for its intended audience. They thereby, incidentally, add to our own knowledge of the intellectual resources of particular groups in the Carolingian world, quite apart from enlarging our understanding of the reception of late antique Christian texts in early medieval Europe. The Vercelli canon law book in particular shows how the image and understanding of the history of the church was based not only on the compiler's readings of ecclesiastical history but also on the way a very particular perception of the history of the church was expressed on a number of key issues. What appears to be reflected in both these manuscripts and the wider cultural context they represent is an historical understanding of the Christian faith, formed by reading, expressed in written and pictorial form, but for which written texts provide the principal inspiration.

---

[50] T. Tobler and A. Molinier (eds.), *Itineraria hierosolymitana*, I (Geneva 1879/80), pp. 353–9. (Munich, Bayerische Staatsbibliothek Clm 22053 not used by P. Geyer (ed.), *Itineraria et alia geographica*, *CCSL*, CXXV (Turnhout, 1965), pp. 114–25). This version is apparently textually related to Wolfenbüttel, Herzog-August Bibliothek, Weissenburg 99, fols. 144r–152v, which is a famous illustrated copy of the eighth century and contains the catholic epistles.

12 Conclusion: History and its audiences in the Carolingian world

The Franks' interest in history is distinctive in early medieval Europe as a whole. Their complex relationship with the past was articulated in many different contexts and a host of different kinds of historical and chronologically ordered texts, many of which were created for the first time by the Franks in the Carolingian period. It is evident in their extensive copying and preservation of histories of Roman antiquity, of the early Christian church and of the barbarian successor states to Rome. It is dramatically expressed in their own contemporary histories. All these have been discussed in the preceding chapters of this book. Yet history for the Franks was not just about the distant past, but also concerned the way in which contemporary memory is transmuted into history. It is on this that I focus in this concluding chapter.

The crisis of 817: contemporary memory and history

In the autumn of 817, Hetti, archbishop of Trier, wrote to inform Frothar, bishop of Toul, of an order sent by the Emperor Louis the Pious. Frothar was to prepare all those in the diocese liable for military service for an expedition to Italy, where, inspired by Satan, King Bernard was preparing to rebel against Louis. Louis, and Hetti, as legate, had received intelligence not of a rebellion already in progress but of preparations for it.[1] The letter survives in a collection dated to the ninth century, possibly in the lifetime of Frothar himself, who died in 847. It is now in the miscellany volume, Paris, BnF lat. 13090.

---

[1] Frotharius of Toul, *Epistolae*, no. 2, ed. K. Hampe, *MGH Epp.*, V (Berlin, 1899), pp. 285–327, at p. 277–8, also edited with French translation and a new study of the manuscript by M. Parisse and his Séminaire de latin médiéval, Université Paris I Panthéon-Sorbonne, *La correspondance d'un évêque carolingien. Frothaire de Toul (ca 813–847)* (Paris, 1998), no. 28, pp. 136–7. See also L. Morelle, 'Enquête sur le manuscrit', *ibid.*, pp. 57–79. On Frothar's own connection with the court of Louis the Pious see P. Depreux, *Prosopographie de l'entourage de Louis le Pieux (781–840)*, Instrumenta 1 (Sigmaringen, 1997), pp. 204–5.

At face value Hetti's letter witnesses to the receipt of news and orders from the central government and to the forming of contemporary attitudes: King Bernard was inspired by Satan to rebel. Hetti made sure that Frothar, whether of like mind or not, would be clear that this, if not the official opinion, was certainly Hetti's. Yet the letter is also a consequence of the knowledge and understanding of the context and implications of information received. Because Hetti clearly knows more than he tells, his letter enables us to see the beginnings of both the creation of an historical memory and the identification of an audience.

If we turn to the contemporary historians' accounts of the ensuing rebellion of Bernard of Italy against his uncle Louis, we may also be able to reconstruct the knowledge underlying the letter. The historical narratives in their turn raise questions about the formation of a collective memory of events as well as of that elusive and inadequate notion: 'public opinion'. Both of these then need to be considered in relation to the work of Frankish historians and to their contemporary and subsequent audiences.

The earliest extant narrative about the events of 817 and King Bernard's rebellion is that of the *Annales regni francorum*. The text of the annals, as previously mentioned, is generally acknowledged to be a more or less official, court-based record.[2] As I have already explained, the precise allocation of blocks of year entries in the *Annales regni francorum* to any one author is largely on stylistic grounds and is still disputed. The customary, though unprovable, attribution of the year entries for 820–9 to Hilduin of St Denis would make the entry for 817 the work of someone else shortly before 820. The text also indicates that between 816 and 817 someone may have made a new start, for the new writer in 817 reiterated in different words material about the envoys from Spain that was included at the end of the entry for 816. Although detailed analysis of the process of composition of the later portion of the Frankish annals which includes the entry for 817, as well as its relationship with the revised or 'E' version of the annals, must wait for another occasion, my surmise is that the entry for 817 could have been made as early as 818. It is thus a directly contemporary comment designed to inform both a present and a future audience.

The annals' entry for the year 817 in which Hetti's letter was written explains that envoys from the Abd-ar-Rahman, the ruler of Muslim Spain, the Byzantine emperor Leo, the Danes and the pope were received in turn by the Emperor Louis at Aachen. After Easter and a hunting trip near

---

[2] See above, chapters 1 and 4.

Nijmegen, Louis convened a general assembly at Aachen:

on this occasion he crowned his first born son Lothar and shared with him the name of emperor. His other sons he appointed kings, placing one over Aquitaine and one over Bavaria.[3]

That done, Louis went hunting again. This time he rode to the Vosges, though he was obliged to stop on the way to receive more envoys from Byzantium at his palace at Ingelheim near Mainz (from whom he learnt no more than from the previous Greek envoys), and to arrange for the defence of his northern borders against a revolt of the Obodrites in alliance with the Danes. Somehow Louis squeezed in his hunting trip (he was quite adept at doing this) and it was only at Aachen thereafter that the annals report that he was informed that his nephew Bernard, king of Italy, 'on the counsel of some depraved men', was planning to set up an unlawful regime and that Bernard had already blockaded the Alpine passes into Italy and received homage from all the cities of Italy. This, the annalist observes, was 'partly true and partly false'. Such a comment is a telling indication of the author's sense of purpose; he was not setting out simply to record events but also to control the understanding of the events he reported.

The emperor, the annalist continues, hastily prepared to enter Italy with a host 'gathered from all over Gaul and Germany in order to nip these movements in the bud'. Bernard was defeated, the conspirators, who included many noblemen and bishops among them, were identified, and the following year the ringleaders were condemned to death. This sentence was commuted to blinding or, in the case of the bishops, deposition. The rest of the rebels were exiled or tonsured and confined in monasteries.[4]

The anonymous life of Louis the Pious, attributed to 'The Astronomer' and written between 840 and 843,[5] follows the annals' account but adds some circumstantial information to this dreadful story, notably the significant details that Louis had been Charlemagne's chief adviser in making Bernard king of Italy, that Bernard had been received by Louis at Aachen

---

[3] *Annales regni francorum*, ed. F. Kurze, *MGH SRG*, VI (Hannover, 1895), p. 146; English translation B. Scholz, *Carolingian Chronicles* (Ann Arbor, 1970), pp. 102–3.

[4] *Ibid.*, s.a. 817 and 818, pp. 147–8.

[5] Astronomer, *Vita Hludowici imperatoris*, ed. E. Tremp, *MGH SRG*, LXIV (Hannover, 1995). Tremp makes the case for the winter of 841, pp. 66–8. For a persuasive case for the composition of the Astronomer's life in the context of the political settlement of 843 and under the patronage of Drogo, bishop of Metz, see H. Doherty, 'The maintenance of royal power and prestige in the Carolingian *regnum* of Aquitaine under Louis the Pious' (unpublished M.Phil. dissertation, University of Cambridge, 1998).

soon after Louis' accession and had been showered with gifts and that Bernard had died as a result of his blinding.[6]

A biography of Louis the Pious, written by Thegan of Trier in 837, that is, three years before Louis' death,[7] claims that Bernard had sworn an oath of fidelity to Louis on his visit in 814, that he had visited Louis again at the general assembly in 815,[8] and that when Bernard rebelled in 817 it was because he wished to expel Louis from his Italian kingdom. Thegan highlights Bernard's illegitimate birth by saying he was merely the son of a concubine.[9] He also tries to imply that Louis was reluctant to carry out the blinding as well as the death sentence and stressed that Louis was full of grief at Bernard's death.[10]

Nithard, a grandson of Charlemagne and supporter of Louis the Pious's youngest son, Charles the Bald, king of the West Franks (840–77), gives an entirely different slant in his Histories, which he completed in the spring of 843. He states simply that Bernard had been granted the kingdom of Italy by Louis, had defected from Louis soon thereafter, was taken prisoner and deprived of his sight and his life by Bertmund, governor of the province of Lyons. Out of fear that his younger brothers might stir up the people as Bernard had done, Louis had them tonsured and put in monasteries per libera custodia.[11]

What all these historical accounts apparently omit is a full explanation for Bernard's rebellion. As we have seen, they convey by one means or another that Bernard was in the wrong and that he had been led astray by depraved men or by Satan, a rather too active protagonist in the affairs of the Frankish empire as far as the Astronomer was concerned. Instead, they spell out the immediate failure of the conspiracy and the fate of the rebels.

But in fact none of the three accounts does omit the reasons, for what they have already told us is about the assembly in 817 at which Louis had made arrangements for the succession to his vast realm. Fortunately,

---

[6] Vita Hludowici imperatoris, ed. Tremp, c. 29, pp. 382–4.
[7] Thegan, Gesta Hludowici imperatoris, ed. Tremp, and see the discussion of the date, pp. 5–7.
[8] J. Jarnut, 'Kaiser Ludwig der Fromme und König Bernhard von Italien. Der Versuch einer Rehabilitierung', Studi Medievali 30 (1989), pp. 637–48, especially p. 639.
[9] See K.-F. Werner, 'Hludowicus augustus: Gouverner l'empire chrétien – idées et réalités', in P. Godman and R. Collins (eds.), Charlemagne's heir: new perspectives on the reign of Louis the Pious (814–840) (Oxford, 1990), pp. 3–123, at pp. 34–5.
[10] Vita Hludowici imperatoris, ed. Tremp, cc. 12 , 14, 22; pp. 192, 194, 210–12.
[11] Nithard, Historiarum libri IIII, ed. R. Rau, Quellen zur karolingischen Reichsgeschichte, I (Darmstadt, 1974), I, 2, p. 388; and P. Lauer, Nithard. Histoire des fils de Louis le Pieux (Paris, 1964), I, 2, pp. 6–8. On Nithard see J. L. Nelson, 'Public histories and private history in the work of Nithard', Speculum 60 (1985), pp. 251–93; reprinted in J. L. Nelson, Politics and ritual in early medieval Europe (London, 1986), pp. 195–237.

there is a formal record of this assembly's decisions, namely, the *Ordinatio imperii*, dated July 817. In addition to the allocation of Aquitaine to Pippin and Bavaria to Louis (the German) clause 17 states:

May the kingdom of Italy be subject to our son Lothar in everything, if God wishes him to succeed us, just as it was to our father and as it is subject to us, God willing at the present time.[12]

In an earlier piece of legislation, however, the *Divisio regnorum* of 806, Louis' father Charlemagne had divided his empire (unequally) between his then still living three sons and had provided for the inheritance of each of the separate kingdoms by a son of his sons, provided the people over whom he was to rule found him acceptable. Italy had been allocated to Pippin.[13] By 811, however, Louis' brothers had predeceased their father. Louis had therefore inherited the entire kingdom and Charlemagne had conferred the imperial title on him and crowned him in 813 for good measure.[14] Charlemagne's arrangements, therefore, were definitively set aside by Louis in his legislation of 817 in favour of his own sons and at the expense of his brothers' sons simply by omitting all reference to Bernard and his offspring. A very difficult political decision, and the degree to which it failed to command universal support within the empire, thus underlies the rising of Bernard and his supporters.[15] Einhard's treatment of Bernard's position in the *Vita Karoli* is also a reflection of the sensitivity of the court to Bernard's position in the light of Charlemagne's recognition of his kingship: 'when his son [Pippin] died [Charlemagne] saw

[12] *Ordinatio imperii* (817), ed. A. Boretius, *MGH Cap.*, I, no. 136, pp. 270–3. For an English translation see B. Pullan, *Sources for the history of medieval Europe* (Oxford, 1966), pp. 37–42.
[13] *Divisio regnorum* (806), ed. Boretius, *MGH Cap.*, I, no. 45, pp. 126–30. For an English translation see P. D. King, *Charlemagne. Translated sources* (Kendal, 1987), pp. 251–5. For commentary on 806 see Y. Hen, 'The annals of Metz and the Merovingian past', in Y. Hen and M. Innes (eds.), *The uses of the past in the early middle ages* (Cambridge, 2000), pp. 175–90, and his references.
[14] W. Wendling, 'Die Erhebung Ludwigs des Frommen zum Mitkaiser in Jahre 813 und ihre Bedeutung für die Verfassungsgeschichte des Frankenreiches', *Frühmittelalterliche Studien* 19 (1985), pp. 201–38.
[15] For a summary of the scholarship to 1974 on the revolt of Bernard and its legal base see T. F. X. Noble, 'The revolt of King Bernard', *Studi Medievali* 3, series 15 (1974), pp. 315–26. T. F. X. Noble, *The republic of St. Peter. The birth of the papal state, 680–825* (Philadelphia, 1984), p. 201 adds a note about Bernard in Italy. See also P. Depreux, 'Das Königtum Bernards von Italien und sein Verhältnis zum Kaisertum', *Quellen und Forschungen aus italienischen Archiven und Bibliotheken* 72 (1992), pp. 1–24; M. Innes, 'Charlemagne's will: piety, politics and the imperial succession', *EHR* 112 (1997), pp. 833–55, at pp. 842–8, and his references to the different modern interpretations; and B. Kasten, *Königssöhne und Königsherrschaft. Untersuchungen zur Teilhabe am Reich in der Merowinger- und Karolingerzeit*, *MGH* Schriften 44 (Hannover, 1997), especially pp. 163–8. For maps indicating the territorial divisions allocated in 806 and 817 see McKitterick (ed.), *NCMH*, pp. 113 and 114.

to it that his grandson [Bernard] succeeded his father [as king of Italy] and he arranged for his granddaughters to be raised alongside his own daughters'.[16]

The royal Frankish annalists, the Astronomer and Thegan clearly assumed knowledge of the *Ordinatio imperii*, of the various members of the Carolingian royal family, of the various expectations of succession and inheritance laid out by Charlemagne in the *Divisio regnorum* of 806, and of the events of the years 810–13. Such knowledge also appears to be behind even Hetti of Trier's brusque injunction to Frothar. The narrators are, in other words, reliant for the effectiveness of their narratives on an already existing historical knowledge on the part of their audience within the Frankish realm.

How might their audience have come by such knowledge? Oral circulation of information, discussions and exchanges of news at the annual assemblies, gossip, letters, and casual references as royal officials went about their business, and as the royal entourage itself travelled from one residence or hospitable royal monastery to another, could account for some of it. Yet we also have to reckon with the systematic dissemination of legislation and information in the Frankish empire. In the case of the royal capitularies, for example, we can reconstruct some of the process of distribution of royal instructions around the kingdom and the role of the royal chancery in this.[17] Certainly someone in as prominent a position as Archbishop Hetti[18] would have known of the *Divisio regnorum* and *Ordinatio imperii*, but no extant manuscript of either text can be linked to Trier. Only five manuscripts of the *Divisio regnorum* survive, two from the tenth century and the other three from the fifteenth and sixteenth centuries. The *Ordinatio imperii* survives only in the version preserved in Paris, BnF lat. 2718 made in Louis' chancery. Much of the manuscript is written in tironian notes, that is, shorthand.[19]

---

[16] Einhard, *Vita Karoli*, c. 19, p. 24, ed. Rau, *Quellen zur karolingischen Reichsgeschichte*, I, p. 190, English translation: P. Dutton, *Charlemagne's courtier: the complete Einhard* (Peterborough, Ontario, 1998), p. 29. This delicacy is, to my mind, a further indication of the early date of *c*. 817 for Einhard's *Vita Karoli* as argued in Innes and McKitterick, 'Writing of history', pp. 203–8.

[17] On gossip see C. Wickham, 'Gossip and resistance among the medieval peasantry', *Past and Present* 160 (1998), pp. 3–24. On the availability and circulation of administrative material see J. L. Nelson, 'Literacy in Carolingian government', in R. McKitterick (ed.), *Uses of literacy*, pp. 258–96; McKitterick, *Carolingians and the written word*, pp. 25–37; and 'Zur Herstellung von Kapitularien: die Arbeit des Leges-Skriptoriums', *MIÖG* 101 (1993), pp. 3–16.

[18] Depreux, *Prosopographie de l'entourage de Louis le Pieux*, pp. 244–6.

[19] See H. Mordek, *Bibliotheca capitularium regum francorum manuscripta. Überlieferung und Traditionszusammenhang der fränkischen Herrschererlasse*, MGH Hilfsmittel 15 (Munich, 1995), pp. 119, 152, 231, 638, 863; and p. 245.

There is also an indication, in the fragment of the annals in the revised or 'E' version, produced in the court scriptorium of Louis the Pious, and mentioned above in chapter 1, that the court played a role in the dissemination of the annals as well, if not of other contemporary historical commentary.[20]

The three narratives in the *Annales regni francorum*, the Astronomer and Thegan, provide a laudatory account of a mighty emperor's dealings with rebellions and revolts of all kinds against Carolingian and Frankish rule. The case of Bernard, however, is aberrant, for it is a family affair and within, rather than from without, the empire. It is Nithard who is most sensitive to this family dimension, for Bernard's revolt is mentioned in the context of how Louis first made his little brothers, Drogo, Hugo and Theodoric, companions of his table and then shut them up in monasteries to reduce the possibility of their gaining political support. As it happened, moreover, Bernard's revolt had extraordinary long-term political consequences for Louis.[21] Although these are not my immediate concern, it is clear that the Astronomer, Thegan and Nithard wrote about the events of 817 and 818 with hindsight. Their understanding of the trauma of 817–18, the public penance undertaken by Louis in 822 and its political reverberations thereafter,[22] meant that they placed far more weight on the event itself and Bernard's position than the Royal Frankish annalist had done. Thegan in particular is over-anxious to cast Bernard in an unfavourable light and stress the legitimacy of Louis' actions. Because the author of this entry in the *Annales regni francorum* was writing before all the consequences became apparent, and because the succession issue was such a delicate matter, he presented it as simply another rebellion of a kind that had happened before. He was at pains to reduce its immediate significance. Indeed, he notes that one of the conspirators was Reginhar, son of Count Meginhar, whose maternal grandfather Hardrad 'once conspired in Germany with many noblemen of the province against the Emperor Charles'.[23] Reginhar's was a family with a tradition of rebellion against the Carolingian family therefore, but also with a history of

---

[20] B. Bischoff, 'Die Hofbibliothek unter Ludwig dem Frommen', in B. Bischoff, *Mittelalterliche Studien* 3 (Stuttgart, 1981), pp. 171–86, at p. 185. Note that the fragment's shelfmark has changed from Capsula 34,1 to Historisches Archiv des Erzbistums Köln, Best. Stift St Maria im Kapitol A II 184; for further details see above, chapters 1 and 6.

[21] Godman and Collins (eds.), *Charlemagne's heir* (especially the essays in Part I); and E. Boshof, *Ludwig der Fromme*, Gestalten des Mittelalters und der Renaissance (Darmstadt, 1996).

[22] See M. de Jong, 'Power and humility in Carolingian society: the public penance of Louis the Pious', *EME* 1 (1992), pp. 29–52

[23] *Annales regni francorum*, ed. Kurze, *s.a.* 817, p. 148.

defeat at Carolingian hands over three generations. We should also note that the Astronomer talks of Count Meginhar's special relationship with Louis, which makes his son's part in the revolt all the more significant for those familiar with the background.[24]

As I have stressed throughout this book, moreover, the *Annales regni francorum* are far more than a record of events. The narrative is a very skilfully constructed piece of political ideology, with a strong political message about the benefits of Frankish rule, the legitimacy of particular Carolingan rulers and the success of the Franks.[25] As we have seen, the fact that the *Annales regni francorum*, together with Thegan and the Astronomer (and Einhard's *Vita Karoli*), were so widely disseminated across the entire Frankish empire, and often as part of the same composite history book, with a concentration of manuscripts copied during the reigns of Charlemagne's grandsons,[26] is an indication of the recognition accorded the message of all these texts in the mid- and later ninth century. Image making and opinion forming, in other words, is as high on the agendas of the annalists as the imparting of information.

Whether directly contemporary or writing within decades of the event, therefore, these Frankish historians[27] were not so much supplying full information and record as providing an interpretative gloss and understanding. They created an image of the past for immediate and future transmission. No doubt to some readers or hearers, their narrative was entirely new. For the most part, however, these writers relied initially for the effectiveness of their interpretations on their audience's memory of these same events and their context. Their narrative then manipulates these memories which subsequently may then get recorded within a new ordering of the past without the special knowledge of the immediate contemporary audience. Without that special knowledge it can then be read very differently. Memory becomes history. Yet it is a selective memory and may become a distortion of the past to serve present concerns. The Frankish historians, like all historians, wrote to a particular agenda and selected and highlighted that which they wanted to impress upon the

---

[24] Astronomer, *Vita Hludowici imperatoris*, c. 7, ed. E. Tremp, *MGH SRG* 64 (Hannover, 1995), p. 306.

[25] Chapters 4 and 5.

[26] E. Tremp, *Die Überlieferung der Vita Hludovici imperatoris des Astronomus*, *MGH* Studien und Texte 1 (Hannover, 1992). Nithard's *Histories* survives from the ninth century in one manuscript only.

[27] Such an enormous range of forms of historical writing has little to do with the historical alienation that Richard Southern suggested, in his classic presidential address to the Royal Historical Society, was behind the English historical writing of the period 1090–1130, 'Aspects of the European tradition of historical writing IV The sense of the past', *TRHS*, 5th series, 23 (1973), pp. 243–64; and see above, chapter 9.

minds of their particular targeted audiences, whether in their own time or for posterity. As Einhard wrote in the preface to his *Vita Karoli*:

I thought it would be better to write these things down [namely, what Einhard had witnessed], along with other widely known details, for the sake of posterity, than to allow the splendid life of this most excellent king, the greatest of all the men of his time, and his remarkable deeds, which people now alive can scarcely equal, to be swallowed up by the shadows of forgetfulness.[28]

Posterity has indeed received Einhard's account, and the histories written by so many of his contemporaries. Frankish history formed a component of later presentations of French and German history, either as the beginning section of new histories or in new copies of the Carolingian texts made throughout the middle ages. Many Frankish historical texts, including Einhard and the *Annales regni francorum* were among the new editions printed in the first century after Gutenberg,[29] as well as the first to be produced by the *Monumenta Germaniae Historica* at the beginning of the nineteenth century.[30] The dependance to this day of modern historians and their audiences on texts and interpretations of their past prepared by Frankish writers for audiences within the Frankish empire in the eighth and ninth centuries remains very great.[31] It is essential, therefore, that we understand the dynamic relationship, involving memory, experience, knowledge and texts, between historians and their original audiences.

Historical mindedness in the Carolingian period

It is to the concept of an audience in posterity, and its context, that I now turn. Why should anyone wish to know about anything other than contemporary events? An understanding of immediate events and their political implications in relation to past decisions does not rely simply on knowledge and memory. It also implies a sensitivity to a place in time and a sense of historical process. The remarkable volume of production of contemporary history in the Carolingian period from which I have selected the most obvious examples was for an audience with an already-formed habit of historical reference, and with an historical understanding or historical mindedness, which I have documented in this book. I have been concerned with the following questions: what contributed to the

---

[28] Einhard, *Vita Karoli*, preface, ed. Rau, *Quellen zur karolingischen Reichsgeschichte*, I, p. 164; English trans. Dutton, *Charlemagne's courtier*, p. 15.
[29] Both were edited, for example, by Hermann von Neuenar in Cologne in 1521.
[30] Ed. G. Pertz, *MGH SS*, I and II (Hannover, 1826 and 1829).
[31] See above, chapters 5 and 6.

Franks' sense of their place in historical time? What did the Franks use to construct their past? How did their own immediate history relate to this longer past? By way of conclusion let me rehearse the main points which have emerged.

I have documented in some detail the resources of the Franks in terms of their history books; the collections formed at the monasteries of Fulda, Lorsch and St Amand were particularly striking. How this might be reflected in the work of an individual scholar of the Carolingian period is evident in the work of someone like Lupus of Ferrières. He commented in 837 in a letter to Abbot Bun of Hersfeld, for example, about a biography he had just completed of the Anglo-Saxon Wigbert of Fritzlar that not being contemporary with the events he was describing did not prevent him, any more than it had prevented other historians, from writing about them:

> Let no one consider this little work inaccurate because I am writing it in the 836th year of our Lords' Incarnation, and the 14th indiction, and seem to be recalling things which took place ninety years ago, for surely anyone with the slightest education knows that Sallust and Livy narrated not a few things which had occurred long before their time, and which they had learned, partly from hearsay and partly from *reading*.[32]

Lupus here neatly sums up the resources of any historian: what they have heard and what they have read. In other letters, Lupus quotes from his own reading of history from, or mentions the texts of, many Roman and Christian historians, such as Justinus, Pompeius Trogus, Livy, Aurelius Victor, Caesar, Sallust, Eusebius' *Ecclesiastical History* translated by Rufinus, Josephus and Suetonius.[33] Educated at Ferrières in the Loire valley as well as at Fulda under Hraban Maur, Lupus clearly had had access to the contents of Fulda's library. It may have been there that he encountered Einhard's *Vita Karoli*.[34]

From library catalogues, extant manuscripts and the citation of earlier historians made by Carolingian authors, it has been possible to establish the rich resources of history books the Franks had at their disposal.[35]

---

[32] My emphasis: Lupus, *Epistolae*, ed. L. Levillain, *Loup de Ferrières. Correspondance*, Les Classiques de l'histoire de France au Moyen Age 10 (Paris, 1964), no. 6, I, pp. 52–4; English trans. G. W. Regenos, *The letters of Lupus of Ferrières* (The Hague, 1966), p. 18. Walafrid Strabo, in his preface to Einhard's Life of Charlemagne, on the other hand, has a more positive view about the importance of first-hand experience as a guarantee of accuracy: O. Holder-Egger (ed.), *Vita Karoli magni, MGH SRG*, VI (1911), pp. XXVIII–XXIX.

[33] Lupus, ed. Levillain, *Loup de Ferrières*, nos. 6, 8, 9, 33, 35, 46, 101, 104; I, pp. 52–4, 68, 78, 152, 156, 196; II, pp. 124, 130.

[34] He praises it in a letter to Einhard, *Ibid.*, no. 1, I, p. 4.   [35] See above, chapter 9.

Various Carolingian libraries had different emphases. In some, contemporary Frankish history or Jewish and Christian history predominated. In others, Roman history books are more numerous. Particular histories became part of the canon of required knowledge. They are recorded in the extant library catalogues of the ninth century and listed in the standard bibliographical guides of Jerome-Gennadius, *De viris illustribus* and Cassiodorus' *Institutiones*, used by the Franks.[36]

Thus it is a fairly straightforward matter to document the existence of history books in the Carolingian world, the concentrations of texts or categories of history book in particular libraries and the production of new copies of older histories.

From the citations of examples from, and use made of histories by, other authors, as well as from ninth-century annotations in the manuscripts of those history books which I have been able to examine so far, moreover, it is quite clear that history books were read. The reading and ownership of history books was not confined to monasteries. The famous libraries of the Frankish lay aristocrats Eberhard of Friuli and Eccard of Mâcon are cases in point. Eberhard bequeathed to his son Berengar, later to become king of Italy and even, in 915, emperor, a *Gesta francorum*, a *Gesta pontificum romanorum* and Orosius' *Seven books of history against the pagans*. In his will, Eccard gave to Bishop Ansegis of Sens his copies of Paul the Deacon's *Historia langobardorum*, and Gregory of Tours' *Historiae*, which recounted the deeds of the Frankish kings to the end of the sixth century.[37] History was not read simply to acquire knowledge. Historical works, such as the *Chronicle* dedicated to the young Charles the Bald by Freculf of Lisieux, were suitable for the education of young princes.[38] Kings were exhorted to read history for inspiration. For King Charles the Bald of the west Franks it was the deeds of the Roman emperors: as Lupus of Ferrières wrote to him in 844:

I have had a very brief summary of the deeds of the emperors [probably a reference to the *Epitome* of Aurelius Victor] presented to your majesty so that you may readily observe from their actions what you should imitate or what you should avoid. I especially commend to your consideration, however, Trajan and

---

[36] I document the creation of a canon of knowledge in the Carolingian period in McKitterick, *Carolingians and the written word*, pp. 165–210.

[37] Eberhard's will: I. de Coussemaker (ed.), *Cartulaire de l'abbaye de Cysoing et de ses dépendances* (Lille, 1885), p. 3; Eccard's will: M. Prou and A. Vidier (eds.), *Recueil des chartes de l'abbaye de Saint-Benoît-sur-Loire*, Documents publiés par la Société historique et archéologique du Gâtinais 5 (Paris, 1907), I, p. 59. See P. Riché, Les bibliothèques de trois aristocrates laïcs carolingiens', *Le Moyen Âge* 69 (1963), pp. 87–104.

[38] J. L.Nelson, 'History writing at the courts of Louis the Pious and Charles the Bald', in Scharer and Scheibelreiter, *Historiographie*, pp. 435–42.

Theodosius, because you can most profitably find many things among their deeds to imitate.[39]

The interest in Roman history was also closely connected with the Roman imperial and early Christian past which Carolingian rulers undoubtedly sought to emulate. Yet Carolingian rulers, like all Franks, were also deeply familiar with biblical history with its spiritual message of God's revelation of himself to humanity and the more practical indication of God's hand in history for the benefit of kings. The Emperor Lothar, Louis the Pious's eldest son, for example, wrote to Hraban Maur, archbishop of Mainz, stating that he could not always take the entire wealth of commentaries, historical and allegorical, with him on all military campaigns, 'when it was often difficult enough to have merely the *bibliotheca historiarum* at hand'.[40] As Mayke de Jong has established, this *bibliotheca historiarum* is most probably a collection of Old Testament texts, possibly embedded in commentary. It is to be seen, moreover, in the context of Hraban Maur's voluminous exegesis on the historical books of the Old Testament written for or dedicated to a number of Carolingian kings and queens: commentaries on the four books of Kings for the Emperor Louis the Pious; on Chronicles and Maccabees for King Louis the German; on Joshua for the Emperor Lothar; and on Judith and Esther for the Empress Judith, with the volume on Judith also being dedicated later to Lothar's wife, the Empress Irmingard.[41]

If we simply document what history was read and by whom, in the Carolingian period, therefore, we open up the entire Judaeo-Greco-Roman past. To that should be added the Franks' own records of their history and such early medieval authors as Jordanes on the Goths, Paul the Deacon on the Lombards, Bede on the English and Gregory of Tours on the Franks.[42] These were quite clearly accessible to the literate and educated, whether laymen and laywomen, or clerics. They were a source of inspiration, edification, information and entertainment. The Franks' reading would encourage them to see their past not just as an immediate past but placed in the context of human history since the Creation.

The perception of time itself is also crucial. This did not come only from history books but was also imparted in the course of the arithmetical

---

[39] Lupus, ed. Levillain, *Loup de Ferrières*, no. 37, I, p. 164; English translation, Regenos, *The letters of Lupus of Ferrières*, no. 37, p. 55.

[40] Hraban Maur, *Epistolae*, ed. E. Dümmler, *MGH Epp.*, V (Berlin, 1899), no. 49, p. 503, lines 38–51.

[41] Mayke de Jong, 'The empire as *ecclesia*: Hrabanus Maurus and biblical *historia* for rulers', in Hen and Innes (eds.), *Uses of the past*, pp. 191–226.

[42] See Walter Goffart, *The narrators of barbarian history (A.D. 550–800): Jordanes, Gregory of Tours, Bede, and Paul the Deacon* (Princeton, 1988).

instruction and time reckoning within the Carolingian school curriculum known as *computus*. As we have seen in chapter 4 above, one of the objects of such instruction was to enable students to draw up calendars and calculate the date of Easter in advance. On the other hand, Frankish authors of the Carolingian period had shown a marked preference for dating according to the year of the Incarnation in their contemporary annals, even while using an administrative sequence of regnal years for dating documents, experiencing liturgical and cyclical time throughout the year and charting cyclical time in their calendars and necrologies. Perceptions of time could overlap. One reader at least of Bede's *On the reckoning of time* in northern Francia added Christian era dates where appropriate in the margin of his copy, now in London, and a Fulda copy of Bede's Reckoning of time juxtaposed the short contemporary annals of Fulda, Easter tables, and Bede's text with its world history.[43]

The implicit placing of a people within the chronology of world history is not peculiar to the Franks. Within the Byzantine historiographical tradition of the eastern Mediterranean, the correct calculation and interpretation of Byzantine events explicitly within this wider chronological context is of crucial importance. Both traditions arguably developed out of the reception and extension of the *Chronicle* of Eusebius.[44] In terms of placing in time, there are also many interesting comparisons to be drawn with the Islamic historiographical tradition. It has been claimed that the Islamic historiographical tradition had a unique preference for concentrating on the activities of mankind over a specific space of time, though such a claim makes little sense if early Islamic historiography is compared with aspects of the western tradition in the same period.[45] Nevertheless, the extraordinary range of historical texts (narratives, cartularies, *Libri vitae*, martyrologies, law collections) created by the Franks, their concentrated activity in assembling and copying the histories of Roman antiquity, of the early Christian church and of the barbarian successor states to Rome, and their own contemporary annals, are strikingly distinctive in comparison with their contemporaries in Byzantium and Anglo-Saxon England.

[43] British Library, Cotton Vespasian B,VI. and Kassel, Gesamthochschulbibliothek, 2o Ms astron.2.
[44] See B. Croke, 'The early development of Byzantine chronicles', in E. Jeffreys (ed.), *Studies in John Malalas*, Byzantina Australiensia 6 (Sydney, 1990) pp. 27–8.
[45] See A. al-D. al-Duri, *The rise of historical writing among the Arabs*, ed. and trans. L. Conrad (Princeton, 1983), p. 75. But see also A. Noth, *The early Arabic historical tradition: a source critical study*. 2nd edn in collaboration with L. Conrad, trans. M. Bonner (Princeton, 1994); F. Donner, *Narratives of Islamic origins. The beginnings of Islamic historical writing*, Studies in Late Antiquity and Early Islam 14 (Princeton, 1998); and C. H. Robinson, *Islamic historiography* (Cambridge, 2003).

In Byzantium in the eighth and ninth centuries there is almost a complete dearth of historical writing, let alone either historical works that can be associated with the court or which recount the deeds of the rulers. Nor is there the enormous variety of historical and chronologically ordered work such as we find in the Carolingian realms. Not only is there little evidence for the preservation or dissemination of the works of the ancient historians, there is very little in the way of historical writing from the middle Byzantine period. The composition of classicising histories had ceased in Byzantium by the middle of the seventh century.[46] Although there are some historical texts produced in the eighth and ninth centuries, the supposed 'renewed interest' in history does not amount to very much compared with the Franks' concentrated activity.[47] There are some 'succinct chronologies': the *Chronographikon syntomon* of Nicephorus, and the Chronicle of Theophanes covering the years 284–813 and continued to 842 by George the monk in the 870s.[48] It is not until the tenth century that historical works under imperial patronage, as well as independent narratives, are produced. Jonathan Shepard has discussed why the maintenance of a continuous historical record up to the present (such as we are accustomed to finding in the Frankish texts) does not seem to have been a high priority for the members of the Byzantine establishment in the eighth and ninth centuries. He suggests that Byzantium had no incentive to assert the continuity of the empire or its manifest destiny in the form of officially sponsored annals or historical narratives. He associates the fall-off in history writing with the loss of the eastern provinces, the Byzantines' change to a defensive strategy, and the confining of the likely readership to the capital. In the middle Byzantine period, diplomacy served to maintain the *status quo*: there was no pressing political need for a general rewriting of history or for triumphalist narratives. In other words, the Byzantines simply lacked the same incentives that drove the Franks to create historical records.[49] In the tenth century a new sense

---

[46] See B. Croke and A. Emmet, 'Historiography in late antiquity: an overview', in B. Croke and A. Emmet (eds.), *History and historians in late antiquity* (Sydney, 1983), pp. 1–12; M. Whitby, 'Greek historical writing after Procopius: variety and vitality', in A. Cameron and L. I. Conrad (eds.), *Studies in late antiquity and early Islam*, I, *The Byzantine and early Islamic near east*, 1, *Problems in the literary source material* (Princeton, 1992), pp. 25–80.

[47] C. Mango, 'The tradition of Byzantine chronography', *Harvard Ukrainian Studies* 12/13 (1988/9), pp. 360–72; and I. Sevčenko, 'The search for the past in Byzantium around the year 800', *Dumbarton Oaks Papers* 46 (1992), pp. 279–93.

[48] See C. Mango and R. Scott, *The Chronicle of Theophanes Confessor. Byzantine and near eastern history AD 284–813* (Oxford, 1997).

[49] J. Shepard, 'The uses of "history" in Byzantine diplomacy: observations and comparisons', in C. Dendrinos, J. Harris, E. Harvalia-Crook and J. Herrin (eds.), *Porphyrogenita. Essays on the history and literature of Byzantium and the Latin east in honour of Julian Chrysostomides* (Aldershot, 2003), pp. 91–115.

of the past informs the 'Macedonian Renaissance', which appears to have been a conscious reappropriation of the world of late antiquity and the models provided by Constantine and Justinian.[50] The focus of attention also appears to shift to the individual biography, and the emergence of what Athanasios Markoupoulos has called the 'professional writers in the service of the powerful'.[51]

The evidence of Anglo-Saxon historical writing in the eighth and ninth centuries is a little more substantial than for Byzantium and it takes familiar forms. There is, nevertheless, very little historical narrative material (not even saints' Lives after *c.* 800) that can be dated between the completion of Bede's *Historia ecclesiastica gentis anglorum* in the first half of the eighth century and the compilation of the *Anglo-Saxon Chronicle* and Asser's Life of King Alfred at the end of the ninth century.[52] From north Wales there is the *Historia brittonum*, a Chronicle running from the Creation to the 680s, and usually dated *c.* 829 or 830, but it is only known in later redactions.[53] Blaming the absence of ninth-century historical writing on the Vikings is hardly persuasive, for it is far too convenient for the Vikings to have been so selective in their destruction and to have left seventh-, eighth- and late ninth-century material relatively unscathed. Claims about the Viking impact on ninth-century English culture rest in any case on the possibly mistaken assumption that there was much to destroy. There are some genealogies.[54] There is also an indication of Northumbrian annals being compiled until *c.* 802. Given the possible connection with Alcuin, these 'Northern' annals in themselves might

---

[50] P. Magdalino 'The history of the future and its uses: prophecy, policy and propaganda', in R. Beaton and C. Roueché (eds.), *The making of Byzantine history. Studies dedicated to Donald M. Nicol* (Aldershot,1993), pp. 3–34; P. Magdalino, 'The distance of the past in early medieval Byzantium (VII–X centuries)', in *Ideologie e pratiche del reimpiego nell'alto medioevo*, Settimane 46 (Spoleto, 1999), I, pp. 115–146; and P. Magdalino, 'A history of Byzantine literature for historians, in *Pour une "nouvelle" histoire de la littérature byzantine. Actes du colloque philologique Nicosie, 25–28 mai 2000*, Dossiers byzantins 1 (Paris, 2002), pp. 167–84.

[51] A. Markopoulos, 'Byzantine history writing at the end of the first millennium', in P. Magdalino (ed.), *Byzantium in the year 1000*, The Medieval Mediterranean: Peoples, Economies and Cultures, 400–1500, 45 (Leiden, 2003), pp. 183–98.

[52] On historiography at the court of King Alfred, see A. Scharer, *Herrschaft und Repräsentation. Studien zur Hofkultur Königs Alfreds des Großen*, MIÖG Ergänzungsband 36 (Vienna and Munich, 2000), especially pp. 49–108; and A. Scharer, 'The writing of history at King Alfred's court', *EME* 5 (1996), pp. 177–206.

[53] D. N. Dumville, '*Historia brittonum*; an insular history from the Carolingian age', in Scharer and Scheibelreiter (eds.), *Historiographie*, pp. 406–34.

[54] D. N. Dumville, 'Kingship, genealogies and regnal lists', in P. Sawyer and I. N. Wood (eds.), *Early medieval kingship* (Leeds, 1977), pp. 72–104; and 'The Anglian collection of royal genealogies and regnal lists', *Anglo-Saxon England* 14 (1985), pp. 23–50. See also C. R. Davis, 'Cultural assimilation in the Anglo-Saxon royal genealogies', *Anglo-Saxon England* 21 (1992), pp. 23–36.

have been influenced by Frankish annal writing. This is in addition to the signs of connections between Francia and England in the assembly of news and the compilation of the 'York annals' (an account of the years 732–802) or 'First set of Northern annals' to which Joanna Story has drawn attention.[55]

Frankish influence in England is also strong in the ninth century, and may be behind the compilation of the Durham *Liber vitae* (*c.* 840), as well as the composite set of annals that forms what is known as the *Anglo-Saxon Chronicle*. This is associated with the court of the royal house of Wessex *c.* 890 and was written in English.[56] Although the gathering of momentum in the *Anglo-Saxon Chronicle*'s entries at the end of the eighth century coincides with the production of the *Annales regni francorum* and other Frankish annals, its narrative strikes the reader as a strong and very particular vision of history from the vantage point of late ninth-century Wessex. It has a triumphalist agenda and a very clear political and ideological message about the pre-eminence of the kings of Wessex to communicate.

It remains conceivable that the account in the *Anglo-Saxon Chronicle* of the early developments of the Anglo-Saxon kingdoms draws in some way on earlier and now lost source material relating to Kent, Sussex, Mercia and Wessex. Just as we saw in the case of the Frankish annals, however, that a set of annals chooses to start in the early 700s is no guarantee of the original record dating from thence. The probable means by which the *Chronicle* was circulated, with a multiplication of copies emanating initially from the court and each copy then providing a basis for further continuations in particular localities, offers many parallels to what we have seen of the dissemination of the *Annales regni francorum*. Similarly, later authors drew on it. Asser, in his *Vita Alfredi regis*, for example, drew on the *Anglo-Saxon Chronicle*, just as Einhard drew in his *Vita Karoli* on the *Annales regni francorum*.

The manuscript evidence for the copying of older histories accords with the meagre amount of literary evidence in indicating that there was simply not the widespread and actively creative interest in the past that we have observed from the Frankish realms.[57] There are no surviving copies of historical texts written in Anglo-Saxon England between the

---

[55] J. Story, *Carolingian connections: Anglo-Saxon England and Carolingian Francia, c. 750–870* (Aldershot, 2003), pp. 93–134.

[56] *Anglo-Saxon Chronicle*, manuscript A, ed. J. Bately, *The Anglo-Saxon Chronicle: a collaborative edition* 3 (Cambridge, 1986); J. Bately, *The Anglo-Saxon Chronicle: texts and textual relationships*, Reading Medieval Studies Monograph 3 (Reading, 1991).

[57] H. Gneuss, *Handlist of Anglo-Saxon manuscripts: a list of manuscripts and manuscript fragments written or owned in England up to 1100* (Tempe, Arizona, 2001). Gneuss records, nos. 2.2 and 137, a ninth-century (second quarter) copy of the *Historia tripartita* from

eighth and the tenth centuries apart from a ninth-century copy of Bede's *Historia ecclesiastica gentis anglorum*. There is nothing to compare with the concentrated copying activity of Roman, early Christian, barbarian or papal history that we have observed on the continent.

In contrast to Byzantium and Anglo-Saxon England, the sense of historical and chronological place also resulted in consistent and constant reference to past biblical and Roman imperial precedent and inspiration in every sphere of public life, notably in the legislation of the Carolingian kings.[58] The approach and frame of reference of many Frankish intellectual enterprises was fundamentally historical. At Fulda it is particularly to be associated with Hraban Maur, abbot of Fulda (824–42) and archbishop of Mainz (847–56). He, like Lupus of Ferrières, provides an indication of one Frank's sense of history. The writing of contemporary history at Fulda integrated local events into the history of the Frankish empire as a whole.[59] It was also under Hraban's aegis that a dossier for the life of Boniface, the English archbishop of Mainz in the eighth century, a key figure in Fulda's history, was compiled. An earlier bishop of Mainz, Lull, had commissioned the *Vita* by Willibald and prepared a collection of Boniface's letters in two groups, represented in two extant manuscripts.[60] A third collection of letters, extant in Vienna, ÖNB cod. 751, is attributed to Hraban Maur's interest. Further it was Hraban who devised a Martyrology, organised in historical sequence and with careful details supplied as to when and where each martyr had lived.[61]

All this contributes to a more general phenomenon of the reception of a host of ideas and their precise location in time and space right across the

north-east France (in fact a fragment thereof), now Winchester Cathedral Library MS. XXV (formerly Brockenhurst [Hants] Parish register) and an excerpt from Eusebius-Rufinus *Historia ecclesiastica* in a codex of the second third of the ninth century from 'E. France' now Cambridge, Pembroke College MS 108, but there is no indication of when they might have arrived in England.

[58] See, for example, J. L. Nelson, 'Translating images of authority: the Christian Roman emperors in the Carolingian world', in M. M. Mackenzie and C. Roueché, *Images of authority. Papers presented to Joyce Reynolds on the occasion of her 70th birthday*, Proceedings of the Cambridge Philological Society, Supplementary volume, 16 (Cambridge, 1989), pp. 194–205; reprinted in J. L. Nelson, *The Frankish world, 750–900* (London, 1996), pp. 89–98; and M. Garrison, 'The Franks as the new Israel? Education for an identity from Pippin to Charlemagne', in Hen and Innes (eds.), *Uses of the past*, pp. 114–161.

[59] For historical writing at Fulda see also Richard Corradini, *Die Wiener Handschrift Cvp 430*. *Ein Beitrag zur Historiographie in Fulda im frühen 9. Jahrhundert*, Fuldaer Hochschulschriften 37 (Frankfurt am Main, 2000).

[60] Munich, Bayerische Staatsbibliothek Clm 8112, a copy of an original collection, dating from the end of the eighth century copied at Mainz, and probably at Fulda by the eleventh century. A second collection, represented by Karlsruhe, Badische Landesbibliothek Rastatt 22, was also produced on Lull's commissioning, compiled at Mainz and a copy of it made at Fulda.

[61] *Rabani Mauri Martyrologium*, ed. J. McCulloh, CCCM, XLIV (Turnhout, 1979).

Carolingian empire. Historical consciousness is manifest in the creation of many new kinds of book and new categories of historical text in which historical orientation is a guiding principle.

Although I have so far concentrated on the placing in time and on the presentation and interpretation of events, one further issue needs to be addressed. This is the role of history in the formation of the identity of its audiences. Many of the histories I have mentioned in this book concern, or are interpreted to concern, the Frankish people. I have highlighted the vigorous image-building of the authors of the *Annales regni francorum* and the way in which the Trojans are invoked as ancestors of the Franks in the *Liber historiae francorum*. I have emphasised the role of such historical associations in the formation of identity.[62] I have also considered how local history and local commemoration, both essential elements of local identities and senses of belonging, fitted into a wider perception of the past, the present and eternity. In this respect the Carolingian cartularies and *Libri vitae* have proved of crucial importance. The cartularies served as a memorial and record of associations, personal friendships and obligations. Their record of all the places of importance to the abbeys who preserved these documents, however small, meant that a sense of the history of the community was built into the legal and memorial functions of each charter collection. They are thus very specific expressions of a community's identity. In the Carolingian cartularies there was a conjunction of an historical sense of the past, attachment to geographical place, commemoration, record and writing. They represent written forms other than narrative in which the past was remembered and commemorated. Their audience was the community whose memories and affairs they recorded.

A more obviously commemorative text was the *Liber vitae*, first produced in the Carolingian period, which I interpreted as history books of a very particular kind. The *Libri memorialis* of Remiremont can be recognised as an embodiment of the effort to pray for a living community and the souls of the dead, as a preserver of collective memory and as very special rendition of the past of the community as a whole. In addition, the Salzburg *Liber vitae* demonstrated how the distinctive historical record represented by a confraternity book can reflect not only cultural assumptions but also specific political affiliations and social communities. In its juxtaposition of the ancient biblical as well as early Christian past with Salzburg's present, the community was also placed in the longer perspective of Christian history. The Salzburg book constitutes, therefore, an expression of both local and of universal identity. *Libri vitae*, such as

---

[62] M. Innes, 'Teutons or Trojans? The Carolingians and the Germanic past', in Innes and Hen (eds.), *Uses of the past*, pp. 227–49.

these two from Remiremont and Salzburg, mirror the interplay between audience, memory, forms of historical record and the writing of history. Prayers for the dead, the *Libri vitae*, *Libri memoriales* and the Carolingian cartularies provide an immediate conjunction between past and present time, in that the dead are remembered in terms of the commemoration of their anniversaries and their benefactions in the present. Such texts also convey a very particular sense of the historical past in which chronology and place in time have crucial roles to play.

History has many manifestations and as many audiences. For the Franks an understanding of the past worked at several levels and was manifested to them in a number of different textual contexts. A sense of the past could express a much more general cultural affiliation and identity within which a sense of time and chronology played a role. As we have seen in this book, the Franks' sense of the past was a composite one. Alternatively one might need to think in terms of different overlapping sequences: of different local and institutional senses of identity expressed in terms of their own communities' foundations, property, associations, dead members and others remembered with some association with a particular place, and of benefactors; of the chronological progression of Jewish and Christian history; of being heirs of both imperial and Christian Rome; of their own sense of achievement as Franks, expanding ever eastwards and imposing their own composite culture on others. A wider knowledge and understanding of the past created an essential interdependence of the history and memory of the Franks in the Carolingian world. A sense of the past was deeply integrated into the sense of identity possessed by the audiences for history in the Carolingian world. The Franks defined themselves in terms of their history.

Bibliography

PRIMARY SOURCES

Abbo of St Germain-des-Prés, *De bello parisiaco*, ed. H. Waquet, *Abbon: le siège de Paris par les normands* (Paris, 1964)

Actus pontificium cenomannis in urbe degentium, ed. G. Busson and A. Ledru, Archives historiques du Maine 2 (Le Mans, 1901)

Admonitio generalis, ed. A Boretius, *MGH Cap.*, I (Hannover, 1883), pp. 52–62

Aethicus Ister, *Cosmographia*, ed. O. Prinz, *Die Cosmographie des Aethicus, MGH Quellen zur Geistesgeschichte des Mittelalters* 14 (Munich, 1993)

Alcuin, *Disputatio de rhetorica et de virtutibus sapientissimi regis Karli et Albini magistri*, ed. and trans. W. S. Howell, *The Rhetoric of Alcuin and Charlemagne* (Princeton, 1941)

Alcuin, *Versus de patribus, regibus et sanctis euboricensis ecclesiae*, ed. and trans. P. Godman, *The bishops, kings and saints of York* (Oxford, 1982)

Andrew of Bergamo, *Historia*, ed. G. Waitz, *MGH SRL* (Hannover, 1878)

Angelbert, *Versus de bella quae fuit acta fontaneto*, ed. E. Dümmler, *MGH Poetae*, II, (Berlin, 1884), pp. 138–9

Agnellus of Ravenna, *Liber pontificalis ecclesiae Ravennatis*, ed. O. Holder-Egger, *MGH SRL* (Hannover, 1878), pp. 265–391

Anglo-Saxon Chronicle, ed. B. Thorpe, Rolls Series (London, 1861), English trans. G. N. Garmonsway (London, 1953); and *Anglo-Saxon Chronicle*, manuscript A, ed. J. Bately, *The Anglo-Saxon Chronicle: a collaborative edition* III (Cambridge, 1986)

Annales Bertiniani, ed. G. Waitz, *MGH SRG*, V (Hannover, 1883); ed. R. Rau, *Quellen zur karolingischen Reichsgeschichte* II (Darmstadt, 1972); and eds. F. Grat, J. Vielliard and C. Clémencet, *Annales de Saint-Bertin* (Paris, 1964); English trans. J. L. Nelson, *The Annals of Saint-Bertin* (Manchester, 1991)

Annales flaviniacenses et lausonenses, ed. G. Pertz, *MGH SS* III (Hannover, 1839), pp. 149–52

Annales fuldenses, ed. F. Kurze, *MGH SRG*, VII (Hannover, 1891); ed. with German trans. R. Rau, *Quellen zur karolingischen Reichsgeschichte* III (Darmstadt (1960), pp. 19–117; English trans. T. Reuter, *The annals of Fulda* (Manchester, 1992)

Annales laureshamenses, ed. G. Pertz, *MGH SS*, I (Hannover, 1826), pp. 22–39; ed. E. Katz, *Annalium laureshamensium editio emendate secandum codicem St. Paulensum*, Separatabdruck vom Jahresbericht des Öffentlichen Stifts-Untergymnasium der Benedictiner zu St Paul (St Paul, 1889)

Annales mettenses priores, ed. B. von Simson, *MGH SRG*, X (Hannover and Leipzig, 1905)

Annales mosellani, ed. I. M. Lappenberg, *MGH SS*, XVI (Hannover, 1859), pp. 494–9

Annales regni francorum, ed. F. Kurze, *MGH SRG*, VI (Hannover, 1895); English trans. B. Scholz, *Carolingian Chronicles* (Ann Arbor, 1970)

Annales sancti Amandi, Tiliani, Laubacenses, Petaviani, ed. G. Pertz, *MGH SS*, I (Hannover, 1826), pp. 6–10

Annales vedastini, ed. B. von Simson, *MGH SRG*, XII (Hannover, 1909)

Annales xantenses, ed. B. von Simson, *MGH SRG*, XII (Hannover, 1909)

Annals of Inisfallen, ed. S. MacAirt (Dublin, 1951)

Annals of the kingdom of Ireland by the four masters, ed. J. O'Donovan, 7 vols. (Dublin, 1851)

Annals of Ulster, I, ed. S. MacAirt and G. MacNiocaill (Dublin, 1985)

Arbeo of Freising, *Vita Corbiniani*, ed. F. Brunhölzl, H. Glaser and S. Benker, *Vita Corbiniani, Bischof Arbeo von Freising und die Lebensgeschichte des hl. Korbinian* (Munich, 1983)

Arbeo of Freising, *Vita Haimhrammi episcopi*, ed. B. Krusch, *MGH SRG*, XIII (Hannover, 1920); ed. B. Bischoff, *Arbeo, Vita et passio Haimhrammi Martyris: Leben und Leiden des hl. Emmeram* (Munich, 1953)

Ardo, *Vita Benedicti abbatis anianensis*, ed. G. Waitz, *MGH SS*, XV, 1 (Hannover, 1887), pp. 200–20

Asser, *Vita Alfredi regis*, ed. W. H. Stevenson, *Life of King Alfred* (Oxford, 1904), repr. by D. Whitelock (Oxford, 1959); English trans. S. Keynes and M. Lapidge, *Alfred the Great, Asser's Life of King Alfred and other contemporary sources* (Harmondsworth, 1983), pp. 67–110

Astronomer, *Vita Hludowici imperatoris*, ed. E. Tremp, *MGH SRG*, LXIV (Hannover, 1995); English trans. A. Cabaniss, *Son of Charlemagne* (Syracuse, N.Y., 1961)

Bede: ed. C. W. Jones, *Bedae opera didascalica*, 2, *CCSL*, CXXIIIB (Turnhout, 1977); ed. T. Mommsen, *Chronica minora*, 3, *MGH AA*, XIII (Hannover, 1898), pp. 247–327; English trans. F. Wallis, *Bede: the reckoning of time* (Liverpool, 1999)

Bede, *Historia abbatum*, ed. C. Plummer, *Venerabilis Bedae opera historica* (Oxford, 1896)

Bede, *Historia ecclesiastica gentis anglorum*, ed. and trans. B. Colgrave and R. A. B. Mynors, *Bede's ecclesiastical history of the English people*, Oxford Medieval Texts (Oxford, 1969); facsimile ed. P. Hunter-Blair, *The Moore Bede*, Early English Manuscripts in Facsimile 9 (Copenhagen, London and Baltimore, 1959)

Benedict of Nursia, *Rule of Benedict*, ed. and English trans. J. McCann (1952)

Brescia, San Salvatore: ed. A. Valentini, *Codice necrologico-liturgico del monasterio di S. Salvatore o S. Giulia in Brescia* (Brescia, 1887)

Brescia, San Salvatore: ed. D. Geuenich, and U. Ludwig, *Der Memorial- und Liturgiecodex von San Salvatore/Santa Giulia in Brescia, MGH Libri memoriales et necrologia, nova series*, 4 (Hannover, 2000)

Breves notitiae, ed. F. Losek, '*Notitia arnonis* und *Breves notitiae*', *Mitteilungen der Gesellschaft für Salzburger Landeskunde* 130 (1990), pp. 5–192

Capitularia regum francorum, ed. A. Boretius and V. Krause, *MGH Leges sectio* 3, 2 vols. (Hannover, 1883–97)

Capitularia: ed. C. Azzara and P. Moro, *I capitolari italici. Storia e diritto della dominazione carolingia in Italia* (Rome, 1998)

Cartularium saxonicum, ed. W. Birch (Oxford, 1885)

Cassiodorus, *Institutiones*, ed. R. A. B. Mynors, *Cassiodorus senatoris institutiones* (Oxford, 1937); English trans. L. W. Jones, *Cassiodorus Senator: an introduction to divine and human readings* (New York, 1946)

Cassiodorus, see also under Epiphanius

Catalogi bibliothecarum antiqui, ed. G. Becker (Bonn, 1886)

Catalogi: ed. P. Lehmann, *Mittelalterliche Bibliothekskataloge Deutschlands und der Schweiz, I, Die Bistümer Konstanz und Chur* (Munich, 1918)

Chronicle of 754, ed. E. López, *Cronica mozarabe de 754: edición critica y traducción* (Zaragoza, 1980)

Chronicle of Alphonso III, ed. J. Giull Fernández, J. L. Moralejo and J. Ruiz de la Peña, *Crónicas Asturianas* (Oviedo, 1985)

Chronicon aquitanicum, ed. G. Pertz, *MGH SS*, II (Hannover, 1829)

Chronicon centulense, see under Hariulf

Chronicon laurissense breve, ed. H. Schnorr von Carolsfeld, 'Das Chronicon Laurissense breve', *Neues Archiv* 36 (1911), pp. 13–39

Chronicon moissiacensis, ed. G. Pertz, *MGH SS*, II (Hannover, 1829), pp. 282–313

Clausula de unctione Pippini, ed. B. Krusch, *MGH SRM*, I (Hannover, 1885); English trans. B. Pullan, *Sources for the history of medieval Europe from the mid-eighth to the mid-thirteenth century* (Oxford, 1966), pp. 7–8; and ed. A. Stoclet, 'La "Clausula de unctione Pippini regis"', *Francia* 8 (1980), pp. 1–40

Codex epistolaris carolinus, ed. W. Gundlach, *MGH Epp.* III (Hannover, 1892); facsimile ed. F. Unterkircher, *Codex epistolaris Carolinus*, Codices selecti 3 (Graz, 1962)

Codex lauershamensis, ed. K. Glöckner, Arbeiten der historischen Kommission für den Volkstaat Hessen 3, 3 vols. (Darmstadt, 1929–36)

Collectio canonum hibernensis, ed. F. W. H. Wasserschleben, *Die irische Kanonen-sammlung*, 2nd edn (Leipzig, 1885)

Collectio canonum Remedio Curiensis episcopi perperam ascripta, ed. H. John, *Monumenta Iuris Canonici*, ser. B: Corpus Collectionum 2 (Vatican City, 1976)

Collectio concilii secundi Arelatensis, ed. C. Munier, *Concilia Gallia A. 314–A. 506*, *CCSL* CXLVIII (Turnhout, 1963), pp. 111–30

Collectio dacheriana, ed. L. d'Achery and L. F. J. Le Barre, *Spicilegium sive collectio veterum aliquot scriptorum qui in Galliae bibliothecis delituerant*, I (Paris, 1723)

Collectio Dionysio-Hadriana, ed. J. Hartzheim, *Concilia Germania*, I (Cologne, 1759)

Collectio herovalliana, *PL*, LVI, cols. 11–354

Collectio hispana et Collectio hispana systematica, ed. G. Martinez Diez, La Coleccion canonica hispana (Madrid, 1966)

Collectio quesnelliana, *PL*, LVI, cols. 359–74

Collectio sangermanensis, ed. A. J. Nürnberger, 'Über eine ungedruckte Kanonessammlung aus dem 8. Jahrhundert', *Bericht der Wissenschaftlichen Gesellschaft Philomathie in Neisse vom Oktober 1888 zum Oktober 1890* (Neisse, 1890), pp. 125–97

Collectio veronensis, ed. E. Schwartz, *Publizistische Sammlungen zum Acacianischen Schisma*, Abhandlungen der bayerischen Akademie der Wissenschaften phil.-hist. Abteilung, Neue Folge 10 (Munich, 1934)

Collectio vetus gallica, ed. H. Mordek, *Kirchenrecht und Reform im Frankenreich* (Berlin, 1975)

Columbanus, *Epistulae*, ed. G. S. M. Walker, *Sancti Columbani opera*, Scriptores Latini Hiberniae 2 (Dublin, 1970)

Concilia: ed. C. Munier, *Concilia africae, a. 345–a. 535, CCSL* CXLIX (Turnhout, 1974)

Concilia: ed. W. Hartmann, *Die Konzilien der karolingische Teilreiche 843–859*, *MGH Conc.*, III, *Concilia aevi Karolini 843–859* (Hannover, 1984)

Conversio bagoariorum et carantanorum, ed. H. Wolfram (Vienna, 1979)

Council of Aachen 809: ed. H. Willjung, *Das Konzil von Aachen 809, MGH Conc.*, II, Supp. 2 (Hannover, 1998)

De ratione computandi, ed. D. Ó. Cróinín and M. Walsh, Studies and Texts (Toronto, 1988)

Dionysius Exiguus, ed. H. Wurm, *Studien und Text zur Dekretalsammlung des Dionysius Exiguus*, Kanonistische Studien und Texte 16 (Bonn, 1939; reprinted Amsterdam, 1964)

Diplomata: ed. E. Mühlbacher, *MGH Diplomatum Karolinorum*, I, *Pippini, Carlomanni, Caroli magni diplomata* (Munich, 1979)

Divisio regnorum (806), ed. A. Boretius, *MGH Cap.* (Hannover, 1883), I no. 45, pp. 126–30; English trans. P. D. King, *Charlemagne. Translated sources* (Kendal, 1987), pp. 251–5

Durham: *Liber vitae ecclesiae dunelmensis*, ed. J. Stevenson, The Publications of the Surtees Society 136 (London, 1923)

Eberhard of Friuli's will, ed. I. de Coussemaker, *Cartulaire de l'abbaye de Cysoing et de ses dépendances* (Lille, 1885)

Eccard of Mâcon's will, eds. M. Prou and A. Vidier, *Recueil des chartes de l'abbaye de Saint-Benoît-sur-Loire*, Documents publiés par la Société historique et archéologique du Gâtinais V (Paris, 1900–7), I, p. 59

Eigil, *Vita Sturmi abbatis fuldensis*, ed. P. Engelbrecht, *Die Vita Sturmi des Eigils von Fulda: literarkritische-historische Untersuchung und Edition* (Marburg, 1968); English trans. C. H. Talbot, *The Anglo-Saxon Missionaries in Germany*, London (1954), pp. 181–202

Einhard, *Opera*, English trans. P. Dutton, *Charlemagne's courtier. The complete Einhard* (Peterborough, Ontario, 1998)

Einhard, *Translatio sanctorum Marcellini et Petri*, ed. G. Waitz, *MGH SS*, XV, 1 (Hannover, 1887), pp. 238–64

Einhard, *Vita Karoli*, ed. O. Holder-Egger, *MGH SRG*, XXV (Hannover, 1911); reprinted R. Rau (ed.), *Quellen zur karolingischen Reichsgeschichte*, I (Darmstadt, 1974); English trans. Paul E. Dutton, *Charlemagne's courtier. The complete Einhard* (Peterborough, Ontario, 1998)

Ekkehard IV, *Casus sancti galli*, ed. H. F. Haefele (Darmstadt, 1980)

Epiphanius: eds. W. Jacob and R. Hanslik, *Cassiodori-Epiphanii, Historia ecclesiastica tripartita, CSEL*, LXXI (Vienna, 1952)

Erchempert: ed. G. Waitz, *Historia langobardorum beneventana, MGH SRL* (Hannover, 1878)

Ermold the Black (Ermoldus Nigellus), *In honorem Hludovici pii christianissimi caesaris augusti*, ed. and trans. E. Farral, *Ermold le Noir: poème sur Louis le Pieux*, 2nd edn (Paris, 1964)

Eusebius-Rufinus, *Historia ecclesiastica*, eds. E. Schwartz and T. Mommsen, *Eusebius Werke*, II, *Die Kirchengeschichte*, ed. E. Schwartz, *Die lateinische Übersetzung des Rufinus*, ed. T. Mommsen, Die griechischen christlichen Schriftsteller der ersten drei Jahrhunderte: Eusebius 2, 1 and 2, 2, 2 vols. (Leipzig, 1903 and 1908); English trans. W. H. Freemantle, *Life and works of Rufinus with Jerome's apology against Rufinus*, A Select Library of Nicene and Post-Nicene Fathers 3 (Oxford and New York, 1890); and trans. P. R. Amidon, *The church history of Rufinus of Aquileia, books 10 and 11* (New York and Oxford, 1997)

Eutropius, *Breviarium*, ed. H. Droysen, *MGH AA*, II (Hannover, 1871); ed. F. Rühl, *Eutropii brevarium ab urbe condita* (Leipzig, 1887); ed. C. Santini, *Eutropii Brevarium ab urbe condita*, Bibliotheca Scriptorum Graecorum et Romanarum Teubneriana (Leipzig, 1979); and English trans. H. W. Bird, *The Brevarium ab urbe condita of Eutropius*, Translated Texts for Historians 14 (Liverpool, 1993)

Flavigny: ed. C. B. Bouchard, *The Cartulary of Flavigny 717–1113*, Medieval Academy Books 99 (Cambridge, Mass., 1991)

Flodoard of Rheims, *Historia remensis ecclesiae*, ed. J. Heller and G. Waitz, *MGH SS*, XIII (Hannover, 1881), pp. 405–599

Folcuin, *Gesta abbatum Lobiensium*, ed. G. Pertz, *MGH SS*, IV (Berlin, 1841), pp. 54–74

Folcuin, *Gesta abbatum sancti Bertini Sithiensium*, ed. J. Heller and G. Waitz, *MGH SS*, XIII (Hannover, 1881), pp. 600–35

Fredegar, *Chronicarum quae dicuntur Fredegari scholastici libri IV cum continuationibus*, ed. B. Krusch, *MGH SRM*, II, (Hannover, 1999), pp. 1–193; ed. and trans. J. M. Wallace-Hadrill, *The fourth book of the Chronicle of Fredegar and its Continuations* (London, 1962)

Freising: ed. T. Bitterauf, *Die Traditionen des Hochstifts Freising*, Quellen und Erörterungen zur bayerischen und deutschen Geschichte NF 4 and 5, 2 vols. (Munich, 1905)

Frotharius of Toul, *Epistolae*, ed. K. Hampe, *MGH Epp.*, V (Berlin, 1899), pp. 285–327; and M. Parisse (ed.), *La Correspondance d'un évêque carolingien. Frothaire de Toul (ca 813–847)* (Paris, 1998)

Fulda: E. F. J. Dronke, *Codex diplomaticus fuldensis* (Aalen, 1962 reprint of 1850 edition)

Fulda: E. E. Stengel (ed.) *Urkundenbuch des Klosters Fulda*, I, 1 (Marburg, 1913) and I, 2 (Marburg, 1956)

Genealogy: G. Pertz, *MGH SS*, II (Berlin, 1829), pp. 308–12

Gesta fontanellensis coenobii, ed. P. Pradié, *Chronique des abbés de Fontenelle (Saint-Wandrille)* (Paris, 1999); and *Gesta sanctorum patrum fontanellensis coenobii*, ed. F. Lohier and J. Laporte, *Mélanges de la société de l'histoire de Normandie* (Paris and Rouen, 1936)

Gesta pontificum autissiodorensium, eds. M. Goullet, G. Lobrichon and M. Sot, *Les Gestes des évêques d'Auxerre* (Paris, 2002)

Gregory of Tours, *De cursu stellarum*, ed. B. Krusch, *MGH SRM*, I (Hannover, 1885), pp. 854–72

Gregory, *Historiarum libri decem*, ed. B. Krusch, *MGH SRM*, I (Hannover, 1885), and revised R. Buchner (Darmstadt, 1977)

Hariulf, *Chronicon centulense*, ed. F. Lot, *Hariulf, Chronique de l'abbaye de Saint-Riquier Ve siècle–1104* (Paris, 1894)

Hegesippus, see under Josephus

Hilderic, *Epytaphium Pauli diaconi*, ed. G. Waitz, *Pauli Historia langobardorum*, *MGH SRG*, XLVIII (Hannover, 1878), pp. 15–16, and *MGH SRL* (Hannover, 1878), pp. 23–4

Hilduin of Saint-Denis, *Gesta Dagoberti*, ed. B. Krusch, *MGH SRM*, II (Hannover, 1888), pp. 396–425

Historia langobardorum beneventanorum, ed. G. Waitz, *MGH SRL* (Hannover, 1878)

Hodoeporicon, see under Hugeburc

Honorius Augustodunensis, *De luminaribus ecclesiae*, *PL*, CLXXII, cols. 197–234

Hotman, F., *Francogallia* (Geneva, 1573): *Francogallia by François Hotman*, ed. and trans. R. E. Giesey and J. H. M. Salmon (Cambridge, 1972)

Hraban Maur, *Epistolae*, ed. E. Dümmler, *MGH* Epp., V (Berlin, 1899)

Hraban Maur, ed. J. McCulloh, *Rabani Mauri martyrologium*, *CCCM*, XLIV (Turnhout, 1979)

Hugeburc of Heidenheim, *Hodoeporicon*, ed. O. Holder-Egger, *MGH SS*, XV, 1 (Hannover, 1887), pp. 86–117; English trans. C. H. Talbot, *The Anglo-Saxon missionaries in Germany* (London, 1954), pp. 152–77

Isidore of Seville, ed. C. C. Merino, *El 'De viris illustribus' de Isidoro de Sevilla. Estudio y edicion critica*, Theses et Studia philologica Salamanticensia 12 (Salamanca, 1964).

Isidore of Seville, *Etymologiae*, ed. W. M. Lindsay, *Isidori hispalensis episcopi, Etymologiarum sive originum libri XX* (Oxford, 1911)

Itineraria: ed. T. Tobler and A. Molinier, *Itineraria hierosolymitana*, I (Geneva 1879/80); ed. P. Geyer, *Itineraria et alia geographica*, *CCSL*, CXXV (Turnhout, 1965)

Jerome-Gennadius: ed. A. Ceresa-Gastaldo, *Gli uomini illustri = De viris illustribus* (Florence, 1988); ed. C. Bernouilli, *Hieronymus-Gennadius De viris illustribus* (Freiburg i. Br. and Leipzig, 1895); ed. E. C. Richardson, *Hieronymus, Liber de viris inlustribus. Gennadius de viris inlustribus*, Texte und Untersuchungen zur Geschichte der Altchristlichen Literatur (Leipzig, 1896); English trans. E. C. Richardson, *Theodoret, Jerome, Gennadius, Rufinus: historical writings*, in H. Wace and P. Schaff (eds.), A Select Library of Nicene and Post-Nicene Fathers of the Christian Church, second series, 3 (Oxford and New York, 1892)

John Skylitzes, *Synopsis historiarum*, ed. I. Thurn (Berlin and New York, 1973)

Jonas of Orléans, *De institutione regia*, ed. J. Reviron, *Les Idées politico-religieuses d'un évêque du IXe siècle: Jonas d'Orléans et son De institutione regia* (Paris, 1930), pp. 119–94

Josephus: ed. V. Ussani, *Hegessipi qui dicitur Historiae libri V*, *CSEL*, LXVI (Vienna, 1932);

Josephus, *Antiquitates*, ed. F. Blatt, *The Latin Josephus (Antiquitates lib. I–V)* (Aarhus and Copenhagen, 1958)

Landolfus Sagax, ed. A. Crivellucci, *Landolfo sagax Historia romana*, I (Rome, 1912)

Leo of Ostia and Peter the Deacon, *Chronica monasterii casinensis*, ed. H. Hoffmann, *MGH SS*, XXXIV (Hannover, 1980)

Lex alemannorum, ed. K. Lehmann, *MGH Legum sectio I. Leges nat. germ.*, V, 1 (Hannover, 1885)

Lex baiwariorum, ed. E. von Schwind, *MGH Leges nat. germ.* V, 2 (Hannover, 1926), pp. 198–203

Liber historiae francorum, ed. B. Krusch, *MGH SRM*, II (Hannover, 1888), pp. 241–328; reprinted in a revised edition by A. Kusternig under the direction of H. Wolfram, *Quellen zur Geschichte des 7. und 8. Jahrhunderts*, Ausgewählte Quellen zur deutschen Geschichte des Mittelalters 4a (Darmstadt, 1982); English trans. R. Gerberding, *The rise of the Carolingians and the 'Liber historiae francorum'* (Oxford, 1987), pp. 173–81

Liber pontificalis, ed. L. Duchesne, *Le Liber pontificalis texte, introduction et commentaire*, 2 vols. (Paris, 1886 and 1892); English trans. R. Davis, *The book of the pontiffs (Liber pontificalis to 715)* (Liverpool, 1990); *The lives of the eighth-century popes (Liber pontificalis)* (Liverpool, 1992); *The lives of the ninth-century popes (Liber pontificalis)* (Liverpool, 1995)

Liudger, *Vita Gregorii abbatis trajectensis*, ed. O. Holder-Egger, *MGH SS*, XV 1 (Hannover, 1887), pp. 66–79

Lorsch, ed. K. Glöckner, *Codex laureshamensis*, Arbeiten der historischen Kommission für den Volkstaat Hessen 3, 3 vols. (Darmstadt, 1929–36)

'Lorsch' annals: see under *Annales laureshamenses*

Lull, *Epistulae*, ed. M. Tangl, *Die Briefe des heiligen Bonifatius and Lullus*, *MGH Epp. Sel.*, I (Berlin, 1916)

Lupus of Ferrières: ed. with French trans. Leon Levillain, *Loup de Ferrières, Correspondance*, Les Classiques de l'histoire de France au moyen âge 10 (Paris, 1964); *Epistulae*, ed. P. K. Marshall (Leipzig, 1984); English trans. G. W. Regenos, *The letters of Lupus of Ferrières* (The Hague, 1966)

Martyrology of Tallaght, ed. R. I. Best and H. J. Lawlor (London, 1931)

Mondsee: ed. E. Rath and E. Reiter, *Das älteste Traditionsbuch des Klosters Mondsee*, Forschungen zur Geschichte Oberösterreichs 16 (Linz, 1989)

Murbach: W. Milde, *Der Bibliothekskataloge des Klosters Murbach aus dem 9. Jht. Ausgabe und Untersuchung von Beziehung zu Cassiodors Institutiones*. Beihefte zum *Euphorion. Zeitschrift für Literaturgeschichte* 34 (1968)

Nithard, *Historiarum libri IIII*, ed. E. Müller, *MGH SRG*, XLIV (Hannover, 1907); ed. R. Rau, *Quellen zur karolingischen Reichsgeschichte*, I (Darmstadt, 1974); French trans. P. Lauer, *Nithard. Histoire des fils de Louis le Pieux* (Paris, 1964); English trans. B. Scholz, *Carolingian Chronicles* (Ann Arbor, 1970)

Notker Balbulus: ed. E. Rauner, 'Notker des Stammlers "Notatio de illustribus viris"', *Mittellateinisches Jahrbuch* 21 (1986), pp. 34–69

Notker Balbulus: ed. E. Dümmler, *Das Formelbuch des Bischofs Salomo III von Konstanz* (1857, reprinted Osnabrück, 1974)

Notker Balbulus, *Gesta Karoli magni imperatoris*, ed. G. Pertz, *MGH SS*, II (Berlin, 1829), pp. 726–63; ed. H. F. Haefele, *MGH SRG*, n.s. 12 (Berlin, 1959); ed. and German trans. R. Rau, *Quellen zur karolingischen Reichsgeschichte*, III

(Darmstadt, 1975), pp. 322–426; English trans. L. Thorpe, *Two Lives of Charlemagne* (Harmondsworth, 1969)

Ordinatio imperii (817), ed. A. Boretius, *MGH Cap.*, I, no. 136, pp. 270–3; English trans. B. Pullan, *Sources for the history of medieval Europe* (Oxford, 1966), pp. 37–42

Origo gentis langobardorum. Introduzione, testo critico, commento, ed. A. Bracciotti, Biblioteca di cultura Romanobarbarica 2 (Roma, 1998)

Orosius: ed. C. Zangemeister, *Historiarum adversum paganos libri VII* (Leipzig, 1889); ed. M. P. Arnaud–Lindet, *Histoires (contre les païens) Orose*, 3 vols. (Paris, 1990–1); English trans. I. W. Raymond, *Seven books of history against the pagans*, Columbia Records of Civilization, Sources and Studies (New York, 1936); R. J. Deferrari, *Orosius, seven books of history against the pagans*, Fathers of the Church 50 (Washington, D.C., 1964); ed. J. Bately, *The Old English Orosius*, Early English Text Society SS 6 (Oxford, 1980)

Paul the Deacon, *Gesta episcoporum mettensium*, ed. G. Pertz, *Liber de episcopis mettensibus*, *MGH SS*, II (Berlin, 1829), pp. 260–8

Paul the Deacon, *Historia langobardorum*, ed. G. Waitz, *MGH SRL* (Hannover, 1878); English trans. W. D. Foulke, *Paul the Deacon, History of the Lombards* (Philadelphia, 1907); ed. with Italian trans. L. Capo, *Paolo Diacono Storia dei Longobardi* (Verona 1992)

Paul the Deacon, *Historia romana*, ed. A. Crivellucci, Fonti per la Storia d'Italia 51 (Rome, 1913)

Paulinus of Aquileia, ed. D. Norberg, *Paulini Aquileiensis opera omnia pars I: Contra felicem libri tres*, *CCCM*, XCV (Turnhout, 1990)

Rainogala and Alagus, *Gesta pontificum autissiodorensium*, ed. L. Duru, *Bibliothèque Historique de l'Yonne* (Auxerre, 1850), I, pp. 309–57; ed. G. Waitz, *MGH SS*, XIII (Hannover, 1881), pp. 394–400, and XXVI (Hannover, 1882), pp. 584–6; and see under *Gesta pontificum autissiodorensium*

Rau, R. (ed.), *Quellen zur karolingischen Reichsgeschichte*, 3 vols. (Darmstadt, 1972, 1974, 1975)

Regino of Prüm, *Chronicon*, ed. F. Kurze, *MGH SRG*, L (Hannover, 1890); ed. with German trans. R. Rau, *Quellen zur karolingischen Reichsgeschichte*, III (Darmstadt, 1975), pp. 180–318

Reichenau: J. Autenrieth, D. Geuenich and K. Schmid (eds.), *Das Verbrüderungsbuch der Abtei Reichenau*, *MGH Libri memoriales et necrologia, nova series* 1 (Hannover, 1979)

Remiremont, *Liber memorialis von Remiremont*, eds. E. Hlawitschka, K. Schmid and G. Tellenbach, *MGH Libri memoriales*, I (Munich, 1981)

Richer, *Historiae*, ed. H. Hoffmann, *Richer von Saint-Remi, Historiae*, *MGH SS*, XXXVIII (Hannover, 2000)

Rimbert, *Vita Anskarii*, ed. G. Waitz, *MGH SRG*, LV (Hannover, 1884); English trans. C. H. Robinson, *Anskar, the apostle of the north* (London, 1921)

Rudolf of Fulda, *Vita sanctae Liobae*, ed. G. Waitz, *MGH SS*, XV, 1 (Berlin, 1887), pp. 127–31

Rufinus, see also under Eusebius

Rufinus: English trans. P. Amidon, *The church history of Rufinus of Aquileia, books 10 and 11* (New York and Oxford, 1997)

Salerno: ed. U. Westerbergh, *Chronicon Salernitanum. A critical edition with studies on literary and historical sources and on language*, Studia latina Stockholmensia 3 (Stockholm, 1956)

Sedulius Scottus, *Liber de rectoribus christianis*, ed. S. Hellmann, *Sedulius Scottus, Quellen und Untersuchungen zur lateinischen Philologie* 1, 1 (Munich, 1906), pp. 1–91

Sigebert of Gembloux, *De viris illustribus*, ed. R. Witte, *Lateinische Sprache und Literatur des Mittelalters*, I (1974); and also in *PL*, CLX, cols. 547–88

Sozomen, *Ecclesiastical history*, II, 1, Greek ed. R. Hussey (Oxford, 1860); English trans. H. Wace and P. Schaff, *A select library of Nicene and post-Nicene fathers of the Christian church*, second series (Oxford and New York, 1891); and ed. J. Bidez, B. Grillet, G. Sabbah and A.-J. Festugière, *Sozomène Histoire ecclésiastique*, Sources Chrétiennes 306 (Paris, 1983)

St Gallen: ed. P. Piper, *Libri confraternitatum sancti galli, augiensis, fabariensis, MGH Necrologia germaniae* [Supplementum] (Munich, 1983, reprint of 1884 Berlin edition).

St Germain-des-Prés: ed. R. Poupardin, *Recueil des chartes de l'abbaye de Saint-Germain-des-Prés*, I (Paris, 1909)

Thegan, *Gesta Hludowici imperatoris*, ed. E. Tremp, *MGH SRG*, LXIV (Hannover, 1995)

Theodoret, *Kirchengeschichte*, ed. L. Parmentier, revised by F. Scheidweiler, Die griechischen christlichen Schriftsteller 44 (Berlin, 1954)

Theodulf of Orléans, ed. A. Freeman, *Opus caroli regis contra synodum* (*Libri carolini*), *MGH Conc.*, II., Suppl. 1 (Hannover, 1998).

Theophanes, *Chronographia*, English trans. C. Mango and R. Scott, *The Chronicle of Theophanes Confessor. Byzantine and near eastern history AD 284–813* (Oxford, 1997)

Victorius, ed. T. Mommsen, *Victorius aquitanus cursus paschalis CCCVII, MGH Chronica minora*, I (Berlin, 1892), pp. 676–84

Vita Lebuini, ed. A. Hofmeister, *MGH SS*, XXX, 2 (Hannover, 1934), pp. 789–95

Walafrid Strabo, Preface to ed. O. Holder-Egger, *Einhardi Vita Karoli magni, MGH SRG*, XXV (Hannover, 1911), pp. XXVIII–XXIX

Walafrid Strabo, ed. A. L. Harting-Correa, *Walafrid Strabo's Libellus de exordiis et incrementis quarundam in observationibus ecclesiasticis rerum. A translation and liturgical commentary* (Leiden, 1996)

Widukind of Corvey, *Rerum gestarum saxonicarum libri*, III, ed. A. Bauer and R. Rau (Darmstadt, 1969)

William of Jumièges, *Gesta normannorum ducum*, ed. and trans. E. M. C. van Houts, *The Gesta normannorum ducum of William of Jumièges, Orderic Vitalis and Robert of Torigny*, Oxford Medieval Texts, 2 vols. (Oxford 1992–95)

Willibald, *Vita sancti Bonifatii*, ed. W. Levison, *MGH SRG*, LVII (Hannover, 1905); ed. with German trans. R. Rau, *Briefe des Bonifatius, Willibalds Leben des Bonifatius nebst einigen zeitgenössischen Dokumenten* (Darmstadt, 1968); English trans. C. H. Talbot, *The Anglo-Saxon missionaries in Germany* (London, 1954), pp. 25–62

Winchester: ed. S. Keynes, *The Liber vitae of the New Minster and Hyde Abbey, Winchester*, Early English manuscripts in facsimile 26 (Copenhagen, 1996).

Zacharias, ed. W. Gundlach, *Epistolae merovingici et karolini aevi, MGH Epistulae*, III (Hannover, 1892), pp. 479–87

SECONDARY LITERATURE

Affeldt, W., 'Untersuchungen zur Königserhebung Pippins. Das Papsttum und die Begründung des karolingischen Königtums im Jahre 751', *Frühmittelalterliche Studien* 14 (1980), pp. 95–187

Airlie, S., 'Bonds of power and bonds of association in the court circle of Louis the Pious', in Godman and Collins (eds.), *Charlemagne's heir*, pp. 191–204

Airlie, S., 'Narratives of triumph and rituals of submission: Charlemagne's mastering of Bavaria', *TRHS* sixth series 9 (1999), pp. 93–120

al-D. al-Duri, A., *The rise of historical writing among the Arabs*, ed. and trans. L. Conrad (Princeton, 1983)

Allen, M. I., *Frechvlfi lexoviensis episcopi opera omnia. Prolegomena. Indices, CCCM*, CLXIX (Turnhout, 2002)

Althoff, G., *Amicitiae and Pacta. Bündnis, Einung, Politik und Gebetsgedenken im beginnenden 10. Jahrhundert*, MGH Schriften 37 (Hannover, 1992)

Althoff, G., 'Zur Verschriftlichung von Memoria in Krisenzeiten', in Geuenich and Oexle (eds.), *Memoria*, pp. 56–73

Amory, P., 'A prosopography of Goths in Italy, 489–554', in Amory, *People and identity*, pp. 348–485

Amory, P., *People and identity in Ostrogothic Italy, 489–544* (Cambridge, 1997)

Angenendt, A., 'Das geistliche Bündnis der Päpste mit den Karolingern (754–796)', *Historisches Jahrbuch* 100 (1980), pp. 1–94

Anton, H. H., *Fürstenspiegel und Herrscherethos in der Karolingerzeit*, Bonner Historische Forschungen 32 (Bonn, 1968)

Aston, M. and P. Biller (eds.), *Heresy and literacy, 1000–1530* (Cambridge, 1994)

Atsma, H. (ed.), *La Neustrie. Les pays au nord de la Loire de Dagobert à Charles le Chauve, 650 à 850*, Beihefte der Francia 16 (Sigmaringen, 1989)

Attridge, H. W. and G. Hata (eds.), *Eusebius, Christianity and Judaism* (Detroit and Leiden, 1992)

Auzépy, M.-F., 'Francfort et Nicée II', in Berndt (ed.), *Das Frankfurter Konzil von 794*, I, pp. 279–300

Backus, I. (ed.), *The reception of the church fathers in the west. From the Carolingians to the Maurists*, 2 vols. (Leiden, 1997)

Ballou, S. H., *The manuscript tradition of the Historia augusta* (Leipzig and Berlin, 1914)

Banniard, M., 'Language and communication in Carolingian Europe', in McKitterick (ed.), *NCMH*, pp. 695–708

Banniard, M., *Viva Voce: communication écrite et communication orale du IVe siècle en occident latin* (Paris, 1992)

Barlow, J., 'Gregory of Tours and the myth of the Trojan origin of the Franks', *Frühmittelalterliche Studien* 29 (1995), pp. 86–95

Bartlett, R., 'Symbolic meanings of hair in the middle ages', *TRHS* sixth series 4 (1994), pp. 43–60

Bately, J., *The Anglo-Saxon Chronicle: texts and textual relationships*, Reading Medieval Studies Monograph 3 (Reading, 1991)

Bately, J. and D. J. A. Ross, 'A check list of manuscripts of Orosius *Historiarum aduersum paganos libri septem*', *Scriptorium* 15 (1961), pp. 329–34

Beasley, W. G. and E. B. Pulleybank, *Historians of China and Japan* (Oxford, 1969)

Becher, H., 'Das königliche Frauenkloster San Salvatore/San Guilia in Brescia im Spiegel seiner Memorialüberlieferung', *Frühmittelalterliche Studien* 17 (1983), pp. 299–392

Becher, M., *Eid und Herrschaft. Untersuchungen zum Herrscherethos Karls des Großen*, Vorträge und Forschungen, Sonderband 39 (Sigmaringen, 1993)

Beeson, C. H., *Lupus of Ferrières as scribe and text critic* (Cambridge, Mass., 1930)

Beiträge zur Geschichte des Klosters Lorsch, 2nd edn, Geschichtsblätter für den Kreis Bergstraße, Sonderband 4 (Lorsch, 1980)

Bellingham, J., 'Musical thought in antiquity and in the medieval west to the end of the Carolingian era' (unpublished D.Phil. thesis, University of Oxford, 1998)

Bernard, P., *Du chant romain au chant grégorien (IVe–XIIIe siècle)* (Paris, 1996)

Berndt, R. (ed.), *Das Frankfurter Konzil von 794. Kristallisationpunckt karolingischer Kultur*, 2 vols., Quellen und Abhandlungen zur mittelrheinischen Kirchengeschichte 80 (Mainz, 1997)

Bernhardt, J. W., *Itinerant kingship and royal monasteries in early medieval Germany, c. 936–1075* (Cambridge, 1993)

Berschin, W., *Greek letters and the Latin middle ages* (Washington, D. C., 1988)

Berschin, W., *Biographie und Epochenstil im lateinischen Mittelalter*, Quellen und Untersuchungen zur lateinischen Philologie des Mittelalters 8–10, 12, 4 vols. (Stuttgart, 1986–99)

Bertolini, O., 'Il *Liber pontificalis*', in *La Storiografia altomedievale*, Settimane 17 (Spoleto, 1970), pp. 387–455

Bethmann, L., 'Die Evangelien Handschrift zu Cividale', *Neues Archiv* 2 (1877), pp. 111–28

Bethmann, L., 'Paulus Diaconus Leben und Schriften', *Archiv der Gesellschaft für ältere deutsche Geschichtskunde* 10 (1851), pp. 247–334

Beumann, H., *Ideengeschichtliche Studien zu Einhard und anderen Geschichtsschreibern des frühen Mittelalters*, 2nd edn (Munich, 1969)

Bickerman, E., *Chronology of the ancient world* (London, 1980)

Bidez, J., *La Tradition manuscrite de Sozomène et la Tripartite de Théodore le lecteur*, Texte und Untersuchungen zur Geschichte der altchristlichen Literatur 32 (Leipzig, 1908)

Bierbrauer, K., *Die vorkarolingischen und karolingischen Handschriften der Bayerischen Staatsbibliothek. Katalog der illuminierten Handschriften der Bayerischen Staatsbibliothek*, I (Wiesbaden, 1990)

Bierbrauer, K., 'Konzilsdarstellungen der Karolingerzeit', in Berndt (ed.) *Das Frankfurter Konzil von 794*, II, pp. 751–65

Bilde, P., *Flavius Josephus between Jerusalem and Rome. His life, works and their importance. Journal for the Study of Pseudepigrapha*, Supplement series 2 (Sheffield, 1988)

Biller, P. and M. A. Hudson (eds.), *Heresy and literacy, 1000–1530* (Cambridge, 1994)

Binding, G., *Deutsche Königspfalzen von Karl dem Grossen bis Friedrich II (765–1240)* (Darmstadt, 1996)

Bischoff B., 'Hadoardus and the manuscripts of classical authors from Corbie', in Prete (ed.), *Didascaliae* pp. 41–57, with a revised German version in Bischoff, *Mittelalterliche Studien*, I, pp. 49–63

Bischoff, B., 'Panorama der Handschriftenüberlieferung aus der Zeit Karls des Grossen', in Braunfels (ed.), *Karl der Grosse*, II, pp. 233–54, revised version in Bischoff, *Mittelalterliche Studien*, III (Stuttgart, 1981), pp. 5–38; English trans. M. Gorman, 'Manuscripts in the age of Charlemagne', in Bischoff, *Manuscripts and libraries*, pp. 20–55

Bischoff, B., 'Die Hofbibliothek Karls des Grossen', in Braunfels (ed.), *Karl der Grosse*, pp. 42–62, revised in Bischoff, *Mittelalterliche Studien* 3, pp. 149–69; English trans. M. Gorman, 'The court library of Charlemagne', in Bischoff, *Manuscripts and libraries*, pp. 56–75

Bischoff, B., 'Die Kölner Nonnenhandschriften und das Skriptorium von Chelles', in Bischoff, *Mittelalterliche Studien*, I (Stuttgart, 1966), pp. 16–34

Bischoff, B., *Mittelalterliche Studien*, 3 vols. (Stuttgart, 1966, 1967, 1981)

Bischoff, B., 'Frühkarolingische Handschriften und ihre Heimat', *Scriptorium* 22 (1968), pp. 306–14

Bischoff, B. (ed.), *Sammelhandschrift Diez B. Sant 66. Grammatici latini et catalogus librorum*, Codices selecti 42 (Graz, 1973)

Bischoff, B., *Die sudostdeutschen Schreibschulen und Bibliotheken in der Karolingerzeit*, 3rd edn, I; *Die bayrischen Diözesen* (Wiesbaden, 1974), II, *Die Vorwiegend Österreichischen Diözesen* (Wiesbaden, 1980)

Bischoff, B., 'Die Hofbibliothek unter Ludwig dem Frommen', in J. J. G. Alexander and M. T. Gibson (eds.), *Medieval learning and literature. Essays presented to Richard William Hunt* (Oxford, 1976), pp. 3–22, reprinted Bischoff, *Mittelalterliche Studien*, III (Stuttgart, 1981), pp. 171–86; English trans. M. Gorman in Bischoff, *Manuscripts and libraries*, pp. 76–92

Bischoff, B., 'Bücher am Hofe Ludwigs des Deutschen und die Privatbibliothek des Kanzlers Grimalt', in Bischoff, *Mittelalterliche Studien*, III (Stuttgart, 1981), pp. 187–212

Bischoff, B., *Paläographie des römischen Altertums und des abendländischen Mittelalters*, 2nd revised edn (Berlin, 1986); English trans. from the 1986 2nd revised German edn D. Ó Cróinín and D. Ganz, *Latin palaeography: antiquity and the middle ages* (Cambridge, 1990)

Bischoff, B., *Die Abtei Lorsch im Spiegel ihrer Handschriften*, 2nd edn (Lorsch, 1989)

Bischoff, B., trans. M. Gorman, *Manuscripts and libraries in the age of Charlemagne*, Cambridge Studies in Palaeography and Codicology 1 (Cambridge, 1994)

Bischoff, B., *Katalog der festländischen Handschriften des neunten Jahrhunderts (mit Ausnahme der wisigotischen). Teil I: Aachen-Lambach* (Stuttgart, 1998), II: *Laon-Paderborn* (Stuttgart, 2004)

Bischoff, B. and J. Hofmann, *Libri sancti Kyliani. Die Würzburger Schreibschule und die Dombibliothek im VIII. und IX. Jahrhundert* (Würzburg, 1952)

Bloch, H., 'The structure of Sallust's Historiae: the evidence of the Fleury manuscript', in S. Prete (ed.), *Didascaliae*, pp. 61–7

Blumenthal, U.-R. (ed.), *Carolingian essays* (Washington, 1983)

Borgehammar, S., *How the Holy Cross was found: from event to medieval legend*, Bibliotheca theologiae practicae 47 (Stockholm, 1991)

Borgolte, M., D. Geuenich and K. Schmid, *Subsidia Sangallensia*, I, *Materialien und Untersuchungen zu den Verbrüderungs Büchern und zu den älteren Urkunden des Stiftsarchivs St Gallen*, St Galler Kultur und Geschichte 16 (St Gallen, 1986)

Borst, A., 'Alkuin und die Enzyklopädie von 809', in Butzer and Lohrmann (eds.), *Science in Western and Eastern civilization in Carolingian times*, pp. 53–78

Borst, A., *Die Karolingische Kalendarreform*, *MGH* Schriften 46 (Hannover 1998)

Boshof, B., *Ludwig der Fromme*, Gestalten des Mittelalters und der Renaissance (Darmstadt, 1996)

Bouchard, C. B., *Sword, miter and cloister. Nobility and the church in Burgundy, 980–1198* (Ithaca and London, 1987)

Bougard, F., 'La Justice dans le royaume d'Italie aux IX–Xe siècles', in *La Giustizia nell'alto medioevo (secoli IX–XI)*, Settimane 44 (Spoleto, 1997), pp. 133–76

Bougard, F., *La Justice dans le royaume d'Italie de la fin du VIII siècle au début du XI siècle*, École Française de Rome (Paris, 1995)

Bourgain, P. and M. Heinzelmann, 'L'Œuvre de Grégoire de Tours: la diffusion des manuscrits', in Gauthier and Galinié (eds.), *Grégoire de Tours*, pp. 273–317

Bowman, A., and G. Woolf (eds.), *Literacy and power in the ancient world* (Cambridge, 1994)

Braunfels, W. (ed.), *Karl der Grosse. Lebenswerk und Nachleben*, I, *Persönlichkeit und Geschichte*, ed. H. Beumann (Düsseldorf, 1965)

Bresslau, H., *Handbuch der Urkundenlehre*, 2 vols. (Berlin, 1931)

Briggs, C. F., 'Historiographical essay. Literacy, reading, and writing in the medieval west', *Journal of Medieval History* 26 (2000), pp. 397–420

Brown, G., 'Introduction: the Carolingian Renaissance', in McKitterick (ed.), *Carolingian culture*, pp. 1–51

Brown, G., 'Politics and patronage at the abbey of St Denis (814–898). The rise of a royal patron saint' (unpublished D.Phil. dissertation, University of Oxford, 1989)

Brown, W., *Unjust seizure: conflict, interest and authority in an early medieval society* (Ithaca, 2001)

Brugnoli, G., *Curiosissimus excerptor: gli 'Additamenta' de Girolamo ai 'Chronica' de Eusebio* (Pisa, 1995)

Brühl, C., *Palatium und Civitas I, Gallien* (Cologne, 1975)

Brunhölzl, F., *Histoire de la littérature latine au moyen âge, I/I, L'Époque mérovingienne* (Turnhout, 1990)

Brunhölzl, F., *Histoire de la littérature latine du moyen âge, II, De l'époque carolingienne au milieu du onzième siècle*, revised trans. from the 1992 German edn by H. Rochais (Turnhout, 1996)

Brunner, K., *Oppositionelle Gruppen im Karolingerreich* (Vienna, 1979)

Buchner, M., *Die Clausula de unctione Pippini, eine Fälschung aus dem Jahre 880*, Quellenfälschung aus dem Gebiete der Geschichte, 1 (Paderborn, 1926)

Buchner, M., 'Zur Überlieferungsgeschichte des *Liber pontificalis* und zu seiner Verbreitung im Frankenreich im IX. Jahrhundert: zugleich ein Beitrag zur

Geschichte der karolingischen Hofbibliothek und Hofkapelle', *Römische Quartalschrift* 34 (1926), pp. 141–65

Bullough, D., 'Ethnic history and the Carolingians: an alternative reading of Paul the Deacon's *Historia langobardorum*', in Holdsworth and Wiseman (eds.), *The inheritance of historiography*, pp. 85–106

Bullough, D., '*Europae pater*: Charlemagne's achievement in the light of recent scholarship', *EHR* 85 (1970), pp. 59–105

Burgess, R. with W. Witakowski, *Studies in Eusebian and post-Eusebian chronography* (Stuttgart, 1999)

Cammarosano, P. and S. Gasparri (eds.), *Langobardia* (Udine, 1990)

Canisius, H., *Antiquae lectiones*, III (Ingolstadt, 1603)

Capo, L., 'Paolo Diacono e il problema della cultura dell'Italia Longobarda', in Gasparri and Commarosano (eds.), *Langobardia*, pp. 169–235

Capo, L., 'Paolo Diacono e il mondo franco: l'incontro di due esperienze storiografiche', in Chiesa (ed.), *Paolo Diacono*, pp. 39–74

Cappuyns, M., 'Les *bibli Wulfadi* et Jean Scot Erigène', *Recherches de Théologie Ancienne et Médiévale* 33 (1966), pp. 137–9

Carruthers, M., *The book of memory. A study of memory in medieval culture* (Cambridge, 1990)

Cavadini, J., *The last Christology of the west. Adoptionism in Spain and Gaul, 785–820* (Philadelphia, 1993)

Cavallo, G. and R. Chartier (eds.), *A history of reading in the west* (Oxford, 1999)

Cervani, R., *L'Epitome di Paolo del 'de verborum significatu' di Pompeo Festo. Struttura e metodo* (Rome, 1978)

Cessi, R., 'Di due miscellanee storiche medioevali', *Archivio Muratoriano* 13 (1913), pp. 69–96

Chatelain, E., *Les Classiques Latins*, II (Paris, 1894–1900)

Chavannes-Mazel, C. A. and M. M. Smith (eds.), *Medieval manuscripts of the Latin classics: production and use* (Los Altos Hills and London, 1996)

Chazelle, C. (ed.), *Literacy, politics and artistic innovation in the early medieval west* (Lanham, Md., 1992)

Chazelle, C. and B. van Name Edwards (eds.), *The study of the Bible in the Carolingian era*, Medieval Church Studies 3 (Turnhout, 2003)

Chesnut, G. F., 'Eusebius, Augustine, Orosius and the later patristic and medieval Christian historians', in Attridge and Hata (eds.), *Eusebius, Christianity and Judaism*, pp. 687–713

Chesnut, G. F., *The first Christian histories. Eusebius, Socrates, Sozomen, Theodoret and Evagrius* (Paris, 1977, and Macon, Ga., 1986)

Chiesa, P. (ed.), *Paolo Diacono: uno scrittore fra tradizione longobarda e rinnovamento carolingio* (Udine, 2000)

Chiesa, P., 'Caratteristiche della trasmissione dell' "Historia langobardorum"', in *Paolo Diacono e il Friuli altomedievale*, I, pp. 45–66

Christensen, T., *Rufinus of Aquileia and the Historia ecclesiastica lib. VIII–IX, of Eusebius*, Historisk-filosofiske Meddelelser 58 (Copenhagen, 1989)

Christensen, T., 'Rufinus of Aquileia and the *Historia ecclesiastica*, lib. VIII–IX, of Eusebius', *Studia Theologica* 34 (1980), pp. 129–52

Coens, M., 'Les litanies bavaroises du "Libellus precum" dit de Fleury (Orléans MS 194)', *Analecta Bollandiana* 77 (1959), pp. 373–91

Coens, M., 'La Provenance du MS Bruxelles 7666–71', in J. P. Gumbert and M. J. M. de Haan (eds.), *Litterae textuales. Varia codicologica. Essays presented to G. I. Lieftinck*, I (Amsterdam, 1972), pp. 25–34

Coens, M., 'Litanies carolines de Soissons et du Psautier de Charlemagne', in *Recueil d'études bollandiennes*, Subsidia Hagiographica 37 (Brussels, 1963)

Coffin, B., 'The production of the *Codex carolinus* in its historical context' (unpublished M.Phil. essay, University of Cambridge, 2003)

Coleman, J., *Ancient and medieval memories. Studies in the reconstruction of the past* (Cambridge, 1992)

Collins, R., 'Deception and misrepresentation in early eighth-century Frankish historiography: two case studies', in Jarnut, Nonn and Richter (eds.), *Karl Martell*, pp. 227–48

Collins, R., *Fredegar*, Authors of the Middle Ages 4, no. 13 (Aldershot, 1996)

Collins, R., 'The "Reviser" revisited: another look at the alternative version of the *Annales regni francorum*', in Murray (ed.), *After Rome's fall*, pp. 191–213

Collura, P., *La precarolina e la carolina a Bobbio*, Fontes Ambrosiani 22 (Milan, 1943)

Connolly, S., *Bede on Tobit and on the Canticle of Habakkuk* (Dublin, 1997)

Constable, G., 'The *Liber Memorialis* of Remiremont', *Speculum* 47 (1972), pp. 261–77

Contreni, J. J., *The cathedral school of Laon from 850 to 930. Its manuscripts and masters*, Münchener Beiträge zur Mediävistik und Renaissance Forschung (Munich, 1978)

Contreni, J. J., 'Carolingian biblical studies', in Blumenthal, *Carolingian essays*, pp. 71–98, and reprinted in Contreni, *Carolingian learning*, chapter 5

Contreni, J. J., *Carolingian learning, masters and manuscripts* (Aldershot, 1992)

Contreni, J., 'The Carolingian renaissance: education and literary culture', in R. McKitterick (ed.), *NCMH*, pp. 709–57

Cordoliani, A., 'Une encyclopédie carolingienne de comput: les Sententiae in laude computi', *Bibliothèque de l'École des Chartes* 104 (1943), pp. 237–43

Cordoliani, A., 'Les Traités de comput du haut moyen âge (526–1003)', *Archivum latinitatis medii aevi* 17 (1942), pp. 51–72

Cordoliani, A., 'Contribution à la littérature du comput ecclésiastique au moyen âge', *Studi Medievali* 3rd series, 1 (1960), pp. 107–37, and 2 (1961), pp. 169–73

Cornford, B., 'The idea of the Roman past in early medieval Italy: Paul the Deacon's *Historia romana*' (unpublished Ph.D. dissertation, University of Cambridge, 2003)

Corradini, R., *Zeit und Text. Studien zum Tempus-Begriff des Augustinus*, Veröffentlichung des Instituts für Österreichische Geschichtsforschung 33 (Munich, 1997)

Corradini, R., *Die Wiener Handschrift Cvp 430*. Ein Beitrag zur Historiographie in Fulda im frühen 9. Jahrhundert*, Fuldaer Hochschulschriften 37 (Frankfurt am Main, 2000)

Corradini, R., M. Diesenberger and H. Reimitz (eds.), *The construction of communities in the early middle ages: texts, resources and artefacts*, The Transformation of the Roman World 12 (Leiden, 2003)

Corradini, R., 'The rhetoric of crisis: *computus* and *liber annalis* in early ninth-century Fulda', in Corradini, Diesenberger and Reimitz (eds.), *The construction of communities in the early middle ages*, pp. 269–321, plates 1–5

Costambeys, M., 'The monastic environment of Paul the Deacon', in Chiesa (ed.), *Paolo Diacono*, pp. 127–38

Cramer, F. H., 'Book burning and censorship in ancient Rome. A chapter from the history of freedom of speech', *Journal of the History of Ideas* 6 (1945), pp. 157–96

Crick, J., 'An Anglo-Saxon fragment of Justinus' Epitome', *Anglo-Saxon England* 16 (1987) pp. 181–96

Crivellucci, A., 'Per l'edizione della Historia Romana di Paolo Diacono', *Bullettino dell'Istituto Storico* 40 (1921), pp. 7–103

Croke, B. and A. Emmet, 'Historiography in late antiquity: an overview', in Croke and Emmet (eds.), *History and historians in late antiquity*, pp. 1–12

Croke, B. and A. Emmet (eds.), *History and historians in late antiquity* (Sydney, 1983)

Croke, B., 'The early development of Byzantine chronicles', in E. Jeffreys (ed.), *Studies in John Malalas*, Byzantina Australiensia 6 (Sydney, 1990) pp. 27–8

Curtius, E., *Europäische Literatur und lateinisches Mittelalter* (Bern, 1948); Eng. trans. W. Trask, *European literature and the Latin middle ages* (London, 1953)

Czapla, B., *Gennadius als Litterarhistoriker. Ein Quellenkritische Untersuchung der Schrift des Gennadius von Marseille. De viris illustribus*, Kirchengeschichtliche Studien 4, 1 (Münster, 1898)

Dahlhaus-Berg, E., *Nova antiquitas et antiqua novitas. Typologische Exegese und isidorianisches Geschichtsbild bei Theodulf von Orléans* (Cologne, 1975)

Davis, C. R., 'Cultural assimilation in the Anglo-Saxon royal genealogies', *Anglo-Saxon England* 21 (1992), pp. 23–36

Davis, J., 'The conception of kingship in Charlemagne's capitularies' (unpublished undergraduate thesis, Harvard University, 1997)

Davis, J., 'Conceptions of kingship under Charlemagne' (unpublished M.Litt. dissertation, University of Cambridge, 1999)

de Jong, M., 'Power and humility in Carolingian society: the public penance of Louis the Pious', *EME* 1 (1992), pp. 29–52

de Jong, M., 'Old law and new-found power: Hrabanus Maurus and the Old Testament', in J. W. Drijvers and A. A. MacDonald (eds.), *Centres of learning: learning and location in pre-modern Europe and the near East* (Leiden, New York and Cologne, 1995), pp. 161–76

de Jong, M., *In Samuel's image: child oblation in the early medieval west* (Leiden, 1996)

de Jong, M. (ed.), *The power of the word. The influence of the Bible on early medieval politics*, special issue, *EME* 7 (1998)

de Jong, M., 'The empire as *ecclesia*: Hrabanus Maurus and biblical *historia* for rulers', in Hen and Innes (eds.), *The uses of the past*, pp. 191–226

de Jong, M., 'Monastic prisoners or opting out? Political coercion and honour in the Frankish kingdoms', in de Jong, Theuws, with van Rhijn (eds.), *Topographies of power in the early middle ages*, pp. 291–328

de Jong, M. and F. Theuws with C. van Rhijn (eds.), *Topographies of power in the early middle ages*, The Transformation of the Roman World 6 (Leiden, 2001)

de Nie, G., *Views from a many-windowed tower. Studies of imagination in the works of Gregory of Tours* (Amsterdam, 1986)

Declercq, G., *Anno domini. Les origines de l'ère chrétienne* (Turnhout, 2000)

Delisle, L., *Le Cabinet des manuscrits de la Bibliothèque impériale* (I) *nationale* (II and III), 3 vols. (Paris, 1868–81)

Delogu, P., 'Longobardi e Romani: altre congetture', in Cammarosano and Gasparri (eds.), *Langobardia*, pp. 112–67

Delogu, P., 'Lombard and Carolingian Italy', in McKitterick (ed.), *NCMH*, pp. 290–319

Delogu, P., 'The writing of history in the middle ages', trans. M. Moran, in P. Delogu, *An introduction to medieval history* (London, 2002)

Depreux, P., 'Das Königtum Bernards von Italien und sein Verhältnis zum Kaisertum', *Quellen und Forschungen aus italienischen Archiven und Bibliotheken* 72 (1992), pp. 1–24

Depreux, P., 'Tassilon III et le roi des Francs: examen d'une vassalité controversée', *Revue Historique* 593 (1995), pp. 23–73

Depreux, P., *Prosopographie de l'entourage de Louis le Pieux (781–840)*, Instrumenta 1 (Sigmaringen, 1997)

Deshusses, J., 'Chronologie des grands sacramentaires de Saint-Amand', *RB* 87 (1977), pp. 230–7

Deshusses, J., *Le Sacramentaire grégorien* (Fribourg, 1971)

Dobias-Rozdestvenskaja, O. A. and W. W. Bakhtine, *Les Anciens Manuscrits latins de la Bibliothèque publique Saltykov-Ščedrin de Leningrad, VIIIe–début IXe siècle* (Paris, 1991)

Doherty, H., 'The maintenance of royal power and prestige in the Carolingian *regnum* of Aquitaine under Louis the Pious' (unpublished M.Phil. dissertation, University of Cambridge, 1998)

Donner, F., *Narratives of Islamic origins. The beginnings of Islamic historical writing*, Studies in Late Antiquity and Early Islam 14 (Princeton, 1998)

Dopsch, H. and R. Juffinger (eds.), *Virgil von Salzburg. Missionar und Gelehrter* (Salzburg, 1984)

Draak, M., 'Virgil of Salzburg versus "Aethicus Ister"', *Dancwerk. Opstellen angeboden aan Prof. Dr D. Th. Enklaar ter gelegenheid van zijn vijfenzestigste Verjaardag* (Groningen, 1959), pp. 33–42

Drijvers, H. and J. W., *The finding of the true cross. The Judas Kyriakos legend in Syriac* (Louvain, 1997).

Drijvers, J. W., *Helena Augusta, the mother of Constantine the Great and the legend of her finding of the true cross* (Leiden, 1992)

Dubois, J., *Les martyrologes du moyen âge latin*, Typologie des sources du moyen âge occidental 26 (Turnhout, 1978)

Dumville, D. N., 'Kingship, genealogies and regnal lists', in Sawyer and Wood (eds.), *Early medieval kingship*, pp. 72–104

Dumville, D. N., 'The Anglian collection of royal genealogies and regnal lists', *Anglo-Saxon England* 14 (1985), pp. 23–50

Dumville, D. N., '*Historia brittonum*; an insular history from the Carolingian age', in Scharer and Scheibelreiter (eds.), *Historiographie*, pp. 406–34

Dutton, P. E., *The politics of dreaming in the Carolingian empire* (Lincoln, Neb., and London, 1994)

Dutton, P. E. and H. L. Kessler, *The poetry and paintings of the first Bible of Charles the Bald* (Ann Arbor, 1997)

Ebner, A., *Die klösterlichen Gebetsverbrüderungen bis zum Ausgange des karolingischen Zeitalters. Eine kirchengeschichtliche Studie* (Regensburg, New York and Cincinnati, 1890)

Edwards, C., 'German vernacular literature', in McKitterick (ed.), *Carolingian culture*, pp. 141–70

Eggert, W., 'Zu Inhalt, Form und politischer Terminologie der 'Frankischen Reichsannalen', in Erkens (ed.), *Karl der Große*, pp. 122–34

Eggert, W. and S. Patzold, *Wir-Gefühl und Regnum Saxonum bei frühmittelalterlichen Geschichtsschreibern* (Berlin, 1984)

Ehlers, J. (ed.), *Deutschland und der Westen Europas im Mittelalter*, Vorträge und Forschungen 56 (Stuttgart, 2002)

Erkens, F.-R. (ed.), *Karl der Große und das Erbe der Kulturen* (Berlin, 2001)

Everett, N., *Literacy in Lombard Italy, c. 568–774* (Cambridge, 2003)

Ewig, E., 'Résidence et capitale pendant le haut moyen-âge', *Revue Historique* 230 (1963), pp. 25–72, reprinted in E. Ewig, *Spätantikes und fränkisches Gallien*, I (Munich, 1976), pp. 362–408

Ewig. E., 'Descriptio Franciae', in Beumann (ed.), *Karl der Grosse*, I, pp. 143–77

Ewig, E., 'Saint Chrodegang et la réforme de l'église franque', in *Saint Chrodegang* (Metz, 1967), pp. 25–53

Fentress, J. and C. Wickham, *Social memory* (Oxford, 1992)

Ferrari, M., *Il 'Liber sanctae crucis' di Rabano Mauro. Testo-immagine-contesto* (Bern, 1999)

Fichtenau, H., 'Abt Richbod und die *Annales Laureshamenses*', in *Beiträge zur Geschichte des Klosters Lorsch*, 2nd edn, Geschichtsblätter für den Kreis Bergstraße, Sonderband 4 (Lorsch, 1980), pp. 277–304, a reprint with Afterword of H. Fichtenau, 'Karl der Große und das Kaisertum', *MIÖG* 61 (1953), pp. 287–309

Fischer, B., 'Bibeltext und Bibelreform unter Karl dem Grossen', in W. Braunfels (ed.), *Karl der Grosse. Lebenswerk und Nachleben*, II, *Das geistige Leben*, ed. B. Bischoff (Düsseldorf, 1965), pp. 156–216

Fleckenstein, J., 'Clausula de unctione Pippini', in R. Auty and R.-H. Bautier (eds.), *Lexikon des Mittelalters*, II (Munich and Zürich, 1983), cols. 2134–5

Flint, V. I. J., 'The place and purpose of the works of Honorius Augustodunensis', *RB* 87 (1977), pp. 97–127

Foot, S., 'The making of Angelcynn: English identity before the Norman conquest', *TRHS* 6th series (1996), pp. 25–49

Forstner, K., *Das Verbrüderungsbuch von St Peter in Salzburg. Vollständige Faksimile-Ausgabe im Originalformat der Handschrift A1 aus dem Archiv von St Peter in Salzburg* (Graz, 1974)

Forstner, K., 'Das Salzburger Skriptorium unter Virgil und das Verbrüderungsbuch von St Peter', in Dopsch and Juffinger (eds.), *Virgil von Salzburg*, pp. 135–40

Fouracre, P. and R. Gerberding, *Late Merovingian France: history and hagiography 640–720* (Manchester, 1996)

Fouracre, P., 'Frankish Gaul to 814', in McKitterick (ed.), *NCMH*, pp. 85–109

Gamble, H., *Books and readers in the early church. A history of early Christian texts* (New Haven, 1995)

Gameson, R. (ed.), *The early medieval bible: its production, decoration and use* (Cambridge, 1994)

Gandino, G., 'La dialettica tra il passato e il presente nelle opere di Paolo Diacono', in *Paolo Diacono e il Friuli altomedievale*, pp. 67–98

Ganshof, F. L., 'L'Historiographie dans la monarchie franque sous les Mérovingiens et les Carolingiens. Monarchie franque unitaire et Francie occidentale', in *La storiografia altomedievale*, Settimane 17 (Spoleto, 1970), pp. 631–85

Ganshof, F. L., 'Einhard, biographer of Charlemagne', in F. L. Ganshof, *The Carolingians and the Frankish monarchy*, trans. J. Sondheimer (London, 1971) pp. 1–16

Ganz, D., 'Humour as history in Notker's *Gesta Karoli magni*', in E. B. King, J. T. Schaefer and W. B. Wadley (eds.), *Monks, nuns and friars in medieval society*, Sewanee Medieval Studies 4 (Sewanee, 1989), pp. 171–83

Ganz, D., *Corbie in the Carolingian renaissance*, Beihefte der Francia 20 (Sigmaringen, 1990)

Ganz, D., 'The *Epitaphium Arsenii* and opposition to Louis the Pious', in Godman and Collins (eds.), *Charlemagne's heir*, pp. 537–50

Ganz, D., 'Theology and the organization of thought', in McKitterick (ed.), *NCMH*, pp. 758–85

Ganz, D., 'Lucretius and the Carolingian age: the Leiden manuscripts and their Carolingian readers', in C. A. Chavannes-Mazel and M. M. Smith (eds.), *Medieval manuscripts of the Latin classics: production and use* (Los Altos Hills and London, 1996), pp. 91–102

Ganz, D., 'The preface to Einhard's "Vita Karoli"', in H. Schefers (ed.), *Einhard. Studien zu Leben und Werk* (Darmstadt, 1997), pp. 299–310

Garrison, M., 'The Franks as the new Israel? Education for an identity from Pippin to Charlemagne', in Hen and Innes (eds.), *The uses of the past in the early middle ages*, pp. 114–61

Gauthier, N. and H. Galinié (eds.), *Grégoire de Tours et l'espace gaulois. Actes du congrès international Tours, 2–5 novembre 1994*, 13e supplément à la *Revue Archéologique du Centre de la France* (Tours, 1997)

Gautier Dalché, P., *Géographie et culture. La représentation de l'espace du VIe au XIIe siècle* (Aldershot, 1997)

Geary, P., *Phantoms of remembrance. Memory and oblivion at the end of the first millennium* (Princeton, 1994)

Geary, P., 'Land, language and memory in Europe, 700–1100', *TRHS* sixth series 9 (1999), pp. 169–84

Geith, K. E., *Carolus Magnus. Studien zur Darstellung Karls des Großen in der deutschen Literatur des 12. und 13. Jarhrhunderts*, Bibliotheca Germanica 19 (Bern and Munich, 1977)

Genet, J.-P., 'Cartulaires, registres et histoire: l'exemple anglais', in Guenée (ed.), *Le Métier d'historien au moyen âge*, pp. 95–129

Gerberding, R. A., *The rise of the Carolingians and the Liber historiae francorum* (Oxford, 1987)

Gerberding, R. A., 'Paris, Bibliothèque Nationale latin 7906: an unnoticed very early fragment of the "Liber historiae francorum",' *Traditio* 43 (1987), pp. 381–6

Gerchow, J., *Die Gedenküberlieferung der Angelsachsen*, Arbeiten zur Frühmittel-alterforschung 20 (Berlin, 1988)

Geuenich, D., and O.-G. Oexle (eds.), *Memoria in der Gesellschaft des Mittelalters*, Veröffentlichungen des Max-Planck-Instituts für Geschichte 111 (Göttingen, 1994)

Gibbon, E., *The decline and fall of the Roman empire*, ed. J. B. Bury, 7 vols. (London, 1898)

Gillett, A. (ed.), *On barbarian identity. Critical approaches to ethnicity in the early middle ages*, Studies in the Early Middle Ages 4 (Turnhout, 2002)

Glenn, J., *Politics and history in the tenth century: the world and work of Richer of Reims* (Cambridge, 2004).

Gneuss, H., *Handlist of Anglo-Saxon manuscripts: a list of manuscripts and manuscript fragments written or owned in England up to 1100* (Tempe, Arizona, 2001)

Godman, P. and R. Collins (eds.), *Charlemagne's heir: new perspectives on the reign of Louis the Pious (814–840)* (Oxford, 1990)

Goetz, H.-W., *Strukturen der spätkarolingischen Epoche im Spiegel der Vorstellungen eines zeitgenössischen Mönchs. Eine Interpretation des Gesta Karoli Notkers von Sankt Gallen* (Bonn, 1981)

Goetz, H.-W., J. Jarnut and W. Pohl (eds.), *Regna* and gentes. *The relationship between late antique and early medieval peoples and kingdoms in the transformation of the Roman world*, The Transformation of the Roman World 13 (Leiden, 2003)

Goffart, W., 'Paul the Deacon's *Gesta episcoporum mettensium* and the early design of Charlemagne's succession', *Traditio* 42 (1986), pp. 59–94

Goffart, W., *The narrators of barbarian history (A.D. 550–800). Jordanes, Gregory of Tours, Bede, and Paul the Deacon* (Princeton, 1988)

Goffart, W., *Rome's fall and after* (London, 1990)

Gorman, M., 'Peter of Pisa and the *Quaestiunculae* copied for Charlemagne in Brussels II 2572', *RB* 110 (2000), pp. 238–60

Gotoff, H., *The transmission of the text of Lucan in the ninth century* (Cambridge, Mass., 1971)

Grant, M., *The ancient historians* (New York, 1970)

Grant, R. M., *Eusebius as church historian* (Oxford, 1980)

Graus, F., 'Troja und trojanische Herkunftssage im Mittelalter', in W. Erzgraber (ed.), *Kontinuität und Transformation der Antike im Mittelalter* (Sigmaringen, 1989), pp. 25–43

Green, D. H., 'Orality and reading: the state of research in medieval studies', *Speculum* 65 (1990), pp. 267–80

Green, D. H., *Medieval listening and reading: the primary reception of German literature 800–1300* (Cambridge, 1994)

Grégoire, R., *Homéliaires liturgiques médiévaux. Analyse des manuscrits* (Spoleto, 1980)

Grierson, P. and M. Blackburn, *Medieval European coinage, I, The early middle ages (5th–10th centuries)* (Cambridge, 1986)

Grosjean, P., 'Virgile de Salzbourg en Irlande', *Analecta Bollandiana* 78 (1960), pp. 92–123

Guenée, B., *Le Métier d'historien au moyen âge*, Publications de la Sorbonne, Série 'Études' 13 (Paris, 1977)

Halbwachs, M., *La Mémoire collective* (Paris, 1950)

Halbwachs, M., *Les Cadres sociaux de la mémoire* (Paris, 1925)

Halphen, L., *Études critiques sur l'histoire de Charlemagne* (Paris, 1921)

Hammer, C., *Charlemagne's months and their Bavarian labors. The politics of the seasons in the Carolingian empire*, BAR International series 676 (Oxford, 1997)

Hammer, C., 'The social landscape of the Prague Sacramentary: the prosopography of an eighth-century mass book', *Traditio* 54 (1999), pp. 41–80

Hammond, C., 'A product of a fifth-century scriptorium preserving conventions used by Rufinus of Aquileia', *Journal of Theological Studies* 29 (1978), pp. 366–91

Hammond-Bammell, C., 'Products of fifth-century scriptoria preserving conventions used by Rufinus of Aquileia', *Journal of Theological Studies* 30 (1979), pp. 430–61

Hammond-Bammell, C., 'Products of fifth-century scriptoria preserving conventions used by Rufinus of Aquileia', *Journal of Theological Studies* 35 (1984), pp. 347–93

Hannig, J., *Consensus fidelium. Frühfeudale Interpretationen des Verhältnisses von Königtum und Adel am Beispiel des Frankenreiches* (Stuttgart, 1982)

Hardwick, M. E., *Josephus as an historical source in patristic literature* (Atlanta, 1989)

Harrison, K., *The framework of Anglo-Saxon history to A.D. 900* (Cambridge, 1976)

Hartmann, W., *Die Synoden der Karolingerzeit im Frankenreich und in Italien* (Paderborn, 1989)

Häse, A., *Mittelalterliche Bücherverzeichnisse aus Kloster Lorsch. Einleitung, Edition und Kommentar*, Beiträge zum Buch- und Bibliothekswesen 42 (Stuttgart, 2002)

Haselbach, I., *Aufstieg und Herrschaft der Karolinger in der Darstellung der sogenannten Annales Mettenses Priores. Ein Beitrag zur Geschichte des politischen Ideen im Reiche Karls des Grossen*, Historische Studien 412 (Lübeck, 1970)

Hauck, K., 'Von einer spätantiken Randkultur zum karolingischen Europa', *Frühmittelalterliche Studien* 1 (1967), pp. 3–93

Heckel, W. and J. C. Yardley, *Justin. Epitome of the Philippic history of Pompeius Trogus books 11–12: Alexander the Great* (Oxford, 1997)

Hedrick Jr, C. W., *History and silence: purge and rehabilitation of memory in late antiquity* (Austin, 2000)

Heidecker, K. (ed.), *Charters and the use of the written word in medieval society*, Utrecht Studies in Medieval Literacy (Turnhout, 2000)

Heinzelmann, M. and P. Bourgain, 'L'Œuvre de Grégoire de Tours: la diffusion des manuscrits', in Gauthier and Galinié (eds.), *Grégoire de Tours et l'espace gaulois*, pp. 273–317

Heinzelmann, M., *Gregor von Tours (538–594): 'Zehn Bücher Geschichte' Historiographie und Gesellschaftskonzept im 6. Jahrhundert* (Darmstadt, 1994), trans. C. Carroll, *Gregory of Tours: history and society in the sixth century* (Cambridge, 2001)

Hellgardt, E., 'Zur Mehrsprachigkeit im Karolingerreich. Bermerkungen aus Anlaß von Rosamond McKittericks Buch "The Carolingians and the Written Word"', *Beiträge zur Geschichte der deutschen Sprache und Literatur* 118 (1996), pp. 1–48

Hen, Y., *Culture and religion in Merovingian Gaul, AD 481–751*, Culture, Beliefs and Tradition. Medieval and Early Modern Peoples 1 (Leiden, 1995)

Hen, Y., *The royal patronage of liturgy in frankish Gaul to the death of Charles the Bald (877)*, HBS Subsidia 3 (London, 2001)

Hen, Y., 'The Annals of Metz and the Merovingian past', in Hen and Innes (eds.), *The uses of the past*, pp. 175–90

Hen, Y., 'Paul the Deacon and the Frankish liturgy', in Chiesa (ed.), *Paolo Diacono*, pp. 205–21

Hen, Y. and M. Innes (eds.), *The uses of the past in the early middle ages* (Cambridge, 2000)

Hennig, J., 'Scottorum gloria gentis. Erwähnungen irischer Heiliger in festländischen Liturgietexten des frühen Mittelalters', *Archiv für Kulturgeschichte* 52 (1970), pp. 177–91

Herren, M., 'Theological aspects of the writings of Paul the Deacon', in Chiesa (ed.), *Paolo Diacono*, pp. 223–36

Herrin, J., 'Constantinople, Rome and the Franks in the seventh and eighth centuries', in J. Shepard and S. Franklin (eds.), *Byzantine diplomacy* (Aldershot, 1992), pp. 91–108

Herrin, J., *The formation of Christendom* (London, 1985)

Hlawitschka, E., *Studien zur Äbtissinnenreihe von Remiremont*, Veröffentlichungen des Instituts für Landeskunde des Saarlandes (Saarbrücken, 1963)

Hodges, R., *Light in the dark ages: the rise and fall of San Vincenzo al Volturno* (London, 1997)

Hoffmann, H., *Untersuchungen zur karolingischen Annalistik*, Bonner Historische Forschungen 10 (Bonn, 1958)

Hoffmann, H., 'Der Historien Richer von Saint-Remi', *DA* 54 (1998), pp. 445–552

Holdsworth, C. and T. P. Wiseman (eds.), *The inheritance of historiography, 350–900* (Exeter, 1986)

Holtz, L., 'L'école d'Auxerre', in Iogna-Prat, Jeudy and Lobrichon (eds.), *L'École carolingienne*, pp. 131–46

Howard-Johnson, J. and P. A. Hayward (eds.), *The cult of saints in late antiquity and the early middle ages. Essays on the contribution of Peter Brown* (Oxford, 1999)

Hubert, J., J. Porcher and W. Volbach, *Europe in the Dark Ages* (London, 1969)

Hubert, J., J. Porcher and W. Volbach, *Carolingian art* (London, 1970)

Huth, V., 'Die Düsseldorfer Sakramentarhandschrift D 1 als Memorialzeugnis. Mit einer Wiedergabe der Namen und Namengruppen (Tafs. XIV–XXXII)', *Frühmittelalterliche Studien* 20 (1986), pp. 213–98

Innes, M., 'Charlemagne's will: piety, politics and the imperial succession', *EHR* 112 (1997), pp. 833–55

Innes, M., 'The classical tradition in the Carolingian Renaissance: ninth-century encounters with Suetonius', *International Journal of the Classical Tradition* 3 (1997), pp. 265–82

Innes, M., 'Memory, orality and literacy in an early medieval society', *Past and Present* 158 (1998), pp. 3–36

Innes, M., 'Teutons or Trojans? The Carolingians and the Germanic past', in Hen and Innes (eds.), *The uses of the past*, pp. 227–49

Innes, M., *State and society in the early middle ages 400–1000* (Cambridge, 2000)

Iogna-Prat, D., 'Lieu de culte et exégèse liturgique à l'époque carolingienne', in Chazelle and Edwards (eds.), *The study of the Bible*, pp. 215–44

Iogna-Prat, D., C. Jeudy and G. Lobrichon (eds.), *L'École carolingienne d'Auxerre de Murethach à Remi 830–908* (Auxerre, 1991)

Jacob, W., *Die handschriftliche Überlieferung der sogenannten Historia tripartita des Epiphanius Cassiodor*, Texte und Untersuchungen 59 (Berlin, 1954)

Jahn, J., *Ducatus Baiuvariorum. Das bairische Herzogtum der Agilolfinger*, Monographien zur Geschichte des Mittelalters 32 (Stuttgart, 1991)

Jahn, J., 'Virgil, Arbeo and Cozroh: Verfassungsgeschichtliche Beobachtungen an bairischen Quellen des 8. und 9. Jahrhunderts', *Mitteilungen des Gesellschaft für salzburger Landeskunde* 130 (1990), pp. 201–91

Jakobi, F.-J., 'Diptychen als frühe Form der Gedenk-Aufzeichnungen. Zum "Herrscher-Diptychon" im Liber memorialis von Remiremont', *Frühmittelalterliche Studien* 20 (1986), pp. 186–212

Jarnut, J., 'Kaiser Ludwig der Fromme und König Bernhard von Italien. Der Versuch einer Rehabilitierung', *Studi Medievali* 30 (1989), pp. 637–48

Jarnut, J., '*Gens, rex* and *regnum* of the Lombards', in Goetz, Jarnut and Pohl (eds.), *Regna and* gentes, pp. 409–27

Jarnut, J., U. Nonn and M. Richter (eds.), *Karl Martell in seiner Zeit*, Beihefte der Francia 37 (Sigmaringen, 1994)

Jones, C. W., 'The Victorian and Dionysiac paschal tables', *Speculum* 3 (1934), pp. 408–21

Jones, C. W., *Saints' lives and chronicles in early England* (Ithaca, 1947)

Jones, L. W., *The script of Cologne from Hildebold to Hermann* (Cambridge, Mass., 1932)

Kaiser, R., *Untersuchungen zur Geschichte der Civitas und Diözese Soissons in römischer und merowingischer Zeit*, Rheinisches Archiv 89 (Bonn, 1973)

Kantorowicz, E. H., *Laudes regiae: a study in liturgical acclamations and medieval ruler worship* (Berkeley, Calif., 1946)

Kasten, B., *Königssöhne und Königsherrschaft. Untersuchungen zur Teilhabe am Reich in der Merowinger- und Karolingerzeit*, MGH Schriften 44 (Hannover, 1997)

Keefe, S., *Water and the word*, 2 vols. (Notre Dame, 2002)

Kelley, D. R., *Foundations of modern historical scholarship* (New York and London, 1970)

Kelly, S., revised edition of P. H. Sawyer, *Anglo-Saxon Charters. An annotated list and bibliography*, typescript (Cambridge, 1994) and http://www.trin.cam.ac.uk/chartwww

Kempshall, M. S., 'Some Ciceronian apects of Einhard's life of Charlemagne', *Viator* 26 (1995), pp. 11–38

Kéry, L., *Canonical collections of the early middle ages (ca. 400–1140). A bibliographical guide to the manuscripts and literature*, History of Medieval Canon Law (Washington, D.C., 1999)

Kessler, H. L., 'A lay abbot as patron: Count Vivian and the First Bible of Charles the Bald', in *Committenti e produzione artistico-letteraria nell'alto medioevo occidentale*, Settimane 39 (Spoleto, 1992), pp. 647–76

Kessler, H. L., *The illustrated bibles from Tours*, Studies in Manuscript Illumination 7 (Princeton, 1977)

Keynes, S., 'Anglo-Saxon entries in "Liber Vitae" of Brescia', in J. Roberts and J. L. Nelson, with M. Godden (eds.), *Alfred the Wise: studies in honour of Janet*

Bately on the occasion of her sixty-fifth birthday (Cambridge, 1997), pp. 99–119

King, P. D., *Charlemagne. Translated sources* (Kendal, 1987)

Klaussen, M., *The reform of the Frankish church: Chrodegang of Metz and the Regula canonicorum in the eighth century* (Cambridge, 2004)

Kleinklausz, A. J., *Eginhard* (Paris, 1942)

Knight Bostock, J., *A handbook on Old High German literature*, 2nd edn (Oxford, 1976).

Knoeppler, H., '*De viris illustribus* and Isidore of Seville', *Journal of Theological Studies* 37 (1936), pp. 16–34

Koehler, W., *Karolingische Miniaturen*, I, *Die Schule von Tours* (Berlin, 1935), II, *Die Hofschule Karls des Grossen* (Berlin, 1958), and III, *Die Gruppe des Wiener Krönungsevangeliar. Metzer Handschriften* (Berlin, 1960)

Koep, L., *Das himmlische Buch in Antike und Christentum. Eine religions-geschichtliche Untersuchung zu altchristliche Bildersprache*, Theophaneia. Beiträge zur Religions- und Kirchengeschichte des Altertums 8 (Bonn, 1952)

Kolarova, L., 'The transmission and dissemination of Carolingian annals' (unpublished M.Phil. dissertation, University of Cambridge, 1995)

Kottje, R., 'Die Lex Baiuvariorum – das Recht der Baiern', in H. Mordek (ed.), *Überlieferung und Geltung normativer Texte des frühen und hohen Mittelalters*, Quellen und Forschungen zum Recht im Mittelalter 4 (Sigmaringen, 1986), pp. 9–24

Kottje, R., 'Zum Geltungsbereich der Lex Alamannorum', in H. Beumann and W. Schröder (eds.), *Die transalpinen Verbindungen der Bayern, Alemannen und Franken bis zum 10. Jahrhundert*, Nationes, Historische und philologische Untersuchungen zur Entstehung der europäischen Nationen im Mittelalter 6 (Sigmaringen, 1987), pp. 359–78

Krüger, K. H., 'Neue Beobachtungen zur Datierung von Einhards Karlsvita', *Frühmittelalterliche Studien* 32 (1998), pp. 124–45

Krusch, B., 'Ueber eine Handschrift des Victorius', *Neues Archiv* 9 (1883/4), pp. 269–82

Krusch, B., 'Das älteste fränkische Lehrbuch der dionysianischen Zeitrechnung', in *Mélanges offerts à Emile Chatelain* (Paris, 1910), pp. 232–42

Krusch, B., 'Die Übertragung des H. Alexander von Rom nach Wildeshausen durch den Enkel Widukinds 851. Das älteste niedersächsische Geschichts-denkmal', in *Nachrichten der Gesellschaft der Wissenschaften zu Göttingen* II, 13 (Göttingen, 1933), pp. 405–36

Krusch, B., 'Studien zur christlichmittelalterlichen Chronologie', *Abhandlungen der Preußischen Akademie der Wissenschaften, phil. hist. Klasse* 8, 1937 (Berlin, 1938)

Kurze, F., 'Ueber die Karolingischen Reichsannalen von 741–829 und ihre Ueberarbeitung 1: Die handschriftliche Ueberlieferung', *Neues Archiv* 19 (1894), pp. 295–339, and 'Zur Ueberlieferung der karolingischen Reichsannalen und ihrer Ueberarbeitung', *Neues Archiv* 28 (1903), pp. 619–69

La Giustizia nell'alto medioevo (secoli IX–XI), Settimane 44 (Spoleto, 1997)

La Rocca, C., *Pacifico di Verona. Il passato carolingio nella costruzione della memoria urbana*, Istituto storico italiano per il medio evo, Nuovi studi storici 31 (Rome, 1995)

La Rocca, C. (ed.), *Italy in the early middle ages* (Oxford, 2002)

Lanciotti, S., 'Tra Festo e Paolo', in Chiesa (ed.), *Paolo Diacono*, pp. 237–50

Landes, D., *Revolution in time, clocks and the making of the modern world* (Cambridge, Mass., 1983)

Le Goff, J., 'Time, merchant's time and church's time in the middle ages', in J. Le Goff, *Time, work and culture in the middle ages*, trans. A. Goldhammer (Chicago, 1980), pp. 29–42

Lee, A. D., *Pagans and Christians in late antiquity: a sourcebook* (London, 2000)

Lehmann, P., 'Erzbischof Hildebold und die Dombibliothek von Köln', *Zentralblatt für Bibliothekswesen* 25 (1908), pp. 153–8

Le Jan, R. (ed.), *La Royauté et les élites dans l'Europe carolingienne du début du IXe siècle aux environs de 920*, Centre de l'Histoire de l'Europe du Nord-Ouest 17 (Lille, 1998)

Leonardi, C., 'Anastasio bibliotecario e la tradizioni dal greco nella Roma alto medievali', in M. Herrin (ed.), *The sacred nectar of the Greeks: the study of Greek in the west in the early middle ages* (London, 1988), pp. 277–97

Leonardi, C., 'La figura di Paolo Diacono', in *Paolo Diacono e il Friuli altomedievale*, pp. 15–24

Levillain, L., 'Les Nibelungen historiques et leurs alliances de famille', *Annales du Midi* 49 (1937), pp. 337–407

Levillain, L., 'De l'authenticité de la *Clausula de unctione Pippini*', *Bibliothèque de l'École des Chartes* 88 (1927) pp. 20–42

Levison, W., *England and the Continent in the eighth century* (Oxford, 1946)

Levy, K., *Gregorian chant and the Carolingians* (Princeton, 1998)

Lewis, B., *History – remembered, recovered, invented* (Princeton, 1975)

Lhotsky, A., *Quellenkunde zur mittelalterlichen Geschichte Österreichs*, MIÖG Ergänzungsband 19 (Vienna, 1963)

Licht, T., 'Additional note on the "Library catalogue of Charlemagne's court"', *Journal of Medieval Latin* 11 (2001), pp. 210–13

Lieftinck, G. I., *Manuscrits datés conservés dans les Pays-Bas. Catalogue paléographique des manuscrits en écriture latine portant des indications de date*, I, *Les manuscrits d'origine étrangère (816–c.1550)* (Amsterdam, 1964)

Losek, F., 'Notitia Arnonis und Breves Notitiae', *Mitteilungen der Gesellschaft für Salzburger Landeskunde* 130 (1990), pp. 5–192

Lowe, E. A., 'An eighth-century list of books in a Bodleian manuscript from Würzburg and its probable relation to the Laudian Acts', *Speculum* 3 (1928), pp. 3–15, reprinted in Lowe, *Palaeographical papers 1907–1965*, I, pp. 239–50

Lowe, E. A., *Palaeographical papers 1907–1965*, ed. L. Bieler (Oxford, 1972)

Löwe, H., 'Studien zu den Annales Xantenses', *DA* 8 (1950), pp. 59–99

Löwe, H., 'Regino von Prüm und das historische Weltbild der Karolingerzeit', *Rheinische Vierteljahrsblätter* 17 (1952), pp. 151–79

Löwe, H., 'Ein literarischer Widersacher des Bonifatius. Virgil von Salzburg und die Kosmographie des Aethicus Ister', *Abhandlungen der Akademie der Wissenschaften und der Literatur in Mainz. Geistes- und sozialwissenschaftliche Klasse 1951* (Wiesbaden, 1952), pp. 899–988

Löwe, H., 'Die Entstehungszeit der *Vita Karoli* Einhards', *DA* 39 (1963), pp. 85–103

Löwe, H., 'Die Geschichtsschreibung der ausgehenden Karolingerzeit', *DA* 23 (1967), pp. 1–30

Löwe, H., 'Das Karlsbuch Notkers von St. Gallen und sein zeitgeschichtliche Hintergrund', *Schweizerische Zeitschrift für Geschichte* 20 (1970), pp. 269–302

Löwe, H. (ed.), *Wattenbach-Levison. Deutschlands Geschichtsquellen im Mittelalter. Vorzeit und Karolinger 6. Die Karolinger vom Vertrag von Verdun bis zum Herrschafts-antritt der Herrscher aus dem Sächsischen Hause. Das ostfränkische Reich* (Weimar, 1990)

Lozovsky, N., *'The earth is our book'. Geographical knowledge in the Latin West ca. 400–1000* (Ann Arbor, 2000)

Lundström, S., *Übersetzungstechnische Untersuchungen auf dem Gebiete der christlichen Latinität* (Lund, 1955)

Lynch, J. H., *Godparents and kinship in early medieval Europe* (Princeton, 1986)

Maassen, F., *Bibliotheca latina iuris canonici manuscripta* (Vienna, 1866)

Maassen, F., *Geschichte der Quellen des canonischen Rechts im Abendlande bis zum Ausgange des Mittelalters* 1 (Graz, 1870)

Magdalino, P. (ed.), *The perception of the past in twelfth-century Europe* (London, 1992)

Magdalino, P., 'The history of the future and its uses: prophecy, policy and propaganda', in R. Beaton and C. Roueché (eds.), *The making of Byzantine history. Studies dedicated to Donald M. Nicol* (Aldershot,1993), pp. 3–34

Magdalino, P., 'The distance of the past in early medieval Byzantium (VII–X centuries)', in *Ideologie e pratiche del reimpiego nell'alto medioevo*, Settimane 46 (Spoleto, 1999), I, pp. 115–146

Magdalino, P., 'A history of Byzantine literature for historians', in *Pour une "nouvelle" histoire de la littérature byzantine. Actes du colloque philologique Nicosie, 25–28 mai 2000*, Dossiers byzantins 1 (Paris, 2002), pp. 167–84

Magdalino, P. (ed.), *Byzantium in the year 1000*, The Medieval Mediterranean: Peoples, Economies and Cultures, 400–1500, 45 (Leiden, 2003)

Mango, C., 'The tradition of Byzantine chronography', *Harvard Ukrainian Studies* 12/13 (1988/9), pp. 360–72

Marenbon, J., 'Carolingian thought', in McKitterick (ed.), *Carolingian culture*, pp. 171–92

Marincola, J., *Authority and tradition in ancient historiography* (Cambridge, 1997)

Markopoulos, A., 'Byzantine history writing at the end of the first millennium', in Magdalino (ed.), *Byzantium in the year 1000*, pp. 183–98

Markus, R. A., 'Church history and early church historians', in D. Baker (ed.), *The materials, sources and methods of ecclesiastical history*, Studies in Church History 11 (Oxford, 1975), pp. 1–17

Markus, R. A., *Bede and the tradition of ecclesiastical history*, Jarrow Lecture, 1975, reprinted in *From Augustine to Gregory the Great* (London, 1980)

Markus, R. A., 'Chronicle and theology: Prosper of Aquitaine', in Holdsworth and Wiseman (eds.), *The inheritance of historiography*, pp. 31–44

Martin, H.-J., and J. Vezin (eds.), *Mise en page et mise en texte du livre manuscrit* (Paris, 1990)

Masai, F., 'Observations sur le Psautier dit de Charlemagne', *Scriptorium* 6 (1952), pp. 299–303

Mason, E., *St Wulfstan of Worcester c. 1008–1095* (Oxford, 1990)

Matthews, J., *The world of Ammianus Marcellinus* (London, 1989)

McCarthy, D. P., 'The chronology and sources of the early Irish annals', *EME* 10 (2001), pp. 323–41

McCluskey, S. C., 'Gregory of Tours, monastic timekeeping and early Christian attitudes to astronomy', *Isis* 81 (1990), pp. 9–22

McCormick, M., *Les Annales du haut moyen âge*, Typologie des sources du moyen âge occidental, fasc. 14 (Turnhout, 1975)

McCormick, M., 'Byzantium and the west, 700–900', in McKitterick (ed.), *NCMH*, pp. 349–80

McCormick, M., *Origins of the European economy. Communication and commerce AD 300–900* (Cambridge, 2001)

McKitterick, R., *The Frankish church and the Carolingian reforms, 789–895*, Royal Historical Society, Studies in History 2 (London, 1977)

McKitterick, R., 'Charles the Bald and his library: the patronage of learning', *EHR* 95 (1980), pp. 28–47, reprinted in McKitterick, *Frankish kings and culture*, chapter 5

McKitterick, R., 'The study of Frankish history in France and Germany in the sixteenth and seventeenth centuries', *Francia* 8 (1981), pp. 556–72, reprinted in McKitterick, *Frankish kings and culture*, chapter 13

McKitterick, R., *The Frankish kingdoms under the Carolingians, 751–987* (London, 1983)

McKitterick, R., 'Knowledge of canon law in the Frankish kingdoms before 789: the manuscript evidence', *Journal of Theological Studies*, n.s. 36 (1985), pp. 97–117, reprinted in McKitterick, *Books, scribes and learning*, chapter 2

McKitterick, R., *The Carolingians and the written word* (Cambridge, 1989)

McKitterick, R., 'The diffusion of insular culture in Neustria between 650 and 850, the implications of the manuscript evidence', in Atsma (ed.), *La Neustrie*, pp. 395–432, reprinted in McKitterick, *Books, scribes and learning*, chapter 3

McKitterick, R., 'The Anglo-Saxon missionaries in Germany: reflections on the manuscript evidence', *Transactions of the Cambridge Bibliographical Society* 9 (1989), pp. 291–329, reprinted in McKitterick, *Books, scribes and learning*, chapter 4

McKitterick, R. (ed.), *The uses of literacy in early mediaeval Europe* (Cambridge, 1990)

McKitterick, R., 'Text and image in the Carolingian world', in McKitterick (ed.), *Uses of literacy*, pp. 297–318

McKitterick, R., *Anglo-Saxon missionaries in Germany: personal connections and local influences*, Vaughan Paper 36 (Leicester, 1991), reprinted in McKitterick, *Frankish kings and culture*, chapter 1

McKitterick, R., 'Nuns' scriptoria in England and Francia in the eighth century', *Francia* 19/1 (1992), pp. 1–35, reprinted in McKitterick, *Books, scribes and learning*, chapter 7

McKitterick, R., 'Knowledge of Plato's *Timaeus* in the ninth century: the implications of Valenciennes, Bibliothèque Municipale MS 293', in H. J. Westra (ed.), *From Athens to Chartres. Neoplatonism and medieval thought* (Leiden, 1992), pp. 85–95, and reprinted in R. McKitterick, *Books, scribes and learning*, chapter 10

McKitterick, R., 'Zur Herstellung von Kapitularien: die Arbeit des Leges-Skriptoriums', *MIÖG* 101 (1993), pp. 3–16

McKitterick, R., *Books, scribes and learning in the Frankish kingdoms, 6th–9th centuries* (Aldershot, 1994)

McKitterick, R., 'Women and literacy in the early middle ages,' in McKitterick, *Books, scribes and learning*, chapter 13

McKitterick, R. (ed.), *Carolingian culture: emulation and innovation* (Cambridge, 1994)

McKitterick, R., *The Frankish kings and culture in the early middle ages* (Aldershot, 1995)

McKitterick, R. (ed.), *The new Cambridge medieval history*, II, *c. 700–c. 900* (Cambridge, 1995)

McKitterick, R., 'Unity and diversity in the Carolingian church', in R. Swanson (ed.), *Unity and diversity in the church*, Studies in Church History 32 (Oxford, 1996), pp. 59–82

McKitterick, R., 'Essai sur les représentations de l'écrit dans les manuscrits carolingiens', in F. Dupuigrenet Desroussilles (ed.), *La Symbolique du livre dans l'art occidental du haut moyen âge à Rembrandt*, Revue française d'histoire du livre 86–7 (Bordeaux, 1995), pp. 37–64

McKitterick, R., 'Das Konzil im Kontext der karolingischen Renaissance', in Berndt (ed.), *Das Frankfurter Konzil von 794*, II, pp. 635–76

McKitterick, R., 'Gibbon and the early middle ages in eighteenth-century Europe', in R. McKitterick and R. Quinault (eds.), *Edward Gibbon and empire* (Cambridge, 1997), pp. 162–89

McKitterick, R., 'Perceptions of justice in western Europe in the ninth and tenth centuries', in *La Giustizia nell'alto medioevo (secoli IX–XI)*, Settimane 44 (Spoleto, 1997), pp. 1075–1102

McKitterick, R., review article of K. Levy, *Gregorian chant and the Carolingians* (Princeton, 1998), *Early Music History* 19 (2000), pp. 279–90

McKitterick, R., 'Kulturelle Verbindungen zwischen England und den fränkischen Reichen in der Zeit der Karolinger: Kontext und Implikationen', in Ehlers (ed.), *Deutschland und der Westen Europas*, pp. 121–48

McLaughlin, M., *Consorting with saints. Prayer for the dead in early medieval France* (Ithaca and London, 1994)

McMullen, D., *State and scholars in T'ang China* (Cambridge, 1988)

Merrills, A., *History and geography in late antiquity* (Cambridge, 2004)

Milde, W. (ed.), *Der Bibliothekskatalog des Klosters Murbach aus dem 9. Jahrhundert. Ausgabe und Untersuchungen von Beziehungen zu Cassiodors 'Institutiones', Euphorion, Zeitschrift für Literaturgeschichte*, Beiheft 4 (Heidelberg, 1968)

Miles, R. (ed.), *Constructing identities in late antiquity* (London, 1999)

Molitor, S., 'Das Traditionsbuch: zur Forschungsgeschichte einer Quellengattung und zu einem Beispiel aus Südwestdeutschland', *Archiv für Diplomatik* 36 (1990), pp. 61–92

Momigliano, A., 'Pagan and Christian historiography in the fourth century A.D.', in A. Momigliano (ed.), *The conflict between paganism and Christianity in the fourth century* (London, 1962), pp. 79–99

Mordek H., *Biblioteca capitularium regum francorum manuscripta. Überlieferung und Traditionszusammenhang der fränkischen Herrscherlasse*, MGH Hilfsmittel 15 (Munich, 1995)

Mordek, H., *Kirchenrecht und Reform in Frankenreich: Die Collectio Vetus Gallica, die älteste systematische Kanonensammlung des fränkischen Gallien. Studien und Edition*, Beiträge zur Geschichte und Quellenkunde des Mittelalters 1 (Berlin and New York, 1975)

Moreton B., *The eighth-century Gelasian sacramentary. A study in tradition* (Oxford, 1976)

Morghen, R., 'Il palinsesto Assisiense dell "Historia Langobardorum" di Paolo Diacono', *Bullettino dell'Istituto Storico Italiano* 38 (1918), pp. 7–23 and plates 1–26

Morse, R., *Truth and convention in the middle ages: rhetoric, representation and reality* (Cambridge, 1991)

Mortensen, L. Boje, 'The texts and contexts of ancient Roman history in twelfth-century western scholarship', in Magdalino (ed.), *The perception of the past in twelfth-century Europe*, pp. 99–116

Mortensen, L. Boje, '*Impero romano, Historia Romana e Historia langobardorum*', in Chiesa (ed.), *Paolo Diacono*, pp. 355–66

Mortensen, L. Boje, 'Stylistic choice in a reborn genre: the national histories of Widukind of Corvey and Dudo of St Quentin', in P. G. A. degli'Innocenti (ed.), *Dudone de S. Quintino* (Trento, 1995), pp. 77–102

Mosshammer, A. A., *The Chronicle of Eusebius and Greek chronographic tradition* (Lewisburg, 1979)

Mostert, M. (ed.), *New approaches to medieval communication*, Utrecht Studies in Medieval Literacy (Turnhout, 1999)

Mostert, M., 'The tradition of classical manuscripts of Fleury, Appendix: Latin classics from the Fleury library', in Chavannes-Mazel and Smith (eds.), *Medieval manuscripts of the Latin classics*, pp. 19–40

Mostert, M., *The library of Fleury. A provisional list of manuscripts* (Hilversum, 1989)

Müller, K., *Q. Curtius Rufus Geschichte Alexanders der Großen* (Munich, 1954)

Murray, A. C. (ed.), *After Rome's fall: narrators and sources of early medieval history. Essays presented to Walter Goffart* (Toronto, 1998)

Nagel, H., *Karl der Grosse und die theologischen Herausforderungen seiner Zeit*, Freiburger Beiträge zur mittelalterliche Geschichte. Studien und Texte 12 (Bern, 1998)

Nees, L. (ed.), 'Approaches to early medieval art', *Speculum* 72 (1997), pp. 959–1143

Neff, K., *Die Gedichte Paulus Diaconus, Quellen und Untersuchungen zur lateinischen Philologie des Mittelalters*, III, 4 (Munich, 1908)

Nelson, J. L., 'Legislation and consensus in the reign of Charles the Bald', in Wormald (ed.), *Ideal and reality*, pp. 202–27

Nelson, J. L., 'Public histories and private history in the work of Nithard', *Speculum* 60 (1985), pp. 251–93; reprinted in Nelson, *Politics and ritual*, pp. 195–238

Nelson, J. L., *Politics and ritual in early medieval Europe* (London, 1986)

Nelson, J. L., 'Translating images of authority: the Christian Roman emperors in the Carolingian world', in M. M. Mackenzie and C. Roueché (eds.), *Images of authority. Papers presented to Joyce Reynolds on the occasion of her 70th birthday*, Proceedings of the Cambridge Philological Society, supplementary volume, 16 (Cambridge, 1989), pp. 194–205; reprinted in Nelson, *The Frankish world*, pp. 89–98

Nelson, J. L., 'Literacy in Carolingian government', in McKitterick (ed.), *Uses of literacy*, pp. 258–96

Nelson, J. L., 'The Annals of St. Bertin', in Nelson and Gibson (eds.), *Charles the Bald*, pp. 23–40, reprinted in Nelson, *Politics and ritual*, pp. 173–94

Nelson, J. L., 'Perceptions du pouvoir chez les historiennes du haut moyen âge', in M. Rouche (ed.), *Les Femmes au moyen âge* (Paris, 1990) pp. 77–85

Nelson, J. L., *Charles the Bald* (London 1992)

Nelson, J. L., 'History writing at the courts of Louis the Pious and Charles the Bald', in Scharer and Scheibelreiter (eds.), *Historiographie*, pp. 435–42

Nelson, J. L., 'Kingship and empire in the Carolingian world', in McKitterick (ed.), *Carolingian culture*, pp. 52–87

Nelson, J. L., 'Kingship and royal government', in McKitterick (ed.), *NCMH*, pp. 383–430

Nelson, J. L., *The Frankish world, 750–900* (London, 1996)

Nelson, J. L., 'Gender and genre in women historians of the early middle ages,' in Nelson, *The Frankish world*, pp. 183–97

Nelson, J. L., 'Making a difference in eighth-century politics: the daughters of Desiderius', in Murray (ed.), *After Rome's fall*, pp. 171–90

Nelson, J. L., 'Aachen as a place of power', in de Jong and Theuws with van Rhijn (eds.), *Topographies of power*, pp. 217–42

Nelson, J. L. and M. Gibson (eds.), *Charles the Bald. Court and kingdom* (2nd edn, London, 1990)

Netzer, N., *Cultural interplay in the eighth century. The Trier Gospels and the making of a scriptorium at Echternach* (Cambridge, 1994)

Nichols, S. G. (ed.), 'The New Philology', *Speculum* 65 (1990), pp. 1–108

Niederkorn, M. and A. Scharer (eds.), *Arn von Salzburg* (Vienna, 2004)

Niederkorn, M., 'Das sanctorale Salzburgs um 800. Liturgie zwischen Norm und Praxis', Habilitationschrift Universität Wien (Vienna, 1999)

Nineham, D., 'Gottschalk of Orbais: reactionary or precursor of the Reformation', *Journal of Ecclesiastical History* 40 (1989), pp. 1–18

Noble, T. F. X., 'The revolt of King Bernard', *Studi Medievali* 3, series 15 (1974), pp. 315–26

Noble, T. F. X., *The republic of St. Peter. The birth of the papal state, 680–825* (Philadelphia, 1984)

Noble, T. F. X., 'A new look at the *Liber pontificalis*', *Archivum Historiae Pontificiae* 23 (1985), pp. 347–58

Noble, T. F. X., 'Tradition and learning in search of ideology: the *Libri carolini*', in R. E. Sullivan (ed.), '*The gentle voices of teachers': aspects of learning in the Carolingian age* (Columbus, Ohio, 1995), pp. 227–60

Noble, T. F. X., 'Paradoxes and possibilities in the sources for Roman society in the early middle ages', in Smith (ed.), *Early medieval Rome*, pp. 55–84

Nonn, U., 'Zur Königserhebung Karls und Karlmanns', *Rheinische Viertel-jahrsblätter* 39 (1975), pp. 386–7

Noth, A., *The early Arabic historical tradition: a source critical study*, 2nd edn in collaboration with L. Conrad, trans. M. Bonner (Princeton, 1994)

Ó Cróinín, D., 'Early Irish annals from Easter Tables: a case restated', *Peritia* 2 (1983), pp. 74–86

Oexle, O.-G., 'Memorial und Memorialüberlieferung im früheren Mittelalter', *Frühmittelalterliche Studien* 10 (1976), pp. 70–96

Oexle, O.-G., 'Die Gegenwart der Toten', in H. Braet and H. Verbeke (eds.), *Death in the middle ages* (Louvain, 1983), pp. 19–77

Oexle, O.-G. (ed.), *Memoria als Kultur*, Veröffentlichungen des Max-Planck-Instituts für Geschichte 121 (Göttingen, 1995)

Oexle, O.-G. and K. Schmid, 'Voraussetzungen und Wirkung des Gebetbundes von Attigny', *Francia* 2 (1975), pp. 71–122

Otten, W., 'The texture of tradition: the role of the church fathers in Carolingian theology', in Backus (ed.), *The reception of the church fathers in the west*, pp. 3–49

Oulton, J. E. L., 'Rufinus's translation of the church history of Eusebius', *Journal of Theological Studies* 30 (1929), pp. 150–74

Pani S., 'Aspetti della tradizione manoscritta dell'Historia Langobardorum', in Chiesa (ed.), *Paolo Diacono*, pp. 367–412

Paolo Diacono e il Friuli altomedievale (secc. VI–X), Atti del XIV congresso internazionale di studi sull'alto medioevo, 2 vols. (Spoleto, 2001)

Parkes, M. B., *Pause and effect: punctuation in the west* (London, 1992)

Parkes, M. B., *Scribes, scripts and readers. Studies in the communication, presentation and dissemination of medieval texts* (London, 1991)

Partner, N. F. (ed.), 'Studying medieval women', *Speculum* 68 (1993) pp. 305–471

Paxton, F. S., *Christianizing death. The creation of a ritual process in early medieval Europe* (Ithaca, 1990)

Pearson, K., *Conflicting loyalties in early medieval Bavaria: a view of socio-political interaction, 680–900* (Aldershot, 1999)

Pecere, O. and M. D. Reeve (eds.), *Formative stages of classical traditions: Latin texts from antiquity to the renaissance* (Spoleto, 1995)

Peitz, W. B. M., *Dionysius Exiguus Studien* (Bonn, 1960)

Peters, E., *The shadow king. Rex inutilis in medieval law and literature 751–1327* (New Haven and London, 1970)

Platelle, H., *Le Temporel de l'abbaye de Saint-Amand des origines à 1340* (Paris, 1962)

Pohl, W., 'Tradition, Ethnogenese und literarische Gestaltung: eine Zwischenbilanz', in K. Brunner and B. Merta (eds.), *Ethnogenese und Überlieferung. Angewandte Methoden der Frühmittelalterforschung* (Vienna and Munich, 1994), pp. 9–26

Pohl, W., 'Paulus Diaconus und die *Historia langobardorum*; Text und Tradition', in Scharer und Scheibelreiter (eds.), *Historiographie*, pp. 375–405

Pohl, W. and H. Reimitz (eds.), *Strategies of distinction. The construction of ethnic communities, 300–800*, Transformation of the Roman World 2 (Leiden, 1998)

Pohl, W., 'History in fragments: Montecassino's politics of memory', *EME* 10 (2001), pp. 343–74

Pohl, W., 'Paolo Diacono e la costruzione dell'identità longobarda', in *Chiesa* (ed.), *Paolo Diacono*, pp. 413–26

Pohl, W., *Werkstätte der Erinnerung: Montecassino und die Gestaltung der langobardischen Vergangenheit* (Vienna, 2001)

Polfer, M., (ed.), *L'Évangelisation des régions entre Meuse et Moselle et la fondation de l'abbaye d'Echternach (Ve–IXe siècle)* (Luxembourg, 2000)

Poole, R. L., *Chronicles and annals: a brief outline of their origin and growth* (Oxford, 1926)

Pratt, D., 'Problems of authorship and audience in the writings of King Alfred the Great', in P. Wormald (ed.), *Learned laity in the Carolingian era* (Cambridge, forthcoming).

Prete, S. (ed.), *Didascaliae. Studies in honor of Anselm M. Albareda* (New York, 1961)

Quadri, R. (ed.), *I collectanea di Eirico di Auxerre* (Fribourg, 1966)

Quinn, P., *Better than the sons of kings: boys and monks in the early middle ages*, Studies in History and Culture 2 (New York, Bern, Frankfurt am Main and Paris, 1989)

Raajimakers, J., 'Sacred time, sacred space: history and identity at the monastery of Fulda (744–856)' (Ph.D. thesis, University of Amsterdam, 2003; akademisch proefschrift)

Rajak, T., *Josephus: the historian and his society*, 2nd edn (London and Philadelphia, 2002)

Rand, E. K., 'On the history of the *De vita Caesarum* of Suetonius in the early middle ages', *Harvard Studies in Classical Philology* 37 (1926), pp. 1–48

Ranke, L. von, 'Zur Kritik fränkisch-deutscher Reichsannalen', *Abhandlungen der königlichen Akademie der Wissenschaften* (Berlin, 1854), pp. 415–56

Rankin, S., '"Ego itaque Notker scripsi"', *RB* 101 (1991), pp. 268–98

Rankin, S., 'Carolingian music', in McKitterick (ed.), *Carolingian culture*, pp. 274–316

Rappmann, R. and A. Zettler, *Die Reichenauer Mönchsgemeinschaft und ihr Totengedenken im frühen Mittelalter*, Archäologie und Geschichte. Freiburger Forschungen zum ersten Jahrtausend in Südwestdeutschland 5 (Sigmaringen, 1998)

Reeve, M. D., 'The place of P in the stemma of Livy 1–10', in Chavannes-Mazel and Smith (eds.), *Medieval manuscripts of the Latin classics*, pp. 74–90

Reimitz, H., 'Social networks and identities in Frankish historiography. New aspects of the textual history of Gregory of Tours' *Historiae*', in Corradini, Diesenberger and Reimitz (eds.), *The construction of communities in the early middle ages*, pp. 229–268

Reimitz, H., 'Ein fränkisches Geschichtsbuch aus Saint-Amand und der Codex Vindobonensis palat. 473', in C. Egger and H. Weigl (eds.), *Text-Schrift-Codex. Quellenkundliche Arbeiten aus dem Institut für Österreichische Geschichtsforschung*, *MIÖG* Ergänzungsband 35 (Vienna and Munich, 2000), pp. 34–90

Reimitz, H., 'Der Weg zum Königtum in historiographischen Kompendien der Karolingerzeit', in J. Jarnut and M. Becher (eds.), *Historiographie und Identität in den fränkischen Regna der Merowinger- und Karolingerzeit* (forthcoming)

Remensnyder, A., *Remembering kings past: monastic foundation legends in medieval southern France* (Ithaca, 1995)

Reuter, T., 'Saint Boniface and Europe', in T. Reuter (ed.) *The greatest Englishman* (Exeter, 1980), pp. 69–94

Reynolds, L. D. (ed.), *Texts and transmission. A survey of the Latin classics* (Oxford, 1983)

Riain-Raendel, D. O., 'Aspects of the promotion of Irish saints' cults in medieval Germany', *Zeitschrift für celtische Philologie* 39 (1982), pp. 1–15

Richards, E. G., *Mapping time: the calendar and its history* (Oxford, 1988)

Riché, P., 'Les Bibliothèques de trois aristocrates laïcs carolingiens', *Le Moyen Âge* 69 (1963), pp. 87–104

Richter, M., *The formation of the medieval west. Studies in the oral culture of the barbarians* (Dublin, 1994)

Ridyard, S. J. (ed.), *Reading and the book in the middle ages*, Sewanee Medieval Studies 11 (Sewanee, 2001)

Rissel, M., *Rezeption antiker und patristischer Wissenschaft bei Hrabanus Maurus. Studien zur karolingischen Geistesgeschichte* (Bern and Frankfurt, 1976)

Robinson, C. H., *Islamic historiography* (Cambridge, 2003)

Robinson, R. P., *The Germania of Tacitus* (Middletown, Conn., 1935)

Robinson, R. P., 'The Hersfeldensis and the Fuldensis of Ammianus Marcellinus', *University of Missouri Studies. A quarterly of research* 11 (1936), pp. 118–40

Rohrbacher, D., *The historians of late antiquity* (London, 2002)

Rose, V., *Die Handschriftverzeichnisse der Königlichen Bibliothek zu Berlin. Verzeichnis der lateinischen Handschriften*, II, part 3 (Berlin, 1905)

Rosenwein, B., *To be the neighbor of St Peter. The social meaning of Cluny's property, 909–1049* (Ithaca and London, 1989)

Saint Chrodegang (Metz, 1967)

Sassel, J., 'L'organizzazione del confine orientale d'Italia nell'alto medioevo', in *Aquileia e le Venezie nell'alto medioevo*, Antichità altoadriatiche 32 (Udine, 1988), pp. 107–14

Sawyer, P. and I. N. Wood (eds.), *Early medieval kingship* (Leeds, 1977)

Sawyer, P. H., *Anglo-Saxon Charters. An annotated list and bibliography* (London, 1968) (see also under Kelly)

Scharer, A. and G. Sheibelreiter (eds.), *Historiographie im frühen Mittelalter*, Veröffentlichungen des Instituts für Österreichische Geschichtsforschung 32 (Vienna and Munich, 1994)

Scharer, A., 'The writing of history at King Alfred's court', *EME* 5 (1996), pp. 177–206

Scharer, A., *Herrschaft und Repräsentation. Studien zur Hofkultur Königs Alfreds des Großen*, MIÖG Ergänzungsband 36 (Vienna and Munich, 2000)

Schefers, H. (ed.), *Einhard. Studien zu Leben und Werk* (Darmstadt, 1997)

Schiaparelli, L., *Il codice 490 della biblioteca capitolare di Lucca e la scuola scrittoria Lucchese (sec. VIII–IX). Contributi allo studio della minuscola precarolina in Italia*, Studi e testi 36 (Vatican City, 1924)

Schieffer, R. (ed.), *Schriftkultur und Reichsverwaltung unter den Karolingern*, Abhandlungen der Nordrhein-Westfälischen Akademie der Wissenschaften (Opladen, 1996).

Schieffer, R., 'Charlemagne and Rome', in Smith (ed.), *Early medieval Rome*, pp. 279–96

Schmid, K., 'Über das Verhältnis von Person und Gemeinschaft im früheren Mittelalter', *Frühmittelalterliche Studien* 1 (1967), pp. 225–49

Schmid, K., 'Ein karolingischer Königseintrag im Gedenkbuch von Remiremont', *Frühmittelalterliche Studien* 2 (1968), pp. 96–134

Schmid, K. (ed.), *Die Kloster Gemeinschaft von Fulda im früheren Mittelalter*, Münstersche Mittelalterschriften 8 (Munich, 1978)

Schmid, K., 'Probleme der Erschließung des Salzburger Verbrüderungsbuches' in E. Zwinke (ed.), *Frühes Mönchtum in Salzburg*, Salzburg Diskussionen 4 (Salzburg, 1983), pp. 175–96

Schmid, K., *Gebetsgedenken und adliges Selbstverständnis im Mittelalter: ausgewählte Beiträge, Festgabe zu seinem 60. Geburtstag* (Sigmaringen, 1983)

Schmid, K. and O.-G. Oexle, 'Voraussetzungen und Wirkung des Gebetbundes von Attigny', *Francia* 2 (1974), pp. 71–122

Schmid, K. and J. Wollasch, 'Die Gemeinschaft von Lebenden und Verstorbenen in Zeugnissen des Mittelalters', *Frühmittelalterliche Studien* 1 (1967), pp. 365–405

Schmid, K. and J. Wollasch, *Memoria. Der geschichtliche Zeugniswert des liturgischen Gedenkens im Mittelalter*, Münstersche Mittelalterschriften 48 (Munich, 1984)

Schreckenburg, H. and K. Schubert (eds.), *Jewish historiography and iconography in early and medieval Christianity* (Assen and Minneapolis, 1992).

Schreckenburg, H., *Die Flavius-Josephus-Tradition in Antike und Mittelalter* and *Rezeptionsgeschichtliche und textkritische Untersuchungen zu Flavius Josephus*, Arbeiten zum Literatur und Geschichte des hellenistichen Judentums 5 and 10 (Leiden, 1972 and 1977)

Schwab, U., *Die Sternrune im Wessobrunner Gebet. Beobachtungen zur Lokalisierung des clm 22053, zur Hs. BM Arundel 393 und zu Rune Poem V. 86–89*, Amsterdamer Publikationen zur Sprache und Literatur 1 (Amsterdam, 1973)

Selzer, W., 'Ein alt-Salzburger Fragment der Kosmographie des Aethicus Ister aus dem 8 Jht', *MIÖG* 100 (1992), pp. 132–49

Semmler, J., *Der Dynastiewechsel von 751 und die fränkische Königssalbung*, Studia humaniora. Düsseldorfer Studien zu Mittelalter und Renaissance, series minor 6 (Düsseldorf, 2003)

Semmler, J., 'Zu den bayrisch-westfränkischen Beziehungen', *Zeitschrift für bayerische Landesgeschichte* 29 (1966), pp. 372–85

Sevčenko, I., 'The search for the past in Byzantium around the year 800', *Dumbarton Oaks Papers* 46 (1992), pp. 279–93

Shepard, J., 'The uses of "history" in Byzantine diplomacy: observations and comparisons', in C. Dendrinos, J. Harris, E. Harvalia-Crook and J. Herrin (eds.), *Porphyrogenita. Essays on the history and literature of Byzantium and the Latin east in honour of Julian Chrysostomides* (Aldershot, 2003), pp. 91–115

Sichard, D., *Le Liturgie de la mort dans l'église latine des origines à la réforme carolingienne* (Münster, 1978)

Siegmund, A., *Die Überlieferung der griechischen christlichen Literatur*, Abhandlungen der Bayerischen Benediktiner Akademie 5 (Munich, 1949)

Smidt, W., 'Ein altes Handschriftenfragment der "Viri illustres" Isidors von Sevilla', *Neues Archiv* 44 (1922), pp. 125–35

Smith, J. M. H., 'A hagiographer at work: Hucbald and the library of Saint-Amand', *RB* 106 (1996) pp. 151–71

Smith, J. M. H., 'Fines imperii: the marches', in McKitterick (ed.), *NCMH*, pp. 169–89

Smith, J. M. H. (ed.), *Early medieval Rome and the Christian west. Essays in honour of Donald Bullough* (Leiden, 2000)

Somfai, A., 'The transmission and reception of Plato's *Timaeus* and Calcidius's Commentary during the Carolingian Renaissance' (unpublished Ph.D. dissertation, University of Cambridge, 1998)

Sorabji, R., *Time, creation and the continuum* (London, 1983)

Sot, M., 'Historiographie épiscopale et modèle familial en occident au IXe siècle', *Annales ESC* 33 (1978) pp. 433–69

Sot, M., 'Le *Liber de episcopis mettensibus* dans l'histoire du genre "Gesta episcoporum"', in Chiesa (ed.), *Paolo Diacono*, pp. 527–50

Sot, M., 'Les dix livres d'Histoire chez les écrivains carolingiens', in Gauthier and Galinié (eds.), *Grégoire de Tours*, pp. 319–30

Southern, R., 'Aspects of the European tradition of historical writing. I. The classical tradition from Einhard to Geoffrey of Monmouth', *TRHS* fifth series 20 (1970), pp. 173–96

Southern, R., 'Aspects of the European tradition of historical writing. IV The sense of the past', *TRHS* fifth series 23 (1973), pp. 243–64

Speyer, W., *Büchervernichtung und Zensur des Geistes bei Heiden, Juden und Christen*, Bibliothek des Buchwesens 7 (Stuttgart, 1981)

Spiegel, G. M., *The past as text: the theory and practice of medieval historiography* (Baltimore, 1999)

Spilling, H., 'Angelsächsische Schrift in Fulda', in A. Brall (ed.), *Von der Klosterbibliothek zur Landesbibliothek. Beiträge zum zweihundertjährigen Bestehen der Hessischen Landesbibliothek Fulda* (Stuttgart, 1978), pp. 47–98

Spilling, H., 'Die frühe Phase karolingischer Minuskel in Fulda', in G. Schrimpf (ed.), *Kloster Fulda in der Welt der Karolinger und Ottonen*, Fuldaer Studien 7 (Frankfurt, 1996), pp. 249–84

Stella, F., 'La poesia di Paolo Diacono: nuovi manoscritti e attribuzioni incerte' in Chiesa (ed.), *Paolo Diacono*, pp. 551–74

Stevens, W., *Bede's scientific achievement* (Newcastle, 1986), revised version in Stevens, *Cycles of time*, chapter 2

Stevens, W., *Cycles of time and scientific learning in medieval Europe* (Aldershot, 1995)

Stiegemann, C. and Wemhoff, M. (eds.), *799 Kunst und Kultur der Karolingerzeit. Karl der Große und Papst Leo III in Paderborn* (Mainz, 1999)

Stock, B., *The implications of literacy: written langauge and models of interpretation in the eleventh and twelfth centuries* (Princeton, 1983)

Stoclet, A., *Autour de Fulrad de Saint-Denis (v.710–784)* (Geneva and Paris, 1993)

Story, J., *Carolingian connections: Anglo-Saxon England and Carolingian Francia, c. 750–870* (Aldershot, 2003)

Syme, R., *Ammianus Marcellinus and the Historia Augusta* (London, 1969)

Tangl, M., 'Studien zur Neuausgabe der Briefe des hl. Bonifatius und Lullus Teil I', in M. Tangl, *Das Mittelalter in Quellenkunde und Diplomatik. Ausgewählte*

Schriften, I, Forschungen zur mittelalterlichen Geschichte 12 (Berlin, 1966), pp. 60–175

Tellenbach, G., 'Der Liber Memorialis von Remiremont. Zur kritische Erforschung und zum Quellenwert liturgische Gedenkbücher, *DA* 25 (1969), pp. 64–110

Tellenbach, G., 'Liturgische Gedenkbücher als historische Quelle, *Mélanges E. Tisserant* 5, Studi e testi 235 (Rome, Vatican City, 1964), pp. 389–99

Temps, mémoire, tradition au moyen âge, Actes du XIIIe Congrès de la Société des historiens mediévistes de l'enseignement supérieur public, Aix-en-Provence, 4–5 juin 1982 (Aix-en-Provence, 1983)

Testo e immagine nell'alto Medioevo, Settimane 41 (Spoleto, 1994)

Thacker, A. and R. Sharpe (eds.), *Local saints and local churches in the early medieval west* (Oxford, 2002)

Thelamon, F., *Païens et chrétiens au IVe siècle: l'apport de l'histoire ecclésiastique de Rufin d'Aquilée* (Paris, 1981)

Thomas, H., 'Die Namenliste des Diptychon Barberini und der Sturz des Hausmeiers Grimoald', *DA* 25 (1969), pp. 17–63

Till, R., *Handschriftliche Untersuchungen zu Tacitus Agricola and Germania* (Berlin-Dahlem, 1943)

Tillotson, M., 'Carolingian sub-kings and kingship, 781–864' (unpublished M.Phil. essay, University of Cambridge, 2003)

Tillotson, M., 'Frankish diplomatic relations in the reign of Louis the Pious' (unpublished M.Phil. dissertation, University of Cambridge, 2003)

Tischler, M., *Einharts Vita Karoli. Studien zur Entstehung, Überlieferung und Rezeption*, 2 vols., *MGH* Schriften 48 (Hannover, 2001)

Traube, L., 'Perrona Scottorum', in L. Traube, *Vorlesungen und Abhandlungen*, II, *Kleine Schriften* (Munich, 1920), pp. 95–119

Treitler, L., 'Homer and Gregory. The transmission of epic poetry and plainchant', *The Musical Quarterly* 60 (1974), pp. 333–72

Tremp, E., 'Thegan und Astronomus, die beiden Geschichtsschreiber Ludwigs des Frommen', in *Charlemagne's Heir*, pp. 691–700

Tremp, E., *Studien zu den Gesta Hludowici imperatoris des Trierer Chorbischofs Thegan*, *MGH* Schriften 32 (Hannover, 1988)

Tremp, E., *Die Überlieferung der Vita Hludowici imperatoris des Astronomus*, *MGH* Studien und Texte 1 (Hannover, 1991)

Turner, C. (ed.), *Ecclesiae occidentalis monumenta iuris antiquissima, canonum et conciliorum graecorum interpretationes latinae*, 2 vols. (Oxford, 1899)

Twitchett, D., *The writing of official history under the T'ang* (Cambridge, 1992)

Ullmann, W., *Principles of government and politics in the middle ages*, 2nd edn (London, 1966)

Unterkircher, F. (ed.), *Das Wiener Fragment der Lorscher Annalen, Christus und die Samariterin. Katechese des Niceta von Remesiana. Codex Vindobonensis 515 der Österreichischen Nationalbibliothek Facsimile Ausgabe*, Codices Selecti 15 (Graz, 1967)

van Caenegem, R. C., *Guide to the sources of medieval history* (Oxford, Amsterdam and New York, 1978)

van der Horst, K., W. Noel and W. C. M. Wüstefeld (eds.), *The Utrecht Psalter in medieval art* (Utrecht, 1996)

van Engen, J. (ed.), *The past and future of medieval studies*, Notre Dame Conferences in Medieval Studies 4 (Notre Dame, 1994)

van Houts, E. (ed.), *Medieval memories: men, women and their past 700–1300* (London, 2001)

van Rhijn, C., *Shepherds of the lord: priests and episcopal statutes in the Carolingian period* (Utrecht, 2003)

van Uyhtfanghe, M., 'Histoire du Latin, protohistoire des langues romanes et histoire de la communication. À propos d'un recueil d'études, et avec quelques observations préliminaires sur le débat intellectuel entre pensée structurale et pensée historique', *Francia* 11 (1983), pp. 579–613

Vansina, J., *Oral tradition. A study in historical methodology*, trans. H. M. White (London, 1965)

Vansina, J., *Oral tradition as history* (Madison, 1985)

Villa, C., 'Die Horazüberlieferung und die "Bibliothek Karls des Grossen": zum Werkverzeichnis der Handschrift Berlin, Diez B. 66', *DA* 51 (1995), pp. 29–52.

Villa, C., 'La traditione di Orazio e la "biblioteca di Carlo Magno": per l'elenco di opere nel codice Berlin Diez B. Sant. 66', in O. Pecere and M. D. Reeve (eds.), *Formative stages of classical traditions: Latin texts from antiquity to the Renaissance* (Spoleto, 1995), pp. 299–322

Villa, C., 'Cultura classica e tradizione Longobarde; tra latino e volgari', in *Chiesa* (ed.), *Paolo Diacono*, pp. 575–600

Villa, C., 'Lay and ecclesiastical culture', in La Rocca (ed.), *Italy in the early middle ages*, pp. 189–203

Vogel, C., 'Saint Chrodegang et les débuts de la romanisation du culte en pays franc', in *Saint Chrodegang*, pp. 91–109

Vogel, C., *Medieval liturgy. An introduction to the sources*, revised edn and translation of the 1981 edn, by N. K. Rasmussen and W. G. Storey (Washington, D.C., 1986)

von Borries-Schulten, S., *Die romanischen Handschriften der Württemburgischen Landesbibliothek Stuttgart. Teil 1: Provenienz Zwiefalten* (Stuttgart, 1987)

von den Steinen, W., *Notker und seine geistige Welt* (Bern, 1948)

von Dziatowski, G., *Isidor und Ildefons als Litterarhistoriker. Eine Quellenkritische Untersuchung der Schriften De viris illustribus des Isidor von Sevilla und des Ildefons von Toledo*, Kirchengeschichtliche Studien 4.2 (Münster, 1898)

von Euw, A., *Liber Viventium Fabariensis. Das Karolingische Memorialbuch von Pfäfers in seiner Liturgie- und Kunstgeschichtlichen Bedeutung*, Studia Fabariensia. Beiträge zur Pfäferser Klostergeschichte 1 (Bern and Stuttgart, 1989)

Voss, J., *Das Mittelalter im historischen Denken Frankreichs. Untersuchung zur Geschichte des Mittelalterbegriffs und der Mittelalterbewertung von der zweiten Hälfte des 16. bis zur Mitte des 19. Jahrhunderts* (Munich, 1972)

Waitz, G., 'Ueber die handschriftliche Ueberlieferung und die Sprache der Historia Langobardorum des Paulus', *Neues Archiv* 1 (1876), pp. 533–66

Wallace-Hadrill, J. M., *The Long Haired Kings and other studies in Frankish history* (London, 1962)

Wallace-Hadrill, J. M., 'History in the mind of Archbishop Hincmar', in R. H. C. Davis and J. M. Wallace-Hadrill (eds.), *The writing of history in the middle ages: essays presented to Sir Richard William Southern* (Oxford, 1981), pp. 43–70

Walter, C., 'Les dessins carolingiens dans un manuscrit de Verceil', *Cahiers Archéologiques* 18 (1968), pp. 99–107

Wattenbach, W., W. Levison and H. Löwe, *Deutschlands Geschichtsquellen im Mittelalter*, II, *Vorzeit und Karolinger* (Weimar, 1953)

Wehlen, W., *Geschichtsschreibung und Staatsauffassung im Zeitalter Ludwigs des Frommen* (Lübeck and Hamburg, 1970)

Weinrich, L., *Wala. Graf, Mönch und Rebell. Die Biographie eines Karolingers* (Lübeck, 1963)

Weisengruber, F., *Epiphanius Scholasticus als Übersetzer zu Cassiodorus-Epiphanius Historia ecclesiastica tripartita*, Österreichische Akademie der Wissensschaften, phil.-hist. Klasse Sitzungsberichte 283, Veröffentlichungen der Kommission zur Herausgabe des Corpus der lateinischen Kirchenväter, ed. R. Hanslik, Heft 5 (Vienna, 1972)

Wendling, W., 'Die Erhebung Ludwigs des Frommen zum Mitkaiser in Jahre 813 und ihre Bedeutung für die Verfassungsgeschichte des Frankenreiches', *Frühmittelalterliche Studien* 19 (1985), pp. 201–38

Werner, K.-F., 'Zur Arbeitsweise des Regino von Prüm', *Welt als Geschichte* 2 (1959), pp. 96–116

Werner, K.-F., 'Gauzlin von Saint-Denis und die westfränkische Reichsteilung von Amiens (März 880). Ein Beitrag zur Vorgeschichte von Odos Königtum', *DA* 35 (1979), pp. 395–462

Werner, K.-F., '*Hludowicus Augustus*: Gouverner l'empire chrétien – idées et réalités', in Godman and Collins (eds.) *Charlemagne's heir*, pp. 3–123

Westerbergh, U., *Beneventan ninth-century poetry*, Studia latina Stockholmensia 4 (Stockholm, 1957)

Whitby, M., 'Greek historical writing after Procopius: variety and vitality', in A. Cameron and L. I. Conrad (eds.), *Studies in late antiquity and early Islam*, I, *The Byzantine and early Islamic near east*, 1, *Problems in the literary source material* (Princeton, 1992), pp. 25–80

White, H., *The content of the form. Narrative discourse and historical representation* (Baltimore and London, 1987)

White, H., 'The historical text as literary artefact', in R. H. Canary and H. Kozicki (eds.), *The writing of history: literary form and historical understanding* (Madison, Wis., 1978), pp. 41–62

Whitelock, D., *After Bede* (Newcastle, 1960)

Whitrow, G. J., *Time in history. Views of time from prehistory to the present day* (Oxford, 1988)

Wickham, C., 'Gossip and resistance among the medieval peasantry', *Past and Present* 160 (1998), pp. 3–24

Wilken, R., 'Eusebius and the Christian holy land', in Attridge and Hata (eds.), *Eusebius, Christianity and Judaism*, pp. 736–60

Wilken, R. W., *The land called holy: Palestine in Christian history and thought* (New Haven and London, 1992)

Williams, P., *The organ in western culture, 750–1250*, Cambridge Studies in Medieval and Renaissance Music (Cambridge, 1993)

Willsdorf, C., 'Le Monasterium scottorum Ettonau et la famille des ducs d'Alsace au VIIIe siècle. Vestiges d'un cartulaire perdu', *Francia* 3 (1975), pp. 1–87

Winkelman, F., 'Das Problem der Rekonstruktion der *Historia ecclesiastica* des Gelasius von Caesarea', *Forschungen und Fortschritte* 38 (1964), pp. 311–14

Winkelman, F., *Untersuchung zur Kirchengeschichte des Gelasios von Kaisareia*, Sitzungsberichte der deutschen Akademie der Wissenschaften zu Berlin (Berlin, 1966).

Winter, J. M., *Sites of memory, sites of mourning. The Great War in European history* (Cambridge, 1995)

Wolfram, H., 'Political theory and narrative in charters', *Viator* 26 (1995), pp. 39–52

Wolfram, H., 'Der heilige Rupert und die antikarolingische Adelsopposition', *MIÖG* 80 (1972), pp. 7–34

Wolfram, H., *Grenzen und Räume. Geschichte Österreichs vor seiner Entstehung* (Vienna, 1995)

Wolfram, H., *Salzburg, Bayern, Österreich. Die conversio Bagoariorum et Carantanorum und die Quellen ihrer Zeit* (Vienna, 1995)

Wood, I., *The missionary life. Saints and the evangelisation of Europe 400–1050* (London, 1999)

Wood, I., *The Merovingian kingdoms, 450–751* (London, 1994)

Wood, I. N., 'Defining the Franks: Frankish origins in early medieval historiography', in S. Forde, L. Johnson and A. V. Murray (eds.), *Concepts of national history in the middle ages* (Leeds, 1995), pp. 47–59

Wormald, P. (ed.), *Ideal and reality in Frankish and Anglo-Saxon society* (Oxford, 1983)

Wright, N., 'Knowledge of Christian Latin poets and historians in medieval Brittany', *Études Celtiques* 23 (1986), pp. 163–85

Wright, R., *Late Latin and early Romance in Spain and Carolingian France* (Liverpool, 1982)

Wright, R., 'Complex monolingualism in early Romance', in W. J. Ashby (ed.), *Linguistic perspectives on the Romance languages: selected papers from the 21st linguistic symposium on Romance languages* (Amsterdam, 1993), pp. 377–88

Wright, R. (ed.), *Latin and the Romance languages in the early middle ages* (London, 1991, and Philadelphia, 1996)

Zechiel-Eckes, K., *Die Concordia canonum des Cresconius. Studien und Edition*, Freiburger Beiträge zur mittelalterlichen Geschichte 5 (Frankfurt am Main, 1992)

Index of manuscripts

General index

WITHDRAWN